Jonathan Fenby has written eighteen books, including the acclaimed *On The Brink: The Trouble with France* and *The General: Charles de Gaulle and the France He Saved*, hailed by the *New York Times* as 'a magnificent book ... learned, incisive and gripping' which 'turns breadth and depth into enthrallment'. In half a century of covering France, he was Paris bureau chief for *Reuters* and *The Economist* as well as writing on the country for many other publications and editing both the *Observer* and the *South China Morning Post*. He has been awarded the Légion d'honneur and the Ordre national du Mérite by the French state.

Praise for *The History of Modern France*:

'Brave and ambitious' Robert Tombs, *Times Literary Supplement*

'Highly readable. A great story told with accuracy and dash'
Lord Patten, Chancellor, Oxford University

'Fenby writes with the authority of experience, and his book is affectionate, admiring and exasperated ... There is much to enjoy in Fenby's fluently written history and much to learn from it too' Allan Massie, *Literary Review*

'Jonathan Fenby's engaging *History of Modern France* charts the country's journey over more than two centuries from the 1789 Revolution, through the Terror, the Napoleonic years, onwards towards the Fall of France and today's Fifth Republic, founded by de Gaulle in 1958' Bruno Waterfield, *The Times*

'Jonathan Fenby positively gallops through a comprehensive account of France from 1789 until now. He has not selected only the juicy bits – the Revolution, Napoleon, the First World War, De Gaulle, 1968. He fills in what happens in between so that events are joined up and the narrative complete' Mary Dejevsky, *Independent*

'A well-told narrative ... [Fenby] is at his best when he teases out the tensions between the republican unifying ideal and the enduring divisions that periodically emerge to challenge the French nation'
The Economist

'Detaile ... nsight
into ... ine

Also by Jonathan Fenby

ALLIANCE

THE GENERAL

GENERALISSIMO

THE SINKING OF THE LANCASTRIA

TIGER HEAD, SNAKE TAILS

THE HISTORY OF
MODERN FRANCE

FROM THE REVOLUTION TO
THE WAR WITH TERROR

JONATHAN FENBY

**SIMON &
SCHUSTER**

London · New York · Sydney · Toronto · New Delhi

A CBS COMPANY

First published in Great Britain by Simon & Schuster UK Ltd, 2015
This paperback edition published by Simon & Schuster UK Ltd, 2016
A CBS COMPANY

1 3 5 7 9 10 8 6 4 2

Simon & Schuster UK Ltd
1st Floor
222 Gray's Inn Road
London WC1X 8HB

www.simonandschuster.co.uk

Simon & Schuster Australia, Sydney
Simon & Schuster India, New Delhi

A CIP catalogue record for this book
is available from the British Library

Paperback ISBN: 978-1-4711-2930-8
Ebook ISBN: 978-1-4711-2931-5

Typeset in Baskerville by M Rules
Printed and bound by CPI Group (UK) Ltd, Croydon, CR0 4YY

*To Ella Grace
and, as always, to Renée*

CONTENTS

PART 4 VICHY, DE GAULLE AND
THE UNLOVED REPUBLIC 1940–1958

PART 5 THE FIFTH REPUBLIC 1958–2015

Prologue

A REPULIC AT WAR

The twenty-first century has not been kind to France. Politically, economically and socially the country has come under increasing strain, breeding a loss of self-confidence and a sense of gloom that sat ill with its view of itself as a beacon for the world. There were complaints about 'French bashing' from foreign commentators, but the mood, known as *morosité*, was pervasive at home; a global barometer of hope and happiness in fifty-four countries put France second to bottom. The country that was meant to incarnate *joie de vivre* was increasingly ill at ease as challenges piled up on all sides, most dramatically with the terrorist attacks which killed 150 people in early and late 2015 and injured more than 360, facing the nation which sees itself as the heir of the Enlightenment and the rule of reason with the reality of home-grown jihadism and the disenchantment felt by millions of its inhabitants with the way the supposedly inclusive republic works in practice.[1]

The first wave of attacks which killed eleven people at the satirical magazine *Charlie Hebdo* and five (including the attacker) at a Jewish supermarket in January produced a huge demonstration of national unity with marches by four million people across the country proclaiming '*Je suis Charlie*' ('I am Charlie'), echoed by rallies in other cities around the world including Berlin, Washington, London, Montreal and Madrid. The November attacks which took at least 130 lives in Paris hugely deepened the sense of shock. So did the fact that the eight attackers were French or Belgian citizens and that five of them had gone to fight for the ISIS-Daesh 'caliphate' in Syria; most had been on police records but had still been able to return to kill, using mobile telephones and encrypted communications to avoid detection. It emerged that 11,700 people were on police lists as having links to radical Islamic groups while French citizens made up the largest contingent among Europeans fighting for the Islamists in Syria and Iraq.

After the January attacks, President François Hollande had sought the reasons for the outrages, talking of social exclusion and the defects of policy; visiting an estate in Grigny, outside Paris, where 60 per cent of children were in families below the poverty line and youth unemployment was 40 per cent, Hollande spoke of 'unbearable discrimination'. He was booed and asked by one young man, 'When are things ever going to change here?'[2]

Now he adopted a martial tone, declaring the country 'at war with terrorism'. It was not simply a matter of the horrific death toll in restaurants, cafés and a concert hall. In words echoed by other political leaders, Hollande called the attacks 'an aggression against our ... way of life'. National values inherited from the two and a quarter centuries since the first Revolution and embodied in the republics that had ruled since 1870 were at stake. France would fight back, the president told parliament, because it was 'a country of freedom, because we are the fatherland of the Rights of Man ... France is always a light for humanity. And when she is attacked, the world finds itself for a time in the penumbra ... We will eradicate terrorism because we are bound to freedom and to the lustre of France in the world.'

A year of terror

On 7 January 2015, two brothers wielding assault rifles attacked the offices of the unbridled satirical magazine *Charlie Hebdo* which had published irreverent cartoons of the Prophet Mohammed (as well as other religious figures).The gunmen, Chérif and Saïd Kouachi, were French citizens born to Algerian immigrants, orphaned at an early age and later gravitating to petty crime. They joined a gang that frequented a mosque in the Buttes-Chaumont district of northern Paris and were radicalised by an Islamic preacher who talked to them in the privacy of his home and who sent jihadists to fight in Iraq, among them Saïd.*[3]

Identifying themselves as belonging to al-Qaeda in Yemen, the brothers shot dead eight of the magazine's staff, including celebrated cartoonists, two police officers and two others, as well as injuring eleven. After they fled in a car, they were tracked down by police to an industrial estate north of Paris where they held out in a company office for two days before security forces stormed the building and killed both of them.

The day after the attack on *Charlie Hebdo*, their associate, Amedy Coulibaly, shot and killed a woman police officer in the road in a Paris suburb and critically injured a street sweeper. Son of an immigrant from Mali, Coulibaly had met Chérif Kouachi in jail where he had been radicalised by a well-known jihadist who was a fellow prisoner. On 9 January, he went to the Hypercacher supermarket at the Porte de Vincennes on the eastern edge of the capital armed with a sub-machine gun, an assault rifle and two pistols. Saying he was fighting for the Islamic State, he killed four people in the supermarket and took others hostage, talking to the Kouachis on his mobile telephone as they were surrounded by police and warning he would kill hostages if the brothers came to harm. A Muslim shop assistant helped hide people in a refrigerated room before escaping himself and aiding police to plan their assault. Storming the shop, they killed Coulibaly and freed fifteen hostages.

The link with the Middle East offered a fresh and highly worrying aspect after earlier outrages, including gun attacks in 2012 by a radicalised petty criminal of Algerian descent who killed three soldiers and four people, including three children at a Jewish school in the south west. 'We have become public enemy number one for Islamic State,' warned Marc Trévidic, France's leading anti-terrorist magistrate until September 2015. Terrorist networks grew amid social and family connections which provided support and protection. New media and mobile telephones added a new dimension to the attacks and to the radicalisation of young Muslims. Prison was a significant breeding ground – according to Reuters, as many as 60 per cent of the 70,000 inmates of France's jails had Muslim origins. Brussels provided a base outside France itself, with movement facilitated by Europe's Schengen free passage treaty.[4]

---

* For more on the brothers, see pp. 475-7.

In February, an Arab assaulted three soldiers guarding a Jewish community centre in Nice as he tried to get inside. In April, an Algerian tried to attack two churches in a Paris suburb, killing a woman. In June, a Muslim delivery driver of North African descent, believed by police to have links with ISIS-Daesh, beheaded his employer at a small industrial plant outside Lyons.

Two months later, a Moroccan who had worshipped at a radical mosque while living in Brussels opened fire with an assault rifle on a train from Amsterdam to Paris as it travelled through northern France. He also carried a pistol and a bottle of petrol. His initial burst of fire wounded three people, after which he turned his pistol on a passenger who tried to stop him, seriously wounding him in the neck. His rifle then jammed and three Americans, two of them off-duty members of the air force, overpowered him. Police classed the attack as an Islamic terrorist incident; the attacker said his motive was robbery caused by hunger and that he had found the weapons in a suitcase in a Brussels park.

Polls showed growing concerns about law and order. For the first time in thirty years a majority of people told pollsters that they favoured the return of capital punishment. At the first round of departmental elections in March, the National Front got 25 per cent of the votes, well ahead of the mainstream right and almost twice as many as the Socialists. The second round was more balanced, with the regular right raising its score to five million while the Front fell back to four million. With 16 per cent of the second-round vote, the Socialists paid the price for being an administration in which few outside the party faithful had much faith.[5]

Social and communal tensions rose. Jewish buildings were put under heavy guard. The number of anti-Semitic and Islamophobic incidents increased. In the first half of 2015, 508 anti-Jewish offences were registered, an increase of 84 per cent on a year earlier, while more than 400 incidents 'of an Islamophobic nature' were recorded compared to 133 in the same period the previous year. (France is home to just under half a million Jews, with an estimated Muslim population of some five million, or 8 per cent of the total population.)

The Jewish community – more than 70 per cent from France's former North African possessions – had come under attack earlier as pro-Palestinian demonstrations degenerated into attacks on Jewish property and synagogues in some places. Now, it felt more broadly threatened. Emigration to Israel nearly doubled between 2013 and 2014 and increased further in 2015 (though a third of those who went subsequently returned or went elsewhere, finding their new home uncongenial). Motivated by communal tension as well as by upward mobility, Jews moved from outer-city districts of Paris where they had Muslim neighbours to safer districts inside the capital and to more middle-class suburbs. In Saint-Denis, where Muslims are estimated to make up 40 per cent of the population, there used to be 500 Jewish families but now, a Jewish observer remarked, it was hard to get enough men together for the Yom Kippur service. The Jewish population of the capital's bourgeois 17th arrondissement soared to 30 per cent of residents, with twenty-nine kosher restaurants and delicatessens specialising in North African dishes.[6]

A group of intellectuals who saw multiculturalism as a communitarian threat to the integrity of the republic set off a debate about national identity. Philosopher Alain Finkielkraut, a one-time leftist who had been elected to the Académie française the previous year, came out in support of a former minister who had been dropped from the main right-wing list for regional elections after she insisted that France was 'a white race' country. Michel Onfray, a popular thinker and author of eighty books, took a resolutely politically incorrect stance ranging from a revisionist view of the 1789 Revolution to questioning immigration. It was all part of the twenty-four-hour rolling media cycle that needed feeding in a country that delights in the play of ideas. But the effect was to ratchet up the tension, with critics accusing the philosophers of playing the National Front's game and them replying that they were only confronting reality.

More important than such jousting was the way in which France appeared to have become the principal target for terrorists, and the issue of its ability to cope as government spending cuts affected the police and security forces. More and more identified Islamic radicals were arriving every day, 'and we're already unable to maintain surveillance of people flagged as potentially dangerous', a senior security official remarked. 'Given the scale of the threat and diverse forms that it can assume, our counter-terrorism system has become permeable, weak, and is no longer as efficient as it was before,' Marc Trévidic warned in September 2015. Two months later, the warnings were borne out in three bloody hours in Paris.[7]

13 November 2015

9.20 p.m. The first sign of trouble comes at Gate J of the Stade de France sports stadium in the Paris suburb of Saint-Denis. President Hollande is among the crowd watching a friendly football match between France and Germany. As a French player passes the ball to a colleague twenty minutes into the game, an explosion sounds at an entrance to the 80,000-capacity stadium. Some fans raise a cheer for what they think is a firework.

A bodyguard leans over the president's shoulder to tell him a suicide bomber has blown himself up outside. The man had a ticket for the game and a routine check at the entrance as he tried to get in fifteen minutes into the match exposed his explosive suicide vest. As he backs away from security guards, he detonates it, killing himself and three others. A Syrian passport in the name of Ahmad al-Mohammed, aged twenty-five, is found at the scene, but it was probably fake, though the prosecutor's office says fingerprints from the corpse are of a man who passed through Greece with refugees from the Middle East in October.

Hollande looks straight ahead for a moment, raises his gaze to the sky and walks to the stadium's control room to confer by telephone with Interior Minister Bernard Cazeneuve. Concerned that the crowd might panic if it realises what was happening, the president decides the match should continue and that nothing should be announced about the attack. He goes back to his seat but does not join in the cheering when France striker Olivier Giroud scores. At half-time, Hollande is flown by helicopter to central Paris where he goes to the Interior Ministry basement situation room to plan the response. Thousands of people are moved on to the pitch as the game ends, waiting for the all-clear to leave; as they are escorted from the stadium, some sing the Marseillaise. The two teams sleep at the stadium on mattresses on the floor.

9.25 p.m. A black car pulls up outside the Carillon bar near the Canal Saint-Martin in the 10th arrondissement, a traditionally working-class area favoured by young people for its reasonably priced housing and as a good place for a night out. This Friday, which is warm for the time of year, café terraces, bars and restaurants are crowded.

Getting out of the vehicle, two men spray the Carillon bar's terrace with automatic gunfire then walk across the road to shoot people in Le Petit Cambodge restaurant. Police say one shouts '*Allahu akbar*' ('God is great'). They kill fifteen people and badly injure ten.

9.30 p.m. A second suicide bomber outside the Stade de France blows himself up; he is a twenty-year-old born in France but living in Belgium who was believed to have gone to fight with ISIS. He posted pictures of himself on Facebook carrying weapons with the message 'Hit the pigs in their communities so that they no longer feel safe even in their dreams'. The third, who is unidentified, blows himself up twenty minutes later. Police speculate that the plan was for the first attacker to set off his explosion inside the stadium and for the other two to cause carnage among fleeing spectators outside.

9.32 p.m. A gunman in the black car fires burst from a Kalashnikov rifle into the Bonne Bière bar in the rue du Faubourg du Temple by the Place de la République. Five people die and eight are injured. The car is later found abandoned in the suburb of Montreuil with three AK-47 rifles inside.

9.36 p.m. Two men rake the terrace of La Belle Équipe restaurant on the rue de Charonne with gunfire, killing nineteen and leaving nine in a critical condition.

9.40 p.m. Brahim Abdeslam, thirty-one, sits down at a table in the Comptoir Voltaire café near the Place de la Nation and places an order. He is wearing an anorak on top of a coat with a fur trim. He turns to other customers with a smile, apologises for any disturbance he had caused – and then detonated the explosive vest hidden below his bulky clothing, killing himself and injuring fifteen people. Born in France but living in Belgium, he had driven to Paris in a rented car and taken a small house in the suburb of Bobigny as a safe house before the attacks. Like the other terrorists, the explosive he carries is peroxide-based triacetone triperoxide (TATP) which can be made from ingredients of everyday products such as hair bleach and nail polish remover.

9.40 p.m. At the same time, a black Volkswagen Polo with Belgian licence plates pulls up outside the Bataclan rock concert venue, a mid-nineteenth-century building on the Boulevard Voltaire built in Chinese style as a home for operettas. Its Jewish former owners, who sold it in 2015, had been a target for anti-Zionist activists and threats from extremist Islamic groups because of the pro-Israel events they staged.

More than a thousand people jam the place; some wearing T-shirts, others stripped to the waist, they are dancing and listening to an American rock band, Eagles of Death Metal. Three men in dark clothing get out of the car, carrying assault rifles. They toss a mobile telephone into a refuse bin; later it will be shown to contain a floor plan of the Bataclan and a message to confederates in a suburban hotel room: 'Off we go; here we go again.'

Two of the men walk into the main hall, a third covers the emergency exit. All three have been in Syria. Samy Amimour, twenty-eight, a one-time bus driver from the Paris suburb of Drancy, is subject to an international arrest warrant. Ismaël Omar Mostefaï, twenty-nine, who lived at his parents' home in Chartres with his wife and baby, had been arrested eight times for petty crimes but never jailed. The third attacker, Foued Mohamed-Aggad, had joined ISIS in 2013 with a group of young men from his home city of Strasbourg; several had been killed in the fighting in the Middle East while others, deterred by the atrocities they witnessed, had left the ranks of the Caliphate, but the experience appears to have further radicalised Foued.

As the band launches into its anthem 'Kiss the Devil' – 'Who'll love the Devil? Who'll sing his song?' – the terrorists open fire on people standing at the bar; the barman dies with a bullet in his head. Some of the crowd think it is a pyrotechnic display to go with the pounding music. 'But then I turned around and saw someone who had just taken a bullet in the eye,' one man recalled.[8]

Shouts of '*Allahu akbar*' are heard above the firing as the attackers throw grenades. They appear calm and determined, reloading their guns several times. The positions they take and their regular firing shows their training.

People take refuge in toilets and offices in the building or crawl on to the roof; two hang from a window over the street. Fifty escape to an adjoining flat. Some lie on the floor feigning death as the men walk round shooting as they go. People who try to get out through the emergency exit are turned back by the third gunman positioned there. The band gets out unscathed.

The attackers kick people lying on the floor and, if they move, shoot them in the head. One says this is 'only the start of a war that will go on'. The main ballroom is silent now except for the shots and the ringing of mobile telephones of relatives and friends of those inside trying to contact them. One person who escaped compared the scene to a slaughterhouse – 'I was wading through blood. It was a centimetre deep in places. I had to clamber over dead bodies to get out.'[9]

10.00 p.m. The terrorists single out dozens of people as hostages, threatening to behead one every five minutes. 'This is because of all the harm done by Hollande to Muslims all over the world,' one says. They use a hostage's mobile telephone to send a text message. One of the attackers pulls out a laptop which appears to have encryption software. Samy Amimour, the former bus driver who has an explosive belt strapped round him, walks to the orchestra pit and plays a xylophone there, 'laughing sadistically', a survivor will recall. A lone policeman enters the building. Coming face to face with a terrorist, he fires his pistol; the terrorist's explosive belt detonates, killing the wearer.[10]

10.15 p.m. The police intervention brigade arrives at the scene, but does not launch an immediate assault, trying to get an idea of the situation inside the Bataclan first. They are told by a hostage through a closed door that they are being held by two men wearing explosive vests. The police are passed a mobile telephone number by hostages acting as go-betweens. They speak to the terrorists several times, and conclude that a massacre of hostages in front of the media is planned.[11] 'I want you to leave the country (Syria),' one gunman tells police over the telephone. 'I want you to remove your military. I want a piece of paper signed that proves it.' Otherwise, he goes on, 'I'm killing a hostage and throwing him out of the window.'

00.18 a.m. The brigade, some of whom had stormed the Jewish supermarket in January, launches its assault. Its men move behind a big metal shield which is hit thirty times. They shine torches ahead of them and throw grenades as they advance. The attack lasts three minutes. One terrorist is shot; the other blows himself up. One of the police describes the scene in the ballroom as being from Dante's circles of Hell. 'There were bodies, people hidden in every nook and cranny, phones vibrating, and blood, a lot of blood,' another officer recalled.

00.22 a.m. The president goes on television to announce a state of emergency and the closure of France's frontiers. He is then driven to the Bataclan. Brussels is put on high alert amid growing concern of an attack in the Belgian capital.

The overall death toll of the previous three hours is 130, 89 at the Bataclan. The Health Ministry says 352 were hurt, including 41 in intensive care. The victims come from some twenty-six countries. As news spreads, governments around the world express solidarity and bathe their famous landmarks in the French national colours of blue, white and red. President Obama says the attacks were 'on all humanity and the universal values we share'; David Cameron vows that Britain and France will stand together 'in sorrow but unbowed'. Five million people visit Hollande's Twitter account during the night.[12]

14 November. In the early hours, Salah Abdeslam, a twenty-six-year-old Belgian citizen from the heavily immigrant-populated Molenbeek district of Brussels, wanders the streets of the suburbs of the French capital. He will be reported to be a key organiser of the Paris attacks; his brother blew himself up on the Boulevard Voltaire. The two of them had been known in Molenbeek as drinkers and gamblers who ran a bar before they turned to religion in 2014. The previous month, he appeared on a list of individuals suspected of terrorist involvement provided to Belgian federal police by the mayor of Molenbeek.

Video footage from a petrol station showed Salah Abdeslam and another man getting out of a black Golf Polo on the road from Brussels to Paris on 11 November. He booked rooms in a suburban hotel in the French capital through a website at a suburban flat – police found pizzas and syringes there. He was believed to have driven the car in which the terrorists arrived at the Stade de France and to have taken others to the Bataclan, as well as supplying weapons and explosive belts.

From the suburb of Montrouge, he telephones a contact being held in a Belgian jail who arranges for two men to take a car to pick him up and drive him across the border.

'Don't leave me in the lurch. Please help me,' he reportedly tells them when they make telephone contact. One of them told Belgian police later that he was 'crying like a 12-year-old child'. They agree to pick him.[13]

Police check the car at the frontier but let it through, though they smell marijuana. The lawyer for one of the contacts who drove Abdeslam to Belgium says police checked the car three times. The Belgian interior minister says information linking him to the attacks arrived at the frontier post fifteen minutes after he was driven off.

In Brussels, a confederate drives Abdeslam to the district of Schaerbeek where he rents an apartment under a false name. The next day, his brother issues a televised message urging him to give himself up. Belgian police carry out raids in Molenbeek. They arrest seven people, but their main quarry remains at liberty.

16 November. Mourners pay tribute to the dead outside the Bataclan. The Place de la République near the scene of the killings becomes a shrine to the dead, the base of the statue of Liberty garlanded with flowers, candles and expressions of mourning and defiance, including some from Muslims saying they do not recognise their religion in the attack. Many European countries hold a minute's silence. In Britain, the French and British flags are flown at half-mast over public places and government offices. When England play France in a friendly football match at Wembley the following day, fans sing the Marseillaise before a minute's silence; the French national anthem is then played before every English Premier League game at the weekend.

Muslim organisations condemn the attacks, though they lack a single powerful voice. Sales of the French tricolour rise sharply and are flown from apartments and offices on a day of mourning. Recruitment to the French army increases tenfold, and the government publishes a guide in cartoon form on how to survive a terrorist attack. Residents of Damascus write an open letter stating, 'We extend our hands to all the people that love peace and freedom, most of all the French people.' Gun sales are reported to have risen significantly in Switzerland.

17 November. Terrorism would 'not destroy the Republic for the Republic will destroy it'. Hollande tells a joint session of the National Assembly and Senate at Versailles. Portrayed as an indecisive figure and compared by satirists to a wobbly flan, the sixty-one-year-old president metamorphoses into a war leader. He orders increased aerial bombardment of 'Islamic State' bases and sends France's aircraft carrier the *Charles de Gaulle* to the eastern Mediterranean, tripling the country's military capability in the region. The first air raid, on 15 November, destroys a command centre, an ammunition depot and a training camp in the ISIS stronghold of Raqqa in Syria. The goal is not to contain the movement, Hollande declares, 'It is to destroy it.'[14]

Sweeping emergency powers are introduced to allow police to conduct raids and searches without warrants and place people under house arrest without the normal judicial process; more than a hundred such detentions follow immediately. Former president Nicolas Sarkozy, a hardliner on law and order whom Hollande defeated in the 2012 election, welcomes 'an unexpected, unprecedented and spectacular change of course'. Big public gatherings are restricted. Troops are deployed to guard buildings and patrol streets. Plans are drawn up to install bollards and video systems to protect schools. The government announces the recruitment of 5,000 more police. Hollande launches a global diplomatic effort to strengthen the coalition to eradicate ISIS-Daesh. Visiting seven capitals to enlist support, he gets considerable sympathy and some help, but many governments are wary of going as far as he has – Italy, its foreign minister says, is ready to back France, but this 'does not mean Italy should feel itself at war'.[15]

Prime minister Manuel Valls insists that the European Union Commission must take France's security spending into account in its budget stabilisation target of cutting the deficit to below 3 per cent by 2017. *Charlie Hebdo* runs a cover of a man drinking champagne which flows out through bullet holes in his body – 'They've got the weapons,' the caption reads. 'Screw them, we've got the champagne.' The magazine's circulation has risen nearly ten times to 280,000 since January, but there is infighting and depression among staff.

18 November. 4.20 a.m. Police raid a shabby apartment building in Saint-Denis where Abdel-Hamid Al-Abaaoud, believed to have been a principal organiser of the 13 November carnage, has rented a flat; the owner said that, when he pointed out there were no mattresses or beds, he was told, 'They just want water and to pray.' From Molenbeek, Abaaoud was accused earlier in the year of organising an attempt to kill a Belgian policeman which ended with two confederates being gunned down. He had also been in contact with the terrorist arrested for shooting dead four people at the Jewish Museum of Belgium in Brussels the previous year and with the attacker on the Amsterdam–Paris train. Though sentenced *in absentia* to twenty years in jail in Belgium for recruiting jihadists, and the subject of an international arrest warrant, he had been able to cross to France without being detected and move about freely there. After the Paris attacks, he had abandoned his rental beside a motorway in the eastern outskirts of Paris; he was caught on a surveillance camera walking nearby wearing orange sneakers. Now, he is brought food and water by a cousin, a 26-year-old woman who was contacted by telephone from Belgium with his whereabouts. She and a friend then pick him up in a car. According to a French security report, he tells them he got back to Europe from Syria among the flood of refugees fleeing the war there. He says that ninety terrorists had followed the same path and were waiting to go into action in France. He gives his cousin, Hasna Aït Boulahcen, money to buy him a suit.

Police were already following her in a drugs investigation. Said by the security report to have been smitten with Abaaoud for years, she had been a vodka drinker who wore jeans, cowboy hat and boots and once tried to join the French army; her brother said later that he had never seen her open a copy of the Koran. But recently she adopted Islamic dress with full veil. Now police spot Abaaoud entering the building with her and before dawn take up position outside.

'Where's your boyfriend,' a policeman shouts.

'He is not my boyfriend,' Boulahcen cries back.

A volley of shots comes from inside. A bang is heard.

'Help me, help me, help me,' Boulahcen shouts.

Police tell her to raise her hands.

After another burst of firing from inside, police unleash a fusillade; in all they fire 5,000 bullets. Among the three killed as they storm in is Abaaoud, his body riddled with bullets and grenade shrapnel, still wearing his orange sneakers. Boulahcen dies, too. There is speculation that she was killed when an explosive belt was detonated beside her. A third, unidentified, body is also found. In the debris are several dozen boxes of mobile telephones still in their packaging.

The interior minister says Abaaoud had been planning an assault on the Paris business district of La Défense. He visited Britain the previous August and his mobile telephone contains images of a shopping centre in Birmingham.[16]

20 November. Islamist militants take 170 hostages and kill twenty of them at a western hotel in Bamako, capital of Mali, where France had deployed its armed forces to defend the regime. The attackers say they are working with al-Qaeda.

22 November. Brussels remains on high alert, with soldiers patrolling the streets, the underground railway system closed, shops and museums shut and concerts and football matches cancelled or postponed. Police raid a building in Molenbeek but it proves fruitless. Officials warn that terrorists are threatening to commit a 'very dangerous act'.

10 December. Police raid the flat in the Schaerbeek district of Brussels rented by Abdeslam; they find his fingerprint and traces of explosives.

16 December. Belgian police enter another apartment where Abdeslam is believed to have hidden. The raid is held up by a law limiting forcible entry into a home between 9 p.m. and 5 a.m. and to avoid any risk towards children at a neighbourhood school and worshippers at a nearby mosque.

22 December. Two young men are detained in Orleans accused of planning to attack a local police station. The interior minister says 3,400 people have been turned back at French frontiers as security risks since 13 November.

7 January 2016. Police shoot dead a man carrying an axe and wearing what looks like an explosive belt (but is not) as he approaches a police station in an immigrant district of Paris.

14 January 2016. President Hollande authorises the security services to monitor the communications of the 11,700 people on the watch list for contact with radical Islamic groups.

15 March 2016. Belgian police searching for Abdeslam ring the door-bell of a flat in the Brussels suburb of Forest, close to Molenbeek. They are met with a hail of gunfire. In the ensuing fire fight, one man inside is killed by a police sniper. Three of the police are injured. Two brothers who have been linked with violent crime in the area are arrested. A Kalashnikov rifle and a large amount of ammunition are found inside, together with a book on Salafism and an ISIS flag. Abdeslam's fingerprints are detected, but he and another man escape across the roof.

16-17 March, 2016. After a tip-off from an acquaintance of Abdeslam in Brussels, police tap telephones and focus on a house in Molenbeek, their suspicions strengthened by an unusually large number of pizzas ordered by one of its resident.

18 March, 2016. Heavily-armed police storm the house. Abdeslam is wounded in the leg in an exchange of gunfire. Dragged out, his head covered with a white hood, he is bundled into an unmarked car and taken to hospital and then to a maximum security prison in Bruges. His lawyer says he is ready to stand trial in France. The prosecutor's office in Paris says he told police he had been due to join the three attackers at the Stade de France, but had backed out at the last minute – Abdeslam's lawyer says his client would sue the prosecutor for abuse of the judicial process.

'Though this arrest was an important step, it is not the final result,' Hollande says. 'There will be further arrests. We know the network is extensive in Belgium, France and other countries.' Security forces believe that more than thirty people were involved in the planning and execution of the Paris attacks, including networks of friends and families. Two men suspected of playing important roles in planning and logistics are still on the run.

22 March, 2016. Terrorists set off bombs in Brussels at the airport and in an underground railway station near the European Union headquarters. Thirty-two people are killed and more than two hundred injured. ISIS claims responsibility. Two of the airport terrorists blow themselves up. A third is the target of a major manhunt. Police carry out a string of arrests in Belgium, France and the Netherlands. They report finding a growing number of links between the Brussels terrorist network and the Paris attacks, underlining the Europe-wide threat. Airports, transport links and public buildings across the continent are put on high alert.

La Morosité du jour

For all the huge demonstrations of unity in January and the shock and horror of November, it was not long before more familiar tensions and insecurities re-emerged. Surveys at the beginning of 2016 found that the

French were more worried about unemployment than terrorism. The 'war' and the state of emergency did nothing to address deep social problems; indeed, they made it easier to avoid them. At the first session of the National Assembly after the November attacks, the opposition blamed the administration for having failed to step up security. They drowned out the prime minister's speech with catcalls and abuse and refused to join in when he called on the chamber to stand in homage to the police and fire services. While opinion polls showed that 70 per cent of those questioned rated Hollande as 'credible in the struggle against terrorism' and approved the emergency measures, only 22 per cent thought his administration's policies as a whole were sound.

There were demonstrations, sometimes turning violent, by everybody from teachers to Breton farmers, hospital workers to air traffic controllers. The president and the government seemed at a loss as to how to cope. 'France is blocked,' the main Sunday newspaper warned in a front-page headline, adding in the accompanying article, 'Society is not far from suffocation'.[17]

Some military experts asked if air strikes alone could destroy the would-be caliphate in Syria and Iraq, warning that only ground troops could do that – sending them in was out of the question for the administration. A leading French strategic thinker, François Heisbourg, pointed out that 'in a war, people expect a beginning, a middle and an end. But the struggle against terrorism is pretty endless.' Opposition leader Alain Juppé, a former prime minister and foreign minister, called the international coalition against ISIS ineffective and urged reconsideration of the policy of refusing to have anything to do with Syrian leader Bashar al-Assad. There was also the possibility that the French reaction might be just what the terrorists wanted if, as Gilles Keppel, an expert on terrorism and Islam argued, they wanted 'to unleash a civil war' and provoke a backlash against Muslims to gain further recruits.[18]

Moving beyond *morosité*, the French were sunk in what one of the early 2016 surveys described as *lassitude*. Inevitably, concern about security increased – in a poll in early 2016, 65 per cent of respondents backed greater powers for the police (83 per cent among supporters of the main right-wing party, the Republicans). The same poll found that 54 per cent thought there were too many immigrants, 52 per cent thought Muslims and Islam had too many rights and 45 per cent agreed that 'we no longer feel at home in France'.[19]

The sour mood and the decline in national self-confidence in a nation that always sees itself as a beacon to the world had been building since the late twentieth century. In the 1990s, France had become one of the world's biggest consumers of tranquillisers and mood-altering drugs. The suicide rate was double that of Britain or Spain. 'The fact of living in France reduces by twenty percent the probability of declaring oneself very happy,' economist Claudia Senik wrote on the basis of a study conducted in 2011.[20]

Icons of French life weakened, accentuating the sense of a country losing its traditional bearings. Cafés closed, wine consumption dropped, sales of packaged sliced bread boomed in place of baguettes and French cyclists failed to win the Tour de France for more than three decades. The economy was at the core of the national mood. Quarterly growth dropped to 0.2 per cent at the end of 2015, investment remained low and France kept to its habit of missing its budget deficit targets with a budget gap of 95 per cent of GDP. Unemployment stayed stubbornly at 10 per cent – a record 3.6 million at the start of 2016 with a rise of 600,000 in the three years after Hollande took office. The European Commission forecast that the rate would stay above 10 per cent in 2017 due to the slow increase in investment.[21]

France had not expanded its workforce outside the civil service since 2001 though the number of retired people had swollen by 30 per cent. By 2015, two-thirds of new employees were on contracts lasting for a month or less and the chances of converting a temporary position into a permanent one had fallen to 25 per cent. Nineteen per cent of young people were not in education, training or employment, almost twice as many as in Germany. Just under half those aged between fifty-five and sixty-four were at work compared to two-thirds across the Rhine.[22]

The principal reason for the continuing level of unemployment lay in the inflexible regulations in a 3,000-page labour code which made employers reluctant to offer long-term engagements since it was difficult to lay off workers if their companies ran into trouble. Those in work and the trade unions – which were numerically quite weak but could still exert considerable muscle in the state sector – clung on to the protection provided by the legislation. The result was a two-speed system of rigidity at the centre and what was called 'hyper-flexibility' on the margins.

The difficulty of shedding surplus labour and high welfare contributions dragged down companies and reduced international competitiveness. The balance of payments stayed obstinately in the red; though the steep fall in oil prices reduced the deficit in 2015 and aircraft sales were healthy, exports of industrial goods fell by more than 20 per cent. France had only one company in the top global fifty by value and 430,000 firms had gone out of business since the economic crisis of 2008. Some of its celebrated enterprises were sold to foreigners; others looked small by global standards.*[23]

The Hollande administration drew up plans to simplify the code and to encourage management and unions to work together on pay and conditions instead of the traditional recourse to strikes. It soon retreated in the face of opposition from Socialists, unions and students as Hollande sought to shore up his electoral base. Instead, it fell back on the old panacea of trying to buy its way out of what was a structural problem by subsidising the creation of half a million vocational jobs and apprenticeships.[24]

'I am not deaf,' the president assured the French. 'I hear the anger. I see the dissatisfaction, and I have to go faster.' But most people thought the politicians did not listen to them, especially at the national level. Jockeying for position – in this case for the presidential election of 2017 – took precedence over advancing and implementing real solutions for real problems. The frequency of elections and the way in which uncommitted voters regularly switched sides – voting one party in and then turning against it – made for instability and short-term political calculations; in the nation of Racine and Proust, the sound bite ruled.[25]

The rise of the National Front added to the confusion. Founded by Jean-Marie Le Pen in 1972 as a home for nostalgic colonialists, small shopkeepers and veterans of the Vichy collaborationist wartime regime, it had broadened out into the main party of the working class and of protest in general, filling, in part, the role taken by the Communist

* This theme is explored in detail in Chapter 24.

Party in the past. Marine Le Pen, Jean-Marie's daughter who succeeded him in 2011, played a savvy game to 'de-diabolise' it by appealing to young professionals and to rural voters who felt left behind by the nation's evolution. It attracted growing support from the police – a survey published in early 2016 showed more than 40 per cent approval in several centres of the gendarmerie including those from which men had taken part in anti-terrorist actions. Marine's public row with her father over his Holocaust denial helped win some Jewish votes from those fearful of Islamic violence.*[26]

The party's anti-European rhetoric of enhancing national sovereignty, protectionism and strengthening the state might make little sense on examination, but that did not matter. Its appeal sprang not from logic, rather from the emotions of those who felt betrayed by the political establishment and sought a new champion whom they could imagine understood their everyday concerns. It depended on a lot of people feeling fed up, and, so long as that continued to be the case, could expect to play a big political role. But its development was curbed by the political system against which it inveighed. Drawing in protest votes as well as its own growing army of dedicated followers, it could come first or second at the initial round of France's two-stage elections, especially when other parties ran several candidates. But that was not enough to clinch victory at the run-off to decide who actually gets to govern.

This had been the case in the first round of the presidential election of 2002 when, in a highly fragmented vote, Jean-Marie Le Pen came second to the incumbent, Jacques Chirac, ahead of Socialist Lionel Jospin, who was eliminated. In the run-off, the Front's founder increased his share of the vote by just one percentage point as voters rallied to the republic to give the president the biggest victory margin of the Fifth Republic. Thirteen years later, in regional elections a month after the November attacks, the Front polled strongly in the first round in the north-east and south-east, but was then blocked when the Socialists withdrew their candidates to give the centre-right a clear path to victory at the run-off, the prime minister warning that it fostered divisions which 'could lead to civil war'.[27]

* For the 2015 election see p. 460.

That manoeuvre served the mainstream's immediate purpose, but reflected poorly on the major parties and raised the question of why they had not been able to succeed on their own, enabling Le Pen to claim that her movement was the only true opposition. Polls repeatedly showed her in the leading place among likely contenders for the 2017 presidential election, but the expectation was that 'republic unity' would prevent her getting to the Élysée; an opinion survey in 2016 found that 56 per cent of people considered the party a danger to democracy.[28]

Disdain for politicians showed in electoral abstention rates that rose as high as 50 per cent. It had been building up for decades as electoral promises were repeatedly broken At the end of the 1950s, Charles de Gaulle had given the country a new political system, the Fifth Republic, as well as introducing major measures to modernise the economy. But, from the time of François Mitterrand and his grandiosely impractical visions as the first president of the left in 1981, politicians of all stripes offered France turning points which did not turn once they had won office. When faced with difficulties, they inevitably chose the easy way out, delaying reform and pandering to interest groups as if afraid that the spirit of the revolution of 1789 might sweep them to the tumbril. The right was in continual disarray as contending barons battled for leadership while the Socialist Party was an uncomfortable melange of modernising social democrats and traditional left-wingers most at home with Marxism. An additional problem was the way in which support for Hollande collapsed even faster than that of his predecessors; his approval rating went as low as 12 per cent after his first year in office and, even after his reincarnation as a war president, reached a ceiling of 33 per cent.

Given the quasi-monarchical nature of the presidency, this created a vacuum at the heart of the Fifth Republic, widened by the all-powerful nature of the state. Regulations constricted activity rather than acting as protection against predatory forces. A journalist recalled seeing a whiteboard in the office of a senior government aide in which somebody had written, in a jest that rang all too true, 'If it moves, tax it. If it still moves, regulate it. If it doesn't move, subsidise it'. The gulf between the ruling elite and the population was a constant sore; gravitating smoothly between politics, administration and business, the top brass was drawn from graduates of the *grandes écoles* colleges which housed 1 per cent of the country's higher education students, only 4 per cent of them from working-class families. As a quip went, they knew about everything except everyday life.[29]

One area in which many people thought their theoretical schemes had failed was immigration. Surveys showed that people thought there are three times as many immigrants in France than there actually were. But it was the perception than counted rather than the reality as regions which had few immigrants began to vote for the National Front.

The rise of Islam was a particular issue. In 2012, a poll published by Le Figaro reported that 43 per cent of respondents regarded the religion as a threat, 60 per cent thought it had too much importance in national life and only 18 per cent favoured the building of mosques. Asked why they took a hostile attitude, 68 per cent said it was because of Muslim 'refusal to integrate into French society' and 52 per cent cited 'too large cultural differences' together with 'the rejection of western values'.[30]

On the other side of the divide, rejection of the republic and its norms grew in the new century among immigrants. On outer-city housing estates where youth unemployment could reach 40 per cent, there was little attachment to the values inherited from the nation's history since the Revolution of 1789. Citizenship could ring hollow to those who felt excluded from a system that insisted that everybody must conform to the one-size-fits-all republic. In a small but telling illustration, a television crew filmed a class of mainly immigrant sixteen–seventeen-year-olds in a Paris suburb in early 2016; asked if they were French, nearly all the pupils raised their hands but, asked if they felt French, hardly any did so.[31]

La belle France

There were, of course, many positive aspects to the nation which had been the home to so much of the world's culture, arts and ideas. France remained a permanent member of the United Nations Security Council. A nuclear power, it deployed troops to fight Islamic extremists in Africa where it intervened in Mali in 2012 and then set up a 3,000-strong rapid reaction force in Chad. The Chirac administration had led opposition to the invasion of Iraq in 2003, and earned credit for that as the operation went wrong, even if the US Congressional canteen renamed French fries as Freedom fries in protest. Now, the Hollande administration's robust reaction to terrorism made it Washington's favoured security partner in Europe and, to express its opposition to Russia's annexation of Crimea, it took the economically onerous step of cancelling warship orders by Moscow in 2015. Booming sales of other armaments, notably military jets, cemented the country's place as a major global weapons supplier, including a $7 billion contract for military jets and missiles to Qatar to tighten links with the Gulf state which had bought heavily into luxury Paris property and owned the country's dominant football team, PSG.

France was the second-ranking power in the European Union and played a big role in coping with the euro debt crisis – if the outcome was hardly satisfactory, it did at least prevent the break-up of the common currency. Its economy was the sixth largest in the world. As soon as sanctions on Iran were lifted in 2016, it clinched the sale of 118 Airbus planes along with an oil contract and a big deal to manufacture cars in the Islamic Republic. Even if he had to backtrack under the impact of economic reality and German pressure, Hollande's initial anti-austerity programme won him a troop of admirers. His administration then played a major role in steering through a global climate deal sealed at a 198-nation conference in Paris at the end of 2015.

France's epic history stretches back to the Gauls who resisted the Roman legions of Julius Caesar and is peopled by great figures: Joan of Arc, the 'Sun King' Louis XIV, Napoleon and de Gaulle. It was central to the Enlightenment of the eighteenth century, which provided the ideas for its first revolution. Its cultural flourishing in the nineteenth and early twentieth centuries was unparalleled – Balzac, Flaubert, Baudelaire, Hugo and Proust in literature, the Impressionist painters and those who followed them, the sculptor Rodin. Until the Second World War, Paris was the creative capital of the world, while the French were at the forefront of the development of aviation and the motor car, and led advances in medicine and science with Pasteur and the Curies.*

Much of that radiance had evaporated by the end of the twentieth century, but the country that invented the moving picture housed a vibrant cinema industry. Frenchmen won Nobel prizes for literature

* See Chapter 10.

and economics in 2014. Economist Thomas Piketty's dense book on wealth and inequality, *Capital in the Twenty-First Century*, became an unexpected global bestseller in 2014, moving on 1.5 million copies.

The Hexagon between the Alps and the Atlantic, the English Channel and the Mediterranean was the world's leading international tourism destination. For many of its people, the French way of life remained without parallels, underpinned by extensive welfare services. Paris was still home to major fashion houses and retained a special sense of style. If French cuisine was no longer acknowledged as the world leader, a chef from the Charente-Maritime department cooking in Switzerland was voted the best chef on earth (though he shot himself dead six weeks later for as yet undetermined reasons).

Hourly productivity was higher than in Germany or Britain, even if the thirty-five-hour working week meant that it fared less well on a monthly basis. The birth rate was high for much of the twenty-first century (though falling off in 2015). Premature deaths among the middle aged fell by 25 per cent in a decade. France boasted a transport infrastructure that put many countries to shame. It was home to cutting-edge new technologies and ranked second to only the United States in developing the web-connected 'internet of things' that enable objects and machines to communicate with one another. All of which moved Manuel Valls to insist soon after becoming prime minister that 'French bashing' was 'honestly unsupportable' for such a 'very great country'.[32]

The state of the state

Once the initial shock had worn off, however, the terror set off a fresh bout of national soul-searching slotting into the wider malaise that counter-balances Valls' optimism. The division of France's security services into ten separate, and sometimes competing, organisations created loopholes and lack of co-ordination – but, bowing to the power of the intelligence baronies and the fear of creating too powerful a central overlord, Hollande decided to leave the structure in place. There were pointed questions about co-operation between European police and why the French authorities had not followed up on advance evidence from foreign intelligence services. Turkish officials said they had sent three alerts in the previous thirteen months, naming one of the Bataclan bombers, but that Paris had not responded. The day before the attacks, Iraqi intelligence warned that ISIS had ordered a campaign in Europe and that a sleeper cell was active in France; officials in Paris said the information was not specific enough for serious investigation. It then emerged that, in early November, a Montenegrin motorist was stopped by Bavarian police who found grenades, automatic weapons, dynamite and ammunition in his car; his navigation system was set for an address in Paris. The Germans did not inform the French. 'We have open borders, but not open information,' as a diplomat in Brussels told the *Financial Times*.[33]

Many of the terrorists – most of whom were petty criminals who had been arrested at one time or another – had been on lists of people to be kept under surveillance but had been able to journey to and from Syria. This raised doubts about the Schengen open borders system and the failure to control people coming into the European Union, especially given the huge refugee exodus from Syria. Opposition parties made much of their calls for tighter security and the way they had been rebuffed.

In practical terms, the closure of the frontiers announced by Hollande in the early morning of 14 November did not prevent Abdeslam's escape. In its first two months in operation, use of the emergency powers led to 2,700 police raids but only twenty-eight sentences, though more would be put under house arrest. In January 2016, thousands of people, mainly from far-left-wing groups, marched in Paris calling for an end to the state of emergency, but opinion polls showed far more supporting it though United Nations special rapporteurs on human rights expressed concern about 'excessive and disproportionate restrictions on fundamental freedoms'.[34]

There were also deeper arguments in France reaching to the heart of the state constructed since the first revolution. The issue of immigration and integration policies challenged traditional assumptions about the meaning of citizenship drawn from 1789 and developed by the subsequent revolutions of 1830 and 1848 and, above all, during the seventy years of the Third Republic from 1879 to 1940. The definition of the republic by the nineteenth-century philosopher Ernest Renan as 'a daily plebiscite' of people living together seemed to apply less and less. A nation that thought of itself as based on reason and common cultural norms found it hard to cope with citizens who preferred to occupy distinct communities and questioned those norms.

It was impossible to know how many first- and second-generation immigrants thought that the values of the republic in whose defence Hollande said the country was at war were not being properly applied to them as regards freedom, equality and fraternity. An amalgamation between Muslims as a whole and those who rejected the republic was clearly wrong, as moderate Islamic leaders insisted. But, equally clearly, there were those who regarded the French integrationist model as a form of servitude. That view might be voiced only by a small radical contingent but it certainly reached more widely; after the January attacks, the prime minister had spoken of a 'territorial, social, ethnic apartheid' and daily discrimination in the 'ghettos' of outer city areas.[35]

Religion and secularism became a central issue in what was really a far wider debate about national identity and should have been more about social conditions and inter-communal relations. The debate bred more intolerance. Members of radical Islamic groups harangued the education minister and Alain Finkielkraut. What was named the 'muslimisphere' became a feature of social media; when the Socialist deputy mayor of Avignon, a practising Muslim son of Algerian immigrants, criticised a co-religionist woman who violently censured the philosopher at great length on television, he was subjected to a flood of hate messages on Twitter, including one which said his address was being forwarded to ISIS.[36]

In a book which caused another storm, and aroused the prime minister's ire, the sociologist Emmanuel Todd categorised the solidarity marches after the *Charlie Hebdo* rallies in January as a great lie, not the deeply felt gesture of social, ethnic and religious unity in defence of tolerance but a display of middle-class domination, prejudice and Islamophobia, 'a sudden glimpse of totalitarianism' by a 'zombie Catholic' elite that wanted to despise Islam. The marchers, he went on, preferred authoritarian values to egalitarian ones, and were 'the new reactionaries shaping France's cultural politics' in demonising Muslims.[37]

There was fresh controversy at the end of the year. A proposal by Hollande to alter the constitution to strip French citizenship from those of dual nationality born in the country who were convicted of terrorist crimes aroused protests across the political spectrum from Socialist deputies to former centre-right prime minister François Fillon. Opinion polls showed 80 per cent support for the measure. Its impact would be minimal; terrorists about to launch an attack were unlikely to be deterred by the prospect of losing their French nationality. But critics saw it as an infringement of the universal nature of French citizenship and the Justice Minister, Christiane Taubira, a standard bearer for the left who would have had to steer the measure through parliament, was so affronted that she resigned from the government. Failing to unite his party behind him, in the spring of 2016 a grim-faced Hollande abandoned the measure. It was a major defeat, and his approval rating sank five points to 15 per cent as unemployment showed a record increase just a year before the 2017 presidential election.[38]

The debate and the question of whether the French were becoming Islamophobic had been brewing for years, given a special edge by the banning of religious symbols in public places, which seemed to be aimed especially against women wearing Muslim face coverings. As the Education Minister Najat Vallaud-Belkacem acknowledged in 2016 when she announced an overhaul of the way secularism was taught in schools, some pupils felt it was 'an aggressive attack on who they were'. All too easily the republic's core doctrine of secularism, or *laïcité*, which had been meant to ensure the freedom of all religions without a single dominant creed in a lay state, became a weapon against Islam.[39]

The left was horribly split. Secularism and republican values had long been its lay religion. But many prominent Socialists recoiled from the idea of being termed Islamophobes for criticising the religion invoked by the terrorists as they mowed down people in the Bataclan – the deputy mayor of Avignon had to wait for a week for grudging sympathy from his party. Valls, however, joined those who argued that 'Islamophobia' was being used as a cover for extremism, criticising the head of the official Observatory on Secularism, former Socialist minister and long-time presidential chief of staff Jean-Louis Bianco, for having put his name to an appeal for cross-religious unity whose signatories also included not only the Chief Rabbi but also people alleged to be close to the Muslim Brotherhood. 'You cannot co-sign calls, including calls that condemn terrorism, along with organisations that I view as participating in this atmosphere,' the prime minister told a Jewish conference.

To which Bianco responded by criticising those who sought 'to turn *laïcité* into an anti-religious and anti-Muslim instrument'. A sociologist who headed another watchdog body on religion then joined in to say that the stance taken by Valls meant 'you cannot say you are anti-Semitic but you can legitimately say you are Islamophobic'. The National Front seized on the debate to present itself as the great defender of secularism – though it was notable that it had nothing to say about traditionalist Catholics who held public prayer meetings against gay marriage and abortion approved by the state. (The mayor of Béziers, elected with Front support, paraded round the southern city's bullring in 2015 behind an effigy of the Virgin Mary to reaffirm the country's religious roots.)[40]

The dispute, however deeply felt, was far from the real problems France faced. It was hard to see when the terrorist danger would ebb. In early 2016, a senior counter-terrorism official told the French news agency AFP that the November attacks had been only a 'dress rehearsal' for wider terror offensive of simultaneous co-ordinated outrages in several countries. Valls said the emergency measures must remain in place 'until we can get rid of Islamic State'. As long as the threat was there, the prime minister added, 'we must use all means at our disposal' in 'a total and global war to the final defeat of the Isis-Daesh terrorist movement'.[41]

The material impact stretched into 2016. The presence of armed troops in city streets became a fact of life. Despite an international advertising campaign based on the French title of Ernest Hemingway's celebration of the city, *Paris est une fête* (*A Moveable Feast*), tourist numbers dropped sharply and business at the capital's restaurants, hotels and cafés fell significantly, as did attendance at theatres. The city's New Year fireworks display was even cancelled.[42]

Past and present

The triptych inherited from the first revolution of liberty, equality and fraternity no longer had quite the same ring. On the first of the cardinal principles France proclaimed as its bedrock, police could raid homes without a warrant or judicial procedures. On the second, a yawning gap separated those with jobs from those without them made all the more divisive by the high level of unemployment among the immigrant community and the discrimination felt by many of its members – anecdotes surfaced of Arabs and Africans finding it much easier to get job interviews when they applied under false European names, though prospective employers might be surprised when they turned up. Fraternity meant less with the growth of divisions in the supposedly unitary republic. In the new context, the concern of the president and prime minister about the 'apartheid' suffered by immigrants vanished in favour of a narrative that evoked, rather, the wars to defend the revolution of the 1790s, with ISIS improbably, replacing the royalist European powers of that epoch. In a sign of the new resolve, the government finally resorted to force in early 2016 to try to solve the long-running problem of the 'jungle' camp outside Calais inhabited by thousands of immigrants trying to get to Britain, sending in riot police to raze the shanty town.

But the fact that most of the terrorists and their helpers had been born and brought up in France or Belgium raised the question of how the 'war' was to be conducted. Bombing ISIS bases was simple; dealing with the seedbed for terrorism and the networks it spawned was far more complex. It was a matter that administrations of left and right had avoided for decades. They had always insisted on the need for immigrants and their offspring to integrate into the national way of life of the republic but riots by Arab and African youths had erupted repeatedly since the 1970s on housing estates in the outer suburbs of big cities, the *banlieues*, which counted some 4.4 million inhabitants by 2015 and became known as the 'lost territories of the republic' with high crime rates, frequent clashes with police and the ritual burning of thousands of cars at New Year. In the spring of 2016, the prime minister put the number of people who had gone to join ISIS by then at 600 – 170 had been killed and 300 had returned. Eight hundred more wanted to go, he added. Just over 2,000 French citizens belonged to Jihadist networks. These numbers raised the question of how much effect the increased bombing of ISIS bases in Syria would have on the terrorist threat since so much of the danger was now in France, itself. (There was also a lurking issue – which the government studiously avoided – of links with Gulf states that bought large quantities of French arms and invested in upmarket assets in the Hexagon while alleged to fund radical groups in the Middle East.)

What was plain was the way in which the year 2015 had not only faced the country with the stark challenge of terrorism but had also deepened questions about the nature of the republic and of society. The values under attack, drawn from the legacy of its modern history, were key to the nation's identity. But the questioning went beyond the killings and the challenges they posed .The way France was run and the way its people saw themselves and their nation was under examination.

In the aftermath of the student riots and general strike of May–June 1968, the new prime minister, Jacques Chaban-Delmas, had taken office with a speech warning that 'we live in a blocked society' which he attributed to three causes – 'the fragility of our economy, the often defective way the state works, the archaic nature and conservatism of our social structures'. He castigated 'proliferating regulation', 'ideological extremism' and self-protective castes.

Nearly half a century later, this analysis still rang true in the strength of a traditional mindset, highly attractive in many ways but ill-suited to deal with the harsher realities of the changing world around it. More than most nations, France carries the weight of its history in its view of itself. Here, the past is not another country but is vitally present, making its modern history crucial to understanding the France of today.

Introduction

THE LASTING LEGACY OF
THE REVOLUTION

The Revolution changed everything and forever, though not in the way its proponents intended; the heritage was far more complex. As it played itself out in the decade before Napoleon took power, this was, as Charles Dickens put it, the best and the worst of times. 'Bliss was it in that dawn to be alive,' wrote William Wordsworth in 1789. But the sequel three-and-a-half years later, as the king was executed and the Jacobins unleashed the Terror, created a fearsome warning of where populism directed by a ruthless political class could lead, the self-proclaimed guides of the people justifying themselves with claims to superior merit and wisdom in a manner that pre-figured twentieth-century totalitarianism to legitimise violence against foes, real or imagined. The Revolution was marked from its early days by factionalism made all the more murderous by the claims of the competing groups to embody ultimate goodness and reason. It all ended in the imperial rule of Bonaparte followed by the restoration of the Bourbon monarchy. Yet the Revolution gave France a new image of itself and set a template which would make the nation a beacon for progressives across Europe, with the overthrow of later Bourbon monarchs in 1830 and 1848 sparking revolts across the continent – and the countervailing evolution of conservative thinking that hardened into reaction.

The storming of the Bastille on 14 July 1789, and the events that followed, bred national narratives that gave France's modern history its ideological complexion over two centuries. Sovereignty passed from a monarch claiming to rule by divine right to the people, however defined.

The monarchical order, dating back thirteen centuries, was replaced by the rule of citizens that was secular, not religious. The certainties of the revolutionaries and the bitter opposition they aroused implanted mutual intolerance and a taste for conflict; vilification of opponents could be justified in the name of the search for virtue and truth or in defence of values held to be at the core of the national character and greatness. When a date for the main national holiday was chosen in the late nineteenth century, it was 14 July, Bastille Day, not 20 August, the Declaration of the Rights of Man. The national anthem, the Marseillaise, calls for patriots to soak the furrows of fields with the 'impure blood' of enemies. The republican figure of Marianne was anything but an apostle of fraternity or sorority as she led revolutionary heroes on the battlefield in Delacroix's iconic painting of the Second Revolution of 1830. The cockerel acts as another national symbol, rather than a less strident animal. In the home of reason, the two most celebrated French leaders of the twentieth century, Georges Clemenceau and Charles de Gaulle, are both celebrated for their achievements in wartime as much as in peace.[1]

France's enduring divisions – between left and right, Catholics and proponents of the secular state, centralisers and devolutionists – have deep roots in the mindsets of those who have seen 1789 and the ensuing events as the start of a new and glorious era and those who view it as having led to a distortion of the rule of reason*. There have, of course, been moments of great national unity around republican values – at the Liberation, against the military coup attempt in Algeria in 1961, in opposition to the success of the far right National Front at the presidential election of 2002, and in the huge nationwide demonstrations after the killing of seventeen people in Paris by Islamic terrorists in January 2015, including staff at the satirical magazine *Charlie Hebdo* and then customers at a Jewish supermarket, followed by the national outrage when 130 died and 380 were injured in a coordinated wave of attacks the following November. But these moments were rare and bred by shock, giving way to divisive politics within a relatively short time. More often, political and cultural certainties and behavioural patterns

---

* It is perhaps no coincidence that France was the main European home of Manichaeism, put down by crusaders who told their soldiers to 'kill everybody, God will recognise his own'.

developed since 1789, along with the cynicism bred from rhetorical overkill and the failure of politicians to deliver, have impeded constructive compromise, marking France's distance from the proposition of the British political thinker, Edmund Burke, that all government, benefits and enjoyment are 'founded on compromise and barter'.

Fundamental questions remain. Who has the right to rule and on the basis of what legitimacy? If politics are primordial, what form should they take – and in what framework? How can democracy coexist with effective executive government, and which should be given precedence? Does citizenship encompass the right of street protest by anybody choosing to claim to speak for the people? Is violence justified in the pursuit of revolutionary ideals or in suppressing them, as in the domestic conflicts of the nineteenth century, which took at least 60,000 lives? When do the people become the mob? Can the Rights of Man be implemented by force and does the pursuit of revolutionary purity justify purging opponents? Indeed, can one speak of 'man' as a generality in quest of improvement, or was the Savoyard, Joseph de Maistre, who took revolutionaries to be the servants of Satan, correct when he wrote that he had met Frenchmen, Italians, Germans and Russians but 'as for Man, I've never met one in my life'. Such issues apply to other countries, but, thanks to the Revolution, they have a lasting and special meaning in France that gives a special character to how the country functions.[2]

Left and right – 'a messy reality'

The left, which seeks its roots in the Revolution and the Enlightenment that preceded it, and the right, which was restored with the Bourbons in 1814–15, are political churches containing many different mansions. A Socialist prime minister, Michel Rocard, sought a simple division of the left into two different schools – one drawing on the centralising, strong state heritage of the Revolutionary Jacobins to enforce change, the other opting for decentralisation and regionalism with strong communities and local enterprises. A more recent writer, Jacques Julliard, in a 942-page book published in 2012, posited four strands – the liberal left, the Jacobin left, the collectivist left and the libertarian left. He then added 'the tranquil left' before identifying yet more lefts rooted in

Jesuitism and the seventeenth-century creed of Jansenism based on the idea of original sin, human depravity, predestination and the need for divine grace. On top of that were left-wing movements drawing on Voltaire, Rousseau, Robespierre, Danton and, from the second half of the twentieth century, Pierre Mendès France and François Mitterrand. Through such complexity, the core conflict remains between individual liberty and the search for a more egalitarian society.[3]

On the right, monarchism faded during the nineteenth century after the ousting of two Bourbon kings, but Napoleon III restored the Empire and some forceful republican leaders have been anything but of the left. For four years, the Vichy regime tried to impose a reactionary collectivist administration headed by a soldier in his dotage surrounded by a gang of conspirators of the right, some of whom sent Frenchmen to fight alongside the Wehrmacht on the Eastern Front. The demarcation between left and right has often been blurred; a general from a traditional background presided over widespread nationalisations and a big extension of the welfare state after the Liberation of 1944 while a Socialist-led government stepped up the war to keep Algeria French. If the Revolution itself was a confused process, so its lasting heritage in France's republicanism is, as one historian has put it, 'a messy reality'.

The execution of Louis XVI, the spectre of the guillotine (adopted at the urging of the doctor-politician Joseph-Ignace Guillotin in 1792 as a humane and egalitarian means of execution) and the totalitarian slaughter of the Terror directed by Maximilien de Robespierre mask the fact that by far the majority of those who perished between 1789 and 1815 did so in warfare with foreign nations, as France defended itself from anti-revolutionary powers and then launched its own campaigns culminating in the Napoleonic bid for European hegemony. In all, perhaps 1.5 million French people died; more than a third of boys born between 1790 and 1795 were killed or wounded. Compared to that, less than 1 per cent of the nobility were put to death.

For all the legacy of street action and the mob unruliness of the *sans-culottes*, the primary beneficiaries of the Revolution were the bourgeoisie, in their several forms, and richer peasants. They bought land confiscated from the nobility and the church cheaply and made the most of the relaxation of the commercial and professional restrictions of the old regime. Under the Directory, which followed the Terror, making money and keeping down the workers was the ruling group's prime concern. While claiming to defend the revolutionary heritage, Bonaparte's meritocratic autocracy ushered in a gilded society for the new rich who amassed assets and titles.

Although Enlightenment reasoning contained an atheistic strand and the church came under violent attack during the Terror, France remained a primarily Catholic nation. Despite the image of the *tricoteuses* sitting at the foot of the guillotine and knitting revolutionary caps between executions and despite the passage of a liberal divorce law, the revolutionaries and their successors saw women as belonging to the private sphere while men ran affairs of state. Olympe de Gouges, a butcher's daughter who published the *Declaration of the Rights of Women and the (Female) Citizen* in 1791, proclaimed that 'Woman is born free and remains equal to man in rights . . . the exercise of Woman's natural rights has no limits other than the tyranny of Man's opposing them', but ended up guillotined.[4]

The cost of recurrent wars tested state finances and boosted inflation, encouraging speculation and hindering capital investment in modernisation outside military suppliers. Old patterns of influence on local politics persisted. Some highly placed officials showed remarkable survival capacities as regimes succeeded one another, demonstrating how ideology coexisted with personal flexibility. The regicide Joseph Fouché became Napoleon's police chief and then a leading minister of the restored Louis XVIII in 1815, while Charles Maurice de Talleyrand, excommunicated as Bishop of Autun for his revolutionary activities, served as Bonaparte's foreign minister and as Louis XVIII's head of government before becoming Grand Chamberlain and ending up as ambassador to London after the Second Revolution of 1830. The Prefect of the Marne *département* held office from 1800 to 1838 and was made a baron by Bonaparte and a viscount by the restored monarchy. The longest distance runner of all, Nicolas Jean-de-Dieu Soult, fought as a commander in many of the emperor's great battles and was rewarded by being made Duke of Dalmatia, before rallying to Louis XVIII in 1814, re-joining Bonaparte as his chief of staff during his short-lived bid to regain power the following year and turning his coat once more to declare himself a dedicated royalist under the restored Bourbons. They, in turn, raised him to the rank of Marshal General of France, before he changed sides once more to ally with their successors under whom he became war minister and then served for ten years as chief minister. Finally, when the Second Republic was declared in 1848, he proclaimed himself a convinced republican and retired to his south-western estate to die in his castle at the age of eighty-two.

Despite the Jacobin search for greater national unity and centralisation, the France that emerged from the Revolution remained highly diverse, its heartlands living separately from one another, their inhabitants following ingrained traditions and conversing in patois. Western France and Eastern Alsace-Lorraine kept a conservative, Catholic identity, the central *départements* were moderate, parts of the south harboured dissidence on left and right, and Paris was potentially revolutionary.

The story of the Revolution might seem like a circular one with a Bourbon Louis back on the throne in 1815. But the quarter of a century after 1789 buttressed the claim to *l'exception française* that sets this nation apart from others with a distinct stamp which permeates at many levels to this day. The Hexagon between the Alps and the Atlantic, the Channel and the Mediterranean, Flanders and the Pyrenees saw – and sees – itself as the home of ideas and ideals with a global message to all those who seek liberty, equality and fraternity.

As well as giving us such everyday innovations as the metric system, the Revolution set out to forge a new kind of human being with the opening proclamation of the Rights of Man that 'Men are born and remain free and equal in rights' and its declaration that 'Liberty consists in the ability to do anything which does not harm others' as well as the statement, crucial for the concept of nationhood and popular rule, that 'the principle of all sovereignty resides in the nation. No body of men, and no individual, can exercise authority which does not emanate directly from it.'[5]

But the reality hardly lived up to such high ideals as the Revolution evolved in a series of hectic changes from constitutional monarchy, to the First Republic with the execution of the king and the Jacobin Terror, to the brief and more moderate Thermidorian interlude and the Directory to the Consulate in which Napoleon asserted his authority, leading in turn to his First Empire of 1804 to 1814, followed the next year by his attempted comeback in the Hundred Days. In all this, there was no Lenin, no Mao, but an unruly procession of leaders, feuding factions and shifting patterns of multi-faceted politics. That disruptive political pattern continued as Bonaparte gave way to the restored monarchy after which came another republic, the Second Empire, and then finally, with the four-year hiatus of the Vichy collaborationist regime during the Second World War, the installation of a republican system which became synonymous with the nation and has been described by the latest president as 'our most precious possession' founded on 'virtue, honesty and honour'.

Despite all the vicissitudes and upheavals of two centuries, this book will argue that common themes run through France's modern history, the main one being that a nation which takes its revolutionary and republican legacy as constituting its core values has never, in fact, fully digested that heritage because it has never wanted to shed its other, more conservative character. Look no further than the seat of the legislature which represents the republic – the National Assembly sits in the Palais Bourbon, with statues of *ancien régime* dignitaries facing the Seine; were it not for the tricolours, one might wonder if the building was not perpetuating the pre-revolutionary era. The past is a constant element in the present especially for a country as aware of its history as France and which so prides itself on its exceptionalism. But bringing the two into harmony is a problem hardly any easier at the start of the twenty-first century than it was at the end of the eighteenth.

The monarchy turns rotten

Never, wrote the nineteenth-century historian and politician Alexis de Tocqueville, 'was an event so inevitable and yet so completely unforeseen' as the Revolution. In the late eighteenth century, France was still the 'Great Nation' with a population of 26 million, more than twice that of Britain. It had the continent's largest army and had begun industrial modernisation with an extensive programme of road building. The court at Versailles still radiated the glory of the era of the Sun King, Louis XIV, who had died in 1715, even if his successor, Louis XV, was, in the words of one historian, 'a perpetual adolescent called to do a man's job'.[6]

Behind the pomp of Versailles, the regime had grown essentially stagnant and was embroiled in religious disputes and confrontations with the rising middle class, at the same time ceding territory abroad and suffering from insufficient tax revenues aggravated by multiple exemptions for the nobility and the Catholic church. Though there was progress in some sectors, France's economic dynamism fell behind that of Britain; manufacturing tended to be at the high and low ends of the market without the reliable mass-consumer goods being turned out across the Channel. Heavy protection of traditional sectors undermined technological innovation. The system generated resentment both from entrepreneurs who wanted commercial liberalisation and from the middle class who resented the way in which its social ascension was blocked by aristocratic privileges. There was deep anger at price manipulation by holders of state monopolies and by speculators. For the mass of the population, the *corvée* system of forced labour that subjected most males aged between twelve and seventy to work on building roads for up to forty days a year was widely hated, particularly when nobles gave priority to the construction and maintenance of roads to their châteaux. Country dwellers demanded the end of church tithes and of feudal laws restricting hunting and fishing.

But those who possessed old rights were determined to hold on to them and the upper clergy formed a bulwark of reaction. At the urging of two highly intelligent, energetic chief ministers, Anne-Robert-Jacques Turgot and the Swiss-born Protestant former banker Jacques Necker, the next king, Louis XVI, tried to strengthen central power. This ran into the opposition of the largely hereditary members of centuries-old regional *parlements*, which had been suspended since 1628, but now wished to re-assert themselves in defence of the rights of their members against more effective exercise of royal authority. So long as the throne had not interfered with them, the local nobility were prepared to accept absolutism, but the attempt to render centralised rule was highly unwelcome. The *parlement* in the Dauphiné in eastern France set the pace, with a meeting near Grenoble in the summer of 1788 to reject increased taxation and declare a regional constitution.

Faced with such a challenge and the bankruptcy of the state caused by the cost of intervention in the wars of American independence (the new republic refused to settle its debts), Louis showed what historian William Doyle sums up as his 'gaucheries and stupidities', abetted by the feckless, extravagant and 'lethally silly' Queen Marie-Antoinette in a system grown 'chaotic, inconsistent and self-contradictory'. As the salon hostess, Madame de Staël, put it, the monarch had a 'naturally timid intellect' and 'lacked the strength necessary to hold on to his power [making] people doubt his courage every time he was in need of it to drive his enemies back'. The classic novel *Les Liaisons Dangereuses*, by Pierre Choderlos de Laclos, cast a revealing light on libertine aristo-cratic morality, as did the Marquis de Sade and his sworn enemy in sexual fantasy, Rétif de la Bretonne.[7]

The elite of the nobility lived in a courtly bubble round the king at Versailles cutting itself off from its roots in the rest of the country and failing to establish links with the worlds of industry, commerce and finance. The monarchical system proved unable to deal with the evolu-tion of society and ideas, especially among the middle class, which absorbed the dissident ideas of the Enlightenment and wanted to exert its rights. The critical writings of Voltaire, Diderot, Rousseau, Montesquieu and other thinkers provided intellectual fodder for change and opposition to royal despotism, leading the historian Jonathan Israel to argue that the 'Radical Enlightenment' was the one 'big' cause of the events of 1789 and beyond, by providing the political and philosophical foundation for the revolutionary current.

This interpretation, and the importance ascribed to the political and ideological movement by the leading French historian François Furet, run counter to the earlier Marxist emphasis on economic issues such as the price of bread. But Furet was doubtful that the Revolution put into effect Enlightenment ideas, seeing its influence rather in the institu-tions that underpinned change, and regarding the Terror as inherent rather than a perversion by authoritarian populists. Another French writer, Roger Chartier, who sees the Revolution as the culmination of de-Christianisation and the creation of a 'public sphere' outside the authority of the state, wonders if it invented the Enlightenment, rather than the other way round. There is no final answer. Ideas, events, economics and institutions came together in a potent mix that the monarchy had neither the ability nor the will to resist.[8]

Its sacred status was subverted by pamphlets depicting scandalous conduct at court. Publication of allegations about the private lives of members of the royal family, ministers, mistresses and other public figures were part of the politics of character assassination. The king was alleged to be unable to satisfy his sexually voracious wife, who was accused of manifold personal immorality, depicted in cartoons as a cruel foreigner with the body of a tiger and a head writhing with serpents, or as an ostrich (in pun on the word Österreich referring to the queen's Austrian heritage) who 'could easily swallow silver but not the constitution' and loathed the people of France. A particularly juicy scandal broke over the affair of the 'queen's diamonds' involving a penniless aristocratic lady acting on behalf of a cardinal anxious to curry favour with Marie-Antoinette by presenting her with a 647-jewel necklace, a Sicilian confidence trickster and a prostitute impersonating the queen by moonlight.[9]

Popular disaffection was compounded by a string of bad harvests in different regions between 1784 and 1788–9 which doubled the price of bread. That reduced what people had left to spend on consumer goods and plunged manufacturing and industry into crisis. A free trade agreement concluded with Britain had a terrible impact on foreign commerce; the textile industry was particularly hard hit. Salaries were cut, unemployment shot up and demand fell further. Bankruptcies multiplied.

Riots against the price of bread spread across the country in early 1789 amid bitterly cold weather. Granaries and grain transports were pillaged. Farms, merchants and officials were attacked. Châteaux were assaulted. In Paris, a mob stormed the mansion of a wallpaper manufacturer, Jean-Baptiste Réveillon, who advocated lower bread prices that would allow wages to be cut and reduce manufacturing costs to stimulate demand.

Louis and his ministers sought to bypass the *parlements* with an assembly of selected dignitaries. But noble delegates refused to go along with this as a threat to their powers. Instead, they proposed the convocation of the Estates General, a body that had not met for two centuries, representing the aristocracy, the church and the Third Estate of the upper bourgeoisie and professionals, a quarter of them lawyers.

Seeing that this could produce a blocking coalition against reforms, Louis and Necker rejected the idea for a year, but then gave way. Meeting at Versailles in May 1789, the Estates divided into two camps, the representatives of the 25,000 members of the aristocracy ranged with the upper clergy against the Third Estate. The latter rested its case on a manifesto by a liberal priest, the Abbé Sieyès, who argued that it represented the nation and so was entitled to take France's destiny in hand; if the two other groups objected, they should be overruled.

The Third Estate was joined by 150 clerical delegates and 47 nobles including Philippe, Duke of Orléans from the cadet branch of the Bourbons, swelling it to 810 members. The throne declared the Assembly's resolutions null and void. A court official tried to get it to dissolve. 'We will leave our places only when forced to do by bayonets,' declared a forceful southern member, Honoré-Gabriel Rignetti Mirabeau. A crowd of Parisians converged on Versailles, where soldiers refused to fire on them.

To try to surf the growing storm, Louis ordered the nobles and clergy to join the Third Estate – only to change course once more by exiling Necker and replacing him with a favourite of the queen, the Baron de Breteuil, a vain aristocrat who, according to Madame de Staël, 'walked with a great noise, banging his feet as if he wanted to summon up an army from the ground'.[10]

Concerned about the threat of anarchy in the streets, the Assembly delegates formed what amounted to a provisional government and organised a National Guard to maintain order, headed by 'the hero of two worlds' the Marquis de Lafayette, who had played a notable role in the American Revolution. A mob attacked the customs wall round the city where taxes were levied on goods entering the capital. An angry crowd bearing looted arms marched on the mediaeval fortress of the Bastille, a symbol of royal power. Though guards opened fire, the governor surrendered, only to be beheaded. There were just seven prisoners inside.

News of events in Paris sparked revolt in a dozen provincial cities. Peasants pressed their demands for the ending of feudal privileges. Rumours of royalist troops marching to enforce the old order set off attacks on châteaux in order to destroy records kept inside which formed the legal basis for rents, restrictions and forced labour. The

National Assembly announced that it would end these aristocratic pre-rogatives; though peasants had to pay compensation and final abolition did not come till 1793.

In October 1789, six to seven thousand women armed with swords, pistols, muskets, lances, pitchforks and broomsticks marched on Versailles to protest at the price of bread (though it was now finally falling). They were followed by the National Guard. The king ordered increased grain supplies to the capital and approved decrees on the Rights of Man issued by the National Assembly. Wanting more, the crowd obliged Louis to return to Paris, which became the arbiter of the nation's politics.

The royalist camp imploded. The king's youngest brother, the Count of Artois, fled across the Alps to Savoy while the middle brother, the Count of Provence, decamped to the Austrian-ruled Netherlands. Executing yet another turn, the monarch donned the revolutionary red, white and blue cockade. The victors set up a committee to elaborate a constitution; to guard against the unbridled power of the people, martial law and a degree of press censorship were imposed. Further rebellion was punishable with death.

Though he had declared 'war on privilege and the privileged', Mirabeau tried to act as bridge between the king and the Assembly, taking money from court for his attempts to preserve some royal powers; his friend, the Abbé Grégoire, remarked that he had 'splendid talents and great vices'. A popular figure, Mirabeau died of natural causes in 1791. The limits of political change were evident in a city like Lyons where the electorate was restricted to 4,000 people of whom one-third were from the nobility or the professions, one-third made up of big merchants and one-third consisting of shopkeepers and artisans; less than 1 per cent of the workforce in the city's extensive silk industry were eligible to vote.[11]

France faced a slave revolt in its Carribean colony of Saint Domingue in April 1791, which would lead to the creation of the independent state of Haiti twelve years later. A good harvest helped to achieve temporary stabilisation and a degree of relaxation – the restaurateur Méot opened a luxurious Parisian establishment in a former ducal palace with more than fifty red and white wines. But the revolutionaries were running out of money to pay for government and meet debt obligations. They hit on the idea of raising funds by issuing bonds, known as *assignats*, to reflect the value of confiscated church properties. Intended to introduce 'freedom of money', there was no control of how many were printed, so they soon exceeded the real worth of the land on which they were meant to be based and lost their value as they stoked inflation.[12]

Then Louis made yet another ill-considered move on the night of 20 June 1791, trying to flee to lead a counter-revolutionary movement. Caught at Varennes in the Marne and returned to the Tuileries, he was pardoned on the spurious grounds that he had been abducted. Revolutionary leaders were divided over whether to keep him on the throne. Militia fired on demonstrators who were calling for his abdication, killing or wounding sixty.[13]

The constitutional committee had no alternative to monarchy; so it was Louis who proclaimed the new order three months after his attempted flight. This aimed to end royal despotism, eliminate aristocratic privileges and limit church power; priests became state employees. The document set out the notion of the general will, citizenship and the sovereignty of the nation. France's 40,000 Jews were emancipated, though colonial slavery continued. There was to be an elected parliamentary assembly. Institutions 'injurious to liberty and equality of rights' would be abolished. 'The revolution is over,' the king declared.

The First Republic

Far from it. The following year, to spread the gospel of change, to defend what had been achieved and to foster national unity, France declared war against Austria, the symbol of old Europe. What the historian Simon Schama has termed 'militarised nationalism' became a major strand of the Revolution, with a war economy and the raising of mass conscript armies accompanying growing radicalisation and calls for a republic. Fighting for the nation became a part of citizenship. Nationalism clashed with the ideal of universal harmony. If others did not like them, the principles of the Revolution had to be imposed by force which was justified by their inherent virtues. Negotiations had no place in the messianic mission; Lazare Carnot, the 'organiser of victory', proclaimed only two alternatives in war – one should 'wage it *à outrance*' (to excess) or go home'.[14]

The opening stage of hostilities was unpromising for the new regime in Paris. Prussia allied with Austria and a royalist army under the Prince de Condé based in Coblenz. Counter-revolutionaries staged risings inside France. One of the leaders of the royalist forces, the Duke of Brunswick, declared that the invasion was on behalf of 'the sane portion of the French nation'. The National Guard and revolutionaries stormed the Tuileries. Louis was deposed. France became a republic.[15]

Victories over the Prussians at Valmy and over the Austrians at Jemmapes safeguarded the young republic. A referendum with universal male suffrage approved the constitution. Yet renewed economic strains increased; a fresh rise in food prices provoked riots and looting as the *assignats* lost most of their value. In an outbreak of mindless violence, armed gangs massacred more than a thousand political prisoners, priests and convicts in Paris jails.

The rigorous adherents of the Jacobin Club, named after its meeting place in a convent, grew increasingly powerful under Maximilien de Robespierre, an unbending lawyer from Arras known as 'the incorruptible' who opposed the war. His associates in the revolutionary assembly of the Convention formed a cohesive group based on Parisian deputies, including the Duke of Orléans. Dubbed the 'Mountain', because of their seats in the upper tiers of the parliament, they were outnumbered by more moderate delegates of the 'Plain' lower down. But, better organised and more determined, they bested the more moderate main faction on the Plain, the federalist-minded Girondins or Brissotins – so named, in the first case, because leading members came from around that south-western river or, in the second, from their chief, Jacques Pierre Brissot, a lawyer and enthusiast for revolutionary war.

The fraught atmosphere and increasing radicalisation made the king's execution inevitable. For the cartoonists, he and his family had moved from being depicted as pigs to being shown as wild animals fit to be hunted down and slaughtered. 'Louis must die so that the nation may live,' Robespierre declared. The Convention voted for his death by 361 to 288, with seventy-two backing delaying measures – for revolutionary purists, the institution of monarchy needed to be liquidated; 'no one can reign innocently,' the Jacobin Saint-Just proclaimed. Among those voting for regicide was the Duke of Orléans, who had taken the name Philippe

Égalité and whose son fought in the revolutionary army at Valmy. From a crumpled piece of paper, he read a declaration of his concern to do his duty. The overall majority for execution was just one vote.[16]

On the morning of 21 January 1793, Louis was guillotined in the Place de la Révolution, his head held up as the crowd cheered – his wife went to the scaffold in November after a trial at which one accusation was that she had had sexual relations with her son. The heir to the throne was held in prison where he died in 1795, regarded by royalists as Louis XVII though he never reigned.

The king's execution heightened tension with royal European powers while the Jacobins stepped up their political purge, backed by a 20,000-strong revolutionary militia. The murder of the fiery Jacobin, Jean-Paul Marat, stabbed by the Girondin Charlotte Corday in the bath where he spent much of his time because of his severe skin disease, heightened the radicalism of Robespierre and the Committee of Public Safety, the main organ of government. A new constitution enshrined popular sovereignty and expanded social rights. The tricolour, in use since 1789 and combining the royal white with the red and blue ensign, was formally adopted as the national flag.[17]

There were positive moves in a focus on education, the abolition of slavery and a guarantee of secret voting at elections. Price controls were introduced to fight inflation. People addressed one another as '*tu*' in the second person singular. New terms entered the language as an instrument of linguistic politics and to reflect changing conditions*. Place names were changed to eliminate references to saints and kings. The use of French was promoted in place of the patois tongues which were held to foster reaction – a report by the Abbé Henri Grégoire propounded linguistic unification to make French the 'universal language' for Europe.

But the leadership perverted the thinking of the Enlightenment in the conviction that it had the right to impose one perfect fate for mankind, decided by any means it chose. Character assassination was used to bring down opponents accused of failing to live up to revolutionary requirements of virtue, selflessness and transparency. The

---

* For instance, the word 'aristocracy' which had previously applied to Greek and Roman antiquity.

accused were deprived of the right to defence lawyers or witnesses. The Terror can be traced, in part, to the paramount search for virtue and morality, but, more important than such high-minded reasons for mass 'punitive violence', was the desire of the rulers to establish a regime of fear in which nobody would dare to oppose them. The resulting paranoia, which assumed that anybody might be an enemy beneath a mask of virtue and hence deserve death, barely concealed ruthless power games.[18]

The main execution site in the capital moved from the Place du Carrousel in front of the Louvre to the Place de la Concorde and the Place de la Bastille before ending up at the Place du Trône-Renversé (Place of the Overthrown Throne, now Place de la Nation). Some 2,600 prisoners left the mediaeval Conciergerie prison between the beginning of 1793 and July 1794, to meet their deaths, 1,306 of them in forty days during the Terror, their bodies buried in mass graves in the garden of a nearby convent. Among those who perished at that time was Orléans, despite a desperate attempt to deny his royal birth by claiming he was the offspring of his father's coachman – when his son urged him to flee to America, he had replied 'Live with black men! Oh no ... at least here one has the Opera.'

The country went on to a war footing externally and internally. The *chouans** of the Army of Saints in the Vendée marched with primitive guns and pitchforks, wearing religious badges under white flags decorated with lilies and royalist slogans. After fighting twenty-one pitched battles against the revolutionaries in Paris who had ditched Catholicism for the state creed of the Cult of the Supreme Being, the rebels attacked Normandy in October 1793, their 30,000-strong army followed by hundreds of thousands of civilians. They headed for the port of Granville, where they thought a British fleet was waiting to join up with them. But there were no ships, and the ensuing retreat through the winter cold was a desperate affair with huge loss of life as the *chouans* were picked off by revolutionary troops under the ruthless General Westerman, and their civilian companions massacred. 'The Vendée is no more,'

---

* The term was taken from the nom de guerre, Jean Chouan ('the silent one'), adopted by a counter-revolutionary leader from the Mayenne department, Jean Cottereau.

Westerman told Paris. 'I have buried it in the woods and marshes ... I have trampled the children beneath our horses' feet; I have massacred their women ... I do not have a single prisoner to reproach me. I have exterminated them all.'[19]

The power of the central government greatly increased. A revolutionary calendar was introduced. Robespierre and his colleagues, including Saint-Just, the 'Angel of Death', declared the primacy of the 'Single Will' interpreted by them to guide the nation. Private life was taken over by the state – children 'belong to the Republic before they belong to their parents', as Georges Danton put it before he lost his head, accused of having conspired against the Revolution, a man who certainly had dubious associations but who became a victim of the paranoia and blood lust driving the Incorruptible and his fellow zealots. Brissot went to the scaffold, with twenty-one colleagues from the Plain. Official records put the death toll at 16,500; many more perished before execution.

Central government emissaries were sent out with draconian powers to beat the provinces into line, especially where they had shown federalist tendencies that countered the Jacobin drive for centralisation. In some departments, the agents from Paris seized grain and farm animals, provoking famines while arresting priests and melting down church bells. In the Ardèche, anybody travelling without a passport or staying with hosts without informing the authorities was subject to arrest. In Arles, the local committee wrote of the crusade against federalist foes that 'One must be without pity for scoundrels of this type.' Several thousand priests were starved to death on prison hulks in the harbour of Rochefort. In Nantes, the hard-drinking Jean-Baptiste Carrier had 2,000 captured rebels shot or guillotined; to speed things up, 4,000 more were put on boats sunk in the Loire to drown them. Another 3,000 died of typhus in jail.

The reaction was fierce and widespread, showing the complex strands of national life. Lyons, France's second city, was a particular problem for Robespierre and his colleagues. Voters there gave 80 per cent backing to a Girondin mayor, but he resigned when confronted with a Jacobin majority on the municipal council. While some local priests made their peace with the regime, others organised resistance to anti-church measures decreed from Paris, leading crowds of mainly female faithful in meetings which Jacobins tried to break up. The Temple of Liberty was attacked and the bust of Rousseau removed as demonstrators chanted 'Long live Louis XVI! Down with the council!' In the early summer of 1793, the Girodins set up their own local administration, put Jacobins in jail and went into open opposition, declaring adherence to 'a one and indivisible Republic, Resistance to oppression, Full and free national Representation'.

An army sent by Paris besieged the city, occupied the high ground on its outskirts and forced the surrender of the rebels in October. One of Robespierre's most zealous associates, the former seminarist turned violent anti-clerical Joseph Fouché, supervised a reign of terror in which 2,000 people died following summary trials without any appeals. After the executions and the tearing down of 'the buildings of the rich', Fouché announced 'Lyons made war on Liberty. Lyons no longer exists'. The city lost some 20,000 manufacturers and workers. The surrounding region was prey to anarchy and lawlessness. The legacy was one of alienation from the Revolution and a rejection of Parisian centralisation that flared up through the following decades.[20]

There were also federalist risings against the Jacobins in Bordeaux and Marseilles, where a counter-revolutionary council took charge, guillotined a dozen followers of Robespierre and established links with Nîmes, Toulouse and other rebellious centres. Troops from Marseilles captured Avignon, which changed hands four times before being brought under control by forces loyal to Paris. Aix-en-Provence also veered into insurrection. In the summer of 1793, royalists in Marseilles conducted negotiations with the British fleet. But a Jacobin army took Aix and then surrounded the port city where anti-royalist groups fought the guards in a series of clashes which observers noted were suspended at meal times. At the end of August, the defenders of Marseilles gave up and the royalists fled. Hundreds were executed.[21]

Along the coast in Toulon, royalists took over, proclaiming allegiance to the king's brother, the Count of Provence. But they had little popular support and came under growing British influence; their agreement to hand over the major naval port to the English cast them as traitors. A revolutionary army marched on the city, pummelling it with cannon fire directed by the rising young officer, Napoleon Bonaparte. At the end of 1793, the attackers took Toulon and exacted revenge – the number of people shot has been put at anywhere from 600 to 1,100 while 2,500 fled.[22]

Some regions escaped such rigours. In the Dauphiné in the east, the jails were filled with political prisoners, but only two priests were guillotined in Grenoble and the father of the writer Stendhal, who was sought as an enemy of the regime, merely hid in his grandfather's home for the duration. 'In the High Alps,' as a local historian remarked, 'moderation turned into lukewarmness'. In Périgord, expelled priests returned to their parishes where the people welcomed them; the guillotine in the square in Périgueux executed only twenty enemies of the revolution.[23]

Still, Fouché declared that 'Terror, salutary terror, is the order of the day. We are causing much impure blood to flow, but it is our duty to do so, it is for humanity's sake.' Mercy, declared Westerman, was 'not a revolutionary sentiment', a statement he might have recalled when he, too, was beheaded. The model of a modern totalitarian terrorist state had been born in a terrible perversion of the ideal of the perfectibility of mankind.[24]

But there was a limit. When Robespierre pleaded for another round of bloodletting to the Convention in July 1794 with a wild speech which suggested he intended to launch a purge of his colleagues, he was met with an ominous silence. Fouché and Carrier both turned against him as a coup took shape within the Convention against its leader. 'The Revolution is frozen,' said Saint-Just. 'All its principles are grown weak. There remain only intriguers sporting the red cap of liberty.' The following day, 'the Incorruptible' and his lieutenant were arrested, and executed twenty-four hours later. As the reaction gathered force, the most rigorous phase of the revolution was over, and France went into one of the political shifts that would mark the next two centuries as the new rulers adapted the constitution to suit them.

The date in the revolutionary calendar gave the new phase its name, 9 Thermidor. Ninety leading Jacobins were executed and others were deported to the penal colony of Guyana. Hundreds more in prisons in southern cities were massacred. Robespierre was vilified as a monster guilty of everything from cannibalism, orgies and torture to making shoes of his victims' skins and feasting on expensive exotic fruits at times of shortages; his northern accent, provincial ways and excessive long speeches were mocked. After four months, a five-man Directory concluded peace agreements in the Vendée that allowed freedom of worship and guaranteed property – peasants who signed up were given back their cows.[25]

The new rulers installed an administration to benefit themselves and their principal supporters, notably by guaranteeing the purchase of property confiscated from nobles or the church by landowners, businessmen and professionals. The *assignats*, which had become virtually worthless, were replaced by *mandats*, a currency in the form of land warrants, and price controls were lifted, leading to a new bout of hyperinflation. Universal male suffrage was swapped for a more restricted franchise. A bicameral legislature was established with a controlling Council of Elders. The economy was liberalised; when price rises sparked a revolt in Paris, 20,000 troops imposed order and the leaders of the rebellion were bought off. The link between wealth and political rights was explicit. 'We must be governed by the best men; those most suited to govern are men of good education and endowed with great concern for the maintenance of order,' as François-Antoine Boissy d'Anglas, a prominent spokesman for the new order, explained. 'You will rarely find such men outside the ranks of those who hold property.'

The Directory's prescription was in tune with a nation exhausted by the events of the past five years. Smart salons flourished in Paris. One was hosted by the beautiful Thérésa Tallien, whose survival reflected the vicissitudes of the age. At fourteen, she had been married to an Old Regime aristocrat described as 'old, red and ugly', and was then saved from the guillotine by a commissioner of the Convention whose mistress she became and whom she subsequently wed – a flamboyant character of a liberal disposition, she was said to bathe in the juice of strawberries and appeared at the Opera with no underwear beneath her white silk dress. Juliette Récamier, whose marriage to a rich banker thirty years her senior as a fifteen-year-old was unconsummated, held more intellectual and literary gatherings, nurturing friendships that lasted over three decades with the Swiss woman of letters, Germaine de Staël, the political thinker Benjamin Constant and the royalist-romantic writer and politician François-René de Chateaubriand. Young followers of fashion adopted affectations to set themselves apart from the common people including dropping the use of the letter 'r' from their speech since they considered it vulgar.

A landing by royalists in Brittany and a royal rising in Paris got nowhere. On the other side of the spectrum, a conspiracy led by the proto-Communist Gracchus Babeuf was easily quashed – thirty plotters were summarily shot and Babeuf guillotined. A march by 12,000 Jacobins from Toulon to try to free comrades imprisoned in Marseilles was met with a wave of arrests, murders and summary trials.

Constitutional monarchists were big winners in elections in 1797. Some nobles who had fled abroad felt it safe to return. But the administration's economic policies, its self-interest and the widespread corruption made it increasingly unpopular. Leading royalists were arrested. The Jacobins staged an electoral revival. Orléanist Bourbons plotted.

The return of empire

The army became increasingly important with victories in Italy and the Netherlands against a coalition of Russia, Britain, Turkey, Sweden and Austria. The campaign of the rising young Napoleon Bonaparte in Egypt, following his decisive intervention to regain the port of Toulon from the British and a successful campaign in Italy, added an exotic note, carefully spun by its commander for positive publicity. Abbé Sieyès, originator of the philosophy of the supremacy of the Third Estate and who had become a director in May 1799, schemed for a *coup d'état* fronted by the military, which would then retreat to its barracks. He was joined by Joseph Fouché, the one-time Terrorist, and Talleyrand.

After two generals rejected their scheme, the thirty-year-old Napoleon took up the role proposed by the Abbé. The epitome of a man on a white horse arriving to save his nation, he was unabashed by the relative failure of his expedition to Egypt with its inconclusive outcome on land and Britain's naval victory in the Battle of the Nile. His brother, Lucien, got parliament to adopt a constitution creating a three-man Consulate to which the Directory transferred power. Asserting himself as the dominant figure, Bonaparte was confirmed as First Consul by a referendum in February 1800 – the official approval rate was 99.9 per cent. 'The Revolution is established on the principles which began it,' the consuls declared in an echo of Louis XVI nine years earlier. 'It is ended.'

However, as he moved from consul to emperor and launched endless military campaigns to assert French hegemony, Napoleon presented himself as the heir of 1789 who would spread the universal values of the Revolution across the continent. He sought popular approval through plebiscites to assert the popular basis for rule laid down in the Rights of Man, however rigged the vote. But he was also ready to compromise to buttress his position.

He reached a Concordat with the Vatican, which recognised Catholicism as 'the religion of the great majority of the French people' while providing a quid pro quo in state control over bishoprics and parishes. Though a man of war, he made diplomatic accords when it suited him, such as the division of Europe with Russia at his meeting with the Tsar on a raft on the River Niemen in 1807 and his marriage three years later to Marie-Louise of Austria, after he had jettisoned the love of his life, the childless Josephine de Beauharnais, in quest of an heir born to a wife from an older empire. Their religious wedding reproduced the last royal marriage, of Louis XVI, down to the last detail, in keeping with the upstart's desire to buttress his claims by drawing on the past.

The son of minor Corsican nobility, Bonaparte was the first modern nationalist despot. Enamoured of war, he asserted authority through the machinery of the state, run by a highly efficient staff. Teetering on the edge of megalomania at times, he became the template of ambition: 'What a novel my life has been!' he exclaimed. He might have used the rhetoric of national liberation, but his huge empire was always dominated by France, with some constituent parts ruled by members of his family and expected to adopt French ways. His energy was formidable and his ambition meant he was unable to accept that anything was beyond him. His unequalled heritage included the legal code, which became the core of the way France worked, the prefectorial administrative system, the central bank, the national audit office and elite administrative colleges; half the administrative rules still in force date from his era. The franc was introduced, ending the spiral of inflation. Grand buildings went up, including the church of La Madeleine and the palace that would become the National Assembly, together with covered markets, fountains, canals and slaughterhouses.

State schooling was expanded by *lycées* run from Paris. The *départements* created in 1790 to replace the old regions became more important administrative instruments under their imperial Prefects. The nation's top decoration, the *Légion d'honneur*, was first awarded to 2,000 troops at a grand ceremony in the camp outside Boulogne set up for the planned invasion of Britain. His claims briefly reached as far away as Australia, where an imperial fleet named the south-east coast Napoleon's Land with a gulf called after him and another dedicated to Josephine.[26]

The Corsican's great victories were military masterpieces, and still give their names to Parisian landmarks. Fifty of his sixty battles ended in victory. His meteoric rise from the rank of captain at the age of twenty-two to emperor at thirty-five, at the head of a highly personalised regime that sought to conquer Europe, created the image of a superman and bequeathed a powerful Napoleonic cult. Only Russia, Britain, Scandinavia and the European domains of the Ottomans escaped his imprint at one time or other. His greatest victory, at Austerlitz in 1805 against a coalition of Austria, Britain, Russia and their smaller allies, led the following year to the end of the Holy Roman Empire as it ceded territory in Italy and Bavaria to France, which reorganised wide areas of central Europe to its liking.

However, his ambition and the fear he aroused meant he faced formidable coalitions of opponents backed by British cash and naval supremacy, even if such alliances were hard to hold together. He lusted for battle – as one historian has put it, he could never see a jugular without going for it in his quest to make himself the equal of Caesar and Alexander. However, his brilliant individual victories did not translate into successful long-term campaigns – rather akin to his amorous performance, if rumour was to be believed. He had to have everything and rejected opportunities to consolidate gains with a lasting settlement because, in the words of one recent biographer, he 'simply could not bring himself to accept what he saw as a humiliating peace'.[27]

Napoleon's constant military ventures exhausted France and resulted in the deaths of the vast majority of more than a million French people killed in wars and internal violence between 1789 and 1815. The cross-Channel landing, for which more than 120,000 men were assembled in 1805, was never undertaken – the army marched south instead to win its greatest victory at Austerlitz. His protectionist measures weakened the economy and were countered by a stronger British blockade. The invasions of Spain and Portugal ended in defeat. Napoleon's treaties were short-lived. Agreement with the Tsar at Tilsit did not prevent the invasion of Russia in 1812 with more than half-a-million men, which became a disaster in the face of the elusive enemy tactics, the terrain and the winter – just under 100,000 came back. Marriage did not stop Austria joining the sixth coalition against France and sending forces to the Battle of Leipzig in 1813, the biggest European encounter before the First World War, at which the imperial army suffered 45,000 dead or wounded.

By then, the economy was paying a big cost for two decades of hostilities. Desertions increased; when British troops marched on Toulouse in 1814 they were welcomed and the defenders had to retreat. The novelist Henri Beyle, better known as Stendhal and an admirer of the emperor, saw a nation 'profoundly ill at ease with itself'. Still, Napoleon continued to pursue victory until his marshals turned against him as Allied forces entered France. His one-time foreign minister, Talleyrand – 'the shit in the silk stocking' as the emperor put it – was now Chairman of the Senate and negotiated with the enemy on his own account. Cornered, Bonaparte abdicated on 6 April 1814. In return, he kept his imperial title, was granted an annual income of 2 million francs and was given sovereignty over the Mediterranean island of Elba for which he sailed at the end of the month.[28]

PART 1

RESTORATION AND REVOLUTION

1815–1848

1

RESTORATION

Since both the republican and imperial models were discredited and unacceptable to the victorious Allies, a royal restoration was inevitable; the victor of Waterloo, the Duke of Wellington, warned that there would be no peace in Europe unless the Bourbons mounted the throne again. The Congress of Vienna, held to define European frontiers after two decades of war, reversed Napoleon's conquests but was otherwise generous to France after Talleyrand inserted himself into the deliberations; in a sign of flexibility among recent adversaries, Britain and Austria allied with France to block a Prussian attempt to absorb Saxony.

However, the new monarch who called himself Louis XVIII in deference to his nephew who had died in prison two decades earlier, made a poor fist of it on his return from exile in Britain in May 1814. The corpulent 59-year-old king surrounded himself with appointees who had been out of government business for more than two decades. His principal minister, the Count of Blacas, was a minor noble who devoted himself to building up a fortune, arousing wide unpopularity and lacking authority. The army was alienated by the appointment of royalists for loyalty rather than ability, and the sacking of veterans who had borne the standard of Napoleonic glory. The monarch's influence was undercut by his reactionary brother, the Count of Artois, and his circle of supporters set on revenge for the Revolution. Louis was unperturbed. As Paris amused itself with balls, he said he slept as well as in his youth.

This complacency was shattered on 26 February 1815, when Bonaparte escaped from Elba to stage an attempted comeback, reaching Paris on 20 March after getting a mixed but generally not unfriendly reception across the country. Louis fled as Napoleon raised a 125,000-strong army and attracted figures who had temporarily sided with the king. A referendum approved a constitution drawn up by the political theorist, Benjamin Constant, though the abstention rate was very high. Seeing a quick and decisive battlefield victory as the way to gain recognition from the Allies, Bonaparte launched his army across the north-eastern border to confront the British and Prussians. The resulting battle at Waterloo on 18 June 1815, was, as Wellington remarked, 'the nearest run thing you ever saw in your life', but defeat dethroned France as a great European power. The universe changed direction, Victor Hugo would judge. More to the point, France had had enough of its emperor. Even if he had not lost at Waterloo, Bonaparte's days would have been numbered. His enemies were simply too strong, France too weakened and his political support too frayed.[1]

Escaping from the rout of his army, Napoleon regained Paris and put on as brave a face as he could. 'All is not lost,' he declared while taking a bath in the Élysée Palace. But the Chamber of Deputies obliged him to abdicate, and he threw himself on the mercy of the British, ending up in his second exile on the bleak South Atlantic outpost of St Helena.

The universe changes direction

The crowds cheered as Louis XVIII was driven in his carriage to the Tuileries Palace in the centre of Paris on 8 July 1815 with a small escort of old followers. The king wore a white wig and his face looked red and glum. A National Guardsman kissed his hand. Referred to by supporters as *le Désiré* (the Desired One), Louis made his Parisian palace, with its succession of halls and apartments stretching down what is now the rue de Rivoli to the Louvre, facing gardens laid out by the great designer Le Nôtre, the centre of festivities that summer. Balls were held at night outside – when the authorities tried to stop them to protect the lawns, the monarch called from the window 'Dance on the grass!' The surrounding buildings were illuminated at night. There were firework displays. Musicians strolled the streets and a charity kitchen fed the poor in the Saint-Antoine district. The Treaty of Paris signed with the victorious Allies assured Parisians that they would 'continue to enjoy their rights and liberties'.

The restored monarch went to see plays at the Comédie-Française and, each morning, courtiers gathered to listen to his stories as he sat in a large armchair and gave them every opportunity to agree with his high appreciation of his wit. Rejecting Napoleon's view that he should exercise despotic rule, he fancied himself as father of the people, refusing to be 'king of two Frances'. A royal proclamation issued a week after Waterloo set out his intention 'to call round our paternal throne the immense majority of Frenchmen whose fidelity, courage and devotedness have brought such pleasing consolation to our heart'.[2]

With a charter setting out rights for the richer sections of society, Louis sought to win over bourgeois liberals and some Bonapartists, though democracy was still far off with an electorate limited to 75,000 men. A police report told him that barely 10 per cent of the French favoured a return of the *ancien régime*. As the writer Charles-Louis Lesur put it in 1817, however deplorable its excesses, the Revolution would 'leave for ever great models as well as salutary lessons'.[3]

Voting for the Chamber of Deputies was on a rolling basis with staggered five-yearly polls. A new upper house mixed old and new figures. Civil rights, religious toleration and press freedom were guaranteed. Conservatives were reassured that 'abuses' would be controlled by Article 14 of the Charter, which enabled the crown to decree ordinances for state security in times of danger. Most important for the middle class and richer peasants, the purchase of land taken from aristocrats and the church was left in their ownership.

Still, the king showed the limits of his tolerance by insisting on the white royal flag in place of the tricolour and dating his reign from the death of his nephew. Royal statues were restored. Streets and squares reverted to old names. Church building underlined the monarchy's identification with Catholicism. The column erected by Napoleon to his glory in the Place Vendôme was torn down.

Louis insisted all power had to devolve from the throne, even if he chose to allow others to exercise it on his behalf. Citizens were to revert to being subjects. It was he who granted the constitution rather than accepting one drawn up by parliament. Ministers needed majority backing in the Chamber but, when they presented proposals to the throne, they said simply, 'Here is our opinion' to which the sovereign replied, 'Here is my will'.

Property owners might be reassured but the outlook was distinctly unpromising for their fellow countrymen. The army, wounded and humiliated, was kept south of the Loire by the Allies. The demobilisation of hundreds of thousands of troops swelled the underclass. Ex-soldiers joined outlaw bands that roamed the countryside.

The restored king and his ministers were subject to the dictates of the Allies, represented in Paris by Wellington and Castlereagh for Britain, Metternich for Austria, the Tsar Alexander for Russia and the 72-year-old Prussian Marshal Blücher whose intervention had been decisive at Waterloo. They had at their command an occupation army of 150,000 men. The tents of the invaders stretched along the Champs-Élysées and frequently drunken British troops reeled through the streets mocking Louis as 'an old bloated poltroon' or referring to his liking for oysters by calling him 'Louis des huîtres'.

Some foreign national treasures, which French armies had seized on their conquests, were reclaimed; a French observer recorded Wellington mounting a ladder to help take pictures down from walls. The Allied commander also annoyed farmers by importing his pack of hounds and hunting with them over fields without warning or compensation for the damage caused; eventually, when protests swelled, he gave the dogs to Louis XVIII.

The Prussians were the most set on revenge, looting at will. Occupying the Place du Carrousel at the end of the Louvre, they trained their cannons on the royal palace. Blücher proposed to blow up the Pont d'Iéna over the Seine commemorating Napoleon's victory over Prussia in 1806, but Louis XVIII said he would go to the bridge to share its fate; hurrying to the scene, Talleyrand offered to change its name to the Pont de l'École Militaire, calculating that, once the invaders were gone, it could revert to Iéna. Most tellingly, Wellington

Louis XVIII: Le Désiré

Louis Stanislas Xavier Bourbon, grandson of Louis XV and brother of Louis XVI, became heir to the throne when Louis's ten-year-old son died in prison in 1795, probably of tuberculosis. Born in 1755, he had been a frustrated figure as Count of Provence, dabbling in business but politically powerless. Fleeing Paris in 1791, he joined émigrés across the Rhine who participated in the abortive invasion of France. Then came fifteen years wandering round Europe, including two years in remote Courland in the Baltic, after which he came to rest for seven years in England.

Always interested in money, he returned to France in 1814 with a British loan arranged by the Rothschilds. After his second Restoration, he received 25 million francs a year voted by the Chamber of Deputies as well as owning six palaces and royal workshops such as the porcelain factory of Sèvres.

A heavy eater whose only exercise was whist and billiards, he grew extremely fat. His eyes were strikingly black. Though usually calm, he could fly into sudden violent rages. In his sixties, he suffered from diabetes, severe gout, varicose veins and skin ulcers.

His marriage to Marie-Joséphine of Savoy was a distant, childless affair – she suffered two miscarriages. An intelligent woman with a sharp tongue, she was ugly, washed rarely and became a heavy drinker. Her husband had a succession of close and witty women friends including the clever Madame de Balbi, whose husband was in a lunatic asylum and who shared his taste for cards, and the well-rounded, amusing and somewhat fierce Countess of Cayala. A contemporary observer quoted the queen as saying that these relationships remained chaste. When asked to give sexual instruction to a royal duchess, she commented, 'If I tell her only what the King taught me, she will not know much.'

Louis was essentially an Old Regime moderate who wanted to avoid trouble. For the writer-politician René de Chateaubriand, his virtue lay in his patience and how he let events come to him – 'he understood his age and was a man of his time'. But Byron wondered if Louis really wanted:

To rule a people who will not be ruled.
And love much rather to be scourged than schooled?[4]

posted a British soldier on the bridge, correctly guessing Blücher would not risk blowing him up.[5]

The economy was in a sorry state, aggravated by financial indemnities to the Allies including meeting the cost of the occupation. Parts of eastern France had been ruined by fighting; in the historic centre of Laon, 280 of 350 homes had been destroyed. National output was below that of 1789; production in Marseilles was 25 per cent lower than at the outbreak of the Revolution. Farming was stagnant. The beetroot industry, encouraged by Napoleon to ensure home-grown supplies of sugar, went bust as imports from the West Indies resumed. There were few big factories; the most advanced city, Paris, was a web of small workshops and artisans doing piecework. Annual coal output was 800,000 tons compared to 17 million tons in Britain. Metallurgy remained stuck where it had been in 1789. British entrepreneurs used their techniques to set up a thriving lace industry round Calais, and an iron foundry and gas works outside Paris.

Barter was common in rural areas. For the better-off, income from land and interest from state securities took precedence over other forms of investment. Trade was at half the level of the mid-1780s. High duties raised the price of imports and manufactured goods were generally not competitive abroad. Falling exports hit port cities hard – the population of Bordeaux had dropped by a third since pre-Revolutionary days and grass grew on the quays. Industrial production in Marseilles was 25 per cent lower than at the outbreak of the Revolution, but the port still received several thousand cargo ships a year and its energetic Greek merchant community conducted commerce with the Levant in cotton, wool, horses, wheat and dried vegetables; one trader, who had a concession from the Pasha of Egypt, made a million francs in profit in 1817.[6]

Banking and finance were hindered by regulation and an unadventurous spirit. Only seven shares were quoted on the Paris stock exchange. When the banker, Jacques Laffitte, proposed to create a company to take deposits to fund credit, the Conseil d'État rejected the idea. Though the state debt was low, government credit was limited and capital remained scarce. The new regime was obliged to raise funds by a forced loan and pawning royal forests, but still faced a budget deficit of 300 million francs and its ability to pay the indemnity to the Allies was in doubt, meaning that the occupation would drag on.[7]

The Catholic church had been the biggest loser of the Revolution in terms of property and influence; nearly all its 4–5 million hectares of land holdings had been confiscated and mainly sold off, compared to an estimated half of those of the nobility. The priesthood had been reduced by more than 20,000 during the anti-Christian crusade from 1789 to 1793 and had not recovered significantly. So it now lost no time in seeking to restore its ranks. Ordinations rose from 900 to 2,500 a year and the number of nuns doubled to 25,000.[8]

Some felt that the church should ally itself with the cause of liberty and progress – the prominent priest and philosopher Hugues-Félicité de Lamennais preached theocratic democracy. But most clergy were loyal to the traditional fusion of church and royal state as the priesthood played a role similar to that of the army under Napoleon in terms of jobs and career advancement for young men without wealth to support them. The importance of the family was stressed. Divorce was banned in 1816; a right-wing deputy castigated it for creating 'a veritable domestic democracy [which] allows the wife, the weaker sex, to rise up against marital authority.'[9]

Despite its sufferings and exile during the Revolution, the nobility still possessed at least a fifth of all land – some aristocrats who fled abroad had used agents to secretly buy property requisitioned from their peers or from the church. On their estates, they tapped in to pro-royalist sentiment among peasants and smallholders who had been alienated by taxation and conscription under the Jacobins and the Empire. In regions like the Gard, Ardèche, Aveyron and Lozère, as well as the Vendée, they drew on rural anti-capitalist, anti-bourgeois, anti-Protestant sentiment, conjuring up rose-coloured memories of paternalistic *ancien régime* welfare to buttress their authority while cutting themselves off from progress.

In towns and villages alike, life was harsh for most people, 60 per cent of whom were illiterate. Bad water and lack of hygiene spread disease. Despite the efforts of the Jacobins to encourage national education, most people outside the Paris area communicated in the local patois; the port city of Toulon was known as 'the northern colony' because it was the only southern town where the national language was spoken by a majority of inhabitants. There were great empty, silent spaces. Stepping down from a coach at a staging post only thirteen miles from the provincial capital of Bourges in central France, Stendhal was struck by the sense of 'complete isolation' while, a little later, the German poet, Heinrich Heine, found Brittany 'a wretched, desolate land where mankind is stupid and dirty'. The Landes in the south-west was known as 'our Sahara', a great deserted region where a travelling official recorded that 'for several hours, I saw nothing but flat country varied by thickets of briar, and now and then, by a forest of pines on the horizon ... the only inhabitants a few rare shepherds perched on their long stilts.'[10]

Rural people faced the continuous threat of bad harvests and hunger. Much of the countryside, where 90 per cent of the population lived, was a backward patchwork of small farms, hamlets and country towns, isolated by poor communications, high hills and mountains, wide rivers, swamps and forests. Lack of transport and paved roads impeded the distribution of food and goods, and farmers held on to what they had for fear of famine. Meat was rare – a pig had to last a family for a year. Peasants depended on the local nobility or teachers and priests to mediate with the authorities on their behalf and lacked the concept of a world beyond their immediate surroundings. Some men escaped to become day labourers in towns or travelling pedlars, but women were confined to the most humdrum, restricted existences.

Poverty and backwardness was most marked south of a line from the border of Normandy and Brittany at St-Malo across to Grenoble in the Alps. North and east of this, people were generally taller, fitter and better educated. They also had better road communications. But even in this more evolved half of France, disparities were great and poverty widespread. Most inhabitants of big cities died without leaving any assets. Urban workers huddled in slums, prey to disease and exploitation or, in the capital, in filthy shanty towns for migrant workers outside the city walls.

Diplomatic recovery

From the British embassy on the rue du Faubourg-Saint-Honoré, Wellington acted as a pro-consul. He oversaw the choice of a government headed by Talleyrand, despite the king's dislike for him. Given his sinuous record as servant of the Revolution and Empire and then a go-between with the Allies, nobody trusted the gout-ridden survivor, but he seemed the best pilot in uncertain times. Wellington also ordered the appointment as police minister of Joseph Fouché, who had stage-managed the king's entry into Paris after Waterloo. Louis had to accept, even if he remarked that he was handing over his virginity. Seeing Talleyrand making his way to a royal audience leaning on Fouché's arm, Chateaubriand described the pair as 'vice leaning on the arm of crime'.

While these two escaped paying the price for their pasts, revenge was sought against some who had served the Republic or the Empire. Those who had committed revolutionary crimes merited 'chains, executioners, torture,' proclaimed François-Régis, Count of Bourdonnaye, an overbearing deputy from western France known as the 'white Jacobin'. Fifty thousand officials lost their jobs and 12,000 officers were put on half pay. Members of the Convention who had voted for the execution of Louis XVI were banished, though a blind eye was turned to Fouché who now showed his habitual lack of scruple by drawing up a list of people to be purged – 'he forgot none of his friends' Talleyrand remarked.[11]

In the region of Lyons, where Napoleonic sentiment still ran high, a portable guillotine was moved around rural areas. When General Charles de la Bédoyère, one of the last commanders to have left the Waterloo battlefield, went to see his wife on his way to exile in Switzerland, he was recognised, arrested and shot. Marshal Ney, 'the bravest of the brave' in Napoleon's phrase, who had rallied to Louis XVIII in 1814 and denounced Bonaparte as a lunatic, but then joined him at Waterloo, was sentenced to death. Following a failed escape attempt, he was executed near the Luxembourg Gardens in Paris after himself giving the order to the firing squad to shoot – one of the twelve crack marksmen aimed wide.

The widespread violence by royalists and local criminal gangs led Fouché to warn the king that 'France is at war with itself. We are threatened by all the ills which can be born from an upsurge of passions and the clash of opinions.' The 'White Terror' in the Midi region in the south, where savagery between rival factions dated back to the struggles of two decades, saw brigands murdering and pillaging at will. Violence spiralled out of control in Marseilles and turmoil spread to Nîmes, Béziers, Uzès and other towns. A Napoleonic marshal, Guillaume Marie-Anne Brune, was murdered when he passed through Avignon; his body was among dozens pitched into the Rhône. In Toulouse, ultra-royalist gangs ran amok. Western France was dominated by leaders who looked back to the *ancien régime* and whose peasants were described by a police report as 'credulous, simple, ignorant'. The east of the country, which had suffered from foreign invasions, was at best lukewarm to the Restoration and contained plenty of Bonapartists.

The election of the Chamber of Deputies in August 1815, gave 'Ultra' loyalists to the throne 350 of the 402 seats. The new Chamber of Deputies was, the king remarked, more royalist than he was – he called it *la Chambre Introuvable* (the Unobtainable Chamber). The Ultras looked to his brother, the Count of Artois, as their leader and anticipated the day when he would succeed the childless and increasingly infirm monarch. Their dislike of Talleyrand and Fouché led to the pair being dropped. The former bishop was given the consolation prize of being made Grand Chamberlain, allowing him to attend court whenever he wished; he settled into the role of elder statesman waiting for a turn of events to bring his recall. The regicide was sent as ambassador to Saxony – he died in exile in Trieste in 1820.

To head the new government, Louis chose Armand de Vignerot du Plessis, fifth Duke of Richelieu, a grey haired, 48-year-old pipe-smoker with a yapping voice. He was a favourite of the Tsar after fighting in the Russian army against his fellow countrymen and serving as governor of the Crimea; he wore black boots and a black cravat in the Russian style. Having spent twenty-four years abroad, he did not know any of his ministers and was at the mercy of the Ultras who pushed through legislation favouring the old nobility and clergy, and instituting press censorship.

At the end of November 1815, a white-faced Richelieu signed the definitive peace agreement dictated by the Allies, lamenting that 'all is finished [by] this fatal treaty'. But, despite two decades of war, the conditions were far less draconian than hoped for by the Prussians. Border modifications were minimal though France lost some colonies to Britain. French frontier fortresses were to be dismantled but were not taken over by the victors. The indemnity was set at 700 million francs plus settlement of claims from individuals who had suffered from France's invasions. The occupation army was to remain for three to five years under Wellington's command, its food paid for by France. The Allies reserved the right to cooperate against any revival of 'revolutionary principles'. Russia, Prussia and Austria proclaimed a Holy Alliance and Britain joined them in the Quadruple Alliance.

Though still an outcast, France did find a friend in Russia after Louis invited the Tsar to stay at the royal Élysée Palace and served up three sumptuous banquets; the cooking was done by thirty-five chefs under the direction of the great food impresario Antoine Carême, a Bonapartist who reflected that he had 'never done anything so beautiful; anger made me a genius'. Alexander worried that the Ultras would provoke fresh revolution by undoing the Restoration, and his lobbying ensured that France held on to Burgundy, Alsace, Lorraine and Franche-Comté in the treaty. 'If France is still France, it is thanks to the Russians,' wrote Count Molé, another political survivor who had been Napoleon's justice minister but then held office under the Bourbons. Faced with Britain, Austria and Prussia, Russia 'had every interest in our remaining a power of the first order', as Molé noted.

Britain held off from such continental stratagems but Wellington harboured no ill will towards the French though he, too, feared that the Ultras would bring down the Bourbons. With two of the Allies taking such a view, Louis felt strong enough to call new elections, which reduced the ranks of the Ultras to ninety deputies as against 150 moderate royalists. Richelieu remained head of the government. Protests broke out in Lyons, Champagne and the Brie region east of Paris after a bad harvest sent the price of wheat up by 85 per cent, causing near famine in some parts and having the usual knock-on effect as households spent all their cash on food and stopped buying manufactured goods.

Clashes between Allied troops and local people suggested that occupation would become an increasingly onerous task. Wellington was the target of several assassination attempts. It was time for the Allies to come to the aid of the monarch. A 100-million-franc loan was raised by the pre-eminent London finance house Barings, working with a French banker, Ouvrard.

Everybody was happy. French finance and the country's credit rating perked up. The Allies got their cash. Investors, many from Britain, received higher interest rates than at home and Barings made between £620,000 and £725,000 a year. Under the influence of the salon hostess Germaine de Staël, who appealed to him to 'become the greatest man, not of our time but of all times, and give us back France', Wellington softened his position when Richelieu travelled in the autumn of 1818 to Aachen (Aix-la-Chapelle) for a congress to determine his country's fate.[12]

France was re-integrated into the European system with a reduced payment to the Allies who withdrew their occupying troops. The remarkably quick diplomatic recovery reflected the country's continental importance, the need the Russians felt to have it inside the tent to balance the other great powers and Britain's greater flexibility, though London predictably opposed a Russian idea of developing a pan-European system tying together royal, Christian nations. Instead, the conference accepted a proposal by Metternich to create a secret Concert of Five with France as a member. Three-and-a-half years after Waterloo, the country of the Revolution was back at the top table.*

---

* The gastronome Jean-Anthelme Brillat-Savarin attributed France's revival to the taste which foreigners had acquired for its food and drink during the occupation. 'These intruders ate in restaurants, in hotels, in taverns, at street stalls, and even in the streets. They stuffed themselves with meat, fish, game, truffles, pastry and, above all, with our fruit. Their thirst was as insatiable as their appetite ... The true Frenchman laughed and rubbed his hands, saying "They are under a spell, and by tonight they will have paid us back more crowns than the Treasury handed over to them this morning" ... if our public bonds are in favour, it is due not so much to the high rate of interest they carry as to the instinctive confidence everybody inevitably feels in a people in whose midst gourmands are happy.' (Brillat-Savarin, *Psychologie du Goût*, p. 136).

Royalisation

After the settlement with the Allies and with greater stability at home, underpinned by the Barings loans, Richelieu thought it time to take a rest, and was succeeded as head of government by another noble, the Marquis Dessolles. But the dominant figure was a lawyer turned civil servant from the Gironde, Élie Decazes, who became chief minister after a year.

Having served the Empire, he turned royalist in 1814 and stayed loyal during the Hundred Days, being rewarded by his appointment as Paris police chief in 1815. Elected as a deputy, he defined his aim as being 'to royalise France and nationalise the monarchy'. Socially adroit and elegant, he was the favourite of the childless king, who arranged for him to marry well. Louis said he would raise him 'so high that the greatest lords will be envious'. Still, like a watchful father, he also noted that the man he called 'my son' suffered from 'mental laziness'.[13]

Under Decazes, the liberals advanced, financed by sympathisers such as the banker Laffitte and drawing inspiration from a political grouping known as the Doctrinaires led by the deputy and salon thinker Pierre-Paul Royer-Collard, who sought to reconcile elected government and the less extreme revolutionary heritage with the restored monarchy around a *juste milieu* (middle path). The voting law was changed to try to prevent an Ultra revival. Fourteen prefects and thirty sub-prefects were replaced by more liberal men. To overcome the opposition of the upper house of the legislature, where the hard right held the majority, sixty new peers were created.

Censorship was eased. Competition was introduced for some military posts. State primary schools were set up to compete with Catholic establishments. Bonapartists and republicans did well at by-elections, some backed by Ultras who wanted to weaken Decazes and the king. Laffitte and another leading banker, Casimir Perier, joined the Chamber of Deputies, followed by Lafayette and the writer and liberal thinker Benjamin Constant, framer of the Hundred Days constitution and lover of Madame de Staël. Louis-Philippe, of the Orléanist branch of the royal family, considered it safe to return from England and benefitted from the financial support of the Rothschilds, who saw him as a good long-term hedge.

Growth started to pick up though it remained well below that of Britain. Reform of state finances began. Gas lighting was introduced in the capital – one of the first places to use it was the gallery built near the Palais-Royal by two *charcutiers* as a dry, safe place in which to eat and shop, with painted ceiling panels and triangular glass skylights. Plans were drawn up to build roads over the Alps, to develop canals and link the Rhine and Rhône rivers. The beetroot sugar industry revived. Charles Lesur, the writer who also held a post as inspector of the Paris lottery, saw France:

'Bent like the reed by the storm, it stands up again like the oak tree in its forests.

Black and blue from its wounds, overwhelmed by its setbacks,

It nonetheless appears as a colossus in the eyes of posterity.'[14]

There was fresh thinking about society, with an emphasis on the importance of private life. François Guizot, a senior civil servant prominent in the Doctrinaire group, argued that power should be entrusted to an elite of paternalist organisers who, though the central figure in families, should have constant democratic discussions with their kin. The prototype socialist, Henri de Saint-Simon, combined mysticism with an attempt to map out a cooperative technocratic state in which politics would be aligned with industry and science, which would replace religion. He foresaw a new aristocracy made up of people, primarily intellectuals, who had shown their ability to organise production and who would eradicate poverty by progress. Saint-Simon's own attempts to build an industrial career did not get far; he suffered from recurrent illness and made a suicide attempt in which he shot himself six times in the head, losing the sight of one eye but failing to kill himself. His ideas would, however, live on through the mid-century.

But the relaxation steered by Decazes had unpleasant repercussions for him and his adoring king. Elections in the autumn of 1819 for fifty-five seats returned thirty-five opposition deputies, mostly Bonapartists, including two of the emperor's generals. Even worse, Grenoble voted for Abbé Henri Grégoire, a revolutionary who had approved of the execution of Louis XVI and was elected with the help of Ultras out to embarrass the government. Louis wrote to Decazes that Grégoire's election was a scandal, and the new Chamber excluded him.

The hard royalist right and its main secret society, the *Chevaliers de la Foi* (Knights of Faith), coalesced even more than before round the handsome, physically fit Count of Artois in his headquarters at the Pavillon de Marsan in the Tuileries. Their publications depicted supporters of the Charter as two-faced opportunists pretending to be concerned for the public good while concealing their true nature as revolutionaries. 'There is no middle ground between the kings and the executioners' wrote one.[15]

Unlike Louis, Artois had two sons, the Duke of Berry and the Duke of Angoulême, offering the continuation of the senior Bourbon line. The elder, the fleshy-faced Berry, was known for his hot temper, bad manners and womanising – he had fathered two daughters while in exile in Britain and had a son by a fashionable dancer. On the night of 13 February 1820, he was stabbed in the heart outside the Paris Opera by a disgruntled Bonapartist. The family, including the dying man's pregnant wife, her dress covered with blood, clustered around him in a chamber at the Opera as doctors tried to save his life. At 6 a.m., he died.

The Ultras blamed the deed on the liberalism of Decazes. Ready as always with an assassin's phrase, Chateaubriand wrote that the chief minister's foot had 'slipped in blood'. Artois and Angoulême demanded his dismissal. Louis tried to protect his 'dear son', but the Ultras insisted. Units of the National Guard threatened to take action. Angoulême's forceful wife went on her knees to beg Louis to get rid of Decazes. Against his heart, Louis agreed. He wrote that, had he been an absolute monarch, he would have kept the son he had never had. But he felt he had to give way. So the favourite was raised to the rank of duke and sent as ambassador to Britain. Louis hung his portrait in his private office and wrote him a note telling of his broken heart and ending 'I kiss you a thousand times.'

With the backing of Artois, with whom the king was on testy terms, Richelieu returned to head the government. Detention without trial was introduced. Censorship tightened again. The richest electors were given a double ballot and voting was organised on a district basis to increase the influence of local nobles. Wealth requirements restricted the number of candidates.

As a result Ultras did well in elections in the early 1820s; by 1823 there were only nineteen liberal deputies in the Chamber. More than a hundred deputies belonged to the *Chevaliers de la Foi*. Richelieu was ready to go and the political equation called for a new head of government. The appointee was Count Jean-Baptiste de Villèle, who had spent the revolutionary years in the West Indies and Réunion. A meticulous conservative and mayor of Toulouse when it was a hotbed of reaction, he reflected the views of the rural nobility of Languedoc from which he sprang and which rejected both the values of the Revolution and the mechanisation of the economy – he refused to invest in industry and lobbied for compensation for land confiscated from the aristocracy and the church. Enjoying the backing of influential figures including the king's close friend, the Countess of Cayala, he was careful with his money and was known as a good father and devoted husband. He and his wife were described as being 'like lovebirds'; when she had to go to the countryside with the family for health reasons, he had a life-sized portrait of himself sent to her.[16]

Chateaubriand, who longed for a more muscular exercise of kingship, became foreign minister. The government paid off France's foreign debts after raising a large domestic loan for which the Paris Rothschild bank was the highest bidder, despite Villèle's desire to 'get out of the hands of those gentlemen'.

Any direct Bonapartist threat receded when Napoleon died on St Helena from stomach cancer in May 1821; his son was held by the Austrians. However, two Bonapartists, who had got to know members of the Masonic-linked Carbonari secret society in Italy, set up a group called the Charbonnerie to bring down tyrants, starting with the Bourbons. Building up a membership estimated at 60,000, they formed branches throughout the country and infiltrated the army. In February 1822, they staged a rising in Saumur, which fizzled out. Another unsuccessful attempt at insurrection led to many arrests and a dozen executions.

Artois's second son, the Duke of Angoulême, lacked the panache of his slain brother; he often seemed ill at ease and walked round making facetious remarks and waving his arms in the air. But Ultras could take comfort in his reliably reactionary views. His wife, the former Marie-Thérèse de France, the daughter of Louis XVI, was even more conservative, harbouring opinions to be expected from somebody who had been held as a teenager in the Temple Tower in Paris with her family for three years during the Revolution and was the only one to survive. A stickler for etiquette, she made ladies at court wear lappet flaps of lace on either side of their heads and heavy mantilla shawls. At her social gatherings, guests might find themselves obliged to watch her engaging in her favoured pursuit of embroidery.

The Angoulêmes, who rose at dawn and lit the fire in their apartment themselves, were childless. This gave considerable status to the widowed Duchess of Berry, Princess Carolina of Naples, especially when she gave birth to a son seven months after the assassination of her husband. The boy was dubbed *l'Enfant du Miracle* and hailed by the then-royalist Victor Hugo as 'the tender flower that rises from a tomb'. The birth came very suddenly and caused the mother great pain, but she insisted on keeping the baby attached to her by the umbilical cord until it had been seen by several senior figures of the royal household to show that the infant was hers and had not been smuggled in to provide an heir.

Louis gave her a cluster of diamonds, saying, 'That is for you.' 'And this is for me,' he added as he took the baby on his knees, following a tradition dating back to Henri IV by rubbing a clove of garlic on the infant's lips and pouring a few drops of Jurançon wine into his mouth. When the cannons thundered just before dawn, the crowd outside the Tuileries cheered enthusiastically at the thirteenth salvo indicating that the child was a boy.

Holding the baby up to the throng, the Duchess of Angoulême dropped her usual severe expression as she called out, 'Look at him! At last we have drained the cup of adversity and can count on divine justice.' Fireworks and the distribution of 10,000 packets of sweets marked the baptism in Notre-Dame. Described at the age of six as small, ugly, lively and very friendly, the Duke of Bordeaux, as he became, was brought up in strict court ritual, with religious education and a servant whose only job was to shine his shoes.

His mother was a spirited figure, a small woman with pale skin whose lack of learning and Neapolitan dialect had shocked courtiers when she arrived in Paris. She was determined, brave and had a mind of her own. She pioneered sea bathing at Dieppe; a cannon sounded and a formally dressed bathing inspector stepped forward as she was carried into the water by attendants and dropped into the waves, wearing a fur hat, woollen dress, cardigan and boots in case crabs were lurking. There were rumours that she was having an affair with her riding master, a toothless fifty-year-old who, the Duchess told a friend, 'smelled like a dead rat'. Yet he had won her affection when he caught her in his arms as she tumbled from her horse. However, the king appears to have lost patience with her melodramatic ways when she produced a letter threatening her and her son after a barrel of gunpowder exploded on a secret staircase in the palace; her confessor confided that she admitted writing the note herself.[17]

Louis's close friend, the Countess of Cayala, engineered a reconciliation between the royal brothers, which involved Louis taking a pinch of snuff from Artois and sighing, 'I will now have peace in the royal house.' But he had a major cause for concern in his own health; his body lost all shape, covered with varicose veins and ulcers, his legs puffed up, his sight and hearing going. He dozed at meetings. Death obsessed him.[18]

In addition, his vision of a united country was under growing strain. There were worker demonstrations in support of wage demands in Paris, Chartres, Marseilles, Libourne, Bordeaux and Rouen. Factory employees, masons, staff at sawmills and jewellery makers formed associations to press for improved pay and conditions. But the electoral system with 110,000 voters, 60 per cent of them landowners, was so rigged that none of this affected elite politics, and Ultras made further progress in elections in February 1824.

Civil servants suspected of not supporting extreme royalism were dismissed. A press law required official authorisation to set up a publication. Criticism of Catholicism was banned. Nineteen bishops and archbishops became peers. A senior priest from the church of Saint-Sulpice in the capital, much in vogue among the nobility, was put in charge of education. Despite the misgivings of the king, the nationalist, legitimist right pushed France into its first post-1815 foreign foray in Spain, where civil war had broken out in 1822 after the Bourbon King Ferdinand VII sought to re-establish the absolute monarchy he had been forced to renounce by a constitution ten years earlier.

Austria, Prussia and Russia backed French intervention and Louis did an about-turn saying, 'a hundred thousand French are ready to march invoking the god of St Louis to keep the throne of Spain for a descendant of Henri IV'. Angoulême commanded the army that advanced to Madrid in May 1824, took Seville and Cadiz, and freed Ferdinand to launch a ferocious counter-revolution. In November, Angoulême returned to a hero's welcome, leaving behind an occupying force of 45,000 men that was not fully withdrawn until 1828. Though he likened the expedition to an episode from *Don Quixote*, Ultras celebrated not only victory but also the restoration of absolute monarchy in Spain. For them, France had paid its dues in the counter-revolutionary alliance directed by Metternich from Vienna.

At the end of August 1824, King Louis XVIII took his last carriage drive through Paris, his body shrunken and bent, his voice so low that visitors had to move close beside him to hear. His hand was that of a skeleton. He had to be moved around in a wheelchair. When he attended mass at Notre Dame, the bandages came off his leg and liquid oozed onto the floor. But it was not until September that the Countess of Cayala dared to suggest he take the last sacraments. After some hesitation Louis agreed. The following day, he was put to bed in the Tuileries in great pain; he had difficulty breathing, toes came off his right foot as his body rotted. The Bourse closed – one of the king's last concerns was that his death would affect government stocks. A huge crowd gathered outside the palace. Princes, princesses, officials, diplomats and politicians filled the royal apartments.

Talleyrand remained without rest by the royal bedside assailed by the stink of gangrene and performing what he called 'the most disgusting duties'. At 4 a.m. on 16 September, the king died. After the

family and courtiers had withdrawn, Decazes prostrated himself at the
bedside, fainting at one point in his lamentations. Then the bed curtains were closed and cleaners moved in to sweep the room, singing and
whistling. The twice restored monarch who had tried his best but not
done enough was buried in the royal cathedral at St-Denis, Talleyrand
propping himself up at the catafalque, grasping the white Bourbon
emblem.[19]

2

REACTION AND REVOLUTION

On 20 September 1824, Artois made his formal entry into Paris in the rain as the new monarch, Charles X. He rode a horse, the first monarch to enter the capital in that way since Louis XIV. After being greeted by municipal officials at the Étoile, he led an impressive parade to Notre-Dame for mass. The crowd cheered. As a pun put it, '*le jour de l'entrée du Roi il a plu partout*' (The day of the King's entry, it rained/he pleased everywhere).

In keeping with the new monarch's views, Villèle's government passed fresh laws favouring the nobility and the clergy. Those whose estates had been confiscated during the Revolution were promised compensation. Anti-sacrilege legislation was enacted. The National Guard set up during the Revolution was disbanded after one of its members shouted 'Down with the Jesuits' during a review by the king – but its members were not disarmed. Appointments to top civil service and army posts were heavily populated with old aristocratic families, frustrating middle-class aspirants. Ultras sent to run provincial administrations were often unfriendly to local business needs – in Limoges the new mayor allocated money for roads to his château and spent nothing on developing the city's infrastructure.

As liberal criticism rose, the chief minister tried piecemeal moderation. But he ran into ferocious opposition from the right led by Chateaubriand, who had been sacked as foreign minister after repeated clashes over his interfering in matters outside his departmental remit. A European economic depression in 1825 hit the textile industry hard as cotton prices gyrated wildly and the big Paris banks had to step in to bail out manufacturers. Legislation limiting the traditional access of peasants to forests to safeguard aristocratic rights sparked revolts including the 'war of the Demoiselles' in the Ariège *département*, in which men in long shirts and bonnets attacked landlords, police and forest guards with guns and axes.

Dancing on a volcano

At the top, a complex power game set in between the king and the liberals, replaying themes inherited from the Revolution. Charles began by naming seventy-six new peers to keep control of the Upper House and dissolving the Chamber of Deputies to strengthen the Ultras. But the outcome of the voting favoured the opposition. When the victors tried to hold celebratory banquets, they were banned. Two days of protests in Paris were met with the intervention of mounted police who killed four demonstrators.

Further elections in 1828–9 gave fifty of the seventy-five seats at stake to the opposition. After Villèle spent a sleepless night trying to work out the future, the king sacked him and appointed as prime minister Jules, Prince of Polignac, who combined hard-line politics, extreme religious devotion and occasional visions. Son of an unpopular favourite of Marie-Antoinette, he spent a dozen years in exile during the Revolution and, after being allowed back to France, was imprisoned for nine years for being implicated in a plot to assassinate Napoleon. After the Restoration, he refused to vote for Louis XVIII's Charter. Being regarded as a hate figure by liberals was a badge of honour. 'I am made only for storms,' he declared. 'I have my old ideas ... I will go ahead with them.' The king compared him to a horse in blinkers; the Duchess of Angoulême called him 'the most presumptuous man I know'.[1]

Bourdonnaye, the verbose 'white Jacobin' deputy who had called for the torture and execution of revolutionaries, became Minister of the Interior, insisting the throne faced an anti-royalist plot that required drastic action. The war ministry went to General de Bourmont, who had led *chouan* anti-revolutionary forces in the Vendée. At the opening of the

The Bourbon Who Learned Nothing

Charles X, who was sixty-seven when he ascended the throne but looked younger, had drawn a different lesson to his brother from the vicissitudes of their lives. He told the more liberal Louis-Philippe d'Orléans that those who opposed his vision of royal rule wanted a republic and the end of the monarchy, but I will not allow my neck to be cut like Louis XVI.'

He put his faith in absolutism and the Catholic church; his piety was said to have set in after the death of his mistress in 1804. The link between throne and altar was underlined by his consecration in the cathedral at Reims, the thirteenth-century church where French monarchs were traditionally crowned, but which Louis XVIII had avoided as too provocative. In Paris, he had an Expiatory Chapel built on the burial site of Louis XVI and Marie-Antoinette.

An elegant widower capable of great charm who cut a fine figure in his dress uniforms, the new monarch assumed that it was the duty of his subjects to follow his will. He surrounded himself with a court that harked back to the *ancien régime* and was notable for its lack of intellectual quality. For all his assumption of royal authority, he was a weak character with an empty mind bereft of the imagination or the courage to enforce his will when the test came.

He operated through trusted officials whom he left to get on with the job, remaining true to his own convictions and alienating those misled by his courtesy into imagining they had made an impression.

Unlike his brother Louis, Charles ate sparingly and preferred simple fare, dining with his family at 6 p.m. and then playing chess with the Duke of Angoulême or whist with his spectacles perched on the end of his nose, insulting other players when he was trumped and trying to stamp under the table on Talleyrand's club foot. At cabinet meetings after mass on Wednesdays and Sundays, the king cut sheets of paper into unusual shapes. The chief minister doodled in exercise books. The finance minister, an Auvergnat count, stabbed balls of wax with an awl. If one of them fell asleep, the monarch woke the offender by pushing his snuffbox at him.

parliamentary session in March 1830, Charles told deputies and peers that, if his government encountered obstacles, he would overcome them. Ultra deputies shouted '*Vive le roi!*' There was silence from other parts of the chamber. Five days later, deputies presented a response, which insisted on the right of citizens to intervene in public policy. 'Go back to your meeting room,' the king told them. 'My ministers will let you know my intentions.'

But economic and social discontent was rising further outside the self-enclosed world of the court and the Ultras. There was a credit crunch and the Bourse came under pressure. The young bourgeoisie resented the lack of official jobs open to non-nobles. Polignac was also rumoured to be planning to exclude businessmen from the franchise. The children of known liberals had a hard time from religious school-teachers, and the prince promised further power for the priesthood. A bad harvest sent grain prices up, provoking riots. Unemployment rose. There was a further irritant in Paris when the police chief, a religious man, banned trading and soliciting by prostitutes on Sundays. The republican Lafayette received a hero's welcome in Lyons. Polignac called fresh elections but the right did even worse as bourgeois electoral networks proved effective.

The opposition had a powerful weapon in the press so long as it could evade censorship – its newspapers sold four times as many as those backing the throne. Able journalists, such as Adolphe Thiers, knew how to build on a swell of discontent among skilled artisans and others who harked back to the tradition of 1789. Among the critical journals were those funded by the financier, Casimir Perier, who joined Laffitte in promoting reform, and by Talleyrand's main lady friend of the time, backed by the wily old man who, as always, had his nose to the wind. Even some conservatives saw Polignac as danger-ously misguided. Under Chateaubriand's influence, the *Journal des Débats* wrote of 'the Court with its old rancours, the émigrés with their prejudices, the priesthood with its hatred of liberty ... Turn [the gov-ernment] round whichever way you like; from every side, it frightens, from every side it angers ... Squeeze it, wring it; all that drips out are humiliations, misfortunes and dangers ... What have we done for our king to separate himself from us? Unhappy France! Unhappy king!'[2]

Charles's position was badly weakened by the presence of a ready royal alternative in the person of Louis-Philippe, head of the Orléanist branch of the royal family, who was living in a château in Neuilly outside Paris and spending bucolic summers at his sixteenth-century château at Eu in Normandy. Though a Bourbon, he had been associated with the early leaders of the Revolution, fought in its army in 1791–2 and was a moderate with whom liberals were comfortable. 'Despite the danger of freedom pushed a little far, I prefer it to absolute authority which I regard as the greatest of misfortunes, both for those who exercise it and those who are subject to it,' he said. At the end of May 1830, he presided over a grand ball for 3,000 people in his family's headquarters at the Palais-Royal in honour of the king and queen of Naples, appearing on the terrace to cries of '*Vive le Duc d'Orléans!*' The festivities went on until 5 a.m. There were few cheers for the king. Strolling through the salons, a politician remarked, 'We are dancing on a volcano.'[3]

Before the eruption, Charles tried a diversionary move by launching the Restoration's second foreign adventure with an invasion of Algeria whose repercussions would live on for 130 years and end in national trauma. The *casus belli* dated from 1827. Under financial pressure, the ruler in Algiers, the Dey, asked for the repayment of a loan made to Paris under Napoleon. When France's consul refused, the Dey hit him with a flywhisk, calling him 'a wicked, faithless, idol-worshipping rascal'. Denouncing Algiers as a 'nest of pirates', France blockaded the coast across the Mediterranean. Despite British objections, Paris had the support of Austria, Russia and Prussia – extending royalist, Christian influence was the order of the day for the Holy Alliance. On 2 March 1830, Charles X announced an expedition to avenge the flywhisk insult and claim Algeria for Christianity.

A force of 37,000 troops left Toulon and entered Algiers two weeks later. The Dey agreed to leave after the French commander promised to respect Islam and local customs, though a mass in Notre-Dame celebrated 'the victory of the Cross over the Crescent'. Public rejoicing in France was restrained; most people viewed the operation as the political expedient it was and the expeditionary force soon ran into difficulties in mountains south of Algiers. But France came to regard Algeria as part of itself and merchants in Marseilles saw the opportunities for trade. By 1839, 25,000 Europeans had moved across the sea; just 11,000 of them were French. As the historian Martin Evans has noted, France stumbled into Algeria with no grand design. It would still be there more than a century later fighting 'a savage war of peace' until Charles de Gaulle drew a line under the whole enterprise.[4]

Unimpressed by the government's foreign foray, the Chamber of Deputies passed a bill to make ministerial office dependent on parliamentary support rather than that of the monarch. Charles took offence at this attack on his prerogatives and at the 'false fears and unworthy suspicions' aroused about him. But fresh elections in June–July brought an even larger opposition majority. 'If I give in this time,' the king remarked, 'they will finish by treating me as they treated my brother.' He proposed to reply by using Article 14 of the Charter, allowing government by decree.

Polignac drew up four ordinances to dissolve the Chamber, tighten censorship, limit the franchise to the richest citizens and call fresh elections. At a cabinet meeting at the château of Saint-Cloud outside Paris after Sunday mass on 25 July, Charles read out the decrees and asked his son what he thought. 'When a danger has become inevitable, it must be addressed head-on,' Angoulême replied. 'One perishes or saves oneself.'

Ministers signalled that they agreed. Charles leaned forward to read the documents again, his head bent, his left hand shielding his eyes. When he looked up, his face was red, his breath short. 'The more I think about it, the more I remain convinced that it is impossible for me to do anything else,' he said – and signed. 'The king has spoken; we are joyous,' a duke wrote. If there was opposition, 19,000 royal troops in the Paris region would deal with any discontent.[5]

The July Days

Monday, 26 July 1830 was hot. Charles went to Rambouillet to hunt with Angoulême. As he left, the Duchess of Berry threw herself at his feet saying 'You reign at last!'

In Paris, the opposition rejected the king's right to invoke Article 14. Liberal politicians met to discuss the situation. Critical newspapers went on publishing in defiance of orders to shut down; Adolphe Thiers of *Le National* led forty-three journalists in a declaration of revolt with an editorial stating that the government had lost its legality and that it was for 'France to judge how far it should extend its resistance'. In Neuilly, Louis-Philippe walked into the dressing room where his wife was doing her hair. Putting down a copy of the newspaper in which the decrees were printed, he said, 'Well, my dear, it's done. There's the *coup d'état.*'

When police raided a printing works and seized copies of liberal newspapers, a mob outside shouted '*À bas les Bourbons!*' (Down with the Bourbons!) and '*Vive la Charte!*' (Long live the Charter!). Brokers at the Bourse refused to lend money. Unemployed workers gathered in the streets. A hostile crowd stoned the foreign ministry.

The royal hunt went badly. The dogs pursued a hind rather than a stag; when another stag was released, they were too tired to chase it. 'This is an unhappy day,' Charles said, ordering everybody back to the château of Rambouillet where he played billiards absent-mindedly and dined before returning to Saint-Cloud. The head of the Royal Guard, Auguste de Marmont, a former aide-de-camp to Napoleon, reported that there was 'a lot of uncertainty and agitation' in Paris. Charles asked how state bonds were doing; down 4 to 5 per cent, the marshal replied. The king went to bed.

Tuesday, 27 July was the day when the protestors took over the centre of the capital in beautiful summer weather. 'Crowds were hurrying through the streets, many of the shops were closed, and not above three or four carriages were to be seen,' noted the Irish writer, the Countess of Blessington, who was living in an *hôtel particulier* on the Left Bank. 'Never did such a change take place in the aspect of a city in so few hours! ... Scarcely a person of those termed fashionable is to be seen. Where are all the household of Charles the Tenth, that vast and well-paid crowd who were wont to fill the anterooms of the Tuileries on gala days, obsequiously watching to catch a nod from the monarch? ... Can it be that they have disappeared at the first cloud that has darkened the horizon of their sovereign ... showing that they have not the courage to meet it?'

The only backing for the throne came from Marmont's troops who took up positions round the Tuileries, Place Vendôme and Place de la Bastille. Patrols fanned out across the city. At dusk, people pelted them with paving stones, roof tiles, flowerpots, furniture and anything else to hand. The soldiers first fired in the air but then lowered their guns – twenty-one people were killed. The crowds shouted '*Mort aux ministres!*' (Death to ministers!) and '*À bas les aristocrates!*' (Down with aristo-crats!).

The clashes destroyed the street lamps and the soldiers marched back to barracks in the dark. Opposition leaders proposed a settlement if the king agreed to withdraw the decrees. But royalist reports reaching Saint-Cloud painted a reassuring picture for Charles and the Court. An officer brought word that troops had opened fire. 'Willingly?' asked the Duchess of Berry. Getting an affirmative answer, she told him, 'I must kiss you.'

Wednesday, 28 July saw even bigger crowds out on the boulevards waving tricolour flags. There was shooting round the Louvre. A huge barricade went up on the rue de Seine on the Left Bank. State armouries were raided and weapons distributed. A Jesuit centre was pillaged. Marmont's troops were fired on from windows.

Looking out from a window, Blessington watched fifty boys march along the street towards a detachment of mounted soldiers, waving flags, wooden swords and lances with nails for points, crying '*Vive la Charte! Vive la liberté!*'. Amused, the soldiers allowed them to get close, but then 'the urchins, rushing among the horses, wounded several of the poor animals quite severely, and effected their retreat before the sol-diers were aware of what had occurred.'

'Sire, this is no longer a riot, it is a revolution,' Marmont, personally liberal but deeply loyal to the throne, wrote to the king. 'It is urgent for Your Majesty to take pacification measures. Tomorrow, perhaps, there will be no more time.' The message reached Saint-Cloud as mass was starting. It lay on a stool for an hour before Charles read it. 'There is no reply,' he said. At nightfall, Marmont left the streets to the protestors, withdrawing to regroup in the Tuileries and the Louvre, where the gov-ernment had taken refuge.

In Neuilly, Louis-Philippe and his family were kept informed by emissaries. Not wishing to commit himself and fearing demonstrators might come to fetch him, the ever-cautious duke moved into a small building at the end of the grounds.

At Saint-Cloud, the king declared a state of siege for Paris and said he would not deal with the rebels. Through a telescope from the second floor of the château, the Duchess of Berry watched the city and offered to ride into town to try to restore order, a suggestion not taken up. 'What a shame to be a woman,' she remarked.

When a visitor warned of the gravity of the situation, the king replied, 'Polignac had visions last night promising help, demanding perseverance and assuring full victory.' He played whist after dinner while the Duke of Angoulême concentrated on his chessboard. The gates at Saint-Cloud were locked. A cache of royal jewels was brought from the capital. The Princess of Polignac dissolved into tears.

Thursday, 29 July put the royalists in an ever more perilous position as protests swelled. National Guardsmen and ruffians marched shoulder to shoulder with graduates and workers, some in elegant clothes and uniforms, others in rags. The tricolour had become the city's flag. Barricades blocked the streets; nearly all the trees in central Paris had been chopped down and paving stones dug up. As demonstrators attacked the Louvre, ministers hurried to Saint-Cloud, escorted by lancers. Royal soldiers began to desert.

Marmont rode to tell the king Paris was lost. Weary, dusty soldiers who accompanied him sat in the palace courtyard where servants brought them lemonade and biscuits – 'Do you think we have come from a ball?' a colonel shouted. 'Bring us meat and wine.' Charles said he did not want to be taken to execution in a cart, but to leave on a horse. 'I fear, Sire, that the moment to mount is not far off,' Marmont replied.

Charles made a moderate noble, the Duke de Mortemart, chief minister. A delegation went to Paris to announce the new administration. The municipal council refused to receive it or to recognise the monarch; the liberals were adamant – the decrees must be cancelled and parliament be called into session. Returning to Saint-Cloud at 1.30 a.m., the envoys and Mortemart woke the king to tell him what had

happened. When they proposed to agree to re-establish the National
Guard as the municipal council demanded, Charles refused, sitting up
in bed in his cotton nightcap. In the corridor outside, Polignac, in dress
uniform and carrying a white plumed hat, lamented that 'my sword has
been broken in my hand.'

The protestors took the Louvre, Hôtel de Ville and Tuileries Palace
where a corpse was placed on the throne. A man appeared at a window
wearing one of the Duchess of Berry's ball gowns. A crowd set out for
Neuilly. Learning of this, Louis-Philippe left for another of his homes.
At 2 a.m., a group of liberal politicians seated at a round table in
Laffitte's house drew up a proclamation stating that, since Charles X
had shed the blood of his people and a republic was impossible, the
only course was for Orléans to take the throne at the behest of the
people, stating that he was 'devoted to the cause of the Revolution'.

Thiers went to Neuilly but the Duchess told him she did not know
where her husband was. The journalist-politician explained that a constitutional, representative dynasty was needed. Convinced, the Duchess
sent a general to fetch Louis-Philippe from his hiding place. At 9 p.m.,
by the artfully crafted family account, he set out on foot for the city,
wearing ordinary street clothes and a tricolour emblem in his hat.
Reaching the Palais-Royal, he told an aide-de-camp to call in Mortemart.
Then he lay down on a mattress, two candles burning beside him.

When Mortemart arrived at 3 a.m., Louis-Philippe gave him a letter
for Charles saying he would rather be torn to pieces than take the
crown. Still, he accepted the post of Lieutenant General of the
Kingdom, which the deputies had voted to him. To confirm the
appointment, he had to go to the parliament sitting in the Hôtel de
Ville. The procession, which set out from the Palais-Royal in the early
afternoon, was a ramshackle affair, but, at the City Hall, everything
went smoothly. Wrapped in a tricolour, Louis-Philippe was embraced on
the balcony by Lafayette. The large crowd cheered. Celebrations
erupted through the city.

At Saint-Cloud, tempers frayed as courtiers discussed a retreat to the
Loire or the Vendée. Angoulême and Marmont came to blows. Alarmed
that compromising letters would be found in her desk in the Tuileries,
the Duchess of Berry sent a guardsman in disguise to retrieve them.

Seized by a crowd, he said he flung the bundle into the Seine; some time later an Austro-Hungarian diplomat wrote that he had dissuaded journalists from publishing the documents in which 'the Princess was extremely compromised'.

On 2 August, having moved for safety's sake to Rambouillet, the king signed an act of abdication in favour of his grandson, the Duke of Bordeaux. Angoulême refused four times to do the same but finally agreed, and fell into a state of despair, walking around aimlessly and then suddenly smiling and laughing. The Duchess of Berry was appointed regent. Amid rumours that royalists were planning to march on Paris, 15,000 people advanced on Rambouillet. A general rode ahead to warn Charles, who set off for the coast of Normandy. In Paris, Louis-Philippe was proclaimed king by 219 of the 252 members of the Chamber of Deputies.

The flight of the king

The death toll of the July Days amounted to around 650 – 150 soldiers and 500 protestors, mainly skilled workers aged between twenty-five and thirty-five. Those who had served the restored senior Bourbons met varied fates. Polignac disguised himself as a servant to a noblewoman and headed for the Channel, but his large diamond ring and the way his supposed employers cared for him when he fell ill aroused suspicions; arrested and sentenced to life imprisonment, he was amnestied in 1836. Chateaubriand refused to swear an oath of loyalty and renounced his state pensions. Marmont accompanied the king and forfeited his rank of marshal; he wandered round Europe before settling in Vienna and Venice. Villèle devoted himself to his memoirs while Bourdonnaye retired to his old-world fiefdom in western France, angry and ill. Decazes developed a mining concession in a town in the Aveyron *département* that took his name. Talleyrand rallied to the new order.

Charles's third journey into exile in 1830 was a slow one in extremely hot summer weather. He and his party lodged in the châteaux of royalists, closely watched by the local police. They sometimes stopped for roadside picnics; there were cheers in a few places, but they were generally greeted with silence. The deposed king seemed resigned.

Angoulême and his wife were downcast. The new regime in Paris sent an envoy to seek to induce the Duke of Bordeaux back to the capital; his mother would have none of that. Red in the face and wearing trousers, waistcoat, a green redingote coat and a man's hat, with two pistols at her waist, she intended to see her son enthroned as Henri V. When the party boarded two steamers at Cherbourg to cross to Britain, she reverted to women's clothes, but kept her pistols.

Charles lived first in Dorset and then at Holyrood Palace in Edinburgh. After two years, he moved to Prague at the invitation of the Austrian emperor, later going to Görz* on the Mediterranean, where he took walks along the shore. After mass on his seventy-ninth birthday in 1836, he became feverish and vomited. He had cholera. As his grandson came to his bedside, a cardinal performed the final rites. The last monarch of the senior Bourbon line was buried in a Franciscan monastery where his tomb was laid on soil brought from France.

Chateaubriand judged that he would have been a reasonable enough king for ordinary times, but was a loser in an extraordinary epoch. It was a charitable verdict. Charles and those who shared his convictions were doomed by the evolution of the nation and their narrow-mindedness, though their top-down ideas would live on in many different forms as the long confrontation between revolution, republicanism, conservatism and reaction played out through the coming decade.

* Now Gorizia in northern Italy, on the border with Slovenia.

3

CITIZEN KING

In his iconic painting *Liberty Guiding the People*, Delacroix depicted France's second revolution, and its third regime change in four decades, as the triumph of the forces of popular progress led to victory by the bare-breasted symbol of Marianne. Royal autocracy had been overturned once more, but this time, elite bourgeois liberalism had taken the street protests in hand to ensure France avoided what Thiers called the 'generous folly' of a republic. What was to follow was, however, unclear.

Despite its fate under Charles X, the Restoration had not been without merit. France had re-joined the community of nations and there had been striking technological advances – the first photographic image was produced in 1822 by Nicéphore Niépce. Frenchmen identified quinine and invented the stethoscope, Braille, the sewing machine and the pencil sharpener. But the attempt by Charles X to turn the clock back after the introduction of a more responsible monarchy by his brother had fallen foul of the evolving power of the upper bourgeoisie, who sent the revolutionary crowds home and took charge under a congenial monarch.

The July Monarchy

The new regime belonged to well-placed establishment figures who saw the folly of Charles X's policies, bankers like Laffitte and Casimir Périer, and middle-way politicians like François Guizot and Adolphe

Thiers, plus some imperial survivors. Louis-Philippe, the 'Citizen King', was expected to play along with their vision of society; a 'normal' ruler in tune with the times, claiming office as the incarnation of constitutionalism as defined by those who put him there, reconciling safe progressive values with respect for property, wealth and stability, a monarch who sang the Marseillaise with his hand on his heart but would defend the interests of the class that had brought him to the throne. What people feared, he had told Charles X, was 'to lose representative government which, alone, can provide repose and happiness'.

Yet, new order's legitimacy was open to question, given the street unrest that had driven out Charles X. Metternich noted that the July Monarchy was a hybrid creature lacking the popular force of the Revolution, the military glory of the Empire or the legitimacy of the Restoration. Talleyrand warned that France was 'moving towards an unknown world without a compass or pilot [in which] only one thing is certain. It will all finish with a wreck'. He put a portrait of the deposed monarch beside that of one of his mistresses and saluted it each morning.

There was, however, no doubting the change of tone. This was to be a practical regime; 'the misfortune of our country is that we never stop thinking,' the king reflected. 'No one is prepared to see things as they really are.' In place of doctrinal disputes, the king 'preferred cunning to force and always tried to turn obstacles rather than attack them frontally,' as Guizot recalled. Making money became a hallmark of the July Monarchy under a king who was one of the richest men in France, with personal assets estimated to bring in 18 million francs a year. The Palais-Royal became an employment exchange for those with the cash to buy official positions. Membership of the National Guard was restricted to those who paid direct taxes and could afford to purchase uniforms.

The Citizen King was businesslike and well organised – a card index of everybody he met was kept so that he could ask after their families and show familiarity with their lives. The number of courtiers was sharply cut. The king and queen shared a secretary. The civil list was cut from 30 to 12 million francs. Louis-Philippe decided that his family

The Normal Monarch

Louis-Philippe's backstory was very different from those of his predecessors. After fighting in the early revolutionary army and then
fleeing France as the Terror gathered pace, he taught at a boys'
school on the Upper Rhine where he insisted on wearing a clean
shirt every day and fathered an illegitimate child by the school's
Italian cook. Leaving with a certificate of competence as a teacher,
he travelled through Scandinavia and spent four years in the United
States, giving French lessons and living in rooms above the Oyster
House restaurant in Boston as well as visiting New York, Maine and
Nashville. In 1800, he went to London and settled in High Shot
House in Twickenham by the Thames.

Nine years later, he married a kinswoman of the Duchess of
Berry, Princess Marie-Amélie of Naples and Sicily who described
herself as 'tall and well-built' with a rather long face, blue eyes,
golden hair, well-set teeth and 'a good leg but rather long feet'. Her
husband was 'of medium height, rather stout, neither ugly nor
handsome ... polite and very learned'. They played with their six
sons and four daughters in the evening and drove about with them
in a coach with room for a dozen people. They called themselves
the Bobinettes. Showing visitors the large royal bed, the monarch
remarked, 'the king sleeps with his wife.'

He was diligent in attending to state affairs. After balls and receptions which ended at 10 p.m., the king worked in his rooms until 2
or 3 a.m. at a maple wood desk that had belonged to Napoleon. He
slept for only a few hours in a bed with a horsehair mattress on a
wooden plank, the lamp burning all night and two loaded pistols on
the table.

would keep the name of d'Orléans and not switch to the traditional de France. He was agreeable company, erudite and courteous, often walking to appointments in middle-class clothes – blue jacket with gold buttons, pale yellow trousers, white waistcoat and grey top hat with a tricolour symbol, and a large umbrella, which he tucked under his arm when there was no rain.

The monarch rose between 7 and 8 a.m., and had his hairdresser fix his wig. After donning a floor-length dressing gown, he received officials, read British newspapers, and worked on state documents, annotating them in his large, spidery handwriting. He shaved and, at 11 a.m., ate boiled rice and a waffle washed down with a glass of water. Then he talked to his family before setting off for a walk, sometimes going as far as his old home in Neuilly, where he picked violets in the spring and shook hands with passers-by.

In the afternoon, he presided over cabinet meetings, discussed affairs of state and received delegations before dining at 6 p.m. At royal dinners for sixty or more guests, he was presented with four or five soups, which he mixed together, a glass of Spanish wine, a slice of roast meat, a little ragout, a few vegetables and a dish of macaroni. After which, he went to a reception or a ball for which jackets, breeches and white stockings could be rented at kiosks set up outside, with the palace taking a cut.

The tricolour was re-established as the national flag. Ministers became Monsieur instead of Excellence or Monseigneur. The Napoleonic column in the Place Vendôme was rebuilt and a new statue of the emperor installed on top. The other major column in the city, at the Place de la Bastille, was dedicated to the July Days, rather than to 1789.

In his inaugural address from the throne, Louis-Philippe declared his support for the middle way championed by Guizot's Doctrinaires. The electorate for national elections was raised to 166,000 and more than two million men were entitled to vote in local government polls. The proportion of nobles sitting in parliament fell from 60 per cent to 40 per cent. Still, less than 1 per cent of the population had the right to vote for the Chamber of Deputies, compared to 14 per cent in Britain after the 1832 Reform Act.

The new order made sure it enjoyed command of the administration with a purge in which 83 per cent of prefects and sub-prefects were replaced. Seven million francs was voted in compensation for those injured or widowed or orphaned during the July Days. Laws enforcing Catholicism were replaced and the Ultra legislation against sacrilege, which had never been used, was undone. Censorship was lifted. The National Guard paraded to greet the new order; Louis-Philippe regarded its mainly bourgeois members as a guarantee of loyalty from the capital's middle class.

Religious salaries and spending were reduced and the appointment of ultramontane bishops, who exalted papal powers, was discouraged. The big Parisian church of Sainte-Geneviève was returned to its revolutionary role as a secular temple, the Panthéon. The Archbishop of Paris went into hiding for a time, the press reporting he had with him a treasure trove of gold and diamonds. While 300,000 people attended mass in Paris, only 50,000 were reckoned to be true believers; shops were allowed to open on Sunday because, as one official put it, 'the people being generally without belief, it would be an act of sheer tyranny to shut them.'[1]

For those who profited it was a comfortable regime that offered an alternative to the roller-coaster ride of the previous four decades. But there was no shortage of critics. De Tocqueville saw the king as having consigned France to being 'a little bourgeois stew pot'. It had once been a great nation, the historian François Mignet lamented, but 'now only wishes to be a prosperous nation'. Karl Marx, who lived in Paris for a time, described the July Monarchy as a joint stock company for the exploitation of national wealth with dividends shared among ministers, parliamentarians and their adherents. 'The religion of money is the only one today which has no unbelievers,' noted the writer Théophile Gautier. The leading historian of the day, Edmond Michelet, condemned 'the reign of gold, of the Jew'. The caricaturist Honoré Daumier portrayed the monarch as a Gargantua figure; consuming sacks of cash carried up to his mouth by ragged citizens.

The king's authority was evident in his first government, which had no chief minister to compete with him. It contained men who would reoccur throughout the July Monarchy, some of whom had navigated the transfer from empire to monarchy and were now set-tled into the elite political establishment. Guizot was interior minister. Another Doctrinaire, Victor, Duke of Broglie, took respon-sibility for education and religious instruction. The foreign minister, Count Louis-Matthieu Molé, an elegant if lugubrious figure, had served Napoleon and been naval minister under Louis XVIII; he har-boured a deep antipathy for Guizot whom he described as having 'an unbridled[2] thirst for power, ambition without limits or brakes, a taste for all the vanity of grandeur'.

The finance ministry was handed to a remarkable technician, Baron Louis, a one-time priest ennobled under the Empire who had overseen the rebuilding of state finances during the Restoration. The war minis-ter, Count Étienne Maurice Gérard, had fought as a senior officer for Napoleon. The bankers, Jacques Laffitte and Casimir Perier were min-isters without portfolio. Thiers had to be content to be under-secretary to the Treasury, but he was only thirty-three.

Talleyrand went to London as ambassador, wearing a hat with an enormous tricolour cockade, and immediately played a key role in the new monarchy's first major foreign affairs test, set off when liberals and Catholics in the southern Netherlands, which had been put under Dutch rule by the Congress of Vienna in 1815, revolted against their Protestant king, in part emboldened by the overthrow of Charles X across the border.

Louis-Philippe was anxious not to be provocative; France, he said, was 'concerned only with her own internal prosperity ... and wishes only for the happiness and repose of her neighbours'. So he resisted calls to intervene as King William of the Netherlands took a hard line. But, after the rebels repulsed Dutch troops and declared a provisional govern-ment in October 1830, France was one of five states that recognised the new nation and guaranteed its independence at a conference in London. Louis-Philippe turned down the idea that the throne should go to his son, the Duke of Nemours; it was awarded instead to Prince Leopold of Saxe-Coburg. When the Dutch tried to regain their posses-sion by force, the guarantee from the major powers meant France was free to send in troops to drive them out. The king's cautious diplomacy had worked and there was no opposition from other powers when his daughter, Louise, married Leopold.

Pleasing as this foreign policy success was, the July Monarchy faced two oppositional poles – the Legitimists and the Parisian streets; the first saw Louis-Philippe as a usurper and the second as having stolen the Revolution. The prominent lawyer and outstanding orator, Pierre-Antoine Berryer, castigated the new monarchy as an unnatural creature founded on broken oaths and incompatible with France's traditions. Legitimists who advocated universal suffrage and social progress found a leader in the Abbé de Genoude, a former businessman who had made a lot of money under the Restoration and joined the priesthood after his wife died; he read editorials from his newspaper, *La Gazette de France*, from the pulpit. There was also opposition in some provincial centres, including Marseilles which repeatedly returned Berryer to parliament. Many people in the port city remained loyal to Charles X – a man who resembled him was presented with free garlands by flower sellers and the clergy rejected the new regime.[3]

Scornful royalists in the Faubourg Saint-Germain across the Seine from the Tuileries called the monarch 'Fipp the First – king of the boulevards'. Their newspaper, *La Mode*, which referred to him as *Untel* (So-and-so), reported that he had set up a stall at the entrance to the Tuileries to hire out umbrellas and walking sticks. The Legitimists worked up rumours against the new regime, alleging that Louis-Philippe was the child of a prison guard conceived during a visit to Italy, and that the queen was fond of the bottle and had a liaison with a general.[4]

A juicy scandal appeared to have emerged when the head of the illustrious Condé family, his Serene Highness Louis Henri de Bourbon, was found dead in his locked bedroom at the family château outside Paris a month after Louis-Philippe ascended the throne. The prince had been strangled by a scarf round his neck attached to a window catch. He could not have tied the scarf himself because of a fractured shoulder and an injury that had cost him three fingers from his right hand. The assumption was that he had been murdered.

The discovery of a secret passage between his room and that of his mistress, an Englishwoman called Sophie Dawes, pointed the finger at her. They had met while he was in revolutionary exile in London where she worked as a maid at a brothel he frequented in Piccadilly. Returning to France at the Restoration, he took her with him and got her married to a French soldier while maintaining their relationship. After Charles X banned her from Court, she gravitated into the Orléanist circle. Condé's will left her 10 million francs, but 66 million went to Louis-Philippe's son, the Duke of Aumale. Legitimists suggested a murder plot by Dawes and the Orléanists to get the money. But the scandal deflated when it turned out that Dawes practised erotic asphyxiation on the aged nobleman, which, on this occasion, had gone sadly wrong. With her cash, she left for London as the Orléans family fortunes swelled even more.[5]

The Duchess of Berry tried to raise the flag of revolt by landing near Marseilles calling for an insurrection on behalf of her son. Attracting little support, she headed for the Vendée and had no more luck there, as scattered attacks by her ill-armed followers were easily crushed. Fleeing to Nantes in peasant clothes and a chestnut-coloured wig, she hid in the home of two royalist ladies. A double agent betrayed her to the interior ministry. When police arrived, she hid in a priest's hole behind an attic chimney-piece. The searchers failed to find her, but two stayed behind and, by chance, lit a fire in the attic, forcing her out, covered in soot and half-suffocated. Held in prison, she was found to be pregnant, and, after her release, married the father of her second child, an Italian count.

On the other side of politics, republicans could draw some comfort from the continued prominence of Odilon Barrot, the Prefect of the Seine, who believed in giving the street its head, and of Lafayette as commander of the National Guard. But true radicals congregated in secret societies and clubs such as those animated by Auguste Blanqui, the incarnation of revolutionary violence who was described by Chateaubriand as having 'wan, emaciated cheeks, white lips, a sickly, wicked and repulsive expression, a dirty pallor, the appearance of a mouldy corpse; he wore no visible linen; an old black frock-coat tightly covered his lean, withered limbs; he seemed to have passed his life in a sewer and to have just left it.'[6]

At the end of 1830, violent demonstrations broke out demanding the execution of Polignac and three other former ministers of Charles X; the king felt obliged to withdraw a proposal to abolish the death penalty though, in the event, the four were given long prison terms. The loyalty of the National Guard came into question when some of its members fraternised with the demonstrators; a republican firebrand officer, Godefroy Cavaignac, was among those arrested for siding with the crowd they were meant to be holding back.

The king named Laffitte as head of a new government, which the banker pledged would seek '*mouvement*', the term used by those who saw the July Revolution as the launching pad for change. The banker also took over the finance ministry but was singularly ineffective. At the war ministry, Gérard gave way to his fellow Napoleonic marshal, Soult, who introduced military reforms and legislation creating the Foreign Legion. Anxious to burnish his popular credentials, Laffitte pushed through a proposal to replace the fleurs-de-lis as the royal symbol with an image of a shield and open book with the wording '*Charte de 1830*'. That displeased the king who got his revenge when the Chamber voted to abolish the post of emergency commander of the Guard held by Lafayette; Laffitte made every effort to placate the 'hero of two worlds', but the king insisted. Cavaignac and nine other republicans were accused of plotting a revolt but were acquitted and carried in triumph through the streets by thousands of supporters. Then, the most serious trouble the regime had faced erupted in Paris in protest at a royalist mass to commemorate the eleventh anniversary of the assassination of the Duke of Berry, starting a series of insurrections that would mark the reign ushered in by street action eight months earlier.

A mass held in the church of Saint-Germain l'Auxerrois by the Louvre on 14 February 1831, was bound to be a provocative act coming after a string of anti-clerical demonstrations in the capital. A mob surged into the church screaming 'Death to priests', or 'Death to Louis-Philippe!' The Austro-Hungarian diplomat, Rodolphe Apponyi, watched 'a huge crowd, men with axes, clubs, spears, their sleeves rolled up, their bodies daubed in red paint, brandishing torches' saw through the cross on the altar which collapsed amid triumphant cries.[7]

The following day, the mob gave similar treatment to the head-quarters of the archbishopric of Paris, throwing the furniture, books and sacred objects into the Seine and parading vestments and religious artefacts through the streets as they sang obscene songs. Demonstrators tried to hoist the cross on the main altar in Notre-Dame and drop it to the floor to destroy it, but it was too solid and heavy to budge. A wild procession then set off led by a man carrying a cross and another with a bowl of muddy water into which he dipped a sprinkler and showered the crowd, shouting 'There, sacred water for nothing!' That night, word spread that a republic was about to be declared. 'It's terrible but let's dance,' Apponyi's partner said to him at an all-night ball at James de Rothschild's mansion. 'If we are really going to have a republic tomorrow, it will be the end of parties and balls for a long time.'

On 17 February, the mob invaded the Palais-Royal; the youngest of the royal princesses had a nervous seizure. Louis-Philippe came out holding a large tricolour flag and persuaded the crowd to disperse. Some demonstrators attacked a Jesuit centre. Lafayette held court in his house while demonstrators flowed through the streets outside. When a big concert was held at the Palais-Royal to suggest that normality had returned, noise from the mob outside drowned the music before troops drove them away. 'Always the same madness,' Apponyi noted. 'They dance in the salons; they fight in the streets; one is in the midst of revolution. Everything seems to crumble; we are on a volcano.'

Laffitte fell after his cabinet, reflecting royal wishes, declined to back him in urging French intervention on behalf of nationalists in Italy. The banker said he now rued his role in putting Orléans on the throne. Leaving a budget deficit of 51 million francs and failing to be elected president of the Chamber of Deputies, he went into eclipse; forced to wind up his financial affairs, he became known by the punning name of *Monsieur Faillite* (Mr Bust). To replace him, Louis-Philippe called on his rival, Casimir Perier, leader of the conservative *Parti de la Résistance* who, with his brother, had founded France's first savings bank and invested in industry, canals, coalmines and insurance as well as developing the suburb of Neuilly.

A highly strung, short-tempered workaholic, with thin lips, little hair and black thickets of eyebrows, the new chief minister was firm in his pursuit of a policy of order at home and peace abroad. His insistence that he alone was in charge of government was not to the king's liking, but he yielded in the face of the politician-banker's competence. However, tensions rose as fighting killed a hundred National Guardsmen and sixty-nine insurgents when silk workers in Lyons staged a rising to protest at reduced rates for piecework. The mayor and the local army commander fled. The government sent in an army that entered the city without bloodshed. Ninety insurgents were arrested but only eleven were prosecuted and all were acquitted. A National Assembly motion depicted the insurrection as a bid to prevent 'the freedom of commerce and industry'.

The first half of 1832 saw trouble in Picardy, the Alpine region and Carcassonne. A riot broke out in Grenoble after the prefect cancelled the annual carnival because revellers sported an insulting mask of the king. A police spy said he had uncovered a scheme by a royalist group to take over the Tuileries and massacre the Orléans family.

A major cholera epidemic raged for three months in Paris in beautiful, clear weather. Twenty thousand died. The artisans' quarter of Saint-Antoine was worst hit. The stink of putrefaction was everywhere as carts piled high with bodies in white sacks trundled to communal burial pits. Many of the rich fled the city. Priests promised consecrated rosaries would ward off the malady. Wrapping oneself in flannel was regarded as a good protection; the king wore a belt of the fabric. When the authorities sent in teams to clean the streets, rag pickers protested at being deprived of the rubbish that provided their living. Ill and exhausted, Casimir Perier succumbed in May after visiting hospitals.

The epidemic came amid failing harvests that set off the familiar cycle of rising food prices and declining demand for consumer goods. Foreign revolutionary refugees joined the secret societies of the left. 'Something terrible was brewing,' wrote Hugo in his novel on the period, *Les Misérables*. 'One could make out the still indistinct and ill-lit features of a possible revolution.' If it did come, it could arise only in the city that had earned its revolutionary spurs in 1789 and 1830.[8]

Paris: head of the world

With its 800,000 inhabitants, Paris contained less than one-thirtieth of France's population, but it was the fulcrum for events that determined the fate of national regimes, its newspapers shaping opinion. Balzac called it 'the head of the world, a brain exploding with genius, the leader of civilisation, the most adorable of fatherlands'. The hub of power lay on either side of the Seine in the middle of the capital – the royal palace of the Tuileries on the right and, across the river, the Palais Bourbon that housed the Chamber of Deputies. Nobles clustered in their stately mansions in the Faubourg Saint-Germain, keeping their distance from the new rich of the Right Bank where the Chaussée-d'Antin district became the centre for finance and business. Up the hill at Montmartre, in a sign of technological progress, a telegraphic relay station linked with Lille. Gas lamps lit the streets, installed by a company in which a major shareholder was an enterprising Englishman, Daniel Wilson, who pioneered gas meters.[9]

There were increasing opportunities for the middle class to spend its gains, from home appliances to the racecourses at the Champ-de-Mars and Chantilly. Glass-roofed shopping galleries grouped together selected retailers. Restaurants burgeoned – the Café Anglais, the Maison d'Or and the Café de Paris along the fashionable boulevards, Grignon in the Galerie Vivienne and the establishments under the arcades of the Orléanist headquarters in the Palais-Royal; at the most celebrated of these, Véry, Balzac had a meal in which he was served a hundred oysters followed by a dozen lamb chops, a duckling, two roast partridges, a sole and a dozen pears. For those who wanted to eat at home, top-class grocers provided large spreads – the sign of the fashionable Corcellet outlet in the Palais-Royal showed a contented man at a table tucking into a large meal from the shop.

With its marble-topped tables and passing procession of dandies, Tortoni, on the Boulevard des Italiens, was celebrated for ice creams. Some restaurants set aside *cabinets particuliers* with private entrances for discrete meetings especially of married men with women other than their wives; females, it was thought, were bound to lower their defences in such places. Satirical drawings showed men arriving with their companions and telling the waiter to bring the food after an hour had elapsed. Those with a more direct approach to sex could choose between 200 registered brothels.

Despite losing treasures reclaimed by the Allies in 1815, the Louvre was the greatest museum and gallery in the world, while Paris was the centre of the international art trade. Pleasure gardens, cafés and dance halls were strung along the boulevards, brothels and gambling dens in the streets behind. Two studios offered the first personal photographic services, at 25 francs a frame. Factories sprang up on the outskirts. Traffic along the Seine and on the Canal Saint-Martin made Paris France's busiest port. Ambitious young provincials headed for the city to make their way in the world. Migrant workers from poorer regions formed communities speaking native patois and specialising in different trades – coal merchants and café owners from the Auvergne, stonemasons from the Creuse, domestic helpers from Normandy and Brittany.

The Boulevard du Temple in the east of the city housed half-a-dozen theatres; its nickname, Boulevard du Crime, did not refer to misdemeanours committed there but to the melodramas on its stages. A little way away, weekend crowds watched fights between dogs and boars, stags, bulls and bears by the Canal Saint-Martin; at the Barrière du Combat people played darts with rats as targets. Les Halles was France's biggest food market, while in a pattern which still persists today, the 2nd *arrondissement* was the centre for the textile and clothing trade and the rue Saint-Honoré for luxury goods. Foreign artists and intellectuals added to the city's cultural allure – Chopin, Liszt, Heine.

The capital was run not by mayors but by prefects, two of who dominated the period from 1815 to 1848. Gilbert Joseph Gaspard, Count of Chabrol de Volvic, held office from the Restoration to 1830 and Claude Philibert Barthelot, Count of Rambuteau, was in charge at the city hall for fifteen years from 1833. Both improved streets and pavements, water supply and drainage, street lighting and open spaces – 'True politics consists of making life comfortable and people happy,' Chabrol said, while Rambuteau believed in 'Air, water and shade'.

But most Parisians still lived in insalubrious homes in filthy streets with garbage piled up around them and sewage running straight into the Seine, creating evil-smelling swamps. Disease was common. Police were harsh. Welfare was rare. Outside the encircling walls, many people huddled in primitive conditions surrounded by health-destroying tanneries and unhygienic slaughterhouses. One per cent of the population owned 80 per cent of the wealth. Seventy per cent left nothing at death. Half were reckoned to be indigent. Paris was thought to contain 30,000 thieves. One in every forty-two inhabitants of the Saint-Honoré district was a prostitute. The maze of twisting streets and alleys housing an array of small workshops in the Faubourg Saint-Antoine in the east of the city was described as 'the crater from which the lava of revolution most often escaped'. As Hugo wrote of 1832, 'France looked to Paris, and Paris looked to the Faubourg Saint-Antoine [which] was coming to the boil.'[10]

Revolt and Infernal Machines

The spark came with the funeral procession for a Napoleonic commander, Jean Maximilien Lamarque, a leading critic of the July Monarchy. At the Place de la Bastille, a demonstrator held up a red flag emblazoned with the words '*La Liberté ou La Mort*' ('Liberty or Death'). Students joined workers as the crowd took over eastern districts of the capital in heavy rain. Soldiers and the National Guard moved in to isolate the rebels behind their barricades. A final redoubt in the Saint-Merri cloister held out for three days against troops who for the first time used artillery against protestors, followed by summary executions.

Showing his habitual personal courage, the king rode through the city to visit National Guard posts; he kept a fixed smile to inspire confidence but his face was flabby and yellow and he wore a three-cornered hat with a front flap that hung over his forehead giving him what the poet Heine, who watched standing on an upturned bath tub, called 'a very unfortunate appearance'. The toll was put at 93 dead and 291 wounded among the insurgents and 73 and 344 respectively among soldiers and guardsmen. There were widespread arrests. State bonds rose by 10 per cent as investors took comfort at the restoration of order.[11]

Louis-Philippe appointed a new government headed by Marshal Soult with de Broglie as foreign minister, Thiers at the interior and Guizot in charge of education. A public works programme was launched to stimulate the economy and Guizot put through legislation providing for a primary school for boys in each commune. But fresh violence broke out in 1834 with protests against legislation to curb left-wing political clubs and a second rising by the silk workers of Lyons angry at their treatment by the manufacturers; Thiers sent in troops who regained control in fighting that took between one and two hundred lives. There were unsuccessful republican revolts in half-a-dozen provincial centres. Barricades went up again in Paris but this fresh revolt was soon suppressed. As order returned, troops were fired on from a house in the rue Transnonain in a central working-class area. Police rushed inside and massacred eleven men, women and children, inspiring one of Daumier's most celebrated lithographs.[12]

Two thousand people were arrested; while only 160 were charged, they included many of the main republican leaders who were jailed or deported. Parliament voted to enlarge the army to fight domestic rather than foreign foes. In the midst of all this, Lafayette died at his country estate, lying on soil he had brought from America so as to die in a free land, his dream of becoming France's George Washington unrealised.

After almost two years in office, Soult resigned as his cabinet grew increasingly disjointed and government became chaotic. The king installed a government under the other Napoleonic marshal, Gérard, and called elections at which Orléanist loyalists fared poorly. Louis-Philippe sent the Chamber on an extended holiday before appointing as chief minister the Duke of Bassano who was so in debt that his creditors seized his pay and his government resigned en masse. Another imperial veteran, Marshal Mortier, stepped in but resigned on health grounds after four months. Finally, in March 1835, de Broglie returned to head the government with Guizot and Thiers at their accustomed places at the education and interior ministries.

Three months after the new government was formed, the king rode out of the Tuileries at the head of a military and civilian procession, which made its way through the city for the rest of the morning. Among those behind him were the royal princes; de Broglie; his predecessor,

Mortier; the Paris Prefect, Rambuteau; and Thiers, a poor horseman. An informer had warned the police of an assassination attempt but a search of the area found nothing.

Loudly applauded by watching crowds, the procession passed along the boulevard and turned into the Boulevard du Temple. A fusillade erupted as if a company of soldiers was firing. 'This is for me,' the king exclaimed, his sons closing ranks round him. A bullet grazed his forehead; another wounded his horse. Mortier fell dead across Rambuteau's mount. Seventeen others were killed and many hurt. Riding forward, Louis-Philippe stood up in his stirrups, waved his plumed hat and shouted 'Here I am!' Cries of '*Vive le roi!*' came back from the crowd.

The plot was the work of a Corsican desperado, Giuseppe Fieschi, who had been presented to the king in 1830 as one of the street revolutionaries of the July Days. He was joined by Pierre Morey, an inveterate plotter with a nostalgia for the Terror. A successful but stupid shopkeeper, Théodore Pépin, provided the money to build an 'infernal machine' and rent a house overlooking the parade route. Designed by Fieschi, the machine fired a score of rifles simultaneously. It was hidden behind the closed curtains of the house; if Fieschi had drawn them a few seconds earlier and activated the machine, the king would probably have been killed. Fieschi was lucky to survive since Morey, not wanting to leave a witness, had fixed the apparatus so that it blew up when fired. As it was, he was horribly injured, but doctors saved his life so that he could be executed with his two co-conspirators.

This was the most dramatic of more than half-a-dozen known attempts to kill Louis-Philippe between 1830 and 1848, including the construction of a similar machine to Fieschi's by a mechanic who was arrested before he could put it into operation and hanged himself in his prison cell. A 26-year-old anarchist shot at the monarch as he leaned out of the window of his armoured coach when leaving the Tuileries for Neuilly. In 1836, a commercial traveller narrowly missed with a shot from a rifle disguised as a walking stick; arrested, he said 'Jesus Christ was a democrat like me and if it had been necessary he would have become a regicide.' A disgruntled gamekeeper took a shot at the monarch in Fontainebleau forest. The king's son, the Duke of Aumale, was also the target of a point-blank shooting which managed to miss him.

Louis-Philippe, who disliked capital punishment, kept a sorrowful list of people he had not been able to reprieve, including most of the would-be assassins. But he did manage to spare the life of a young man who fired into his coach as he and his sons drove to the Chamber of Deputies, explaining his action by saying that 'the Orléans have always made France unhappy'. The king revoked the death sentence and the young man went to live in the United States with a small royal pension.

The search for stability

The scale of the Fieschi attack deeply shocked public opinion. The powers of the public prosecutor were increased, simple majority voting by juries replaced the two-thirds majority previously required; the press, which was blamed for having fanned the flames of revolt, was banned from discussions about the king, his family and the constitutional monarchy. The de Broglie government suffered from the usual internal rivalries and fell in early 1837 after it tried to lighten the public debt in ways that would have affected the value of bonds, into which the French liked to sink their savings.

It was now the turn of Thiers to try to put together a majority. The son of a locksmith from a small southern village, he showed his roots by eating olives in cabinet meetings and spitting out the stones. He had recently married a sixteen-year-old, two decades his junior, and was the object of allegations that he and other ministers had indulged in a drunken orgy at a château during which they stood naked on the billiard table to deliver parodies of political speeches. As well as his journalism and politics, he had made his name with a ten-volume history of the Revolution arguing that republicanism was the central theme of contemporary French history. Believing that the king should rule but not govern, he was quite content to head a royal government under a monarch who amused himself by keeping police reports on the politician's amorous affairs.

Thiers enjoyed the support of rich patrons whom he repaid with state preferment. Short, vain and with a nasal voice, he was hard to pin down. The British prime minister Lord Melbourne called him 'a strange quicksilver man'. He inspired 'an indefinable feeling of aversion and disgust' in Victor Hugo while Karl Marx described him as a 'monstrous gnome' who was 'the most consummate intellectual expression of bourgeois class corruption ... having entered his first ministry poor as Job, he left it a millionaire'.[13]

He achieved little, failing to negotiate a marriage for the dauphin – a tall, slender man with what Heine described as a 'rosy, healthy, blooming, youthful face' – to an Austrian archduchess as the king greatly desired. He pressed for military intervention in Spain to support the royal family against a rightist Carlist revolt, but Louis-Philippe demurred and Thiers stepped down after seven months. Molé, who enjoyed the favour of the monarch's influential sister, took over, but Guizot and Thiers buried their rivalry to oppose him. In a marathon string of parliamentary debates at the beginning of 1839, the three men made thirty-two often-lengthy parliamentary speeches between them in twelve days, and Molé managed to emerge victorious, much to the king's pleasure.[14]

Instead of an Austrian marriage, the Duke of Orléans wed Princess Hélène of Mecklenburg-Schwerin, which pleased Louis-Philippe since he saw the union as marking the acceptance of the Orléanist clan into the European court establishment. There were other reasons for royal satisfaction. The Château of Versailles was restored and turned into a national museum. The economy improved and the army reported success in the conquest of inland Algeria, conducting *razzias* to deny the native population food or shelter while officers grabbed booty and appropriated land for personal estates.[15]

A general amnesty was extended to political prisoners, but the government also made a gesture to Catholics by having crucifixes re-established in courtrooms and allowing the church of Saint-Germain l'Auxerrois in Paris to resume its cultish religious practices. There were, however, two more assassination attempts and Napoleon's nephew, Louis-Napoleon Bonaparte, attempted to foment a rising at Strasbourg. When this flopped, he was bundled off without trial on a ship to the USA.

Louis-Philippe and Molé decided to hold elections but government supporters were left in a minority and the Guizot-Thiers coalition prevented the formation of a stable government. At the opening of the parliamentary session in the spring of 1839, a mob rioted around the Chamber of Deputies as Soult, returning as head of government, failed to impose order.

A secret society, the innocuously named *Société des Saisons* (Society of the Seasons), led by Blanqui and other radicals, staged a rising in the Parisian districts of Saint-Denis and Saint-Martin, raiding a gun shop for arms and sending gangs of men running through the city. They briefly seized the Chamber and the City Hall, but failed to raise popular support. Falling back on the working-class area east of the city centre, they put up a final stand around the Saint-Merri cloister as they had before in 1832, but were, once more, overcome by troops. Blanqui and his fellow serial conspirator, Armand Barbès, were given death sentences, which were commuted; they were locked up in Mont Saint-Michel in Normandy.

When Soult's government collapsed for lack of a solid parliamentary majority in March 1840, the king's only recourse was to call in Thiers. Guizot was sent off as ambassador to London. The new chief minister played his cards more judiciously this time, appealing to the centre-right to put together a comfortable majority. He sought to draw on the glorious past with the completion of the Arc de Triomphe and by bringing Napoleon's ashes from Saint Helena for burial in a tomb set on a plinth under the great dome of Les Invalides in Paris; huge crowds watched the procession. Having returned from the United States, Louis-Napoleon tried a fresh rising, this time in Boulogne. Again, it failed. Tried by the Chamber of Peers, he was given a life sentence and locked up in the dark, dank fortress of Ham in north-east France.

Thiers continued his patriotic line by taking a tough stance in a dispute with Britain, Prussia and Russia over the pro-French pasha of Egypt. He threatened to send the army across the Rhine, but was restrained by the king and the high command, which was well aware of the country's military weakness. Unabashed, the chief minister dusted off old plans for a ring of fortifications round Paris in case of war. When completed in 1843, this stretched for thirty kilometres and included seventeen military strong points – '*les fortifs*' as they would be known. They deprived the people of Paris of unhindered access to the countryside.

But the king, always keen on construction projects, welcomed them for providing work.[16]

However, Thiers lost ground as liberals staged big demonstrations for reform, there was another attempt to assassinate the monarch and the economy stalled. Bourse prices fell. Textile and building workers went on strike. Furniture makers in the Faubourg Saint-Antoine put up barricades. Thiers sent in the National Guard and banned public meetings.

To show his disapproval, the king refused to make a speech drafted by the government declaring that no sacrifice would be too great to keep France's position in the world. Thiers and his ministers resigned and in October 1840 Soult was called back a third time at the age of seventy-one. However, Guizot at the foreign ministry was the guiding force in the new administration, which lasted for an unprecedented seven years in an alliance between the king and the Doctrinaire that dominated the last half of the July Monarchy.

The austere, aloof Calvinist from Nîmes was the king's favourite politician; Louis-Philippe called him 'the last Roman' in contrast to those who had 'a superabundance of courage and audacity when in opposition but, when in office, prove to be featherweights'. An excellent parliamentary debater, he left no doubt about his moral and intellectual superiority; Heine described him 'an almost German pedant'. He believed change had gone quite far enough; the aim should be to protect the status quo in a royal state that left the lives of citizens to themselves and God. If people wanted to get the vote, they should enrich themselves through work and saving to meet the qualifications.[17]

There were reforms, notably in increasing the number of schools; pupil numbers rose by 50 per cent. The salt tax was abolished. Legislation was passed to reduce the use of child labour, though it was often evaded. Serious-minded followers of the early socialist theorist Saint-Simon, seeking a new model for society and politics, applied his ideas to industry and banking (though most attention was grabbed by a 'charismatic' group headed by the eccentric, fez-wearing Barthélemy Prosper Enfantin who had himself declared its Père, advocated free love and propagated his ideas through a newspaper, *Le Globe*, until his group was banned). Still, in the name of economic freedom, the ban on trade unions continued and many of those employed in factories and workshops were supplied by contractors who kept wages down so that their cut from employers was as large as possible.

Guizot shared the monarch's caution in foreign policy, so they turned a deaf ear to pressure for action to help nationalists in Poland and Italy. Queen Victoria wrote of a 'gay and happy' visit to the king at his Norman château of Eu in 1843, the first to France by a British monarch since Henry VIII. At a picnic in the woods, Louis-Philippe produced a large pocket knife to peel her a peach, remarking that, 'When one has been like me a poor devil living on forty sous a day, one always carries a knife in one's pocket.' The king made a reciprocal visit to Britain the following year, staying at Windsor, visiting his old home at Twickenham and receiving the Order of the Garter. A member of his suite noted that, once he left France, he became more regal and majestic, treating with Victoria as one great sovereign to another.[18]

The foreign secretary, Lord Aberdeen, spoke of 'a cordial good understanding', while Louis-Philippe, echoing Guizot, said they were in a spirit of '*cordiale entente*', an expression taken up by Victoria in an address to parliament. She noted the French sovereign's 'vast knowledge upon all and every subject' and 'his great activity of mind', finding him 'thoroughly French in character, possessing all the liveliness and talkativeness of that people'. But his 'tricks and over-reachings' led him to take 'pleasure in being cleverer and more cunning than others, often when there was no advantage to be gained by it' she added.[19]

The king's cheery demeanour was sorely tested in July 1842, when the popular dauphin, whom many saw as the hope for a reformist monarchy, was killed after jumping from his open carriage when the driver lost control of the horses; his head was fractured as he hit the pavement. The body was laid on a couch in a nearby house. The queen sobbed uncontrollably on her knees while the king stared silently at the corpse; Thiers judged that the death meant he was 'no longer the same man'. There was widespread public mourning of an heir who had appeared ready to enlarge the Orléanist franchise beyond the limits set by his father.

His widow, the German Hélène de Mecklenburg, ordered her husband's room in the Tuileries to be left unchanged, with a newspaper from the day of his death beside the armchair. The new dauphin was the dead man's four-year-old son, the Count of Paris. The queen suspected his German mother of promoting her own interests against those of Louis-Philippe. Sharing such suspicions, the Chamber voted the regency to the king's second son, the Duke of Nemours, a keen athlete who hid his timidity behind a wall of protocol, insisting that visitors wear silk knee-breeches and telling off guests who turned up for balls in trousers.[20]

SHARPENING THE KNIFE

For all the regime's conservatism, Paris was enjoying a cultural boom and had become a haven for refugees from authoritarian states and political thinkers on the left, including Karl Marx, until he was expelled in 1845. Music, art and literature evolved from the classicism of the Restoration towards romanticism in 'an attempt to recapture the realm of fancy, the tension, the eloquence and the high feats that had been banished by the realm of fact'.[1]

While the Italian composer Gioachino Rossini increasingly devoted himself to food, the German Meyerbeer triumphed with grand historical operas. Two pianists and composers from Eastern Europe who settled in Paris, Liszt and Chopin, caused a sensation with their virtuosity. Offenbach came from the Rhineland, Donizetti from Lombardy and Bellini from Sicily. Paganini performed at the Opera. After a spell in Italy, Berlioz returned to France for his most productive period. The star singer Laure Cinti-Damoreau dominated operatic roles.

The appetite for music was such that there were said to be more pianos in Paris than in any other city on earth while piano makers in Marseilles turned out 400 a year, 150 for export. At a popular level, the dance halls of Montparnasse saw the quick ballroom gallop movement develop into a routine involving high kicks and flailing arms and legs, which was fused with the splits performed by the celebrated entertainer, Charles Mazurier, to produce the cancan.[2]

Stendhal's masterpiece, *The Red and the Black*, with its piercing analysis of society under the Restoration, appeared in 1830; it sold only 1,500 copies in its first two editions. Victor Hugo had provoked scuffles between classicists and romantics in the Comédie-Française at the opening of his rule-breaking drama *Hernani* just before the July Revolution; after the rumpus in the theatre, he and his friends crossed the Palais-Royal to dine at the Café de Chartres on his favourite dish of vermicelli, mutton and white beans. He published *The Hunchback of Notre-Dame* in 1832, and became a central figure of the cultural establishment, being made a peer before moving towards republicanism and setting himself to write, with a long interruption, *Les Misérables*.[3]

The alcoholic dandy, Alfred de Musset, librarian at the interior ministry, established the Romantic school of poetry, sipping a mixture of absinthe, brandy and beer in the Divan Lepelletier. Alphonse de Lamartine, who combined verse with politics and pantheism, wrote the iconic romantic work *Le Lac*. The Romantic Gérard de Nerval led his pet lobster round the Palais-Royal because 'it does not bark and knows the secrets of the sea' – he preferred the 'spirit world' to the one lived in, and suffered repeated breakdowns before committing suicide; Alfred de Vigny had a great success with his drama *Chatterton*, which set a fashion for young poets to choose death (or the idea of it) when rejected by philistines; he then withdrew to his ivory tower at the family property near Angoulême.

This was an age of prolific authors. Starting with *Les Chouans* in 1828, Honoré de Balzac published a novel a year in the 1830s, including the great *Comédie Humaine* studies of society and human life. Alexandre Dumas *père*, founded a production studio staffed by an army of underlings known as his *nègres* who would write under his editorial guidance. His avalanche of novels, serialised with great success, included *The Count of Monte Cristo* and *The Three Musketeers*. Eugène Sue painted a dramatic, often melodramatic, picture of working-class life and the underworld in his best-selling series, *Les Mystères de Paris*, offering bourgeois readers vicarious contact with the heaving popular districts of the capital. In a very different vein, George Sand chronicled rural life around her estate in central France as part of an outpouring of books, plays, political texts and literary articles which took an increasingly political tone as she called for reform and proclaimed that 'There is only one happiness in life, to love and be loved.' The dramatist Eugène

Scribe employed a troop of assistants to help him write 182 well-plotted, witty and lightly satirical works for the Gymnase Theatre while also providing librettos for operas.

Bourgeois theatre blossomed as the classicism of the Comédie-Française fell out of fashion in the face of Romanticism. The middle class flocked to waltz nights at the Salle Valentino on the rue Saint-Honoré and to promenade concerts on the Champs-Élysées and in the Turkish Gardens. Leading artists, musicians and writers met in *cercles*, such as the monthly sessions of the Club des Hashischins (Club of Hashish Users), in a hotel on the Île Saint-Louis attended by Dumas, de Nerval, Gautier and the young Charles Baudelaire. Some marked themselves out through striking dress. The poet, dramatist and travel writer Théophile Gautier attended the premiere of *Hernani* as part of Hugo's fan club in a pink satin doublet and pale grey trousers with black velvet bands down the seams. George Sand caused a stir by appearing in public in men's clothes – and smoking. Others, like de Nerval, stayed up all night or set out to shock as when the young Baudelaire approvingly compared his well-done fillet steak to a child's brain.

Bohemians, including the poet Théophile Dondey de Santeny, who adopted the anagrammatical pseudonym of Philothée O'Neddy, met in the homes of patrons such as the Italian Princess Triulzi-Belgiojoso, who rejoiced in thirteen first names and shrouded her main drawing room in dark brown velvet and her bedroom in Spanish leather. The accomplished and beautiful singer, Apollonie Sabatier, mistress of a rich Belgian businessman, consorted with Berlioz, Gautier and de Nerval at the home her lover provided for her on the lower slopes of Montmartre. The writer Henry Murger immortalised this anarchic group in his *Scènes de la Vie de Bohème*, stories that would form the basis for Puccini's opera.

In painting, Delacroix and Géricault had passed their high points while, as a regicide and associate of Robespierre, the neo-classical master David had gone into exile on the fall of Napoleon, dying in Brussels in 1825 after being hit by a carriage. But Millet was starting to make an impression with his paintings of rural scenes that would grow into the Barbizon School while Courbet was developing his depictions of everyday reality, including striking self-portraits. It was a golden

age for caricature even if it attracted censorship and a warning by
Thiers that 'there is nothing more dangerous than scandalous carica-
tures, than seditious drawings'. Charles Philipon gave them wide
publication in his magazines, *La Caricature* and *Le Charivari*. Put on
trial for insulting the king in a series of critical lithographs, he argued
that anything could be depicted as resembling the king, and proved
his point by drawing a series of distortions of Louis-Philippe ending
with the image of a pear. Perhaps because of a certain natural resem-
blance or because the slang meaning of the word *poire* is simpleton or
bungler, the nickname stuck with the king who was known thereafter
as '*La Poire*'.[4]

Prominent women used their own political salons to attain a degree
of influence denied to them in the world of male politics. One of the
most celebrated was hosted by the Baltic German Princess Lieven, who
moved to Paris after a long spell as wife of the Russian ambassador to
London and formed a close association with Guizot. Marie-Madeleine
Poutret de Mauchamps used her drawing room to press the case for
greater freedom for women to pursue artistic activities and, with her
husband, edited the *Gazette des femmes*. The Countess of Agoult, who had
separated from her husband and wrote not very good novels before
becoming an excellent recorder of contemporary events, held regular
receptions attended by leading figures of the epoch, the men in white
tie and tails paying court to elegantly gowned ladies. The countess
believed that 'flirtation has become a science as deep as the science of
politics. Since society leaves [women] outside real action, they have
easily learned to make use of a man's desire to make him, at least temporarily, their slave.'[5]

Newspapers flourished: Émile de Girardin of *La Presse* introduced a
new business model in which advertising revenue enabled him to
reduce the cover price and boosted sales by serialising popular novels,
while Charles Havas founded the world's first news agency, and
employed a German, Paul-Julius Reuter, who went on to set up the
company that bore his name in London.

Louis Daguerre invented the photographic process called after him,
the daguerreotype, while Hércule Florence, an intrepid traveller who
emigrated to Brazil, developed camera imagery and coined the term

photographie in 1834. French pioneers came up with a vehicle propelled by compressed air, isolated codeine and discovered polyvinyl chloride (though PVC would not be introduced industrially for a century). French luxury goods producers set the global style standard. Furniture was designed with clear lines and good wood for the middle classes, offering comfort, good value and practicality by melding traditional craftsmanship and large-scale production.

The 'social question'

The situation in the mid-1840s appeared sustainable to Guizot, Soult and the king with annual economic growth of 2.5 to 3.5 per cent. Though land remained the major source of wealth, mechanised production expanded. Paris developed as a financial centre dominated by big banking houses. The banks, often run by Protestants or Jews, constituted a powerful financial aristocracy which inter-married and enjoyed political links, including with the king. Foremost were the Rothschilds – Gautier wrote of the 'century of the Rothschilds' – who enjoyed a bonanza from their early involvement in the northern railway network that served industry, the Channel ports and the weekend tourism region outside the capital.

Other entrepreneurs flourished, prominent among them Charles Auguste Louis Joseph de Morny, a descendant of Napoleon's family. His investments and speculations ranged across the business world and agriculture, helped by the advice and intervention of his beautiful and rich mistress, the wife of the Belgian ambassador. Deputy for the Auvergne capital of Clermont-Ferrand, he backed the July Monarchy but was far from enamoured of the parliamentary system; when asked what he would do if the Chamber was swept clean, he is said to have replied, 'Put me on the side of the broom handles.'

Under the Railway Law of 1842, the state laid down most lines and sold operating concessions to companies. This enabled ministers to determine where expansion occurred. There was a military aspect to this but it was also important politically – 'you could put up a horse as a candidate so long as we get a railway', as a saying went. British entrepreneurs, squeezed by competition at home, built the first long-distance line from Paris to the Channel coast followed by one from the capital to Tours and Bordeaux. In 1845 alone, fifty companies were established in London to invest in French railways, their prospectuses garlanded with endorsements of French aristocrats, deputies and generals. In all, Britain is estimated to have provided half the capital to fund French railways up to 1847.[6]

For the home team, the Saint-Simonist Péreire brothers financed the line between Paris and Saint-Germain – they asked Louis-Philippe to inaugurate it but the government thought he should not take risks with such an unknown form of transport and the queen did the job instead; after she had travelled safely, her husband also tried the train. People marvelled at being able to get from Paris to Orléans or Rouen in only three-and-a-half-hours. Sceptics complained about noise and smoke and the danger of being trapped; some pundits warned that travelling too fast could ruin the digestion. Fears deepened when two locomotives pulling a crowded train on the Paris-Versailles line derailed and caught fire in 1842. More than fifty people died, mainly because the doors of the compartments were locked to stop passengers jumping on and off between stations.

Elections in 1846 appeared to vindicate Guizot and Louis-Philippe. The government got a hundred-seat majority – half its deputies were civil servants and they ensured that a bill to enlarge the franchise to 450,000 by lowering the tax requirement was defeated by a large margin. 'Those who are not content with the actions of the cabinet can go over to the camp of the opposition,' Guizot remarked. His complacency proved ill-founded as the following two years brought another of the recurrent switchbacks of modern French history.

The reasons were evident to anybody who bothered to look. Guizot's *juste milieu* avoided what was known as the 'social question', despite increasing awareness of pauperism and the growing wealth gap. 'A very great silence reigns here,' Heine noted in the capital in 1842. 'All is silent as a winter night wrapped in snow. Only a little mysterious and monotonous noise, like falling drops. This is the interest on capital, falling into the strongboxes of the capitalists and almost spilling over. The continual swell of the riches of the rich can be distinctly heard. From time to time there is mixed with this dull ripple, the sob of a low voice, the sob of poverty. Sometimes you can also hear a light metallic noise, like that of a knife being sharpened.'[7]

Living conditions were still deplorable for most of the population; Rambuteau's introduction of street lights, drains and public urinals as well as parks with fountains and wider streets still left much of Paris a filthy place. The streets of Toulouse, it was noted, were only clean when there was a storm, though the inadequacy of the drains meant horses were sometimes seen swimming in flood waters. Charles Dickens was so repelled by conditions in Lyons that he swore to make a detour 'to avoid coming across it again'. In the southern city of Montauban, there were 300 beggars as wages dropped by 20 per cent, factories closed and food prices rose. The homes of many peasants were little better than hovels, their diet consisted mainly of potatoes and bread, and a report from the Nièvre *département* in central France told of peasants who in winter 'take to their bed and spend their days in it, pressed against each other to keep warm and to eat less'.[8]

Despite reforms boosting the number of school pupils to 3 million, anywhere from one-third to half the recruits to the army were illiterate. France's demographic supremacy was affected by a rapid fall in the birth rate as contraceptive methods spread in the countryside. Yet some rural regions were still over-populated given their low output. Three million people were registered to receive charity in the 1840s. Writers recorded their astonishment at the solitude and backwardness of areas not far from Paris. Superstition was rife. Michelet regarded Brittany as 'a country quite different from ours ... scarcely French'; as for the Midi, it was 'a country of ruins' marked by a record of 'murderous violence'. Stendhal wrote of 'that fatal triangle which stretches between Bordeaux, Bayonne and Valence. There they ... cannot read and do not speak French.' As Balzac noted in his novel, *Les Paysans*, 'you don't have to go to America to see savages.'[9]

Credit was tight as money supply expanded more slowly than overall growth. Provincial banking was highly fragmented between hundreds of small, primitive establishments, many carrying doubtful loans and short of capital. After a flirtation with freer trade, protectionism was re-imposed; still, a small trade surplus in the 1830s turned into a deficit in the following decade because of high production costs, the weakness of the merchant fleet and the lower costs of competitors, particularly the British. Manufacturers relied overwhelmingly on the domestic market.[10]

In industry, there were still many old charcoal furnaces and much small-scale metallurgy. Textiles and silk depended on piecework. Only 7 per cent of workshops in Paris employed more than ten workers. 'France is a nation of divided industry, of small workshops,' the Society for the Encouragement of National Industry noted, seeing this as evidence of the democratic spirit expressed in 'work done in small establishments with the direct involvement of the worker who naturally applies himself to objects destined to satisfy the demands of the upper classes.'[11]

The growth in agricultural output was slowing and larger-scale farming remained rare outside north-eastern France. Conflicts over grazing rights and access to wood in forests continued; police enforced laws in favour of landlords. A poor cereals harvest in 1845–6 set off riots and raids on granaries and wagons carrying grain. There was heavy flooding of the Loire River. A potato blight increased prices fourfold.[12]

The downward cycle in agriculture hit consumption and manufacturing once more. Wages were cut but the price of bread and other foodstuffs soared. When controls on grain imports were lifted, speculators made a killing. Government purchases of expensive wheat from Russia widened the trade deficit. Rural riots were accompanied by strikes and machine breaking. Seven hundred thousand people lost their jobs in 1847. Workers at the naval arsenal in Toulon caused a shock by staging a strike which gained them partial satisfaction. Building workers in Montauban stoned the home of the mayor, shouting 'Work and bread!'

France was caught up in a major financial crisis after the collapse of the railway boom in Britain. As investors pulled out, the government took over some projects, but the stock market slumped, as did the price of state bonds in which many middle-class people put their savings. A string of smaller banks collapsed. Gold reserves dropped by two-thirds. The Bank of France had to borrow from Britain and raise the discount rate, driving more companies out of business. Public works were suspended. Heavy manufacturing output plummeted. Mining contracted.

Public affairs, private profit

At this volatile moment, a set of scandals tarnished the elite. The news-paper editor and deputy, Émile de Girardin, who had taken money from the government not to vote against it but then fell out with Guizot, alleged he had been offered a seat in the upper house in return for support. The justice minister died after his taste for sex with girls of ten to twelve had been revealed – the cause of death was given as apoplexy, but rumours flew that he had killed himself. A former public works minister was convicted of having taken a 94,000-franc bribe to grant a salt mine concession, with a former war minister acting as inter-mediary.

A member of the royal household, the Duke of Choiseul-Praslin, killed his wife, with whom he had had eleven children, with fifteen stab wounds after she threatened to go to court over his affair with their off-spring's female tutor; the duke was found dead of arsenic poisoning in prison and the authorities were said to have killed him to hush up the scandal. The French ambassador in Naples, who was close to the king, cut his throat, probably because of domestic difficulties. Officials were found to have used public money to speculate in grains. A senior court figure was caught cheating at cards.[13]

De Broglie and Molé joined Lamartine in expressing concern about the effect on the regime. Hugo compared Guizot to a respectable woman who found herself running a brothel. De Tocqueville asked his fellow deputies if they did not scent revolution in the air, and joined those charging the administration with acting 'like a private business, each member thinking of public affairs only in so far as they could be turned to private profit'. The king's third son, the Duke of Joinville, wrote to his brother, Nemours, to express concern at 'events which I see piling up on all sides' and the way in which everything depended in the end on their septuagenarian father 'who wishes to govern but who lacks the strength to make a firm resolution ... You know my respect and affection for him; but I can't help looking into the future and it rather frightens me.'[14]

Probably not by coincidence, these severe economic difficulties coin-cided with an unusual exhibition of assertion abroad on the part of

Louis-Philippe in a series of conflicts with Britain as he sought to show he could stand up for his nation. These involved London's declaration of its right to search French ships for slaves, affairs in the Middle East where the British were anxious to restrain French influence and in North Africa where Paris made military moves against Morocco which was harbouring the leader of Algerian nationalists. An unlikely clash erupted in the South Pacific after a French admiral tried to get the queen of Tahiti to put herself under France's protection. This was strongly opposed by a local British missionary, George Pritchard, alleged by the admiral to be the queen's priest, minister and lover. The French had Pritchard incarcerated and deported to London. The incidents deflated in time, but Queen Victoria wrote to the Belgian king that 'the French keep us constantly in hot water.'[15]

After the Francophobe Lord Palmerston took over the Foreign Office in 1846, a fresh crisis erupted over the marriage of Queen Isabella of Spain. Palmerston's predecessor had indicated that he would accept an agreement worked out by Guizot that she should wed a member of the House of Bourbon, either from her own country or Naples. Fearing this would bring Spain into France's dynastic orbit, the foreign secretary expressed his preference that a prince of Saxe-Coburg and Gotha related to the British royal family become Isabella's husband. It was France's turn to get alarmed since another prince from the German duchy had been installed on the throne of Belgium, and Paris might find itself with British-aligned kingdoms on both its south-western and north-eastern borders. After French counter-lobbying, the queen, aged sixteen, married her Bourbon cousin, the Duke of Cádiz, rumoured to be impotent and homosexual, while her sister wed Louis-Philippe's youngest son, the Duke of Montpensier. If the queen could not have a child, the throne would pass to their offspring.

This victory for Louis-Philippe came at a price. Relations with London were wrecked; Queen Victoria was particularly outraged and suspended her correspondence with the Citizen King. The British embassy disinvited Guizot from a grand ball in Paris and developed relations with Thiers instead. The link with reactionary royal regimes further alienated liberals at home and weakened support for the throne.

The February revolution

In January 1848, the *Gazette de France* noted that 'there is great disquiet in Paris. Bond prices are falling every day. In politics, people have stopped being reasonable. They are overcome by the consequences of their principles and dragged along in their wake. Now it is events that speak loud. For seventeen years, efforts have been made to stop revolution breaking out in France, and now revolution is feared everywhere.'[16]

The swell of discontent took in a stream of young men from social studies institutes established by the regime who were alert to the problems of the population at large, while progressive Catholics attacked the indifference to the plight of the poor. Skilled workers in the capital set up self-help and self-improvement associations, which, if not overtly political, brought them together and often backed strikes. Others, attending what were ostensibly social gatherings, discussed the state of the nation and ways of making life better, which bred growing organisation of political opposition; republicans headed Masonic lodges at Beaune, Chalon-sur-Saône, Toulon and Le Mans.

Flora Tristan, who had been shot and wounded by her husband, pressed for women's rights and launched a workers' union to build premises that would provide employment and education, and quarters for the old and ill. She toured the country preaching revolution but enjoyed little success except in Toulon where she backed strikers at the naval arsenal. The newspapers, *Le National* and *La Tribune*, kept up pressure for political reform, abetted by publications such as the *Revue Indépendante*, co-edited by George Sand. The republican cause was championed in the Chamber by a small but impressive group of deputies including the scientists François Arago and François-Vincent Raspail, a one-time member of the Carbonari secret society.

Sitting with them was a successful businessman, Louis-Antoine Garnier-Pagès, and the lawyer Alexandre-Thomas Marie, a leading defender of newspapers and militants. Adolphe Crémieux, another prominent lawyer much concerned about human rights, moved steadily away from the regime as did Lamartine, one-time royalist and spokesman for the colonial sugar trade, who came to believe France needed a crisis to galvanise it. Fear of republicanism was lessened by the way in which historians, led by Michelet, presented the Revolution in a favourable light not to be obscured by the Terror. The First Republic was identified with patriotic memories of the fight against reactionary invaders commemorated in the national anthem and a panel at the newly completed Arc de Triomphe.

With Guizot assured of a parliamentary majority, the opposition sought other channels to protest, notably at huge and lengthy banquets where, after much wine and food, the virtues of reform were celebrated in speeches that drew inspiration from the history of the Revolution as airbrushed by Michelet. The first such occasion, in Paris in July 1847, was attended by 1,200 people. Seventy events of various sizes were then staged across the country, attracting some 17,000 in all. In his constituency of Mâcon, Lamartine said the regime risked being brought down by 'the revolution of public conscience and the revolution of contempt.'[17]

Most of the banqueters came from the less affluent middle class – shopkeepers, artisans and farmers – who resented their exclusion from the national franchise. Blanqui continued his revolutionary crusade. Secret groups, such as the proto-Communist *Société Dissidente*, plotted uprisings, though they were usually infiltrated by police spies. Saint-Simonians extolled the virtues of a new state run by enlightened technocrats. Louis Blanc, an accomplished journalist and writer, extremely short and with the little red cheeks of a schoolboy, advocated cooperative workshops and associations that would ensure 'from each according to his abilities, to each according to his needs'. At a banquet in Dijon, he warned the rulers that 'when the fruit is rotten, it needs only the wind to remove it from the tree'.

The loud-voiced lawyer, Alexandre-Auguste Ledru-Rollin, who had made a speciality of defending republicans in court, preached democratic socialism and was elected deputy for the independent-minded town of Le Mans. He got into legal trouble himself for his speeches and was sentenced to four months in jail, but then escaped on a technicality. After marrying a half-English heiress, he devoted himself to politics, financing the newspaper, *La Réforme*, appealing to workers, calling for universal suffrage and coining his celebrated phrase about the working people, 'I am their leader; I must follow them.'

A former commercial traveller, Charles Fourier, who is credited with the first use of the word 'feminism', denounced the effects of competition and called for harmony and cooperation. He pictured communities where men and women would work for mutual benefit, swap partners at will and have children do the dirty work since the little ones enjoyed getting filthy. (He also believed that in 15,000 years human beings would develop a tail with an eye in it.) The socialist, Étienne Cabet, who ran a cheap newspaper, *Le Populaire*, described a society in which everybody would share equally in a land of plenty with absolute equality – all homes would be exactly the same down to the bathroom.

Pierre Leroux, who was thought to have introduced the word 'socialist', enjoyed popularity among younger people, as he championed the idea of solidarity between workers and the middle class. Fat and red-faced with bushy, wild hair, he was elected to parliament where he put forward a bill for constitutional reform so eccentric that it was rejected by all the other deputies. Philippe-Joseph-Benjamin Buchez, a one-time Saint-Simonian, argued that the key to progress for workers lay in moral regeneration, and set up cooperatives, one of which had eight branches in the jewellery trade in Paris. The prolific Pierre-Joseph Proudhon is best remembered for his statement that 'property is theft' though he meant this only to apply to those who had obtained it without having earned it. He wanted life to become more independent and self-reliant for the masses, and he ranged far and wide in writings that filled fifty volumes; among many other things, he thought women were inferior to men and should be content with chaste lives in submission to their husbands.

Though they argued constantly among themselves, these thinkers of new and not-so-new thoughts plumbed the growing malaise after eighteen years of the July Monarchy. 'We were like people who were bored with having been so well off,' as the painter Delacroix reflected. The government reacted to the criticism with a few repressive measures, most notably in cancelling lectures by Michelet and other historians who celebrated the Revolution. It took little notice of liberalising moves by the King of Prussia and anti-regime agitation in Italy and Switzerland. Guizot was as serene as ever. 'For the moment there is nothing,' he

remarked. 'No grave questions, no embarrassing event [only] superficial and puerile effervescence.' The 74-year-old king was afflicted by the
death of his sister, Adélaïde, the only person to whom he spoke frankly;
she left him 60 million francs.

The monarch dismissed 'agitation which fosters blind passions of
enmity' and declared that 'France enjoys all the advantages of peace
and prosperity'. Still, the campaign of banquets was seen to need
counter-action and, on 21 February 1848, Guizot and the Paris Prefect
banned a banquet due for the next day in the 12th *arrondissement* of the
capital. Thirty thousand troops were ordered into the city. Though radical newspapers called for a mass march to the event, the organisers
decided to cancel it. 'I was sure they would give way,' the king told a visitor, since 'one does not make a revolution in wintertime.'

Tuesday, 22 February 1848 was cold and rainy. Crowds massed on the
boulevards from early morning, stirred up by veterans from previous
insurrections. Several hundred students marched to the empty
Chamber of Deputies; they wandered through the building and chanted
pro-reform slogans outside until dispersed by cavalry. Crossing to the
crowded Place de la Concorde, they mingled with workers in overalls
and a sprinkling of agitators. Children threw stones at mounted soldiers
and a barricade went up at the bottom of the Champs-Élysées. Cavalry
with drawn sabres drove the crowd back, but could not disperse it. The
Countess of Agoult watched as an officer returned his sword to its scab-
bard, 'material force yielding to moral force'. The Bourse closed.[18]

By 4 p.m., the crowd had grown bad-tempered, pulling down the
railings round the church of Saint-Roch behind the Tuileries to use as
spears. People ransacked gun shops and built barricades of paving
stones, overturned carriages and furniture grabbed from houses. The
troops did not move and, as night fell, most of the crowd went home.
Radicals of the *Société Dissidente* convened in the wine shops of Les Halles
and, after one of their members handed out weapons, surged down the
boulevard but were turned back by cavalry.

The king remained relaxed; 'The Parisians know what they are
doing,' he told the police prefect. 'They are not going to give up the
throne for a banquet'. The nobility held balls that night as if nothing

untoward was happening. But only half the thirty-six guests turned up to a dinner given by the finance minister.

Wednesday, 23 February brought even heavier rain from the clouds covering the capital. Troops occupied strategic points, while secret revolutionary societies distributed weapons and demonstrators threw up fresh barricades. When soldiers attacked one on the square in front of the city hall, they met heavy gunfire, which killed sixteen of them. Many demonstrators were teenagers. Children broke bottles and spread the glass across the streets to cut the feet of cavalry horses. A red flag was hoisted over a barricade on the rue Montmartre. After hesitating all morning, the Austrian embassy decided at 2 p.m. to cancel the ball it had been due to hold that night in its elegant eighteenth-century *hôtel particulier* on the rue de Grenelle, instead, distributing the food to the poor.

When the police prefect called out the National Guard, most shouted reform slogans. In three places, they used bayonets to force back mounted soldiers trying to disperse the crowds. Members of the *Société Dissidente* got Guards' uniforms from clothes shops and paraded in front of the Tuileries shouting '*À bas Guizot!*' (Down with Guizot!). The king, who had regarded the Guard as a loyal symbol of the regime, finally woke up to what was happening as the shouts of protest sounded through the palace windows. Receiving the interior minister, Charles Duchâtel, he evoked the resignation of Guizot. The queen, listening from the next room, burst in to say that the Doctrinaire could render a last service to the throne by stepping down. Louis-Philippe asked Duchâtel to fetch him from the parliament building across the river; as the minister left, soldiers in the palace courtyard shouted in protest, watched by the king from the window above.

Half an hour later, Guizot arrived, pale and stiff. Louis-Philippe told him that necessity and the safety of France demanded his departure. The chief minister accepted the decision. As he left, Louis-Philippe said, 'To you the honour, to me the shame.' Guizot crossed the Seine to announce his departure to the Chamber; he held his head high so as not to bow to events. The streets erupted in celebration. Louis-Philippe asked Molé to take over.

A crowd gathered outside the offices of the opposition newspaper, *le National*. A tall, long-haired, yellow-coated man, who posed for painters as a model for Jesus, shouted 'Forward, my friends!' Holding aloft a torch, he led the crowd carrying red and yellow paper lanterns on long poles down the Boulevard des Capucines. They got as far as the foreign ministry, long Guizot's headquarters. When soldiers stopped them, the man in the yellow coat argued with the officer in charge, singeing his moustache with the flames of the torch. A sergeant shot him dead. The rest of the troop joined in, killing fifty-two people. 'There we were, a hundred people, lying, fallen, rolling on the ground, on top of one another, with screams and sobbing,' wrote the diplomat, Apponyi, who had gone to the scene and was wounded in the face. A second fusillade rang out before the wounded could be taken away.

Protestors loaded bodies into a commandeered cart, a partly dressed female corpse on top. Dripping blood, the vehicle was drawn by a white horse through the streets. Beneath the monumental column of the Bastille, the torch-waving crowd called for vengeance. Finally, the bodies were laid in the courtyard of a municipal building, the semi-naked woman prominently displayed. 'The phantom of the Republic hovered over those sinister shadows,' the Countess d'Agoult wrote. 'The monarchy was tottering. The dead had killed the living. At that moment the cadaver of a woman had more power than the most valorous army in the world.'

Thursday, 24 February brought the last act. Walking along the boulevards, de Tocqueville noted how empty they were except for men cutting down trees and toppling police sentry boxes for barricades; during the day 1,500 such obstacles went up through the city. Troops he saw by the Madeleine hung their heads 'shamefaced and frightened'. Molé gave up trying to form a government. The king called in Thiers at 1 a.m. and grudgingly accepted his list of ministers.

Marshal Bugeaud, who had headed the colonialisation of Algeria and was a hate figure to the masses of Paris because of his role in suppressing revolts, was put in charge of a military crackdown. After starting well, his drive to pacify the city ran into stiff resistance in Montmartre. Thiers persuaded the king to end the military action and appoint the popular General Lamoricière to command the National

Guard, but when he rode out of the Tuileries, the crowd called on him to lead it against the throne. He refused; as he headed back to the palace, protestors fired, wounding his horse.

There was fighting round the fountains of the Château d'Eau – by today's Place de la République – where blood mixed with water flowed into the street. Another battle broke out round the Place de la Concorde when the troops who had been stopped at Montmartre were set on by the throng. Inside the Tuileries, the king took dinner with the queen, their sons and Thiers who advised a retreat to Saint-Cloud, from where a massive attack could be mounted on the capital. But Louis-Philippe chose to put on his uniform and review what remained of the National Guard outside the palace. After guardsmen shouted '*Vive la réforme!*' and '*À bas le régime!*' he went back inside and sat silently in an armchair. A succession of uninvited guests arrived at the Tuileries. One, the editor de Girardin, said that, unless the king abdicated, there would be no France and no monarchy left.

'Yes, abdicate,' chipped in the youngest of the royal sons, the Duke of Montpensier. 'There is no other way of preserving the throne for the family.'

'Is that what you want?' Louis-Philippe asked as bullets ricocheted off the walls of the palace and broke some windows. 'Well, so be it, I abdicate.'

He got up heavily and walked to the next room where his wife threw herself into his arms and then watched as he wrote his abdication letter at his maple wood desk. He passed the crown to the Count of Paris, the son of his dead elder son. Seeing the widow, the queen cried out, 'Well, Hélène, be happy; you have achieved your aims.'

The one-time Napoleonic marshal, Gérard, wearing a black uniform and round civilian hat, mounted the king's white horse to take the abdication letter across the Seine to parliament. He held the document in one hand and a laurel branch in the other. But, when his reins became mixed up, he got down from the saddle to proceed on foot. Demonstrators grabbed the paper from him and threw it to the ground.

Calling out for a republic, the crowd pressed in on the Tuileries where panic reigned. After burning his papers, the king headed to the Place de la Concorde with his wife, abandoning a fortune in the drawers of his desk – he was said to have just 15 francs in his pocket. As he went, he called out, 'My keys! My briefcase!' Valets carried the royal grandchildren behind them. The Duchess of Orléans was left behind with her two sons.

The transport summoned for the now former king had been unable to get through the crowds and the burning barricades. So his son, Nemours, arranged for three carriages to be brought up. Louis-Philippe got into one with his wife and three grandchildren. Somebody closed the door behind them. 'Thank you,' said the ever-courteous abdicator. 'Think nothing of it,' the man replied. 'I've been waiting for this for eighteen years.' With a mounted guard on either side, the carriages drove off to Saint-Cloud.

*

From Paris, Louis-Philippe and his wife went to the town of Dreux in Normandy to pray at the family mausoleum. Learning that a republic had been proclaimed, they decided to head to the Channel coast under the names of Monsieur and Madame Lebrun; other members of the family made for Belgium. Louis-Philippe removed his wig, and donned a black cap and dark glasses. He and the former queen stopped at Évreux where a royal agent gave them lunch of onion soup and an omelette, and loaned them a thousand francs. Travelling by night along back roads, in freezing cold and heavy rain, they reached the coast near Honfleur, where they hid in a sympathiser's house. 'Worse than Charles X, a hundred times worse,' the deposed monarch lamented.

After the captain of a cross-Channel steamer refused to accept them, they were told of a boat that might take them from Trouville. But it was grounded by a storm. So they lodged in a house found by a general escorting them – only to be warned that they had been spotted. Slipping out of the back door, Louis-Philippe ran into a man who told him, 'Sire, a faithful subject is here to conduct you to a place of safety.' This turned out to be the home of a supporter where Louis-Philippe conversed with friendly locals.

At dawn on 2 March, a member of the British consulate at Le Havre arrived to say the steamer was available. The ex-monarch adopted a new alias, William Smith, a supposed relative of the consul. He shaved his side-whiskers, donned a greatcoat and goggles, and spoke loud English. As he and his wife sailed off in foul weather, police arrived at their lodgings. The consul recalled it as 'a hair-trigger affair altogether'.

Landing in Newhaven, the couple put up at a hotel from where Louis-Philippe wrote to Queen Victoria to express his desire to find 'a refuge and peaceful retreat'. If he had died in 1844, the queen noted, 'he would have deservedly gone down to posterity as a great monarch. His fate is a great moral.' His son-in-law, King Leopold of Belgium, lent him his gloomy mansion at Claremont in Surrey. Money was tight. Polluted drinking water killed three of the entourage and obliged a move to London, where they stayed initially at the Star and Garter pub in Twickenham. A story has it that, as the ex-king walked in the London suburb the landlord of another pub shook his hand and said he might remember him from his time in the area during the Revolution. 'I've kept the Crown,' the local said. To which he got the quick-fire response 'That's more than I did.'

Louis-Philippe was in ill health, with liver disease. Guizot, a fellow refugee, found him 'thin as a sheet of paper, his face fallen in, but his eye is bright, his complexion clear, his voice firm and his mind as quick and serene as ever.' He spoke wistfully of a restoration; 'perhaps people will miss me,' he said. In August 1850, the Citizen King died after a pleurisy attack.

The republic is proclaimed

The death toll of the third revolution was put at 289 insurgents and 72 of the king's men with some 500 injured in all. Louis-Philippe had not ordered the regular army to fire at the mob that chased him from the throne. Had they done so, they probably could have dispersed the protestors on the Place de la Concorde. But the king had lost the will to exercise power, leaving the dynamic of street protest to take on its own momentum. The collapse of the July Monarchy was literally a pushover. A well-meaning man had been undermined by his own self-satisfied caution and overtaken by events, ending up, as the Duchess of Maillé put it in her memoirs, 'neither loved nor respected'.

As he fled Paris, mobs invaded the Palais-Royal, the château at Neuilly and the main target, the Tuileries, where they burned the grand chambers and, in the cellars, hacked open the wine barrels – several people were drowned. A boy took away a pot of jam for his sick grandmother. A prostitute was decked out as the symbol of freedom. The royal bed was fouled and the king's yellow carriage pitched into the Seine. The throne was taken to the Place de la Bastille to be burned.

Dressed in black, the Duchess of Orléans and her children were escorted to the relative safety of the Chamber of Deputies. There were a few shouts of '*Vive la Duchesse d'Orléans! Vive le Comte de Paris!*' However, after a shambolic session during which a drunken agitator mistook Lamartine for Guizot and tried to shoot him and then an equally chaotic meeting at the Hôtel de Ville, a republic was proclaimed.

The duchess took her son to Germany. The royal dukes of Aumale and Joinville joined their father in England, as did Nemours, who sought a rapprochement between the two lines of the ousted monarchy so that they could work together for a restoration. But the Duchess of Orléans would have none of it; nor would Charles X's heir, the Count of Chambord. Guizot took up residence for a year in Kensington before returning to Paris to write history books and nine volumes of memoirs before dying in 1874. Thiers became leader of the conservative republicans. Soult declared himself a republican and returned to his country domain where he died in 1851. Count Molé stayed on in parliament for a short time but then stepped out of public life.

Claiming their entitlement to change regimes which they had assumed in 1789, the people of the Parisian streets had ensured that France finally shed its monarchy for good. What was to follow was uncertain, beyond the insistence of the revolutionaries that they would not be cheated of their prize. As the left-wing politician, Odilon Barrot, noted, the workers 'imagined they had beaten the bourgeoisie' and looked to a new dawn of the inheritance of the Revolution.

PART 2
REPUBLICANISM AND EMPIRE

1848–1870

THE IMPOSSIBLE DREAM

The immediate outcome of the third revolution took the form of outbreaks of violence and work stoppages. The Rothschild mansion at Suresnes was pillaged. A mob invaded the home of the former prefect, Rambuteau, throwing furniture and silverware out of the windows. In Lyons the silk workers attacked monasteries where poor people, given shelter, were producing goods that undercut them. Parisian carriage drivers went on strike, as did street cleaners wanting to work by day rather than at night. Workers wrecked machines threatening their livelihoods. Carriage drivers and boatmen tore up railway tracks and burned stations. Peasants attacked tax collection offices and reclaimed common land taken over by landowners. Blanqui, who had been moved from the grim prison at Mont-Saint-Michel to a hospital in Tours at the end of the July Monarchy, joined a stream of released leftists who made for the capital where he became a symbol of suffering on behalf of the cause, wearing his prison rags, spitting blood, his hands trembling.

The revolution shocked the governments and crowned heads of Europe, even more so as revolts broke out across the Hapsburg lands and there was an upsurge in national identity politics in Germany, Italy, Hungary and elsewhere. 'We could speak of nothing else,' Queen Victoria noted in her diary after hearing the news from Paris. However, the presence of Lamartine and his colleagues at the National Assembly reassured the bourgeoisie and at least some of the upper class. The politician-poet went without food and sleep as he struggled to draw up a constitution. There was agreement on the need for social progress, action to help the poor and the implementation of universal suffrage, which was seen as a panacea, though only for men. But there was no political group to take charge and the seven ministers appointed by the acclamation of the crowd outside the Palais Bourbon on 24 February 1848 were a varied group.[1]

At their head, nominally at least, was Jacques Charles Dupont de l'Eure, who had first sat in parliament under the Directory. At eighty-three, he was too old to be more than a figurehead. The outspoken lawyer and newspaper proprietor, Ledru-Rollin, became interior minister. Lamartine took the foreign ministry. Other posts were filled by the scientist Arago, the republican businessman Louis-Antoine Garnier-Pagès, and the lawyers Alexandre Marie and Adolphe Crémieux. A well-respected if irascible banker, Michel Goudchaux, became finance minister to assuage the business world – he and Crémieux were the first practising Jews in senior ministerial posts in France.

A crowd outside the office of the radical newspaper *La Réforme* added four left-wing names – the socialist Louis Blanc, two newspaper editors, Armand Marrast and Ferdinand Flocon, plus a prominent working-class militant and secret society member, Alexandre Martin, known as 'Albert the Worker'.

Five of those on the lists could be counted as moderates – Marie, in charge of public works, Crémieux, the justice minister, Arago, Minister of the Marine, Garnier-Pagès, who became mayor of Paris, and Marrast, a bachelor of no fixed abode who played an indeterminate role. Blanc and Albert of the hard left drew their strength from representing the workers. Though his taciturnity made it hard to know where he stood, Flocon's newspaper had been the voice of uncompromising opposition and given space to socialist views. Lamartine and Ledru-Rollin stood in the middle. The first benefitted from his literary prestige and speech-making prowess but could be seen as too idealistic. The second was a bombastic tribune known among Parisian workers, in a pun on the first part of his name, as 'the tough one'. There were said to be Auvergnat peasants who thought France was being run by a dictator called Le Dru who had two mistresses, La Martine and La Marie.

Though the example of the Paris revolt helped to incite a rash of revolutions across Europe, the men in charge lacked a grand design, except for the utopianism of Blanc and Albert. As Proudhon put it, the provisional government was 'a farrago of conservatives, doctrinaires, Jacobins, socialists, all talking their own private language.' Lamartine disavowed some of the instructions with which Ledru-Rollin showered the commissioners of the Republic, as prefects were now renamed. Utopian Socialists pressed schemes for a new society but the job creation they promoted depended on the public works ministry run by Marie, a moderate.

The provisional government faced little organised opposition. There was no agitation in favour of the Orléanist monarchy. The army did not move. The deposed king's son did not seek to use his position as governor of Algeria to raise resistance there, handing his command to the republican Louis-Eugène Cavaignac. The church rallied, the archbishop of Lyons telling clergy, 'Give a lead to the faithful in obedience and submission to the Republic.' Writers and intellectuals bored with the July Monarchy rejoiced at the prospect for a new and more stimulating chapter in national life.

Some immediate measures were simple, such as the abolition of noble titles and an end of the death penalty for political offences – a comfort to those who feared a new Terror. Laws muzzling the press were suspended. Michelet was reinstated and the Bourse reopened. A veteran republican, Marc Caussidière, who had fought on the barricades and whose colossal body contrasted with his uncertain manner, was appointed prefect of police for the capital; he created a People's Guard. Imprisonment for debt was ended. Crémieux realised his ambition of getting slavery made illegal in the colonies.

Amid this wave of change, Lamartine argued successfully against an attempt by radicals to replace the tricolour with the red flag and issued a circular to reassure other powers that Paris would not export revolution. 'War,' he declared, 'is not a principle of the French Republic.' Still, Poles living in France were allowed to form a legion and marched off to fight vainly for the independence of their nation.

Fading illusions

The revolution did not alleviate the economic problems that had dogged the last years of Louis-Philippe. The distress of the poor sharpened.

Unemployment rose to 50 per cent in Paris. There were fresh bankruptcies. A reduction in indirect taxation provoked a government crisis at the beginning of March that led the finance minister, Goudchaux, to resign; he was replaced by Garnier-Pagès, with the newspaper editor Marrast becoming mayor of Paris. The Bourse took fright. The bond market collapsed. Money was very tight. Gold disappeared from circulation. Treasury reserves dropped sharply and tax revenue declined. A bank closed; two others warned that they were in danger of doing so.

The government authorised the new finance minister to seize royal lands, diamonds and other possessions valued in all at 150 million francs. Garnier-Pagès used the proceeds as backing for a state loan which, together with cash issuances by the Bank of France, stabilised the situation. A 45-centime supplementary tax was added to existing payments, a measure particularly resented by peasant owners of small farms who found the new regime even more onerous than its predecessor, though exemptions meant the tax brought in only half its potential revenue.

As illusions faded, 250 political clubs sprang up, many demanding radical action. Posters called for the establishment of popular assemblies and the promotion of Robespierrean values. Blanqui told the people to 'wait a few days more – then the revolution will be ours!' Armed workers burst in on a meeting of the government to demand the right to work, forcing it to pledge to guarantee employment for all and set up national workshops. A commission in the Luxembourg Palace chaired by Blanc and Albert with a majority of workers' delegates oversaw labour policies. Subcontracting was abolished and a maximum working day fixed at ten hours in Paris and eleven in the provinces. A mobile guard made up of unemployed young men was created, its members given green epaulettes to distinguish them from regular guardsmen. Many were feckless and rootless, not particularly committed to the republic but ready to mete out violence in return for the pay, cheap mercenaries for Ledru-Rollin and his colleagues.

Elections were set for April. Blanc, Blanqui and others on the left wanted them to be put off until there was time to educate voters in republican ways. But a majority of ministers resisted and only a small delay was permitted. Divisions widened further when workers' meetings coalesced into a demonstration that marched on the Hôtel de Ville demanding 'the end of the exploitation of man by man'. The middle-class National Guard stood firm and the day ended peacefully with Lamartine noting in his diary that it was the happiest day of his life as 'factions were more than vanquished ... society was re-established.'

Ledru-Rollin instructed the commissioners to do all they could to ensure that the old republican camp came out on top at the election in which all men aged over twenty-one were eligible to vote in a secret ballot – a movement to enfranchise women got nowhere. The leader-ship's message was modulated according to the audience – priests were told that Christ had been a great republican, schoolteachers that the new regime was on the side of education, small landowners that the 45-centimes tax would be reviewed, and lawyers that their jobs would be safe. Voting on Easter Sunday, 23 April, brought a very high turnout of 84 per cent as people relished their first opportunity to choose 900 members of parliament. Rural people thought nothing of walking for several hours to the ballot box. Priests headed their congregations on treks to the polls after mass.

Blanc's forebodings had been correct and Ledru-Rollin's instruc-tions did not bear fruit as rural France stayed set in its ways, impervious to the message from the capital and loyal to old, localised ties. The influence of the provincial nobility and big farmers remained strong while peasants, to quote the ever-acute Eugen Weber, saw themselves as belonging to 'a way of life with its own hierarchies of the old-fashioned sort'.[2]

Though all provisional ministers were returned in the *département* of the Seine, Albert and Blanc were only in twenty-first and twenty-sev-enth places. The hard left generally did badly – Blanqui and Cabet failed to win seats. Just 285 of the new deputies, less than one-third, were pre-1848 republicans as against 439 who had rallied opportunistically to the cause after the fall of the July Monarchy. There were also 56 unre-pentant Legitimist royalists. The introduction of universal male suffrage had thus rebounded to the disadvantage of its proponents by showing up the schism between the nation as a whole and its leaders in the cap-ital, reflecting the continuing dichotomy between the heritage of the first Revolution and a more conservative France.

Blanc and Albert were dropped from the government which was now run by a five-man executive commission made up of (in order of the support they received from the National Assembly) Arago, Garnier-Pagès, Marie, Lamartine and Ledru-Rollin, who was only included when the politician-poet made this a condition of his own membership. The defence minister was General Cavaignac, who had returned from Algeria and won a parliamentary seat. The Second Republic was proclaimed on 4 May 1848 and work began on a constitution.

'Bread or death'

Festivals were held to celebrate fraternity but workers revolted in Rouen, where several dozen were killed by the forces of law and order, and in Limoges. The political clubs of Paris prepared for street action. On 15 May, an armed crowd, including workers from the national workshops, surged towards the Palais Bourbon where parliament was in session. Led by Blanqui, Albert, the scientist Raspail and the radical Armand Barbès, the march was ostensibly to demand help for Polish nationalists but, when the crowd burst unopposed into the Chamber, it developed into a direct challenge to the new order. Shocked deputies watched as the sweaty, dirty, raucous throng, many in rags, surged round them and ran to the upper floor. 'Throwing their legs over the balconies, hanging by their arms from the cornices that they might slide down on the heads of the representatives, they poured into the hall with flags, dust, cries and confusion, forming a true and atrocious image of an invasion of barbarians upon civilised society,' Lamartine recalled.

Raspail read out a proclamation in favour of the Poles. Next up was Blanqui, shirtless in his usual filthy black topcoat, who drew a connection between Poland and France. Then Barbès, described by the Duchess of Maillé as having 'a fine featured and military face, active, vehement but with a mad air', proposed a tax of a billion francs on the rich. A police secret agent who had infiltrated the leftist ranks called for the dissolution of the Assembly. As the chaos grew, the deputies left the Chamber and guardsmen arrived to clear the place.

For the moderate republicans, *Le National* depicted this as a plot against the nation and an assault on the sovereignty of the people, but there were strong suggestions that it was a trap by the authorities to ensnare the far left. Caussidière was sacked as prefect of the Paris police. Albert, Barbès, Blanqui and Raspail were among 130 people arrested after the National Guard restored order. Showing the wide reach of the left, the charge sheet listed men of letters, lawyers, doctors, watchmakers, masons, cobblers, coachmen, cooks, an organist and a woman 'who called herself religious'. Some were detained for having sung songs in favour of Louis-Napoleon or shouted slogans in his support. Blanc was molested by guardsmen. Several radical political clubs were disbanded by force. Three months after its creation, the new regime had its first political prisoners.

Travelling south to Vichy in mid-June, the Duchess of Maillé found only discouragement among those she met. In the capital, street agitation and strikes continued unabated. In the poor working-class faubourgs, people secretly prepared munitions. A gunpowder factory was hidden off the Faubourg-Saint-Antoine, a cannon was put together in the Faubourg-du-Temple, bullets were moulded in thimbles and a locksmith's foundry made guns and ammunition.

The Luxembourg Labour Commission operated at will, to the disadvantage of enterprises that found it hard to attract workers as the national workshops took on 100,000 men and 20,000 women drawn not only from the jobless but from the ranks of carpenters, masons, jewellers, printers, furniture makers, metalworkers and tailors. The closure of the workshops was decided on 21 June. Alternative work was offered building railways or draining the marshes of the Sologne south of Paris. If the men would not leave the city voluntarily, the government warned, 'we shall compel them by force'. Thousands marched through the capital, denouncing the government, refusing to go to the Sologne, which they likened to Siberia, and, in some cases, shouting slogans in support of Louis-Napoleon. 'Liberty or Death!' the working-class leader Louis Pujol called out at the Place de la Bastille. Placards had a more down-to-earth message, 'Bread or Death'. At night, the protestors converged at the Place du Panthéon, strategically located on a hill on the Left Bank and a familiar spot since it was where the national workshops wages were handed out. Pujol advised them to spend the night setting up barricades and to meet again in the morning.

Fighting escalated from the morning of Friday, 23 June. Tens of thousands of well-armed protestors entrenched themselves behind more than two hundred barricades in the narrow streets below the Panthéon, in the Poissonnière district across the Seine and in the traditional home of revolt in the Faubourg-Saint-Antoine and Bastille area. Lines of communication were set up through houses, gardens and courtyards. Troops pitched triangular white and blue tents along the Boulevard du Temple by the workers' district in the east of the city. The street urchins joined in too. After troops failed to dislodge the demonstrations, the government minister, Arago, walked to the barricade at the Panthéon ahead of a squadron of dragoons. The protestors refused his entreaties to disperse. 'These men are senseless; I can do nothing more; it will have to be decided by force,' he told the troops. A cannon was brought up. Down the hill towards the Seine, savage fighting broke out at a big barricade after a barrage followed by a bayonet charge.

Across the river, guardsmen marching to the beat of drums were met with a fusillade on the Boulevard Bonne Nouvelle. The rebel leader stood on an overturned carriage waving a flag until fatally hit by a bullet. A good-looking young woman with dishevelled hair and naked arms, a prostitute according to Hugo, grabbed the flag and waved it. When soldiers cried out for her to leave, she shouted back at them, raising her skirt and daring them to shoot her in the belly. When she was hit, another woman, younger, even better looking and also a prostitute in Hugo's account, ran forward to support her with one hand while throwing stones with the other. She, too, was brought down by more bullets. A military doctor hurried forward to find that the two were dead. The soldiers stormed the barricade.

The insurgents took over houses and fired from windows commanding crossroads and narrow streets. Troops and guardsmen smashed doors and plunged into hand-to-hand fighting inside the buildings. The bravery of their opponents amazed them. One military detachment broke through five barricades in the Faubourg-Saint-Denis in half an hour, the air full of smoke, bullets and explosions. A thunderstorm followed by lightning filled the sky. Then heavy rain washed pavements covered with the blood of corpses.

'Society cut in two'

The revolt sprang from the abysmal living conditions of the poor and growing population pressure as migrants moved in from parts of France hit by the economic downturn. The death rate in Paris was the highest of any region of France. A third of births were illegitimate and a tenth of newborn babies were abandoned in foundling hospitals – 60 per cent died before reaching their first birthday. The mark of the city was, as Balzac put it, the division between rich and poor, felt all the more keenly by the latter because of the glittering life on the boulevards, which they could watch but not share; the great mansions of the wealthy, the bustle of business round the Bourse and the Chaussée d'Antin, the fashionable social haunts and brothels. In stark contrast, 'there are in Paris, in these faubourgs of Paris,' as Hugo wrote, 'streets, homes, sewers in which families, whole families, live on top of one another, men, women, girls and boys only having for bedding, for covering, I almost said for clothing, infected and fermenting rags, gleaned in the mud, the dunghill of the city, where human creatures bury themselves alive to escape the winter cold.' A floating population of people seeking day jobs lived in *chambres garnies* described by one visitor as 'up a crazy, moth-eaten staircase with a greasy cord as support ... usually containing five to ten beds ... each bed consisting of nothing better than a species of straw palliasse, destitute of sheet, blanket or any covering whatsoever. These miserable beds are usually let by the month or, if by the night at the rate of two sous. It frequently happens that one mattress is occupied by two persons'. Such bedding, 'swarming with vermin', naturally bred pestilence.[3]

No wonder that this led, once more, to violent revolt, which the new leaders felt they had to suppress. 'Society was cut in two: those who had nothing united in common envy; those who had anything united in common terror,' in de Tocqueville's words. He saw the rising as 'the greatest and strangest [insurrection] that had ever taken place in our history or perhaps in that of any other nation; the greatest because for four days more than a hundred thousand men took part in it ... the strangest because the insurgents were fighting without a battle cry, leaders or flag, and yet they showed wonderful powers of coordination

and a military expertise that astonished the most experienced officers.' Skilled workers provided leadership for the revolt rather than
Blanqui, Barbès and the other tribunes of the political clubs. A giant
barricade erected on the Place La Fayette was commanded by a
draughtsman who had deserted from the National Guard; other barricades were overseen by journalists, engineers, railway workers, a
68-year-old shoemaker, a naval officer, a hat maker, a horse dealer and
a builder.

Between them, the insurrectionists make a troubling counter to
France's narrative of republican progress based on the principles of the
First Revolution. As a result, they have been pushed into the background
of history, their rising an uncomfortable reminder of how eminently
respectable republicans turned the troops on their own people motivated primarily by the desire for a decent livelihood and the right to
share in the ideals of liberty, equality, fraternity. They stood outside the
conventional themes of political debate, their aim, de Tocqueville wrote,
'not change the form of the government, but to alter the organisation of
society'. As such they were more dangerous than royal reaction.[4]

The war minister, Cavaignac, sent in three columns of soldiers for the
fiercest fighting of any of the conflicts the capital had seen. The Mobile
Guard, with their green epaulettes, seemed exhilarated by the sound
and fury as they stormed forward; they 'resembled weasels with their
snouts in blood', a contemporary writer of the left recalled. General
Lamoricière, whom Louis-Philippe had tried to summon to his aid in
February, went to the front on a large horse, driving the troops on.

Fighting ebbed and flowed throughout 25 June round the faubourgs
and the Panthéon. Ninety cannon shots were needed to break through
a barricade in the Faubourg-Saint-Denis. The insurgents took the
mayor's office in the Place des Vosges with its arsenal of 15,000 sabres
and ammunition. They advanced on the Hôtel de Ville but were beaten
back. Troops took the Panthéon in hand-to-hand fighting with heavy
losses on both sides. The commander of the government offensive on
the Left Bank was fatally wounded in an attack on a barricade – one of
five generals killed. When he fell, a young guardsman jumped on the
barricade, shot an insurgent dead and returned to the ranks where he
broke down in sobs.

Another general was shot after going to try to reason with insurgents behind their barricade. A bullet hit the archbishop of Paris in the kidney when he walked into an angry crowd carrying a cross and preaching peace. Neither side showed any mercy. After a group of deputies forced their way into the room where the Commission was meeting and demanded its resignation, the political leadership gave Cavaignac full military authority. Meeting Hugo, Lamartine told him, 'we're fucked'.

Government reinforcements and ammunition arrived by railway. Lamoricière executed a sweeping movement to take barricades on the edge of the city and urged pursuit of total victory rather than negotiating with a peace delegation from the rebels. When the delegates returned to the faubourg, great cries rose – 'Death to Cavaignac!', 'Death to the executioner of the people!' Lamoricière's cannons opened up and his soldiers charged. A young man jumped on top of the barricade waving a white handkerchief as if in sign of surrender. It was too late. The charge swept on. An eighteen-year-old member of the Garde Mobile who had plucked a flag from a barricade (and perhaps killed an insurgent with his sword) was taken to the Chamber of Deputies where Cavaignac put his own *Légion d'honneur* on the youth's chest.[5]

Diehard rebels fell back to Belleville, La Chapelle and La Villette where they were overcome or forced to flee by advancing troops. In the Chamber, the deputy speaker read out a proclamation from Cavaignac that 'the revolt is destroyed.' Four thousand people had been killed and another six thousand wounded. Hundreds who had surrendered or been taken prisoner were massacred, some while being marched to jail; some were thrown into the Seine and shot in the water while others were killed after getting to prison. Public gardens became execution grounds. Crossfire from Mobile Guards deployed on quays on either side of the Seine mowed down captives on a bridge. In the centres of the revolt, bodies were pitched into pits. Hospitals overflowed with wounded; in some, rebels and soldiers fought and had to be put into straitjackets. Those in prison risked starvation or being shot through the bars if they made any noise. The number detained was put officially at 25,000 with 11,000 in long-term custody. Thousands were deported to Algeria. Sporadic provincial risings were suppressed, though protests spluttered on in the Massif Central and the south against the 45-centime tax.

Le National depicted a battle in which 'on one side there stood order, liberty, civilisation, the decent Republic, France; and on the other, barbarians, desperados emerging from their lairs for massacre and looting, and odious partisans of those wild doctrines for which the family is only a word and property naught but theft.' Young men from the Garde Mobile were invited to smart parties and balls and magazines depicted them as 'the sweethearts' of Parisian women, lolling in their boudoirs while they kept their husbands at bay.[6]

France might have got rid of royalty for a second time, but it was clearly set on the path dictated by the bourgeoisie with remnant aristocratic characteristics, a military streak, and a conservative countryside which balanced the streets of Paris. 'What we are seeing is certainly not the Republic,' the left-wing Catholic seer Lamennais wrote. 'Around its tomb is the saturnalia of reaction.'

FROM PRINCE PRESIDENT TO EMPEROR

A new constitution provided for both 'a democratic, united and indivisible Republic based on the principles of Liberty, Equality and Fraternity' and a regime based on 'the Family, Work, Property and Public Order'. An executive president would be chosen by universal suffrage for a single four-year term. He would select ministers, who, like him, would be responsible to the Assembly. Revision of the system could only take place if backed by three-quarters of the deputies three times in a special session.

Cavaignac seemed best placed to win the post, but, despite an overwhelming vote by the legislature lauding his suppression of the revolt, he insisted on a scrupulous exercise of his powers, which worked against him. The right-wing parliamentary majority regarded him as insufficiently tough while, for liberals, he was a man of blood. Lamartine's day had waned. Ledru-Rollin commanded little respect. Instead, the rising figure was a man whose past failures might have seemed to disqualify him as a serious contender but whose very name aroused wide public support in the new context of universal male suffrage.

Louis-Napoleon was the son of the brother of the Emperor, who had made him King of Holland, and Hortense, daughter of Bonaparte's wife, Josephine. His mother had a number of extra-marital affairs and had borne an illegitimate son. As a boy, he played in the Tuileries and became a favourite of his uncle. Expelled from France at the Restoration, Hortense took her son to live in a castle in Switzerland, which became a haven for Bonapartists. Devoted to his mother, the boy was pleasant, timid and given to laziness. His father instructed that he should wash his feet once a week, wear large shoes, abstain from coffee, clean his head with a dry sponge, and be limited to a quarter of a bar of chocolate a day. His mother took him on her frequent trips to Italy where he became involved in the Carbonari movement against Austrian rule before travelling to France to mount his first abortive rising against the July Monarchy in Strasbourg. After being expelled to the United States, he went to England to live for two years in Leamington Spa and then landed with fifty followers at Boulogne for his second failed coup.

Arrested and sentenced to life imprisonment in the fortress of Ham in the Somme, he fathered two children by a local seamstress and wrote political works, notably a book entitled *The Extinction of Poverty* that criticised the economic system and proposed wage rises and settlements for the unemployed on wasteland. He escaped from Ham in 1846 after exchanging clothes with a mason. Going back to England, he lived in St James's and began a relationship with a red-haired would-be actress, Harriet Howard, who had inherited a fortune from an earlier lover. She was described as having 'a face from an antique cameo, a superb figure, a lively intelligence and the talent of a brilliant Amazon'.[1]

Back in Paris after the 1848 revolution, the prince sent a letter to Lamartine pledging his loyalty to the provisional government. The reply was curt; he should leave the city until the elected assembly was constituted. Though re-crossing the Channel, he won a seat in a by-election in absentia. Returning to Paris once more, he installed himself in a two-floor suite at a hotel in the Place Vendôme and was charming and sociable to visitors, all things to all men, though keeping himself aloof from the Assembly and its golden-tongued debaters; he was a poor public speaker, with a thin voice and a German accent.

Though the establishment dismissed him – Thiers called him a cretin – some politicians kept from office under Cavaignac were ready to work with the prince. He had an energetic campaign manager in the ardent Bonapartist, Jean-Gilbert-Victor Fialin, who had taken part in the attempted coups and retained his conspiratorial ways, operating under pseudonyms and changing hotels frequently. He brought over influential press proprietors. Some monarchists gave calculated support, reckoning that he could be used to serve their anti-republican interests. Charles de Morny, Hortense's illegitimate son, whose business empire had been ruined by the fall of the July Monarchy, rallied to his half-brother.

Louis-Napoleon put himself forward as the friend of the workers on the basis of his writings while in Ham; 'his name is very often on the workers' lips,' a police report noted. But he also vowed to assure order, so the right was ready to back him. Relatively young at forty, he was a new face and offered an escape from the hermetic world of Parisian politics for the enlarged electorate. His name brought nostalgia for the imperial epoch, fanned by the stirring retro songs of the composer Béranger sung in cafés and bars – the Emperor was remembered fondly in rural areas and civil servants cherished the Napoleonic state.

A Bonaparte returns

The result of the election, in December 1848, was a walkover. The prince got 5.4 million votes, compared to 1.4 million for Cavaignac, 400,000 for Ledru-Rollin, 37,000 for Raspail and 8,000 for Lamartine. He won an absolute majority everywhere except in Brittany and the far south-east. In a largely rural area like the Périgord, he got 88.5 per cent of the vote. Universal male suffrage had once more shown the gulf between the electorate and the political chieftains in the capital.[2]

The veteran centre-left politician, Odilon Barrot, became chief minister, and de Tocqueville moved to the foreign ministry on the Quai d'Orsay. The education portfolio went to Alfred de Falloux, a former Legitimist who advanced legislation to extend state primary education to girls but also lobbied for greater religious influence over schools. Despite his triumph, the new head of state knew how to bide his time in a context he could exploit to his advantage as the economy deteriorated and demonstrations broke out in Paris – establishing himself as a man of order, the Prince President rode between key strategic points as the protests were suppressed, drawing cries of support. Parliamentary elections in May 1849 showed the strength of the right, which took 500 of the 900 seats.

Forming a group known as *la Montagne*, with echoes of the First

Republic, the left-wing *démoc-socs* led by Ledru-Rollin, Arago and other survivors of the first 1848 government promised to deliver the French from ignorance and hunger. But they won only twenty parliamentary seats and needed a cause round which to rally support.[3]

They thought they had found one in Italy after nationalists forced the Pope to flee the Vatican in early 1849 and a French military expedition was sent to Rome to forestall Austrian intervention to restore him. The Italian nationalists had agreed to a referendum under French protection, but the strong showing of the Catholic right in the May elections led Louis-Napoleon to order the expeditionary force to put the Pope back in the Vatican. This contravened a provision in the constitution on respecting the internal affairs of foreign nations and, in an impassioned (though some thought ridiculous) speech in the Assembly, Ledru-Rollin called for the impeachment of the president and the government.

A demonstration by *la Montagne* in Paris on 13 June was dispersed by cavalry, and the left got scant popular support when it tried to set up a 'National Convention'. Troops flooded the boulevards. The president turned out once more on horseback. The whole affair was over by nightfall in Paris, though serious clashes continued in Lyons where cannons were deployed and scores died. 'The time has come for the Good to find reassurance and the Wicked to tremble,' Louis-Napoleon declared. Ledru-Rollin fled to London.

Having pleased Catholics, particularly the ultramontane Catholics, the Prince President showed his habitual taste for trimming by urging the Pontiff to be less reactionary. This provoked a parliamentary crisis and brought down Barrot. In the midst of an outbreak of cholera that took the life of the celebrated salon hostess Madame Récamier, a government was installed under a figurehead general containing several of the president's friends. This saw through legislation drawn up by the departed Falloux that pleased the Catholic right by providing for the expansion of religious schools and enabling the church to operate at university level. But the social volatility continued and the left staged a resurgence in by-elections, which led the government to cut the electorate from 9.6 million to 6.8 million, mainly by disqualifying itinerant workers. There was a crackdown on political clubs. Press controls were imposed. Hundreds of *démoc-soc* mayors were dismissed. Martial law was imposed in some places. The bourgeois *Revue des Deux Mondes* warned of 'ferocious hordes ... coming out from under the streets in the hours of anguish' and a more polemical pamphleteer warned of 'bullets being made ... knives being sharpened in the shadows, victims being marked out, the spoils of the vanquished divided in advance'.[4]

Louis-Napoleon was still underrated by the establishment, a verdict encouraged by his indolent style. Rising at 10 a.m., he met ministers in the middle of the day and then spent time with his mistress. Described by her lover as 'a person of such pure devotion and high character', Miss Howard took up residence in the rue du Cirque by the Élysée with his two sons and a child she had borne to her late English lover.

The Prince President promised to care for the welfare of the people at large but also backed authority, religion and the pursuit of respect abroad. He appealed to the fears of the bourgeoisie by hinting that France faced an insurrection from 'red' plotters, while seeking the support of workers by attacking the restrictive electoral law of 1850. Setting a tone that would become the leitmotif of real and imagined strong men of French politics, he pledged 'a precise and energetic direction', placing himself above the competing parties and the familiar political actors. With government reshuffles, he installed his own men in ministerial posts while close supporters planned a takeover. 'We need men devoted to my very person, from deputies to police inspectors,' he said, adding that the memory of his uncle was 'the only sentiment by which subversive ideas can be fought'. Financial backing came from rich supporters plus Miss Howard's fortune. The army commander, who wore a wig and corset, was elbowed out in favour of Armand de Saint-Arnaud, a libertine ready to do the prince's bidding, a veteran of Algeria where he liked to drive nationalists into caves and asphyxiate them with smoke.

Crossing the 'Rubicon'

The disarray of the Assembly became evident in November 1851, when it considered a motion asserting its right to call in the army. Fearing that Thiers and the right-wing majority might use such powers to restore the monarchy, republicans voted with the president's supporters against the bill. At that, Louis-Napoleon considered it time to usher in the fourth change of regime in France since his uncle had been packed off to Saint Helena thirty-six years earlier.

After the guests dispersed from the Élysée at the end of the usual Monday reception on 1 December, he huddled in a room filled with cigarette smoke with his stepbrother Morny, the inveterate conspirator Fialin, General Saint-Arnaud and Charlemagne-Émile Maupas, a prefect known for his readiness to ignore legal constraints. At midnight, the president gave the order to launch a coup. It was a do-or-die affair, 'all or nothing', as he told a visitor a week later. His dossier for the affair was entitled 'Rubicon'.[5]

Soldiers took up strategic positions in central Paris. Troops occupied republican newspaper offices. Eighty politicians were arrested including Thiers, Lamartine, Crémieux, Falloux and Cavaignac, who was held in the same cell at Ham where the new ruler had once been detained. Workers at the national print office were summoned to turn out a decree dissolving the Chamber, proclaiming full universal suffrage and calling for a new assembly to grant the president a ten-year term. Watched by guards, they produced the document in small sections so that none could know its full message. 'The present situation cannot continue,' it explained. 'Each day that passes increases the country's dangers.' The Assembly was accused of being 'a hotbed of sedition', of 'forging weapons for civil war', of 'fostering every wicked passion' and trying to interpose itself between the president and the people. 'I invite the whole people to adjudicate between it and me,' the prince concluded.

Morny became interior minister. Maupas took the Paris police prefecture. A military assault cleared the Palais Bourbon. Royalist deputies tried to rally at the mayor's office, but were arrested. The plotters grabbed 24 million francs from the Bank of France; Fialin disbursed some of it to troops and others who needed to be bought over. At 7 a.m. on 2 December, he told the head of state the coup had been a complete success.

He was premature. The army met opposition as it moved in the ever-turbulent eastern faubourgs of the capital. Barricades went up; cannons took hours to demolish one in the rue Saint-Denis. Republican deputies in the streets urged resistance. The troops burst into houses, restaurants and cafés, slashing and shooting as they went. When shot at from windows, they fired back indiscriminately. Lancers charged along the boulevards, mowing down people with swords and concentrated fire. In the prosperous rue Le Peletier windows were smashed and walls pierced by shots, while undertakers gathered to take away bodies. The Rothschild family watched the fighting from the windows of its house.

A *démoc-soc* deputy was killed in the street. Prisoners taken to the Champ-de-Mars were executed on the spot. Near their home on the rue Saint-Georges, the Goncourt brothers saw troops picking off passers-by. After their exertions, some of the soldiers relaxed on the quais of the Seine where the diarist brothers recorded them piling up their rifles, 'sausages and flasks of wine littering the benches, feasting in a public and praetorian fashion, drunk from the morning and the night before'.[6]

Receiving the Austro-Hungarian diplomat Apponyi on the evening of 12 December, Louis-Napoleon told him that he was the only rampart against disorder. To buttress his position, he would restrain the press and crush the 'demagogic party'. Lighting a cigar, he strode up and down so briskly that his visitor had trouble keeping up with him. Then he stopped and declared, 'If the revolution raises its head once more, I will precede the battle with the rolling of drums and cannon shots to warn peaceful citizens to go home and close their doors and windows. After that, too bad for those who stay in the streets.'[7]

Though resistance was repressed in Paris, old antipathies boiled over in the provinces, less for the defence of a republic with which few people sympathised than in an opportunity for peasants to assert their rights and attack the bourgeoisie. There were pitched battles in the south-east as peasant columns marched in semi-military formations on sub-prefectural towns. A state of siege was declared in half the *départements*. Armed bands occupied sixteen towns. The authorities spread fearsome stories of wild excess, pillage and looting, known as the *jacquerie*. Waves of troops suppressed the protestors and those arrested were taken before summary tribunals. Morny ordered the mass replacement of local officials.

Most of the political leaders detained on the night of the coup were released quite soon, but they were given no chance to organise opposition. After being held briefly at Ham, Thiers was taken to the Belgian border and spent time in Brussels before being allowed to return to France the following summer. Victor Hugo went into exile, ending up in the Channel Islands. A regulation required an oath of loyalty from holders of public offices. Professors were forbidden to wear beards since these were 'symbols of anarchy'. Michelet lost his post again.

A constitution giving the head of state a ten-year term and making ministers dependent on him alone was submitted to a plebiscite. Voting produced 7.5 million in favour and 640,000 against with 1.5 million abstentions. Even Paris was recorded as having approved by 132,000 to 80,000 with 75,000 abstentions. The Prince President said he had 'only departed from legality to return to the law' and the vote 'absolved' him.

The National Assembly was cut to 300 members. The press was subjected to controls. An army of official electoral candidates was chosen, mainly by the new regime's prefects. Mayors were given the job of ensuring that the right men won; their jobs often depended on it. They represented muscular state power at local level, the channel by which villages and communes could be assured of subsidies if they voted the correct way.

The aim was to create a new political class to replace the men who had held sway under the July Monarchy. This was not easy given the lack of suitable candidates. Though the regime based itself on mass support, the Prince President did not want to pack the legislature with nostalgic Bonapartists but to recruit a new class of notables and self-made businessmen. Since members of the new Assembly were not paid, this would be a parliament of rich men whose loyalty sprang from self-interest rather than conviction.

Fialin took over the interior ministry after growing tension between the president and Morny led to the latter's resignation over a decision to nationalise the 30-million-franc fortune of the Orléans family – he was soon back in the leader's circle, however. Better known to history under the noble title of Persigny, the new minister was a demanding taskmaster with a sharp temper and a straightforward view of politics – 'anything that delays the fusion of parties into the great family of the state delays the enjoyment of freedom', the task of government being to eradicate 'passions hostile to the established order'.

To that end, he supervised the imprisonment, expulsion or deportation to the colonies of Guiana or Algeria of 14,000 people arrested after the coup. The prince showed his approval of the 44-year-old Bonapartist with a gift of half-a-million francs when he married the eighteen-year-old granddaughter of Marshal Ney and the banker Laffitte. Persigny described his wife as 'a precious diamond' but her taste for luxury and high society put a strain on her husband, who disliked going out and lived frugally. He irked colleagues by acquiring authority beyond his brief and, in time, Louis-Napoleon proposed that he should become minister without portfolio. Persigny resigned and went as ambassador to London. But he had set the mould for the administration.

At the core were the prefects, most of them highly educated, efficient, upper-class administrators, rather than the corrupt despots depicted by republican writers. They ranged from conservatives who worked with the old elites to those who wanted to initiate social and political reform. They generally sought understandings with the dominant political groups in their departments, creating a patchwork of power that stood in the way of a full-blown dictatorship even if Louis-Napoleon had aimed at that – which he did not, dreaming rather of a system in which the mass of the people would rally to him of their own accord.

New-old path

Of 9.8 million registered voters, 6.2 million went to the polls in the two-round parliamentary election in February and March 1852. The rigging was blatant; mayors were sent slips with the names of official candidates to hand to trusted electors and reminded that only those designated by the regime would be in a position to look after local interests. Government candidates got 5 million votes, the opposition 820,000 (and eight seats). Still, a high abstention rate meant government candidates received the votes of only 53 per cent of registered electors, with low turnouts in major cities. Orléanists and *démoc-socs* boycotted the polls. Government candidates gained the support of less than half the registered electorate in legitimist Brittany, the Vendée and the left-leaning south-east. The new ruler's strength lay in a broad sweep of rural constituencies in central and eastern France and the south-west; even areas where there had been violent opposition to the coup rallied to the new regime which, in Marx's analysis, became the representative of a rural population unable to enforce its interests itself, the defender of peasants against both rich landowners and the cities.[8]

However, the parliamentary majority contained plenty of local magnates, old-style royalists and survivors from the July Monarchy. Persigny lamented that 'we have handed the legislative body to the upper classes.' The proportion of civil servants fell but they still constituted the single biggest bloc by background. Businessmen played less of a role than the new rulers had hoped.

Still, industrialists and financiers had every reason to back the new administration. Railways boomed after the first line (to the north) was opened in 1845; traffic through the Gare du Nord in Paris was so heavy the original building had to be torn down and a new station opened in 1860 – the original was re-erected in Lille. Consolidation of firms produced the Paris, Lyon, Méditerranée (PLM) company which built the 'imperial line', taking travellers between France's three biggest cities and becoming the country's biggest freight carrier. Its lines linked to colonial sea traffic to Africa and the Middle East and reached through the Alps to Italy and Switzerland. Its elegantly fitted carriages provided passengers with hot-water bottles for cold journeys. Financed by the Rothschilds, the firm was headed by an outstanding Saint-Simonist railway engineer, Paulin Talabot. He had been to Britain to meet Robert Stephenson whose skills he set out to replicate in France as well as becoming involved, in the spirit of the age, with other engineering projects including plans for a canal through the Isthmus of Suez.

Marseilles saw the launch of several big shipping companies. One of the largest, the *Messageries Impériales*, was capitalised at 20 million francs. Steamships linked the Mediterranean port with the Americas. Regular lines took passengers and freight between the PLM railway terminus and North Africa. The number of ships using the port rose from 8,670 in 1860 to 12,019 ten years later and the volume of cargo from 2 million tonnes to 3.5 million. Talabot supervised the expansion of the harbour with financial participation by the Rothschilds, Schneider and other big business figures.[9]

As the European economy improved, credit became easier; mutual insurance companies were encouraged and urban renovation pursued. Eugène Schneider began the development of his great industrial bastion at Le Creusot in Burgundy. In October 1852, Louis-Napoleon laid out a sweeping vision – 'we have huge uncultivated territories to clear, roads to open, ports to dig, rivers to render navigable, canals to finish, and our network of railways to complete.'

The national mood improved. The state of siege was lifted. The Prince President threw lavish balls at the Élysée, giving his arm to favoured ladies. When he toured central and southern France in the autumn of 1852, the interior ministry told prefects to distribute flags emblazoned 'Long Live the Emperor'. In Bordeaux, run by the ambitious Georges-Eugène Haussmann, Louis-Napoleon announced that what France wanted was an Empire.

A gerrymandered referendum produced a vote of 7.8 million in favour of this to 250,000 against. On 2 December, a year after the coup and on the forty-eighth anniversary of his uncle's coronation, the Second Empire was proclaimed. The Prince President became Napoleon III (Bonaparte's son, who died in 1832, had been the second holder of the title). France could dream of new glory and many felt more comfortable with a ruler on a throne rather than the messy republic. But some were concerned about the new-old path, and not only divided royalists and routed republicans. Though his bank profited handsomely from a bull market set off by the new regime, James de Rothschild wrote to his nephews: 'How would you like a French constitution for two sons? They're being sold in the streets for that.' He worried that the ruler was 'an ass – who would end up turning the world against him', as he liked 'nothing more than to play the little soldier'.[10]

THE OPPORTUNISTIC EMPIRE

Napoleon III had a bad press in his lifetime. If the Austrian statesman Metternich called him a sphinx, the Prussian Bismarck snorted that he was 'a sphinx without riddles'. Victor Hugo dismissed him as 'Napoleon the Little'. Karl Marx saw him as an example of history repeating itself as farce. Baudelaire wrote that 'he showed how anybody at all, if only he gets hold of the telegraph and the printing presses, can govern a great nation.' Critics portrayed him as a mountebank who ran an empty show played to the catchy but often superficial tunes of its most popular composer, Jacques Offenbach, with the burgeoning of finance, urban development and the glittering social life of the capital hiding a deeply degenerate, unjust society as the numbers of poor in the cities swelled and the peasantry was left 'soaked in mud up to our knees', in the words of one rural observer.[1]

Despite such disdain, the second emperor ruled for nearly eighteen years, restoring France's international standing for a time, opening up the economy, and introducing political reform when he had to. Embodying the hypocrisies of government, he escapes easy definitions, a political innovator constantly juggling with the possibilities of personal rule, not admirable to be sure, yet searching to reconcile the contradictions of his country at the head of a complex and all too human administration.

His flexibility deprived his empire of a moral compass; appropriately, an early exponent of psychiatry, Dr Bénédict Morel, published a 'Treatise of the Physical, Intellectual and Moral Degenerations of the

Human Race' in 1857. Conventional morality declined. Morny, who split his time between politics, business and the social whirl and built himself an extremely *grand maison* close to the Élysée,* was described by the Goncourt brothers in their diary as typifying a time when people were 'all doing shady deals, selling something of everything, selling even their own wives ... steeped in corruption ... a vulgar libertine, the mind of Paris'. A rake who was said to keep a box by his bedside containing images of his mistresses, usually naked and with flowers on their genitals, the emperor's half-brother was not only a profiteer but also a patron of the arts, amateur librettist and promoter of Deauville as an upmarket holiday resort with its racecourse and railway line.

Despite his marriage to the Spanish noblewoman, Eugénie de Montijo, and his courting of the Catholic church, Napoleon had multiple affairs; a rumour reported by the Goncourts had it that, when he fancied a woman, she would be driven to the Tuileries in a cab, undressed and taken to see the ruler, also naked, by the imperial chamberlain who told her she could kiss him anywhere except on the face. Whether there was any truth in this was beside the point; the fact that such stories circulated said much about the times.

Miss Howard flew into a rage when she learned of his marriage, but she was made Countess of Beauregard with a château near Versailles and repayment of her loans with interest. The emperor went on to liaisons involving a cousin, celebrated actresses and a strikingly attractive Italian countess sent by the nationalists in Turin to win hearts in Paris, which she duly did at the very top, communicating with her employers in code.

In 1862, he began an affair with Justine Marie Leboeuf, known as Marguerite Bellanger, a former acrobatic dancer and bareback circus rider. She was twenty-five, he fifty-four. Zola mentions her in his novel, *Nana*, and Manet may have used her in part for the naked figure in his painting, *Olympia*. Napoleon provided her with two houses in the outskirts of Paris, a château near Meaux, fine horses and a smart carriage in which she drove proudly past that of the empress in the Bois de

* Now a luxury hotel.

The 'Liberal' Emperor

Napoleon III lived for the day, making the most of the chances that came his way, turning on a centime piece, unscrupulous but also not without human feelings, seeking to evoke the memory of his uncle but lacking in application and vision to meet the task. 'What is the Empire?' he asked a diplomat. 'It's only a word.'

Self-contained and secretive, he showed little of himself and his intentions to others. He suffered from the awareness that other European leaders regarded him as a parvenu. His physical appearance did not help in an age that liked its leaders to be imposing figures. His large nose, pointed moustaches and goatee beard made his face seem even longer than it was. Five-and-a-half-feet tall with short legs, he had what Queen Victoria described as 'a head and bust which ought to belong to a much taller man'. His face was pale, his blue-grey eyes glassy with either 'a smiling and kindly expression' or 'a dull, staring look which is rather peculiar', in the words of the court doctor.

He could be dreamy, distracted, preoccupied and sink into silence that resembled melancholy – or fall into fits of laughter during which he sometimes came close to crying, often at one of his own jokes which, the doctor noted, were 'not always of the finest sort'. As a rule, he walked slowly, his toes turned out.

His heavy smoking affected his health. He had trouble with his kidneys and prostate, haemorrhoids and, as he aged, gout and arthritis. He suffered from headaches and found it increasingly difficult to urinate because of his bladder disease. His rooms were overheated to ease rheumatic pain; sometimes he took to his bed by day to keep warm.

In 1856, a British consultant diagnosed 'nervous exhaustion' after the emperor said he had woken in the middle of the night in a fit, wetting his bed; the specialist thought he risked becoming an epileptic and told him to work less, eat two light meals a day and take better care of himself.[2]

Boulogne. When she bore a son, paternity unsure, he gave him a château.

She was said to walk into the bedroom on her hands. Flaubert said he had heard that Napoleon put on a paper hat to decorate the house he bought for her at Saint-Cloud, with a concealed entrance for his use. Noting how exhausted her husband was after weekends with his mistress, the empress went with a court functionary to see her. 'If he comes to me, it is because you bore and annoy him,' Marguerite told her. As the two women shouted at one another, the official withdrew. When silence intervened, he returned to find them laughing together. After the affair ended, Marguerite kept her property, marrying a Prussian serving in the British army and dying in 1886 after catching a cold walking in the gardens of her château.[3]

The court, with its constant balls and receptions, was a sexual bazaar reflecting the capital city, which the puritanical English historian of the Revolution, Thomas Carlyle, denounced as 'nothing but a brothel and gambling hell'. The 'lions' of the elite Jockey Club competed to show off their horses and mistresses. A deaf-mute photographer Bruno Braquehais, made a speciality of female nude shots and pornographic images of intercourse. The Goncourts recorded overhearing two important officials debating whether decorations should be worn when visiting a brothel; one, a former prefect and future senator, said it was advisable because, if you did, 'they give you women who don't have the pox'. The English courtesan known as Cora Pearl, née Emma Crouch, appeared near nude at a masquerade ball and had herself served at dinner covered only by parsley on a huge silver dish. Starting out as a street prostitute, she became the mistress of the Duke of Rivoli, kept a stable of sixty horses and was famed for her ability to 'make bored men laugh'. Her lovers included the emperor's cousin, Prince Napoleon, who bought her a palace, les Petites Tuileries.[4]

Marie-Anne Detourbey, a bottle washer in Champagne before moving to the capital, became another lover of Prince Napoleon who installed her in an apartment by the Champs-Élysées where she held a literary salon. Nearby, an extremely rich Silesian aristocrat built a marble palace encrusted with gold and precious stones for Esther

Pauline Lachmann, daughter of Russian Jewish émigrés who took the name of La Pavia and married her lover. After she died, he kept her corpse in embalming fluid, weeping in front of it for hours – despite having remarried.

A 'good despotism'

The imperial constitution of 1852, drawn up by the influential conservative Eugène Rouher, stipulated the emperor's direct link to the people, and gave him all executive power. He named members of the Council of State, which proposed laws, and the Senate. Ministers reported directly to him. The Assembly, elected by popular suffrage, was reduced to a rubber stamp to approve the executive's measures. It met for three months a year and proceedings were reported only in official summary form. It could not vote in detail on the budget and was not empowered to name its own president. The government could disregard its amendments. 'This country is so tired of revolutions that all it wants today is a good despotism,' Morny observed. 'That's just what it's got.'[5]

The regime sat on a huge web of patronage overseen by Rouher, a man with an enormous capacity for work who served at various times as president of the council of state and minister of agriculture, public works and commerce, as well as pushing railway development and free trade. The civil service doubled in size to 265,000. Below the powerful prefects, mayors named by the state ran a network of constables, tax collectors, gamekeepers (who outnumbered teachers) and postmen and postmistresses (a rare civil service job open to women). Those dependent on licences for their trade, such as operators of hostelries, bars and cafés, were counted on to toe the line. Fire brigades were Bonapartist bastions: 'the emperor is the father of all firemen!' declared one prefect.

Anybody suspected of opposition activity was watched. Police strength was increased. The gendarmerie of former non-commissioned military officers under the war ministry maintained order in the countryside. The press was required to lodge caution money and subject to official warnings on coverage and comment. Though most newspapers in Paris were republican, Orléanist and Legitimist, two hundred in the provinces were loyal to the regime.

Behind this hard-line front, the ruler and those around him were, for the most part, more supple than the system they had erected. Commercial regulations were reduced and laissez-faire economics encouraged. Some prefects worked with local royalists as in the case of Eugène Janvier de la Motte, who ran the Eure *département* in cooperation with powerful Orléanists while gaining popular support through lavish banquets and festivities. To win over workers, the emperor granted the right to strike in 1864. Though no fan of the Industrial Revolution, he encouraged urban job creation and manufacturing. A third of the confiscated fortune of the Orléans family went to fund workers' housing and as much to subsidise mutual societies pooling savings for welfare and other services – by 1870, they had 500,000 members.[6]

The ministers and advisers round the emperor were too different in personality, background and interests to form a cohesive power elite. Morny presided over parliament and made it more important than it might otherwise have been. Achille Fould, finance minister from 1852 to 1867, had an Orléanist background and belonged to a prominent banking rival to the Rothschilds. Édouard Drouyn de Lhuys, foreign minister from 1852–5 and 1862–70, had been in Barrot's government under the Second Republic. The Marquis de Chasseloup-Laubat, son of an imperial general, promoted colonialism. Count Walewski, who served as both foreign minister and minister of state, was an illegitimate son of Bonaparte and a Polish countess; his wife was one of the emperor's mistresses. The stout and libidinous Prince Napoleon, known from the childhood pronunciation of his name as 'Plon Plon', urged his cousin to be 'revolutionary' abroad and anti-clerical at home while advocating 'progress towards liberty through dictatorship'. As the ruler put it, 'The empress is a Legitimist, Morny is an Orléanist, Prince Napoleon is a Republican, and I, myself am a Socialist. There is only one Bonapartist – Persigny – and he is mad!'[7]

Flowering of the arts

Despite its meretricious character, the Empire saw a considerable flowering of the arts. The emperor helped innovative painters by sponsoring the Salon des Refusés for works rejected by the official Salon and showed concern for the nation's history by encouraging the writer Prosper Mérimée and the architect Viollet-le-Duc to undertake the protection of historic buildings, ensuring the preservation of such jewels as the abbey at Vézelay, Mont-Saint-Michel and Carcassonne, which was extensively rebuilt.

Starting to write at 9 p.m. after a busy day of eating, socialising and strolling, Gustave Flaubert established the modern novel, advising that artists should live in bourgeois style and save their bohemianism for their work. The publication of *Madame Bovary* in serial form in 1856 led to his trial and acquittal for obscenity. In 1869, he followed with *L'Éducation Sentimentale*. His good friend, Amantine Lucile Aurore Dupin, writing as George Sand, produced forty-six books and eleven plays plus literary criticism and political essays.

At eighteen she had married a baron by whom she had two children before breaking with him and conducting liaisons with several writers, including de Musset and Mérimée, the socialist Louis Blanc and the actress Marie Dorval. From 1837, she had a ten-year affair with Chopin; but they fell out two years before he died in 1849 and she was not among the 3,000 mourners at his funeral in Paris and his burial at the Père Lachaise cemetery in Paris. Sitting next to her at dinner, the Goncourts were struck by her 'beautiful and charming head which, with age, becomes each day like that of a kind of mulatto'. Her celebrated country home at Nohant in central France was described by Théophile Gautier as being 'as amusing as a Moravian monastery'; the hostess, resembling 'a ghostly automaton', came down to breakfast at 10 a.m., woke up over a game of bowls, retreated to write for three hours and played silent patience after dinner.

Sand had a volatile relationship with the less-remembered Marie, Countess of Agoult, who also wrote under a male pseudonym, Daniel Stern. The two were initially great friends and shocked society by

smoking in public, Daniel cigars and George cigarettes. After separating from her unfaithful husband, Marie moved to Switzerland to
live with the star pianist and composer Franz Liszt. Though they did
not wed, they had three children – the middle one, Cosima, married
Richard Wagner. She fell out with Sand over her promiscuity, disliked
Chopin, and suspected her friend of having designs on Liszt with
whom, however, she split to return to France, where she wrote plays
and stories and a fine account of the 1848 revolution, enjoyed friendships with prominent Second Empire figures, visited the Wagners in
Switzerland and died in 1876, three months before Sand.

The ultimate Parisian flâneur, Charles Baudelaire published the first
volume of *Les Fleurs du Mal* in 1857, aweing many of his fellow artists;
Flaubert told him that he had rejuvenated Romanticism, though *Le
Figaro*'s critic inveighed against it, saying that 'Everything in it which is
not hideous is incomprehensible, everything one understands is putrid.'
The leading critic, Charles Augustin Sainte-Beuve, was appointed professor of Latin at the Collège de France, but resigned after being
heckled by anti-imperial students; he later became a senator and
pleaded for press freedom.

Balzac had died a year before Napoleon's coup – Hugo reportedly
slipped into the grave while delivering the eulogy at the cemetery. But
the elder Dumas remained a venerable figure; returning home in 1861
after joining the struggle for Italian unification. His son, also called
Alexandre, as painstaking a writer as his father was prolix, was the leading playwright of the epoch and enjoyed great success with his novel *La
Dame Aux Camélias*, the basis for the play and Verdi's opera, *La Traviata*.
Starting with his highly successful five-act farce, *Un Chapeau de Paille
d'Italie*, Eugène Labiche spun a series of comedies that delighted boulevard audiences. As well as his works with monuments, the scholarly,
officious Prosper Mérimée wrote the story *Carmen*, on which Bizet based
his opera. The leading actor of the day, Philibert Rouvière, dominated
the male stage with his black-clad Hamlet while former street singer
Mademoiselle Rachel (real name Élisa Félix) was queen of the
Comédie-Française, less than five feet tall but overpowering audiences
with her stagecraft and her imperious bearing before she burned out at
the age of thirty-eight.

The realistic painter Gustave Courbet made his mark at the Salon of 1850–1 with his great works, *A Burial at Ornans* and the *Stone Breakers*. Championing socialist and anarchist ideas, he presented himself as an ignorant peasant epitomising his art in his life, and created fresh waves with his depiction of two prostitutes at the Salon of 1857 followed by a series of erotic paintings leading to the image of female genitalia in *L'Origine du Monde* not shown publicly for more than a century. Edgar Degas established himself during the Empire as did Édouard Manet, who developed a new aesthetic of modernity drawing on Spanish and Dutch old masters. His *Déjeuner sur l'Herbe* was a sensation at the Salon des Refusés, which also saw an exhibition of Paul Cézanne's work in 1863 though he was rejected for the next five years.

While popular café-concerts flourished, offering entertainment, drinks and flirtation, a string of major operas at the Place du Châtelet by the Seine included Gounod's *Faust*, Bizet's *Les Pêcheurs de Perles* and Berlioz's *Les Troyens*. Playing at the church of the Madeleine in Paris, Camille Saint-Saëns was called the world's greatest organist by Liszt. His pupil, Gabriel Fauré, spent most of the 1860s at the church organ in Rennes. The pianist and organist Juliette Godillon was a hit with her improvisations, which melded classic, opera and peasant themes while she preached the need for stricter morality. Popular entertainment thrived. Tight-rope walker Charles Blondin earned an international reputation crossing Niagara Falls on a highwire, blindfolded, on stilts, in a sack, carrying his manager on his back or stopping midway to cook and eat an omlette. The tuneful, dandyish German-born Offenbach captured the spirit of the times with his catchy melodies, gentle satire and innuendo in eighteen operettas, including *La Belle Hélène*, *La Vie Parisienne* and *La Périchole* as well as *Orpheus in the Underworld*, a satire on the imperial court in which Cora Pearl appeared half-naked.[8]

Industrial and commercial expansion

The Empire created the basis of a modern capitalist system alongside its attempt to enforce a voluntarist social policy. The emperor's principal economic adviser, the Saint-Simonian Michel Chevalier, declared that the stability of state and society required everybody to get a better return for their work and be 'better nourished, clothed, heated, lighted and furnished'. Assets that had lain unused in drawers were to be mobilised for investment. Government policy was to encourage industrialists and businessmen to raise workers' pay. The administration and business worked hand in glove. Self-made tycoons, such as the iron master Schneider, as well as financiers like the Péreire brothers, sat in parliament. Bankers expanded their operations, developing joint stock operations and indulging in fierce rivalries. Morny had close links with financiers ready to pay him for favours. Manufacturers encouraged colonial expansion to provide new markets for their goods while merchants welcomed exotic imports that appealed to the new rich.[9]

The heads of traditional manufacturing companies branched out into new fields – in Lyons, silk-making families went into banking, transport and chemicals. Deficit financing of big projects was used to encourage economic development. Protectionism gave way to free trade policies, including a commercial treaty with Britain. France backed a Latin Monetary Union, agreeing with Italy, Belgium, Switzerland, Spain and Greece to harmonise their currencies and make them freely interchangeable.

Growth rose strongly before a slump in 1857. Thereafter, expansion was steady except for a downturn in 1866–7. National income is estimated to have gone up by more than half under the Second Empire with a 40 per cent increase in wages. Though there were significant loopholes, the easing of restrictions on labour organisation represented progress for workers. Communications advanced. The number of telegraph stations went from seventeen to 1,500. The iron and steel industries benefitted from railway expansion. Improved transport of goods created a national market and made Paris the centre of the food trade.

Some sectors of agriculture did well from land reclamation. In the north-east, the growing of beetroots which had been promoted by the First Emperor underwent a revival as the Caribbean sugar industry costs were hit by the emancipation of slaves. Mills paid 'fabulous' dividends – a seven-kilometre tunnel was built to channel the juice and one enterprise near Laon reimbursed its shareholders within a year.[10]

Major infrastructure programmes were launched in big cities, with wide roads dedicated to the emperor, palatial railway stations and chambers of commerce. Lyons and Marseilles both got broad '*rues impériales*' and the average width of new Parisian streets doubled. A new town was built outside the fortifications surrounding Toulon, its broad roads lined with palm trees. A fresh style of architecture emerged for middle-class apartment buildings, monumental but with all manner of decorations, from classical figures holding up street doorways to delicate flowery motifs. A horse-drawn omnibus service was launched in the capital in 1856; a year later it carried more than 100 million passengers a year on its 347 buses.

The visionary city planner, Hector Horeau, imagined zoning, moving slaughterhouses, cemeteries, hospitals and hospices out of city centres, suburban transport links and houses with hollow walls that could be moved between estates. His peer, Eugène Hénard, envisaged roads and railways superimposed on one another to facilitate urban movement. Little of this was put into practice but it reflected the spirit of the age and laid the basis for future town planning.[11]

The number of coal mines increased nearly 50 per cent under the Empire. Iron steamships replaced wooden vessels. The population in urban centres with more than 50,000 inhabitants doubled. A catastrophic decline in the silk industry in Lyons after epidemics wiped out silkworms bred in France was solved by the import of hundreds of thousands of boxes of eggs from Japan. The marshes of the Sologne were drained and the vast moors of the south-western Landes were planted with pines; Napoleon bought 20,000 acres for a model farm.[12]

The popular press flourished and book publishing boomed with printing techniques that enabled the use of thinner paper and smaller type – nearly 14,000 new titles were appearing each year by the mid-1860s. The Lévy brothers took a risk in bringing out *Madame Bovary* but scored a much bigger seller with Ernest Renan's *Life of Jesus*. Louis Hachette's business ranged from dictionaries to station bookstalls and a papermaking venture with Morny. Literacy rose sharply; by the end of the Empire, 18 million French people could read; nearly 700,000 attended adult education courses. The number of public libraries tripled.

Industrial consolidation made inroads into the traditionally fragmented nature of manufacturing. The metals and mining industries formed powerful federations to regulate their industries and protect their interests. Consumerism led to the development of department stores. After a slump in 1847–9, the property market expanded rapidly, boosted by the rebuilding of city centres. Limited liability firms sprouted. The Paris stock market expanded as the money supply rose and industrial groups floated shares; the Bourse, said Alexandre Dumas *fils*, was the 'cathedral' of the age. Savings accounts trebled to two million. Major new banks such as the Crédit Lyonnais were created.[13]

The Péreire brothers moved out of the shadow of the Rothschilds to found the Crédit Mobilier and the Crédit Immobilier banks, which took deposits from the general public and invested in industry, breaking the small circle of big financial institutions. They invested in rail and shipping, gas, insurance, a newspaper and property, including the development of the Parc Monceau area in Paris as an upmarket residential district – the Camondo banking family moved there from Turkey and built up a great collection of *ancien régime* treasures in a palace with a kosher kitchen and an elaborate green fountain where dinner guests could wash their hands before going to table.

The Wendels expanded their metals group connected to Belgian coalmines and coke furnaces; by 1870, they employed 7,000 workers producing 245,000 tons of iron a year. Jean-Baptiste Godin, who started work in a foundry at eleven, built a fortune making cast-iron stoves and adopted the idea put forward by Charles Fourier that factories would function best in cooperative communities with staff housed in big complexes. His large apartment development, *le Familistère*, for his workers beside his factory in northern France, was complete with ventilation, rubbish chutes, water fountains, bath-houses, a 'culinary workshop' and regular cleaning services. The coal company at Montceau-les-Mines took boys under its wing, paid for their education, gave them rooms with heating, employed them for thirty years and guaranteed a pension. Jean-Félix Bapterosses looked after everything from childcare to old age for his thousand employees making porcelain buttons and artificial pearls.[14]

The red-faced iron and steel master Eugène Schneider's industrial empire at Le Creusot in Burgundy employed 12,500 people, some occupying detached company houses. His business was greatly boosted by railway work and a monopoly contract to supply weapons to the army. As well as sitting in the Chamber of Deputies, he was a Regent of the Banque de France, the privately owned central bank. One of his associates at Le Creusot was the English businessman Daniel Wilson, who branched out from supplying the gas lighting system for Paris into investments in railways, metallurgy and property including two mansions in Paris and a 557-hectare estate outside the capital where he housed a collection of 248 works of art and a cellar of 1,500 bottles of the finest wine. Schneider was an avid collector, too, in his case of Dutch art stored in a locked room, the key to which he kept with him at all times and he admitted nobody else. Wilson's estate was worth 6 million francs at his death, Schneider's 10 million.[15]

The financial sector grew increasingly important, split between the conservative Rothschilds, whose business focussed on underwriting loans, and more adventurous operators like the Péreire brothers. James de Rothschild built the most lavish château of the nineteenth century at Ferrières, east of Paris, which was graced in 1862 by a visit from the emperor who walked in the 1,500-hectare park, planted a cedar tree and took breakfast off silver plate and Sèvres porcelain before joining a shooting party which killed a thousand head of game; he caused his host embarrassment by pausing on the grand staircase to sniff the air – Baron James had the kitchens moved underground outside the château.[16]

The Banque de France was controlled by the 183 Regents, later expanded into *les deux cents familles* said by conspiracy theorists to run the country; the central bank's capital increased from 100 million francs in 1851 to 2.5 billion in 1870. Financiers ranged across every part of the economy at home and abroad and bred a new group of entrepreneurs who founded careers on their ability to raise and use cash. The Bourse boomed as savings were unlocked and great schemes were unfolded.

Son of the owner of a small watch shop, Jules Isaac Mirès moved to Paris as a youth. Self-educated, he worked his way up via the press and judicious investments, often in partnership with a fellow Bordelais, Moïse Polydore Millaud. Their best-selling newspaper, *Le Petit Journal*, set a trend by concentrating on crime and human-interest stories, serials and popular columnists. Associated with the Péreires, who like him had Portuguese Jewish roots, Mirès enjoyed entrée to the imperial court, paying commissions to Morny for help. In 1852, he got a loan of 50 million francs from the city of Paris, bought property on the Champs-Élysées and created a bank to raise capital from the public for investments. He financed railway lines and mines, rebuilt the Marseilles docks and obtained a concession to light the city – Napoleon III presented him with the *Légion d'honneur* on a visit to the port.

His partner, Millaud, put out his first newspaper in Bordeaux at the age of twenty. Moving to Paris in 1836, he launched a journal sold outside theatres, followed by other papers, including one that supported Louis-Napoleon and was banned under the July Monarchy. In the mid-1850s, he made a fortune from real estate. Lavish receptions and dinners at his mansion on the rue Saint-Georges became celebrated, and he joined Mirès to launch *Le Petit Journal* followed by a string of other popular publications, while also dabbling in the theatre.

Daniel Iffla, given the name of d'Osiris by imperial decree, earned his spurs with Mirès and Maillaud, bought five Parisian mansions and built a fortune of 50 million francs. Frugal, he ate in humble restaurants and refused to have electricity installed in his main home. After his Christian wife died, he distinguished himself through charity for the poor of Paris. An avid collector of Napoleonic memorabilia, he restored the royal domain of Malmaison and paid for a statue of Joan of Arc in Nancy after failing to buy her birthplace. The target of anti-Semitic campaigns, he had synagogues built beside his home in Paris and in other cities – the Second Empire marked a heyday of synagogue construction in France. He lived to the age of eighty-two, dying in 1907 and leaving much of his wealth to fund medical research.[17]

Aristide Boucicaut, son of a hatter, and his wife, originally a laundress, built up the Bon Marché store from an enterprise with twelve staff to one employing 1,700 with a turnover above 70 million francs. Their fellow retailer, Félix Potin, from a farming family, abandoned legal studies to found a cut-price grocery business, which boomed with its own processing factory, selling wine imported from North Africa and a home-delivery service, his motto being to 'sell cheap but sell a lot', a recipe that worked well enough for the eponymous shops, often with ornate façades, to become city landmarks.* The Menier chocolate factory produced 4,000 tons a year and expanded operations to London and New York. The family patriarch, Émile Justin, constructed a 20-hectare town of two-family houses for workers with water fountains and privies coated with cocoa leaf, cheap stores, restaurants, schools, medicines and sick pay.[18]

The most successful property developer of the era, Alexandre Chauvelot, a one-time strolling singer, launched his career by trading plots of land in Paris, and then built suburban houses outside the ring of fortifications erected by Thiers. They catered for the new class of commuters using improved transport facilities, with a large pleasure garden for their diversion. A philanthropist like a number of his peers, he operated a soup kitchen for the poor.

There were significant downsides to this image of progress. Heavy spending on modernising major cities meant that there was less money left to expend on other developments – the budget for rural roads fell by a quarter in the 1850s. The rapid expansion of the financial system contained its own weaknesses. The Péreires, who poured money into a competitive château of their own within hailing distance of the Rothschild palace at Ferrières, were squeezed, particularly by competition from the Rothschilds who broadened their activities and joined with other banks and transport companies to set up the Société Générale in competition with them. After his main company collapsed, Mirès was sentenced to five years in jail, though the verdict was overturned and Morny got him shares in a Spanish railway. Caught up in financial scandals in the early 1860s, Millaud retreated from public life.

Manufacturers used to protection found it hard to cope with foreign competition while lower duties led to rising imports. For all the expansion of the coal industry, imports from Britain increased. Despite urbanisation, 90 per cent of the population still lived outside the main centres. Regions like the Auvergne and parts of Brittany and the Southern Alps remained very poor. Official figures in 1863 showed that a quarter of the population

* A particularly fine example can still be seen at the corner of the Boulevard de Sébastopol and the rue Réaumur in Paris.

did not understand French, as many were illiterate. Though Paris, with its two million inhabitants, housed 15 per cent of industrial workers, only a tenth of them worked in factories and large enterprises. Growing wealth was unevenly distributed; while wages rose significantly, profits increased far faster. Three million people worked at the bottom of the pile as day labourers, farm hands and household servants while the rural exodus added further to overcrowding in slums untouched by the urban renovation led by the prefect who had organised Napoleon's visit to Bordeaux in 1851, in which he had told France it needed to restore the Empire.

Imperial plans

'The Empire means peace' Napoleon declared in his speech at Bordeaux setting out his imperial plan. In fact, he brought recurrent wars as he sought to rally the nation behind him by rebuilding French glory on Bonapartist tradition.* 'The Empire,' he told a visitor, 'will be for or against Europe according to how it is received.' His belief in a 'policy of nationalities', backing the creation of unified nations out of the hodge-podge of countries such as Italy, was bound to lead to conflict with conservative powers. He felt no fondness for the Tsar, who declined to address him as a royal 'brother' or for Austria, which he said 'thwarts me everywhere'. His first aim was to disrupt the understanding between the four states that had triumphed over his uncle. In that, he had to cope with the deep-seated suspicion of France harboured by Palmerston, the leading British politician of the time, but in the Crimea the two countries found common cause against Russian designs on the Ottoman Empire.

Confrontation with the Tsarist Empire would enable Napoleon to flex Gallic muscles against the nation that had driven the First Emperor back from Moscow, pleasing the army, republicans and those who viewed Russia as the home of reaction and obscurantism. Catholics could only be pleased by a campaign aimed at ensuring access to the Holy Places. Above all, Crimea offered the prospect of a British alliance, which Napoleon saw as key to his planned disruption of the anti-French Concert of Europe.

---

* His military adventures also provided a fresh batch of names for Paris boulevards – Alma, Sébastopol, Magenta.

The Demolition Artist

Georges-Eugène Haussmann aimed to make Paris 'the capital of a powerful Empire, the residence of a glorious sovereign.' From 1853, he effected the most wide-ranging transformation the capital had ever seen, a process continued by the Third Republic and evident in the layout of the city today.

His work was needed. With little improvement from the conditions that had helped to set off the 1848 insurrection, the city was on the point of becoming uninhabitable; the political economist Victor Considérant described it in 1848 as 'a foul hole where plants wilt and perish and four out of five children die within their first year.'

Haussmann believed better conditions would boost business, attract tourists and increase tax revenue as well as provide jobs. He was a top-down authoritarian who called himself 'the demolition artist' and brooked no delay – 'get those warts off my face,' he said of old districts about to be torn down. Though not ennobled, he was known as Baron Haussmann.

His long broad avenues had the strategic advantage of making it easier for cavalry and cannons to put down revolts, while property developers lined their pockets from the new apartment buildings.

The rue de Rivoli was enlarged as a major thoroughfare, and the Sébastopol, Strasbourg, Saint-Germain and Saint-Michel boulevards laid out, lined with buildings for the middle and upper classes – as well as the boulevard named after the *faux* Baron. The mileage of roads in Paris doubled. The Étoile became the heart of a network of avenues commemorating the First Emperor's victories.

The Île de la Cité round Notre-Dame was turned into an administrative centre. Les Halles market, 'the belly of Paris', was rebuilt and a new opera house was started. The sewage and water systems were modernised and four big parks opened – Napoleon gave the city the land of the Bois de Boulogne and Bois de Vincennes.

The capital's surface area was doubled to 8,000 hectares and the population increased by the same proportion. But the cost led to Haussmann being driven from office in 1870 after a campaign exposed the financial legerdemain of his schemes. Following the scandal, he devoted himself to writing his memoirs before dying in 1891.

So, when Russia got the Ottomans to reject French demands on the Holy Places, the emperor despatched France's most modern warship, the *Charlemagne*, to the Black Sea, followed by a larger naval task force. When Russia made the next move by occupying the Danubian principalities, a British fleet joined in and the Sultan in Istanbul declared war on St Petersburg. After the Ottomans suffered a naval defeat, London and Paris issued an ultimatum to Russia to pull out of the principalities. This being ignored, they declared war, the first conflict among major European powers for almost half-a-century.

A French force marched south to the River Alma on the road to the port city of Sevastopol. A division scaled cliffs towering above the waterway and drove back the defenders. However, reinforcements were lacking and two units, including one commanded by the emperor's cousin, Prince Napoleon, were halted by the terrain and Russian fire. After often chaotic fighting, the British advanced and the Russians were routed. Further allied victories included the taking of Sevastopol after a lengthy siege.

Napoleon celebrated the new entente with Britain by visiting Windsor and receiving Victoria and Albert in France. Austria's unwillingness to join the conflict drove a wedge between it and Russia, which felt badly done by, given the aid it had provided for Vienna against the rising by Hungarian nationalists four years earlier – Austrian fear of Russian control of the Danube outweighed any sense of gratitude for the helpful intervention in 1849. For Napoleon this was a welcome indication of success in his policy of splitting the alliance that had brought down his uncle and reversing the settlement of 1815.

But inefficient logistics bogged down the Crimean expedition. War weariness grew; French public opinion saw the fighting as being driven mainly by British interests. In April 1855, the emperor had to face down a revolt by ministers who warned that war was putting the domestic peace of the country at risk and dangerously depleting the treasury. The despatch of so many men was affecting agriculture and causing food shortages. Prefects warned of unrest. The provincial press turned critical.

More than 300,000 French troops had gone to fight a war whose purpose was out of proportion with its cost. Nearly a third were killed on the battlefield or by cholera, scurvy and typhus and deficient medical care. The soldiers were restive and the prospect was for an unending war at Britain's behest. As opinion against the conflict mounted across the Channel, too, peace negotiations were launched at a conference in February 1856 held at the foreign ministry on the Quai d'Orsay – a sign of France's international renaissance. The resulting Treaty of Paris did not make major territorial changes, though the Russians undertook not to establish naval or military arsenals on the Black Sea coast and the integrity of the Ottoman Empire was guaranteed. It was an outcome unworthy of the loss of life involved but Napoleon could take comfort in the disruption of the Concert of Europe and his own increased authority in foreign affairs. Next, it was time to turn to the country where he had joined revolutionaries in his youth.

He had always been attached to Italian nationalism, in part because of his desire to end Austrian rule in Lombardy and Venice, and in part from his belief that Europe should be organised on ethnic lines. If he could be the patron of Italian nationalism while also safeguarding the Pope's position in Rome, he could win the backing of both left and right in France and mark another step in restoring France's position in Europe. But his way of going about this was typically sinuous and, in the end, too clever by half.

At the end of July 1858, the emperor took a carriage ride in the Vosges Mountains with Count Camillo Benso di Cavour, prime minister of the kingdom of Sardinia, as the region of Piedmont was known. Cavour was in France secretly on a false passport. Driving through the woods, they agreed to provoke a war in Italy in which Austria would appear the aggressor. France would intervene and, after victory, Italy would be split into three kingdoms with the Turin-based regime represented by Cavour holding the upper hand. France would get Nice and Savoy. Far from uniting Italy, the emperor aimed to keep it divided, with France as the dominant power.

Napoleon did not inform his government, but Cavour was spotted and news leaked out, causing the French ruler to delay. He sent his cousin to Russia to get the Tsar to agree not to support Austria in the event of a war in return for support from Paris for the revision of the Black Sea clauses of the treaty ending the Crimean war. He then planted an anonymous article in the official newspaper denouncing Austrian rule in Italy while saying publicly that he wished to avoid military conflict and proposing his favourite device of a European congress on the issue. Vienna turned this down and invaded the North Italian kingdom. France went to war, the emperor taking personal field command.

The French army, with a small Piedmontese contingent, won victories at the battles of Magenta and Solferino, the latter a particularly bloody encounter. To the surprise of the Piedmontese, Napoleon then called off the war and engaged in negotiations with the Austrians in which he persuaded them that their best course was to relax their grip on their Italian possessions. The Emperor Franz Joseph agreed to cede Lombardy while retaining Venetia. Napoleon's success was vitiated, however, when he tripped himself up in attempting a double game on the papal lands. Though France got Savoy and Nice in June 1860, Garibaldi outflanked him with his campaign to liberate the south of the country. When Italy voted overwhelmingly for national union, Napoleon decided he had done enough meddling in its affairs and withdrew.[19]

Nor was he able to do anything about Poland, another nationalist cause which resonated in France, but where the conservative powers that divided the country between them proved intransigent; or in the complex crisis over Schleswig-Holstein, despite strong pro-Danish sentiment in France in the face of the first exhibition of North German military prowess. So he looked further afield, encouraging expansion in Algeria, sending an expedition to Syria to protect Catholic Maronites and expanding France's colonial presence in West Africa. After the murder of a missionary, French troops joined the British in a punitive expedition to China in 1860 that included sacking the Summer Palace outside Peking and won France a naval concession in the south of the country. Imperial forces invaded Cochinchina in southern Vietnam, established a protectorate in Cambodia and staged an unsuccessful naval attack on Korea. The import of Japanese silkworm eggs to save the silk industry was followed by arms sales, the despatch of naval instructors, supervision of the building of a shipyard and the launch of a shipping line between Marseilles and Yokohama.[20]

Looking west, the emperor met representatives of the Confederacy in the United States and sent an ironclad warship to help their cause. He cherished the idea of establishing a French-backed monarchy to replace the republic in Mexico and seized on a refusal by that country to honour its debts to send in an army – the Civil War prevented the US from intervening to apply the Monroe Doctrine to keep European powers out of its hemisphere and Napoleon banked on acquiescence from a victorious Confederacy. The French were defeated at first at the Battle of Puebla in 1862. But they then made progress in league with Mexican right-wingers. Urged on by his wife, Napoleon installed a Hapsburg prince, Maximilian, as emperor. But republicans put up stout guerrilla resistance, backed by Washington after the Civil War ended. Faced with an American naval blockade, Napoleon pulled out his forces in 1866. He appealed to Maximilian to flee, but the ruler he had installed insisted on staying. His empress, a Belgian princess, called on Napoleon and Eugénie at the Tuileries to ask for help, which was refused. Maximilian was taken prisoner by republicans and then shot – Manet's painting of the execution was refused by the Salon and lithographs of it were banned. The princess went mad.

A more successful projection of influence was provided by Ferdinand de Lesseps, who had been forced out of the diplomatic service as the scapegoat for French fumbling in Italy in 1849. As a young man, he had befriended the son of the self-styled khedive of Egypt and Sudan who succeeded his father as ruler in 1854. Lesseps had long nurtured the idea of driving a canal through the Suez Isthmus and obtained the rights from his friend Sa'id Pasha to carry this out. After long years of fund-raising and political sparring, particularly with the British, the canal was opened in 1869 by Sa'id's successor Ismai'il Pasha, with ceremonies attended by Eugénie, Emperor Franz Joseph of Austro-Hungary and Henrik Ibsen.

For all its activity, the emperor's foreign policy forays had brought few concrete results beyond the colonial conquests. Though he had established himself as an international figure, his reputation and influence were far from living up to his ambitions. He still had to find a role for France in a world where the power structure was shifting; simply avenging 1815 was not enough.

8

REFORM AND DISASTER

In the Bonapartist tradition, the emperor constantly put on shows at home to convince everybody that his was a modern regime in touch with its people. He was a master at using public occasions to involve citizens in the new-old narrative, replacing the martial Marseillaise with a ballad hymning the virtues of patriotism and self-sacrifice and promoting a style that combined modernity with exhibitionism on a scale meant to impress the French with the achievements of empire, even if it often descended into vulgar excess. That said; there was a lot to be proud of.

Grand Exhibitions showed off French technology, inventions, manufacturing products and the arts, attracting such eminent guests as the Tsar from Russia, the Prince of Wales from Britain and King William and Bismarck from Prussia. The visitors went to a comic operetta by Offenbach and were served a special dinner at the Café Anglais consisting of escalopes of turbot, sole fillets, chicken, lobster, duckling, ortolans and eight wines. Paris became a major tourist destination for travellers from across the Atlantic as well as from Europe. New hotels boasted lifts and ice-making machines.

The Second Empire saw Louis Pasteur's discovery of the technique that bore his name, Zénobe-Théophile Gramme's building of the first continuous-current electric generator and Léon Foucault's pendulum to show the rotation of the earth. The mathematical economist Léon Walras developed the theory of the general equilibrium of markets. French scientists and inventors came up with margarine, the dry cell battery, the hypodermic needle, the bicycle and a submarine powered by compressed air.

The first glider to fly higher than its departure point was launched by Jean-Marie Le Bris in 1856. Henri Giffard flew a steam-powered airship over Paris in 1852, while Louis Charles Letur tested a parachute-glider in the first heavier-than-air flight controlled by a pilot. In 1863, another aviation pioneer, Félix Tournachon, built a big red balloon in which he took fifteen paying passengers for a perilous trip that narrowly missed a train, got tangled in telegraph wires and bounced along the ground for ten miles before stopping in a clump of trees; nobody was killed but all on board were injured. Under the name of Nadar, he also developed photographic portraiture.

The emperor presided at military parades on horseback and at grand balls in the Tuileries. Favoured guests were invited to weekend parties at the imposing château at Compiègne north of Paris. To meet citizens and reach into *la France profonde*, Napoleon and the empress travelled round the provinces reviewing delegations of local people, attending mass at cathedrals and greeting crowds in towns and cities decked with triumphal arches – on a visit to Brittany in 1858, a journalist described 'an almost continuous arch from Paris to Cherbourg, Cherbourg to Brest, Brest to Auray, Auray to Rennes to Paris.' A month-long journey in 1860 took the imperial couple to Dijon, Lyons, Grenoble, Annecy, Marseilles and Algiers. Priority was given to regions where support was low, such as in the west.

The emperor hurried to the scene of disasters to reassure his public and made a point of attending farm shows; a crowd of 150,000 gathered when he graced one in Orléans. Between the major centres, the imperial train would make short stops to enable country dwellers to catch a glimpse of the imperial couple; on one such halt in Normandy in 1863, Napoleon was given a taste of the local cheese and liked it so much that he ordered a regular supply for the Tuileries, launching Camembert as a national product.

These trips were written up enthusiastically in loyal newspapers and by authors paid to turn out laudatory books. The emperor frequented spas at Vichy and Plombières, and joined his wife as she turned Biarritz into a social centre, travelling to the south-west with his entourage in the

The Last Empress

At the beginning of 1853, Doña María Eugenia Ignacia Augustina de Palafox-Portocarrero de Guzmán y Kirkpatrick, more familiarly known as Eugénie de Montijo, wrote to her younger sister that she was prey to 'a certain terror' at mounting 'one of the greatest thrones of Europe'. At her wedding to Napoleon III on 29 January, she added subsequently, her face was paler than the jasmine flowers she wore to set off her pink dress.

Known as Eugénie in France, she counted on her beauty to keep him faithful. They were happy for a time. But, only four months after the wedding, in another letter to her sister, the Duchess of Alba, she reflected that, though she had gained a crown, this merely made her 'the first slave of my realm'. A fervent Catholic of the ultramontane persuasion, she was politically reactionary. During two spells as regent when her husband was out of the country she tried to advance conservative causes and work with the Austrians, but had little influence.

Writing in 1856, a doctor described her as having 'fine sensitive features [which] reflect her feelings both keenly and rapidly ... every part of her body displays a remarkable purity and delicacy of construction ... her bosom, which she displays a little too much and too frequently, is beautifully placed and modelled'.

Eugénie delighted in bullfights and made Biarritz, close to the border with her native land, a social centre, opening the windows of her seaside palace as soon as she arrived to gaze down the coast. She invited a Scottish medium, a thin, sickly 21-year-old called Hume, to visit; according to her letter to her sister, he conjured up 'hands' which took bells held by ladies round the table, and made an accordion held by the emperor play of its own accord. Her aversion to intercourse was strengthened by a miscarriage early in the marriage and a warning from doctors after she had given birth to a son that a future pregnancy risked being fatal – she probably did not sleep with her husband again. 'Do not suppose that I have not always been aware of that man's infidelities,' she told friends. 'I have tried everything. I have even tried to make him jealous. It was in vain.'

She lived to ninety-four, spending most of her time in England (Chislehurst, Farnborough and the Isle of Wight with trips to the spa at Bournemouth) and at her villa in the South of France.

eight-carriage imperial train. This had a principal salon with sofas, chairs, armchairs and a long folding table. The windows were of the finest plate glass, the seats upholstered in brown and green leather, with golden arabesques. There was a separate smoking room, lavatory and pantry. Dr Barthez of the imperial medical staff found the train, which went up to fifty miles an hour, 'admirably driven, avoiding all shocks and sudden stoppages'.

The 'liberal' empire

The emperor might flatter himself that he was winning hearts and minds, but opposition persisted among Legitimists, Orléanists and republicans, even if they had scant representation in the legislatures; elections in 1857 were so rigged that they gave little real reflection of discontent at an economic downturn. His reverses in foreign policy bred criticism. Thiers called for the restoration of a parliamentary regime and the return of 'the necessary freedoms'.

In January 1858, three revolutionaries led by Felice Orsini, a heavily bearded, charismatic Italian member of the Carbonari, to which the emperor had once belonged, threw bombs at the imperial couple as they arrived at the Paris opera house in the rue Le Peletier to see Rossini's *William Tell.* Orsini believed that Napoleon III was the main obstacle to Italian independence and had gone to Britain to get bombs made by a gunsmith before travelling to Paris – Morny stigmatised England as 'the laboratory of crime'.[1]

When the first bomb went off, the coachman whipped the horses forward. There was a second explosion and 'we heard the vehicle breaking beneath us', Eugénie wrote to her mother. A third bomb killed one of the horses. The two doors flew open. The emperor and empress got out of the carriage into a crowd of people covered with blood who cried '*Vive l'Empereur, Vive l'Impératrice*' – he had a slight scratch on the end of his nose, she a tiny bomb fragment in one eye. Keeping to the role of the imperturbable ruler, Napoleon walked into the theatre with his wife. Eight people were killed and 140 wounded during the incident.[2]

Orsini returned to his lodgings where he was arrested the following day. During his trial, which ended in a death sentence, a letter by him to Napoleon was read out saying the future of Italy was in the hands of the emperor – there has been speculation that the missive was actually the work of the ruler himself. According to the British ambassador, Napoleon told him he had the greatest sympathy for the terrorist, and wondered if he could commute the sentence. The Paris police chief, a Corsican devoted to the Italian cause, lobbied for Orsini's life to be spared. But Eugénie wanted revenge and Orsini went quietly to the guillotine. A new security law provided for internment, deportation or exile of suspects without trial. Elections in 1860 returned just five opposition deputies.[3]

Though Napoleon could take this as a sign of popular support, he saw the need for reform to maintain backing as economic conditions worsened. The American Civil War dragged trade down; the budget deficit hit 100 million francs a year, with an accumulated debt of one billion. State aid was needed to maintain railway expansion. So a political U-turn began two years after the Orsini attack. An amnesty was proclaimed in August 1859. Then parliament was granted the right to hold an annual vote in reply to the speech from the throne. The press was permitted to report debates in place of controlled official summaries. 'March at the head of the ideas of your century, and these ideas follow you and support you,' the emperor declared. 'March behind them, and they drag you after them. March against them and they overthrow you.' The newspaper proprietor, de Girardin, coined the term the 'liberal empire'.[4]

Still, there were disturbances, including a demonstration to commemorate the 1848 Revolution during which those arrested and held for seventy-seven days in prison included a young medical student and political activist, Georges Clemenceau. Critics deplored the way in which centralisation was stifling the provinces and urbanisation was sending up rents while neglecting social improvements. A *Union Libérale* of liberals, republicans and Legitimists won forty seats at elections in 1863. Persigny, who had been recalled to run the poll, was sacked again, though partially compensated with a dukedom; in his letter announcing the decision, the emperor advised him that his position had been harmed by his wife's wild behaviour and extravagance.

Napoleon now embarked on a zigzag course seeking to combine reform and order. The anti-clerical historian Victor Duruy was appointed education minister and oversaw improvements in the living conditions of teachers and an extension of adult education. But the conservative Rouher acquired growing influence, becoming, in the words of one critic, the ruler's 'grand vizier' and France's 'vice-emperor' – and Duruy's efforts to introduce secondary education for girls by male teachers was blocked by the church – his resignation was accepted.[5]

Encouraged by the partial reform measures but unsatisfied by general policy, the opposition regrouped. A moderate Third Party, situated between Bonapartists and republicans, pressed for a parliamentary system and expanded civil liberties. Émile Ollivier, a lawyer and former prefect who had pushed through the trade union legislation and who married one of the Countess of Agoult's daughters, emerged as the leading advocate of reasonable compromise.

Son of a celebrated Carbonarist, Démosthène Ollivier from Marseilles, Émile had initially been a strong republican, serving as prefect of the Var and Bouches-du-Rhône department in 1848. He was banished from France for nine years after Napoleon's coup but, after his return, moved to the centre of politics and refused to join Thiers in advocating greater power for the legislature. Rather, he was ready to accept a system of executive power so long as it was under democratic control.

Accordingly, he offered to work with the emperor if his demands were met. Seeing himself as becoming the 'Richelieu of liberty', Morny favoured this, but the ruler let Rouher delay the implementation of reforms. However, they ran into political headwinds with a plan to double the size of the army to a million men by creating a trained reserve. Republicans and Orléanists feared the use he would make of such a big force while the middle class and richer peasants treasured the opportunities the existing system offered to buy their sons out of service. The generals preferred professional soldiers, and, emboldened by 'pacification' campaigns in Algeria, were satisfied with the army's prowess, backed by modern weapons including the chassepot bolt action, breech-loading rifle, and primitive machine guns.[6]

Offenbach still served up frothy operettas – in 1869, the particularly silly *Vert-Vert,* about a teacher at a girls' school who is enlisted by his pupils to replace their pet parrot – but intellectuals and artists fretted about the world created by the superficial opportunism of the Empire and epitomised by its capital. 'All very beautiful for the moment but I wouldn't give two *sous* to see the last act,' mused de Musset. 'Rarely,' wrote the historian-commentator Hippolyte Taine, 'has a generation lived in all respects through so many changes of mind so quickly.' Flaubert deplored how 'Our lying had turned us into idiots! ... What ignorance, what muddle, what fakery!'[7]

Discontent was fanned by an expansion of the opposition press, including the outspoken newspaper *La Lanterne* run by the shock-haired, fiercely republican Marquis de Rochefort-Luçay. A successful author of vaudeville entertainments, he was repeatedly fined and jailed between duels with political opponents. From exile, Victor Hugo fired salvos against the regime while the forceful radical orator, Léon Gambetta, melded calls for political change with demands for social reform. An election campaign in the spring of 1869 produced big critical public meetings in major cities and rioting in Paris amid government warnings of a 'red terror'. The opposition won 3.5 million votes compared to 4.5 million for pro-government candidates, the worst showing the regime had suffered. Ollivier's Third Party made significant gains. Though rural areas remained Bonapartist, republicans progressed in big cities; Gambetta was elected in Paris on his 'Belleville platform' of democratic and social reform.[8]

Napoleon realised that he needed further change if he was to survive and avoid the fates of Charles X and Louis-Philippe. The political base constructed in the early 1850s was crumbling. Fealty to the emperor and populist plebiscites were no longer enough. Wages were not keeping up with prices and rents. The unequal division of wealth was widely resented. Society had changed. The alliance with the church had frayed.

Strikes broke out in the coalmines of Carmaux and Firminy, among silk workers in the Ardèche, and in textile mills in Normandy and Champagne. Two thousand women at the Lyons silk mills stopped work to demand a pay rise and a cut in the working day from twelve to ten hours; they got the reduction but not the wage increase. Some employers took a tough line towards the labour agitation, with Schneider particularly intransigent. Seventeen people were killed in the summer of 1869 in repression of protesting miners from the enterprise founded by Decazes in the Aveyron, which the ironmaster had taken over.

Napoleon agreed to strengthen the role of parliament, though ministers remained responsible to him and he retained the right to dissolve the Assembly and appeal directly to the people. Rouher resigned, though staying on as president of the Senate. After protracted negotiations, Ollivier became chief minister in January 1870, at the head of a government drawn from parliament. The emperor did not relish this but had no alternative. France would not accept a hard-line Bonapartist administration; he did not want to fall back on the Orléanists or Legitimists whose support was declining in any case and he could not stomach Thiers.

Ollivier told the emperor he was saving the dynasty. Napoleon observed that the head of government was young (forty-four) and talented – 'he believes in me and is the eloquent interpreter of my ideas, especially when I let him think they are his own'. The British ambassador was less confident; the new man was a fine speaker but a poor parliamentarian, he noted, adding that running a government under the emperor 'requires tact, experience, firmness, knowledge of men and a few other qualities in which he seems singularly deficient.'[9]

There was an immediate clash when Napoleon rejected Ollivier's proposal to have mayors elected. Legislators were put out by the appointment of expert commissions, which threatened to bypass the Assembly. But the press laws were relaxed and the 1858 security legislation repealed. Strike leaders were released from jail. Pardoned, Ledru-Rollin returned to France. A dozen prefects were sacked and Ollivier also showed determination in mobilising troops against left-wing demonstrations in Paris, while two dozen striking steelworkers at Le Creusot and leaders of the communist First International were detained.

A new constitution restricted the emperor's authority and increased

Regicide: Execution of Louis XVI, 21 January 1793 – France becomes a republic.

Emperor's end: Waterloo – 18 June 1815 – kills the Napoleonic dream, but not its legacy.

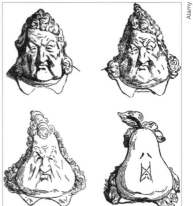

Citizen King: Louis-Philippe reduced to a pear, which gave him his nickname 'La Poire'.

City in ferment: Despite the royal restoration, Paris spawned fresh revolutions in 1830 and 1848.

Empire returns: Napoleon III being sworn in after his coup of 1851.

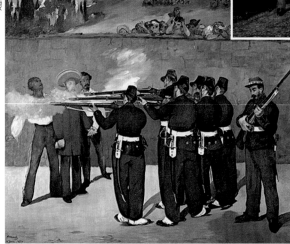

Mexican adventure: Napoleon III's adventurism ended in disaster and one of Manet's greatest paintings.

Bloody week: The Commune was put down savagely, though the death toll may have been less than supposed.

The president: Adolphe Thiers lauded the republic as the regime which least divided the French.

Education first: Promoted by Jules Ferry, lay schooling became the means of spreading republican values.

Le Petit Journal
SUPPLÉMENT ILLUSTRÉ
Hult pages : CINQ centimes

LE TRAITRE
Dégradation d'Alfred Dreyfus

The Affair: The Dreyfus case divided the nation and took more than a decade to put right.

Colonial French values: Republican politicians extolled the spread of civilisation, but France reaped profits as well.

A war of extermination: France repulsed the German advance in 1914 but was then condemned to grinding trench warfare.

The victors: Clemenceau (second from right) with Wilson and the British and Italian prime ministers at the Versailles conference, 1919.

Prime ministerial sextet: From left, Aristide Briand, Georges Leygues, Édouard Herriot, Raymond Poincaré, Paul Painlevé, Louis Barthou – all occupied the Hôtel Matignon in the decades after the First World War.

Victor Hugo: The one-time royalist became the patron saint of the Third Republic.

Remembrance of times past: Marcel Proust's novel became a literary monument.

Nothing regretted: Édith Piaf sang for the emotions of the French for three decades.

The boulevardier: Maurice Chevalier was the epitome of French style in films, on the stage and through his music.

Man of the left: Léon Blum led the Popular Front government in 1936 and epitomised the intellectual in politics.

Savouring victory: Hitler jubilated when he visited defeated Paris the day after France's surrender in 1940.

Partners in collaboration: Pétain and Laval were an unlikely pair to head the Vichy regime.

The Constable: Charles de Gaulle refused to accept defeat and marched in victory down the Champs-Élysées in August 1944.

Colonial quagmire: France's efforts to hold on to its colonies in Indochina ended badly at Dien Bien Phu.

that of ministers and parliament. It was put to the national vote in a plebiscite in May with wording associating Napoleon with reform. This divided the opposition between those who could not oppose changes for which they had campaigned and those who rejected the regime out-right, such as Thiers and Gambetta. Strikes and arrests of communists in an alleged plot to explode bombs and assassinate the Emperor pro-vided a fresh opportunity to appeal to the fear vote.

The emperor surrenders his sword

The plebiscite produced the last great imperial victory at the polls. The constitution was approved by 7.35 million to 1.53 million with 1.9 mil-lion abstentions. That gave the ruler three million more votes than at the 1869 election, with 80 per cent support in the north, south-west, centre and west, which finally rallied to him if the numbers were to be believed. The 'no' vote was concentrated in the south-east, pockets of eastern France and the big cities. Gambetta concluded that the Empire was stronger than ever.

Not so the health of its leader. He had serious bladder trouble, but doctors were unsure how to operate and he was not told of the gravity of his condition. Meeting him in Paris in September 1869, an Austrian prince wrote that Napoleon was very thin, pale and weak 'like a man who has been in bed for weeks'. His concentration went after twenty minutes.[10]

Despite the success of the plebiscite, Napoleon was dissatisfied with Ollivier. But he had failed to bring on a new class of politicians and there was, in any case, a basic flaw in the liberal Empire. Though the government was responsible to parliament, ministers also answered to the head of state. The emperor was held to be the chosen representative of the people as a whole, expressing itself through direct votes rather than through the legislature. So how could he be responsible to the Assembly – and how were ministers to split their responsibilities to him and to parliament? Caught in such domestic quandaries of his own making, the emperor looked abroad for relief and consecration of his status – and met disaster.

The French ruler had been surprised by the speed and scale of

Prussia's rise. Its victory over Austria in the war of 1866 caught him flat-footed. Despite the obvious danger it presented, France was unable to check the increasing unity of the north German states and their preponderance over the Hapsburgs. Napoleon considered working with Austria, suggested a deal with Russia that would have involved removing the independence granted to the Romanians after the Crimean War and sought an alliance with Britain. But St Petersburg preferred Berlin to Paris, relations with Austria remained fragile and Britain was, as usual, unwilling to commit itself on the Europe mainland, remaining suspicious of Napoleon's ambitions and alienated by a row between Paris and Brussels over strategic railway lines in Belgium.

Bismarck, who had been his guest at Biarritz in the early 1860s, concluded not only that the emperor was a sphinx without secrets, but also that he was not as shrewd as people thought – 'he has a succession of *idées fixes* and never knows where they will lead him ... as if he suddenly woke up in charge of a locomotive that he did not know how to drive.'[11]

Though Ollivier declared at the end of June 1870, that 'at no time has the peace of Europe been more assured', the Spanish royal succession again presented a bone of contention. After the abdication of Queen Isabella, the throne was offered to a cousin of King William of Prussia. The prospect of having Hohenzollern monarchs to the east and south was something Napoleon could not accept. So he sought to get the candidacy withdrawn and a promise that the Prussians would not seek the Spanish throne in the future. Political and military leaders in Paris warned that, if France did not gain satisfaction, the only alternative was war.

The strongly anti-Prussian foreign minister, the Duke of Gramont, favoured a hard line. Napoleon secretly lobbied the Spanish, Belgian and British governments to apply pressure to get the prince to withdraw. His policy seemed to have worked when, during his son's absence on holiday in the Alps, William announced he was withdrawing the young man's candidature. Even Thiers was impressed; Guizot hailed it as 'the finest diplomatic victory I have ever seen'.

But Gramont insisted that a more binding withdrawal was required with a guarantee that the prince would not renew his claims. Without consulting Ollivier, the emperor and foreign minister instructed the ambassador to Prussia to get such an undertaking from King William. When the envoy cornered him in the garden at the spa of Bad Ems, the monarch gave the Frenchman a polite brush-off. Bismarck then edited the official account of the conversation to make it sound highly dismissive. The French took offence as he had intended, and public opinion mounted in favour of hostilities. Marshal Leboeuf, the war minister spoke glowingly of the efficiency of French arms. Gramont alluded to secret alliances. Having allowed the war party to grab the initiative, Napoleon got a cabinet meeting to call for his favourite crisis remedy, a European congress. The hawks, led by the war minister Marshal Lebœuf, were incensed. In a sign of how far the emperor's authority had been dented, they forced a second cabinet session, attended by the empress, which took a bellicose position. Ollivier, who had adopted a pacific line at the first session, now favoured calling up the reserves. Napoleon expressed no firm opinion.

Amid cries of '*À Berlin*', France declared war on 19 July 1870, the prime minister replying to criticism from Thiers by saying he accepted war 'with a light heart'. Napoleon had not only stepped into Bismarck's trap, but had done so in such a way that France appeared to be the aggressor and found itself without allies.

Still, at the start of the first of three wars with its neighbour, which would tear Europe apart over the next seventy-five years, French forces were confident of victory. As in Italy, the emperor went to the front, though in severe bladder pain. Taking his fourteen-year-old son with him, he altered the battle plan, adding to the confusion that marked the mobilisation. Poorly organised, French forces were short of everything from food and maps to supply vehicles and ambulances. Failure to enlarge the army meant that, at 200,000 men, Marshal Bazaine's main force was half the projected size. Railway lines jammed up with troop trains in contrast to the well-organised movement of the Prussians. While French rifles were excellent, there was a severe shortage of powerful artillery to match the Krupp guns ranged against them.

Still, all seemed well as the French advanced towards Saarbrücken and shelled the railway station. After a false report of the defeat of the Crown Prince of Prussia and the capture of 25,000 enemy forces, a throng surrounded the Bourse, singing the Marseillaise, led by an opera star standing atop a horse-drawn omnibus. Edmond de Goncourt had never seen such fervour – 'men pale with emotion, children hopping around in enthusiasm and women making drunken gestures.'*

But the French forces were soon on the retreat across the frontier. After a bad-tempered cabinet meeting, Ollivier walked home alone through the night. At the front, the emperor was in such pain that he preferred to dismount from his horse and walk. His disjointed orders made little tactical sense and his presence inhibited field commanders. The defeat of the Army of the Rhine forced the French to fall back on Metz where they were besieged by 150,000 Prussian troops. Napoleon and Field-Marshal MacMahon formed a new army from the available soldiers and headed towards the Belgian border with the idea of turning south to link up with other French forces. The emperor asked his wife, acting as regent in his absence, to call him back to Paris so that he might retrieve the political situation. Ollivier fell after losing a parliamentary vote in which only ten deputies backed him.

The new prime minister and war minister, Charles Guillaume Marie Appollinaire Antoine Cousin Montauban, Count of Palikao, set to work to raise more men to send to the front. Plon Plon Bonaparte went to see the emperor to urge him to return to the capital. Eugénie, who wrote to relatives in Spain that anxiety stopped her eating or sleeping, was intent on keeping him away to enable her to continue to act as regent. Napoleon lamented 'I seem to have abdicated.'[12]

When Palikao sent an army to relieve the siege of Metz, the Prussian field commander, Count Helmuth von Moltke, caught the French in a pincer movement and forced them to withdraw to Sedan where they were surrounded. The battle there involved more than 400 infantry battalions, 300 cavalry units and 1,300 guns. The

---

* Edmond was writing the diary alone now since his brother Jules had died of syphilis that summer.

Prussian artillery proved murderous and von Moltke was able to bring up reinforcements while the French were out of men and energy. Napoleon rode into the fiercest fighting as if seeking death. The French lost more than 17,000 dead and wounded and 21,000 prisoners; Prussian losses were 2,320 killed, 5,980 wounded and 700 captured or missing.

The emperor, who traipsed between humble lodgings, his cheeks rouged to give him some colour, wrote to King William that it only remained for him to surrender his sword. At dawn on 2 September he was driven in a two-horse carriage to meet Bismarck, who was in uniform. The two men spoke of a peace agreement. Napoleon handed over his sword. The Prussian rode off and the defeated ruler went to a small house where he took bread and wine and was reading Montaigne when King William arrived. Both wept. William said he would put a German castle at his prisoner's disposal. That afternoon, he was given permission to telegraph news of the surrender to Paris.[13]

The capital was thunderstruck. 'Who can describe the consternation written on every face, the sound of aimless steps pacing the streets at random, the anxious conversations,' wrote Edmond de Goncourt. 'Then there is the menacing roar of the crowd in which stupefaction had begun to give place to anger.' Furious, Eugénie initially damned her husband for his failure to die on the battlefield to enable her to claim glory in defeat and ensure the succession of their son. Calming down, she sought advice from Thiers and General Trochu, the military governor of Paris. But a crowd invaded the National Assembly and Gambetta and his colleagues proclaimed a republic from the Hôtel de Ville. When a mob stormed the Tuileries, the empress took flight for England.

After six months, Napoleon was released to join his wife and son in England, living in a mock French château in Chislehurst, Kent. A mad old Scottish woman stood at the gate raising a bunch of broom to the sky, calling down prosperity and power on the former ruler. When a German journalist visited him, he complained about the stifling fog and lack of sunshine. Showing a mixture of self-delusion, contradiction and resignation, he declared that, at a single word from him, 'the flag of Empire would be raised in fifty places at once from one end of

France to the other … for I am still the Emperor of the French and my first duty is still to consider the interests of France.'[14]

The Second Emperor died in January 1873 during an operation for a bladder stone. His body was laid in Saint Michael's Abbey in Farnborough, Hampshire, built by his wife as a mausoleum for him. The empress was also buried there together with their son, who died fighting in the British army in South Africa in 1879, stabbed eighteen times in the body and head by assegais in an attack by Zulus during which his fellow soldiers did nothing to save him.

PART 3
THE THIRD REPUBLIC

1870–1940

THE BLOODY WEEK

Evoking the heritage of the revolutionary defence of the nation, Hugo declared, 'Let the lion of 1792 draw itself up and bristle' as the Government of National Defence committed itself to continuing the war. A proclamation drawn up by the 32-year-old Gambetta, who was minister of both the interior and war, blamed defeat on 'twenty years of corrupting power which quashed all the sources of greatness'. Others sought different scapegoats. The church pointed at the moral degeneracy of the Empire. In the Dordogne, peasants rounded on local nobles, burning one young aristocrat to death.[1]

Gambetta's proclamation urged the French to raise their spirits to fight on. But the Germans rolled over northern France and surrounded Paris with a quarter of a million troops.

Most of France's army had either been captured by the Germans or was bottled up in the east where the 160,000-strong force in Metz surrendered at the end of October. The country's heart was not in continuing the war. Gambetta, who flew out of Paris by hot-air balloon to direct the action from Tours, struggled to assert authority over local leaders seeking autonomy for their cities, particularly in Marseilles. The National Assembly decamped to Bordeaux.

The ring of ten-metre high fortifications built round the capital by Thiers in 1840 and since reinforced meant that besiegers had to cover a fifty-mile front, from which they kept up a constant bombardment though it did relatively little damage. The defenders numbered 50,000 professional soldiers plus 90,000 Gardes Mobiles conscripts, 15,000 men from the navy and 8,000 police and firemen. The Paris National Guard was 300,000 strong, but many were ill trained, undisciplined and no match for the invaders.

The siege, from 19 September 1870 to 28 January 1871, cut off man-ufacturers from national and foreign markets. The Germans severed the telegraph lines. To provide food, 250,000 sheep and 40,000 oxen had been brought in to graze in the Bois de Boulogne, but supplies eventu-ally ran short and people turned to other sources of sustenance. Horses were the first to be consumed including two trotters given by the Tsar to Napoleon III. Dogs came next. Then it was rats served in pies at the Jockey Club. The rich ate meat from slaughtered zoo animals; the Café Voisin on the rue Saint-Honoré served a Christmas Eve dinner that included stuffed donkey's head, elephant consommé, bear ribs in pepper sauce, roast cat with rats and truffled antelope terrine, accom-panied by the finest clarets and a 1858 Burgundy.[2]

Sixty-five hot-air balloons flew out of the city with a total of 164 pas-sengers and five dogs; none managed the flight back. Instead, carrier pigeons were used to carry messages from Tours – a microphotography unit there reduced pages to tiny sizes; a pigeon could carry thousands, which were projected on to a screen in Paris and transcribed, but only fifty-nine of the 302 birds from the Loire Valley arrived, some brought down on the way by German falcons.

The ministry of works forged guns in basements on the rue de Rivoli and invented prototypes of weapons that would come into use in the fol-lowing century. Proposals put forward to the scientific committee but never brought to fruition included petroleum bombs to explode above the enemy, shells containing smallpox germs, a 'mobile rampart' much like a tank and a unit of women fighters in black pantaloons with orange stripes, hooded black blouses and black *képis*; they would hold out their hands to the enemy and kill them with embedded pins laced with Prussic acid.

Touring Europe to meet the foreign ministers of Russia, Austria and Britain, Thiers found none ready to back France. So he went to see Bismarck who demanded the ceding of all of Alsace and parts of Lorraine as well as large reparations. The government decided to fight on. The French won a victory near Orléans in mid-November but an attempt to break out of the capital at the end of the month went badly wrong with 4,000 casualties compared to 1,700 for the Germans.

The political orator and anti-Bonapartist, Jules Favre, led fresh negotiations with Bismarck at the Rothschild château at Ferrières*. The French hoped that by offering a large monetary indemnity they would be spared from territorial losses. But the Prussian was unyielding: 'We will talk about the money later, first we want to determine the frontier,' he said. His position was strengthened by four victories in the winter of 1870–1, as severe cold gripped the capital. Famine threatened. Coal, wood and medicines were in short supply.[3]

The victors rubbed salt into French wounds with the declaration of the German Empire under Wilhelm I in the Hall of Mirrors in the Palace of Versailles in January 1871, while acrimonious negotiations continued over territory and money with bitter sessions between Bismarck and Thiers who called in James de Rothschild to help, only for the banker to be subject to a tirade from the Prussian. 'Count Bismarck would seem to have conducted himself with monstrous brusquerie and intentional rudeness,' the German banker Gerson von Bleichröder noted. The treaty was finally signed on 26 February, providing for an indemnity of 5 billion francs and the loss of Alsace and part of Lorraine.[4]

The government, now in Bordeaux, provisionally accepted Bismarck's terms, and got a stipulation that Paris would not be occupied and that regular soldiers would not be taken prisoner. German troops entered the capital only for a victory parade in the Bois de Boulogne and a review by their new emperor on the Champs-Élysées; they did not stay long but it was still a stinging humiliation. The drama now unfolded among the French, once again pitting the two sides descended from the Revolution against one another.

Wednesday, 8 February 1871. A general election returned a large number of conservative, rural and middle-class deputies with twice as many royalists as republicans. Hugo and Gambetta refused to take their

---

* 'No Kings could afford this! It could only belong to a Rothschild,' Kaiser Wilhelm declared when he visited Ferrières.

seats in protest at the loss of Alsace and a chunk of Lorraine where inhabitants were given until October 1872 to decide whether to stay and accept German nationality or to move to French territory with only what they could carry. Patriots lamented the lost lands, with the poet Victor de Laprade urging his compatriots to 'foreswear pity [and] cultivate hatred to the limits'. But only 10 per cent of the population chose to leave.

Friday, 17 February. The new parliament named Thiers as the chief executive of the Republic to restore peace and order. Exhausted, feverish and unable to work with Thiers, Gambetta left for Spain. Once again, Paris was out of step with the nation. At the election, it gave thirty-seven of its forty-two seats to republicans and socialists, among them Louis Blanc, the consumptive old Jacobin Louis Charles Delescluze and Félix Pyat who edited the newspaper *Le Combat*. Blanqui denounced the government and the moderate mayor of Paris, Jules Ferry, for failing to emulate the resistance spirit of revolutionaries of 1792. Riding the wave of electoral success, radicals staged a string of demonstrations calling for a 'democratic and social republic' and the arming of civilians. Marches, in January 1871, ended with shots being exchanged and the arrest of eighty left-wingers. The National Guard, which had played a prominent role in past turbulence in the capital, had not been disarmed by the armistice because the Germans thought it would maintain stability. This proved to be a major misjudgement since the force reflected the capital's radical nature.

Delegates chosen by its 260 battalions elected as their chief the Italian revolutionary, Garibaldi, who declined the post. They created a thirty-eight-member central committee with headquarters near the Place de la Bastille in the area that had been the scene of recurrent revolts earlier in the century. Its first act was to refuse to recognise the authority of the military governor of Paris or of the National Guard commander appointed by the government, which had set up in Versailles. Ferry left for Versailles.

Saturday, 18 March. The Guard clashed with regular soldiers trying to take from them a stock of obsolete bronze cannons set up in the city's parks. On the Butte Montmartre, where 170 of the cannons were located, the confrontation escalated despite attempts to mediate by the local mayor, Georges Clemenceau. Two generals were seized by the National Guard and shot dead. Barricades went up in workers' districts. The army withdrew. In Versailles, Thiers denounced 'an open revolt against national sovereignty'.[5]

In the following days, the National Guard took the Hôtel de Ville, hoisting the red flag. It occupied ministries and police headquarters while Blanquists seized gunpowder stored in the Panthéon and the Gare d'Orléans railway station. Thiers and the government were joined by 40,000 soldiers and Marshal Patrice de MacMahon, the commander of imperial forces who had just been released from captivity in Germany. A delegation led by Clemenceau went to present Thiers with proposals for Paris to gain independent status, but was rebuffed. Relations between the radicals and the district mayors in the capital rapidly deteriorated. Guardsmen seized Clemenceau's office – 'we are caught between two bands of crazy people, those sitting in Versailles and those in Paris,' he remarked.

Sunday, 26 March. Elections for a Commune council, with an all-male franchise, returned a radical majority. Though in prison in Brittany, Blanqui won in several *arrondissements*. Abstention was high in smart districts. The council's membership, reduced from ninety-two to sixty as a number of successful candidates refused to take their seats, included a majority of industrial and office workers who saw themselves picking up the strands of 1848 in what a song termed 'cherry time'.

The council got down to work on a list of long-standing left-wing aspirations, deliberating in secret so as to give nothing away to the authorities in Versailles. It had no president though the absent Blanqui was elected honorary chief. There was some pragmatism. The gold reserves of the Bank of France were protected to ensure that the National Guardsmen were paid. A loan was raised from the Rothschild bank. Publication of pro-Versailles newspapers was banned, but the most popular daily, *Le Rappel*, was not censored when it condemned the killing of the two generals.[6]

Still, the new regime in the city was distinctly radical. Night work was abolished in bakeries. A rent holiday was decreed for the period of the siege. Pawned tools and household items were to be returned free. Commercial debt obligations were postponed with interest waived; employees got the right to take over firms deserted by owners who were, however, guaranteed compensation; workers set up schools and orphanages with free food and clothing and took over local administration.

The red flag replaced the tricolour. The death penalty was abolished. The Revolutionary calendar was restored. The Commune council separated church and state; religious property was taken over and religious education banned in schools. Churches were required to be open for public political meetings in the evening. A series of measures laid the foundations for municipal government catering for the mass of the population, creating a heritage for left-wing local urban government in the future.[7]

Though they had not been given the vote, a number of women figured prominently in the Commune, most famously Louise Michel, the 'Red Virgin' of Montmartre. A women's union called for gender equality, the right of divorce, professional education for girls and the abolition of prostitution. The anarchist Nathalie Lemel set up a cooperative restaurant serving free food for the poor. A Russian exile, Anne Jaclard, founded a newspaper, *Paris Commune*. A female battalion was formed in the National Guard.

Sunday 2 April. Regular forces under MacMahon deployed on the outskirts of the capital, their ranks swollen by prisoners of war released by the Germans after the peace treaty was finalised in Frankfurt. They turned back the National Guard in a skirmish at the Pont de Neuilly after which four guardsmen were summarily shot. Undeterred, the Commune council launched an offensive against Versailles, but the guardsmen were caught in crossfire and fled back to the capital in disarray. Communes in Marseilles, Grenoble, Lyons, Narbonne and Limoges were crushed.

Monday 3 to Wednesday 5 April. The Commune council adopted tougher policies, including a decree by which anyone accused of complicity with the Versailles government could be immediately arrested, imprisoned, and tried by a special jury. If convicted, they would become 'hostages of the people of Paris' and every execution of a Communard by the opposing forces would be followed immediately by the execution of three times as many hostages. The first arrests were of the archbishop of Paris and two hundred priests, nuns and monks. Versailles rejected a proposal to barter Blanqui for seventy hostages and passed legislation allowing military tribunals to mete out punishment within twenty-four hours.

A Committee of Public Safety, modelled on Robespierre's group, was created with the newspaper editor Félix Pyat in a prominent role. It widened the net of arrests, taking in an eighty-year-old general and recent commanders of the National Guard. Following a suggestion by the painter Courbet, backed by Pyat, Napoleon's column in the Place Vendôme was destroyed for a second time as 'a monument of barbarism'; the idea was to replace it with a monument made of melted-down German cannons. Thiers's home was ransacked and demolished; proceeds from the sale of the furniture went to widows and orphans. 'The hour of revolutionary war has struck,' a Commune leader declared. 'To arms, citizens! To arms!' But there was no concealing the weakness of Paris. A fifth of guardsmen were absent without leave. Desertion more than halved the ranks of trained artillerymen.[8]

The night of Friday 7 to Saturday 8 April. A key position south of the capital, Fort Issy, was taken by the army after a see-saw battle; the National Guard commander was sacked as a result and replaced by a journalist without military experience. Many of the troops were smarting from defeat and captivity at the hands of the Germans. Drawn predominantly from conservative rural areas, they were told by their commanders they faced a radical anti-religious rabble of agitators, work-shy ruffians, criminals and foreigners, who did not have the support of the mass of Parisians and would consign the nation to the devil.

Sunday 21 May. Sixty thousand soldiers moved through an undefended section of the fortifications to occupy the Passy and Auteuil districts before taking key points and fighting an artillery duel between the Quai d'Orsay, the Madeleine and the Tuileries. Haussmann's boulevards helped to circumvent barricades and soldiers fired from vantage points on top of the Second Empire's apartment blocks. As in 1848, there was no quarter. Sixteen National Guardsmen captured on the Left Bank were summarily shot; Communards carrying away dead and wounded were peppered with bullets. After a fierce battle at the Madeleine, 300 Communards were caught and shot on the spot. Defiant, the committee of public safety declared that 'Paris, with its barricades, is undefeatable'. But only some 15–20,000 people responded to the call to arms.

Monday 22 May. As fighting swirled in the streets, National Guardsmen burned down the Tuileries Palace after soaking the walls and floors with oil and turpentine, and putting barrels of gunpowder at the foot of the grand staircase and in the courtyard. The 48-hour fire gutted most of the huge edifice. Communards set fire to public buildings along the rue Royale, the Faubourg-Saint-Honoré and other central streets; the Louvre library was destroyed by flames, though the museum was saved.*

Tuesday 23 May. Having established itself in central Paris, the army headed for Montmartre and its hill, the Butte, overcoming the women's battalion on the way. The soldiers pierced the ring of barricades and forts at the bottom of the Butte and by noon had raised their tricolour on the telegraph station at the top. Forty-two guardsmen and several women captured in the fighting were taken to the house where the two generals had been shot, and executed. Louise Michel was captured, thrown into the trench and left for dead; she was still alive and escaped before giving herself up in return for the freedom of her mother.

The following day, fighting in the streets fragmented into localised battles. Communards burned down their headquarters at the Hôtel de Ville. Guardsmen shed their uniforms and many quit the city, leaving a final force to fight on under skies darkened by smoke from the incinerations, which now included the main law courts, the police prefecture the Palais de Justice, theatres and churches.

---

* The pornographic photographer Braquehais took shots of the damage and soldiers – he then went bankrupt and died a broken man owing some 130,000 francs to creditors (McCauley, *Industrial Madness*, pp. 187–93).

Wednesday 24 May. Summary executions continued, the army sometimes using machine guns to mow down prisoners. The head of the committee of public safety killed four prisoners, and was then captured and shot. The archbishop of Paris and five other hostages were executed in the courtyard of their prison. Guardsmen took forty-seven prisoners, including ten priests and twenty-seven policemen from the La Roquette jail, lined them up along a wall and shot them before bayoneting and beating the corpses with rifle butts.

Thursday 25 May. The Communard leader, Delescluze, wearing his outfit of the revolutionary days of 1848 – top hat, frock coat, black trousers and boots – donned his red parliamentary sash, climbed onto a barricade and was shot dead.

Friday 26 to Saturday 27 May. After six hours of heavy fighting, the army took the Place de la Bastille but was still subject to artillery bombardment from Commune strongholds in the Buttes-Chaumont and Père-Lachaise districts. After Foreign Legion troops captured the first, the battle focussed on Père-Lachaise. A savage evening battle ended with the last 150 guardsmen overwhelmed, put against a wall and shot.

'There has been nothing but general butchery,' the American minister to France, Elihu Washburne, wrote. 'The rage of the soldiers and the people knows no bounds. No punishment is too great, or too speedy, for the guilty but there is no discrimination. Let a person utter a word of sympathy, or even let a man be pointed out to a crowd as a sympathiser and his life is in danger. A well-dressed respectable looking man was torn to a hundred pieces ... for expressing sympathy for a man who was a prisoner and being beaten almost to death.'[9]

End of the 'war against Paris'

By Sunday 28 May, the 'Bloody Week' was over. Zola, who approved of the action by the Versailles government, described the city as 'a vast cemetery ... a lugubrious necropolis where the odours of the morgue lingered on the pavements'. The death toll among the insurgents has traditionally been put at 20–25,000, with some estimates going as high as

30,000. The army reported 877 killed, 6,454 wounded and 183 missing in the civil war as a whole. The official record showed 43,522 prisoners, 1,054 of them women and 615 under sixteen. Seventy-eight per cent of those arrested were workers, almost identical with the figure for 1848. In all, 22,727 captives were freed before trial on attenuating circumstances or humanitarian grounds. Nearly 16,000 were put before courts and 13,500 were found guilty with 95 sentenced to death and 251 to forced labour. Among other sentences, 4,316 were deported to French colonies and 4,616 went to prison, 40 per cent for less than a year.[10]

Twenty-five Communard leaders were shot. Louise Michel asked for the death penalty, but was deported to New Caledonia where she worked as a schoolteacher. Courbet was sentenced to six months in prison, and later ordered to pay the cost of rebuilding the Vendôme column; he preferred exile in Switzerland and died there before the first payment was due. Seven thousand people went into exile, half of them to London.

The generally accepted Communard death toll of 20–30,000 was an essential element in the campaign for amnesties for those sentenced to prison or deportation and was then used as a graphic illustration of the ruthless and bloodthirsty nature of the right epitomised by Thiers and the generals. The notion of 'the war against Paris', the title of a book published in 1880, entered folklore. In fact, much of the city was not affected by the fighting. Half the population had abstained from voting for the Commune committee and felt no commitment to the insurrectionists. When a member of a parliamentary enquiry quoted a general as mentioning a figure of 17,000 for those killed in combat or afterwards, MacMahon said it seemed exaggerated and added that the general might have included wounded as well as dead. A paper delivered in 2011, by the historian Robert Tombs, argued that the number killed was in the range of 6–7,500, including some 1,400 Communards executed by the army. Still a large number, but much lower than the figure generally quoted. Tombs's work, based on meticulous examination of the records, is convincing, but is unlikely to shake the central story of 1871, 20–30,000 deaths of Parisians at the hands of an army defending the middle and upper classes, making the Bloody Week of May central to the revolutionary tradition.[11]

Lenin judged the Commune a living example of the dictatorship of the proletariat even if it had 'stopped halfway'. Marx wrote that it would be 'forever celebrated as the glorious harbinger of a new society'. Engels depicted it as a transition to a new order run by and for the workers. It certainly envisaged innovative left-wing measures, but did not have time to implement many. Extreme radicals were always in a minority. The main dynamic was the attempt to assert the special nature and position of Paris against a national government determined not to recognise that. In this respect, it fitted a pattern stretching back to 1789 and followed up in 1830 and 1848. Edmond de Goncourt judged that the repression 'by killing the rebellious part of a population, postpones the next revolution ... The old society has twenty years of peace before it.' He was wrong in his timing; despite recurrent periods of crisis, the regime that followed would stretch for more than three times as long as he thought and then be renewed in much the same form for another fourteen years.

10

A GOOD LITTLE REPUBLIC

The Third Republic saw itself ushering in a free and prosperous society where rational discussion would enhance solidarity and justice. Thiers, who had once dismissed the idea of a republic as a 'generous folly', now saw it as the form of government that 'divides us least'. 'Necessary liberties' inherited from 1789 were to be safeguarded as interpreted by the bourgeoisie. Order was needed after the Commune. The Catholic church would be kept in place by a lay majority. France was to avoid a fresh foreign war. The playbook came straight out of Guizot's *juste milieu*, but sought to create a new notion of nationhood surmounting divisions stretching back nearly a century and based on the supremacy of reason as defined by the victors of 1870. 'The First Republic gave us the land, the Second the vote, the Third knowledge,' claimed Jules Ferry.[1]

Recreating the nation

As it turned out, the divisions inherited from the Revolution proved hard to eradicate, as did the far older differences between France's regions, starting with the linguistic distinction between the north of the country with its *langue d'oïl* and the south with the *langue d'oc*. There were differences of mentalities, architecture, customs, dress and diet both nationally – butter or oil, beer or wine – and within regions – the cassoulets of Toulouse (with sausage and pork, duck or goose), Carcassonne (mutton and partridge) and Castelnaudary (only pork), not to mention the vast numbers of cheeses.

The Third Republic was at heart a moderately conservative regime and, as such, was subject to repeated challenges from left and right. The all-male electorate was quite evenly divided between the broad camps of conservatives and moderate progressives; small movements of voters could produce significant swings in parliament, impeding the formation of durable governments and producing multiple coalitions and deal making. The idea of a 'loyal opposition' was unknown. A close-knit network linked politics, finance, big companies, the press and the elite civil service. Its main actors co-operated at times and competed at others. They were united in belonging to the same microcosm cut off from the bulk of the population, except when elections needed to be won or money raised from everyday savings.

To ensure stability in the unlikely event that the Chamber of Deputies got carried away, veto powers were given to a Senate whose members were initially appointed for life and then elected by local officials to nine-year terms. Seats in both legislative houses were weighted towards conservative rural regions. As a result, social and financial reforms were slow – it was not until the First World War that an income tax was introduced and the Republic depended on loans to supplement archaic and inefficient revenue-raising powers.

The new rulers prided themselves on encouraging meritocracy and opening doors through education; the number of university students quadrupled between 1875 and 1910. The loss of power by the old rural nobility was portrayed as a sign of modernity by a state that stood out as an exception in monarchical Europe. A degree of decentralisation was introduced through elected departmental councils and mayors.[2]

A patriotic narrative of national history and solidarity was developed. Thiers re-engineered the Revolution as having been 'to abolish classes, so that there should be in the nation only the nation itself, the nation united living all together under one and the same law, carrying the same burden, enjoying the same advantages in which, in a word, every man should be rewarded or punished according to his works.'

*

The wave of technological modernisation in the late nineteenth century did not change the economic and social balance of the nation whose tax geography in 1931 was very similar to that of the 1840s. Economic progress was pursued within the bounds of limited democracy and often involved brutal change and conditions for factory workers and new urban residents while life in many rural areas remained harsh and precarious.

Paris predominated in the national landscape in every way. Its average taxable income was more than three times the national mean. Big provincial centres like Lyons and Marseilles, the most cosmopolitan of cities with its mix of European sailors and visitors and immigrants from the Mediterranean, spread out with suburbs but the capital did so even more with new towns like Levallois, Le Vésinet and Issy-les-Moulineaux springing up both for workers and for middle-class Parisians who wanted a second home in semi-rural surroundings. The city and its region were by far the most heavily populated region of France, with a population density in the capital of more than 50,000 per square kilometre. The economic predominance of northern France and the Lyons area was reinforced – the only big factory in Toulouse was the tobacco works.

At the outbreak of the Great War in 1914, only 2 per cent of French people had passed the *baccalauréat* school-leaving examination. Social reform was achingly slow. Women were denied the vote though there were some stirrings of recognition of gender equality as a Masonic order calling itself *Le Droit Humain* (The Human Right) declared that 'women have the same duties as men. They must have the same rights both within the family and society.'*

Some self-made men did rise high, especially in business, epitomised by Louis Dorizon, a grocer's son who entered the Société Générale as a messenger and rose to be its chief executive from 1896 to 1913. But social mobility was low until a significant growth in the lower middle class at the end of the century. Most sons did the same job as their fathers. Half the parliamentary deputies were lawyers followed by doctors and senior civil servants. While denouncing the money politics of the Second Empire, republicans accepted funding from business and leading politicians formed close links with big banks and corporate lobbies.[4]

* Its temple, with Egyptian motifs on the façade, is still 5 rue Jules Breton in Paris.

Deputies might demand reform when in opposition but once in government, they united round the state and the regime – defence of the
Republic covered many failures and sins. They were individualists and
the electoral system, whether by constituencies or party lists, did not
encourage discipline. In the Chamber, change was circumscribed by the
power of members to amend legislation in committees and form ad hoc
coalitions to block bills and look after the interests of their voters and
their own careers, toppling ministries at no political cost and reducing
most governments to the role of reflecting parliament's will rather than
implementing executive leadership.

Political alignments were loose, floating affairs – the main movements, the Radicals and Radical Socialists, did not formally organise as
parties until 1901 and, even then, let members oppose each other at
elections. Regional factors and traditions counted for much – the historian Charles Seignobos noted that the Republic appeared to have
been made by the 'idealism of Paris, the serious elements of the East
and the rowdy elements of the Midi'. In some areas, Bonapartists with
strong local connections held on – they had senators from the Périgord
until 1893.[5]

The revolutionary heritage meant politicians operating under the
banner of movements calling themselves of the left claimed a certain
moral superiority, but the names of political groupings meant little.
When seating at the National Assembly was reorganised in 1914 to place
deputies from left to right according to their beliefs, members of the
Radical Left, the Republican Left and the Democratic Left were put on
the right of the Palais Bourbon hemicycle. As a moderate deputy and
law professor, Joseph Barthélemy, explained, a member of the
Republican Left was 'a centrist who is obliged by the misfortunes of the
times to sit on the right.'[6]

The interests of the many strata of the middle classes had to be
catered for. Foremost were professional men plus richer business people
and middle-to-senior level civil servants. Many worked for their living
but others depended on the regular earnings from their *rentes* – stocks,
bonds, loans or income from land. The gap between richest and poor-
est was about the same as in 1815. At the end of the century, 86 per cent
of the population, 9.5 million people, earned 2,500 francs or less a year

while 0.002 per cent, or 3,000, made 100,000 or more. In the first decade of the twentieth century, 37 per cent of adults died without leaving any inheritance and 40 per cent of assets were in the six *départements* of the Paris region. A 1906 study found that indirect taxation meant labourers paid 10 per cent of earnings to the state while the maximum for the middle class was 11 per cent and for the rich under 12 per cent.

Industrial workers were lowly remunerated, toiled long hours in sometimes dangerous conditions and lived in poor accommodation. Slums persisted in major cities – one area of Rouen which had been condemned as uninhabitable in 1851 had not undergone any improvement at the end of the century. In 1906, 10 per cent of French homes had no external opening, 25 per cent lacked a chimney. A law of 1902 to punish negligent landlords was no more effective than similar legislation passed in 1850.[7]

Welfare, pensions and sickness insurance were lacking. Illegitimacy rates ran at 20 per cent or more in Paris, Lyons, Nancy, Rennes, Rouen, Bordeaux and Grenoble, which was known as a 'voluptuous city'. Infant mortality was high, especially in cities. Though medical discoveries reduced the impact of cholera and there was substantial building of hospitals, outbreaks of disease claimed thousands of lives during the last decades of the nineteenth century.[8]

Local personalities and concerns predominated at departmental level and below bequeathing a tenacious network of vested interests which left its traces into the twenty-first century. Though voting was meant to be secret, electoral booths were not introduced until 1913 – before that voting papers were handed to officials who could easily check on which candidates people had favoured. Farmers were adept at putting pressure on the 'political population' in the legislatures to ensure that agriculture was protected, that roads and railway branch lines were built and that there was a suitable flow of decorations. Professions were protected from competition.

'We are obliged to use the largest part of our efforts in petty errands and unrewarding solicitations,' observed Raymond Poincaré, a conservative mainstay of the regime between 1887 and 1929. 'Under the pressure of local influences we find ourselves considering daily meddling in administrative questions as vital to keeping our seats.' The political elite might congregate in Paris but rural voters were of prime concern to them and, as Ferry noted, they were animated by 'a spirit of conservation and a love of stability'.[9]

The path of rational prudence, which was the regime's hallmark, took account of change but was not going to be swept along by it wherever the pressure came from. The regime claimed to be the heir to the tradition of 1789 but, as the historian Sudhir Hazareesingh has argued, it obscured many key troubling political events of the eighty years that preceded it and rested on 'an invented tradition' which left it with a 'substantive thinness' that contributed to France's 'unfinished democracy'. Episodes such as the Commune or the rising of 1848 were airbrushed from the record. There was no place in its lineage for popular rebellion against the state. The writer Ernest Renan counselled that 'Forgetting, and I would even say historical error, are an essential factor in the creation of a nation.' As one of the more interesting figures of the Third Republic, Joseph Caillaux, noted, voters were well served by 'a good little republic', even if the constitutional laws setting the basis for the longest-lasting republic were passed in 1875 by only a single vote in the Chamber of Deputies.[10]

Recovery

France's recovery from defeat and German occupation was remarkably swift. The first half-billion francs of reparations were paid only a month after the suppression of the Commune. The rest followed by 1873 and the Germans withdrew. Three years after Sedan, the army paraded in all its pomp at Longchamp racecourse. After the damage done during the suppression of the Commune, the Hôtel de Ville was rebuilt in mediaeval style, the 2,156-seat Garnier opera house was finished, Napoleon was put back on the top of his column, and the Tuileries was sold off for property development.

The loss of Alsace-Lorraine was ventilated by politicians as a constant cause for national anger and the region was depicted on maps in violet, the colour of mourning, but the decision of 90 per cent of the

region's inhabitants to remain under German rule indicated that pragmatism outweighed patriotism. For most of the French, the lost lands in
the east were far away and meant little. More important than revenge
were the consolidation and stability that seemed possible after seven
regime changes in less than a hundred years.[11]

Colonialism in Africa and Asia became an important element in
national recovery, justified by the claim to be spreading the virtues of
French civilisation and Christianity. Ferry called such expansion 'a
right for the superior races, because they have ... the duty to civilise
the inferior races.' Missionary zeal and the spreading of French culture were certainly important and affected some younger army
officers who went to serve in faraway lands. But economics was always
a driving force, and there was not much civilisation evident in the
way French manufacturers saw the colonies as captive markets, or in
how native workers were treated in the rubber and rice plantations of
Vietnam or in the development of farms in North Africa, where settlers held 1.6 million hectares by 1890 and used loans from Paris
banks to fund exports of wine, grain, fruit and olive oil across the
Mediterranean.[12]

At home, the republicans reshaped the country – and identified the
regime with material progress – through stimulus programmes, which
gave priority to railways and roads, and also covered rivers, canals and
ports. As voters clamoured to be served by trains, the amount spent
went 50 per cent above budget. Track rose to 19,750 kilometres in
1879 and 26,330 kilometres three years later, while the number of railway workers rose from 172,000 in 1876 to 222,800 in 1881. A law
promoting the construction of rural roads not only linked rural communities but also, vitally, connected them to the rail line. The process
was abetted by emissaries from the centre, be they officials, school-
teachers or trades people. Fruit and vegetables circulated beyond
village barter and local markets. Wine went to the rest of the country
from the big vineyards of the south-west. Factory goods were distributed nationally.[13]

Though parts of France were left behind, the impact of communications advances was enormous, as was the spread of electricity at
the end of the century in urban areas. With the new transport links

came the postal and telegraphic systems; the number of letters, news-papers and other material sent by mail doubled between 1874 and 1884. Though many people still spoke native patois, national culture spread, powerfully aided by expansion of state education on which expenditure rocketed from 27 million francs in 1869 to 209 million in 1899. Being able to read and write was necessary to keep track of the traffic of local goods sent to distant markets and to deal with the complexities of accounting. Railway timetables meant everybody worked to the same clock instead of setting the passage of hours by the sun.

The civil service continued its expansion. In the second half of the nineteenth century, its numbers doubled to 420,000, a third of them teachers, as state intervention in the economy went from 79 million to 206 million francs in the first three decades of the Third Republic. Three thousand senior figures, drawn mainly from wealthy families, kept the administration going whatever the changes of government – at the foreign ministry, 77 per cent of the close-knit diplomatic corps had inheritances of 100,000 francs or more in 1900; family connections and patronage were extremely important and junior staff served their seniors with tea and cakes in the garden each afternoon.[14]

The drive for increasing centralisation was not universally accepted. The writer Frédéric Mistral launched a movement to defend Provençal culture, retiring to a village in the south and extolling regional lan-guages and traditions as a bar to the 'revolutionary virus' of big cities. Others looked back to movements such as the Cathars and the Huguenots of the Cévennes. The Provençal poet, author and critic, Charles Maurras, called for sovereign assemblies in Toulouse, Montpellier, Bordeaux, Marseilles and Aix, to release 'the souls of provinces'. Maurice Barrès, from Lorraine, advocated a more federalist republic. In 1900, a *Fédération Régionaliste Française* was set up to bring together 'decentralisers, regionalists or federalists'.[15]

The radical revolutionary left was boosted by the amnesty for Communards. The Marxist Jules Guesde formed a Workers' Party. Blanquists agitated though their leader stayed in prison. Small groups kept alive the teachings of Proudhon and other mid-century thinkers. Trade union membership more than doubled to 650,000 by the start of the twentieth century. Moderate Socialists won a growing number of Chamber seats and took control of the Bourse du Travail labour council in Paris. But workers were divided between reformers and revolutionaries, and progress was slow.

While retaining strongholds in western and southern France, the old rural nobility saw its influence steadily decline. Aristocratic membership of the Chamber of Deputies fell from 34 per cent in 1871 to a third of that fifty years later. The brighter members of the aristocracy invested in industry and moved to the cities. Big landowners who stayed in the countryside stuck to antiquated farming methods, which reduced their economic clout. Deference declined as elected mayors and provincial councils became the intermediary between peasants and the state. The nobility's political power was diminished by fears among rural voters that electoral victory for the royalists and the church would bring a return of *ancien régime* privileges, the absence of a cohesive message and the split between Legitimist followers of Charles X's grandson, Henri, Count of Chambord, and those loyal to Philippe d'Orléans, the Count of Paris.

Chambord had the superior claim and Philippe agreed to step aside in the expectation that his line would take the throne when the childless senior Bourbon died. But, staying on the wrong side of history, Henri ruined his chances through bull-headedness, insisting he would take the crown only if France abandoned the tricolour for the royal white fleur-de-lis flag. Clemenceau quipped that he was 'France's Washington' – the man without whom the Republic could not have been founded. His death in 1883 left the royalists divided and confused, the Orléanists pressing their case while Legitimists found their best candidate in the Carlist pretender to the Spanish throne.

The greatest challenge for the new regime came from the Catholic church. Defeat in 1870 at the hands of Protestant Prussia sparked a religious surge among those who blamed the debacle on the Empire's lax morality. For them, France was the church's eldest daughter who had strayed from her anointed path and must now make amends. Members of the Assumptionist congregation organised big pilgrimages to holy sites. Each year, half a million people bought donation cards for

the building of the huge white basilica of the Sacré Coeur on the Butte Montmartre, site of the martyrdom of Saint Denis (and the Commune struggle). The church project was declared by the National Assembly to be 'of public utility' in 1873 but it was not finished and consecrated until 1919, having attracted 40 million francs in contributions from the faithful.

Opposition to religious power served as a glue for republican politicians who themselves constructed a lay religion to keep the church out of domains that should be controlled by the state, starting with education. The church was a formidable opponent given the scale of religious adherence in many parts of France. In 1880, 20 per cent of boys and 54 per cent of girls were at church schools nationally, but this rose in a department such as the Ardèche to 47 and 77 per cent. Teachers sent out by the republican regime became missionaries for the state. Schools run by religious orders were closed by order of the government but in the Ardèche, 38 per cent of boys and 69 per cent of girls were still being taught in congregational schools in 1888, plus an unknown number in underground establishments.[16]

The church did not help itself with decrees opposing the regime's values, the support of bishops for the right-wing opposition, loyalty to Rome and the doctrine of papal infallibility which no descendant of the Enlightenment and 1789 could regard as anything but superstition. 'Clericalism – that is the enemy,' Gambetta told parliament (though his letters to his mistress contain plenty of religious references). Freemasonry thrived among committed republicans; all the members of a government formed in 1902 belonged to a lodge.

One reason for refusing the vote to women was that they might cast their ballots as instructed by priests. Some doctors evolved the theory that celibacy led to satyriasis with the build-up of semen turning priests into sex maniacs. The clergy was seen as threatening to undermine the position of the husband and father and learning too much about intimate matters in the confessional. As for female saints venerated by the church, doctors decided that they were, as one put it, 'nothing more than simple hysterics'.[17]

Coming out to play

French society evolved as people became more aware of their status as individuals and as members of groups with common interests that lay beyond the orthodox political and old religious worlds. Tenants banded together to protect their rights in the Anti-Landlord League. Organisations advocated birth control since 'large families engender misery and slavery'. The CGT trade union federation exhorted women to be 'mothers only when you choose to be'. Female workers in Vienne told their employers in 1890, 'We are flesh and blood like you.'

People took to being photographed for individual portraits, which the bourgeois put on their visiting cards. Reading by a better-educated population encouraged the expansion of libraries and the mass distribution of cheap books. More houses had single bedrooms. Though many couples never saw one another naked, marriage became less constrained and more sexualised for the progressive-minded: flirtation was accepted as normal, male and female contraception spread, arcade shops sold condoms. Female sexuality was admitted by some, while the flood of propaganda against masturbation suggests solitary pleasures were also much pursued. But the church was always on watch; Bishop Dupanloup of Orléans agreed that women, who were mainly responsible for the increased demand for books, should read as much as they wished, but insisted that it should be only 'pure and exquisite' material.[18]

For all the straight-laced nature of the bourgeoisie, prostitution thrived in cafés and cabarets, in streets and parks as well as in brothels. Paris became famous for its 'naughty' postcards of naked women. An early film-maker, Edouard Pirou, produced the cinema's first striptease showing the actress Louise Willy in her bedroom, removing layer after layer of underwear down to her slip before a man emerged from behind a screen. Well-kept apartments flourished in major cities where men could meet women who arrived in respectable attire before heading for the bedrooms. They had rich decorations, mirrors, thick carpets, electric lighting, *tableaux vivants* and, for voyeurs, peepholes through the walls. The Monthyron and Chabanais *maisons closes* offered particularly luxurious surroundings – the Prince of Wales bathed in champagne and had a special upholstered chair with foot and arm rests to accommodate his bulk as he took his pleasure.

One estimate had it that 80,000 women became prostitutes each year. At the top of the tree were the *grandes horizontales* headed by Carolina Otero known simply as 'La Belle'. Born in Galicia, she went to France as a dancer and starred with her opulent bosom and dark eyes as an Andalusian gypsy at the Folies Bergère music hall. Her lovers included the heir to the British throne, the Prince of Wales, as well as the kings of Serbia and Spain and Russian grand dukes; six men were said to have killed themselves after she ended their affairs. Her fortune was put at the equivalent of $25 million, but she gambled heavily and died in a one-room flat in Nice in 1950.[19]

Liane de Pougy earned fame on the stage of the Folies Bergère and the Casino de Paris as a courtesan and for her much-spoken-of lesbian relationships. The actress, Alice Regnault, her hourglass figure accentuated by tight corsets, made a fortune from sex. She retired from the game after ten years to publish two novels under the pseudonym Mitaine de Soie, marrying the writer Octave Mirbeau, a leading critic, playwright and author of the biting satire of finance, *Les Affaires sont les Affaires* (*Business is Business*) and the scandalous *Le Journal d'une Femme de Chambre* (*Diary of a Chambermaid*).

The house of the Englishman, Charles Worth, continued as the ultimate arbiter of fashion, employing the innovative French designer Paul Poiret until his clothes alienated the high society clientele. Poiret then set up his own fashion house, freeing women from the tyranny of the corset, launching his kimono coat, staging elaborate window displays and pioneering marketing techniques as he branched out into furniture, decorations and perfume. Jeanne Paquin offered pastel evening gowns taken from eighteenth-century models and tightly tailored day wear, while the clothes Jeanne Lanvin made for her daughter attracted the attention of friends who asked her to do the same for them, setting the foundations of a fashion empire. French perfumiers – Coty, Houbigant, Guerlain, Roger & Gallet – ruled the roost with ever more beguiling fragrances.

Countess Greffulhe, who was also an accomplished painter, a pro-Dreyfusard, an admirer of Clemenceau and an advocate of introducing income tax reigned as the most elegant woman in Paris (and became a model for Proust's character the Duchesse de Guermantes), even if her husband went back to his mistresses soon after their marriage. But elegance and style spread far beyond aristocratic circles. When France celebrated the new century at the Universal Exhibition of 1900, the symbolic figure over the monumental entrance was not Marianne the Republican, but *La Parisienne*, a typical young woman of the city dressed by Paquin. Such figures of the modern age, a journalist wrote, had a special character marked by 'discreet elegance in every aspect of her social life, sobriety, taste, innate distinction and the indefinable blend of bearing and modernity we call chic.' But also with a touch of seduction as in Whistler's portrait of the wife of an artist friend who lets the shoulder strap of her dress slip.*[20]

Cabarets and music halls thrived after a law of 1880 liberalised the opening of public meeting places and outlets selling alcohol. By the turn of the century, the capital had 200 such establishments ranging from small neighbourhood dives to the smart locations of the Divan Japonais and the Bal Tabarin. The culture of the musical hall and of social freedom was celebrated at the Moulin Rouge and the Folies Bergère, where Guy de Maupassant described the barmaids as 'sellers of drink and love'. Paris – the 'wondrous capital' as Henry James called it – became the City of Light, thanks to electricity. There were endless night-time diversions – roller-coaster rides on the boulevards, wrestling shows and street dancers calling themselves Apaches thrilling the bourgeois customers slumming it in Belleville. A modernised lantern show offered moving images at the Théâtre Optique. Musette music featuring the accordion became highly popular and a symbol of French everyday life.[21]

Edward, Prince of Wales, and Sigmund Freud were among the crowds which went to see Jules Pujol, the master of wind, who could play the Marseillaise on an ocarina through a rubber tube inserted into his anus. Artists made Montmartre – where rents were low, vines grew and wine was not taxed – the epicentre of popular culture with

* The exhibition awarded a prize for excellence in design to the Japanese room at the luxury brothel, the Chabanais.

its celebrated cabaret, Le Chat Noir, and the dance hall and restau-rant-drinking garden of the Moulin de la Galette high on the hill. The Moulin Rouge, which opened in 1889, offered the cancan; its great, brazen star, Louise Weber, had a heart embroidered on the front of her panties and a habit of downing drinks from tables as she passed, gaining her the nickname of *La Goulue* (The Glutton). Her promoter, the wine merchant Jacques Renaudin, appeared alongside as Valentin le Désossé (Valentin the Boneless One), tall, cadaverous and double-jointed in a stovepipe hat, frock coat and skin-tight trousers.

The young Mistinguett, real name Jeanne Bourgeois, became a star at the Casino de Paris, having been engaged by the revue's direc-tor after they met on a train. Flamboyant, husky-voiced and with routines that verged on the scandalous, she went on to top the bill at the Folies Bergère and Moulin Rouge, and was said to be the world's highest paid female entertainer. Lucien Guitry, the top actor of the day, returned from a stay in Russia to direct the Théâtre de la Renaissance. At the Comédie-Française, Louise Abbéma was a popu-lar favourite, playing servants and soubrettes and posing for a dozen portraits by Renoir before dying of typhoid in 1890 at the age of thirty. The wittiest writer of the day, Alphonse Allais, deployed his wordplay and deadpan humour in 1,600 newspaper and magazine pieces , writing at café tables as he consumed oceans of absinthe; never seen to laugh, he co-founded the Club of the Hydropaths (those allergic to water).[22]

The Lumière brothers set up their cinemas. Georges Méliès gave the new art form its first masterpiece with his vivid depiction of a trip to the moon. The Pathé brothers founded what became the world's biggest film production company and pioneered newsreels as well as running a huge glittering picture palace on the Place de Clichy. By 1913 Paris had thirty-seven cinemas alongside its forty theatres. Advertising boomed and produced a surge of new poster art; Jules Chéret devel-oped coloured lithographs for images of Moulin Rouge performers, an art carried on by the diminutive Henri de Toulouse-Lautrec as he depicted the dancer Jane Avril, the blonde English singer May Milton, the realist Aristide Bruant with red scarf and black cape and hat, and the *diseuse* Yvette Guilbert, whose daring words contrasted with her still appearance in tight yellow dress and black gloves.

The extraordinary flowering of the Impressionists, who came together for their first group exhibition in 1874, reinforced France's position in the artistic world. After initial rejection, Monet, Sisley, Morisot, and Pissarro won over the public with their celebration of sunlight, colour and spontaneity. Manet, Degas, Renoir and Cézanne added to France's artistic aura. Seurat and Signac developed new techniques and Caillebotte left imperishable images of Paris. Van Gogh came from the Low Countries to exult in the sun of Provence, accompanied for a time by Gauguin before he headed for the South Seas. The dealer Paul Durand-Ruel pioneered the selling of painters as brands with his one-artist shows, promoting Renoir, Degas, Pissarro and, in particular, Monet and Manet, from whom he bought twenty-three canvases on the day they met. As well as offering enthusiasm and moral support, he bought their work in bulk, paid them monthly stipends and settled their rents and bills. In 1885, he opened up modern French art to American collectors, transporting forty-three crates of paintings with him to the US where he achieved quick sales of canvases that took twenty years to be appreciated in France – 'the Americans do not laugh, they buy,' he observed. Late in life, he reflected that 'At last the Impressionist masters triumphed. My madness has been wisdom.'[23]

Rodin became the father of modern sculpture moving into the Hôtel Biron on the rue de Varenne in Paris which was also used by artistic figures including Henri Matisse, Jean Cocteau, Isadora Duncan and Rainer Maria Rilke – rabbits ran in the gardens where the great man exercised his growling German shepherd.* Picasso moved from Spain in 1900 and joined the Modernist school in Montmartre with the Cubist Georges Braque and the Fauvist Maurice de Vlaminck who, with Henri Matisse and Raoul Dufy, gave new meaning to colour. Modigliani, who moved from Italy to Paris in 1906, introduced a new style of elongated faces and figures. Art Nouveau brought close observation of the natural world and whiplash lines – and was taken to the streets with the decorations at the entrances to Paris Métro railway stations.

* It is now the Musée Rodin.

Father Hugo and the Divine Sarah

No two cultural figures were more celebrated in the early decades of the Third Republic than the two long-distance performers, Victor Hugo, whose long career and exile under Napoleon III during which he had published *Les Misérables*, gave him the status of a seer, and Sarah Bernhardt, the outstanding stage performer whose career would stretch to 1925.

Hugo had helped to spear the romantic movement, achieved fame with *The Hunchback of Notre Dame*, been a peer under the July Monarchy and fought for the suppression of the insurrection of the June Days of 1848.

Returning from the Channel Islands in 1870, the writer, who had set off a storm with his convention-busting play *Hernani* four decades earlier, epitomised the humanist aspirations of the Republic. His eightieth year, in 1881, brought a parade that took six hours to pass his home as he watched from a window on the Avenue de Saint-Cloud; the name of the street was changed to the Avenue Victor-Hugo. What he saw in 1848 set him on an unusual trajectory from youthful reaction to left-wing views in older age. When he died in 1885 aged eighty-three, two million joined his funeral procession. He was laid in the Panthéon, the first writer to enter its portals.

Hugo and Bernhardt were friends; she appeared in the role of the queen in his play *Ruy Blas*. She had made her unsuccessful debut in 1862 and gone to Belgium where she became the mistress of a prince by whom she had a son. Her subsequent marriage to a morphine-addicted Greek actor collapsed and she was rumoured to have conducted an affair with the Prince of Wales followed by a lengthy liaison with Louise Abbéma, an impressionist painter nine years her junior. Returning to Paris and the stage, she performed the gamut of classic roles and slept in a coffin with gold fixtures given by an admirer to help her understand tragic roles, or so she said. At her Théâtre Sarah-Bernhardt, she played Hamlet to great reviews, earning the name of 'The Divine Sarah'.

To celebrate the turn of the century, the 55-year-old actress put on a corseted costume for the role of the youthful hero of Rostand's four-hour long play *L'Aiglon*. She travelled to the Americas, where the bishop of Chicago thundered against her – she sent him $200 for the publicity. Her cinema debut, in the two-minute *Le Duel d'Hamlet* in 1900, was followed by ten other films. Performing in Rio de Janeiro in 1905, she injured her right knee onstage; ten years later gangrene set in and her leg was amputated, but she continued to act up to her death in 1925 at the age of seventy-nine from kidney failure followed by uraemia.

Bizet, Fauré and Massenet breathed new life into music. Composing in his head as he walked his regular twelve miles a day, Satie laid the foundations for minimalism. Debussy divided opinion with his opera *Pelléas et Mélisande*. Diaghilev brought his Russian ballet to Paris in 1909; after an initially cool reaction, enthusiasm grew at the extravagant productions and Nijinsky's acrobatic dancing. Stravinsky's *Rite of Spring*, performed in 1913, provoked a riot. Zola's realistic novels made him Hugo's heir, Maupassant crafted the short story in Flaubertian mode. Jules Verne took readers on fantastical journeys, made less improbable by the technological advances of the era. The year before the outbreak of the Great War, Proust – like Flaubert a night writer – published the first volume of his epic and appropriately titled *À la Recherche du Temps Perdu* (Remembrance of Things Past)* and Alain Fournier published his idiosyncratic, haunting masterpiece of young love, *Le Grand Meaulnes*. The prolific symbolist and absurdist Alfred Jarry pointed the way to Surrealism with his play *Ubu Roi*.

The great actor of the day, Jean Mounet-Sully, incarnated classical roles at the Comédie-Française. Edmond Rostand had a huge and enduring hit with *Cyrano de Bergerac* followed by his six-act play on Napoleon's unhappy son, *L'Aiglon*, before he retired to treat his pleurisy at a large self-designed villa in the Basque country. In sixty stage works, Georges Feydeau raised farce to an art form, his giddying pace reflecting the new age of speed while his plots showed bourgeois hypocrisy and helplessness at the complexity of modern life. Georges Courteline's satirical plays bequeathed a treasure trove of *bons mots* as he sent up his main characters – the fat Boubouroche and his over-cunning mistress, the Boulingrin couple martyred by married life, and Monsieur Badin, the victim of inescapable bureaucracy.

Such entertainment catered primarily to the taste of the middle classes, the social force in the Third Republic. They aimed to live a comfortable life in which the home was celebrated and their dinner parties could reflect, in a more sober, bourgeois manner, the traditional banqueting of the aristocracy. An account of the eating habits of a bourgeois family in Paris in the 1870s listed a daily routine of 8 a.m. – coffee,

---

* It was initially turned down at the publisher Gallimard by André Gide who later acknowledged that it had been the biggest mistake of his life.

bread and butter; 11 a.m. – two meat dishes, a vegetable, cheese, dessert and coffee; 3.30 p.m. – children's meal of bread and jam, chocolate, fruit; dinner – soup, entrée, roast, vegetables, sometimes a sweet course, cheese, dessert and coffee followed by tea or a herbal infusion at 9 p.m. A typical dinner party consisted of soup, tuna fish, olives and radishes; sole; quail, roast beef, peas; cheese; dessert washed down with one bottle of white Burgundy, two of red Burgundy, two of claret and two of champagne followed by coffee and liqueurs.[24]

Newspapers flourished and some politicians made sure of a good press by buying shares in them. The *Petit Journal* achieved daily sales of one million copies in the 1890s under the ownership of Hippolyte Marinoni, son of an Italian immigrant and inventor of the rotary printing press. It ran a weekly colour magazine and sponsored major sporting events such as the first long-distance bicycle race from Paris to Brest and back, a road race from the capital to Rouen, a running race from Paris to Belfort and a Paris marathon won by a British bricklayer. The first Tour de France was staged in 1903 by the sports newspaper, *L'Auto* – the leader's yellow jersey reflecting the colour of the paper on which it was printed. The city of Pau, looking out at the Pyrenees and much prized for the quality of its air, became a centre for motor racing and horse racing, as well as for pioneering aviation – the Wright brothers opened a flying school there.

Sporting activity and gymnastics were seen as a way of developing physical prowess and avoiding the debilitation which was blamed for France's defeat in 1870. Soccer and rugby football were brought over the Channel. Shooting clubs proliferated. Bicycling flourished, though the improbably named Dr Ludovic O'Fallowell warned of the danger of women riders falling prey to 'genital satisfaction and voluptuous sensations'. The Bon Marché encouraged its staff to take up fencing. Pierre de Coubertin, anxious to re-establish his country's physical and moral fibre and an admirer of the sporting pursuits of British public schools, established the International Olympic Committee in 1894.[25]

Railways and then motor cars enabled people to get to know their own country better as the French discovered France. The Touring Club of France had more than 100,000 members at the turn of the century.

The faithful could make pilgrimages to far-off places; between 300 and 400,000 people went to Lourdes each year. Luxury villas and palatial hotels went up at smart seaside towns. Parisians took the train to Deauville and Trouville, the latter the most visited resort on the Normandy coast with its two casinos and two big bathing establishments. Le Touquet became a lure for upper-class British after two entrepreneurs from London saw its potential for visitors from across the Channel. At the Channel resort of Le Tréport, according to a contemporary writer, there were 'almost as many bathers as pebbles on the beach'.

Nice and Cannes developed as holiday resorts bringing in visitors from northern Europe in search of the sun. Biarritz retained the elegance of the empress's day. There was also extensive building of simpler accommodation where, as a writer put it in 1883, 'a very modest public can in its turn enjoy the pleasures hitherto reserved for the rich alone'.[26]

By the end of the 1890s, 800,000 visitors patronised 350 thermal establishments, characterised by their elegant light metal architecture and grand hotels. Vichy attracted 100,000 visitors a year while the little village of Vittel in the Vosges grew into a humming resort with a casino, velodrome, racecourse, polo ground and a grand hotel built by a businessman who found its waters soothing for his liver, kidneys and stomach. Each spa publicised its special virtues – Cransac in the southern Massif Central proclaimed that its waters were 'a sovereign remedy' for abdominal problems, constipation, fevers, dyspepsia, dysentery, migraine, gastric ailments, anaemia, liver and kidney trouble, rheumatism and skin ailments, as well as hypochondria; it reassured visitors that the waters could be taken at table and did not affect the quality of the wine.[27]

Invention, construction and consumption

The big banks increased their hold on the financial world, symbolised by the 10,000-square-metre headquarters of the Crédit Lyonnais in central Paris. The consumer society advanced and big department stores took a growing slice of spending. Bourgeois districts of major cities were steadily developed. In Paris, the long-serving public works supervisor, Adolphe Alphand, took up the mantle of Haussmann. A burst of apartment building for the middle classes at the end of the century led to taller buildings, some with flamboyant Art Nouveau façades and bulging windows sticking out over the pavement. Monumental blocks towered over smart parts of the city such as the Champ-de-Mars between the Eiffel Tower and the École Militaire while architects indulged their own and their clients' fancies as in the extra-ordinary edifices round the Square du Temple in the old workers' district topped with cupolas, a spire and a wall given over to gam-bolling naked nymphs. The huge central post office was built on the rue du Louvre as a modern palace and, to show that the past was not forgotten, the Bourse de Commerce was reconstructed in ornate neo-classical style after being destroyed by fire.

The super-wealthy amassed great art collections; the Protestant banker Édouard André, who had been among the promoters of Haussmannian development of the capital and helped to finance the first Paris horse-drawn omnibus service, built a mansion in the 17th *arrondissement* to house the enormous trove of treasures from the ancient regime and Middle Ages that he had accumulated with his artist wife, Nélie Jacquemart*. Grand hotels went up and the Gare de Lyon and Gare d'Orsay stood as proud monuments to the railway age. A new sewer system was laid in the capital, which also saw the establishment by the post office of *la lettre pneumatique*, using compressed air to whizz mes-sages around the city through a series of underground tubes for delivery two hours after despatch. The *théâtrophone* enabled people to listen to stage performances, concerts and the proceedings of the National Assembly from their homes.†[28]

The introduction of buses and trams, some double-decker, brought different strata of society together; 'duchesses and millionaires rub shoulders with cooks and clerks,' a contemporary writer noted. In 1900, the first Paris Métro underground line opened amid dire warnings of

* This is now the Musée Jacquemart-André on the Boulevard Haussmann.
† Proust was a fan of the *théâtrophone*, listening to performances in his cork-lined bedroom on the Boulevard Haussmann (which has been restored and can be visited at number 102).

asphyxiation, electrocution and pickpockets. The number of journeys soared from 15 million in its first year to 312 million in 1909.

Industrial output grew steadily as the economy tilted away from agriculture. The arrival of electricity revolutionised industries in some far-flung regions, such as paper production and metallurgy in the Alps where the Casimir Brenier company pioneered hydro-power turbines; the population of Grenoble grew from 42,000 in 1872 to 77,000 in 1911. By the end of the century, almost one-third of the working population was engaged in industry and manufacturing and there was an equivalent increase in the number in service industries while the proportion of agricultural workers dropped to 43 per cent. Cartels were established for chemicals, steel and coal, driving out small enterprises or those in isolated areas – steel activity in the Vivarais region above the Rhône valley was reduced to a single mill and the workforce fell from 1,760 in 1883 to 175 in 1913. On the other hand, the big Anzin mine in the north increased output from 1.6 million tons in 1870 to 2.6 million in 1889.[29]

The corporate elites established a new lifestyle with big houses and huge apartments, buying châteaux from impoverished nobles, building up antique and art collections and indulging in aristocratic pursuits such as hunting. A web of intermarriages and family connections linked the leading business families while aristocrats were ornaments on corporate boards, and some arranged to marry their daughters to the sons of big capitalists.

An array of engineers from the École Centrale des Arts et Manufactures pushed at the frontiers of progress. Some founded great dynasties: the engineer Gustave Eiffel, whose iron lattice tower that would become the capital's most famous landmark was built for the *Exposition Universelle* of 1889; the aviation pioneer Louis Blériot; the Alsatian Schlumberger brothers in mining; René Panhard and Armand Peugeot in cars with the Michelin brothers to provide the tyres. André Citroën was a graduate of the École Polytechnique, though Louis Renault taught himself by working on engines in the tool shed of his family home in the Paris suburb of Billancourt.

Étienne Lenoir, an immigrant from Luxembourg, had developed the single-cylinder two-stroke internal combustion engine running on coal and gas in 1859 but it was not until 1884 that the first gasoline-powered car was built by Édouard Delamare-Deboutteville who then switched his attention to the family's cotton mill. With a partner, Panhard made the first car with a modern transmission in 1895. After the partner was killed swerving to avoid a dog, his successor, Arthur Krebs, pioneered major design improvements including the steering wheel, shock absorber and multi-disc clutch, followed by the rear-wheel drive – he also piloted the first army airship and the first submarine with periscope and gyrocompass. Peugeot built up France's biggest pre-Great War motor company, making 10,000 cars a year. Louis Renault and his brothers, Marcel and Fernand, intro-duced mass-production techniques as they branched out into lorries, buses and taxis, closely followed by Citroën. The Paris Motor Show was organised by the Marquis de Dion, a noted duellist and the inven-tor of a single-cylinder gas-powered engine that could power a four-wheel car.

In the air, too, France led the world. Félix du Temple staged the first manned flight in 1874 with an aluminium aircraft powered by a steam boiler. The Voisin brothers set up their aircraft company in 1905. Four years later, Blériot flew the Channel. Later in 1909, a week of flying events at Reims was attended by 3,000 British visitors and 2,000 Americans, including the flamboyant Francophile newspaper propri-etor James Gordon Bennett, who offered a prize for the fastest flight. It was won by his compatriot, Glenn Curtiss. Prussian army observers reported that twenty-eight of the thirty-six aircraft taking part were French, and that all but two of the pilots came from France: 'Germany has shamefully little to show in the face of French achievements,' they concluded. In 1912, 800 aviators were flying each day on average in France compared with ninety in the USA.

There was an outburst of intellectual curiosity and inventiveness in which scientists became hero figures, led by Louis Pasteur with his life-saving vaccines and his desire to show French science to be superior to that in Germany. Marcellin Berthelot made ground-breaking discover-ies in chemistry. Henri Poincaré worked out the theory of special relativity well before Einstein. Henri Becquerel identified radioactivity and the Curies developed radium. Exhibits at the Great Exhibition of

1878 included a hot-air balloon that could carry up to fifty passengers. Among many other discoveries and inventions, in the three decades after 1870 French pioneers came up with fluorine, artificial silk, liquid oxygen, the inflatable tyre, the hair dryer and the modern brassiere, which the French continued to call the *soutien-gorge*. The first experiments with radio transmission were staged from the Eiffel Tower in 1897.

The *Hachette Guide to the Universal Exhibition* of 1900 described the nineteenth century as 'the most fertile in discoveries, the most prodigious in science'. The poet Charles Péguy declared in 1914 that the world had changed 'less since Jesus Christ than it has in the last thirty years'.

Food consumption grew steadily and diet became more varied. Meat consumption nearly doubled between the 1840s and the end of the century while the proportion of household budgets spent on bread halved to 9 per cent. The leading chef of the day, Georges-Auguste Escoffier, introduced lighter cuisine and a new system of restaurant management. Adolphe Dugléré, of the Café Anglais on the Boulevard des Italiens, created his classic dish of filets of sole poached with tomatoes and cream sauce. On the rue Royale, Maxim's epitomised the *belle époque* with its velvet-lined Art Nouveau décor and clientele of men in white tie and tails squiring even more elegant ladies, some of whom might even be their wives – one of Feydeau's hit plays was *La Dame de chez Maxim* and the writer had a table permanently reserved for him. César Ritz set up his luxury hotel in the Place Vendôme with Escoffier running the kitchen, en suite bathrooms and telephones in all rooms.[30]

The confidence generated by such evidence of progress and good living for the privileged buttressed the belief that the Third Republic represented a new stage in national life, reconciling reason and revolution with bourgeois characteristics. If governments had short lives that was of little importance because the administrative class would ensure things went on functioning as before. Indeed, the way in which the same cast swapped ministerial posts was a reassuring sign of overall stability.

Haves and have-nots

The decades after 1870 were troubled by recurrent crises involving presidents of the republic, ministers, parliamentarians and shady financiers amid anti-Republican and anti-Semitic sentiment. Anarchist violence killed one president. Others were forced to resign after trying to stage a constitutional coup or when a relative was revealed as having sold honours. One resigned out of frustration at the limits of the job and a fifth died in the arms of his mistress in the Élysée Palace.

Strikes became more common, put down with extreme force in some instances. Fifty thousand workers staged a stoppage in Marseilles in 1904 bringing a lock-out by employers and the intervention of the army; two years later, 1,500 firms were hit by another big strike. In 1907, Paris electricity workers showed the vulnerability of modernity by plunging the city into darkness.

There was a pervasive questioning of progress and concern, especially among intellectuals who fretted at belonging to 'a society about to disappear'. The middle classes worried about nervous strain and physical, intellectual and moral degeneration. The celebrated neurologist, Dr Jean-Martin Charcot, gave packed lectures on epilepsy, hysterical illnesses and syphilitic paralysis, illustrated by the presence of his patients. Jules Ferry warned that 'It is written in the destinies of this country to find its men always inferior to circumstances.' The historian Hippolyte Taine described a seemingly irreversible process of national decline while the philosopher Ernest Renan declared that 'if the leprosy of egoism and anarchy causes our western states to perish, the barbarian will recover his function, which is to rebuild virility in the corrupt civilisations.'[31]

The decline in population growth accelerated. If reproduction was a reflection of national confidence, France was suffering from depression; in the 1870s there were just under a million births annually for a population of 37 million. Proportionately, the rate was the same as in 1789. The ratio of births to people was 1:25 in Germany, 1:30 in Britain and 1:39 in France. In 1870, Germany and France contained about the same number of men aged between 20 and 34; by the outbreak of the next conflict in 1914, the former had 7.7 million to 4.5 million in France. As well as the spread of contraception and the disinclination of farmers to see their land split up among heirs all entitled to a share, other causes included urbanisation, wider education and the rise of the middle class. In his later novels, Zola denounced homosexuals, priests and childless couples for contributing to the lack of people.[32]

Immigrants, mainly Italians crossing to the south-east, Belgians working in the north-east and Jews fleeing persecution in Eastern Europe, were welcomed by the authorities to swell the work force. They were concentrated in Paris, in the mining region of the north-east and in big cities near frontiers such as Nice, Lille and Marseilles where, at the start of the twentieth century, there were 100,000 Italians, and foreigners outnumbered French people moving in from rural areas. If employers liked the cheap labour they provided, the population at large could be less appreciative. The 300,000 Italians, who made up a quarter of all aliens, were the target of recurrent violence – eight died in fighting at a salt works at Aigues-Mortes in 1893. As the historian Eugen Weber noted, the anti-Semitism of the end of the century was 'only one aspect of a broader xenophobia'.[33]

The exodus to cities weakened traditional rural social structures, those left behind isolated in backwardness. Fear of impotence accompanied warnings in medical treatises of the dangers of masturbation and debauchery. Tobacco and alcohol consumption rose. Among a smaller number of people, use of drugs increased, mainly opium and morphine which the younger Dumas called 'the absinthe of women'. Marcel Proust accumulated a formidable medicine chest of a dozen drugs including heroin, morphine and opium; he advised a correspondent always to have the first available and told another of the 'daily necessity of opium'.[34]

Crime rose in the 1890s, with the press going to town on stories such as the *crime passionnel* of Marie Bière, who was acquitted in a sensational trial after trying to kill her rich lover. The fraudster Thérèse Humbert, who gulled investors for twenty years with a tale of having inherited 120 million francs in the will of an American whose life she had saved, provided a popular soap opera with allegations from the right that ministers had taken bribes to protect her; when the safe said to contain the vital documents was opened, it contained some scraps of paper, an Italian coin and a metal button.

Though the number of women going out to work rose to 31 per cent by the end of the century, social attitudes remained conservative. Only in 1886 were women permitted to open savings accounts without their husbands' permission. Adultery was a criminal offence for women, but not punishable for men. Domestic violence was fuelled by rising drunkenness. For some women religious devotion was such that, in the words of one study, 'attendance at Mass was a secondary sexual characteristic of French women'. Child-bearing and looking after the home defined the female condition. Women did not have the vote and were subject to the restrictions of the Napoleonic Code. Though divorce was finally legalised, it was surrounded by restrictions and women found it hard to obtain. Above all an urban phenomenon, with six times as many divorces in towns as in rural areas after the law came into force in 1884 and twice as many in subsequent years, it was seen by progressives as a sign of modernisation and a stream of 'divorce novels' was published to mark the new freedom.[35]

Modernisation was epitomised by the great exhibitions in Paris such as the *Exposition Universelle* or World's Fair in Paris in 1878 which was attended by 13 million people, covering 66 acres with the newly finished Statue of Liberty in its gardens before it was shipped to New York. But such displays left much of France untouched. The adoption of the telephone was halting. Installation was slow and the cost high, boosted by a special tax. Jules Grévy, president of the Republic for eight years, was reluctant to have one in the Élysée. Polite society saw the apparatus as an intrusion into private life. By 1900, only 30,000 telephones had been installed.

In leading cities, prosperous districts were separated from poor areas still lacking basic facilities. Industrial workers changed jobs frequently. Rural migrants moved about seeking temporary employment. In the countryside, many still lived on an unvarying subsistence diet; better produce from farms was sent to market. In some areas, bread was baked only a few times a year and hoarded jealously; in others, corn and oats were consumed instead. Wine was rarely drunk in such places; more common were cider, rotgut alcohol and *piquette* made by pouring water over the skins of grapes after the last pressing.[36]

Rural towns remained without electricity, running water or heating. Sewage poured into the nearest river. In the episcopal city of Rodez, in the Aveyron, a report in 1892 found filthy streets 'where many inhabitants empty chamber pots and kitchen waste'. In some places, pigs roamed in the streets and wolves came in from the countryside during winter. In the Causses by the Cévennes, a traveller in the 1890s came across patois-speaking locals wearing only sheepskins and living on rye bread made from husks, grain, bacon, cheese and potatoes, drinking only water and 'hearing mass only once a fortnight in summer and not at all during the long winter'. On the road outside the departmental capital of Mende in the Lozère, he noted 'wild-looking, weather-worn figures, men, women and girls keeping their half-dozen sheep or goats, patiently turning up the stony soil or getting some tiny crop'.[37]

There was little to do outside the home or workplace, adding to the humdrum nature of life. In rural homes, chickens shared the living space with people and, in the Landes, cattle poked their heads over half-doors to be fed by farmers sitting in their kitchens. In the high southern Auvergnat chestnut country – so called because they were the main ingredient used for flour – communities clung to the religious traditions of the pre-revolutionary era though worms ate away their holy relics and the lack of priests meant they worshipped and fasted under the guidance of family elders.[38]

Though food consumption grew significantly, adulteration was common with consequent dangers for health. Taking a bath or brushing teeth was an occasional exercise while washing clothes was a dilatory matter for many. Some doctors warned that one should bathe only once a fortnight and 'for pale and weak women once a month after their periods'. Others thought bathing aroused excessive sexual desire.

Water had to be carried up to city apartments. Some families rented a bath from time to time, the woman of the house using it first, then her husband and then the children. Marie Talabot, maid, mistress and then wife of the PLM railway engineer, was an exception in practising hydrotherapy in the bathroom of their Paris house, which was fitted with a substantial copper bath, a tub, a bidet and a large basin. But a mansion the Duke of Broglie bought in the capital in 1902 had no bathrooms or flush toilets, and one tap per floor, though the number of communal wash houses in Paris rose from 126 in 1860 to 422 in 1886.[39]

A drive for urban improvement set in at the end of the century but even Paris remained behind the times in some respects. Street hygiene was poor, though the heavily bearded Prefect of the Seine, Eugène Poubelle, appointed in 1883, ordered that home owners should have dustbins which were collected each morning by wagons whose presence was announced with a bugle call – the bins bear his name to this day. The lack of new building for the capital's proletariat to compensate for the destruction of old districts by Haussmann meant that many families lived in overcrowded tenements, subdivided by landlords to maximise revenue, and many bachelor workers inhabited single rooms in lodging houses often run by café owners – Paris housed a quarter-of-a-million renters by 1882. As rents rose steadily, poor people moved frequently.[40]

One result of the crowding at home and of solitary lives in lodgings was that people increased their use of cafés, whose numbers doubled in the 1880s and then enjoyed a boom at the turn of the century with 146,000 opening in the decades to 1914 – many going bankrupt after being set up by artisans whose businesses were hit by foreign and provincial competition. Some cafés offered entertainment, concerts and dancing to attract customers, plus political orators, one of whom was reckoned to have downed 65,820 glasses of absinthe over a twelve-year period. Others had rooms where clients could go with prostitutes – there were seventy-four such establishments in the northern industrial town of Roubaix in 1881, fifty or sixty in Grenoble and Brest, and more than 100 in Béziers. Lyons was estimated to house 5,000 unlicensed prostitutes in 1883 and Bordeaux 2,000. In the steel town of Briey, 325 café staff and 200 female companions of the owners were available for sex at the start of the twentieth century.[41]

Cholera outbreaks recurred, though medical advances reduced the death toll. Smallpox was a big killer before compulsory vaccination was introduced in 1893. Tuberculosis, also known as consumption, phthisis, or the 'white plague', was a major scourge, seen by some as a symbol for the moral disease of the times.

Despite the growth of transport links, the people of regions like Lower Brittany and the Basque country continued to exist in worlds of their own, unable to communicate with outsiders – a version of the parable of the prodigal son was rendered in eighty-eight different patois in 1879. Wages and revenue from land fell or stagnated. Agriculture was hit by a worldwide depression and price competition from the New World. Farm output stagnated between 1875 and 1894 and rose only slowly after that. The price of grain fell by between 19 and 34 per cent in the last quarter of the century and potatoes were down a third. Most holdings were still small family undertakings.

Despite the great industrial and financial barons with their powerful industrial federations, most enterprises remained small in size, many of them family owned. At the end of the century, 62 per cent of firms employed fewer than ten people. Piecework was common. Small firms lacked the resources to exploit the inventions of science. By the turn of the century, real wages had begun to fall, a trend continued to the outbreak of the Great War. Protectionism rolled back the Second Empire's free trade policies. Agriculture was shielded by tariffs while 10 to 30 per cent duties were put on manufactured imports in 1881. Savings went into safe, interest-bearing securities, the *rentes* bought by the middle classes, rather than into productive investments. More and more French money flowed abroad – by 1914, 36 per cent of investment was in foreign assets. Lamenting the 'langour' and 'inertia' affecting business, Alphonse de Rothschild noted that cash had never been more plentiful, and asked, 'Why is this money not utilised for the development of commerce and industry?'[42]

Telling history through its main political actors is not in fashion among historians; social movements and the tide of ideas are held to be more important. The evolution of the nation under the Third Republic certainly reached far beyond the political and administrative world; yet this was a time when leading politicians and their networks epitomised

France after the turbulence it had gone through since 1789. They might not be great figures in the main, but they gave the country a set of identifiable personalities whose imprint lasts to the present day – grand old men, solid provincials, clever lawyers, populists, technocrats, trimmers, rabble rousers, resounding orators and, behind them, the mass of parliamentary foot soldiers. They played in the same political space without organised parties to limit their freedom of manoeuvre. They ensured that the legislature, the base of their authority with its small circle of grandees, remained supreme, decrying executive rule as a betrayal of the traditions of the Revolution. Though some leading figures were urban politicians, more came from the provinces and retained their attachments there.

Most were not short of cash – half of the ministers who died before 1914 left assets of more than 100,000 francs and 29 per cent bequeathed a million or more. Money to meet expenses that considerably exceeded parliamentary pay came from an independent income, lobbyists, benefactors, seats on company boards or a wealthy wife. Some used their position to amass substantial wealth even if they took care not to parade it; the supposedly puritanic president Jules Grévy, from modest origins, left an estate of 7.5 million francs, boosted by investments suggested by his astute son-in-law, a parliamentary deputy, and was surrounded by a political and family clan that did at least as well.

With parliaments elected for fixed terms, there was constant jockeying among the senior occupants of the Palais Bourbon to form new combinations and gain office. Of 561 ministers under the Third Republic, 170 figured in three or more governments and a fifth of the 561 occupied half of all government posts during their careers. Retaining membership of the club was more important than principles declaimed at elections, which were then tucked away in the interests of expediency and personal advantage.[43]

The politicians who headed governments were not necessarily those who figure largest in the French pantheon and have streets and squares named after them. The post of prime minister did not formally exist before 1934 and the occupant of the Hôtel Matignon was usually one who could bring together sufficient support, rather than being a strong leader. Jules Armand Dufaure, of no political grouping, has left scant imprint on history, but was prime minister five times, more than any other head of government between 1871 and 1914. On the other hand, the aggressive tribune Georges Clemenceau had to wait till 1906 to lead a government, while the administration of the great republican Gambetta lasted for seventy-three days. Men like them were too individualist, too discomforting for a regime whose main appeal was summed up by its godfather, Adolphe Thiers, that it would head off 'a new revolution ... the most fearsome of all'.

11

THE MEN OF THE MIDDLE

Short of stature, strong of will, sharp of tongue and impatient of manner, Marie Joseph Louis Adolphe Thiers was the epitome of the self-made man, brimming with self-confidence and energy. From humble origins, he admired the Napoleon of the Consulate and detested Socialism. As well as his political career, he was a famous historian and chairman of the company that owned the large northern coalmine of Anzin. 'Monsieur Thiers', as he was always known, aroused strong antipathies. The left hated his record of repression stretching from the Commune back to the suppression of Parisian revolts under the July Monarchy – he 'charmed the French bourgeoisie for almost half a century, because he is the most consummate intellectual expression of their own class corruption,' wrote Marx.

The bile of his enemies apart, he hardly seemed the ideal first chief for a republic meant to incarnate understanding, reason and fraternity. Some of his close supporters were past their best and he concentrated too much authority in his own hands. But, now in his mid-seventies, Thiers had more experience than anybody else. His opposition to the war against Germany, his determination in suppressing the Commune and his force of character and self-confidence all strengthened his position – and, whatever the cost, he had concluded the negotiations with Bismarck. So he was the sole choice to take the provisional presidency of the still unformed Republic on 30 August 1871.[1]

As well as middle-class supporters, Thiers aimed to rally Orléanists and the rural backers of Napoleon III. A cartoon showed him mixing flasks of red and white wine in a barrel. He used his authority to impose a republican government on the divided royalist majority in the National Assembly. Dufaure, who had proposed him as provisional president, was chief minister, but was clearly subservient to the old warhorse. Another associate, the education minister, Jules Simon, who had been arrested by Gambetta when he agitated for peace with Germany, set out the Republic's great theme of universal free primary education.[2]

The standing of the provisional president was enhanced when, after raising large loans, France paid off its reparations to Germany and Berlin withdrew its occupation forces. The economy recovered from defeat. State revenue rose steadily while expenditure was controlled. The stupidity of the Legitimist pretender, Chambord, undermined the monarchists who did badly at by-elections that brought major gains for republicans.

This emboldened Thiers's opponents on the left, especially when their candidate at a legislative election in Paris easily defeated the foreign minister, the Count of Rémusat. Royalists were horrified by the vote, the Orléanist Duke of Broglie conjuring up the return of the Commune. Fearing that their parliamentary majority might be in danger, they forced out the republican speaker of the Assembly, Grévy. Their next target was Thiers. Broglie, a former foreign minister and the son of Louis-Philippe's chief minister, proposed a motion of no-confidence in the government, which was carried by a small majority, Bonapartists allying with the royalists for the occasion.

Thiers resigned, expecting to be called back. But the royalists had their own candidate, Marshal MacMahon, who did not hide his sympathies with them. The 65-year-old veteran of the Prussian war and the repression of the Commune visited Thiers who recorded him as having 'an air so kind, so friendly, so affectionate that he seemed to me to wish to protest by his attitude against the language of his friends'. But he was elected as the new provisional president with 99.7 per cent of the vote, and declared that 'with the aid of God, the devotion of the army and the support of honest people we are going to proceed to the re-establishment of the moral order.'

Fortunately for the republicans, he was a man of limited intelligence, as he showed when, after four ministries in as many years, he dissolved the Chamber with the approval of the Senate and appointed de Broglie as head of the government. The church strongly backed this 'republic of dukes', which aimed to restore the monarchy and impose MacMahon's 'moral order'. Though he had acted within his constitutional rights, the Marshal's action was widely portrayed as amounting to an attempted coup. To try to achieve victory at new elections, the de Broglie government indulged in the wholesale dismissal of unreliable officials and press censorship. Cafés where political discussions were held were closed. The president toured the country trying to drum up support. Thiers led the opposition but died of a stroke during the campaign, so it was Gambetta and Grévy who upset the plans of the right as republicans won 326 seats to 207 for their opponents. The episode, known by the date of MacMahon's action as *le 16 Mai*, ensured that the regime would be led by its legislative politicians not by the Élysée – that would have to wait for another eighty years.

'Power enlightened by reason'

As well as its strength in cities, rural voters rallied to the Republic. The Minister for Public Works, Freycinet, launched a big programme to stimulate the economy with a state takeover of the railways and the injection of 3 billion francs into new lines, plus a billion on developing canals; voters clamoured for more transport links and, in the words of one French historian, 'from now on, the government would ensure that the state of the railways would be its business.'[3]

Mayoral and Senate elections in 1878–9 brought further centre-left advances. MacMahon finally resigned; it was, said Gambetta, 'the first victory gained by the legislative power over the proceedings of personal power, and that without any revolution, riot or disturbance ... all due to democratic institutions.' The staunchly republican Jules Grévy replaced MacMahon at the Élysée in January 1879. 'Since yesterday, we are in the Republic,' Gambetta declared the following day.[4]

The new president had been detained in the imperial coup of 1851

and opposed the war of 1870. Hailing from the healthy rural department of the Jura, he struck a solid, reassuring note, a man of good
sense and moderation who could be depended on to defend republican values. He was known for his careful way with money; he was said
to save 900,000 francs from his annual salary of 1,200,000 and did not
light the fire even in the depths of winter; he kept his wealth accumulation through financial investments guided by his son-in-law a
close secret. During nearly nine years in office, he saw twelve governments succeed one another. As a believer in the power of the
legislature, he vowed that he would 'never enter into opposition
against the national will expressed by its constitutional organs'. Still,
he retained a strong sense of his own authority. Freycinet noted how,
while not intervening in ministerial discussions, he nodded if he
approved and, if he did not, would 'appear to awake from a light doze
just before the vote' to point to the hostility and dangers a measure
might arouse, concluding, 'But it is your business, gentlemen; it is
you who are responsible. Do as you please.' Ministers often took note
of his reservations.[5]

Grévy's refusal to entrust a government to Gambetta was the most
obvious evidence of his will. The bushy-bearded son of an Italian grocer
from Cahors, the leader of the government of national defence in 1870
was a winning speaker with a strong personality, known as the 'travelling
salesman' of the regime. He called himself ugly, had a glass eye and may
have suffered from syphilis. His party, the *Union Républicaine*, appealed
to the 'new social strata' of office workers, shopkeepers, small industrialists and farmers as he preached social equality and fraternity, aiming
to reconcile radicalism and republicanism by combining 'the strength
of numbers and the power enlightened by reason'. But he was too
strong-willed, too individualistic for the republican establishment – his
problem, Thiers had told him, was that he was a gambler and he was suspected of harbouring dictatorial ambitions.

Grévy preferred sober administrations led by politicians known as
Opportunists, their main platform being to push for educational laws
to replace church influence with that of the secular Republic, along
with colonial expansion. But he was leery of the challenge to his
authority by Ferry and so preferred lesser figures to head governments.

The new premier was William Henry Waddington, naturalised son of an Englishman and the only French minister to have rowed in the British university boat race (in a victorious Cambridge crew). A distinguished archaeologist, he had, as foreign minister, gained British agreement to the expansion of French influence to Tunisia. Backed by Gambetta, he lasted for nine months and was succeeded by the emollient, well-connected Freycinet who steered through an amnesty for the Communards, but lost the support of the left with a compromise course on religious matters. In October 1880, the only choice for Matignon was the leading Opportunist, Ferry, a man marked out by his self-belief and his support for the extension of secular education and colonial expansion.[6]

Raising the nation's status

Apart from economic advantage and missionary activity, the aim of colonial expansion was to raise the nation's status without coming into conflict with Germany, which isolated France by the League of Three Emperors created in 1873 with Russia and Austria-Hungary, followed by the Triple Alliance with Austria-Hungary and Italy. The expansion of French territory amounted to 3.5 million square miles between 1876 and the First World War. 'France is recovering its rank as a great power,' declared Gambetta. It set up its protectorate in Tunisia in 1881 and expanded steadily into North, West, and Central Africa. In Indochina, colonies established under Napoleon III were widened to Annam and Tonkin in central and northern Vietnam and to fresh concessions in China. Bismarck was favourable since he hoped colonial adventures would distract the French from seeking to regain Alsace and Lorraine while he locked in his alliance system in Europe, and there was even a temporary rapprochement between Paris and Berlin.

After his supporters scored strongly at elections in 1881, Grévy was finally forced to call on Gambetta to head a government. But hopes of forming a *Grand Ministère* of republican leaders failed, as other leading figures refused to work with him, fearing his ambitions, disliking his colonial approach, which included joining forces with Britain to dominate

Jules Ferry: Education and Empire

Ferry was not one to court popularity. He was described as being 'always certain of himself, affirmative and peremptory' with his precise dress and mutton-chop whiskers, pedantically superior as he exalted stern bourgeois values – notwithstanding his visits to a blonde seamstress on the rue Saint-Georges. He reconciled his attachment to republican virtues with a belief in spiritualism.

A lawyer and Freemason from the Vosges married to an heiress from Alsace, Ferry made his name criticising Haussmann's financial affairs and headed three governments, concentrating on educational reform and the extension of France's colonies.

Under him, free secular instruction was embedded as a core element in the regime. It was to replace religious teaching in instilling morality but also to act as a guard against revolution. He doubled the number of teachers. Still, standards of basic learning varied hugely and not only between employers and employed, civil servants and those they administered – fishermen were three times and peasants twice as illiterate as industrial workers.

Ferry believed that national and spiritual unity could be achieved only by a republic run by men as dedicated and rigorous as he, so he purged monarchist civil servants, judges and officers. He wanted to hold capitalism in check to balance the interests of the state and business and to avoid aggravating social tensions; he thought universal suffrage a useful force for conservatism since the politics of the peasantry would remain 'local, narrow and self-interested' for a long time.

A convinced colonialist, he oversaw expeditions in West and Central Africa and the occupation of Madagascar. Imperial generals became national heroes. The colonial lobby backed expansion for business reasons. The church welcomed the missionary opportunities and Ferry extolled France's civilising mission. But Clemenceau campaigned fiercely against colonialism as a diversion from the struggle with Germany and the Chamber refused credits for a joint punitive expedition with the British to Egypt in 1882. Still, Ferry pressed action in Vietnam against local forces backed by China with an attack on the old imperial capital of Hue, earning himself the nickname of 'Ferry the Tonkinois' but bringing about his undoing.

Though he lost office in 1885 and failed to win the presidency of the republic, he remained an influential figure as president of the Senate. He continued to attract hostility – a madman tried to shoot him and he suffered from the wounds until his death in 1893.

Egypt, and opposing him on policy for the railways. So his administration was made up mainly of young, inexperienced acolytes.

Buffeted by an economic slump, it lasted for ten weeks. In December 1882, grown stout and red-faced, Gambetta was wounded by an accidental revolver shot at home. It was not life threatening, but, on New Year's Eve, he died from stomach cancer. Five artist friends were at his bedside together with his Creole-Jewish mistress, a former courtesan with whom the politician exchanged more than a thousand letters celebrating the virtues of the heroes of antiquity and expressing disappointment at the times they lived in. He was forty-four.[7]

His place as the main irritant for the Opportunists was taken by Clemenceau at the head of the Radicals. The former mayor of Montmartre, who had moved his political base from Paris to the traditional left-wing southern bastion of the Var, urged France to focus on achieving revenge for the losses of 1870 rather than pursuing colonial ambitions. In a speech in May 1879, he made a vociferous call for the defence of liberties, secular education and tax reform, castigating the Opportunists as men lacking the authority needed to defend republican values. When Ferry denounced him as a scheming, impetuous, facile rabble-rouser, Clemenceau hit back by charging that public morality was worse than under the Second Empire.[8]

The return of Ferry in 1883 at the helm of a government which lasted for two years and two months marked a high point of this first stage of the Republic. But an economic slump brought down a big Catholic bank along with a stock market panic and noisy rallies by the unemployed. Agriculture was hit by falling international prices as exports rose from across the Atlantic. The phylloxera epidemic cut wine output by two-thirds between 1875 and 1889. To reverse falling investment on the railways, the government underwrote the operations of the big companies in return for a large share of any profits; with dividends and loan interest guaranteed, railway companies were a highly attractive investment, ensuring the continuing expansion of the network.

Still there was not enough money to pay for the public works programme as the government heeded middle-class voters and refrained from direct taxation, continuing to rely on loans. Work on digging a tunnel under the Channel was abandoned in 1883 amid British scares that the French might use it to stage an invasion. The agriculture minister, Méline, introduced tariffs on grain in 1882; with the creation of rural credit associations two years later this served to buttress the appeal of the Republic in previously reactionary or Bonapartist regions. There were other significant steps to popularise the regime. Along with the pursuit of lay education as the bulwark of the new order, the Marseillaise was adopted as the national anthem and 14 July fixed as the great annual holiday. Controls on the press, bars and cafés were relaxed.

But Clemenceau was out to make trouble. As a French expedition in Indochina ran into difficulties against local resistance backed by Chinese troops, he tabled a motion calling for the impeachment of Ferry for abandoning the true interests of the nation by pursuing colonial expansion. He warned Opportunist deputies that if they voted against him, they would find themselves opposed by Radical candidates in the next general election in the autumn of 1885.

Legislators from marginal seats took heed and the government lost the vote in the Chamber. Ferry walked out through a hostile mob threatening to lynch him. His fall was ironic since French troops were in the process of winning several victories in Vietnam, leading China to agree to withdraw its forces and the subsequent creation of an Indochinese Confederation of Cochin, Tonkin, Annam, Cambodia and Laos. But news of that success arrived too late to save Ferry and he was succeeded by Freycinet at the head of a 'concentration' government of Opportunists and Radicals.

The next election saw a significant shift in the balance between the Opportunists, who lost nearly half their seats, and the Radicals, who won almost as many. The two groups squabbled over policies and the formation of governments. Matignon changed hands five times in as many years against a background of economic woes. Construction, mining and metal industries slumped, unemployment rose, bread prices increased after a bad harvest, and the state deficit widened.[9]

Nor was the Republic's reputation enhanced by the revelation that Daniel Wilson, son of the English entrepreneur of the same name and Grévy's son-in-law, was selling honours and government contracts from an office in the Élysée. Having inherited half his father's fortune and launched successful enterprises himself, he did not need the money but enjoyed the influence he gained, working with high-level fixers such as a German-American manipulator of business and politics, Cornelius Herz. Though not implicated, the head of state resigned at the end of 1887. Ferry's unpopularity prevented him succeeding to the Élysée which went, instead, to Marie François Sadi Carnot, a former civil engineer, prefect and finance minister under Ferry and Freycinet, with a reputation for integrity and unusually impressive facial hair even for that heavily moustached and bearded era.

Ferry thought that the main danger to the Republic came from the left with Clemenceau as its standard bearer at the head of the Radicals. There was labour unrest and two Socialist parties emerged to press the rights of workers in a republic that operated mainly for the benefit of business and the professions. In fact, the threat that emerged at the end of the 1880s was in the shape of a dashing military man, Georges Ernest Jean-Marie Boulanger, adopted as a standard bearer by disparate groups ranging from royalists and extreme nationalists to Bonapartists and Blanquists who followed the teachings of their leader after his death in 1881.

Along with financial and ideological backing from the right, Boulanger won support in left-wing districts of Paris, though the Socialist Possibilitists and the Marxists opposed him. In his first parliamentary speech, he called for a dissolution and constitutional revision. But only a third of deputies backed him, nearly all royalists. He resigned his seat in protest. A coup seemed only a matter of time.

A big crowd shouting 'To the Élysée' surrounded the restaurant where Boulanger was dining, as his victory in an election in Paris became known. But he hesitated and support ebbed. The death in Brussels of his mistress, to whom he had been devoted, weakened his resolve. The canny interior minister, Ernest Constans, a former manufacturer of lavatory cisterns, spread a rumour that he was going to be arrested for conspiracy and treason. Boulanger fled abroad.

He was stripped of his parliamentary immunity, and the Senate sentenced him and two supporters to deportation and confinement. His backers did badly at elections and the 54-year-old general went to the

The Man on the Black Horse

Appointed war minister in 1886 at Clemenceau's urging, Georges Boulanger introduced popular reforms including allowing soldiers to grow beards. He fought duels and championed anti-German policies that earned him the nickname *Général Revanche* (General Revenge); he had military outposts built on the frontier at Belfort and his popularity soared after he confronted Berlin in a flare-up in 1887.

This brought him into conflict with the peace-minded government and he was sacked. But he got 100,000 votes in a by-election and, when the administration sent him a safe distance away to the garrison in Clermont-Ferrand, ten thousand people tried to stop the train leaving Paris from the Gare de Lyon, plastering it with posters declaring *Il reviendra* (He will return).

Boulanger launched his own movement, gaining backing from conservatives including the rich and generous Duchess of Uzès, a feminist and France's first registered woman car driver; the maverick politician-newspaperman Henri de Rochefort; and the ultra-nationalist, Paul Déroulède, who led the *Ligue des Patriotes* (League of Patriots). He met the Bonapartist heir, and got tacit backing from the Orléanist Count of Paris while the regime suffered from the scandal over the sale of honours and government contracts by Grévy's son-in-law.

Though expelled from the army, he was elected to parliament in a series of by-elections. With his swirling moustache, he became a symbolic figure on his black horse, cheered by crowds. Some 370 songs were written to praise him. His name was used to sell soap, cheese, toys and an aperitif 'containing no German ingredients, putting fire in the belly'.[10]

grave of his mistress Madame de Bonnemains in Brussels where he shot himself in the head in September 1891. He was buried in the same tomb as her. For all the alarm he caused, he was a deeply flawed figure with little political sense. 'He died as he lived: a second lieutenant,' was the verdict of his former backer, Clemenceau.

Though the threat from Boulanger proved short-lived, it showed the range of opposition to the Republic. These opponents were unable to form a united front, but they – and others who knew better than to rally to the general's standard – represented a continuing source of instability in the seemingly solid regime as different currents came into play on all sides. With the encouragement of the liberal-minded Pope Leo XIII, progressive Catholics sought to bring their religion into line with modern thinking to seek reconciliation with the Republic and evolve a political movement on the lines of the British Conservatives. They were soon disappointed. Given their core anticlericalism, Opportunists were not interested in cooperation while rigorous Catholics rejected the idea of reconciliation with the regime – nuns prayed that the Pope would see the light and recant from his dangerous views.

On the socialist left, the Possibilitists, under Brousse, were at odds with Guesde's Marxist *Parti Ouvrier*, which led the trade union movement and was particularly strong in the north-east industrial region. A series of strikes was met with repression – nine people were killed and thirty wounded, including children, when police fired on May Day marchers calling for an eight-hour day in the wool town of Fourmies.

A flare-up of violence from another quarter began after anarchists exchanged shots with police during a May Day demonstration in Paris in 1891. When they were sentenced to jail, an armed robber and accordionist, François-Claudius Ravachol, set off bombs in the homes of the judges. He was betrayed to police and arrested – the restaurant where the informer worked was bombed the day before he went on trial. A celebrated Italian criminologist of the day, Cesare Lombroso, judged that he had the traits of a born criminal – an asymmetrical face, abnormally large eyebrows and an enormous lower jaw, and that he, like most anarchists, was mentally afflicted.[11]

Ravachol was sentenced to life imprisonment and, at a second trial, found guilty of three murders and sent to the guillotine. He became a symbol of revolt and the subject of popular songs; a supporter threw a bomb into the Chamber of Deputies – it injured a deputy. Another bomb, directed by the son of a Communard into the Gare Saint-Lazare hotel, killed one person and wounded twenty. Then, an Italian anarchist fatally stabbed President Sadi Carnot who had rejected a number of clemency appeals on behalf of other anarchists.

Jean Casimir-Perier, president of the Chamber of Deputies, succeeded him, but stepped down after seven months saying he was fed up with being ignored by ministers. The Élysée went to a former follower of Gambetta, Félix Faure, a fine figure of a man made for ceremonial occasions. However, his term was cut short in 1899 by a fatal attack of apoplexy while he and his mistress were making love in the palace. His successor, Émile Loubet, a forceful orator and former interior minister, was the first president to serve his full term to 1906.

As the wave of anarchist violence subsided both from loss of momentum and under the impact of harsh legislation, the legal approach gained strength on the left. There was a degree of progressive legislation – the daily working time of women, and children under eighteen, was limited to eleven hours and children under thirteen were not to work at all unless they had a primary education certificate. The statutory right to one day's weekly rest was established. In practice, these laws were poorly enforced and there were still plenty of reasons for militancy, which led to the development of syndicalism to assert workers' rights through direct action, as advocated by its prophet Georges Sorel.

In the southern mining centre of Carmaux, striking workers won control of the mayor's office after a long confrontation ended with surrender by the mining company; the left-winger, Jean Jaurès, was elected deputy there in 1893. He was one of forty-nine socialists of various stripes returned to the Chamber that year; others included Guesde, René Viviani, elected in Paris, and the lawyer Alexandre Millerand who championed a reformist approach through electoral and trade union work. Two years later, the *Confédération Générale du Travail* (CGT) was set up as an umbrella organisation to coordinate labour action.

Generational change

The large majority won by its supporters at the 1893 election confirmed that the Republic was safe. But it also brought a generational
change as nearly 200 new deputies entered the Chamber. There was
much talk of social and tax reform – though vested interests and the
Senate continued to oppose such a measure, the number of deputies
supporting the introduction of income tax and a social security system
steadily rose. Younger legislators, such as Raymond Poincaré, saw
change as necessary to stave off further progress by the left. Their
hopes were boosted by the appointment as head of the government of
Léon Bourgeois, the son of a watchmaker who had become prefect of
the Paris police and minister of education and then of the interior. He
subscribed to the doctrine of 'solidarism' which held that society as a
whole should work together and that the well-off should help those less
prosperous – its motto was 'Every man his neighbour's debtor'. Loubet
hailed it as a 'higher law', which was 'the great common inspiration'
while Millerand saw in it 'the secret for the material and moral
grandeur of societies'.[12]

Bourgeois was not a socialist and stressed the role of the individual
and individual development. But his was the most left leaning of governments to date. It used subsidies and legal protection to encourage
mutual assistance societies, which attracted more than a million new
members. Bourgeois also proposed a tax of 1–5 per cent on those earning more than 2,500 francs a year. This aroused opposition centred in
departmental councils and the Senate. The economist Paul Leroy-
Beaulieu warned that it would 'poison the whole life of a democracy
[with] a struggle to the death between the treasury and the taxpayers'. As
Charles Péguy noted, non-payment of taxes was the 'dream of every
Frenchman'.[13]

The upper house provoked the fall of the Bourgeois government
after six months by rejecting credits for a military expedition to
Madagascar. Its successor, headed by the political adroit tariff champion
Méline, lasted for two years. The prime minister took a relaxed attitude
to the Catholic church and celebrated France's international status with
a visit to Paris by the Tsar, which attracted a million spectators and was

commemorated by the Pont Alexandre-III over the Seine, a single span feat of engineering adorned with thirty-two huge three-branched lamp posts and four monumental columns with classical statues attached. There were social reforms, such as the establishment of industrial accident compensation. Socialists did well at municipal elections. But the national tone remained conservative and the new threat to the regime was to come from a particularly potent mixture of radical anti-republicanism and racism that split France apart.

12

FROM THE AFFAIR TO WAR

A new form of right-wing activity emerged from the Boulanger legacy: an anti-establishment, anti-capitalist and anti-Semitic movement which one of its backers, the writer Maurice Barrès, called 'national socialism'. Its appearance coincided with fresh strain for the republican consensus from two great end-of-century scandals – the first over the scheme by the iconic Ferdinand de Lesseps to build a canal at Panama, followed by the affair of the alleged German spy, Captain Alfred Dreyfus.

Nobody was more intent on tearing down the republican façade and those he saw as its degenerate agents than the black-bearded, wild-haired journalist and author, Édouard Drumont, whose book *La France Juive* (*Jewish France*) advocated excluding Jews from society. The fact that Dreyfus and three of the Panama money-men were Jewish was manna from heaven to him. Founder of the Anti-Semitic League, he launched a newspaper, *La Libre Parole* (*Free Speech*), to propagate his virulence, drawing on a seam of long-standing prejudice. That paragon of the Enlightenment, Voltaire, had written of the Jew, 'You have surpassed all nations in impertinent fables, in bad conduct and in barbarism. You deserve to be punished, for that is your destiny.' Some Romantics abhorred Jews, epitomised by the Rothschilds, and attacked what Gautier called the 'fever for gold' and the 'religion of money'. Michelet condemned the July Monarchy as 'the reign of gold, of the Jew'. Proudhon wrote that 'the Jew is the enemy of humanity, this race must be sent back to Asia or exterminated.'[1]

The Jewish question

France's Jewish community had more than doubled since the start of the Third Republic because of immigration from Alsace after the defeat of 1870 – Dreyfus among them – and the larger influx of refugees flee-ing pogroms in Eastern Europe. But, at around 50,000, it represented well under 1 per cent of the population. Jews kept a low profile and melded into bourgeois society. Looking back on the Dreyfus affair, Léon Blum wondered whether the prim, proper, eminently bourgeois captain would have been a *Dreyfusard* or would have kept his head down and avoided trouble if he had not been the central figure in his own tragedy. Péguy noted that 'the anti-Semites know nothing about Jews'.

That only made it easier for Drumont and his ilk to appeal to those who sought a scapegoat for everyday concerns – anti-Semitism pros-pered in areas suffering from agricultural depression, social upheavals and decline in regional identity and among those who felt they lost out under the bourgeois Republic. Nobody was better at catering to such fears than the editor of *La Libre Parole*, a Catholic devotee from an earlier age who was also deeply superstitious and believed in palm-istry.[2] His newspaper, with an estimated daily circulation of 200,000 copies in 1892, was augmented by similarly anti-Semitic journals such as *L'Éclair, Le Petit Journal, La Patrie, L'Intransigeant,* and the Assumptionist *La Croix* which pursued a holy war against the Republic and the Jews. At the election of 1898, the hard right won nineteen seats, including four anti-Semites elected from Algeria, Drumont among them; in 1902 their strength rose to fifty-nine.

Drumont played a big role in unmasking the very real scandal of the Panama project. The Suez Canal had made a national hero of the 'Great Engineer' Ferdinand de Lesseps. Some 800,000 people poured 1.8 bil-lion gold francs into his second venture which financiers exploited for profit in a series of opaque manoeuvres. However, his plan was com-pletely impractical since it did not include the locks needed to drive the waterway through difficult terrain. Progress was slow and 25,000 workers, mainly from the Caribbean, died of disease and poor conditions. But de Lesseps continued to present a confident face as he sold bonds to raise cash, including one bond issue approved by parliament and linked to a lottery. He enlisted another eminent figure, Gustave Eiffel, to design the locks he finally admitted were necessary on the canal.

But, in 1892, the Panama company went bust. The main banker involved, Baron de Reinach, who was Jewish, committed suicide. The principal fixer, Cornelius Herz, also Jewish, fled to England as did the Jewish bagman. De Lesseps and his son were convicted of financial infringements; the son went to jail, the father, protected by his Grand Sash of the Legion of Honour, was left to die in his country home. Enemies of the Republic leaped on the affair as an example of the legerdemain of high finance in cahoots with corrupt politicians to plunder the savings of the ordinary French people. It became known that 104 members of parliament, including an array of former ministers, had taken bribes to back the lottery bill. The nationalist leader Paul Déroulède accused Clemenceau of being an associate of Herz, which he was. The two politicians fought a duel in which neither was hurt, but Clemenceau was defeated in the legislative election of 1893.[3]

The following year, Dreyfus, a 35-year-old artillery officer, was found guilty of having passed information about the firing mechanism of French artillery to the German embassy in Paris. His trial, in a closed military court, was farcical – when the lack of evidence against him became obvious, his accusers in the army high command submitted a secret dossier they claimed showed his guilt. Dreyfus was duly sentenced to exile in prison and military degradation. The death penalty for political crimes had been abolished in 1848 and some on the left objected that Dreyfus had escaped with his life – 'A soldier has been sentenced to death and executed for throwing a button in the face of his corporal. So why leave this miserable traitor alive?' the Socialist Jean Jaurès asked.

Newspapers devoted front pages to depictions of the degradation ceremony in the courtyard of the military school in Paris in which a Republican guardsman tore the badges, stripes and cuffs from Dreyfus's jacket while the accused raised his arms and cried out, 'Innocent, Innocent! Vive la France! Long live the Army!' An adjutant broke his sword on his knee and marched the prisoner slowly in front of his former companions. Dreyfus was deported to Devil's Island in French Guiana.

Most people forgot about the affair, but his family kept up a campaign to prove Dreyfus's innocence and inquiries by a new head of military intelligence, Georges Picquart, pointed to forgeries in the evidence at the trial. The writer and polemicist, Bernard Lazare, launched a campaign, which gained momentum when Zola wrote his celebrated polemic under the headline '*J'accuse*' in Clemenceau's newspaper, *L'Aurore*. This appeared at the start of 1898 after the acquittal of an officer who had, in fact, betrayed secrets to the Germans and then participated in mounting the case against Dreyfus. Zola was sentenced to a year in jail and fined for having defamed the army. His trial led to an upsurge of pro-republican feeling, especially among progressive intellectuals. The prominent writers, Octave Mirbeau and Anatole France, advocated a new trial, while Jaurès and his fellow Socialist, Léon Blum, became convinced there had been a miscarriage of justice. A friend of Oscar Wilde, Carlos Blacker, discovered from the Italian military attaché the identity of the real spy, Major Ferdinand Walsin-Esterhazy – Blacker's plan to trap him was undone when the Irish writer divulged his discovery to reporter friends, unleashing a campaign by the anti-Dreyfusards and forcing Blacker to flee the country.[4]

As a result of the Socialist switch from seeing Dreyfus as a privileged traitor spared execution to regarding him as a victim of the military establishment, anti-Semitism became a political preserve of the right. Maurras published a eulogy of the officer, Colonel Henry, who had forged documents against Dreyfus calling him a 'heroic servant of the great interests of the State'. *La Libre Parole* launched a subscription to erect a monument to him; 14,000 people, including fifty-three members of parliament, contributed 131,000 francs. Social groups and households were divided – a celebrated drawing by the cartoonist Caran d'Ache. There was a strongly anti-Dreyfus group among the artists of the day including Cézanne, Renoir, Rodin and the anti-Semitic Degas were anti-Dreyfusards; their differences over the affair contributed to the end of the once close relationship between the former and Zola – though the latter's unsparing portrait in a novel of a shambolic painter who resembled his fellow southerner and Cézanne's marriage to his long-time companion who was considered socially unacceptable by the writer's wife were probably bigger reasons.

The head of government, Jules Méline tried to draw a veil over the matter, telling the Chamber of Deputies, 'There is no Dreyfus affair.'

The election of 1898 was dominated by agriculture, taxes, pensions and religious teaching in schools, as the victorious Méline promised 'neither reaction nor revolution'. There were Dreyfus-linked riots in thirty cities and towns. Protestants as well as Jews were targets since extremists like Drumont considered them almost as suspect.

President Loubet was known to favour a new trial, and the hard right, led by Déroulède's League of Patriots and the Anti-Semitic League, tried to use the state funeral of his predecessor, Félix Faure, to stage a coup. Déroulède deluded himself that he had army support but, when he grabbed the bridle of the horse of the general commanding the funeral escort with the cry 'To the Élysée!', the soldier rode back to his barracks, the politician trotting alongside him. Déroulède insisted on being tried for high treason, and exulted when he was acquitted.

The Marquis de Dion, the motor show founder, dented Loubet's top hat with a blow from his walking stick at the Auteuil racecourse – when the main sports newspaper, *Le Vélo*, criticised the nobleman's action, anti-Dreyfusards, including Édouard Michelin, founded a rival publication, *L'Auto-Vélo*. A demonstration to support the Republic attracted 100,000. The former Gambettist, René Waldeck-Rousseau, formed a government to defend the regime.

A successful commercial law barrister who lived in high style with a rich wife, he wanted to move towards a British system of big, organised political parties, and to get more businessmen and industrialists into the Chamber. Political stability round a broad conservative movement was, he believed, needed to head off a clash between workers and employers and to counter stagnant economic conditions. He appointed as commerce minister the Socialist, Millerand, who was promptly expelled from his party; he created a labour section of his ministry that pushed reforms, including reducing the working day. However, Waldeck-Rousseau was unable to organise a broad political movement or to get business figures to commit to politics, and his efforts towards religious compromise were undercut when secular enthusiasts sharpened his proposals so much that the church refused to cooperate.[5]

In February 1899, Waldeck-Rousseau denounced a 'moral conspiracy' in the Dreyfus affair. The Supreme Court referred the case to a military court in Rennes. Dreyfus sailed back to France in a locked cabin. The Breton capital was in a state of siege as his trial opened; the main defence lawyer, Fernand Labori, was shot in the back as he walked to court. In Paris, police went after a leader of the Anti-Semitic League, Jules Guérin. He held out for twenty-three days with armed supporters in a barricaded house in the rue de Chabrol; captured, he got ten years in jail and the League was outlawed.

The military command stuck to its story and, in September 1899, by a vote of five judges to two, the court found Dreyfus guilty of treason 'with extenuating circumstances'. He was sentenced to ten years' imprisonment and further degradation. Waldeck-Rousseau offered a pardon if he would accept his guilt. Dreyfus accepted and was released. In November, the prime minister tabled an amnesty excluding only Dreyfus himself. This indemnified Zola and Picquart, whose doubts about the case had earned him temporary exile to North Africa, but protected the true culprits.

It was a thoroughly unsatisfactory outcome to a major miscarriage of justice. The weaknesses of the legal system had been shown up, together with the tenacity of the military establishment, which lived a life of its own and was seen by some republicans as a hostile force. In 1905, the Attorney General called for the conviction to be quashed and denounced the army. The following year, the Supreme Court unanimously cancelled the judgment and declared 'the end of the rehabilitation of Captain Dreyfus' since 'in the final analysis of the accusation against Dreyfus nothing remains standing'. He was reinstated as a cavalry major but his promotion was blocked and he resigned from the military. In 1908, during the transfer of Zola's ashes to the Panthéon, a right-wing extremist wounded him with two revolver shots – the attacker was acquitted at his trial, which set off anti-Semitic riots. During the First World War, Dreyfus returned to the military to head an artillery depot outside Paris before being posted to the battlefield of Verdun. Promoted to Officer of the Legion of Honour in 1919, he died in 1935, aged seventy-six.

Separation of church and state

Though the overall government majority increased at elections in 1902, Waldeck-Rousseau's own supporters won only a third of the seats taken by the republican group, which was united round support for secular education but little else. The extreme right made gains; a candidate elected in Paris declared himself 'an anti-Semitic republican' who demanded that 'the 150,000 Jews and their lackeys, the 25,000 Freemasons, stop oppressing and ruining 38 million French.' Waldeck was succeeded by the Radical Émile Combes, the epitome of a provincial politician, describing himself as 'short in stature, with a common face and a common appearance'. Stingy and small-minded, he never went to the theatre or to cafés and was a teetotaller – at banquets he drank red-coloured water. Under his government, which lasted from June 1902 to January 1905, the republicans solidified their grip on both the army and the church.

The war minister, General André, took the promotion process out of the hands of senior officers and handled it directly on political and religious considerations. He set Freemasons to spy on officers. The progress of devout Catholics was blocked. When this came to light, the government was weakened and military morale suffered. Religious tension rose under the new Pope, Pius X, a traditionalist who opposed compromise and worked to retain the advantages the church enjoyed under the Napoleonic Concordat, appointing conservative bishops and beatifying Joan of Arc, a symbol for the right.

Anti-clericals reacted by pushing through legislation removing the annual 40-million-franc subsidy to the church, requiring that parishes be run by local residents' associations and ordering that non-religious property bequeathed to the church should go to the poor. Priests were not allowed to criticise the government or the civil service. Laws on educational establishments were implemented more strictly.

Resistance from the faithful led to soldiers besieging a monastery near Tarascon in the south and clearing three convents in Brittany; sixty-four schools in the department of Finistère were closed by force and 12,000 people attacked a republican march in Quimper. In the Var, 2,000 people sacked a church and burned religious objects to protest at the way the local priest conducted the first communion for children. In the Ardèche, where resistance to anti-clericalism was at its highest, thousands demonstrated against the laws, urged on by the president of the Organisation of Young Catholics who criss-crossed the region on his bicycle. Ten police brigades were needed to restore order in Annonay; but the repression only resulted in a growth in religious devotion and the network of Catholic groups, including a sporting association with members from ten towns.[6]

In Montauban, the bishop, Monsignor Marty, organised religious processions even though they were banned and wrote in his episcopal bulletin that 'Catholics are not obliged to believe in universal suffrage and even have the excellent reasons to not believe in it at all.' In Marseilles, church groups backed by rich families mobilised, including a 10,000-strong women's organisation, and the combative Monsignor Andrieu denounced 'the victory of occult Judeo-Protestant and Masonic powers'.[7]

The Minister for Religions, the rising former Socialist Aristide Briand, was careful not to interfere with freedom of worship, but, by 1904, when a new law banned all teaching by members of religious orders, nearly 10,000 religious schools had shut, among them one which had operated for young ladies in the Hôtel Biron in Paris, enabling Rodin and other artists to move in. The Hôtel du Chatelet, the one-time Austrian embassy on the rue de Grenelle which had been given by Napoleon III to the Archbishopric of Paris to win church favour, reverted to the state and subsequently housed the Ministry for Social Affairs. Thousands of priests and nuns left France.

The following year, a law finally separated church and state. 'We have torn human consciences from the clutches of credulity,' the Socialist Viviani declared. 'With a magnificent gesture we have put out the lights of heaven and they will never be lighted again.' More prosaically, the church lost property worth hundreds of millions of francs and many village priests became nearly destitute.[8]

Combes's radicalism was not enough to maintain the backing of the left and he resigned, though he had not been defeated in the Chamber – he was honoured at a huge banquet as the father of the separation of church and state. Riots over religious policy brought down his successor, Maurice Rouvier, a protégé of Gambetta and a centre-left coalition under a low-key Radical, Jean Marie Ferdinand Sarrien, brought together a bevy of future premiers including Clemenceau, Poincaré, Briand, Gaston Doumergue and Louis Barthou.

As interior minister, Clemenceau reformed the police and, in the spring of 1906, sent 20,000 troops against strikers in the Pas-de-Calais region after a mining disaster that killed 1,099 people. He refused to allow public employees to join trade unions; when post office workers went on strike to claim the right to do so, he sacked 300. He declared a state of siege as the CGT organised a 200,000-strong May Day demonstration for an eight-hour working day, and arrested union leaders: 'Your method is disorder,' he told them. 'My duty is to preserve order.' His harsh reaction to syndicalism made the Radicals acceptable to business and the middle class. When the Sarrien ministry resigned in October 1906, the 65-year-old finally entered the Matignon.

Clemenceau's government included leading figures such as the finance minister Joseph Caillaux, Viviani at the interior, Briand in charge of education and religious affairs, and Georges Picquart from the Dreyfus affair as minister of war. It introduced social and labour reforms and nationalised the Western Railway – the company was in poor shape and the shareholders were overcompensated, but the Radicals earned political support in a part of the country where they had traditionally been weak.

The government faced a major crisis as wine growers in the south demanded subsidies to deal with low prices resulting from their overproduction after the recovery from the phylloxera epidemic and from cheap imports from Algeria, Italy and Spain. Workers whose wages were cut by the big producers and small growers who were being edged out of the market swelled big rallies; half-a-million people joined the biggest protest in Montpellier. Mayors and councils resigned in sympathy. Clemenceau despatched troops who fired on the demonstrators. The movement's main leader, a small wine grower called Marcelin Albert, took fright and fled to Paris where the prime minister spoke to him paternally, gave him his fare home and told him to call off the agitation, which he did.

Troops were also sent in to put down work stoppage by construction workers in the Paris suburbs; two of them were shot dead. A general strike was called after CGT leaders were again arrested but Clemenceau refused to budge. Abroad, he developed the *Entente Cordiale* with Britain, and reached a peaceful outcome in a confrontation with

Germany over Morocco. But, when the government was defeated in a debate on the navy in July 1909, it was time to step down and embark on a lengthy trip to Latin America. In his absence, his successor, Briand, continued his tough policies towards labour, reflecting the conservative social nature of the nation and an electoral system tilted towards rural voters. The Radicals might claim the heritage of the Revolution but they needed to win elections. Briand was, however, subtler than the Tiger – he dealt with a stoppage by 150,000 railway workers by having them conscripted as soldiers and sent back to work as troops of the Republic.

Rise of the hard right

But the political context was changing as the number of industrial workers topped 4 million, and CGT membership grew steadily. The socialists, unified in a single party, the SFIO, won more than a million votes and a hundred seats at the 1910 election, Jean Jaurès declaring that revolution meant not violence but the gradual transformation of capitalism into collectivism through social reform. Briand preached *apaisement* in place of strife to 'make all people love the republic'. But he fell in 1911 and, after a short interim administration, it was the turn of Joseph Caillaux, a clever, arrogant, elegantly dressed economics expert with a billiard-ball skull, monocle and precise gestures; an enthusiast for an income tax who was prone to consort with shady figures in business and journalism, his government lasted for seven months.

The political volatility was evident in a swing to the right in 1910 followed by a centre-left victory four years later. There were eleven governments between the summers of 1909 and 1914 and four in 1913 alone. 'Republican discipline' ensured that the regime was safe but covered such a variety of opinions – from Guesde and Jaurès to Waldeck-Rousseau, Poincaré and Caillaux – that coherence was impossible once victory had been declared in the battle with the church.

The safe ways of those in charge were challenged by the popular philosophy of Henri Bergson, based on *élan vital* (dynamic life force), which put a premium on action based on personal experience and feelings rather than reason. Nationalism fanned militarism and a cult of the

Le Tigre

Georges Benjamin Clemenceau came from the Vendée, still a poor region remote from Paris when he was born in 1841. Though the area had a long history of reaction and religious devotion, his father, a misanthropic, non-practising doctor, was known as an atheist and political activist, devoted to the cause of the Revolution. His son believed in social progress but thought it could best be achieved by aggression. A lonely figure after an acrimonious divorce and a skilled duellist, he defined his approach as: 'My home policy; I wage war. My foreign policy; I wage war. All the time I wage war.' He had 'one illusion – France – and one disillusion – mankind,' John Maynard Keynes wrote.[9]

In his late teens, he left the Vendée to study medicine in Paris and plunged into journalism and politics, but was imprisoned in 1862 for calling for a demonstration against the Second Empire. He went to New York to work as a doctor, writing for a Paris newspaper and teaching French and horseback riding at a Connecticut girls' school. In 1869, he married a student, Mary Eliza Plummer – they had three children before divorcing when he caught her with another man.

Returning to Paris after Napoleon III's fall, he became mayor of Montmartre but his attempt to mediate between the Commune and the government in Versailles led to him falling out with both Thiers and Ferry. Elected to the Chamber of Deputies in 1876, his cutting rhetoric, combativeness and energy made him leader of the Radicals. He was badly embarrassed by his association with the promoter Cornelius Herz in the Panama Affair, losing his parliamentary seat. But few were more active in defending Dreyfus – he wrote more than 650 articles on the subject and, as editor and proprietor of *l'Aurore*, published Zola's '*J'accuse*' article on the front page, claiming the headline was his.

The Tiger lived a comfortable life in the smart Paris district of Passy, dressed in English clothes and ordered his furniture from London. As he aged he grew tubby, but took great care of his health, visiting spas and exercising with gymnastics and horse riding. Elected senator for the Var (though he had earlier called for the suppression of the upper house), his radicalism ebbed and, as interior minister, he became known as 'France's first cop' with his new force of the *Brigades Mobiles* nicknamed *les Brigades du Tigre* after their founder's animal soubriquet.[10]

troops in their scarlet trousers, blue tunics and red-and-blue headgear. The leading military theorist, Colonel Grandmaison, extolled all-out offensive tactics to enable the infantry to sweep all before it, an approach that melded with growing enthusiasm for the army among patriotic politicians and the press.

Anti-republicanism fostered by the Panama, Dreyfus and Boulanger affairs gained a new vehicle in the Action Française movement led by Charles Maurras, a malevolent figure, deaf and solitary, an ardent anti-Semite, propounding 'integral nationalism' that put the country above everything else. For him, the 'anti-France' of Jews, Protestants, Freemasons and foreigners should be banished from a decentralised nation returning to its roots with the central government responsible only for foreign policy, the military, finance and justice. He considered Dreyfus's Jewishness sufficient evidence against him. His influence spread abroad, winning followers ranging from Francisco Franco to T. S. Eliot.

The movement's newspaper, *Action Française*, was edited by the clever, unscrupulous Léon Daudet, a pornographer whose journalistic skills gave its philosophy coherence for a wider public. Its appeal was sharpened by the crash of a big Catholic bank, the Union Générale, which it blamed on the machinations of Jews and Protestants.

Other members of this hard right included the popular historian Jacques Bainville and Maurice Barrès, the one-time Symbolist and royalist who exalted a mixture of 'Nationalism, Protectionism and Socialism'. The extremely rich Countess of Loynes, a faded sixty-something who held a salon in her mansion on the Champs-Élysées, contributed 100,000 gold francs to Action Française while her lover, the nationalist critic and member of the French Academy, Jules Lemaître, headed a League for the French Fatherland. The Archbishop of Lyons, whose family was ruined by the Union Générale collapse, preached against Jews and Protestants.

Action Française had muscle in the form of the *Camelots du Roi*, street fighters whose attacks on opponents gave an impression of greater strength than the movement actually had. It attracted royalists and right-wing Catholics emboldened by Pius X's tough line against reconciliation with the Republic. However, its extremism led the pretender to the throne to disavow it in 1910 and French bishops gave information against it to Rome, leading to it being added to the index of prohibited bodies – though the Pope showed his true feelings by ordering that this should be kept secret.

A less serious but spectacular challenge to law and order came from a revival of violent anarchism in the shape of the *Bande à Bonnot* (Bonnot Gang), a thirty-strong group of desperados, who used stolen cars and revolving rifles to rob banks and private homes in France and Belgium in 1911 and 1912. Jules Bonnot, who provided the group's name, was finally caught after a shootout in a Paris suburban garage. It took 300 police and 800 soldiers to capture two of his associates in another suburban siege in Nogent-sur-Marne. Most of those caught were guillotined.

Amid the turbulence, the reasonable, rational right found a standard bearer in the lawyer turned politician Raymond Poincaré, who succeeded Caillaux in January 1912. A cold advocate of stability and conservative bourgeois values, he was committed to the Republic and was deeply anti-clerical, but was a bête noire for the Radicals as head of the Democratic Republican Alliance, which he founded in 1902. He operated as an aloof technocrat, in contrast to the more supple, humane Briand, the other perennial presence of the first two decades of the twentieth century. Their difference was immediately apparent, Poincaré trim and spade-bearded, Briand thickset and with a luxuriant moustache. The former knew everything and understood nothing, a British diplomat remarked, while the latter knew nothing and understood everything.[11]

World power

Bismarck's pan-European system of alliances had isolated France, leaving it bemused by his diplomacy in which, an ambassador noted, 'the alternation of blows and caresses is ... one of the characteristics of the method of dressage applied by Prince Bismarck to governments he wants to yoke to his policies.' The German banker, Bleichröder, called by Ferry 'the old crocodile', acted as a go-between who expressed the Chancellor's 'friendly sentiments for France' to the Quai d'Orsay, but the alliance system woven by Berlin kept Paris in the box to which it had been consigned by the defeat of 1870.[12]

On the other hand, Bismarck was only too happy for the French to pursue colonial aims, especially since this might lead to tension with its obvious ally, Britain, as London remained generally suspicious of its cross-Channel neighbour; a feeling which was mutual given the memory of eighteenth-century confrontations, the Napoleonic Wars and the way that Britain's free-trading global expansion sat ill with France's protectionist mindset. The French empire was enlarged from Senegal and the Ivory Coast to take in Chad, French Congo, Dahomey, Gabon, French Guinea, Madagascar, Mauritania, Mauritius, Niger, French Sudan and Upper Volta, plus lands in Central Africa, Nigeria and Gambia. Islands in the Indian Ocean and the South Pacific were added, including New Caledonia and French Polynesia. French citizenship was granted in Guadeloupe, Martinique, Guyanne and Réunion and parts of Senegal together with the right to elect representatives to the French Chamber of Deputies, most of whom were white settlers. Elsewhere, there was strict separation between indigenous people and the population of European extraction.[13]

Clashes with other European powers became inevitable, the most dramatic with Britain in 1898, when 132 French soldiers who had journeyed for fourteen months eastwards from Brazzaville in the Congo met a British force at the isolated fort of Fashoda on the White Nile in Sudan. The British, under Herbert Kitchener, had just defeated the forces of the Mahdi at the Battle of Omdurman and were reconquering the Sudan in the name of the Egyptian Khedive. Each side claimed Fashoda but agreed not to fight while they waited for their governments to sort things out. Britain's naval superiority on the scene forced Paris to order a retreat, followed by an agreement to settle the frontiers of the two African empires. It was an eminently sensible outcome but French nationalists were inflamed – Charles de Gaulle, busy playing with his tin soldiers at wars France always won, remembered it as the most traumatic moment of his childhood.

The failure of Bismarck's successor Leo von Caprivi and the Kaiser to renew the treaty with St Petersburg opened the door to the flowering of Franco-Russian relations in reaction to growing German power.

A defensive treaty was signed in 1894 after von Caprivi had allowed Germany's agreement with St Petersburg to lapse. The Tsar visited Paris. Russophilia flourished and 500 million francs of French capital flowed eastwards each year to earn interest from funding the modernisation of the new ally. The French were particularly keen on the development of railways, which would enable the Tsarist forces to move fast in the event of war, obliging Germany to keep large numbers of troops on the eastern frontier. Paris and St Petersburg opened naval talks. Politicians like Joseph Caillaux who urged better relations with Berlin were suspect – he was forced to resign as head of the government in 1912 after it was disclosed that he had held secret talks with Berlin.

In this regime of frequently changing governments, the short, dark-haired Théophile Delcassé represented extraordinary continuity at the foreign ministry on the Quai d'Orsay which he occupied from 1898 to 1906. A pince-nez-wearing native of the out-of-the-way Pyrenean *département* of the Ariège, he set out to win British friendship to go alongside the Russian alliance, championing the pacific outcome of the Fashoda crisis and helped by British alarm at Germany's naval build-up and the negative impact of Kaiser Wilhelm's bombast in a series of crises on Morocco – Britain, Russia, Italy, Spain and the United States backed France's quasi-colonial sway over the North African territory against German efforts to ensure its independence.

Though Italy was linked to Germany and Austro-Hungary in the Triple Alliance, France signed a secret agreement that gave it a free hand in Libya and reached an accord with Spain to fix the boundaries of the two nations' colonial possessions. The development of closer relations with Britain led to an exchange of visits by Edward VII and the signing of the *Entente Cordiale* in 1904 with its agreement on spheres of influence in North Africa, the settlement of conflicting colonial claims and secret military clauses. No wonder that the Kaiser called the apparently insignificant workaholic at the Quai 'the most dangerous man for Germany in France'.

The realignment was taken further by an Anglo-Russian agreement in 1907 and a visit to London by the French president. The *Exposition*

Universelle of 1900 in Paris underlined France's international status; visited by 50 million people, it covered 112 hectares in the centre of the capital which was proclaimed to be 'the showcase of the world'. It displayed all the trappings of modernity – film shows, tinned soup, Art Nouveau designs, the largest telescope ever seen and a 106-metre high Ferris wheel that could accommodate 1,600 people at a time in cabins modelled like railway carriages. A seventy-metre high Palace of Electricity was fitted with 5,000 multi-coloured incandescent lamps. There was a moving platform along the Quai d'Orsay and a diesel engine running on peanut oil. In a gesture to France's ally, the Grand Prix de Champagne went to a Russian sparkling wine. A banquet was thrown by President Loubet for the country's 20,777 mayors; they sat at 606 tables to eat food prepared in eleven kitchens, with the meal coordinated by telephone. To coincide with the exhibition, the first Olympic Games outside Greece were held in Paris, though it was a low-key affair with winners given 100 francs to buy their own medals. The Métro underground railway between the Porte Maillot and the Porte de Vincennes opened three months later, the exterior of its stations decorated in the trademark Art Nouveau style of Hector Guimard.

By 1906, Delcassé was considered to have spent too long at the Quai and was pushed to resign. But Poincaré took up the baton of the Russian alliance, first as both prime minister and foreign minister in his government of 1912 and then as president from 1913, when he used the position to dominate foreign policy. Clemenceau, who returned to the fray after a lengthy trip to South America and a prostate operation, insisted on the need to strengthen France's power. Military service, cut to two years in 1905, was extended back to three years, plus seven in the territorial army and seven more in the reserves.

Caillaux, the outstanding political expert on financial matters and president of the Radical Socialists, led opposition to this. Apart from wishing to avoid conflict with Germany, he did not see how a build-up would be funded. Though the legislation on military service was passed, his campaign helped to bring down the government in the autumn of 1913 and he became finance minister and the dominant figure in the next administration, headed by the Radical Gaston Doumergue. His campaign for an income tax and other socially progressive policies alarmed the right. The main conservative newspaper, *Le Figaro*, published letters Caillaux sent to his future second wife while still in his first marriage. She shot the editor dead in his office. Her husband resigned from the government – his wife was tried but acquitted on the grounds that the murder had been a *crime passionnel*.

Though the principal advocate of friendship with Berlin had been unseated, the parliamentary majority was far from bellicose. The right lost half its seats at the 1914 election, ending up with only seventy-four. In bowler hat and frock coat, Jaurès addressed huge meetings with his anti-militarist discourse. Insisting that war was justified only in self-defence, he negotiated with Caillaux about a possible coalition. Viviani, who had gravitated from the Socialists to the centre, moved into the Matignon, undertaking not to pursue immediate reversal of the three-year military law in return for the lifting of the Senate's veto on income tax.

That settled, Poincaré and the prime minister set out in mid-July 1914 to visit St Petersburg, where Delcassé had become ambassador. There had been accommodation with Berlin over Morocco but the alliances with London and St Petersburg were at the heart of French foreign policy. Poincaré had been to Britain the previous summer and King George V and Queen Mary went to Paris in April 1914 for the tenth anniversary of the *Entente Cordiale*. Tsar Nicholas sent a message associating himself with the celebration.

An unavoidable conflict

Poincaré and Viviani did not consider the assassination of the Austrian Archduke Franz Ferdinand and his wife in Sarajevo at the end of June a reason to put off their Russian trip. They landed back in France the day after Austria-Hungary delivered its ultimatum to Belgrade. Paris regarded this as an unacceptable breach of Serbia's sovereignty and evidence of the imminent danger of aggressive moves by Berlin, which had assured Vienna its army was ready for whatever might transpire. French backing could only encourage Russia's determination to assert itself on behalf of the Serbs. The prime minister declined to give a straight reply to a German request as to what France would do if war erupted between Germany and Russia. There was no widespread agitation for war though a nationalist assassinated Jaurès in a Paris café.

Just as Viviani had equivocated with Berlin, so Britain did not give a clear answer when asked if it would intervene were Germany to attack France. French troops were reinforced on the north-eastern frontier but they were kept ten kilometres from the border to avoid accidental incidents. On 1 August, general mobilisation was declared.

The arguments about responsibility for the start of the Great War continue to this day. France, in alliance with Britain and Russia to check Germany and sort out colonial squabbles, did nothing to restrain its ally in the east and welcomed action in the Balkans which it hoped would restrain the Germans in the west. Its nightmare was that it would be left alone to fight the Reich. Successive governments in Paris were comforted by the *Entente Cordiale* and secret talks with the British at the level of chiefs of staff which began in 1906 and led to the belief that, if war broke out, Britain was sure to abandon its long policy of keeping out of continental entanglements and, acting as the balancer of power, would intervene if war broke out, reducing the need for France to build up its forces.[14]

The die was cast when Germany demanded the right of passage through Belgium and, the next day, moved troops into Luxembourg to start incursions across the French border. On 3 August, Berlin declared war in response to supposed attacks from France – in fact, French soldiers were ordered not to pursue the attackers back across the border. If the Germans had not invaded Belgium or moved only through the Ardennes towards France, the Poincaré-Viviani administration might have found that its assumptions did not play out as expected. But the invasion of a neutral state swung the British cabinet and ensured that Paris was not alone in the west with the Socialists accepting that combat was necessary to defend the nation. Overall, the situation appeared quite clear to the French at the time, bolstered by pride in their army, the desire for revenge for 1870 and the conviction that Berlin alone was the aggressor, the moves of the Russian ally in the east overlooked at the time and the idea of a pre-emptive strike into Belgium rejected.

The belated French military build-up may have led the General Staff in Berlin to conclude that it was running out of time for the quick win the west needed under its Schlieffen Plan for a two-front war. But, though the French commander, Joseph Joffre, was developing a more offensive strategy based on the Russian alliance and planned to 'proceed to battle with all my forces', it is difficult to imagine France or Britain attacking Germany in the way the Kaiser's armies did to their western foe.

The only course Viviani and the president could have taken to avoid being plunged into the conflict would have been to renege on the alliance with St Petersburg, which would have meant accepting German preponderance on the continent. Poincaré argued that dropping the existing alliances to keep the peace would have 'led to the definitive subordination of France, her economic and moral subjugation, her inevitable decadence'. He and his colleagues did not see this as a war of choice but a conflict into which France had been pitched willy-nilly. There was little the politicians in Paris could do in the face of Austria-Hungary's determination to destroy Serbia after the assassination at Sarajevo in 1914, Germany's decision to back Vienna and Russia's impatience to mobilise in defence of the Slav cause and its own ambitions. The government was caught in a momentum from which it saw no reason to seek an escape, with the prospect of regaining lands lost in 1870 a powerful motive to take action.

The country immediately rallied behind the *union sacrée* proclaimed by Poincaré*. Nearly 4 million men were mobilised in August, most of them infantry men known as *poilus*, meaning virile, brave fellows. Only 1.5 per cent of those called up did not join the forces; the High Command had forecast 13 per cent. Streets in the 'Europe' district round the Gare St-Lazare were renamed, rue de Berlin becoming rue de Liège and rue de Hambourg rue de Bucarest, though the rue de Vienne kept its name. Kant was regarded

---

* A copy of the mobilisation decree can be seen on the wall beside Maxim's restaurant in Paris.

with suspicion as a representative of German thought. Pre-war divisions dissolved; if Clemenceau remained outside government, it was because he thought it was not prosecuting the fight with sufficient vigour. Revolutionaries earmarked for arrest in the police *carnet B* were left untroubled. Delcassé was recalled to the Quai d'Orsay and Millerand became war minister. In a sign of national unity, Jules Guesde, the leading Socialist after the killing of Jaurès, joined the government as minister without portfolio. The expectation was for a short conflict, which would be won by the end of the year by the *poilu* infantrymen and their officers implementing Colonel Grandmaison's doctrine of offensive warfare.

However, despite its advances in some sectors, such as aviation, the French faced a generally stronger foe. Germany had more men of fighting age, advanced heavy artillery and a faster-growing industry; its annual steel output was 13 million tonnes compared to 3.3 million in France. The French infantry rifle was little more than a carbine and its red-trousered infantrymen made easy targets. Early advances were turned back and the Kaiser's forces exacted a terrible price on the French, who lost 27,000 men killed and wounded in a single day on 22 August. By September, the Germans were within thirty miles of Paris. The government left for Bordeaux where it stayed for three months. Then, General Gallieni, in charge of the defence of the capital, saw the chance of a flanking attack and unleashed the Battle of the Marne. Joffre's order of the day calling for the army to go on the attack warned that 'no shortcomings can be tolerated at a moment when the battle on which the safety of the country depends is joined.' Troops were ferried to the front in taxis, creating a potent and enduring patriotic symbol though the number of soldiers they carried to the front was small. Paris was saved.[15]

The French and British armies advanced forty miles on a 160-mile line. The 'race to the Channel' produced lines of opposing trenches from which the war of attrition would now be fought. The German chief of staff, Helmuth von Moltke, was reported to have told the Kaiser 'Your Majesty, we have lost the war.' He was dismissed. French troops exchanged their dashing red trousers for duller uniforms that made them stand out less, and donned metal helmets instead of cloth *képis*.

'What is this war except a war of extermination?' Lieutenant Charles de Gaulle asked in a letter to his mother from the front. But, two decades later, as a military historian, he would write of the Battle of the Marne: 'The spell was broken. For the first time in over a hundred years, France had beaten Germany in a big-scale battle. Psychologically, the game was won.'[16]

The victory nearly halved the amount of French territory occupied by the enemy, and liberated such key centres as Amiens and Reims. But the industrial region round Lille and the iron fields of Lorraine were under German control and the Reich's occupation of territory whose loss Paris could not accept meant that the war was bound to grind on until one side or the other caved in from exhaustion.

The cost was already enormous. By the end of 1914, France had suffered 528,000 casualties, fewer than Germany's 800,000 but far more than Britain's 59,000. Though patriotic sentiment remained high, and the government announced that it would not pursue peace until Alsace-Lorraine was recovered, the optimistic spirit of the Republic ebbed; it was hard to have faith in the idea of progress and human values when millions were dying in the grinding slaughter of the 475 miles of trenches stretching from the Swiss border to the North Sea. The social-ist conviction, championed by Jaurès, that workers of opposing nations would not kill one another proved sadly misplaced.

Parliament, in effect, ceded control to Joffre, the hero of the Marne, who was covered politically by Millerand. The cost of the war escalated and France's low tax base meant it financed the fighting by massive borrowing. The demographic weakness of having only 4.5 million men between the ages of twenty and thirty-four compared to 7.7 million in Germany made it dependent on allied troops, from Britain and then the United States.

Joffre launched a series of offensives in late 1914 and early 1915 while 79,000 French troops joined the much larger British force to attack Gallipoli. But the expedition against the Turks ended in disas-ter while the initiatives on the Western Front stalled against the line of enemy trenches. An army corps commanded by the veteran infantry general, Philippe Pétain, did manage a breakthrough in an attack round Artois but the French reserves were too far back to lend the necessary support. Elsewhere the maze of trenches behind forests of barbed wire, some with thirty-feet deep dugouts and concrete pill-boxes, prevented the offensive warfare for which the French army had been trained. The introduction of poison gas and tanks made little difference.

The letters and diary of the future General de Gaulle are telling in their evidence of life at the front for a deeply patriotic young junior officer and his *poilus*. 'For hours, sometimes for days, the artillery barrage pounds positions, and breaks spirits. The survivors are depressed and apathetic. Without sleep, food or water, feeling abandoned by God and man, the soldiers have one hope – that their ordeal should end quickly, no matter how.' He wrote to his mother of 'disastrous areas where every day fresh corpses were piled up in the filthy mud; orders to attack whatever the cost, given over the telephone by a distant command after trifling artillery preparation … assaults carried out without illusion against deep and undamaged networks of barbed wire into which the best officers and men advanced, to be caught and killed like flies in a spider's web.'

Wounded twice and promoted to the rank of captain, de Gaulle recorded how his company 'lived like frogs' in the winter rains. At other times, he offered a reward of five centimes for each rat his soldiers killed. He contrasted 'the long anguish of ever-threatening death and unrelieved misery' of the soldiers with the manoeuvring in Paris and profiteering by civilians 'who enjoyed the things of which [the soldiers were] deprived – comfort, freedom, women'.[17]

Verdun

Though muffled by war, divisive politics did, indeed, soon re-appear in the capital. Viviani's government was brought down in October 1915, by lack of military progress. Briand, his successor, was faced with a crucial military test as the Germans attacked the key military stronghold of Verdun on a bend of the River Meuse in the furthest eastern stretch of territory controlled by the French. The chief of staff, Erich von Falkenhayn, told the Kaiser he would mount an offensive that would draw in most of France's army and 'bleed it to death'.

On 21 February, the Germans unleashed more than a million shells at Verdun and its Douaumont fortress. The phlegmatic Joffre, an old-fashioned figure with a sweeping moustache who declined to use the telephone, appeared untroubled by the attack, going to bed early at his headquarters in Chantilly, north of Paris. But his deputy, Édouard de Castelnau, visited Verdun where he was concerned at the fear and chaos, and urged the appointment of the well-regarded infantry commander, Philippe Pétain, to take charge of the defence. But the general could not be found.[18]

An aide tracked him down to the Hôtel Terminus opposite the Gare de Nord in Paris, where he was seeing his mistress, his presence given away by a pair of yellow military boots outside a bedroom. The aide knocked at the door. The general appeared in his nightshirt, and said he would leave at 7 a.m. Then he returned to his lady.[19]

By the time Pétain reached Verdun through deep snow, the Germans had taken the Douaumont fortress and were within three miles of the city. He issued his war cry – 'They will not pass'. The enemy advance ground to a halt. A troop rotation system, known as the 'mill wheel', was set up to move huge columns of men in an endless procession while shell-shocked survivors were pulled back to recuperate before being sent back into the battle. The route to and from the front became known as the *Voie Sacrée* as the battle took on an iconic character.

Pétain alienated both Joffre, who wanted to concentrate on a battle shaping up on the Somme, and Poincaré, with whom he did not get on when the president visited the front. As a result, he was moved from direct command after two months, though retaining overall authority as the battle on the Meuse stretched for 298 days involving 259 of the country's 330 infantry regiments. In all, France lost 378,000 dead, wounded and missing, while German casualties were put at 337,000.

The battle saw the introduction of flamethrowers and gas but was primarily an artillery duel with the infantry playing the role of victims on a vast scale. It was, the poet Paul Valéry wrote, 'a complete war in itself'. A leading French novel of the First World War, *Le Feu* by Henri Barbusse, described 'men squashed, cut in two, or split from top to bottom, blown into showers by an ordinary shell, bellies turned inside out and scattered anyhow, skulls forced bodily into the chest as if by a blow with a club'.

Verdun was saved by the enormous commitment to defend it and by the decision of the new German high command under Paul von Hindenburg and Erich Ludendorff that the price of continuing the battle was too high. Pétain went down as 'the Victor of Verdun' while his future nemesis de Gaulle was felled by a deep bayonet thrust into his right thigh while leading a charge in a cloud of poison gas and was given up for dead. His obituary notice in the Official Journal recorded Pétain's judgment that the French had lost 'an incomparable officer in all respects'. In fact, he was captured by the Germans and spent the rest of the conflict as a prisoner of war.[20]

Despite the victory at Verdun, the stalemate at the front encouraged politicking in Paris by Briand, who was anxious for a more offensive strategy, while his government defined France's war aims as including control of the east bank of the Rhine and the division of the Middle East with Britain under the Sykes-Picot agreement of 1916. Briand waged a destructive campaign to unseat Joffre in favour of the more dashing and politically connected General Robert Nivelle, who had commanded the recapture of key strong points at Verdun after intense bombardment by 'super-heavy' guns and a creeping artillery barrage. Using the same tactics, he now proposed to launch a massive offensive to break the deadlock on the Western Front.

The British, who liked Nivelle's fluency in English, agreed to put their forces under French overall command. When Briand fell in March 1917, the lawyer-politician Alexandre Ribot, who had sat in parliament since 1878, returned for his fourth spell as prime minister. Cowed by Nivelle's threat to resign if he did not get his way, both Ribot and Poincaré went along with his offensive on the Chemin des Dames ridge in the Aisne department. It was a disaster from the start. The general had forecast 10,000 French casualties; after he blundered into a German trap, 28–32,000 were killed outright, 5,000 died of wounds, 80,000–100,000 were wounded and 5,000 were taken prisoner in nine days, increasing the toll of French military dead to nearly one million.

Mutinies broke out in almost half the French divisions, echoed by scattered civilian strikes against the war. Up to 30,000 soldiers deserted; others refused to go to the front, most of them veterans who saw the war as a futile exercise in mass killing. The repression was immediate as 3,427 courts-martial were held, at which an estimated 2,878 men were sentenced to hard labour with 629 death sentences – of which between thirty and forty-nine were carried out.[21]

Ribot was succeeded by the mathematician-politician Paul Painlevé amid political strife which saw the Socialists refusing to join the government, though still supporting the war. The main argument was over Nivelle's fate. Poincaré did his utmost to escape responsibility for the deadly fiasco on the Chemin des Dames. But Nivelle was doomed, and Pétain became first Army Chief of Staff at the end of April 1917 and then Commander-in-Chief with Ferdinand Foch as his chief of staff. The new military chief took pains to rebuild military morale, granting longer regular leave and halting big offensives until the Americans arrived and tanks were more plentiful. Pétain accepted that a breakthrough was impossible and concentrated rather on targeted short attacks with air and tank support.

The war effort was hit abroad by the Russian revolution and a statement on the Italian front. Left-wing doubts about the war grew. Briand maintained contact with a German baron who wanted to act as a go-between with Berlin and the prime minister was rumoured to have explored the possibility of negotiations through the Austrians. Caillaux began to talk of a compromise with Berlin. There was a scandal involving a parliamentary deputy found in possession of a large cache of money from war contracts and Action Française accused a former interior minister of having betrayed French war plans. The Dutch exotic dancer, Margaretha Geertruida 'Margreet' Zelle MacLeod, known by the stage name Mata Hari and the mistress of industrialist Émile Étienne Guimet, was executed for spying following a trial weighted against her.

The slowness with which the interior ministry acted in such cases was held to show that the minister, Louis Malvy, was lacking in patriotic zeal. He was also caught up in a murky affair involving a left-wing newspaper financed first by his ministry and then by the Germans; its owner was arrested and found dead in his cell. Clemenceau, who estimated that one-third of deputies wanted peace but did not dare to speak out, railed against Malvy for laxness that had allowed the army mutinies and obtained his resignation. When the accumulation of failures and scandals brought down the Painlevé government, it was succeeded by a man with only one idea – absolute victory.[22]

The Father of Victory

Though Poincaré hated the Tiger, now a stout 76-year old, he knew there was no alternative. Taking the war ministry himself and vowing to continue the conflict to 'the last quarter-of-an-hour', Clemenceau defined his war aim quite simply – to win.[23]

He imposed what Maurras termed a 'mon-archie', filling the government with second-raters who would not get in his way. Briand, Ribot and the Socialists were excluded. The prime minister visited the troops and radiated confidence, saying privately that he was 'gambling on American intervention which will bring us such resources that we cannot fail to finish the Germans off'. He put down anti-war strikes in Paris and the weapons factories of Saint-Étienne. His finance minister, Louis-Lucien Klotz, relaxed fiscal policy to allow a degree of inflation which made people feel happier, even if his lack of acumen led Clemenceau to remark that, 'My finance minister is the only Jew in Europe who knows nothing about money.'[24]

Though he relaxed press censorship, saying that 'the right to insult members of the government is inviolable', he got a parliamentary committee to order the arrest of Caillaux, who was sent to prison for three years. An international adventurer, Paul Bolo, was shot after being found to have used large sums from the Germans to influence French newspapers. The feminist, trade unionist and anti-war activist Hélène Brion was arrested for spreading defeatist propaganda and became the subject of a press witch hunt accusing her of being an anarchist, wearing men's clothes, visiting Russia, sheltering strange individuals, corresponding with soldiers and receiving German money. In her defence at her trial by a military court, she said that she was a pacifist because she was a feminist – 'war is the triumph of brutal force; feminism can only triumph by moral force and intellectual worth.' She was given a suspended three-year prison sentence.

The big test came in March 1918 as Hindenburg and Ludendorff deployed German troops freed from the Russian front to advance on the Marne, threatening to split the French and British armies. They launched huge bombardments before the infantry advanced, firing 3.2 million rounds on the first day, a third of them containing chemicals including mustard gas. German aircraft strafed their opponents, though the Allies eventually established aerial dominance with French planes showing their technological mastery and squadrons of up to sixty aircraft in action day and night.

Pétain's natural caution bordering on defeatism surfaced as he proposed a retreat on Paris. Clemenceau told Poincaré he had heard the commander say that 'the Germans will beat the British in open country. After which they will beat us too.' 'Surely a general should not speak or think like that?' the prime minister remarked. The British commander, Douglas Haig, thought Pétain 'had the appearance of a commander who had lost his nerve'. Though the Victor of Verdun was retained, Clemenceau got the conference to agree to appoint Foch as supreme Allied commander at the head of coordinated operations. Pétain was required to report to him. Foch proposed the creation of a big force, to be held in reserve round Amiens, which could be used for an eventual counter-offensive – just the kind of language the Tiger liked to hear.

The Germans launched a fresh advance in Flanders in April followed by the biggest attack of all, advancing thirty miles in three days in May and aiming at Paris as in 1914. They reached the Marne, thirty-nine miles from the capital, at the end of the month. Pétain told the commander there to prepare to evacuate. His troops could not hold their positions, he warned Clemenceau, advising that the government move to Bordeaux. Though French reinforcements arrived from the north, it was a bitter struggle to hold the line. The Germans enjoyed two-to-one numerical superiority. On 1 June, Pétain reported that seventeen divisions were 'completely used up'. The Germans took the railway line between Paris and Nancy, interrupting the flow of metal from the east to the arms factories round the capital. Dining with Foch and his staff, the US commander, General John J. Pershing, recorded that it would be 'difficult to imagine a more depressed set of officers'. He noted that there was 'something akin to panic' in Paris.[25]

A million people fled the capital, and Ludendorff hoped that the offensives would end up by provoking a political crisis in France, leading to collapse. But Clemenceau showed his mettle, refusing to listen to defeatist voices and insisting that the war would still be won, especially with the growing number of American troops reaching the Western Front. The German successes brought a heavy price for them as the front widened, forcing Ludendorff to move seventeen divisions out of the attack force on the Marne. Defending the salient opened up by the offensive trapped German forces and prevented them being deployed in Flanders. Though the Paris-Nancy line was taken, other key railway lines remained in French hands. German munitions ran short. Troops lived off the land and got drunk on wine from ransacked homes. Allied air supremacy had its effect as did the new tank units. The Reich was running out of men, while morale deteriorated.

In mid-June French and American forces counter-attacked and the offensive petered out. Troops from across the Atlantic poured in, more than a million of them by July. Foch launched converging offensives and Allied forces pierced one defensive line after another. On 1–2 November, Canadian troops entered Valenciennes, the last big French town held by the enemy. The Germans fell into a general retreat, sometimes moving so fast that their opponents could not keep up with them. Clemenceau was hailed as *le Père la Victoire* (Father Victory) and France awaited the fruits of its triumph after so much loss.[26]

13

THE TROUBLED PEACE

Triumph after more than four years of war came at a cost to France that would permeate politics, the economy, society and thinking for two decades. There were, to start with, 1.5 million dead; as a proportion of the population, the toll was slightly more than in Germany and twice the level of Britain. If one includes the number of children not born because of the war, the population deficit may have been double that. Of the 6 million survivors, half were wounded, some mutilated, shell shocked or confined to a wheelchair. More than 60 per cent of men born before 1901 had fought in *La Grande Guerre*. With most of France's soldiers drawn from rural areas, the war advanced the breaking down of the isolation of the countryside; some soldiers from poor regions ate meat on a regular basis for the first time in the forces. Memorials listing hundreds of names in the villages and small towns which provided most of the *poilus* bore witness to the scale of the sacrifice; only one of France's 38,000 communes did not lose an inhabitant. Most families had been deprived of a husband, father or son.

Rejecting greatness, returning to confusion

The nation was, in the words of the writer Jean Giraudoux who had been wounded several times, gripped by 'fatigue, fatigue'. Victory brought the recovery of Alsace-Lorraine with its two million people, but there was little joy for returning troops. Social conditions and healthcare remained backward. More than 400,000 died in France during the global influenza pandemic which lasted until 1920 and which killed Edmond Rostand, among so many others.[1]

The birth rate declined further despite the introduction of the *carte famille nombreuse* offering financial benefits to those with three or more children. Four million people were estimated to have syphilis. Known abortions rose to 400,000 a year. A surgeon, Serge Voronoff, attracted considerable attention with repeated – and repeatedly unsuccessful – attempts to transplant testicles from primates to men lacking 'virility'. Regions where the fighting had been concentrated were devastated. In the *département* of the Nord, from which 300,000 people had fled to safer parts of France, mortality was double its pre-war rate. In Lille, described as 'a dead city on the edge of a desert', more than 80 per cent of teenagers were underweight. Farming equipment and animal herds had been lost, stolen or destroyed – a million cattle and as many sheep were killed by the war.[2]

The cost of the conflict had been met largely by loans, increasing France's indebtedness, mainly to the USA and Britain, to $7 billion (equivalent to $1.4 trillion today). Wartime lending from across the Atlantic produced a realignment of the relationship between Europe and America in which France was dangerously exposed. The tripling of public debt meant high interest payments. The trade gap widened and, when Allied financial credits ended in March 1919, the franc plunged. By the next year France was in an economic crisis.

Industrial output was only a little more than half its 1913 level – in metallurgy, it was one-third, while construction was at 16 per cent. The demands of war led to the expansion of large-scale assembly-line manufacturing at such icons of the age as the Renault works at Boulogne-Billancourt on the edge of Paris, the Michelin tyre factory at Clermont-Ferrand in the Auvergne and the shipyards of Saint-Nazaire. But small-scale enterprises remained very numerous. The growth of big firms and national brands inevitably caused tension and demands for protection from the traditional sectors, which, feeling threatened by modernity, became fodder for extremists of right and left. A third of the population was still employed in agriculture in 1919 but the continuing rural exodus and the death toll of country dwellers in the war further tilted the population balance – by 1931 more than half the French lived in towns. Though the Crédit Agricole banking network was set up to help farmers and rural electrification was developed, agriculture remained quite traditional in most regions.[3]

The election of 1919 was a triumph for the right-wing *Bloc National* led by Clemenceau at his most aggressive and Poincaré at his most austere. It campaigned on the slogan 'Germany will pay!' and made much of the dangers of Bolshevism amid a wave of strikes. The winners ended with 433 seats, against 190 for the Radicals and Socialists – another *Chambre Introuvable*, and no easier to deal with than its predecessor under Louis XVIII.

The Tiger had pledged to provide France with security to prevent another war. He got some of what he wanted but not enough. In the treaty signed at Versailles in June 1919, a ceiling of 100,000 men was put on the German army, which was not allowed heavy artillery or an air force. The mining basin of the Saar was placed under international control for fifteen years. Knowing that the Americans and British would not accept Foch's idea of absorbing the Rhineland into France given Woodrow Wilson's pronouncements about national self-determination, Clemenceau settled for demilitarisation of the region with three French bridgeheads on the river for five to fifteen years and a guarantee against future German aggression.

London and Paris respected one another's colonial reach – Britain in East Africa and India, France in West and North Africa and Indochina. In the Middle East, the secret Sykes-Picot agreement of 1916 drew artificial frontiers to create new nations such as Syria, over which France claimed influence. The Sèvres Treaty of 1920 confirmed this splitting of the Ottoman Empire, though there would be tensions between the two European powers, notably over the resurgence of Turkey under Atatürk. France then faced a revolt in Syria that led it to bombard Damascus.[4]

Hard bargaining produced a figure of 132 billion gold marks for reparation to be paid by Germany. But this proved a chimera made up largely of non-existent bonds, and the total handed over up to 1931, when payments were suspended indefinitely, was 20 billion gold marks, worth $5 billion (£1 billion), leading to widespread disillusion in

France and resentment at war debts to the US. It was time to return to classic Third Republic politicking. When Poincaré's presidential term ended in early 1920, Clemenceau expected to get the job. But Briand exacted revenge for his ousting during the war by organising backing for Paul Deschanel, a former president of the Chamber, supported mainly by disappointed nationalists and Catholics who disliked the Tiger's lay beliefs.

The new head of state wanted to continue the active presidential role played by his predecessor, but his mental health deteriorated fast – when schoolgirls presented him with a bouquet, he threw the flowers back at them one by one; he received the British Ambassador wearing only his decorations of his office; he fell through a window of the presidential train after taking sleeping pills and was found wandering in the countryside in his nightshirt. After he left a meeting to walk into a lake, he resigned, but was still elected to the Senate. His successor, Millerand, also wanted to make the Élysée into a centre of real power but ran into strong parliamentary opposition and stepped down in 1924 to be replaced by the inoffensive former prime minister, Gaston Doumergue.

Clemenceau lamented that the French had 'rejected greatness and returned to confusion'. There were forty-two governments in all between the two world wars. As in the previous decades, only a narrow margin separated the number voting for left and right but the electoral system exaggerated the outcome in terms of seats and meant that control of the Chamber swung from one coalition to another. Continuing the pre-war tradition, the same figures remained through all the changes in government – Briand was prime minister eight times between 1921 and his death in 1932 (on top of his three previous spells in Matignon).

At departmental and city levels, local political barons maintained the tradition of continuity as mayors, sometimes combining these posts with national office as in the case of Édouard Herriot (three times prime minister and mayor of Lyons from 1905–42). Others remained largely rooted in their home places, like the redoubtable Marius Escartefigue with his bushy beard and his ability to navigate political currents in the best centrist tradition as mayor of Toulon from 1919–1940, though also winning election to the National Assembly for a time by drawing conservative backing from his support for Poincaré while appealing to the left through his previous incarnation as a Radical Socialist*.[5]

Amid a rolling financial crisis, the years 1920–2 saw four governments. Poincaré then held the Matignon for two-and-a-half years but five more premiers took office in the ensuing two years before he returned to power. Though both remained committed to Marxism, Communists and Socialists split at a congress in Tours in 1920 after the Kremlin demanded obeisance – the Moscow line won a three-to-one majority so the Socialists walked out to chart their own course. A pacifist spirit gripped the nation. 'There is probably no other nation in Europe that is less warlike,' war minister André Maginot noted. The teaching profession, which had suffered disproportionate losses in the conflict, delivered an anti-war message to the young while a flood of memoirs kept alive the horrors of the trenches. The high command adopted a defensive strategy which would 'be more sparing of the blood of soldiers' in the words of Pétain, who was raised to the rank of marshal in 1918. The huge line of defensive fortifications built in the 1930s and bearing Maginot's name was supposed to ensure security.[6]

Making sense of life in the wake of so much death

If a defensive mentality dominated policy and popular thinking, France enjoyed a prime position at the forefront of arts, culture, luxury goods, sport and cuisine. Paris consolidated its position as the world's haute couture capital. Coco Chanel presented the little black dress, made the bob hairstyle fashionable and developed jersey knit in women's clothing. Jeanne Lanvin decorated her couture with elaborate trimmings, embroideries and beaded decorations. Jean Patou offered geometric and Cubist motifs in clothes with clean lines.

---

* It can hardly have been a coincidence that Marcel Pagnol named two of the characters in his Marseilles trilogy Marius and Escartefigue, the latter a sea captain who plays in an epic card game in which he takes an interminable time to pick up César's hints to play hearts, giving rise to some of the most celebrated exchanges in French cinema.

René Lacoste introduced the polo shirt. Along with Henri Cochet, Jacques Brugnon and the 'bounding Basque' Jean Borotra, who appeared on court in his regional beret, Lacoste made up the 'Four Musketeers' of French tennis who won seventeen grand slam titles from 1925 to 1932. Suzanne Lenglen dominated the sport in the decade after the Great War, creating a sensation when she appeared at Wimbledon in a sleeveless dress cut just above the calf, and sipped brandy between sets.

Georges Carpentier won the world light heavyweight championship in 1920, though he was mauled by Jack Dempsey the following year when he tried for the heavyweight title in the first bout to attract a million dollar gate. The 24-hour motor race was held at Le Mans from 1923 and French cars dominated Grand Prix racing.

France's luxury liners were the smartest way to cross the oceans. The country's aviation industry was the biggest in the world, and, after their wartime exploits, its fliers became peacetime heroes. A 1914–18 ace pilot, Jules Védrines, won a 25,000 franc prize offered by the Galeries Lafayette department store for landing on its narrow roof; men grabbed the wings as it landed. In 1927, Charles Nungesser, the epitome of a dashing, high-living pilot, tried to cross the Atlantic, taking off with the navigator, François Coli, in their *L'Oiseau Blanc* (The White Bird) biplane painted with a Great War insignia. They disappeared somewhere in the Atlantic. Two weeks later, Charles Lindbergh successfully crossed in the opposite direction, receiving a hero's welcome from 100,000 people at Le Bourget airfield north of Paris.

French cuisine moved away from the formal dishes of the pre-war era to make greater use of regional ingredients and recipes, led by a quartet of chefs on the holiday route from Paris to the south.* Restaurant guides flourished, headed by the red-covered *Michelin*. The press and radio appointed gastronomic critics.

In painting, the great modernist tradition set before the war developed further in the hands of an extraordinary list of artists augmented by major foreign figures – Picasso, Braque and Matisse, Rouault, de Vlaminck and Dufy, Modigliani, Derain, Léger, Utrillo, Chagall and a

* See page 257.

legion of others spread between Montmartre and Montparnasse. Paris was home to Dadaism, Surrealism and Abstract Expressionism. Photography flourished through the lenses of Lartigue, Brassaï, Willy Ronis, Doisneau and Cartier-Bresson. The French-Swiss Charles-Édouard Jeanneret-Gris, known as Le Corbusier, revolutionised architecture and urban planning with his modernistic apartment blocks and houses dreaming of creating 'streets in the sky'.

Jean Cocteau acted as a cultural gadfly while Antonin Artaud introduced the avant-garde Theatre of Cruelty. Anatole France, Henri Bergson and Roger Martin du Gard won Nobel Prizes for Literature. Alain Fournier's novel *Le Grand Meaulnes*, published just before the outbreak of the war, became a memorial to the old world, its poignancy heightened by its author's death at the front in 1914 at the age of 27 – the body was not identified until 1991.

While pursuing a diplomatic career, the deeply Catholic Paul Claudel developed a unique style of lengthy, linguistically rich blank verse poems and historical plays, some lasting for more than ten hours. André Malraux crafted his globetrotting legend. André Gide sought intellectual honesty in confronting freedom and sensuality with the social and education constraints of conservative France, while François Mauriac examined morality and guilt in a series of often fatalistic novels.

It was an era for serial works – having laid out the scale of human credulity in his hit play *Knock*, Jules Romains produced twenty-seven volumes in his series, *Les Hommes de Bonne Volonté* (Men of Good Will), while Martin du Gard's cycle *les Thibault* consisted of eight books and Proust's *À la Recherche du Temps Perdu* of seven by the time it was finished in 1927 at 4,000 pages and with some 2,000 characters.

Louis-Ferdinand Céline produced a new kind of novel in 1932, with his nihilistic, misanthropic, semi-autobiographical *Voyage au Bout de la Nuit* (*Journey to the End of Night*) in slang-ridden everyday language, its pessimism drawn from his experience in the Great War and from life around him as a doctor in a poor Parisian suburb. Three years later, he pushed his stylistic innovation to the limit in *Mort à Crédit* (*Death on the Instalment Plan*) and then embarked on a series of virulently anti-Semitic works paving the way to his collaboration with the German occupiers in the Second World War.

Four Chefs and a Prince

The development of motoring led to the emergence of national gastro-nomic stars for restaurants in provincial towns made accessible to travellers. Nowhere more so than on the main road from Paris to the south, which was populated by the four greatest chefs of the age. All were early recipients of the coveted three rosettes from the Michelin tyre company's red guide, product of their regions from families steeped in the restaurant tradition.

Fernand Point, a convivial giant (1.9 metres, 165 kilos), held sway for three decades at La Pyramide restaurant in Vienne, south of Lyons. He was a perfectionist – if a client lit a cigarette, the bill was taken to the table. One of the first chefs to run his own business, his dishes were based on the fresh-est produce, with a lot of vegetables and light sauces. In the habit of drinking a magnum of champagne a day, he stocked more than 40,000 bottles in his wine cellar. During the Germans' occupation of France in the Second World War, he closed La Pyramide rather than serve their officers. After his death in 1955, his legacy was carried on by Paul Bocuse, the Troisgros brothers and other exponents of the nouvelle cuisine of the 1960s.

In Valence, André Pic set new standards with his pike sausage, kidneys in sorrel sauce and sea bass with caviar while, in Saulieu, to the north, the rotund Alexandre Dumaine turned an old coaching inn, La Côte d'Or, into a temple of taste while Lyons, France's gastronomic capital, was home to a for-midable group of women chefs known as *les Mères*, headed by Eugénie Brazier. The specialities of these restaurants highlighted dishes made with local pro-duce – crayfish, Charolais beef and poultry with precise flavourful sauces.

On top of this parade of gastronomic excellence sat an array of food writers and critics. Édouard Alexandre de Pomiane, a scientist of Polish origin, was very influential through his radio broadcasts while Maurice Edmond Sailland who called himself Curnonsky (Whynotsky, from the Latin '*cur*' and the French '*non*' plus a Russian suffix) was the leading food critic of the day, preaching that 'in cuisine, as in all the arts, simplicity is the sign of perfection', since 'good cooking is when things taste of what they are'.

France, and Paris in particular, became even more of a mecca for leading foreign writers and artists – Hemingway, Joyce, Borges, Fitzgerald, Nabokov and Brecht among many others, and Ezra Pound before he decided to opt for fascism in Italy. Gertrude Stein held her literary salon and Sylvia Beach published *Ulysses* and other avant-garde works from her Shakespeare and Company premises by the Seine. Beckett and Ionesco wrote in French. Georges Simenon came from Belgium to chronicle the cases of Commissaire Maigret and Henry Miller spent his quiet days in Clichy. From Japan, Foujita created some of the most enduring images of Parisian artistic and café life. Josephine Baker was the toast of the town with her daring banana dance and her declaration that she had two loves, 'Paris and my country'; she received 46,000 fan letters and two thousand marriage proposals in her first two years in France.

Black jazz musicians found a refuge from racism in the French capital where the Quintette du Hot Club de France with Django Reinhardt and Stéphane Grappelli mixed strings and swing, French musette and gypsy music, and Coleman Hawkins and Benny Carter set up mighty riffs in recordings in Paris. Fats Waller played on the 'God box' at Notre-Dame cathedral. The new cabarets, bars and brasseries of the Boulevard Montparnasse – La Coupole, Le Select and La Rotonde – provided haunts for modernist artists and writers in a high-pressure cocoon; just down the Boulevard Raspail, away from all the excitement, a bourgeois couple like the de Gaulles lived a more sedate life, only once visiting a cabaret and feeling uncomfortable.

The pre-war musical-hall star Mistinguett enjoyed great success with her anthem '*Mon Homme*' and resumed her stage career after peace came, insuring her legs for 500,000 francs in 1919. The realist singer Fréhel kept alive the musette tradition despite the ravages of alcohol. The handsome musical-comedy singer and dancer, Maurice Chevalier, became an international star, appearing on Broadway in 1922 and going to Hollywood after the invention of sound pictures for a string of hit films, making sure he kept a debonair French accent despite his excellent English. The singer-composer Mireille Hartuch, known simply by her first name, also travelled to New York and Hollywood where she appeared on screen with Douglas Fairbanks Jr and Buster Keaton.

The private lives of some of these performers were intertwined. Chevalier was the lover of both Mistinguett and Fréhel, whose husband left her for another noted singer, Damia; she appeared at a theatre named after her with a single spotlight trained on her face, bare arms and hands. A nightclub owner, Louis Leplée, discovered Édith Piaf singing in the street and promoted her at his smart club off the Champs-Élysée. Charles Trenet, whose exuberant style earned him the nickname of *le Fou Chantant* (the Singing Madman), formed a duo with the Swiss pianist Johnny Hess to perform at the top nightclubs, record and run a radio show as well as writing for singers such as the highly popular crooner Jean Sablon. Tino Rossi played the Latin lover in a string of films and operettas. Ray Ventura's big band, the Collegians, mixed swing with witty lyrics, reaching its high point with '*Tout va Très Bien, Madame la Marquise*' in 1936, which has a noblewoman being told of a string of calamities by servants who assure her that all is still fine, a metaphor for the national denial of France's problems. Records revolutionised the music business. Radio swept the nation with the first private transmitter, Radiola, starting regular broadcasts in 1922. By 1940, fourteen commercial and twelve public-sector stations were operating.

Cinema blossomed in popularity and artistic achievement. Jean Gabin became a major star, as did Danielle Darrieux and Michèle Morgan. Charles Boyer went to Hollywood as the epitome of the smooth French leading man; Arletty (born Léonie Marie Julie Bathiat) epitomised the down-to-earth Parisienne. One of the top music-hall stars, the horse-toothed Fernandel, made his first film in 1930 and went on to make a stream of movies at home and abroad. Overcoming a bad stammer, the great actor Louis Jouvet moved from theatre to screen for thirty-four films and iconic status. So, in a different mode did the shambling Michel Simon – the two men could not stand one another but gave classic performances in Marcel Carné's two-hander *Drôle de Drame*.

René Clair directed *Sous les Toits de Paris* (*Under the Roofs of Paris*) and the early musical comedy *Le Million*. The perennially popular star, Annabella, played dozens of shy, pretty roles and went to Hollywood where she married the actor Tyrone Power. The enormously popular

Georges Milton, a small, rotund actor and singer, made a national character of Bouboule, a jovial *resquilleur* (cheat) who got the better of his superiors by cunning and clowning. Marcel Pagnol filmed his Marseilles trilogy, *Marius, Fanny* and *César* with the peerless Raimu. Sacha Guitry, son of the great nineteenth-century actor, wrote more than a hundred plays and made five films a year at his peak, many starring his wife Yvonne Printemps who epitomised French elegance and vivacity. Jean Renoir directed the great anti-war film *La Grande Illusion* (*The Grand Illusion*) in 1937 and, two years later, *La Règle du Jeu* (*The Rules of the Game*) which reflected the moral disarray of the last year of peace and was banned on the outbreak of war for its demoralising impact.

Roots of the crash

The pessimism captured by Renoir was heightened by the international situation in which France had good reason for trepidation. Britain was seen as an uncertain ally. Woodrow Wilson's proclamation of what has been described as 'conservative evolutionary liberalism' that required other countries to follow a course laid down by Washington cut little ice in France, especially when the Americans retreated into isolationism, and so played no role in attempting to construct new security arrangements to protect states created by Wilson's policies. Congressional pressure for tax cuts meant there could be no general write-down of war debts contracted by France and others, pushing Paris to pursue the frustrating effort to extract reparations payments from Germany.[7]

The old alliance with Russia was complicated by fear of Bolshevism. A string of treaties with the small states of central and Eastern Europe were unconvincing given France's defensive military stance. A military mission sent to Poland helped to turn back a Soviet advance in 1920, but there was no answer to the fundamental foreign policy issue of what France would do if and when Germany revived.

Policy vacillated between Briand, who sought to reach agreement with Berlin, and Poincaré, the hard man who sent military engineers backed by troops to take over factories and mines in the industrial bastion of the Ruhr in early 1922 when Germany fell behind with reparations payments. This was met with peaceful opposition from the inhabitants and Britain disapproved, but the move was very popular in France especially when the Germans called off their resistance. Their central bank reformed the Weimar Republic currency, swingeing austerity measures were introduced and the Chancellor, Gustav Stresemann, said Berlin would live up to its obligation to supply coal under the reparations programme.

As the mark stabilised, a run on the franc developed and Poincaré had to raise loans from British and American banks, cut civil service jobs and increase taxes. The *Cartel des Gauches* (taking in moderates as well as socialists) ran a strong campaign in the general election of May 1924, on the slogans 'For peace', 'For the ordinary people', 'Against the power of money' and with a pledge to allow government employees to organise trade unions. It took 328 of 582 National Assembly seats. The new prime minister was the third major political figure of the time, the Radical Socialist Édouard Herriot, a canny, cultured, lazy, pipe-smoking fixer – and a gastronome as befitted the mayor of Lyons.

The change of government did nothing to alleviate the financial problems. As so often, the Radicals and the left (without the Communists, whose doctrinal rigidity reduced its appeal and its parliamentary seats to only a dozen in 1928) could come together to win elections. But government cooperation was ruled out by the class-war Marxism of the Socialists and their refusal to serve under non-Socialists, while the Radicals, with their loose coalition of varied interests and belief in small government, found it hard to agree on policies – and even harder to implement them.

The franc fell further. A run on state bonds impoverished the middle classes. Public debt and inflation rose. The government blamed the crisis on the forces of finance – the 'wall of money' – and announced a forced loan from the rich. The moderate wing of the *Cartel* defected. Catholic opposition grew as the government fell back on anti-religious rhetoric. Poincaré delivered a biting speech in the Senate. The government was defeated and resigned.

A series of governments headed by Painlevé, Briand and Herriot followed, before worsening economic conditions brought back Poincaré at the head of a right-wing administration with a conservative social agenda allied to spending cuts and tax increases imposed by decree. The franc doubled in value against the dollar. Gold reserves rose. Tariffs were increased, making industry even more dependent on protected domestic sales.

Defence of the currency became the watchword; the governor of the Bank of France, Émile Moreau, played a highly nationalist game, converting foreign exchange reserves into gold and cutting currency holdings in half between 1928 and 1931. An English observer described him as 'a magnificent fighter for narrow and greedy ends'. The strong franc might be seen as a sign of national virility but the impact on exports was dire – in 1927 a third of cars made in France were exported; in 1930, this was down to 8 per cent. Still, industrial profits continued to grow through the 1920s and the Bourse index was 5.5 times its 1913 level.[8]

Governments of the centre-left and the right united on maintaining colonial rule in North Africa. The native inhabitants there were, according to the official reasoning, being turned into citizens of France enjoying the benefits of metropolitan civilisation. When the Moroccan nationalist Emir Abd el-Krim led rebels out of the Rif Mountains to challenge the French, Marshal Pétain was sent to wage a campaign that achieved an easy victory with heavy artillery and planes.

In Europe, Briand sought to normalise relations with Germany, Britain and the newly created (or restored) states of the centre and east of the continent, and to buttress the League of Nations. Earning the label of the 'Apostle of Peace', he and Stresemann received a joint Nobel Peace Prize for negotiating the Treaties of Locarno of 1925 including the 'Rhineland Pact' by which Germany, France and Belgium undertook not to attack one another and Britain and Italy acted as guarantors, but from which the US and the Soviet Union were both absent. The perennial foreign minister, who held the Quai d'Orsay from 1925 to 1932, proposed a European Federation, which proved premature, and drew up a pact to outlaw war with the US secretary of state Frank Kellogg signed by fifteen countries.

If that was to prove a dream, he did see the end of the Allied occupation of the Rhineland and promoted a plan supervised by the American banker, Arthur Young, to remove the running sore of reparations. Briand had expected to have his career crowned with the presidency of the republic to succeed Doumergue in 1931. But a majority which wanted a weak figure in the Élysée coalesced to elect the 74-year-old president of the Senate, Paul Doumer, a former governor-general of Indochina with an extraordinarily luxuriant white beard. A year into his term, he was fatally shot by a deranged Russian émigré, and was succeeded by the pliant Albert Lebrun, who made do with a fine, sweeping moustache.

A progressive conservative, André Tardieu, sought to inflate the economy with a programme of public works and social insurance, including child benefits, but the hard-line monetarist policies of Poincaré and Moreau were generally continued, even under Herriot when he took office for six months after the electorate swung back behind the Radicals and Socialists in 1932. The centre-left was united only in its opposition to the right. Three governments then came and went, floundering on financial policy, until Camille Chautemps, a man of limited intellect, managed to get a majority of deputies present to vote for a budget including a provision for a 6 per cent cut in official salaries – but only after the Socialists had walked out of the Chamber to avoid having to vote. Becoming prime minister was 'a thing that may happen to anyone in French politics', the British diplomat, Robert Vansittart, remarked.

Moreau's monetary policies shielded France from the initial impact of the Great Slump as international investors put their money in the golden franc and France seemed to be an island of prosperity in an impoverished world. But when the crash did come in 1932, industrial output dropped by nearly a fifth in a year. Agricultural prices collapsed; between 1929 and 1935 grain prices halved and farm incomes fell by a third. Unemployment rose to 1.3 million. More than a hundred banks closed down. The Bourse index plunged to a third of its 1929 value by the end of 1934. Dividends were slashed by 50 per cent in the first half of the 1930s while investment dropped by 37 per cent, company failures doubled and exports fell by 60 per cent. Budget deficits became inevitable as state revenue weakened while spending commitments in pensions, civil service salaries and interest of debts prevented balancing expenditure cuts. France, in the words of the contemporary economist Charles Rist, found itself with 'a vegetating economy at a depressive level'.[9]

Military expenditure was cut by 32 per cent between 1931 and 1935 just as Hitler was getting into his stride. The foreign minister, Louis Barthou, set out a more muscular approach to the rising Fascist powers in Europe including negotiating a Franco-Soviet Treaty and the entry of the Soviet Union into the League of Nations, but he was assassinated by a Bulgarian revolutionary in Marseilles together with the visiting King of Yugoslavia in October 1934. Policy drifted under his successor, Pierre Laval, who, despite his own misgivings, was forced by pressure from ministerial colleagues to conclude a pact of mutual assistance with Moscow but also reached an agreement with Mussolini setting out zones of influence in North Africa. This gave Italy a free hand in invading Ethiopia, though a public outcry undid an agreement with Britain to permit it control of two-thirds of the African country. A plebiscite led to the return of the industrial region of the Saar to Germany. France remained resolutely pacifist; theories of offensive armoured warfare propounded by Lieutenant-Colonel de Gaulle and taken up by the moderate conservative Paul Reynaud were strongly opposed by the military establishment and its figurehead, Marshal Pétain.

Stoking the fires of dissent

Disrespect for the politicians together with rising unemployment and falling living standards spurred increasingly militant protest movements. Henri Dorgères, a butcher's son, organised farmers behind the slogan, '*Haut les fourches!*' (Raise your pitchforks!). He claimed 500,000 members and ran a security force, the Greenshirts. The National Catholic Federation struck an intransigent line against the left and Jews. Though the Vatican, under the moderate Pope Pius XI, condemned the Action Française and banned its members from religious rites, many priests ignored the decree. The influx of 70,000 Jewish refugees from Eastern

Europe between 1927 and 1937 – part of half-a-million immigrants attracted by an easy naturalisation policy to compensate for the low birth rate – created an easy target for anti-Semites. Maurras called them 'appalling vermin ... bringing with them lice, plague and typhus in anticipation of the Revolution'.

The biggest league of ex-servicemen, the *Croix de Feu* (Cross of Fire), led by First World War veteran Colonel François de la Rocque and claiming 400,000 adherents, provided big battalions for anti-republican demonstrations, advocating an authoritarian corporatist system. The champagne baron Pierre Taittinger set up the *Jeunesses Patriotes* (Patriotic Youth) garbed in blue coats and berets. A former agitator for Action Française, Eugène Deloncle, founded a Secret Revolutionary Action Committee, known from the hoods members wore as *la Cagoule*. The perfume baron François Coty launched *Solidarité Française* and funded a newspaper, *L'Ami du Peuple*, which joined other journals with a xenophobic, anti-republican message that had little regard for truth, let alone decency. Despite the presence of some who would have willingly followed Hitler or Mussolini and a significant streak of anti-Semitism, the demonstrators were mainly angry traditionalists rather than fascists, while the French Communist Party (PCF) played an equivocal role, following Stalin's order not to collaborate with the bourgeois regime.[10]

Far right-wing writers provided intellectual fodder – Pierre Drieu la Rochelle with his biting novels attacking the bourgeoisie, the brilliant young polymath Robert Brasillach who came out in support of fascism, and the admirer of masculine strength, Henry de Montherlant, who wrote regularly for the weekly *La Gerbe*, directed by a pro-Nazi novelist and Catholic reactionary Alphonse de Châteaubriant.

There were also anti-regime figures from the left. Jacques Doriot, a prominent Communist and mayor of the Paris working-class suburb of Saint-Denis, was expelled from the party for advocating a common front with the Socialists. Turning against his former comrades, he moved towards fascistic ideas of national socialism at the head of his *Parti populaire français*. Marcel Déat, secretary of the Socialist parliamentary group as a young man, preached collaboration between social classes and national solidarity in a corporatism system with an

Serge, Marthe and Albert

One was a refugee from Ukraine, another from an industrial family in Lille, the third the son of the proprietor of the Ambigu (Ambiguous) café in Carcassonne.

After running various questionable enterprises, and trying out as a café singer and nightclub manager, Serge Alexandre Stavisky, known as *le Beau Sacha* (Handsome Sacha), issued a tide of bonds from the municipal pawnshop he managed in the south-western town of Bayonne. The security for these was allegedly a set of emeralds owned by the former Empress of Germany. In fact, the jewels were made of glass; the bonds were worthless. But the scheme raised 300 million francs.

Arrested, Stavisky bought political protection and newspaper advertising space. His trial was endlessly postponed and he was granted bail nineteen times during which he continued his swindles. At the end of 1933, however, he fled, and was found dying from gunshot wounds in an Alpine chalet. He died the next day. His death was officially classified as suicide but there was immediate speculation that, on government orders, police had killed him to prevent him spilling the beans on his highly placed associates.

Marthe Hanau and her ex-husband Lazare Bloch ran a newspaper that promoted the stocks of shell companies run by associates. She launched a financial news agency and issued bonds that promised 8 per cent interest, raising 120 million francs. When banks began to investigate her activities, she bribed politicians, but she, Bloch and their partners were arrested and went in and out of jail. In 1935, she killed herself with sleeping pills.

Albert Oustric, from Carcassonne, set up a bank that recycled depositors' cash through companies he controlled. The Great Crash brought him down and revealed a web of political connections. He was sentenced to eighteen months in jail and fined 3,000 francs. His banks were 1.5 billion in the red, ruining many small investors. 'A scandal which scandalises nobody,' as a journalist wrote. 'We are used to them.'

authoritarian state replacing the parliamentary system. Expelled from the SFIO in 1933, he led a movement calling itself the Socialist Republican Union with the slogan 'Order, Authority and Nation'. Moving between marginal groups, he was joined by the long-time mayor of Bordeaux, Adrien Marquet, who had also been expelled from the SFIO for dissidence, to urge understanding with Germany and preach strident anti-communism.

Repeating themes from the end of the century, opponents of the regime depicted it as having been sold out by corrupt politicians linked to financial scandals. Clemenceau's wartime finance minister, Klotz, was jailed for passing bad cheques. The fact that, like him, two celebrated swindlers, Serge Stavisky and Marthe Hanau, were Jews and that the incumbent premier, Chautemps, was a Mason, was paraded as proof of moral turpitude and how the Republic had fallen under the sway of 'anti-national' groups.

Buffeted by the Stavisky case, Chautemps stepped down to be replaced by fellow Radical Édouard Daladier, a man of the south whose actions rarely lived up to his reputation as 'the Bull of the Vaucluse' – if he was a bull, it was one with the horns of a snail, a trade unionist remarked. He did take a decisive step by sacking the popular Paris police chief, Jean Chiappe, known for his right-wing sympathies, and a more symbolic one in banning performances of Shakespeare's *Coriolanus* for its anti-democratic message. Chiappe's dismissal provoked mass demonstrations in Paris led by the *Croix de Feu* and Action Française. On the night of 6 February 1934, a crowd of 40,000 tried to storm the National Assembly; the PCF veterans' association stood by, uncertain whether to join in. Six hours of fighting with police took between fourteen and sixteen lives and injured more than a thousand. Deputies came to blows.

The Republic was in peril. Daladier resigned. Cincinnatus-style, Gaston Doumergue came out of retirement at his southern estate at the age of seventy to form a 'government of public safety'. The hard right leagues split, staging separate marches through Paris. The *Croix de Feu* assembled 30,000 followers to join de la Rocque as he laid a wreath at the tomb of the Unknown Soldier at the Arc de Triomphe and went on to Doumergue's home on the Avenue Foch where he climbed on a chair to declare, 'You will smash the forces of revolution. You will save our country.' The prime minister invited the Colonel in for a conversation. The Socialist Party newspaper, *Le Populaire*, denounced 'fascist groups, which think only of a new war and aim for civil war'.

TOUT VA TRÈS BIEN,
MADAME LA MARQUISE

Faced with the threat to the Republic, Radicals, Socialists and Communists put aside their divisions to stage a mass rally in the capital amid fears of a coup by the right – nine people died in clashes with police. The three parties held a joint meeting addressed by Blum, Daladier and the PCF leader Maurice Thorez, and a march of 200,000 supporters on Bastille Day. The dissolution of the Action Française was ordered after *Camelots du Roi* hooligans dragged Blum from his car, beat him severely and probably would have lynched him if police had not intervened. Maurras branded him 'a man to be shot; in the back' and when he became prime minister, the violently anti-Semitic deputy, Xavier Vallat, told him, 'this country is thinking, deep inside, that it is preferable for this country to be led by a man whose origins belong to his soil . . . than by a cunning talmudist.'

De la Rocque staged a parade up the Champs-Élysées. After the violence of 6 February, he insisted on adhering to republican legality and formed the *Parti Social Français*, whose members included the tennis star Borotra. Under the slogan of '*Le social d'abord!*' (Social matters first!), it called for the reform of parliament, cooperation between industries, an alliance of capital and labour, a minimum wage, paid holidays, votes for women and resistance to Germany, while maintaining its xenophobic, anti-republican, anti-Semitic basis. It grew into the country's largest political organisation with groups for women and youth. But for all their activism, the hard-right groups were divided among themselves whereas the left and the Radicals moved closer together, especially after Stalin lifted his anathema on non-Communist parties and advocated anti-fascist unity.

Rise of the left

Blaming France's economic troubles on the *mur d'argent* (wall of money) and the sinister power of the 200 regents of the central bank, the Radicals and Socialists emerged victorious from elections in May 1936. The centre-left took 57 per cent of the popular vote and held 346 of the 610 seats in the Chamber. With 149 deputies, the Socialists outstripped the Radicals' 110. The PCF nearly doubled its vote in the first round of the election, and increased representation in the Chamber from ten to seventy-two. The vote for right-wing candidates was down by only 70,000 on the previous election; the scale of the centre-left sweep was the result of the discipline of the Popular Front in lining up its voters behind the best-placed candidate while its opponents were disunited.

The result was the first real government of the left under Blum. The Communists, with their strength in labour unions, played a canny game, giving support but not taking any ministries so that they could claim credit for reforms while encouraging labour action and criticising the government for not going far enough. In addition, Stalin wanted them to avoid frightening the Radicals and impeding rearmament against Hitler's Germany.

The new administration was greeted with an explosion of rejoicing by workers and progressive members of the middle class – as well as such unusual figures as Élisabeth, Countess of Clermont-Tonnerre, whose ancestor had argued for Jewish equality during the Revolution, and whose views earned her the soubriquet of the 'Red Duchess'. A vast procession to the Place de la Nation in Paris on 14 July was headed by a tall, pale young woman in a red shirt, her black hair streaming behind her. Two million striking workers occupied factories; at the huge Renault plant on the edge of the city, they slept on the seats of half-finished cars and hung red flags in the managing director's office. There was also militancy in parts of the countryside. In the region round Laon, in the east, agricultural workers occupied big farms and châteaux. They were met with the employment of scab labour from extremist right-wing groups in Paris. An agreement was reached which revealed the conditions under which farm labourers worked – as well as pay rises, those who lived on site were assured of fresh sheets once a month.[1]

The government sought to boost demand through wage increases. The franc was devalued to help exports. A marathon negotiating session with employers at the Hôtel Matignon established collective bargaining rights, set the working week at forty hours and granted a 10–12 per cent pay rise. Annual paid holidays of two weeks were guaranteed, giving workers a chance to visit seaside resorts and inducing horror among the privileged at sharing their beaches with the unwashed from the cities. Despite this, the factory occupations continued.

Nationalisation of railways and of arms and aviation factories began. The Bank of France was made more accountable. The school leaving age was raised from thirteen to fourteen. Measures were introduced to help farmers. In Indochina, 7,000 of 10,000 political prisoners held after a Communist-led rising were freed. The Chamber of Deputies approved votes for women but the Senate rejected the bill and it was buried.

Membership of the Socialist SFIO party soared, but economic realities soon made themselves felt. Inflation rose steeply. The franc was devalued. Civil servants and pensioners were alienated as their revenues lagged behind those of industrial workers and they were pinched by rising prices. The inflexible nature of the new labour system and reduction in the working week produced bottlenecks accentuated by a shortage of skilled staff. Output fell. Capital fled France and a ban on private gold transactions halted the inflow of the precious metal.

The economic situation forced the government to declare a 'pause' in its reform programme. Spending on public works dropped. Money was diverted to the military budget after Germany's reoccupation of the Rhineland in March 1936. Blum's caution about aiding the Republicans in the Spanish Civil War alienated some supporters. The Communists urged intervention but the cabinet was divided and the prime minister feared that aiding the Republicans would lose the support of the moderate Radicals, widen the left-right chasm and provoke civil strife.

Man of the Year

André Léon Blum was the incarnation of the intellectual in politics, bringing in historic reforms but caught between his ideology and emotions on the one hand, and the realities of government on the other. Born in 1872 and trained as a lawyer with writer and artist friends, he wrote on everything from Stendhal to socialism. His engagement in public life stretched from the Dreyfus affair to the Fourth Republic after the Second World War, but he remains known primarily for a single year – his premiership of the Popular Front government in 1936–7, which made him the first Socialist and the first Jew to head a French government.

The Dreyfus affair took him into politics, bringing him into contact with Jean Jaurès as he campaigned for the Captain's acquittal. After the assassination of Jaurès, from whom he inherited a deep pacificism and belief in the positive power of labour, Blum became the main Socialist theoretician, a highly intelligent debater whom it was difficult to beat in debate. Though a Marxist, he did not believe in violent revolution or in Moscow's dominance. Deputy from the Mediterranean port city of Narbonne, he also edited the party newspaper, *Le Populaire*, which he used as a platform for his progressive views.

When the reaction to the rise of right-wing extremism at home and Nazi rule in Germany produced the centre-left sweep at the election of June 1936, the walrus-moustached Socialist was the natural choice to enter the Hôtel Matignon. Though physically quite frail, he led from the front with rousing speeches in the tradition of his mentor, Jaurès, falling back exhausted when he finished. The sweeping reform legislation, which marked the ensuing year, made him a hate figure for the right, whose cry became 'Better Hitler than Blum' as it depicted him as a Jew doing Moscow's bidding.

The right's attacks were unceasing, backed by funding from big business. The interior minister, Roger Salengro, committed suicide after a vicious, mendacious campaign claiming he deserted to the Germans in the First World War. On the anniversary of the battle of Verdun in June 1936, Pétain called for a revival of the family and the army. Pierre Laval, who had begun as a socialist lawyer defending strikers and took a pacifist line during the Great War before moving rightwards in two terms as prime minister, said the parliamentary regime could not continue and needed to draw on the Victor of Verdun's prestige.

Popular enthusiasm for the government ebbed. There were fresh right-left clashes. Police fire killed six people and wounded several hundred demonstrating against de la Rocque's party in Paris. The Senate refused Blum's request to impose financial policy by decree. So the prime minister resigned in June 1937, a year after taking office, and Chautemps stepped in for nine months. Blum then returned to office the following March, at the time of Hitler's Anschluss union with Austria, but failed to put together a majority and resigned after three weeks. France moved back to the centre under Daladier.[2]

'Nightmare of Fear'

Despite the rise of Nazi power, most French people were intent on avoiding war even if it meant selling out their allies. Reluctance to include the Soviet Union, if only because of the impact on domestic politics, seriously weakened the system of alliances with nations of central and Eastern Europe. A temporary show of force, which deterred Hitler from taking the whole of Czechoslovakia in 1938, caused panic, with warnings of Paris being obliterated by air raids. People fought for seats on trains. Roads out of the capital were jammed. Mobs attacked Jewish shops shouting 'Down with the Jewish war!'

Calm returned when Daladier joined his British counterpart, Neville Chamberlain, to sign the Munich Agreement ceding the largely German Sudetenland to the Reich in September 1938. He feared hostile crowds on his return to Paris; instead he was welcomed with cheers, leading him to mutter 'Imbeciles! If they only knew what they are cheering.' The Socialists voted for the pact and the critical Communists were branded as warmongers. The serpentine foreign minister, Georges Bonnet, argued that, since France could not compete with Germany, it should buy off Hitler. 'Let us not be heroic,' he advised. 'We are not up to it.' When his Nazi opposite number, Ribbentrop, visited Paris to sign a friendship declaration, he made sure Jewish ministers did not attend the receptions; the arch Nazi Jew-baiter Julius Streicher was awarded the *Légion d'honneur*. The nation lived in 'a nightmare of fear', as the writer Julien Green put it.[*3]

But the inflation of rising prices and falling output was reversed by the Daladier government after the debonair Paul Reynaud became finance minister at the end of 1938 arguing that, since France lived in the capitalist system, it must operate by the laws of profits, individual risk, free markets and growth through competition. The franc was again devalued. Policies were introduced to promote production. Taxes rose to reduce the deficit. Reynaud chipped away at the forty-hour working week. A Communist-led general strike flopped. State finances improved. Industry and investment increased. Unemployment and inflation declined. The franc strengthened and capital began to flow into France.[4]

However, the European situation grew ever more threatening. In January 1939, Franco's forces won the Spanish Civil War. In March, using the pretext of Slovak discontent with rule from Prague, Germany occupied all Czechoslovakia. Italy invaded Albania. Jolted into a show of resolution, Paris joined London in extending guarantees of territorial integrity to Poland and then did the same to Romania and Greece. Hitler showed what he thought of that by invading Poland on 1 September.

Though Marcel Déat published and spoke for appeasers, with his article 'Why Die for Danzig' arguing that France should not go to war with Germany over Poland, public resolve hardened. A defence loan collected six billion francs. Reservists were called up. Communist newspapers were banned. Reynaud formed a government – though it was approved by only one vote. He got an agreement with Britain that

* Despite this, the biggest statue on the Champs-Élysées was erected in 1938 celebrating the resistance of Belgium to Germany in 1914; it showed King Albert I of the Belgians in military dress mounted on a horse.

neither country would sign a separate peace agreement with Germany. But his fragile parliamentary position meant he had to juggle between the factions in his coalition, and put up with Daladier as defence minister. His mistress, the pro-German sardine heiress, Madame de Portes, who had a liaison with the German ambassador and wanted to 'distance herself from Jews and old politicians' as her lover put it, urged him to drop aides who favoured a strong military stance. She read secret documents in bed and, claiming she was speaking for the prime minister, questioned the head of the German section of French intelligence. The suave banker, Paul Baudouin, a protégé of hers and a leading advocate of accommodation with Berlin, became secretary to the war cabinet. Maurice Gamelin, the intellectual commander-in-chief described by Reynaud as 'an old woman', rejected the idea of offensive action.[5]

The last quarter of an hour

The incapacity of the high command's military planning was tragically revealed when the Wehrmacht advanced into Belgium, the Netherlands and Luxembourg at dawn on 10 May 1940 and by-passed the Maginot Line to attack France through the wooded highlands of the Ardennes. French and British forces were cut off as the Germans took Sedan and drove ahead. Reynaud finally sacked Gamelin and dropped Daladier, taking over the defence ministry himself, with the 49-year-old Lieutenant-General Charles de Gaulle as his deputy. Pétain was called back from his ambassadorship in Madrid and the army was put under Maxime Weygand, who had worked with Foch in the Great War, led the expedition to Poland in 1920, and served in the Middle East before becoming Chief of Staff and retiring in 1935. From his days as a strong anti-Dreyfusard, the dapper 73-year-old deeply disliked the Republic he was now appointed to defend. He called the conflict 'sheer madness' since 'we have gone to war with a 1918 army against a German Army of 1939 without adequate reserves and with an erroneous strategy'. To balance the ship, Reynaud appointed as interior minister Georges Mandel, who had begun his political career working with Clemenceau and was the toughest voice in the government for resistance. He had plenty of enemies and, as a Jew, was the target of anti-Semitic attacks.

France's tank forces were 30 per cent larger than Germany's, including the heaviest and most powerful fighting vehicle in the world, the 32-ton Char B1. In the air, the French and British had one-third numerical superiority between them. But the defensive mentality prevailed. Visiting Paris, Churchill found 'utter dejection' on every face. At the front, the historian Marc Bloch recorded a 'tide of despair' among officers, which communicated itself to troops. Threatened by the blitzkrieg advance that brought warfare to their doorstep, millions of refugees fled in the intense summer heat; they were compared by the pilot and writer Antoine de Saint-Exupéry to a great anthill kicked over by a boot.

The population of Lille fell from 200,000 to 20,000. In the eastern city of Troyes, only thirty people were left. Refugees from northern regions slept in the streets in Limoges, Cahors and Pau. The crowd waiting to board trains leaving Paris stretched for a kilometre. Officials at the foreign ministry carted out documents in wheelbarrows to burn them on the lawn. In deference to US isolationist sentiment, Roosevelt declined to respond substantively to an appeal by Reynaud for support. The Dunkirk evacuation roused hostility to 'perfidious Albion'; Pétain told the American ambassador Britain would allow the French to fight to the last drop of their blood and then sign a treaty with Hitler.

Though most of the army disintegrated, there were isolated episodes of resistance – infantry backed by tanks fought for three days for a town near Sedan, which changed hands seventeen times. Before joining the government, de Gaulle had led an armoured force into battle in the east and then outside Abbeville in the north, though German anti-tank weapons and dive-bombers won the day. The 1.95-metre tall general was still on the battlefield when Reynaud offered him a choice – command of all France's tank forces or the post of deputy defence minister. Taking the second, he faced immediate hostility from Weygand, who called him 'a child', Pétain, with whom he had feuded through the 1930s, and Baudouin and others who favoured an armistice.

In his order of the day to the army on 9 June, Weygand declared that the 'last quarter of an hour' had come. De Gaulle was sent to London to try to get Churchill to commit the RAF to the Battle of France; the British rejected the idea – and said the Frenchman told him he was right. The following day, Weygand handed Reynaud a note saying the battle in metropolitan France was lost. The official radio announced that Reynaud was going to join the armies; in fact, he left for the Loire Valley, taking back roads to avoid refugees on the main route. President Lebrun joined him, as did Pétain, aged eighty-four, in his Cadillac. Paris was declared an open city. On 14 June, the Germans entered the capital at dawn – only 700,000 of the 2.8 million pre-war residents were still there. Italy entered the war on the Nazi side.

Churchill made two trips to try to bolster French morale. De Gaulle urged resistance and the replacement of Weygand. The interior minister, Georges Mandel, wanted to go on fighting from North Africa. But the defeatists steadily gained ground as the government moved to Tours in 1870. Pétain insisted that an armistice was 'the necessary condition for the continued existence of eternal France'. The deputy prime minister, Chautemps, proposed using a neutral channel to ask Hitler for terms and decide whether to accept them. Weygand spread a false report of a Communist insurrection in Paris and, when Mandel argued with him, flounced out of the room, crying that the ministers were mad and should be arrested.

His ever-expressive eyebrows twitching, his face jumping with a tic, Reynaud looked 'ghastly, with a completely unnatural expression, still and white', according to Churchill's envoy, Edward Spears. De Portes, described by her lover's private secretary as 'ugly, dirty, nasty and half-demented', stalked the châteaux they occupied as they moved south. Reaching Bordeaux, her first concern was to acquire white tissue wall drapes for their quarters while Mandel's mistress, an actress at the Comédie-Française, ordered furniture and linen to the tune of 9,760 francs for their rooms at the Préfecture. On the night of the government's arrival, de Gaulle saw Pétain in the dining room of the Hôtel Splendide and went to shake his hand. Neither said anything. It was the last time they met.

In the leading Bordeaux restaurant, the Chapon Fin, Laval, his fingers stained with nicotine and his eyelids heavy, said he would conduct negotiations with Berlin after Reynaud had borne the shame of capitulation. Pétain drafted a resignation letter protesting at slow progress towards an armistice, and discussed the composition of a new government with the navy commander, Admiral Darlan. When the Marshal read his letter to the cabinet, President Lebrun talked him out of it, but Pétain said he would quit if Britain did not agree to let France sound out armistice terms.

De Gaulle was despatched on another mission to try to persuade Churchill to commit the RAF to defend France. Shaving in his hotel by Hyde Park on 16 June, he was visited by the ambassador, Charles Corbin, and the international official and banker, Jean Monnet, who was supervising French arms purchases. The two had a proposal for a Franco-British union. The general lunched with Churchill, assuring him that the French fleet would not be handed over voluntarily to the Germans. That afternoon, the British cabinet approved a Franco-British Union, joining the two nations indissolubly in their 'unyielding resolution in their common defence of justice and freedom' with joint defence, foreign, financial and economic policies, and a single war cabinet.

De Gaulle telephoned Reynaud to read out the declaration. Spears, in Bordeaux, described the prime minister taking down the wording with a thick pencil on sheets of paper that flew off his desk as he wrote, his eyebrows shooting up so far that they seemed about to merge with his neatly parted hair. When Churchill came on the line, the Frenchman said he would unveil the plan to his cabinet that evening, and rout the appeasers. Spears saw his face 'transfigured with joy'.

But Weygand had access to military taps on the prime minister's telephone and de Portes read the declaration as it was typed up. Forewarned, Pétain said union would tie France to a corpse; it was all a British plot to absorb France's empire and turn the country into a dominion. The proposal fell without a vote. Reynaud resigned. Lebrun called on Pétain to form a government. Weygand became defence minister Admiral Darlan took the navy. Baudouin got the foreign ministry and sounded out Berlin and Rome on an armistice. 'It is with a heavy heart that I tell you today that the combat must be ended,' Pétain said in a national broadcast, adding that he gave France 'the gift of my person to alleviate its misfortune'. There was nothing to be done with the Marshal, Mandel remarked – 'he is gaga'. The newly deposed minister was Britain's first choice to lead resistance. But he turned down a suggestion from Spears to fly out to London in the morning. Sitting in a large room lit by a single candle, he acknowledged that, as a Jew, he might be in danger if he stayed; but that was why he could not go – 'it would look as if I was afraid, as if I was running away.'

De Gaulle learned of the failure of the union scheme and Reynaud's resignation after flying back to Bordeaux in a British plane. He saw Reynaud at 11 p.m. and said he intended to go to Britain to continue the combat. The next morning, he boarded a two-winged British Rapid Dragon plane, having called in at military headquarters, raised his arms and declared against all the evidence, 'the Germans have lost the war.' He then flew with Spears to London and went to see Churchill to start his ascent to greatness.

Despite the national humiliation, Pétain's appointment was received with rejoicing, if simply because the aged Marshal offered to end the fighting. Mandel, Daladier and others tried to get to North Africa to continue the struggle for French territory there, but were turned back and interned. The armistice, signed on 22 June in the same railway carriage in the forest clearing at Compiègne where Germany had surrendered in 1918, put northern and western France, including Paris, the Atlantic coastline and Alsace-Lorraine, under German occupation. France was required to pay the costs of the occupation forces and hand over political refugees on its territory; leading German socialists were taken back to Germany to their deaths. An Italian invasion of south-east France halted but, with German blessing, Mussolini got control of Corsica and the Alpes-Maritimes and a zone along the frontier containing 28,500 people – demilitarised zones were established for the naval bases of Toulon, Bizerta, Ajaccio and Oran and between the two countries' African colonies.

Two-fifths of national territory came under the Marshal's government, which moved first to Clermont-Ferrand in the Auvergne and then, finding it lacking in facilities and hotel rooms, to the spa of Vichy. France was allowed to keep a 94,000-man army, though without tanks. Apart from ships needed to defend the Empire, the fleet was to be laid up. The Marshal and Weygand pronounced the conditions 'tough but not dishonourable'. The Chamber of Deputies and the Senate, most of their members elected in 1936 when the Popular Front won its majority, ratified the armistice and, by 569 to 80 with 18 abstentions, authorised the cabinet to draft a new constitution. Laval told them: 'Parliamentary democracy has lost the war. It must disappear to give way to an authoritarian regime.'

Three days after the armistice, Hitler visited Paris, which was garlanded with huge Nazi flags. According to the architect Albert Speer, who was with him, the Opera House sent the Führer into ecstasies – he tried to give his French guide a tip but was refused. After driving up the Champs-Élysées and to the Trocadéro and the Eiffel Tower, he stood for a long time at Napoleon's tomb at the Invalides. 'It was the dream of my life to be permitted to see Paris,' he told Speer. That evening he remarked that, when the renovation of Berlin was completed, 'Paris will only be a shadow. So why should we destroy it?'[6]

The Third Republic ended in catastrophic defeat and enormous civil disarray after a persistent refusal to face reality. Pétain became head of state with virtually unlimited powers. The legislature was dissolved. The reign of reason had been undone by military defeat but the seeds of collapse lay much deeper, in the failure to resolve inherent conflicts rooted in the past century-and-a-half and to rally round a narrative which could enable France to live up to its view of itself.

PART 4

VICHY, DE GAULLE AND
THE UNLOVED REPUBLIC

1940–1958

15

TWO FRANCES

The legend that, apart from a small group of Fascists and crooks round the geriatric Marshal, France resisted the Germans for four years is just that. The varnishing of history was adopted when Allied troops liberated the country in 1944 and Charles de Gaulle argued that his Free French movement in London, not the Vichy regime under Pétain, represented the indivisible Republic. For decades, the extent of collaboration was obfuscated and the persecution of the Jews forgotten in favour of a more comforting account of 'passive resistance'. Simone Veil, the concentration camp survivor and future minister, recalled how wounded she had been when she returned to France and found a wall of indifference. The showing on television of the ground-breaking documentary, *Le Chagrin et la Pitié* (*Sorrow and Pity*) about the reality of the Occupation was delayed for a dozen years (Veil, now a minister, was a leading figure in the opposition to showing it – she said on the grounds that the director wanted too much money). It took an American historian, Robert Paxton, to show how the French had done the Nazis' work for them, and it was not until 1995 that a President of the Republic publicly recognised France's responsibility for deporting tens of thousands of Jews to Nazi death camps.

Dedicated collaborators were certainly in a minority, but so were those who actively resisted, at least until the landing of American and British troops on the Channel coast in 1944 swelled the ranks of 'resisters of the last hour'. Members of the National Assembly and

Senate voted almost unanimously for the Marshal to become head of state with legislative and executive powers. Laval warned that, if they did not do so, the Germans would occupy the whole country. Having done as he instructed, parliament was dissolved until the Victor of Verdun saw fit to reconvene it, which he did not.

For most of the French, especially those in the occupied zone, the next four years were a time of ambiguity and of surviving till the country was delivered back to itself by the Allied powers. While there was no shortage of real heroes and villains and occasional strikes and food riots, with widespread evasion of rules and regulations, most people watched and waited, playing both sides of the street if they could, as epitomised by the quintessentially ambiguous future president, François Mitterrand, who accepted a decoration from Pétain but also entered the Resistance.

The divide widens

The years before the debacle of 1940 had greatly accentuated the long-running conflict between the Republic, claiming the inheritance of the Revolution, and its opponents. They saw in Pétain the reactionary father figure France needed, who would preside over the creation of a new political and social system that would represent national values more truly than the Third Republic had done, realising the dreams nurtured by the hard right for three-quarters of a century. Opponents of the republican order jubilated. Maurras said the Marshal's assumption of power was a 'divine surprise' while the poet Paul Claudel wrote that, after sixty years, 'France is delivered from the yoke of the Radical Party and the anti-Catholics (teachers, lawyers, Jews, Freemasons) [with the] hope of being saved from universal suffrage and parliamentarianism.' In 1941, he wrote an ode calling on the French to venerate the old man who spoke to it like a father.[1]

The truth was that the Marshal's capacity to be anything more than figurehead diminished by the month. Not that this made him easier to deal with. While his mental facilities diminished, his pride remained unshakable. While he took the path of passivity when faced with the need to make decisions, he would not give way but held tenaciously onto the legend he had created for himself.[2]

The Resistance, on the other hand, took on a radical left-wing character, especially after the Reich attacked the Soviet Union in June 1941, and the French Communists became its biggest source of recruitment. The violent nature of the period between 1940 and 1944 meant that this latest round in the French ideological struggle took on a particularly acute form, leading to multiple killings by both sides. If the country did not suffer bloodletting on the scale of the First World War, surrender was far from ending the death toll. In all, 600,000 people perished in France. Some 350,000 were civilians, including 68,000 who died in Allied bombing raids and 75,000 Jews, a quarter of the community, deported to concentration camps.

In this process, in the greatest of ironies, the nationalist right allied itself with a foreign occupying power while the left accepted the leadership of a military man with old-fashioned views of authority. Pétain sought a paternalist order based on family, fatherland and work, extolling traditional morality. The word 'Republic' was discarded; the Marshal became the head of the French state as well as chief of government, the regime founded on personal loyalty to him, in Bonapartist fashion. A paternalist Pétainist cult was developed as he urged a renewal of society in a national revolution to eradicate the noxious elements that had brought disaster. But he was showing his age – the American ambassador described him as 'a feeble, frightened old man, surrounded by self-seeking conspirators'.[3]

The first Vichy cabinet under Laval included two Socialists, a Radical and a senior member of the CGT trade union federation. The Radical Socialist leader, Édouard Herriot, who, over a meal of lamb with sorrel sauce, had rejected a British attempt to get him to go to London, appealed to the cabinet to unite around the Marshal 'in the veneration which his name inspires in all' and to 'take care to avoid disturbing the unity established under his authority'.

The condition of the country was, indeed, grave. As well as the hugely demoralising defeat, the official count of refugees reached 6 million. The interior ministry announced that urban centres with more than 20,000 inhabitants would be declared open towns. Washington and Moscow recognised the Pétain government. In Munich, Hitler and Mussolini met to plan the future as the Führer prepared to attack Britain. Stalin remained in alliance with Berlin; Soviet troops completed the occupation of Latvia and Estonia. In Chicago, Roosevelt promised American mothers he would not send their sons to fight in far-off lands.

In a rare display of defiance, a military commander in the Auvergne ordered his men to resist. A Communist member of the National Assembly, Charles Tillon, issued a tract declaring that 'the French people will not bear slavery.' In Chartres, the prefect of the Eure-et-Loir *département*, Jean Moulin, declined to sign a proclamation handed to him by the Germans and tried to kill himself by slitting his throat to avoid giving way under torture. But, for the most part, the French accepted the price of peace.

The new state aimed to be 'national, authoritarian, hierarchical and social', in the words of its ideologue René Gillouin. For Weygand, 'a political regime of Masonic, capitalist and international accommodations, has led us to where we are; France does not want any more of that.' Appointed bodies replaced elected ones; most government departments were run by technocrats, who sought to reorganise the economy with wage and price controls, setting up corporatist organisations instead of trade unions and using industrial committees favouring big firms ready to supply the Nazis.

The price of occupation and collaboration

None of these initiatives proved very effective. Much of industry was disorganised and most resources, together with the richest agricultural regions, lay under German control. The victors requisitioned machinery, materials, food and farm animals, including 700,000 horses. After Alsace and Lorraine were absorbed into the Reich, 200,000 inhabitants were expelled on top of 630,000 who had left in 1939. A zone running from Lille through Champagne to the Swiss border was earmarked for German colonisation. A bad harvest was aggravated by the absence of agricultural workers held as prisoners of war. The black market thrived and barter became common.

The Odd Couple

The two leading figures of the four years of the Vichy regime could hardly have been more dissimilar: Philippe Pétain sought to elevate himself above the fray of politics; Pierre Laval was an inveterate schemer. The Marshal was eighty-four when he became head of state; Laval celebrated his fifty-seventh birthday on 28 June, six days after the armistice. The old man was distinguished and paternal, with startlingly blue eyes but more than a touch of senility. Laval was described by a British diplomat as 'intelligent, olive-skinned and leering' with discoloured teeth and an ever-present white tie sometimes marked with food stains.

Impassive and mediocre, prejudiced and without ideas of his own, subject to the influence of the last person he had spoken to, the Marshal was the glue of Vichy, greeted by crowds chanting '*Maréchal, nous voilà!*' (Marshal, here we are!). Millions of cards were distributed bearing his image. The church offered enthusiastic support. The poet Paul Claudel called on the French to 'listen to this old man who bends over you and speaks to you like a father'.

He occupied the third floor of the Hôtel du Parc in Vichy and went for daily constitutionals by the River Allier, even when snow fell. His appetite was good, and he took red wine with meals.

His long career as a senior military figure and his status as the saviour of Verdun enabled him to appear as a sage, helped by the way he said little. But his life had, in some ways, been at odds with the regime he headed. He attended mass, but admitted he had lost his faith. 'I love two things above all else,' he said, 'sex and the infantry'.

While the old man now lived largely in a world of his own, Laval was a quintessential hands-on politician. Weygand told him he was 'worse than a dog; you roll in shit', but the Auvergnat had grown used to abuse as he navigated from his early socialism to collaboration, making sure of a good income by ventures into property and printing, and using the defeat of 1940 to propel himself to the top, carrying the complaisant old soldier along with him.

Payment of the costs of occupation forces under the armistice absorbed 55 per cent of national revenue. The franc was devalued by 20 per cent, increasing the cost of the occupation and enabling the victors to buy at knockdown prices. A system of forced labour sent 600,000 young men to work in Germany during the war years. France handed to the Nazis the Belgian gold reserves entrusted to it for safe-keeping. A British naval blockade closed off ports, and a British attack seriously damaged the fleet at the North African base of Mers-el-Kébir. Vichy recognised Japanese predominance in Indochina.

As the family was given quasi-religious devotion, women were seen as home-makers whose duty was to bear as many children as possible. Abortion became a capital offence and legislation was introduced against adultery. Divorce was made more difficult. Sanctions punished alcoholism. Physical training schemes were introduced for the young.

Anti-Semitic measures were swiftly introduced. Though some apologists have argued that he tried to moderate them, Pétain, in fact, toughened up the initial legislation. The racial laws were welcomed enthusiastically by Action Française, which had been freed from papal condemnation and thundered against '*métèques*' of non-French birth. Jews were excluded from state employment and jobs in enterprises that received government money. Their property was grabbed by profiteers. A network of camps was set up where Jews, foreigners, gypsies, political prisoners and others regarded as undesirables were held often in harsh and squalid conditions. A commission began to revoke naturalisations granted to foreigners since 1927, mainly Jews. A general commissariat for Jewish issues was set up in 1941, headed by the prominent anti-Semitic parliamentarian, Xavier Vallat. However, he proved too moderate for the SS, and was replaced by the more extreme Louis Darquier de Pellepoix, who combined racial obsession with dissembling self-promotion.[4]

While not conducting a Nazi-style extermination campaign against the mentally ill, the Vichy regime left many of them to die from hunger and neglect. The number remains a matter of controversy, with some estimates running as high as 400,000. Among those who perished was the sculptor Camille Claudel, Rodin's model and lover and the elder sister of the poet Paul Claudel; schizophrenic, she had been confined to an asylum outside Avignon for three decades. Her brother crossed France in her last days of life, but did not manage to see her or attend the funeral.*[5]

The Marshal was particularly hostile towards Freemasons, another target of Action Française. They were barred from public services; a list of suspected Masons contained four times as many names as there were members of French lodges. Leading Third Republic politicians were arrested, among them Mandel, Daladier, Blum and Reynaud, who had been injured in a car crash that took the life of his mistress when a suitcase shot forward and broke her neck. Some were put on trial for their responsibility for defeat by having spent too little on defence, but proceedings were abandoned when Daladier and Blum showed that military expenditure had increased under their governments and that cuts had come under ministries which included Pétain and Laval.

Behind the façade of unity in Vichy, political infighting was evident from the start, as Laval ploughed ahead with collaboration, drawing on anti-British sentiment after the naval attack at Mers. He framed a plot to oust Pétain but was himself deposed, arrested and replaced by Admiral Darlan, who travelled to Germany to assure the Führer of Vichy's desire to pursue cooperation. The admiral, described by Churchill as 'dangerous, bitter ... an ambitious crook', aroused opposition, led by Weygand, because of his willingness to let the Nazis use French bases in Syria. Intriguing with the German ambassador, Laval returned in April 1942 as Darlan stepped down a rung as Commander-in-Chief.

Back in the saddle, the Auvergnat set up a meeting between Pétain and the Führer at the railway station of Montoire-sur-le-Loir, on the demarcation line between the two zones of France, as Hitler went to Spain to try to get Franco to come into the war on his side. The Nazi leader helped the old soldier to climb the steps into his carriage for two hours of talks during which the Vichy leader said Britain was the prime cause of France's defeat. A statement announced that they had agreed on collaboration.

* In 2015, President Hollande agreed to the creation of a memorial to the dead after lobbying by scientists, writers, film makers and philosophers.

The Germans wired the photograph of the two men shaking hands round the world, throwing Churchill into a rage. Pétain tried to limit the damage with a broadcast in which he insisted France remained sovereign but he added that 'in the framework of the active construction of the new European order, I enter today on the path of collaboration.' Laval said he hoped Germany would win the war.

Much as he and the French Fascists might dream of playing a role in a new Europe led by Berlin and justifying themselves by invoking an anti-communist crusade, Hitler had no such intentions and they became prisoners of their own illusions as the tide of war changed, descending into desperate denial and nihilism. 'If necessary, France will cover itself with concentration camps and execution squads will work round the clock,' wrote the politician Marcel Déat. 'The birth of a new regime is carried out with forceps and in pain.'

Laval assumed executive power. Weygand was arrested and moved to Germany. For all his hopes of wheedling France's way to a privileged place at the Nazi table, the cost of occupation and collaboration rose steadily. Hitler reacted to the Allied invasion of North Africa in November 1942, by sending the Wehrmacht to occupy the Vichy zone; Italian troops moved over the south-eastern frontier. Pétain recorded a broadcast saying these were 'the darkest days of my life'. German troops hurried to the radio station and confiscated the disc. Only one Vichy commander refused to accept the occupation, General de Lattre de Tassigny; he was arrested and sentenced to ten years' imprisonment.

The regime's popularity declined steadily, and prefects warned of widespread disaffection; but the Marshal continued to attract big crowds, and the regime had a seductive spokesman in its secretary of state for information, Philippe Henriot, a man whose speeches and broadcasts were described by a British journalist resident in France and sympathetic to Vichy as 'so pungent, so vitriolic, so eloquent ... delivered with a fire, a forthrightness, an effectiveness of utterance that his bitterest enemies cannot deny.' But everyday life grew tougher as rationing and badly managed food supplies exacerbated shortages and inequalities while the incidence of tuberculosis and diphtheria rose and mortality increased by up to 50 per cent in the worst affected regions. There were food riots in Paris and the north.[6]

Annual payments to the Reich amounted to 31 per cent of France's pre-war gross national product, and contributed 9 per cent of German GDP. Young Frenchmen were drafted to work in German factories at the rate of three for every prisoner of war sent home. Most companies collaborated. French factories turned out weapons valued at 31 billion francs between 1940 and 1943. Renault and Citroën supplied 30,000 vehicles a year and France delivered 2,517 military aircraft during the war. Railway rolling stock was sent to Germany or commandeered by occupation forces. Still, a brittle form of high life continued in occupied Paris where the occupiers made sure the top restaurants they patronised had enough food and coal; officers got a 90 per cent discount at the Ritz. Some prominent entertainers such as Sacha Guitry frequented Abetz's embassy while the choreographer Serge Lifar received the German top brass at the Opera. French writers went to see Goebbels.

Leading actors, artists and musicians were feted in the Reich. Coco Chanel and Arletty had affairs with German officers while living at the Ritz. The owner of the newspaper, *Le Matin*, held dinners with table flowers arranged in the shape of a swastika. Prominent film directors continued to work and produced some great cinema such as Henri Clouzot's *Le Corbeau* about poison pen letters in a small town and Marcel Carné's historical fresco *Les Enfants du Paradis*, but other major screen figures preferred to spend the war in Hollywood while Jean Gabin joined the Free French and was decorated twice in North Africa.[7]

Finding Vichy too conservative, ardent Fascists based themselves in Paris where they could work directly with the occupiers. Doriot and Déat set up political movements to agitate for a new order in France and Europe. Though they probably never had more than 20,000 members between them, the two men reached a wider public through radio and the press. Sales of the rabidly anti-Semitic publication, *Je Suis Partout* (*I Am Everywhere*), reached 300,000. Laval asked a First World War veteran, Joseph Darnand, to create a paramilitary force, the *Milice* (Militia), to impose order in association with the Germans. By 1944, Darnand, who swore an oath of loyalty to Hitler and held SS officer rank, commanded 35,000 *miliciens*, many of them young men anxious to avoid labour service in Germany. Doriot, Déat and Darnand formed units to fight alongside the Wehrmacht. One regiment of 2,500 men suffered heavy losses round Moscow in 1941 while others battled partisans in Ukraine. A former Communist, Paul Marion, led the Legion of French Volunteers Against Bolshevism and created an Association of Friends of the Waffen SS.

In the occupied zone, round-ups of Jews began in May 1941. They had earlier been banned from working or frequenting public places and were required in 1942 to wear Star of David patches – for which they were charged two clothing coupons. Camps were set up, including the big centre at Drancy in the Paris suburbs, as staging posts for deportation to death in Eastern Europe. In April 1942, French police took 5,800 women, 4,000 children and 3,000 men from their homes in the capital in an operation planned with the Gestapo and SS by Darquier de Pellepoix and René Bousquet, secretary-general of the national police. In agreement with Laval, Bousquet ordered that children be included. About 7,500 of those detained were herded into the cycling stadium, the Vel d'Hiv, and held for five days in stifling summer heat with one water tap and no lavatories before being moved to Drancy and then to Auschwitz on French state trains*. Laval expressed satisfaction at having got rid of such 'dregs' of society. The Germans gave Bousquet additional arms for the police and greater powers to act against the Resistance.

As the war moved towards its end, the deportations increased – 14,000 Jews went to their deaths in the eight months before the Liberation. In all, 80,000 Jews were sent from France to concentration camps, some 24,000 of them of French nationality and 56,000 more recent arrivals. Three per cent returned alive.

High as the death toll was, it was proportionately considerably lower than in Belgium and Holland, which the historian Jacques Semelin, author of a landmark book on the subject published in 2014, puts down to a range of factors. There was clandestine help from French people who hated the Germans, especially after the Nazis moved into the Free

---

* In all, 11,000 Jewish children were deported from the capital, an act recognised only recently in plaques outside schools where they had studied.

Zone. Some leading Catholics were vocal in their outrage, led by Archbishop Saliège of Toulouse and followed by colleagues in Marseilles, Lyons, Montauban, Bayonne and Albi who denounced the round-ups from the pulpit and through parish letters. Some 7 per cent of French Jews escaped to Spain or Switzerland. But, as the tide of war turned, the main salvation probably lay in the increasing caution of civil servants and policemen about committing themselves to the occupying power as they kept three sets of files – one to show how they had helped the Germans, one to record their services to Vichy and the third to record what they had done for the Resistance, destroying the first two on D-Day.[8]

The Free Frenchman

Few people heard the speech Charles de Gaulle made on the BBC on 18 June 1940, calling for resistance. Among them, according to a relative, was the general's mother, who was living in Brittany. The broadcast nearly did not take place. When they met the previous evening, Churchill had told the general he could use the airwaves. But the Foreign Office under Lord Halifax was hoping to build bridges with the Pétain regime and thought a speech by de Gaulle 'undesirable'. That provoked Edward Spears to get Churchill's agreement that the Frenchman he had brought to London should speak if most members of the cabinet would change their minds, which they did.

'Has the last word been said?' de Gaulle asked. 'Must hope disappear? Is defeat final? No!' He did not actually utter the words 'France has lost a battle, but not the war' – they were appended later – but that was the import of his message. France was not alone in a worldwide struggle. With its overseas possessions, it could align itself with the British Empire and draw on 'the immense industry of the United States'. Lacking any legitimacy – he had been a junior minister for all of twelve days – or backing beyond Churchill's goodwill, and showing insubordination that sat ill with his belief in discipline, the little-known soldier put himself at the head of resistance, claiming to have taken the Republic with him to London and announcing that 'I, General de

Gaulle, am starting this national task here in England. I invite all the French who want to remain free to listen to me and to follow me.' The British establishment was not convinced he was its man. Even de Gaulle had doubts; he said later that he had wondered if he was doing something mad, 'throwing myself into the water without knowing where the bank is . . . I put myself in God's hands.'

But, for all the weakness of his position, his dependence on an ally from which he wished to demonstrate independence, not to mention a death sentence passed on him by a Vichy court, the general insisted from the start on the special nature of his mission – to save France's honour and ensure that he, rather than Pétain, represented the nation. Asked by an associate for the legitimacy of what they were doing, he replied simply, 'We are France.' He wrote in his memoirs, 'It was for me to take the country's fate upon myself'.

The assertion of independence from Britain, which he had always seen as France's foe but on which he depended, was essential, in contrast to the increasingly vassal status of Vichy to the Germans. In place of Laval's efforts to ingratiate himself with the Nazis, the general saw intransigence as the one weapon at his command – 'He had to be rude to the British to prove to French eyes that he was not a British puppet,' Churchill observed. 'He certainly carried out this policy with perseverance.'

Despite their continual sparring, which would lead Churchill to say that the general had gone off his head and that he was 'sick to death of him', the British recognised him as 'Leader of all Free Frenchmen, wherever they may be, who rally to him in support of the Allied Cause'. Churchill told him, 'You stand alone. So what? I recognise you alone.' But the going was sticky to begin with. Though de Gaulle was not privy to this, Britain maintained contact with Vichy through the embassies in Madrid and Churchill dallied briefly with an envoy from the collaborationist regime. Most of the established French figures in London shunned the general, among them the writer André Maurois, and the proponents of the Franco-British Union plan, Ambassador Corbin and Jean Monnet. The committee de Galle established attracted only a tenth of the 2,000 French soldiers evacuated to London plus a number of medical staff, sailors and 150 airmen.

Three weeks after he left France, Britain presented de Gaulle with a major challenge when it attacked the French fleet moored at Mers-el-Kébir base outside the Algerian city of Oran to prevent it falling into German or Italian hands, sinking or badly damaging three big ships and killing 1,285 on board. After an initial private outburst, the general recognised that the attack was inevitable. Speaking on the BBC, he said that all French people felt grief and anger, but that it was better for the ships to have been sunk than to have been used by the enemy since 'no Frenchman worthy of the name can for a moment doubt that a British defeat would seal for ever his country's bondage'. Churchill called him 'magnificent in his demeanour'.

His committee gained two notable recruits that summer. General Georges Catroux, the governor general in Indochina, moved to London after being cashiered by Vichy. Vice-Admiral Émile Muselier escaped from France via Gibraltar with some naval craft on which he flew flags emblazoned with the Cross of Lorraine, originally a form of Byzantine cross, giving the Free French their emblem. Some of the British envisaged the pipe-smoking Catroux as an alternative or co-equal to de Gaulle, but he never challenged for the leadership. Muselier was a different matter, repeatedly bridling at de Gaulle's primacy and using the backing of the British Admiralty to mount a challenge that went awry in 1942. The General had his security men arrest the admiral, telling the British that he was 'a tired man who indulged in drugs [and] was morally unbalanced.' The British withdrew support for Muselier and de Gaulle put him on the retirement list.

The resistance in London, now known as the Free French and with 2,721 members, got a big boost when Britain agreed to pay its European personnel and guarantee funding on a loan basis from the Treasury – de Gaulle's own income came from private donations, mainly by French supporters, such as the head of the Cartier firm in the United Kingdom who put his car at the General's disposition and sometimes acted as his chauffeur. He moved his headquarters into a stately building in Carlton House Gardens by St James's Park and was joined in London by his wife and children who had taken a boat from France. The family settled initially in a house in Kent and then moved to Shropshire, though de

Gaulle stayed in London at the Connaught Hotel, before taking a house in Middlesex and ending up in a large building in Hampstead in north London.

A French community in exile thrived round their club in St James's. There was support from the royal family; Queen Elizabeth was particularly warm, making a broadcast in French to the women of France. The BBC was used to great effect for broadcasts by the General, news of events in France and entertainment from leading figures in exile. Vichy figures showed the audience rising to millions by 1942.

The most important early success came in West Africa where the highly regarded black governor of Chad, Félix Éboué, came out for the Free French, and where two early recruits, Captain Philippe Leclerc and Squadron Leader Hettier de Boislambert, led twenty volunteers to take charge of the colony of Cameroon. The Vichy governor of French Congo was displaced and Free French representatives seized control of the territory of Ubangi-Shari (later the Central African Republic).

This encouraged de Gaulle to stage an attack on the Senegalese capital, Dakar, a key naval base. Churchill was enthusiastic, and agreed that Britain would contribute soldiers and a naval flotilla, which set sail at the end of August. The expedition was a disaster. Vichy sent three cruisers to join its most modern warship, the *Richelieu*, which had sailed to the base in June from Mers-el-Kébir; though it was still under construction and had been damaged in a British air attack, it could serve as a powerful gun battery. The bombardment from the British ships killed 2,000 people, half of them civilians. But the defenders, led by a one-legged Verdun veteran, repelled the naval attack and an attempted beach landing, inflicting heavy losses.

The shock was plain for the Free French and, even more, for its leader. Three separate reports speak of him contemplating suicide. He had set Frenchman against Frenchman, and had failed to achieve his objective. Still, he swiftly recovered, landing in Cameroon for his first *bain de foule* (crowd bath). Moving on to Chad, he drew up a plan with Governor Éboué for a Free French military column to march north through the Sahara to the Mediterranean. In October, Vichy

The Constable

Charles de Gaulle had been preparing for his meeting with destiny for a long time. Born in 1890, he had written in his mid-twenties of the nature of great leaders whom he intended to join one day. They must, he noted, be ready to seize the moment when it presented itself, remain aloof, without friends or entanglements, and pursue their own paths. 'I look down on those who serve me,' an early biographer recorded him as saying. 'As for those who contradict me, I can't put up with them.'

A humanist who appeared distant and often arrogant as he towered above those around him, he was expert at keeping his thoughts to himself and then coming out with *ex cathedra* statements – he had been nicknamed as a young officer '*le Connétable*' (the Constable) who would run the realm. He was devoted to his family – his wife Yvonne, and three children including the youngest, Anne, who had Down's syndrome and to whom he was dedicated. But he was, at the same time, terribly solitary, so alone, he wrote, that he 'had to reach the heights and never come down again'.

Churchill detected the pain behind his impassive façade, pain, above all, for the nation of which he would say he had 'a certain idea'. France's humiliation was a very personal matter for him.

His family background was highly conservative – his parents were both royalists who rejected the Revolution. He believed in old-fashioned morality and the military values of discipline and order, stemming from his early years in the army and his fighting in 1914–16 in the trenches of the Western Front where he was wounded three times before ending up as a German prisoner of war, staging half-a-dozen fruitless escape attempts. Yet he was dedicated to the republican state, despite his disdain for the political parties, and would voluntarily relinquish office twice.

When his time came in the summer of 1940, he threw over all his respect for the order and discipline represented by Vichy and set out a new standard to preserve the honour of his country. He called himself the only real revolutionary among French leaders and, much later, told an aide, 'I always thought that I would be at the head of the state one day. Yes, that always seemed to me evident.'[9]

forces in Gabon capitulated to a Free French unit under Leclerc and Marie-Pierre Koenig; the governor committed suicide. Éboué was appointed governor-general of French Equatorial Africa, and a Council for the Defence of the Empire was created. Free French forces in Africa numbered 20,000. All this did not erase the memory of Dakar, but, as de Gaulle wrote to his wife, 'No storm lasts indefinitely.' He had, he added, become a 'living legend'.

If that was the case, it did not prevent some serious conflicts with the Allies as de Gaulle pursued Free French interests during a victorious joint campaign against Vichy forces in Syria. He flew to the region and clashed repeatedly with British military and civilian officials – Edward Spears, who had been posted to the Middle East and refused to go along with the General's demand that France alone should determine Syria's political future, coined the phrase that the cross Britain had to bear was the Cross of Lorraine. Still, de Gaulle got recognition of France's rights in the Levant; the Free French acquired Vichy military equipment and recruited 6,000 men.

General Auchinleck, Britain's commander-in-chief in the Middle East, thought the Constable 'mad and consumed by personal ambition'. After de Gaulle gave an interview with an American correspondent in which he spoke of an implicit arrangement between Berlin and London in which each made use of Vichy and kept it alive, Churchill exploded. 'No one is to see General de Gaulle,' he ordered. The press was told not to report his return to Britain. A request by the Free French leader to broadcast on the BBC was refused. De Gaulle tried to wriggle out of it by saying his words had been distorted, and the prime minister agreed to a meeting which he began with such heated words that the interpreter fled the room, but which ended with the two men sitting side by side with amiable expressions, smoking cigars and speaking in French.

The entry of the United States into the war after Pearl Harbor, at the end of 1941, led the General to declare that 'the war is finished since the outcome is known from now on. In this industrial war nothing will be able to resist.' What counted now, he remarked, were relations between Washington and Moscow; he feared that, after Germany's defeat, there would be a great war between the United

States and the Soviet Union which the Americans risked losing if they did not prepare in time. He recognised that Churchill's main priority was to maintain friendship with America; 'From now on,' he forecast, 'the British will do nothing without Roosevelt's agreement'. As the prime minister told him on the eve of D-Day, 'every time I have to decide between you and Roosevelt, I shall always choose Roosevelt.'

That presented de Gaulle with a problem, since Roosevelt regarded the Frenchman as a potential military dictator and had maintained relations with Vichy. The verdict of the president and his close advisers (as well as Stalin) that France had been politically and morally bankrupt by 1939 was not far from de Gaulle's assessment, but their belief that Washington had the right to determine its post-war shape certainly was. FDR envisaged an American military governorship and the creation of a new country to be called Wallonia carved out of French-speaking Belgium, Luxembourg and the General's birthplace of Flanders. Characteristically, de Gaulle chose to make matters worse with an assertion of independence, rather than seeking to appease Washington.[10]

On Christmas Eve 1941, seventeen days after Pearl Harbor, a small Free French force of ships and marines occupied the islands of Saint-Pierre-et-Miquelon off Canada. Though Churchill and the Canadians approved, the State Department was outraged; it had just reached an agreement with Vichy to maintain the status quo in all French possessions in the western hemisphere. Secretary of state Cordell Hull denounced the 'arbitrary action', referring to the 'so-called Free French'. After a quick poll showed 90 per cent of the inhabitants backed his movement, de Gaulle replied that the action had been carried out 'to re-establish the independence and greatness of France that is necessary for the equilibrium of the world'. But Hull and de Gaulle's opponents among French exiles in Washington got the Gaullists excluded from the pact creating the United Nations, signed by twenty-six countries soon afterwards in Washington. The General reflected how strange it was 'that, as soon as America entered the war, the Free French were eliminated from the Allied conferences in spite of the military effort which they were making'.

The fortunes of his movement ebbed and flowed. A column under Leclerc forged 600 miles north from Chad to take the Italian-held oasis of Kufra in Libya – de Gaulle hailed this as 'the first decisive step towards victory'. The Free French also scored a notable success in holding back much larger Axis forces in the desert at Bir Hakeim in May and June 1942. Seeking to develop relations with Moscow, the General sent an emissary to the Soviet Union, and met the foreign minister, Molotov, when he visited Britain. He despatched French pilots to the Eastern Front, where they flew 5,000 sorties in Soviet Yak fighters and claimed to have shot down 268 German aircraft. But Stalin had a low opinion of the Free French and thought their nation had to pay for its collapse in 1940.

Fresh trouble broke out with the British after they launched an operation against the French territory of Madagascar in May 1942 without informing de Gaulle, and then made matters worse by trying to negotiate with the Vichy authorities there. The General threatened to dissolve the movement he headed and advised its members to enrol in the Canadian army. Like all such quarrels, it simmered down, but the Levant continued to cause Franco-British tension as the two sides sparred for influence, with Churchill growling that instead of waging war with Germany, de Gaulle had waged war with England and had 'not shown the slightest desire to assist us'.

Resistance is organised

For the first year of the Occupation, the Nazi-Soviet Pact put a straitjacket on the main natural anti-fascist party, the Communists. Though one central committee member, Charles Tillon, immediately advocated resistance and an independent-minded party member, Georges Guingouin, set up a network in the hills of the Limousin, the PCF leader, Maurice Thorez, deserted from the army and went to Moscow, denouncing French support for Poland as imperialist aid for 'the oppressors of the people'. The Party urged fraternisation with the Germans and denounced attempts at industrial sabotage.

In contrast, underground networks sprang up across the political spectrum. One of the first was created by anthropologists and ethnologists at the Musée de l'Homme in Paris, but it was uncovered in

February 1941 and most of its members executed. *Libération-Sud* was created in July 1941 with Socialist support under an aristocrat, Emmanuel d'Astier de la Vigerie, who had begun as an anti-Semitic monarchist but now hoped to bring together Socialists, Communists and trade unionists. The Socialist Christian Pineau launched *Libération-Nord*, which linked with d'Astier's group. Another non-Communist group, *Combat*, was founded in Lyons under Henri Frenay, a former officer disillusioned with Vichy; its newspaper, which bore the unit's name, was edited by the writer Albert Camus. The *Franc-tireur* (Sniper) group, also in the Lyons area, drew members from the far left and far right as the city in central France became the focal point for the growing force of partisans known as *l'Armée des Ombres* (the Army of the Shadows). After initially sympathising with Vichy, Colonel de la Rocque of the *Croix de Feu* set up a resistance unit in 1942 that worked with the British until he was deported to Germany.

Other groups were created at the Sorbonne and by industrialists who wanted to see a British victory. Tillon became head of the military committee of the national *Francs-tireurs* and another Communist, Auguste Lecoeur, organised a strike by more than 100,000 miners in northern France in the early summer of 1941 to protest at stagnant wages, long working hours, rising food prices and shortages; the action was put down after ten days by the occupation forces with 450 arrests and 244 deportations to Germany. There were also resistance bodies further afield, such as those organised by the ethnologist Jacques Soustelle in Latin America and the academic Georges Gorse in Egypt.

The Free French sent its first three agents across the Channel in the late summer of 1940. They were followed by Gilbert Renault, a former Action Française sympathiser and unsuccessful film producer, who took the codename Rémy and established a ring of agents among port officials, merchant shipping captains and railway station managers in western France, who sent information about movements of German troops and supplies to guide British air and sea attacks. The British, who were often in conflict with the Free French intelligence operation in London, had their own network in France called

Alliance that was run by Georges Loustaunau-Lacau, a former member of the far right-wing *Cagoule* movement. After he was arrested and sent to a concentration camp (which he survived), the organisation was headed by Marie-Madeleine Méric, the only woman to hold such a post. A total of 303 of its members were executed and 520 deported to Germany.

When Hitler attacked the Soviet Union in June 1941, Moscow told the PCF to join the Resistance and the party's *Front National* became its largest group, adopting united front tactics to draw in other groups. Hit-and-run assassinations of occupation troops began, bringing savage reprisals; de Gaulle advised against assassinations because it was so easy for the occupying forces to massacre French fighting men in return. His advice was not heeded.

Taking the name *maquisard* from the scrublands of south-eastern France, the underground fighters directed sabotage at the railway network to disrupt enemy traffic. Resistance units stormed several factories and a big power plant in 1942–3 as well as a German artillery depot in Grenoble. Collaborationists were attacked and raids were mounted to free captured fighters. Resistance newspapers, usually consisting of four small pages, blossomed – one count put their number at more than a thousand, the biggest with circulations of more than 100,000, and, in one case, 450,000 by 1944. A song broadcast from London, '*Ami Entends-tu?*' (Friend, Do You Hear?) was adapted as a rallying anthem, '*Le Chant des Partisans*' (The Song of the Partisans). In Paris, young jazz enthusiasts known as '*Zazous*' reacted to the imposition of the yellow star on Jews by sporting similar shaped badges with 'Swing' written in the centre – the amount of their kind of music broadcast by Radio Paris increased sharply at the start of the Occupation before jazz bands and dance halls were banned in 1942.

For the early resisters, de Gaulle was a far-away radio voice. 'We took our first steps without him,' the Socialist Christian Pineau recalled. 'He was not living in national territory and was not sharing our dangers.' That began to change when the former prefect, Jean Moulin, arrived in London via Portugal in September 1941 saying he was the delegate of three Resistance movements. In fact, though he had some contacts with the underground, he represented nobody. But he was a rare recruit from the senior ranks of the French administration and a man of undoubted talent, who was close to the Communists but saw de Gaulle as the necessary rallying point. So he was parachuted into Provence to unite the Resistance under de Gaulle's umbrella, living a double life as a retired prefect and organiser of the *Armée Secrète*.

Henri Frenay and Emmanuel d'Astier de la Vigerie resented the former prefect's authority and went to London to protest. De Gaulle told them simply: 'I shall give the orders.' His leadership was accepted. D'Astier took to referring to him as 'the Symbol'. 'Most of us were prepared to recognise his authority,' Pineau recalled. 'For we needed a flag, if not a guide.'

The resistance groups agreed to come together under the broad umbrella organisation the *Conseil National de la Résistance* (CNR) to act 'with de Gaulle in the fight he leads to set the country free and to give the power of decision back to Frenchmen'. Moulin took overall charge. To organise the fighters in the field, General Charles Delestraint, who had led a tank attack on the Germans in 1940 and then joined Frenay's group, was appointed to head the *Armée Secrète*. Though the prominent Socialist Pierre Brossolette argued for the Resistance to be used to create a left-wing movement to replace the parties of the Third Republic, de Gaulle preferred the broad church approach adopted by Moulin.

The 'most difficult of allies'

The leader of the Fighting French, as they were now known, had cause for shock when 700 Allied ships landed 100,000 troops in Vichy-held North Africa on 8 November 1942, in Operation Torch, without informing him in advance. Roosevelt had vetoed a suggestion from Churchill that de Gaulle should be told of the American-led operation. This was partly because the Americans thought Gaullist participation would stiffen the resistance of Vichy commanders on the spot, but the exclusion stemmed mainly from the president's distaste for the General who flew into a rage when told by an aide. 'I hope the Vichy folk throw them into the sea,' he cried. 'One does not break into France.' Still, as over Mers-el-Kébir, he calmed down to make a BBC broadcast in which he said the Allies did not have territorial designs on North Africa and called on Vichy troops there to ally with them.

The landing provoked Hitler's order to the German army to move into the unoccupied zone, further reducing Vichy to puppet status. Occupation costs were raised from 300 to 500 million francs a day. Seizure of assets ranging from farm machinery to works of art increased. The Germans sent troops towards Toulon to seize the French fleet anchored there. Laval instructed the port commanders not to resist. But an order drawn up by Darlan in 1940 for the ships to be scuttled if they came under threat was implemented and the vessels were blown up.

The big unresolved political issue was Washington's choice of a French partner in North Africa. They went for General Henri Giraud, a handsome, straight-backed 63-year-old who had escaped from captivity in a German castle by sliding down a rope strengthened with wire which his wife sent him hidden in food tins. Travelling with false papers, he went to see Pétain in Vichy where the Americans established contact with him, and then made his way to Gibraltar where he accepted the American commission. But Giraud, nicknamed King Pin by his new patrons, lacked non-military skills, was contemptuous of politics and poor at administration and organisation. Dwight Eisenhower, the US commander, said he was somebody who 'wants to be a big shot, a bright and shining light, and the acclaimed saviour of France' but who turned out to be 'a terrible blow to our expectations'.

As they encountered stiff resistance from troops loyal to the Marshal, the Americans turned to the more powerful if dubious figure of Admiral Darlan, who was susceptible to their approaches after being elbowed aside by Laval and was visiting Algiers to see his son, who was gravely ill with polio. The readiness of the Allies to collaborate with such a prominent member of the Vichy hierarchy caused dismay among the Resistance. De Gaulle protested to the White House, but got no reply. The British foreign secretary, Anthony Eden, was critical, but Churchill went along in the name of Allied solidarity.

Eisenhower reached an agreement with Darlan to get Vichy forces to stop fighting after suffering 3,000 dead or wounded (about the same as Allied losses). The Admiral became high commissioner of a French 'Imperial Federation' and resumed the repressive methods he had pursued at Vichy, harassing Free French supporters and Jews in an atmosphere which Eisenhower characterised as rife with 'petty intrigue with little, selfish, conceited worms that call themselves men'. The State Department warned Roosevelt of a storm of protest at the installation of a 'semi-Fascist' government in the first major territory liberated by US forces.

This episode was brought to an abrupt end when a young French royalist, Fernand Bonnier de la Chapelle, shot the Admiral in the stomach in his office – he died two hours later. The assassin was swiftly tried and shot. There was no direct link between the killing and the Fighting French, but some of the dollars taken to Algiers by an emissary of de Gaulle were found on the assassin and the General mentioned Darlan's disappearance favourably in a conversation with Eden; he called the death an execution.

Giraud was left in charge on the French side, but he and the Americans made a hash of things. Maurice Peyrouton, a former Vichy interior minister who had signed the death sentence for de Gaulle, was put in charge of civil administration. The food situation deteriorated and bad weather bogged down the advance east along the coast. De Gaulle judged that Giraud showed 'extreme political clumsiness'.

The Fighting French leader did not have to wait long for his chance to insert himself into North African affairs and carve out a new operational base there. In mid-January 1943, Roosevelt and Churchill met in the Anfa suburb of Casablanca in Morocco to review the progress of the war, plan the invasion of Italy and bring the two French generals together. Emboldened by further success for Leclerc's column in Libya and the extension of his movement's authority to the East African territory of Djibouti and the islands of Madagascar and la Réunion, de Gaulle played hard to get until Churchill threatened that, if he did not fly to Casablanca, Britain would have to 'review' its attitude and 'endeavour to get on as well as we can without you'.

There was trouble from the moment the Constable arrived. When he saw that the windows of his car were covered with mud, he assumed that his hosts wanted to conceal him from the local people, not knowing that this had been done for security reasons to Roosevelt as well. The intrusive presence of armed US guards on French soil grated. At lunch with Giraud, he refused to sit at the table until French soldiers replaced the American sentries.

Such was American distrust of de Gaulle that when he had his first meeting with Roosevelt, armed secret service men were posted behind the curtains. Speaking French, the president observed that none of the various French groups could claim sole legitimacy; de Gaulle, for instance, had never been elected. To that, the General responded that Joan of Arc had drawn her legitimacy from taking action and refusing to lose hope. FDR did not improve matters by comparing France to 'a little child unable to look out and fend for itself'. De Gaulle told an aide that he had met 'a great statesman. I think we understood one another well.' But Roosevelt's son, Elliott, noted that his father thought the Frenchman determined to establish a dictatorship in France and remarked that 'there is no man in whom I have less confidence' – he also spread a tale that de Gaulle had compared himself to Joan of Arc, Clemenceau and other great historical figures.

The Frenchman had another stormy session with Churchill. However, the prime minister showed his admiration as the Fighting French chief walked away down the path from his villa, telling his doctor: 'His country has given up fighting, he himself is a refugee, and if we turn him down he's finished. But look at him! Look at him! He might be Stalin, with 200 divisions behind his words. Perhaps the last survivor of a warrior race.'

Anxious to present a façade of understanding between the two generals to the press, Roosevelt talked de Gaulle into shaking hands with Giraud for photographers on the lawn outside his villa. But, in the following months, the Constable comprehensively outwitted his rival, setting up a new headquarters in Algiers and gaining control of the French struggle against Vichy and the Germans. When he left London for North Africa in May 1943, he had a meeting with Eden – Churchill was in Washington. The foreign secretary told him in a friendly tone that he was the most difficult of allies. 'I don't doubt that,' de Gaulle replied with a smile. 'France is a great power.'

Preparing for peace

With the post-war era in view, de Gaulle set about shifting the emphasis of his movement from an anti-Vichy, anti-German operation to the nucleus of a government after liberation by creating a national committee in Algiers. This was joined by leading Fighting French figures including René Pleven, with responsibility for economic and financial matters and colonial policy, André Diethelm, Mandel's former chief of staff, and the early Gaullist Jacques Soustelle along with Henri Frenay, Emmanuel d'Astier and Pierre Mendès France, the Popular Front deputy finance minister who had escaped from detention under Vichy. Another former minister, the Radical Socialist Henri Queuille, chaired inter-ministerial commissions, using political skills learned under the old regime to smooth over differences.

Though still keeping his distance from the General, Jean Monnet rallied, and sought to get supplies from the Americans. De Gaulle also gained the support of a prominent military man, Jean-Marie de Lattre de Tassigny, who had been jailed for his opposition to the German occupation of the Vichy zone in 1942 but escaped by using a saw smuggled into his cell to cut the window bars and scale two walls. General Koenig, the victor of the battle at Bir-Hakeim, took command of the *Forces Françaises de l'Intérieur* (FFI) while military affairs in France were delegated to 29-year-old Jacques Delmas, who subsequently added his Resistance pseudonym of Chaban to his name. De Gaulle's family came, too, the General and his wife continually worrying about the condition of their daughter, Anne.

Giraud's defeat was assured when his rival became the sole chairman of the national committee. 'I let myself be beaten without a fight,' he admitted. 'On the political level, I was unbelievably incompetent, clumsy and weak.' The British delegate to North Africa, Harold Macmillan, judged that 'never in the whole history of politics has any man frittered away so large a capital in so short a time.'

A Provisional Consultative Assembly was appointed, including fifty-two representatives of the Resistance, twenty of the old parliament and twelve of the general councils of the Empire. De Gaulle reshuffled the administration to take in six representatives of non-Communist political parties, five Resistance figures plus five officials and generals, including Monnet and General Catroux. Seventeen 'general secretaries' were to run the administration, regional commissioners and prefects below them.

Though de Gaulle refused to let the Communists choose which posts they should hold and banned Thorez from visiting North Africa, the increasingly radical tilt of this 'virtual republic' was evident. The charter drawn up by its National Committee stipulated 'the eviction from management of France's economy of the great economic and financial feudal forces'. After the Liberation, there was to be a minimum wage, full social security, nationalisation of big companies, worker participation in management, and enhanced rights for inhabitants of colonies. De Gaulle said he looked to 'the end of an economic regime in which the great source of riches escape from the nation, where the main production and distribution activities are beyond its control and where the management of firms excludes the participation of workers' organisations on which, however, they depend.'

An official statement in Algiers said civil servants who followed Vichy orders were guilty of 'punishable servility'. An example was made of a former Vichy interior minister, Pierre Pucheu, who had gone to North Africa with what he thought was a safe conduct from Giraud, intending to enlist in the forces fighting the Axis. The Communists were after him for his alleged involvement in handing over hostages, mainly from their party, to the Germans for a mass execution in 1941. After a show trial, he was shot.

Across the Mediterranean, growing expectations of an Allied victory and the unpopularity of forced labour service in Germany bolstered the Resistance. According to a British estimate, the partisans now numbered 150,000, though only 35,000 were properly armed. Partisan groups stepped up their 'immediate action' with increased sabotage of railway lines and strongholds in the Massif Central, Limousin, Brittany, the Lot, the Ain and Savoie.

The Gestapo caught General Delestraint – he was imprisoned in camps in Germany and executed – and then arrested Moulin who died under torture; whether he was betrayed or caught by German detective work remains a matter of controversy. The Socialist Resistance leader, Pierre Brossolette, was also detained, and died jumping from a high window of the Gestapo building in Paris. One of Moulin's close associates, Georges Bidault, a Christian Democrat journalist, held the movement together despite these reverses.

As the Wehrmacht retreated from Italy, the Allies took Corsica and the Germans prepared for a cross-Channel landing, the struggle in the Hexagon sharpened. A Resistance leader, Philippe Viannay, published an article saying there was 'a clear duty to kill' all Germans, French people who helped the occupation forces, and police who were involved in the arrest of patriots. Pétain's mind was unravelling: visiting Lyons, he asked as he walked in front of a welcoming parade, 'Who am I? Where am I? What am I doing?' He sent an emissary to Algiers to propose a rendezvous with de Gaulle at the Arc de Triomphe to transfer his authority. He also offered to put himself in British hands. He received no response to either message.

At the end of September 1944, an anti-Laval group at Vichy unveiled a plan under which a regency council would take over if the Marshal died or stepped down. A month later, Pétain tried unsuccessfully to get rid of the Auvergnat and, as a result, was put under tighter German supervision. Joseph Darnand, head of the *Milice* collaborationist paramilitary, was appointed secretary-general for order. Members of the Resistance were subject to summary courts or were simply shot out of hand. Special German units carried out mass shootings of hostages. An important Alpine base on the Plateau des Glières in Savoy was assaulted by collaborationist forces and German troops and planes; 150 *maquisards* were killed, some after being captured and tortured.

16

LIBERATION

D-Day plunged relations between de Gaulle and the Allies into a fresh crisis as the general was excluded from planning and informed about it only during a visit to Churchill on the eve of the landings. No French forces were to be involved in the first wave. At a stormy lunch, he was further irritated by a US plan to issue special bank notes in France and by the prime minister's suggestion that he go to Washington to seek Roosevelt's benediction. The president had never wanted to see him in the past, he shot back, so why should he now 'lodge my candidacy for power in France with Roosevelt. The French government exists.' Still the two men ended by toasting one another, Churchill raising his glass 'to de Gaulle who never accepted defeat' while his guest drank 'to England, to victory, to Europe.'

But the White House decreed that the Supreme Commander, Eisenhower, was free to deal with any groups he chose in France rather than having to talk to a provisional government Washington did not recognise. A text to be read out on the radio and distributed in leaflets named the American as ultimate authority for the country and omitted any mention of Fighting France, the Resistance or de Gaulle. Shown this, the Frenchman exploded. His anger increased when he learned that he was expected to follow Eisenhower in a post-invasion broadcast, giving the impression of endorsing what had just been said. He refused to speak at all, and withdrew the cooperation of French liaison agents.

That provoked a harangue from Churchill to the cabinet about de Gaulle's misdeeds while the General described the prime minister as a gangster. Summoning a representative of the French leader, Churchill accused him of 'treason at the height of battle'. As usual, de Gaulle calmed down and agreed to speak on the BBC on the landings so long as this was some hours after Eisenhower. He would also supply liaison agents. Churchill was not appeased. From his bed late at night, he dictated an instruction that de Gaulle was to be flown to Algiers 'in chains if necessary'. Eden had the memo burned.

Showing continuing bad temper, the prime minister did not ask de Gaulle to accompany him when he visited Normandy on 12 June. Nor did he attend a dinner the foreign secretary gave for de Gaulle. He also raised objections about de Gaulle's intention to visit France, but the General went ahead, crossing the Channel on 14 June aboard the destroyer, *La Combattante*. Driving inland in a jeep, he stopped to talk to local people who 'cried out with joy', one of his companions recalled.

In Bayeux, the first town liberated, the mayor and municipal council put on a hero's welcome. 'At the sight of General de Gaulle, a kind of stupor took hold of the inhabitants who broke out into cheers or dissolved into tears,' the Constable recorded in his memoirs. Everywhere, he was acclaimed, the public reaction contradicting Roosevelt's insistence that he was not a representative figure, though FDR maintained his reservations when de Gaulle finally visited Washington the following month, describing the visitor to his wife as the 'president of some French committee or other' and an 'egotist'. For his part, de Gaulle was convinced that America was 'already trying to rule the world' and, since Britain would always accede to the US, France had to count on itself, a belief he would nurture till the end of his life.

The brink of civil war

The Allied advance through Normandy took a heavy toll on French people caught up in the fighting or killed by bombing. The retreating Germans massacred hundreds of civilians, shooting eighty detained partisans in Caen prison on the day of the landings. There were also killings of civilians, rapes and pillage by the Allied forces, increasing the disproportion between civilian and military losses in France during the conflict.

The French second armoured division (*la 2ème DB*) under Leclerc crossed the Channel at the end of July to join the advance on Paris once the Allies had broken out of the Normandy pocket. In mid-August, Allied forces, including a division under de Lattre de Tassigny, landed on the Riviera. Resistance fighters proclaimed new 'republics'; 140,000 partisans were estimated to have received weapons through Allied parachute drops on top of arms captured from the Germans and the *Milice*.

Seven thousand partisans mustered in the Morbihan *département* of Brittany. In the Resistance stronghold of the Limousin, the maverick Communist Georges Guingouin led 20,000 men to take over Limoges after the Germans capitulated. Other partisans set up a base in the rugged south-eastern uplands of the Dauphiné region, which brought together farmers and former soldiers, priests, Communists and Jews, mechanics, café owners and local officials in the Free Republic of the Vercors. But they were cut off and did not receive arms drops or bombing support to enable them to ward off a German attack that killed 600 *maquisards* and 200 local inhabitants.

There was lawlessness, vengeance killings and summary trials as France appeared to teeter on the brink of civil war. In Toulouse, Limoges and Montpellier, Jacques Baumel, a Resistance fighter and future Gaullist minister, witnessed 'atrocities comparable to the killings in the Spanish Civil War'. The numbers of those slain in the process and earlier in the war are subject to different estimations. The total of Resistance fighters who died in action, were executed or perished after deportation has been estimated at between 12,000 and 20,000. The interior ministry provided a figure of 9,673 for all summary executions by the Resistance during the war, 4,439 of them during or after the Liberation. A later official committee put the number at 12,000. The revisionist historian Robert Aron arrived at 20,000 for 1944 and 30–40,000 for the war as a whole, a figure contested by other experts.[1]

The *Milice* and the retreating occupation forces became ever more violent. The SS Panzer Reich tank division picked up men in the Corrèze provincial capital of Tulle and killed ninety-nine by hanging them from balconies. It then slaughtered 642 people in the Limousin village of Oradour-sur-Glane, 240 of them women and children burned in the church. At one town in the Loire Valley, the Germans shot dead 124 people, including 44 children; in another massacre, 305 were executed and 732 deported, 405 to their deaths. A *Milice* leader had eighty Jews rounded up and the men buried alive under bags of cement in a well.

Partisans disguised in blue paramilitary uniforms got into the building where the Vichy propaganda minister, Philippe Henriot, was sleeping and murdered him in his bed – big crowds filed past his coffin outside the Hôtel de Ville in Paris before the funeral at Notre-Dame. In retaliation, militiamen took Georges Mandel, who had been handed over to them by the Germans, into the forest of Fontainebleau and killed him. Others led the Popular Front education minister, Jean Zay, from prison, shot him, stripped the body, tore off his wedding ring and flung the corpse into a quarry.

Pétain, who was reported to have reacted to news of D-Day by singing 'It's a Long Way to Tipperary', criticised the *Milice* for imposing 'an atmosphere of police terror unknown in this country until now', but he was now an impotent prisoner of the Germans who moved him to what amounted to house arrest in a château in the northern Auvergne. Laval sought an escape with a plan to revive the Third Republic; he got backing from eighty-seven mayors but failed to win the support of the pre-war premier Édouard Herriot who was brought to meet him from a lunatic asylum where he was being held.[2]

The Germans moved the Vichy leaders to Belfort in eastern France where a phantom administration was set up under Fernand de Brinon, the former Vichy representative to the German High Command in Paris who had used his position to get a pass protecting his Jewish wife. Darnand and Déat were among the ministers. In the autumn of 1944, the Allied advance forced them to flee to a grandiose, gloomy castle on a rocky outcrop on the Danube in the small town of Sigmaringen together with some other leading collaborationists, including the writer Louis-Ferdinand Céline.[3]

Freeing the capital

As the Vichy leadership moved in ignominious retreat, de Gaulle made a triumphant progress through Normandy and Brittany. Church bells rang and the streets were garlanded with flowers. But his relations with the

Allies were still tense. There was yet another row with Britain over Syria and Lebanon, and an argument about who should be responsible for distributing arms to police in France. De Gaulle objected at not being consulted over the Allied destruction of ships at Toulon, Sète and Marseilles. Churchill visited Corsica without telling the French in advance.

In Paris, the Wehrmacht laid explosives in strategic points to destroy the city in keeping with Hitler's order. Eisenhower wanted to avoid a big urban battle, which could delay his advance on Germany, but his hand was forced by a Resistance rising in the capital that began on 15 August, the day that a final convoy of more than 2,000 prisoners left for Buchenwald. Railway workers, led by the Communists, went on strike. Police and staff on the bus and underground transport systems followed. De Gaulle saw the danger of a 'populist government which would encircle my head with laurels, ask me to take a position which it would designate for me and pull all the strings ... until the day when the dictatorship of proletariat was established'.

On 18 August, a general strike was declared in the city. The unified Resistance command, the French Forces of the Interior (FFI) headed by the Communist Henri Rol-Tanguy, told Parisians to mobilise. There were echoes of the popular risings of the nineteenth century as the City Hall, public buildings, railway stations, telephone exchanges and electricity stations were occupied. Barricades went up in the streets and trees were cut down to block boulevards. The Germans blew up a big flourmill, threatening bread supplies. De Gaulle insisted to Eisenhower that there could be 'serious trouble' unless the city was liberated as soon as possible with French troops under Leclerc leading the way.

On the evening of 24 August, French vanguard tanks crossed the Seine south-west of the capital, but the main column was still 5 miles from the main southern gateway into the city, the Porte d'Orléans. Growing increasingly frustrated, the overall field commander, General Omar Bradley, ordered the US 4th Division to join the attack, raising the prospect that French troops would not be alone in liberating the city. That was enough to spur on Leclerc. Cane in hand as he walked through the streets of a southern suburb, he took aside a captain, Raymond Dronne, who had been with him in Chad in 1940–1, and told him 'Head immediately for Paris ... Go fast. Arrive this evening.'

Dronne's tanks crossed the Seine, rolling along the quays on the Right Bank to the Hôtel de Ville. Church bells rang in celebration. The German commander, von Choltitz, decided to surrender. In all, 1,500 resistance fighters died in the freeing of the capital. De Gaulle was driven to Paris where, after calling at the Police Prefecture, he walked through dense crowds to the Hôtel de Ville. There, he made one of his most evocative speeches to proclaim 'Paris! Outraged Paris! Broken Paris! Martyred Paris! But liberated Paris! Liberated by itself, liberated by its people with the help of the French armies, with the support and the help of all France, of the France that fights, of the only France, of the real France, of the eternal France!' Then he went to the window looking down at the crowd below and raised both his arms in a gesture that would become familiar, his height turning him into a monument.

As he staged a triumphal walk down the Champs-Élysées, the throng lining the wide avenue erupted in joy. The tanks of Leclerc's division rolled down from the Arc de Triomphe, but snipers, mainly from the *Milice*, fired from the rooftops on the Place de la Concorde and along the rue de Rivoli when the General boarded an open car to drive to Notre-Dame, where he marched through the church, his shoulders thrown back while bullets ricocheted off the pillars behind which people sheltered, women cuddling children in their arms. When the service ended, the shooting continued, but the General took no notice as he walked out into the sunlight. The bullets may have been from over-excited partisans. In a letter to his wife, de Gaulle suggested that 'certain elements' – he meant Communists – had seized on the occasion to flex their muscles.

The Wehrmacht launched a bombardment that killed 50 people, injured 400 and turned the night red with the flames from burning houses. Electricity was cut off – in the war ministry, de Gaulle's aide-de-camp took the only oil lamp available. In the north and west of the country, 75,000 German soldiers held out; the last Nazi troops were not driven from French territory until early 1945, with the First French Army under de Lattre de Tassigny taking Strasbourg and joining the Allied advance across the Rhine. More than 2 million French people were prisoners of war or labourers in Germany.

The Pétain regime evaporated as if it had never been. But collaborators had to pay, with the exercise of summary popular justice reminiscent of the Revolution and the insurrections and repressions of the previous century. Women who had fraternised with Germans had their hair cropped and were paraded through the streets, daubed with tar, stripped to the waist and painted with swastikas; at least 20,000 were punished in this way. In Paris, some prostitutes who had entertained Germans were kicked to death. In half-a-dozen cities, there were riots to force tribunals to condemn collaborators to death, encouraged by the Communist Party, which claimed the impossibly high number of 75,000 members killed during the war. Elsewhere, mobs simply grabbed those regarded as guilty, torturing and executing some out of hand.

France had emerged from the war on the winning side, thanks largely to de Gaulle's perspicuity and perseverance. But now it had to confront the problems of peace under an unelected leader whose mindset was at odds with the nation's modern history and inclinations. The threat of civil war with the Communists using their muscle to try to usher in a new regime was evident. So was de Gaulle's determination to thwart them in the name of the Republic as he pursued his vision of national unity which would transcend the country's old divisions.[4]

17

SEEKING A NEW COURSE

Though some rural areas had survived on their own resources, much of France was in a devastated condition. Describing the country as 'ruined, decimated, torn apart', de Gaulle, who became prime minister, compared himself to Macbeth peering into the witches' cauldron. Rations in Paris in 1944 provided less than half the necessary calorie intake; long queues became a regular feature of life. Protestors at big demonstrations in Nantes, Le Creusot, Laon and Lyons marched under the banner, 'Our kids are hungry'. In Normandy, bakeries were pillaged. In Tours, a crowd attacked the prefecture to protest at rationing.

The black market was estimated to involve 4 million suppliers and intermediaries. The wheat harvest of 1944–5 was half that of pre-war years. Shortages spurred inflation; retail prices were four times those of 1939. The trade gap widened, as did the budget deficit, which had to bear the cost of providing for men coming home from captivity and forced labour without jobs and sometimes in poor physical condition. Government revenue covered only a third of spending. The state debt was four times that of 1939, and printing of bank notes to pay government bills further exacerbated inflation.

Wartime destruction and German requisitioning meant shortages of industrial equipment, raw materials, vehicles, food and farm machinery and animals. National production in 1944 was 38 per cent of 1938–9. A quarter of the housing stock had been demolished or damaged. Allied bombing had hit 1.3 million houses in more than 1,500 towns and cities, mostly in the north where St-Nazaire was flattened and Le Havre

80 per cent demolished, but also in Paris and the south where 3,000 people perished in raids in May 1944. A million families were homeless. Coal output was 50 per cent of the 1939 level. Half the railway track and a third of the stations were out of service. In all, 7,500 bridges were destroyed and many roads damaged. Telephone services and electricity supply worked only sporadically.

The hopes of some Communists that the Liberation would open the door to an uprising based on the Resistance and directed by the PCF, with de Gaulle reduced to the role of a figurehead who would soon be disposed of, came to nothing. The General was not going to be pushed aside and, on instructions from Stalin to cooperate with the bourgeois parties while the Allies pressed the final stage of the war, Thorez squashed notions of revolution. Instead, he went along when the new prime minister ordered the disbandment of partisan units – de Gaulle called the PCF leaders 'reeds painted as iron'.[1]

Restoring the orderly process of law

Instead of proffering gratitude, de Gaulle instructed partisans to go back to their regular jobs and to stop pretending to be soldiers. The Resistance was 'in no way national', he told his secretary, so it lacked the legitimacy he claimed for himself. The nation, he said, had been 'gravely ill for a long time without diplomacy, without hierarchy . . . and entirely empty of men of government'. As a first step to restoring the state's authority, the disorderly punishment of collaboration had to give way to due process of law.[2]

Some 125,000 people were detained; about half were subsequently released without punishment. In all, 767 were executed. Twenty-three per cent of those tried were condemned to national degradation and 16 per cent sent to prison or otherwise detained. Maurras got both degradation and life imprisonment after a trial at which his attempts to deploy nineteenth-century rhetoric were undone by the forensic arguments of the prosecution and his claim that his anti-Semitism was 'more civilised' than that of the Germans carried no weight; he called the verdict the 'revenge of Dreyfus'. The novelist and critic, Robert Brasillach, who had run the violently anti-Semitic collaborationist journal, *Je Suis*

Partout' was given a death sentence, which de Gaulle refused to commute despite a petition from writers and artists. Drieu la Rochelle committed suicide.

Other prominent figures condemned for collaboration included Louis Renault, who died in prison and the actress Arletty, who had lived with a German officer in the Ritz – in her defence, she declared that 'my heart is French but my cunt is international'. Another prominent woman who had had a German lover, Coco Chanel, headed for the safety of Switzerland. Arletty's friend, the flamboyant writer, director and actor Sacha Guitry, was hustled from his home in Paris wearing yellow pyjamas, green pumps and a Panama hat, and held for sixty days.

Some eminent former Pétainists changed their stance to accord with the situation; to follow his ode to the Marshal of 1941, Claudel published a poem in praise of de Gaulle as the nation's 'son and blood'. Civil servants and the better-off generally escaped lightly from the purge, some claiming convenient contacts with the Resistance, which had been none too evident before the Allied landings. The collaborationist police chief René Bousquet was not tried until 1949 and was then sentenced only to five years of national degradation, which was immediately lifted on the grounds that, after being sacked in Vichy, he had participated in the Resistance. He then occupied senior positions at a major bank and a provincial newspaper, and the rising politician François Mitterrand saw no problem in maintaining their friendship.[3]

The two leading figures of Vichy were brought back to France in the spring of 1945. Wearing a simple blue uniform adorned only with his *Médaille Militaire*, Pétain went on trial for treason in July 1945. De Gaulle did not relish the event; he would have preferred to let the Marshal slip out of history. The ambiguities of the time were shown by the fact that three of the judges had served under the collaborationist regime and taken an oath of allegiance to the accused. The old man recited a statement saying he had sacrificed himself and his prestige for the good of the nation to prepare for the liberation of a country that was 'sad but alive'.

After that, he sat silently, cupping his hand over his ear and dozing as evidence was heard from Reynaud, Herriot, Daladier, Weygand and Blum, who had just returned from a German concentration camp after his guards had decided not to implement an order to execute him. Laval, who had fled from Germany to Spain, only to be sent by Franco to Austria where the Americans delivered him to the French, was brought to take the stand from his prison in a Paris suburb. In a creased suit and discoloured white tie, his moustache nicotine stained, his dark hair plastered flat on his scalp, he played with the court, pretending not to understand what was going on and, at one point, provoking laughter by asking for Vichy water.

The jurors found Pétain guilty by fourteen votes to thirteen, meaning execution. But then they voted that the supreme penalty should not be carried out. De Gaulle, in search of national reconciliation and perhaps in memory of the time when the Marshal had been his military idol, had already decided to commute the sentence. The old man was kept on the desolate Île d'Yeu off the west coast where he was allocated two rooms in a fort, his home until he died in 1951 at the age of ninety-five; his last words were 'I'm hungry'. To commemorate the Victor of Verdun, Presidents of the Republic sent wreaths to be laid on his tomb on each Armistice Day.

The *Milice* leader, Darnand, was shot after a brief hearing. The head of the last collaborationist government, de Brinon, was also executed. Déat escaped to hide in a convent in Italy where he died in 1955. Doriot had been killed in February 1945 when his car was strafed by fighter planes in Germany. Laval's trial in October 1945 was a tragic farce. He argued that ultimate responsibility had lain with Pétain who had just been spared execution, so the supreme penalty should not be applied to him. The court was having none of that. The defence was given so little time to make his case that his lawyers boycotted the hearings. The main judge was heard to hiss at one point, 'He's pissing me off. We've got to finish.' A death sentence was pronounced after four days.

Reynaud and Blum both criticised the conduct of the hearing, the Socialist writing to de Gaulle to say that execution could not take place after such a pantomime. But there was strong pressure from the Communists to go ahead. A few hours before Laval was due to be shot, he swallowed a cyanide pill he carried with him. His stomach was pumped. Two officials went to inform de Gaulle. 'Have the last rites been pronounced?' the General asked. Told they had, he said coldly,

'Then he no longer belongs to us. Let the firing squad do its duty.' After his shoes had been removed, the Auvergnat was taken to a mound behind the jail and strapped to the execution post. 'You wanted this show, you'll have it to the end,' he shouted at watching judges hiding behind a prison van. '*Vive la France!*' he cried as the firing squad was ordered to shoot.

Change on a huge scale

De Gaulle's conceit was that the state had travelled to London with him and that Vichy had been an illegitimate blip in the Republican narrative. When the resistance chief, Georges Bidault, suggested that he proclaim the restoration of the Republic, the General replied that there was no need to do so since it had never ceased to exist. As prime minister, he regarded himself as incarnating a legitimacy that had been accorded to him by history, if not by the electorate.

He presided over an extraordinary swing to the left in the second act of the transformation opened by the Popular Front eight years earlier, providing a fresh swing of the national pendulum between revolution and reaction. The state took over the commanding heights of industry and finance. The welfare system was substantially expanded and access to credit was reorganised to better serve social needs. Measures to encourage families were introduced, boosting the population by 3 million in ten years.

Public ownership was extended to the gas and electricity network, thirty-four insurance companies, shipping and aviation companies, aircraft manufacturers, the Bank of France and four leading financial institutions, including Crédit Lyonnais and Société Générale. Nationalisation of the railways was completed. By 1946, state enterprises employed 1.1 million people, nearly 10 per cent of salaried workers. Tarnished by collaboration, Renault was placed in public ownership, its big plant outside Paris the beacon for trade union activity as car output jumped to double the pre-war level.[4]

The attack on private big business was fuelled by its collaborationist record and was welcomed by de Gaulle who always saw the forces of money as a great enemy. A planning commission was set up under Jean

Monnet. A national scientific research organisation, the CNRS, was given the job of improving university work and making France internationally competitive. A finishing school for civil servants, the *École Nationale d'Administration* (ENA), was opened in the 7th *arrondissement* of Paris. The brainchild of the Gaullist official Michel Debré, it was designed to breed top administrators to build a new France. To give the country a great newspaper, funds were provided to create *Le Monde* under the austere, dedicated Hubert Beuve-Méry. Citroën launched an icon of the age, the 2CV mass market car designed especially for use in the countryside to be able to carry eggs across a ploughed field without breaking any.

This massive programme of change was put through by two pre-war parties, the Socialist SFIO and the Communist PCF, and a new centrist Christian Democratic grouping born from the Resistance, the *Mouvement Républicain Populaire* (MRP), which included prominent Gaullists. With 200,000 members, the new movement called itself 'the party of loyalty' – implicitly to the General; its first president was his wartime spokesman, Maurice Schumann. The logical next step would have been for de Gaulle to have become its leader. This might have set France on the path for a more coherent political system with a single strong non-leftist grouping. But the Constable saw himself as a historic figure operating above political parties while leading MRP figures, such as Bidault and the justice minister François de Menthon, prized their independence and wanted to play their legislative role to the full free from de Gaulle's vision of executive supremacy.

In that, they were at one with the rest of the party spectrum whose chiefs – new and old – insisted that the new political regime must be dominated by the legislature. The Pétain years heightened the regard for parliament, which was bolstered by the return of pre-war figures such as Blum, Reynaud and Daladier. Pierre Mendès France took the economics ministry. Jules Jeanneney, who had been president of the Senate when it voted to grant power to Pétain, was forgiven that as he became the second ranking member of the government as Minister of State. In accepting the backing of the parties while in Algiers, de Gaulle had tied himself to them in a way he could not but resent, however necessary it had been to gain a degree of democratic legitimacy. However,

he rebuffed Communist attempts to gain a major government department – their most senior minister was the early resister Charles Tillon,
in charge of aviation.

A stickler for discipline, despite his own huge act of insubordination
in 1940, the prime minister tried to run cabinet meetings like military
staff sessions; ministers were not allowed to take notes or to question the
prime minister – nor could they light a cigarette before he had done so.
This alienated men like Bidault who told a friend, 'If you only knew
how he treats us.' The General's letters and reflections to his secretary,
Claude Mauriac, make plain his growing disillusion, and he sought relief
in foreign affairs, trying to restore France's international prestige – with
mixed results. A trip to meet Stalin in Moscow resulted only in a vacuous
friendship pact and there was a fresh rebuff when France was excluded
from the Allied conference at Yalta in early 1945. The relationship with
Washington did not improve when Harry Truman succeeded Roosevelt.
Churchill paid a triumphant visit to Paris but there was yet another
Anglo-French crisis over Syria and Lebanon. Accusing London of
'infamy that should never be forgotten', the General sent in three battalions of soldiers on two warships to back French claims. After protest
riots in Damascus, the French general in charge ordered his troops to
fire on the crowd and an aircraft dropped bombs; a thousand people
were killed. The British then intervened with US backing; Truman's
comment to his staff was typically direct – 'Those French ought to be
taken out and castrated.' De Gaulle was forced to retreat, but told the
British ambassador, Duff Cooper, 'You have outraged France and
betrayed the West. That cannot be forgotten.'[5]

He discerned a link between British intervention in the Levant and
Arab demonstrations in Algeria, which degenerated into the killing of
102 people of French origin in two days in the town of Sétif. The local
French commander ordered the artillery and the air force into action
while local people were massacred by troops from French West Africa,
joined by German and Italian prisoners of war pressed into service.
The death toll remains controversial, but was probably around 8,000. De
Gaulle appears to have approved of the repression.

Opinion polls showed strong support for his drive to restore republican order, but the prime minister's demeanour was that of a man

growing increasingly disappointed behind his arrogant mask. He even let himself be swayed into preferring facility to rigour at the start of 1946 when he declined to back tough anti-inflationary measures proposed by Mendès France. The economy minister wanted to tax capital gains, control prices and wages and introduce stricter rationing. He also planned to clamp down on the six-fold expansion in banknotes caused by the printing of money printed in wartime to meet German occupation costs and then to pay for the army and reconstruction. Though backed by the Socialists, this was opposed by farmers and the Communists who had both built up big stocks of notes during the war.

The General sided with the more pliant finance minister, his wartime colleague René Pleven, leader of a small liberal party who allowed inflation to continue. Mendès – the closest thing to a de Gaulle among the parliamentary figures – resigned. Inflation and the deficit continued their upward course. There was a perfectly good reason for the path de Gaulle chose – he wrote in his memoirs that France was 'ill and wounded' and he thought it better not to risk 'dangerous convulsions', so he preferred the soothing Doctor Pleven to Surgeon Mendès wielding his scalpel. But it was an uncharacteristic choice for a man who believed in taking hard decisions for the longer-term national good and, perhaps, a sign that political life was wearing down the Constable.

Leaving for the sake of the country

A referendum was arranged for October 1945, gave 96 per cent backing for a proposal to set up a constituent assembly to draw up the rules of a new regime and determine its make-up; the ballot was particularly notable as it was the first time women were enfranchised. The simultaneous election of the chamber's members showed both the left's strength and the equal division of party strengths at the polls. The Communists, who earned the dividend of their strong organisation, Resistance record and the national appetite for economic and social reform took 26 per cent of the vote to 25 per cent for the MRP and 24 per cent for the Socialists. The Radicals slumped to 9 per cent, with 13 per cent of votes going to moderates and the remainder to small fringe parties.

De Gaulle mused about resigning as the legislature, presided over by the Socialist Félix Gouin, went out of its way to demonstrate its authority by delaying approval of the government for a week though then voting for de Gaulle to continue as prime minister with a single abstention, that of Clemenceau's son.

After stormy negotiations during which de Gaulle was heard to shout 'I've had enough', a new government was formed with Thorez, the Socialist Vincent Auriol and the MRP Francisque Gay as ministers of state, along with the moderate Louis Jacquinot. There were four Socialist ministers and as many from the MRP and the PCF. Economic troubles mounted as the franc was devalued despite a $550 million grant from the US Export-Import Bank. The Communist tribune Jacques Duclos kept up a full-frontal attack from the hard left while the Socialists fought to raise pay increases for civil servants and threatened to table a vote of confidence on military spending. De Gaulle told the Assembly that, if it refused to give the government the means to govern, he would step down.

Though he compromised on the military spending issue, the General wrote in his memoirs that he had made up his mind to resign when he left the Palais Bourbon on the evening of 1 January 1946. Apart from the immediate clashes with parliamentarians, the new constitution was heading in a direction of which he disapproved, with an all-powerful legislature. On 5 January, he set off for a week on the Riviera to meditate on his next move. He was extremely tired, having hardly had a break during the five-and-a-half years since the start of the war. He walked along the rocky Mediterranean inlets in a dark suit and homburg hat, chain-smoking as he went, visited beauty spots and held a press conference to talk up the joys of tourism. In his memoirs, he wrote that, during his Mediterranean retreat in the winter sun, he decided to 'leave in silence … without saying anything about what I would do afterwards.'

Wanting to enter the capital as discreetly as possible, he got off his train at a siding outside Paris. The Socialist transport minister, Jules Moch, drove to greet him, and, as they headed into the city, the General told him 'I've something to tell you' – splitting each syllable, he said it was 'im-pos-si-ble to go-vern wi-th the par-ties.' He went on, 'As I cannot govern as I wish, that is to say with full powers … I am going.'[6]

On Sunday, 20 January, he called a cabinet meeting, arriving in uniform, his back straighter than ever, his features drawn. After shaking the hands of ministers, he told them: 'The exclusive regime of the political parties has reappeared. I disapprove of it. But, short of establishing by force a dictatorship, which I do not want and which, doubtless, would turn out badly, I do not have the means of preventing this. I therefore have to retire.' He would send a letter to Gouin to inform the president of the constituent assembly of his decision. 'I am leaving for the sake of the country,' he added as he walked out.

Moving to a rented villa in the park at Marly, outside Paris, he awaited a call from the country to return. But a poll showed that, while 40 per cent of those questioned said they did not take pleasure in his departure, only 27 per cent wanted him back. De Gaulle slept badly and appeared nervous and tired as he ruminated to his secretary, Claude Mauriac, on the prospects for France – the continuation of 'shambles and mediocrity', the Communists taking power leading to war, 'or my return'. Surprised by the lack of people coming to take a look at his new home, he sent a bodyguard to see if the police had set up barriers on the drive through the park from the main road; there were none. When he went out to the cinema in Paris on 1 April, he attracted little attention.

18

THE UNLOVED REPUBLIC

Despite a strong campaign led by the Communists, the electorate rejected the constitution drawn up by the constituent assembly by 10.58 million votes to 9.45 million with more than 5 million abstentions. De Gaulle was jubilant as the disjunction between the political class and the people was confirmed while, as under the Third Republic, the civil service, strengthened by Monnet's planning commission, got on with the job of running France.

Weak foundations

Though the PCF, the SFIO and the MRP sat together in government, the underlying tension between the Communists and their partners grew steadily. Bidault became prime minister, described by the Gaullist Chaban-Delmas as 'that little man, always with his back arched, always living on his nerves, cutting and jerky' – his heavy drinking led Duff Cooper to note the saying '*In Bido, Veritas*'. A fresh draft of a constitution was finally approved by a referendum in October 1946, in which 53 per cent voted, but one-third abstained, meaning that the text had the backing of 36 per cent of the total electorate.

While enshrining the supremacy of the legislature, it contained provisions aimed at lessening its control over the executive. In practice, however, the new Fourth Republic was little different from the Third with the president relegated to a largely ceremonial role except at a few moments of crisis – de Gaulle sniffed that the inhabitant of the Élysée was good only to open flower shows. Twenty governments succeeded one another over the ensuing dozen years. Though their electoral strength had declined, Radical Socialists headed ten of them while the MRP supplied four prime ministers, the Socialists three and smaller liberal or the conservative, mainly rural *Centre National des Indépendants et Paysans* (CNIP) four. The longest-lived administration, headed by the perennial provincial politician Henri Queuille, lasted for thirteen months.

The first general election held under the new constitution, in November 1946, made the PCF the biggest party with 29 per cent of the vote and 183 parliamentary seats. The MRP did well but the SFIO slumped to 18 per cent of the vote. Two months later, the tubby, bespectacled Socialist, Vincent Auriol, became President of the Republic and Édouard Herriot president of the National Assembly. Despite his party's reverses at the polls, Blum formed a government made up exclusively of Socialists, but it lasted for only five weeks and he was succeeded at the Hôtel Matignon by another Socialist, Paul Ramadier, a Verdun veteran with a tufty beard who slept little, received evening visitors in his carpet slippers and was happy to dine simply on goat's cheese.

Reverting to the Third Republic's big tent approach, he formed a coalition including representatives of the three main parties, Radicals and Independents. Among the latter was the strongly anti-Communist François Mitterrand of the small moderately left-wing *Union Démocratique et Socialiste de la Résistance* (UDSR), who became Minister for Ex-servicemen. The administration confronted growing economic problems and falling output. Pleven's victory over Mendès led to the face value of banknotes in circulation rising from 600 billion francs in 1944 to 900 billion in 1947 (it had been 100 billion in 1939). The value of money fell by a factor of three in the thirty months after Liberation.

The bread ration was cut to 200 grams a day. There was a poor harvest and shortages of coal. The black market flourished. Disputes over colonial policy and a tide of strikes against government policy organised by the Communist CGT labour federation led Ramadier to eject the PCF, which became a powerful political outsider, critical of successive governments, relying on its own resources, polling a quarter of the popular vote, running towns and cities, using trade union muscle to assert its strength, operating organisations – and publishing a cycling magazine. In the PCF's absence from government and despite a persistent hankering for Cold War neutrality by some on the centre-left, expressed most fluently in *Le Monde*, links with the United States strengthened. Help under the Marshall Aid programme amounted to $2.6 billion between April 1948 and January 1952, while the war against the Viet Minh nationalists which France was waging in Indochina was conveniently subsumed into the anti-Communist struggle.

The colonial issue in Asia and North Africa would be one of the persistent weaknesses of the Fourth Republic along with the attitude of the Communists and of de Gaulle and the state of the economy where, despite strong growth and considerable modernisation, inflation led to continual budgetary strain and undermined France's competiveness. Such factors were magnified by the shortage of politicians able to offer strong leadership in a short-term political system which bred reluctance to get to grips with difficult issues. The 'good doctor' Henri Queuille from the rural Corrèze, who was prime minister three times, epitomised the plight of the republic with his advice that 'politics is not the art of settling problems but of shutting up those who pose them.'

De Gaulle was soon back in the fray – the widespread idea that he spent the Fourth Republic in the political wilderness in his country home at Colombey-les-Deux-Églises is a myth. On 16 June 1946, four months before the second constitutional referendum, he travelled to the Norman town of Bayeux, where he had staged his return to France after D-Day. In military uniform, his hair slicked back, he thundered against the party system and the threat to public order, which could unleash dictatorship. France, he added, needed strong democratic institutions to compensate for 'our perpetual political effervescence'. A 'national arbiter' with executive authority was required, standing above daily politics, naming the prime minister and government, issuing decrees, promulgating laws, presiding over cabinet meetings and with the power to dissolve the legislature and call elections 'at times of serious confusion'. When Ramadier made a secret night-time visit to his country house at Colombey-les-Deux-Églises to sound out his intention, the General told the prime minister, 'I will remain the guide for the nation ... I serve only France.'

His forthright assault on the still-unborn republic provoked a Communist allegation that he was seeking 'a plebiscitary dictatorship' on Bonapartist lines, while Blum drew the comparison with a royal pretender to the throne. At the end of March 1947, de Gaulle returned to Normandy to address a rally of 50,000 people on the towering cliffs by the hamlet of Bruneval, declaring the need for reform to get rid of 'sterile games'. Cries of 'de Gaulle to power' rose in response. In Strasbourg the following weekend he told a large crowd that the Republic had to be 'brought out of its tomb' by a movement of the French people. A week later, he announced the launch of a political movement, the *Rassemblement du Peuple Français* (Rally of the French People) or RPF. The country had three choices, its posters declared – the Communists, the parties which were 'burning France's cards' or the 'rally of the mass of French people'.

The RPF was, in the General's mind, a means of bringing the bulk of the French people together rather than being an orthodox political party. Its attempted inclusiveness meant that it was 'like the Métro', de Gaulle's apostle, the writer André Malraux, remarked. It advanced ideas of an association between capital and labour, appealed to those running small businesses and the self-employed, beat the anti-Communist drum and offered to overcome the 'paralysis and disorder' of class warfare and political rivalries. The General said privately that it consisted of 'one third good folk, one third idiots and one third collaborators'. By May 1947, it claimed to have received 810,000 membership applications, an exaggeration but still an indication of its impact. Though saddened by the deaths of his daughter Anne, and of his favourite lieutenant Marshal Leclerc, killed in an air crash in North Africa, de Gaulle plunged into a round of provincial tours, attracting cheering crowds of up to 100,000. In the National Assembly, forty-one deputies formed a parliamentary group to back him.

At municipal elections in October 1947, the Gaullists took 38 per cent of the vote in big cities, winning control of thirteen of the twenty-five main urban centres including Strasbourg, Rennes, Nancy and Bordeaux as well as a majority on the Paris city council, of which de Gaulle's brother, Pierre, became the president. Civil servants made up the single biggest group of its electorate, followed by industrial workers, shopkeepers and artisans. 'The frogs are croaking in desperation,' de Gaulle wrote to his son. Blum warned that the Republic faced a double danger – 'On the one hand, international Communism has openly declared war on French democracy. On the other, a party has been formed in France whose object, and perhaps its only objective, is to remove fundamental rights.'

The PCF launched a wave of strikes on the railways and in northern mines. There was a tough reaction from the new government of Robert Schuman of the MRP, a lifelong bachelor and enthusiast for European construction with a deeply boring speaking style – a leading journalist wrote that 'his audience did not grow impatient; it fell asleep'.

The no-nonsense Socialist Jules Moch, first as transport minister and then at the interior ministry, despatched the army to the coalfields; some strikers were killed when troops opened fire. After the stoppages cut electricity supplies in Paris, the military was sent in again. Rail track sabotage derailed an express, killing twenty-one people. Communists in Marseilles attacked the city hall and the law courts, injuring the mayor. Army reserves were called up. A stormy six-day debate in the National Assembly approved a motion in favour of 'republican defence' to guarantee freedom to work. Sensing the way opinion was moving, the Communist-led CGT union federation ended the strikes while other workers set up a separate labour group, *Force Ouvrière*, with US encouragement.

PCF and RPF militants fought in the streets of Grenoble after a speech there by de Gaulle; one person was killed and more than a dozen seriously hurt as shots were fired and cars set ablaze. In the southern port of La Seyne, Gaullist 'gorilla' security guards threw Communists, including two parliamentary deputies, into the sea. The General's movement claimed 123 of the 320 seats in elections for the upper house of parliament and then took one third of the vote in cantonal polls. The political class consisted of 'wounded beasts who bite and slather,' he told his aide, Georges Pompidou.

Queuille formed a government which included Schuman, Bidault and Moch, and calmed things down as the economy showed signs of improvement thanks to the Marshall Plan and big loans from the International Monetary Fund. Rationing of bread, milk, fats, chocolate and textiles was lifted. At the foreign ministry, Schuman pursued Western European cooperation. The press was squared with a generous law on journalists' tax-free expenses. Against all the evidence, the Minister for the Colonies declared that the army had won the struggle in Indochina, where a conditional independence agreement was signed with the Vietnamese Emperor Bao Dai.

The Soviet blockade of Berlin that led to the airlift to supply the city and the Communist coup in Prague in February 1948 pushed the PCF further into its corner, but that only increased its combativity as Bidault took over as prime minister for ten months. Thorez had gone to the Soviet Union for treatment after a stroke and the party's principal spokesman was the diminutive, spherical Jacques Duclos who launched strident parliamentary attacks, sometimes so violent that fist fights broke out in the National Assembly and the police had to be called. Yet another government, under de Gaulle's one-time associate René Pleven, adjusted the voting arrangements for elections in 1951 in an attempt to do down the RPF and PCF and boost the moderate parties, then known as the Third Force.

The tactic brought the Socialists, now led by Guy Mollet, the MRP, the Republican Left and the CNIP 388 of the 625 seats, but the Communists and RPF emerged as the two biggest groupings with 26 and 22 per cent of the votes respectively. President Auriol approached the Gaullists to try to form the next administration. That set off a crisis within the movement as its secretary-general, Jacques Soustelle, had talks with Pleven, Bidault, Schuman, Reynaud, Queuille, Moch, Mitterrand and Mendès France. The General was furious at this accommodation with the system he despised and upbraided his lieutenant harshly, reducing him to tears on one meeting. Soustelle put it down to jealousy and soon resigned from his RPF post.

In fact, the Gaullist movement was fragmenting organisationally. The General's nationalistic approach to Europe and his doubts about the Marshall Plan and the European Coal and Steel Community negotiated by Robert Schuman sat ill with the spirit of the times as France sought to give a lead to European cooperation. His jeremiad messages were clear but his positive offerings vague. A quarter of the RPF deputies voted for the next government under Antoine Pinay, a prim provincial from the Auvergne with a neat moustache who wore a little round hat with an upturned brim. Leader of the conservative CNIP party, which drew its support from rural and small town voters, he was the epitome of the bourgeois France the General abhorred. But de Gaulle faced dissension within his own party when eighty-one RPF deputies lined up to back the Radical René Mayer who took over from Pinay as prime minister in January 1953. Municipal elections early that year brought fresh evidence of the decline of the *Rassemblement*, which won only 10.6 per cent of the vote. No longer scared of a PCF take-over, the public had 'returned to its usual vomiting', as de Gaulle wrote to his son. In May, he freed the RPF deputies to do as they wished and did go into the wilderness, ending his experiment at heading a political move-ment, which had shown the limitations of his style of leadership. Sixty-two RPF deputies voted for the next government under Joseph Laniel of the CNIP. Five became ministers; de Gaulle cut off contact with them.

Though it had survived the Gaullist offensive and proved capable of containing the Communists, the Fourth Republic was demonstrating the extent of its internal instability. When Auriol stepped down as pres-ident, it took thirteen votes to find a majority for his successor, the far from outstanding René Coty from Normandy. The MRP had failed to live up to its early promise. Support for the SFIO had declined signifi-cantly – its active membership fell from 353,000 to 117,000 in the two decades after the Liberation. The right remained fragmented.

Politics is not everything

In that context, the civil service played an ever more important role. As industry was modernised, Jean Monnet's planning commission super-vised big investments in railways, power, coal and shipping. Along with rising exports and increased productivity, this gave the public the sen-timent that France was, indeed, reviving economically as it entered what are known, misleadingly, as the '*Trente Glorieuses*' (Glorious Thirty Years)*. There were certainly positive indicators. National output rose

* The phrase was originated by the economist Jean Fourastié.

by 46 per cent between 1954 and 1957 and agriculture expanded by 19 per cent. Annual growth ran at an average of 5.5 per cent between 1954 and 1959. Total output in 1957 was 30 per cent higher than 1954.

Internationally, France was a leading force in the ongoing process of European integration which had begun with Schuman's initiatives, and relations were good with the United States.

But the geographical imbalance was enormous – incomes in western France were half of those in the east, where 80 per cent of factories were located.

French ingenuity showed itself alive and well with the development of the Caravelle jet airliner and the Citroën DS automobile, which set new standards for comfort and road handling with its hydro-pneumatic self-levelling suspension – both were launched in 1955. The front-wheel drive Renault 4 followed for the mass market, selling 8 million vehicles. Marcel Bich pioneered the disposable ballpoint pen after buying the patent from the Hungarian László Bíró. Air France served the best meals available in flight.

Paris remained a great world capital of fashion and culture with new figures joining stalwarts from the inter-war period and an array of foreigners. Picasso, Braque and Matisse had continued to work during the war though they exhibited little. After the Liberation, they and other pre-war artists continued on their earlier paths while others turned to abstractionism and action painting in Tachism and *l'art informel*. Dubuffet's childlike drawings, graffiti and cartoons explored different media and Bernard Buffet enjoyed great popular success with more than 8,000 paintings and prints in a fashionable post-Modigliani style.

Philosophical thought became dominated by existentialism with its leading proponent, Jean-Paul Sartre, the epitome of a public intellectual as he plunged into political debates and argued that existence precedes essence and individuals bear sole responsibility for themselves in a godless world 'on the far side of despair'. The gnome-like philosopher and his companion, the writer and feminist Simone de Beauvoir, both of whom had rallied to the Resistance only at the last gasp, became Left Bank celebrities. Eventually, his political posturing grew tiresome and he was elbowed aside by the Structuralists, headed by Claude Lévi-Strauss and Jacques Lacan, who taught that it was the structures around them which determined how people thought and behaved. The semiologist Roland Barthes identified the establishment propaganda to be found in the press, films and advertisements through embedded signs, which buttressed the status quo on behalf of the bourgeoisie.

Avant-garde drama saw works by Eugène Ionesco, Jean Genet, Arthur Adamov, Fernando Arrabal and Samuel Beckett, who drank quietly behind the stained-glass windows of the Falstaff tavern in Montparnasse. The Théâtre National Populaire (TNP) flourished in the capital and the annual Avignon festival was launched in 1947. Local authorities funded theatres in the regions and in working-class urban districts. Mauriac and Malraux continued as literary lions and André Gide was awarded the Nobel Prize for Literature. Romain Gary produced a string of books, winning the Goncourt Prize for *The Roots of Heaven*. Albert Camus, who had made his wartime choice early on in his work for the underground newspaper *Combat*, emerged as perhaps the leading novelist of the era with *The Outsider*, *The Plague* and *The Fall*. Asking if suicide was the right response to an absurd world, he responded that life required revolt and struggle. Awarded the Nobel Prize in 1957, the deeply humanist and honest Camus was a constant critic of totalitarianism, which led to his rupture with Sartre over the other man's failure to denounce the repression of the Soviet Union.

Jean Anouilh wrote a stream of high-class conventional plays and was a recurrent competitor for a Nobel Prize alongside Malraux and Sartre. Alain Robbe-Grillet, Marguerite Duras, Michel Butor, Nathalie Sarraute and Claude Simon, joined by Beckett, developed the *Nouveau Roman* without classic plots or characters. Georges Perec and Raymond Queneau experimented with convoluted word games. The Olympia Press published the work of Henry Miller, Vladimir Nabokov, Jean Genet and William Burroughs, along with a stream of erotica. In the later 1950s, American writers of the Beat generation – Allen Ginsberg, Gregory Corso, William Burroughs and Lawrence Ferlinghetti – congregated on the Left Bank.

George Plimpton founded the influential *Paris Review* mainly to publish expatriate writers. Afro-American writers – Richard Wright, James Baldwin, and Chester Himes – found a refuge from racism in Paris along with jazz musicians headed by the French adoptee, Sidney Bechet. Duke

Ellington defined himself as a 'drinker of Beaujolais'. Josephine Baker staged a triumphant return to the stage at the Folies Bergère in 1949.

Many of the foreigners congregated and feuded on occasion in the cafés of Saint-Germain-des-Prés and Montparnasse, where young French couples gave exhibitions of bebop dancing as if they had invented jiving. Baldwin recalled 'the days when we walked through Les Halles singing, loving every inch of France and loving each other ... the jam sessions in Pigalle, and our stories about the whores there ... the nights spent smoking hashish in the Arab cafés ... the morning which found us telling dirty stories, true stories, sad and earnest stories, in grey workingmen's cafés.'[1]

Françoise Sagan, the 'charming little monster' according to François Mauriac, created a sensation with her first novel *Bonjour Tristesse*, published in 1954 when she was eighteen. Maurice Druon, a wartime Free French broadcaster from London, brought mediaeval history alive with his seven novels published in the 1950s under the title *Les Rois Maudits* (The Accursed Kings). Pierre Daninos won wide popularity with his series of comic books depicting the discovery of France and the French by the bowler-hatted, pipe-smoking Englishman, Major Thompson. Crime fiction enjoyed a boom: alongside the perennial Georges Simenon and his Commissaire Maigret, Léo Malet invented the highly popular, badly behaved detective Nestor Burma. Meanwhile, in works like *Du Rififi chez les Hommes* and *Touchez Pas au Grisbi*, Auguste Le Breton and Albert Simonin pioneered a genre that made the most of slang popular life. The high priest of the *polars* in their distinctive black jackets was Frédéric Dard whose main character, Commissaire San-Antonio, punned and flirted his way through more than seventy books.

The fashion for *noir* naturally infused the popular cinema with films starring the patriarchal Jean Gabin and his gang of tough-guy actors with soft hearts, many of them scripted by the extraordinarily productive and inventive Michel Audiard. A series of hit productions starred the American-born Edward (Eddie) Constantine as the hard-drinking, womanising Lemmy Caution. The role of the director as *auteur* was established by Robert Bresson and Jean-Pierre Melville and their peers. Alongside them went a boom in costume dramas featuring the heartthrob Gérard Philipe and Martine Carol in *décolleté* roles before her position as the top sex star was usurped by Brigitte Bardot. Together with the horse-faced Fernandel, new comics also enjoyed great screen popularity, led by Louis de Funès, Bourvil, Darry Cowl and the hugely talented but anarchic Francis Blanche, for whom 'a day without a joke is like a gruyère without holes', while Jacques Tati pursued his idiosyncratic way with *Jour de Fête, Monsieur Hulot's Holiday* and *Mon Oncle.*

Though facing considerable competition from Hollywood films imported under a 1946 quota agreement, the domestic industry benefitted from box-office levies, the establishment of the Centre National de la Cinématographie, the showings at the Cinémathèque with its enormous archive, and a growth in serious criticism from the magazine *Cahiers du Cinéma.* Audiences reached 423 million in 1947 and still ran at 400 million in the late 1950s before the impact of television was fully felt. A dozen sound stages catered for the work of new directors such as Yves Allégret, Jacques Becker, Robert Bresson, René Clément, Henri-Georges Clouzot, Claude Autant-Lara and Alain Resnais.

Le Corbusier turned his plans into reality with modernistic buildings that paved the way for brutalism, notably with the rough cast concrete twelve-storey *Cité Radieuse* apartment block in Marseilles. Pierre Boulez developed serialised music with his masterpiece for voice and orchestra, *Le Marteau sans Maître* (*The Hammer without a Master*). French popular singers picked up where they had left off (if they had) during the war – Édith Piaf, beset by morphine and alcohol after the death of her lover, the boxer Marcel Cerdan, in a plane crash in 1949, made up to twenty recordings a year. Her protégés, Yves Montand and Charles Aznavour, established themselves as perennial favourites while Juliette Gréco epitomised bohemian life on the Left Bank along with the jazz-loving writer Boris Vian. Maurice Chevalier became the archetypal ageing urbane boulevardier capped by his performance in the musical *Gigi.* Georges Brassens and Jacques Brel (who was Belgian) made poetry popular through their songs. Charles Trenet recorded the song '*La Mer*' in 1946 and was a regular headliner at music halls after returning in 1951 from a six-year stay in the USA.

France was the biggest international tourist destination – Americans made 264,000 visits in 1950 and three times as many by the end of the decade. It was easy to fall back on the clichés of *Gai Paris* as a haven of pleasure not to be easily found at home – a 1951 Gallup Poll reported that the first thoughts of American men on hearing a mention of the French capital was 'dancing girls' and 'leg shows', while women mentioned fashion, perfume and landmarks. A Marshall Plan programme provided for the modernisation of French hotels to make them more acceptable to transatlantic visitors.

Divisions and discontent

There was thus no lack of diversions as France recovered from the war. But there was no denying the extent of everyday worries among its people, and the growing social tension arising from the squeeze which modernisation put on traditional sections of the population. Protectionism sheltered farmers from foreign competition but this encouraged over-production and surpluses, some of which were dumped in provincial towns in the protests that became a regular feature of rural France. The number of tractors was five times that in 1939, but many were bought on subsidised credit and were little used on small farms. Though differences had been reduced by mobility, improved transport, education, mass retailing and broadcasting, social and economic regional differences were still very evident, as was the way in which local power bases were essential for most leading national politicians.

Catholic observance was strongest in Brittany and in a long, broad belt running from the eastern regions down through the Auvergne to the Basque country, while church attendance was low in the north. The population was oldest in the predominantly rural *départements* of the centre and youngest on the north coast. Though a quarter of rural dwellers moved to towns between 1949 and 1954, France still had more people outside urban areas than most other major Western countries. In a dozen *départements* between the Massif Central and the Landes in the south-west and the three *départements* of Western Brittany, a majority of households still lived off farming, fishing and forestry.

Only in the Paris and Lyons areas and the north-eastern border *départements* did more than half the inhabitants work in industry and transport. Sixty-five per cent of national output of goods and services came from twenty-seven of the ninety *départements* according to a survey in 1955. Such divergences were reflected in voting patterns and the degree of political involvement. The abstention rate was lowest in the twenty-seven most productive *départements* where electoral support was higher for the PCF and for those who backed the progressive Radical Mendès France.[2]

Despite the regional differences, the increasing homogenisation of rural and small town life with the advanced urban mainstream meant that people living in the countryside no longer saw themselves as confined to an old world. They wanted to hold on to their way of life but also to share in the new world represented by the Citroën DS, the Caravelle, foreign travel and fashionable Parisians depicted in the press, and, before long, on television.

Their discontent found its demagogue in Pierre Poujade, a shopkeeper from the south-west who headed the *Union de Défense des Commerçants et Artisans* (UDCA) (Union for the Defence of Shopkeepers and Artisans) which started as an anti-tax movement. Its leader thundered against the 'thieving' state and the 'brothel' of parliament with its 'rubbishy pederast' deputies while exalting 'the good little people of France' and 'the humble housewife'. At legislative elections in 1956, it won 12 per cent of the vote, polling up to 22 per cent in southern *départements* and the west. Its score was slightly more than the Radicals or the MRP, and, with fifty-two National Assembly seats, replaced the Gaullists as the main non-Communist foe of the Fourth Republic – the youngest deputy elected on its list was a leader of its youth branch, Jean-Marie Le Pen.[3]

The UDCA was fervently nationalist and xenophobic, picking up themes from the hard right-wing leagues of the 1930s. Poujade told *Time* magazine, apropos of Algerian independence supporters, 'All this is a great diabolic scheme to dismember France. As for those who are against us, I need only say: let them go back to Jerusalem. We'll even be glad to pay their way.' For all his noise, however, he lacked a political programme beyond denunciations of the political class and incitement to tax evasion. When he ran in a by-election in Paris, he flopped and his movement disintegrated, though he popped up again in 1981 to back the presidential candidacy of François Mitterrand, who appointed him to a social and economic government council.

Colonial cancer

From its early days, the Fourth Republic faced recurrent problems with its colonies. Stretching from West Africa and the Caribbean to Indochina and the South Pacific, each component of the empire had a specific role as a producer of raw materials, cotton, minerals or coffee. The theory since Jules Ferry had been that, as well as providing France with such primary products, they would be good markets for goods manufactured in the Hexagon. But most of the profits from their exports were retained by companies in metropolitan France and wages were extremely low for most of their employees. So, while the largely French bourgeoisie of Dakar or Saigon bought Parisian goods, there was relatively little purchasing power overall for metropolitan products.

The empire of almost 13 million square kilometres had been re-named the French Union by the 1946 constitution and some liberal politicians in Paris saw the need to address decolonisation. But force took the upper hand in response to a revolt in Madagascar in 1947, which resulted in the deaths of 550 French people and 1,900 native inhabitants killed by paratroopers; Foreign Legionnaires sent in by the Ramadier government then slaughtered an estimated 80,000 people. There were other risings in African colonies – notably in the Ivory Coast and in Cameroon, where insurrections were violently repressed in the 1950s. But it was Indochina that began the undermining of the Republic from far away.

De Gaulle's Liberation government had set out to recover Vietnam for France after Japan's surrender. But the French forces were weak, the Chinese occupied the north of the country and the US leaned towards the nationalist united front under the Communist-led Viet Minh, which swept the board at elections in early 1946. Ho Chi Minh, as president, reached an agreement with the French emissary, Jean Sainteny, for the country to become a free state with its own government within the French Union and with France retaining 15,000 troops in the country. He flew to Paris in May to finalise the agreement, but de Gaulle's emissary, a glacially superior monk turned admiral, Thierry d'Argenlieu, shunned the Viet Minh and backed South Vietnamese puppets without authorisation from Paris.

After Ho returned home, the Viet Minh, under increasingly firm Communist control, formed its own government, which drew up a constitution that made no mention of any link with France. D'Argenlieu cut off the southern territory of Cochinchina from the Viet Minh and fighting erupted in the northern port of Haiphong where shelling by a French cruiser killed several thousand people. After clashes spread to Hanoi, Hue and other cities, Ho called for a general uprising. The Viet Minh blew up the power station in Hanoi, and mobs massacred French civilians. As the colonial army used its superior firepower to dominate urban areas and the main highways, the Viet Minh retreated into guerrilla warfare. Their successful attacks in the autumn of 1950 threatened Hanoi and produced a major disaster for the French when troops evacuating a base in the north of the country were caught in an ambush in which 4,600 of them were listed as dead or missing. Other outposts in north-east Vietnam were abandoned. Panic set in at the realisation of how well organised and skilful the enemy was.

The Second World War commander, de Lattre de Tassigny, was sent in to retrieve the situation, which he did by throwing in all available troops and bringing heavy artillery and air power to bear. But the cost of the war was a major drain in the already strained state finances and a scandal erupted over currency profiteering on the Indochinese piaster said to involve politicians. Coming after the Communist victory in China and the outbreak of the Korean war, the conflict in Vietnam formed part of a far from cold war, but ministers were unwilling to take a grip; they preferred to let policies be lost in overlapping departmental structures as they sought local puppets such as Bao Dai and left the army to get on with the job.[4]

The military task was made fundamentally impossible by two main factors – the size, ruthlessness and nationalist appeal of the Viet Minh and the way in which the French were trying to control the whole country while being confined to often impractical roads with air support limited by the weather. Governments in Paris increasingly looked for what prime minister René Mayer defined to the new commander, Henri Navarre, in mid-1953 as an 'honourable way out'. A poll in Le Monde showed only 15 per cent support for vigorous military operations; most people favoured either a negotiated withdrawal or a transfer of the matter to the United Nations – or simply wanted to forget about the issue.[5]

Under Joseph Laniel, Mayer's successor, Paul Reynaud took charge of Indochinese affairs and put forward proposals to enable Vietnam, Laos and Cambodia to 'perfect their independence'. The idea was not to give up the fight against the Communists but to get the local administrations to take on the task, with France in a supporting role*. Navarre planned to confront the main Viet Minh force in northern Tonkin and had paratroopers dropped in November 1953 to re-occupy the base of Dien Bien Phu in the wild mountain forests near the border with Laos.[6]

The Viet Minh encircled the base and the battle, from March to May 1954, became an epic struggle between the well-equipped but vulnerable European army and its guerrilla opponents, who were able to deploy greater manpower and weaponry in relentless attacks as air power failed to swing the day. The new prime minister in Paris, Mendès France, who had spoken the previous year of the impossibility of military victory, drew the typically clear conclusion that it was time to abandon the wishful thinking that had characterised the nation's Indochina policy.

On taking office in June, he had set a new pattern by abandoning the tradition of reshuffling the same pack of ministers. Instead, he named a government of largely new men including the Free French figure, General Marie-Pierre Koenig, as defence minister and the Gaullists Chaban-Delmas and Christian Fouchet as Minister of Public Works and for Moroccan and Tunisian Affairs respectively, while sending Jacques Soustelle to Algeria as governor. A conference to try to end the wars in Korea and Vietnam had opened in April in Geneva grouping the US, USSR, China, France and Britain. Mendès used this to reach a ceasefire and an agreement temporarily separating Vietnam into two zones, the north to be governed by the Viet Minh and the south by an administration headed by Bao Dai. A final declaration provided for a general election by July 1956 to create a unified state – this document, issued by the British chairman, was not accepted by the South Vietnamese or the US. France withdrew from Indochina at the end of six-and-a-half years of war costing it 3,000 billion francs and 75,000 lives.

---

* As Richard Nixon and Henry Kissinger were to do at the end of the 1960s.

Seen as a miracle worker, Mendès went to Tunisia, accompanied by Fouchet, for negotiations that led to an agreement to grant independence in 1956, paving the way for broader legislation creating elected local assemblies in French overseas territories. The prime minister was all business – Chaban-Delmas noted the 'sober, effective and rapid' nature of cabinet sessions. But he ran into heavy weather with the proposal launched by his predecessors for a European army as a means of containing German rearmament while decolonisation made him an easy target for the right as the relief of withdrawal from Indochina passed. *Pieds-noirs** suspected him of preparing to make concessions to nationalists in Algeria. Anti-Semitism fuelled attacks on PMF, as he was known – the young deputy, Jean-Marie Le Pen, spoke of his 'patriotic, almost physical repulsion' for the premier. Beetroot farmers in northern France revolted against the abolition of a system under which a third of their crop was bought by the state to be turned into low-quality alcohol. Mendès was not helped by his unbending personality, his lack of political finesse and his insistence that he was correct, not to mention his calls for the French to give up wine for milk.

When he decided to let the European defence plan drop after it was defeated in parliament, he alienated the MRP, which was worried that he might put together a broad non-Communist reform movement that would attract its voters. In February 1955, the government fell after losing the vote in a parliamentary debate on North Africa. 'Men come and go, national necessities remain,' Mendès remarked as he left the Chamber.[7]

Elections at the end of 1955 saw a strong showing by the Communists despite the questions raised by Nikita Khrushchev's denunciation of Stalin earlier in the year; they took 25 per cent of the votes and 150 seats, an increase of forty-seven. It was a disaster for the Gaullists who won only 4.4 per cent and twenty-one seats, a sixth of their score of 1951. The Socialist Guy Mollet, a dry party bureaucrat who hoped to govern with Communist support, formed a government evoking the memory of 1936 with its label of the Republican Front. Mendès France

---

* The name comes from the black shoes or boots worn by settlers in contrast to the natives who went barefoot or wore babouche slippers.

and the Gaullist Jacques Chaban-Delmas were ministers of state, though the first disapproved of the Socialist's economic policy. Félix Houphouët-Boigny from the Ivory Coast, who had participated in national politics since being elected to the post-war constituent assembly, became France's first African cabinet member, as minister delegate. However, the attempt to forge a new left-of-centre unity proved yet another false dawn as a fresh colonial storm gathered pace across the Mediterranean.

THE END OF A REPUBLIC

Encouraged by the Viet Minh victory, the National Liberation Front (FLN) in Algeria launched an organised assault on French rule with bomb attacks and murders in the Aurès Mountains. Paris sent in military reinforcements. 'The only negotiation is war,' justice minister François Mitterrand declared. 'Algeria is France.'[1]

For most of the French, more than a century after Charles X had sent the military expedition across the Mediterranean, the North African territory of 2.4 million square miles was, indeed, not a colony but an integral part of the nation. More than 80 per cent of the one million *pieds-noirs* inhabitants of European origin had been born there; most were from countries other than France. A few of them were very rich, but the bulk were ordinary workers, shopkeepers, civil servants and farmers out in the *bled* (countryside). When they were depicted as a minority, they replied that they were part of the 55 million-strong population of France stretching 'from Dunkirk to Tamanrasset [in the Sahara]', which made Algérie française an indissoluble part of the nation. In a tight parliamentary situation, governments had to take notice of its thirty deputies in the National Assembly.

Algerian morass

Though they controlled 90 per cent of the territory's wealth, the *pieds-noirs* were outnumbered in Algeria nine to one by non-Europeans. Of the 9 million other inhabitants, some 70 per cent were Arabs and the rest mainly Berbers in the rugged mountains of the Kabylie and Aurès regions, plus 600,000 nomads in a million square kilometres of the Sahara. Algerians had served in the French army from the early days of colonialisation – 100,000 died in the First World War. North African soldiers played a significant part in the liberation of southern France and campaigns in Italy and Germany of 1944–5, as well as in the attempt to hold on to Indochina. Known as *harkis*, they were used by the French as lightly armed militia in their home villages and towns after the FLN revolt began, later fighting alongside the regular army as guides and auxiliaries – a role which made them particular targets for the nationalists.

For the French army, which had been humiliated in 1940 and then failed to defeat the Viet Minh, suppressing the FLN was a chance to restore its reputation and self-belief even if this meant using extreme methods. Paratroopers who blamed their fate in Indochina on the politicians in Paris moved to North Africa determined not to let themselves be traduced again, just as the *pieds-noirs* were intent on not being sold out by governments across the sea. Any compromise was suspect – 'announcement of reforms gives the agitators their greatest hope,' a deputy from Algiers told the National Assembly.

International criticism was brushed off as troop numbers across the Mediterranean jumped from 40,000 to 450,000. Despite protests, including some by drafted soldiers, there was cross-party support in the National Assembly for holding on, with dissent only from the Communists and a few brave voices on the left, such as the journalist Claude Bourdet who revealed the army's use of torture. Though Mendès France backed the use of force, he resigned from the government after six months in protest at the way 'the sentiments and miseries of the native population' were being ignored, warning that France would lose throughout Africa unless it dealt with the Algerians in whom it had confidence to 'ensure their gradual emancipation'. The conflict spread to the streets of Paris with incidents between Algerian immigrants and security forces including one clash in the Goutte d'Or district in which fifteen police were hurt, fourteen demonstrators were taken to hospital and forty shops were looted.[2]

Parliament granted Mollet special powers and he flew to Algeria to install his choice as governor general, de Gaulle's wartime colleague, Georges Catroux. But Catroux was suspect to the *pieds-noirs* on account of a plan he had drawn up a dozen years earlier for a degree of devolution of power. They pelted the prime minister with rotten tomatoes and stones amid cries of 'Mollet to the gallows' and 'Throw Catroux in the sea'. The police did not intervene. It was a foretaste of what lay ahead as the army and its supporters on the spot ignored the civilians in Paris who, for their part, usually preferred not to know what was being done in the name of the Republic, as epitomised by Mitterrand's failure to do anything about the use of torture and illegality by the troops.

When Catroux decided not to take the job, it went to the Socialist Robert Lacoste, a thickset, combative politician with slicked-back black hair, who tried initially to reduce the gulf between the settlers and the Arabs but increasingly moved to the side of repression, especially after the shock of an FLN ambush that killed twenty-one young soldiers in a gorge south of Algiers in May 1956, their bodies defiled, castrated and disembowelled. A pattern developed of tit-for-tat attacks with high death tolls. Secret contacts in Rome were broken off after the FLN voted to pursue violence as the way to independence. The French military kidnapped the nationalist leader, Ahmed Ben Bella, after illegally intercepting his aircraft on its way from Morocco to Tunis. Faced with this fait accompli, the government put him in a Paris jail.[3]

The desire to hit back at the Arab cause led Mollet to cooperate with Britain and Israel in the ill-fated operation against the Egyptian leader Gamal Abdel Nasser, after his nationalisation of the Suez Canal in 1956. Though militarily successful, this ended in diplomatic disaster when US opposition and a threat of intervention by Moscow brought it to an abrupt end. But Mollet did make progress in other domains.[4]

France played a major role in the negotiation and signature of the Treaty of Rome establishing the six-nation European Common Market in March 1957. It was also among the founders of the European atomic agency, Euratom. The Minister for Overseas Territories, Gaston Defferre, completed a reform of relations with France's African dominions, to give them a form of internal autonomy under councils headed initially by a French official but then by a local.

The government was, however, brought down in June 1957 by its internal tensions, a spiralling trade deficit and high inflation. The next cabinet, headed by the Radical Maurice Bourgès-Maunoury, lasted for five months and had to endure a demonstration on 13 March by police outside parliament that ended in violence. The disintegration of the political system was evident when it took five weeks to put together a new government under a 37-year-old Radical technocrat, Félix Gaillard, who oversaw a devaluation, spending cuts and tax increases, and ordered a speeding-up of the nuclear weapons programme begun under Mendès France.

The climate in Algeria deteriorated with a fresh series of FLN bombings by young women who left explosives in a milk bar, cafeteria, restaurant and nightclub frequented by Europeans, bringing reprisals by *pieds-noirs*. The Casbah in Algiers was transformed into an armed camp. Lacoste and the French military commander, Raoul Salan, a veteran of Indochina, put a tough, craggy-faced paratroop general, Jacques Massu, who had served in the Free French and also fought in Indochina, in charge of the attack on the nationalist stronghold. A curfew was imposed and the FLN stronghold was invaded street by street as the Battle of Algiers unfolded. A general strike called by the FLN was defeated by strong-arm methods. The army stepped up arbitrary round-ups of Algerians and torture – independent reports put the number of people who 'disappeared' at 3,000.[5]

After ten months, the battle ended with the capture of one of the FLN's leaders and the death of another, blown up as troops penetrated his hiding place. The army had won, but the cost was a further sharpening of the division between French and Algerians, the increased independence of military commanders and the use of illegal methods as paratroopers became heroes for the settlers in contrast to the pusillanimous politicians in Paris.

A fresh crisis broke out when a French air attack killed sixty-nine people in a Tunisian frontier village, near which sixteen of France's soldiers had died in an FLN ambush a month earlier. The Tunisian president Habib Bourguiba demanded the withdrawal of French troops from their base at Bizerta in his country. Paris accepted a mediation effort by America and Britain, but the settler lobby warned that this would lead to foreign interference in Algeria. *Pieds-noirs* set up a 'vigilance

The General's return: In 1958 France was on the brink of civil war
before de Gaulle returned to create the Fifth Republic.

Long road out: Algeria did not gain independence until
1962, after a war that split France.

Artistic stars: Pablo Picasso and Jean Cocteau illuminated France's cultural aura.

Thinking couple: Jean-Paul Sartre and Simone de Beauvoir were icons for the age.

Yé-yé: The 1960s saw an explosion of youth culture and made performers like Johnny Hallyday stars.

Man of his time: Prime minister Georges Pompidou shows the popular touch, complete with cigarette.

The bond: Charles de Gaulle and Konrad Adenauer seal the Franco-German Friendship Treaty, West Europe's most important single bilateral agreement since the Second World War.

Atomic power: De Gaulle travelled to the South Pacific to witness a French atom-bomb test.

Street revolt: Mass demonstrations in May–June 1968 ripped through Paris and other big cities . . .

. . . Rocking the Gaullist administration and shaking the Fifth Republic.

En grève: At the same time as the demonstrations, a general strike brought much of France to a halt before Pompidou negotiated a pay deal with the unions.

Last coup: De Gaulle caused consternation by disappearing for a day.

Rally of the faithful: A huge Gaullist demonstration swelled down the Champs-Élysées led by ministers (from left) Maurice Schumann, Michel Debré and André Malraux.

The new prince: Giscard d'Estaing promised a new and more modern presidency, but won only one term.

Twenty-six years: Between them, Jacques Chirac (left) and François Mitterrand (right) held the presidency for more than a quarter of a century.

Les Bleus: The World Cup victory of France's ethnically mixed team in 1998 fuelled hopes of social harmony – it was not to be.

Banlieue violence: Torching cars has become a feature of the recurrent unrest in France's immigrant districts.

Presidents and partners: Nicolas Sarkozy and his wife Carla Bruni leave the Élysée Palace after he lost the 2012 election, watched by François Hollande and his partner Valérie Trierweiler.

The challenger:
Leading the National
Front, Marine Le
Pen became a major
rival to mainstream
politicians and split
with her father.

Temporary unity: Murderous terrorist attacks on the magazine
Charlie Hebdo and a Jewish supermarket in January 2015 brought
out huge demonstrations of national solidarity.

Paris as terrorist target: Police move in on the Bataclan concert hall
where eighty-nine people died in the assault of 13 November, 2015.

committee' and 30,000 demonstrated to demand military rule. After another protracted round of negotiations, Coty asked the Alsatian MRP leader, Pierre Pflimlin, to try to form a government in May 1958.

Pflimlin, an MRP leader known as 'the Little Plum', formed an administration of five Christian Democrats, nine centrists and four independents. He found that the 'decomposition' of the Fourth Republic was worse than he had realised. Though growth was strong and unemployment low, inflation was raging. The trade deficit widened and Jean Monnet was sent to Washington to raise a $274 million loan. The regime had lost credibility and showed no signs of being able to regenerate itself. There was no shortage of able young technicians, but, as the commentator Pierre Emmanuel noted, 'though they are most competent and full of initiative in their fields ... they have not succeeded in changing the obsolete part of the existing French structures'.[6]

Governments appeared unable to rely on two bastions of the republic, the police and the military. At the beginning of May 1958, right-wing policemen demonstrated outside the National Assembly. Generals in Algeria sent a letter to President Coty warning of a 'desperate reaction' to any surrender to the FLN; the army reported killing 15,000 FLN members in a year as Salan focussed on consolidating control over inhabited areas and using psychological warfare to win over the local population. Soustelle headed a Union for the Safeguard and Renewal of French Algeria (USRAF), which brought together academics, military men, religious figures and others who believed that the territory's best future lay in continued rule by France. Gaullists intrigued to whip up support for a return of the General. Massu privately lamented the incapacity of the politicians in Paris, and thought de Gaulle alone could lead events in the right direction. The main settler newspaper, *L'Écho d'Alger*, published an open letter, calling on the Man of 18 June to emerge from his silence.

Facing the National Assembly for the first time, the prime minister-designate called for institutional reform to strengthen the executive and, echoing the failed policy in Indochina, said negotiations with the nationalists could only follow a French military victory. As he spoke, a general strike in Algiers closed down public buildings, shops, factories, transport, cinemas, cafés and restaurants. A student leader, Pierre

Lagaillarde, a tall, intense figure with a brooding look, harangued a crowd of tens of thousands asking 'Are you going to let Algérie française be sold down the river? Will you allow traitors to govern us?' Dressed in a paratrooper's uniform, he led a mob to attack the main government building; riot police retreated after firing a few cans of tear gas. The demonstrators commandeered a lorry to break down the gates and sacked the building, flinging furniture, typewriters and a blizzard of official papers from the windows. The crowd outside wildly applauded Lagaillarde when he appeared on an upper balcony.

When Massu arrived in a furious temper, the crowd cheered as he called for 'a government of public safety under General de Gaulle'. He became its chairman with a Gaullist who had been intriguing in Algiers all year as his deputy. Demonstrators took over the radio station. Officers plotted an airborne landing in metropolitan France to follow their putsch in Algeria.

In Paris, Pflimlin got the backing of legislators who voted at the end of the National Assembly debate, but the number of abstainers, among them the Communists, deprived him of an overall majority. He formed a government with Mollet as vice-premier, Pleven as foreign minister and Edgar Faure as finance minister. After a delay, Jules Moch took the interior ministry.

The General steps in

14 May 1958. De Gaulle thought the only way to avoid civil war was by the appointment of a figure of national authority, and 'that authority could only be mine.' But a poll the previous year had shown only 1 per cent support for his return to office and most of the press backed Pflimlin. So he needed to move carefully and let the situation deteriorate to the point at which power fell into his hands, making it clear that he was ready to save the nation for a second time but not staging an illegal coup. He did not side with the rebels across the Mediterranean; nor did he condemn them.

17 May. Fighter aircraft flew over Colombey in the formation of the Cross of Lorraine. In his gardens, the General raised his arms in salute.

19 May. De Gaulle held a press conference in Paris in the Hôtel d'Orsay, a once grand building by the Seine. Wearing a dark double-breasted suit, he looked significantly older and stouter than many of the journalists remembered him. He presented himself as a solitary figure who 'could perhaps be useful' because he stood apart from the political parties, 'a man who belongs to nobody and who belongs to everybody'. When the prominent journalist Maurice Duverger asked him if he risked putting public freedoms in danger, he replied 'Why? Do you think that at the age of sixty-seven I am going to become a dictator?'

Mendès France and Mitterrand took severe exception to his refusal to condemn the rebels. An emissary from Salan told him he represented an 'enormous hope'.

20–25 May. The General was driven between Colombey and Paris in his supercharged Citroën, which outran his police followers. In Corsica, paratroopers sympathetic to the rebels, joined by comrades from Algiers, took charge of the island; they swiftly neutralised a force sent in by the interior ministry. In Algiers, officers drew up a plan codenamed '*Résurrection*' to land paratroopers at two Parisian airfields and march on the Champs-Élysées and the National Assembly, raising a mass demonstration to force Pflimlin to resign, occupying government buildings and opening the way for a government of public safety under de Gaulle. In *Le Monde*, Duverger wrote that the General should be called to office 'before the nation is completely torn apart, before it becomes the hostage of one camp or another.'

26 May. De Gaulle sent a letter to Pflimlin proposing a meeting, to which he agreed. The prime minister left Matignon secretly late at night and was taken by a circuitous route to the one-time royal domain of Saint-Cloud at 12.15 a.m. There, de Gaulle assured him that he would not take power 'in a tumult of generals'. Still, he refused to condemn the rebels. 'These people want things to change,' he went on. 'They think the regime is bad and I cannot say they are wrong.'

27 May. The General ignored an agreement with Pflimlin that their encounter should be kept secret, and issued a statement claiming that he had 'begun the regular process necessary for the establishment of a republican government capable of assuring the unity and independence of the country'. He called for public order and told troops to remain under their military leaders. As if in charge of the military, he asked Salan for a list of the forces at his command and instructed him to await orders.

Though Pflimlin got a large majority for a constitutional bill to strengthen the executive, three ministers resigned. At a 2 a.m. cabinet meeting, the foreign minister, Pleven, pointed out that the government was unable to send its Minister for Algeria to Algiers, that the defence minister did not control the army and that police loyalty was breaking down. 'We claim to exercise power,' he added, 'but we do not have it.' Pflimlin said he would step down.

De Gaulle had another midnight meeting at Saint-Cloud with the presidents of the two houses of parliament – the centrist Gaston Monnerville of the Senate was understanding but the Socialist Assembly speaker, André Le Troquer, was sharply hostile and helped to sway his party's National Assembly group to vote 102–3 against supporting de Gaulle if he tried to form a government.

28 May. Panic buying broke out along with scare stories of paratroopers in civilian clothes arriving in Paris carrying heavy suitcases. The Communist-led CGT union federation called a general strike in metropolitan France, and 200,000 people joined a march in the capital headed by the PCF secretary-general, Waldeck Rochet, Mendès France, Mitterrand and Daladier in which participants shouted 'Hang Massu' and 'De Gaulle to the museum'.

29 May. A Gaullist aide, Pierre Lefranc, telephoned Colombey about the prospect of a paratroop landing, and told those around him, 'the General agrees that the operation should be launched without delay.' Six Dakotas took off from Algeria to ferry troops to south-west France.

President Coty announced that, since the country was on the brink of civil war, he was 'turning towards the most illustrious of Frenchmen ... I ask General de Gaulle to confer with the head of state and to examine with him what, in the framework of Republican legality, is necessary for the immediate formation of a government of national security and what can be done, in a fairly short time, for a deep reform of our institutions.'

The military command sent a message to Algiers relaying de Gaulle's instructions that army intervention must be avoided – it was no longer needed but would be resumed 'in case of difficulty for le Grand Charles'.

After calling on Coty at the Élysée, the General asked for special powers for six months as prime minister. He said he would propose a referendum to separate the executive and the legislature; he wanted to 'restore national unity, re-establish order in the state and raise the public authorities to the heights of their duties.'

30–31 May. De Gaulle received party leaders and political veterans, including Daladier, Pinay and Ramadier. When Pflimlin said he did not want to join the new administration, his host replied: 'You cannot say no to de Gaulle.' The only open criticism came from Mitterrand who warned that France was entering an era of Latin American-style military coups. In reply, the General said that 'in certain circumstances, political men should know how to raise themselves to the level of statesmen.'

1 June. De Gaulle was driven to the Palais Bourbon through a violent afternoon storm. A vote of 329 to 224 backed him as he pledged to bring 'unity, integrity and independence'. Among those voting against was Mendès France, who said that he could not approve the new administration since parliament's hand had been forced by insurrection and the threat of a military coup. Mitterrand attacked the new prime minister for associating himself with 'force and sedition'.

4 June. An opinion poll of metropolitan France showed 54 per cent in favour of Algeria's integration and 41 per cent backing independence. The General flew to Algiers where he appeared in uniform on the balcony of the city hall to tell the huge crowd '*Je vous ai compris*' (I have understood you). It was a meaningless phrase, but supporters of Algérie française exploded in joy on hearing it, assuming the new leader was on their side*. They were further reassured when, during a visit to a military

---

* Those four words may have saved him from the first of repeated assassination attempts; a former Pétainist in a building opposite put down his rifle when he heard what he took to be an undertaking to back the *pieds-noirs*.

unit, de Gaulle called out '*Vive l'Algérie française!*' – he said later the phrase had just come out, it was not in his written text. However, when he got back to Paris he told an aide that the 9:1 population ratio meant France could not maintain its grip across the Mediterranean.

From premier to president

Having won his way back to power by legal means, though not with an overwhelming parliamentary majority, de Gaulle continued to work within the system he so despised and intended to replace. His government was designed to reassure the country and ensure maximum support. There were senior posts for leaders of all major non-Communist parties. Mollet became deputy prime minister and Minister of State, a rank also held by Pflimlin and Félix Houphouët-Boigny from the Ivory Coast who had sat in the Assembly since 1945. Pinay was appointed finance minister. There were only three out-and-out Gaullists – the intense Michel Debré at justice with the job of elaborating a new political system, the passionate, mercurial Malraux at information and culture, and, at veterans' affairs, Edmond Michelet, who had distributed tracts calling for resistance in the Corrèze the day before de Gaulle's broadcast on 18 June 1940 from London, and was later deported to Dachau concentration camp. Soustelle soon took over information from Malraux.

Civil servants were given several leading posts with the Quai d'Orsay going to the wiry, highly experienced, golf-playing ambassador in Bonn, Maurice Couve de Murville. Pierre Guillaumat, previously in charge of the atomic research agency, took responsibility for the armed forces under de Gaulle's supervision. The Premier's staff at Matignon acted as a parallel administration under his long-time aide Georges Pompidou, a consummate manager.

The suspension of parliament for six months gave the General vital breathing space and the presence in the government of political leaders like Mollet and Pflimlin denoted a consensus. Some non-Gaullists who backed him may have thought that, once he had dealt with Algeria, things would return to normal, enabling them to pick up the reins of power once more with the return of the legislative-dominated tradition

stretching back more than eighty years. But de Gaulle was intent on radical change in the governing system of the country with which he so
closely identified.

The constitution he put to a referendum clearly separated the executive and the legislature, with a great strengthening of the first in the
presidency of the Republic. Guarantor of national independence and
territorial integrity, the head of state appointed the prime minister and
could take special powers to rule without parliament when 'the institutions of the Republic, the independence of the nation, the integrity of
its territory or the execution of its international commitment are
gravely and immediately threatened and the regular functioning of the
constitutional public authority is interrupted'. Another article permitted him to hold referendums on any bill dealing with the organisation
of government or ratification of a treaty. He was both the arbiter of
national political life and its most powerful player, elected for a seven-
year term by an 80,000-strong college of members of parliament,
departmental councils, the assemblies of French overseas territories
and local councils.

In another sharp reversal of the tradition of legislative supremacy,
parliament would consider laws put to it by the executive when invited
to do so, but would have little power to initiate action or propose spending measures. The government would be able to push through
legislation without amendments, notably on budgetary matters. A constitutional council would vet laws. French overseas territories were to be
allowed to opt for independence.

The main non-Communist parties came out in favour. The PCF
remained strongly hostile, as did Mitterrand and Mendès France, Left
Bank intellectuals and a hard right rag-bag including Poujadists, remnant Pétainists and Catholic diehards who disliked the definition of
France as a secular state. On 29 September 1958, after an extremely lopsided campaign, the text was approved by 78.25 per cent in a record
turnout of 84.9 per cent of the electorate. The 'no' vote of 4.6 million
was well below the 5.45 million won by the PCF alone in 1956; estimates of the number of Communists who voted 'yes' went as high as 1.9
million. In Algeria, where Muslim women voted for the first time and
the army oversaw the campaign, the positive vote was 96 per cent. Ten

French African territories voted to become self-governing members of a Community of States. Only Guinea opted for independence; Paris cut off all assistance, including the country's telephone system.

Legislative elections in November saw a new Gaullist party, *l'Union pour la Nouvelle République* (UNR), win a working majority with its conservative allies in the *Centre National des Indépendants et Paysans.* Chaban-Delmas was elected speaker. The left was routed, and the Poujadists eliminated. The electoral system of single member constituencies with two rounds of voting meant that the Communists ended up with only ten deputies. The centrist electorate rallied massively to de Gaulle; the Radicals were reduced to thirteen seats though the MRP managed to return fifty-six members to the Assembly. All that really counted was the dominance of one man and his promise of change that would sweep away the failings of the previous two republics.

The Fourth Republic had not functioned too badly in terms of the evolution of the nation. It had provided economic growth, albeit with consistently high inflation, and had overseen the post-war process of modernisation. It had seen France retain its position as an intellectual and artistic centre with a special sense of style – in its early years, Christian Dior had launched his New Look line of voluptuous fashion while, as it expired, Yves Saint Laurent took up the reins at the couture house and gave the world the Trapeze Dress. It had housed outstanding writers and film makers and, in *Le Monde,* and the magazines *Elle* and *Paris Match,* seen the perpetuation of the great French media tradition. But the post-war republic had suffered from two major crises in France's overseas territories, the reality of which politicians in Paris had been unable, or unwilling, to confront as they played party games and manoeuvred for office. At *Le Monde* Hubert Beuve-Méry judged that the regime had committed suicide while the cartoonist, Tim, depicted Marianne dropping the guillotine blade on her own head. For the Christian Democrat Robert Buron, the regime established in 1946 simply disappeared little by little, like the Cheshire Cat.

De Gaulle appointed Debré as premier, and announced his candidature for the presidency. He got 78.5 per cent of the votes in the electoral college. At noon on 8 January 1959, wearing a tailcoat, the General was driven to the Élysée where Coty proclaimed him President of the

Republic, declaring that 'the first among Frenchmen is now the first person in France.' The two men laid a wreath at the Tomb of the Unknown Soldier at the Arc de Triomphe. After this, the General was meant to see Coty to his car and then to have been driven behind him down the Champs-Élysées; instead, he murmured '*Au revoir, monsieur Coty*' and plunged into the crowd, a man who had renewed his destiny and was intent on seeking a direct link with the French people that transcended the cleavages born of 1789.

PART 5
THE FIFTH REPUBLIC

1958–2015

NEW REGIME, NEW TIMES

'Basically, the Republic is me,' de Gaulle told Mollet. He was right, and therein lies the long-term problems of the regime he founded, which continue to the present day. He belonged to nobody and yet to everyone, as he put it, or, in Malraux's words, he was a figure from yesterday, today and tomorrow. For seven years, much of it while he was in his seventies, the General was the most successful leader France had in the two hundred years covered by this book, a complex figure behind his monolithic public façade, a man who insisted on rules but was ready to break them when he saw fit.

His achievements in reviving the country, establishing a new political regime, ending the war in Algeria, developing European links, particularly with West Germany, and in giving France a new status in the world make his first seven-year term as impressive an achievement as that of any European democratic leader of modern times.

He had always believed France needed strong executive institutions to deal with what he called 'our perpetual political effervescence'. He imposed them through democracy, albeit of a top-down variety, with himself in control, free of the limitations of collective decision-making, keeping his cards close to his chest, prizing the effect of surprise – nothing strengthened authority so much as silence, he had observed. His close circle of faithful retainers at the presidential palace was more powerful than the government – it included Jacques Foccart, the secretive *éminence grise* for Africa, his wartime aide Geoffroy de Courcel, who ran the administration of the presidential palace, and Albin

Chalandon, a loyalist from the days in London who kept the UNR party under control.[1]

Author, stage manager and star of the new national narrative, the president used provincial tours with their 'crowd baths', carefully orchestrated press conferences and sonorous broadcasts to take his message to the nation over the heads of parliament and parties in keeping with his jibe that politics were too serious to be left to politicians. He emerged from his *bains de foule* with buttons torn, a sleeve ripped, his military *képi* tipped over, but, as Pierre Viansson-Ponté of *Le Monde* put it, his eyes 'shining with pleasure, happy to be alive'. Often despairing of the French as *veaux* – best translated as sheep – unworthy of their nation, he tried to persuade, cajole and frighten this country 'of 246 different kinds of cheese' to unite and live up to his vision, an oracle of great physical stature and historical resonance. Visiting the US in 1959, he told Eisenhower's granddaughter, 'I am an old man – many people have been angry with me . . . but I still have to follow my path.'

His basic values were those of his rigorous, socially aware parents, even if he shared neither their royalism nor their fervent Catholicism – though never missing mass, he seemed bored during the services. For all his lofty mien, he took delight in besting opponents. 'Nobody else would have the nerve to do what I have done,' he remarked to a minister in 1962, and, on a later occasion, told aides he would not only get the better of opponents, but 'I'll get them up their arses.'

His defence of French interests could become too resolute but he enabled the nation to box well above its weight in global affairs, supporting European cooperation, but only on his own terms, and lording over rulers of French-speaking Africa, even after fourteen countries there declared independence in the years after Guinea's break. He set policies with minimal consultation. Ministers were there to implement his instructions. 'Nobody dared to stand up to him,' as Antoine Pinay recalled. Visiting the Élysée office with John F. Kennedy, secretary of state Dean Rusk was taken aback when the prime minister and foreign minister came in and clicked their heels like cadets in front of a superior officer.

De Gaulle: The Republican Monarch

The satirical magazine *Le Canard Enchaîné* entitled its account of events at the Élysée, *La Cour* (The Court), with the head of state as a new Sun King, Louis XIV. De Gaulle certainly played up to the regal aspect of the new regime. He received visitors like a monarch. His press conferences were aptly described as 'high masses'. He could fall into depressions and seek reassurance from old followers, but he was king-pope of the Fifth Republic.

His main physical problem was his eyesight, requiring spectacles with thick lenses. He disliked them as a sign of physical decline but, when he discarded them, could not see clearly the crowds listening to him, was uncertain with the aim of his fork at meals and was sometimes unable to make out the features of people about to be presented to him.

He drew a strict line between his public and his personal lives, paying for the telephone and electricity bills in their apartment at the Élysée. His wife explained to a minister that they did not invite their grandchildren for fear that they might break something that belonged to the state. On another occasion, she regretted to a visitor that the children had been unable to go on a winter sports holiday because they had left it too late and could not get a place on the train; the idea of pulling rank in a personal matter was foreign to them both.

But when it came to the state, expense was no object with grand banquets and ceremonies. The forty-five strong presidential staff were required to work under cover of secrecy and to keep out of the public eye. His interests were omnivorous, ranging from nuclear strategy to the breeding habits of snails: 'he wants to understand everything,' his aide for Africa, Jacques Foccart, noted.

Municipal elections chipped away at the Gaullist triumph as the Communist vote recovered and the UNR failed to win major urban targets such as Lyons, Marseilles and Saint-Étienne. The centre-left gained 40 per cent of Senate seats, with places for Fourth Republic stalwarts such as Mitterrand, Duclos and Edgar Faure; the Upper House speaker, Gaston Monnerville, a native of French Guyana, took an increasingly critical view of the General. But this was marginal, and opinion polls showed that the public was happy with the passage of events even if critics saw him as a Bonapartist or a latter-day Caesar.

The Communists were implacably opposed to the regime at home, though Moscow saw Gaullist foreign policy as a useful tool against Washington and the General hankered after a link with the USSR to balance the Western alliance and give France the position of a global arbiter. The acute left-wing commentator, Gilles Martinet, depicted him as a 'liberal monarch with Stalinist tendencies . . . a brutal realist'. Mitterrand, who inveighed against 'a permanent *coup d'état*', commented that the new regime 'has its own constitution, its government, its majority, its referendum, its television, its nuclear force . . . It has its Europe.' More fanatical opponents staged a dozen assassination attempts from some of which de Gaulle had miraculous escapes. But the new regime brought new hope for a nation which had begun to question its course.

No limits

The economy revived under the plan drawn up by the banker Jacques Rueff and accepted by de Gaulle despite the reservations of the finance minister, Pinay, who, however, gave it his name once it was a success. The planning system provided a rational basis for expansion of industry and infrastructure under the guidance of technocrats turned out by top finishing schools. Total factor productivity increased by 3 per cent in the 1960s while output per worker per hour increased at double that rate. Inflation fell and the currency strengthened as state finances were put on a firmer foundation. Exports to the rest of Europe jumped from 16 to 50 per cent of the total.[2]

There was still a split between sectors behind protectionist barriers and those open to competition, particularly from the Common Market. Still, France's growth rivalled Germany's and exceeded that of Britain and the United States. In its report on France's economy for 1962, the Organisation for Economic Co-operation and Development (OECD) paid tribute to its 'extraordinary vitality' that seemed to ride over the ups-and-downs of the international situation. The 170 leading publicly owned firms played a big role in the expansion of industry plotted by the minister responsible, Jean-Marcel Jeanneney.[3]

Motorway construction expanded and the telephone system was upgraded. Cities like Grenoble pioneered urban development and new towns were built outside Paris. As culture minister, Malraux launched a programme to clean up historic buildings, and established *Maisons de la Culture* in provincial cities. A programme was launched to reduce regional inequalities. The agriculture minister, Edgard Pisani, promoted greater productivity as hard negotiating produced favourable Common Market agreements. Farm output increased steadily and, by the 1970s, would be ahead of Germany and Italy.

Two innovations from the Fourth Republic, the Caravelle airliner and the DS limousine, came into their own. Fighter-bombers from the group headed by the Gaullist Marcel Dassault and Sud Aviation's Alouette made France a leading arms producer. A French train broke the world speed record. The big natural gas field at Lacq in the south provided an important source of energy. The soaring bridge over the Seine at Tancarville kept alive the tradition of Gustav Eiffel. A space programme came up with the first French communications satellite. In February 1961, the president inaugurated the new Orly airport outside Paris; he declared that as 'one of the youngest and greatest' of states, France knew no limits; it even got its first chain of fast food restaurants along the new highways.

The birth rate rose in cities to an average of almost three children per mother. Two million foreign immigrants moved to France, mainly from Italy, Spain and Portugal. The population became younger and more urbanised, with 62 per cent living in towns and cities by 1962 compared to 53 per cent in 1946. In 1960, the total of pupils in secondary education was almost double that of 1950 and university

numbers had increased by 50 per cent. As incomes rose and the proportion of the population employed in industry increased, the
French spent a smaller slice of their earnings on food and clothing
and more on accommodation, health, transport, telecommunications
and culture.

Television changed the way people lived; instead of the café or the
family gathering in the evening, the small screen ruled. Music hall acts
and popular singers of the new generation blanketed the nation.
Television stars like Guy Lux and Léon Zitrone became household
names. In the world of writing, authors developed further the *Nouveau
Roman* while Roland Barthes presented another challenge to orthodox
thinking with theories on semiology and structuralism. Louis
Althusser ardently defended Marxism and Sartre's *Critique de la Raison
Dialectique* (*Critique of Dialectical Reason*) sought to present it in a
humanist form; the philosopher-author turned down the Nobel Prize
to demonstrate his rejection of orthodox values. Claude Lévi-Strauss
became an international celebrity with works stemming from his
anthropological studies, and Michel Foucault published ground-
breaking research on social institutions, psychiatry, medicine and
prisons.

The *Nouvelle Vague* revolutionised the cinema with its stream of fine
directors, and made a new generation of French stars household
names abroad, at least in art house cinemas. Brigitte Bardot became a
global sex symbol. Yves Saint Laurent came back from a nervous
breakdown induced by his treatment by fellow conscripts during a
brief spell of army national service to set up his own fashion house
with his partner Pierre Bergé and launched the first ready-to-wear
collection by a top Paris designer. A new *yé-yé* generation adopted rock
'n' roll, with French characteristics but transatlantic names – Johnny
Hallyday (Jean-Philippe Smet from the family name of his Belgian
father), Eddy Mitchell (Claude Moine from Paris), Dick Rivers (Hervé
Fornieri from Nice) and Richard Anthony (Richard Btesh from
Cairo). France Gall, a Luxembourger singing in French, won the
Eurovision Song Contest. Mireille Mathieu, from a family of fourteen
children in Avignon, blasted her way to fame with her huge voice,
provincial simplicity and echoes of Piaf.

With a few exceptions, such as the prim Mathieu, the new generation brought with it a more relaxed attitude to life and sex, epitomised by the louche *génie maudit*, Serge Gainsbourg, and the relationship between Hallyday and the singer Sylvie Vartan written up in the fast-growing celebrity press. With Bardot as its cheerleader, Saint-Tropez became the epitome of a more hedonist world of which French youth might dream. It was not a way of life with which de Gaulle, let alone his prim wife, could empathise, but was all part of the national renewal he had set in train, enabling him to proclaim that France had 'married its century'.

There were still, of course, significant aspects of national life which remained backward or where the evolution was not positive for some sections of the population. Contraception was illegal, though nobody was prosecuted. Birth control techniques were often primitive; surveys of hospitals showed that a third of pregnancies were not wanted. Abortions were estimated at 500,000 a year. There was no evidence that the low divorce rate – half that of West Germany – meant that French couples were happier than their counterparts across the Rhine. Life for many people became less individualistic. Factories were increasingly dominated by assembly line work. Agriculture became more mechanised, especially in the north of the country. Chain stores and supermarkets edged out traditional shops. Communal village life declined under the impact of television, the growing rural-urban imbalance and the falling birth rate in the countryside. The crush of people moving into big cities produced crowded urban estates and dormitory towns with little life of their own.

A certain idea

Still, in his first years in office, de Gaulle could claim to have made significant progress in reviving the country of which he had 'a certain idea'. To strengthen the state and remedy the weakness from which it suffered under the Fourth Republic involved policies and measures his opponents would condemn as verging on the dictatorial but which played to the recurrent popular desire for strong leadership and always fell within the framework of the regime he had founded. The General's taste for order as defined by himself reigned supreme and he did not brook criticism.

A key element in the myth that surrounded de Gaulle was that he always knew what he was doing, and was always in control. It was an impression he prized – 'One decides on solutions, one chooses them, one decides them,' he told a newspaper editor in 1960. 'They are not imposed on one.' But Algeria was a different matter. He dallied with different solutions – from military victory to a form of self-determination under which an Algeria, led by a 'third force' of moderate Muslims and *pieds-noirs*, would maintain close cooperative links with metropolitan France. He shrank from the logic of abandoning France's last major overseas possession: 'You think [I] was created and put in this world to give up Algeria?' he asked Chaban-Delmas. But he feared that the popular solution of full integration would bring eighty Muslim deputies into the National Assembly, tilting the balance of the legislature; on the other hand, he saw complete independence as leading to disaster and mass killings. Any overt move towards a settlement could propel the Ultras into the streets once more, pushing the majority of Muslims into the arms of the FLN and leading the army to mount a challenge to democracy in favour of a regime in the mode of Franco's Spain.

At one point de Gaulle was led to observe to Edgar Faure that Algeria was one of those problems that had no solution. But that was no answer. He had to act, not simply because of the way in which the quagmire across the Mediterranean was dragging down France but also because it posed an unacceptable challenge to the state he was seeking to rebuild. The *pieds-noirs* and military officers could not be allowed to defy the Republic. It was a painful position.

'You think he doesn't suffer, de Gaulle?' he asked Chaban. Two visits to Algeria in July and September 1958 showed what he was up against. He announced sweeping plans for social and economic development but, when he appealed to the FLN to cooperate to 'open up the future for everybody', members of the Public Safety Committee walked out in protest.

A purge of the army forced some extremist officers to retire and broke up groups formed during the spring revolt. But the deputies from Algeria returned to the National Assembly in November 1958 were all Algérie française supporters.

De Gaulle was not deterred, though his offer of a '*paix des braves*' under which the FLN would lay down its arms went down badly with the nationalists, who saw no reason to accept an agreement that would have been a defeat. At the end of 1958, he replaced Salan with an air force general, Maurice Challe. Helicopter-borne attacks on FLN mountain strongholds reduced the nationalist forces to an estimated 8,000 active *fellagha* fighters in Algeria – though another 10,000 were across the border in Tunisia and Morocco but were cut off when the frontiers were sealed. France seemed on the brink of victory. The FLN was buffeted by internal feuds and the loss of several leaders in the fighting. A million Muslims were herded into 'regroupment' camps. The *harki* forces were expanded to 250,000 men. Abuse of civilians and use of torture by the army increased.

Yet, however many battles the French won, they could not clinch the war and the FLN hit back with savage reprisals including the massacre of more than 100 people in a village which had put itself under the French colours. Paul Delouvrier, who had worked as an economic expert with Jean Monnet, was named Delegate General for civilian affairs in Algeria and opened secret contacts with the nationalists' civilian wing, the GPRA. 'France stays,' he declared on his arrival, but after a tour of the territory, he told de Gaulle Algeria would become independent.

In a newspaper interview, the president remarked that those who shouted loudest for integration wanted to be given back 'Papa's Algeria', 'but Papa's Algeria is dead, and, if one does not understand this, one will die with it.' That summer, a memorandum written by Bernard Tricot, the senior civil servant on his staff dealing with Algeria, argued that the idea Algeria had to remain entirely French was evaporating, and that the heavy economic cost of the war could not be ignored. Nor could the international dimension, with the prospect that the United States might vote against France at the United Nations in the autumn. 'We have to march forward or die. I chose to march, but that does not mean we will also not die,' de Gaulle told the cabinet at the end of a lengthy discussion of Algeria. Visiting Algeria once again he told Massu he was growing fed up with the *pieds-noirs* and declared in one speech that, 'The Algerians will make their own destiny.' On a visit to military headquarters in the Kabylie region, he said the era of administration by Europeans was over, so 'we must act in Algeria only for Algeria and with Algeria in such a way that the world understands.'

In keeping with this approach, de Gaulle told Dwight Eisenhower, who was visiting Paris, of his plan to opt for self-determination, noting that France needed a peaceful Algeria in order for oil companies to be able to continue operations in the Sahara. On 16 September 1959, he went on television and radio to announce that Algeria would be invited to vote on a choice between three alternatives – secession, full Frenchification and the third path 'the government of Algeria by the Algerians, supported by the help of France and in a tight union with her for the economy, education, defence, foreign relations in a federal internal regime which would guarantee the rights of the different communities.' He left no doubt he backed the last course.

The reaction in metropolitan France to his address was overwhelmingly positive; polls showed a steadily increasing desire to get out of Algeria. After a delay of a week, the FLN's civil arm welcomed the recognition of the right of Algerians to decide their own destiny and said it was ready to talk – though it insisted on being the sole representative of the non-European population. The civilian and military Ultras across the sea were horrified. Nine UNR deputies quit the party while eighteen of the seventy members of its central committee abstained on a motion backing the General. A *Rassemblement pour l'Algérie française* (Rally for French Algeria) was created on both sides of the Mediterranean, joined by Georges Bidault, Roger Duchet, leader of the conservative CNIP National Assembly group, and four UNR deputies. Jacques Soustelle, a convinced advocate of Algérie française, stayed in the government for the time being, but did not hide his antagonism.

The political opposition was squashed by a government majority in a parliamentary vote on Algeria. But, across the Mediterranean, the extremists prepared for action amid a new wave of violence by the FLN. The student leader, Pierre Lagaillarde, gathered together his co-conspirators of May 1958, and began to obtain weapons. Another veteran of 1958, Joseph Ortiz, a bar owner, mobilised the *Front National Français* (FNF), which clothed its militants in khaki shirts and armbands decorated with the Celtic cross, a symbol of fascist movements. When Bidault visited Algiers in the middle of December, the FNF fielded 1,500 men as a security force. Ortiz warned the *pieds-noirs* that, if de Gaulle had his way, their only choice was between 'the suitcase and the coffin' – leaving Algeria or being killed by the nationalists. He was backed by a stirring orator, Dr Jean-Claude Pérez, whose practice in the suburb of Bab-el-Oued gave him an audience among the poor Europeans living there, and by a 25-year-old medical student, Jean-Jacques Susini, who provided the ideological arguments for the group veering towards fascism and designed to attract remnant Pétainists.

The key figure was Massu. He was trusted by the army and the *pieds-noirs*, but had a Gaullist history stretching back to the Free French. However, in an interview with a West German newspaper in January 1960, he was reported as saying that part of the army regretted having called de Gaulle back to power, did not understand his policy, and was disappointed that he had become 'a man of the left'. He was immediately stripped of his responsibilities in Algeria and sidelined with a posting to Metz. When he went to see de Gaulle at the presidential palace, aides heard raised voices and, on leaving the Élysée, Massu telephoned Algiers to reverse an order he had given his chief of staff to do nothing.

A general strike was called in Algeria. Lagaillarde established armed positions in the university. Ortiz mobilised his shock force. On 24 January, after police threw tear gas grenades at the rebels, a gun battle killed fourteen members of the security forces and eight demonstrators as well as wounding 200 people. 'The hour has come to bring down the regime,' Susini declared. 'The revolution will start from Algiers and reach Paris.'

An unusually stormy cabinet meeting in Paris, at which Soustelle proposed negotiating with the insurgents and de Gaulle denounced them as 'stupid and criminal', decided to replace the parachute division in Algiers with more reliable troops. Wearing military uniform, the president went on television and radio on 29 January to deploy his greatest weapon – oratory. 'Well, my dear and old country,' he told his audience, 'here we are again facing a heavy test.' Insisting that self-determination was the only way ahead, he called on the army to reject even passive association with the insurrection and instructed it to re-establish order. If the state bowed before the challenge, 'France would be no more than a poor, broken toy floating on an ocean of uncertainty.'

Within fifteen minutes, forty army units in Algeria declared their loyalty. Lagaillarde and his 200 companions were persuaded to leave their stronghold; the leader was flown to prison in Paris. Ortiz slipped out of town. Soustelle was sacked at a two-minute meeting with the president; he and Bidault were banned from going to Algeria. By 441 votes to 75, the National Assembly granted the president the power to rule by decree for a year. Trade unions held a symbolic one-hour strike to back the government. A poll by the IFOP organisation gave de Gaulle a 75 per cent approval rating. There was a further boost when the country's first atom bomb test was conducted successfully in the Sahara on 13 February – 'Hurrah for France,' the General exclaimed.

Going for broke

An attempt at negotiations with the FLN failed, in part because of de Gaulle's insistence that it must end the fighting as a preliminary to discussion – 'one does not have talks unless one has left the knives in the cloakroom,' he remarked at a press conference. Under a new military commander, Houari Boumediene, the nationalists increased attacks on settlers and the GPRA raised the pressure on France within international bodies. Lagaillarde was released by a military tribunal and went with Susini to plot in Spain.

In metropolitan France, the crisis was polarising society. Publications that dared to write about torture by the French army were censored while a few opponents of the war began to assist the FLN. A manifesto by writers and professors declared that desertion was justified. Jean-Paul Sartre was among the signatories, and judicial proceedings were started for his arrest before de Gaulle ordered them stopped – 'One does not imprison Voltaire,' he explained.

The logjam was broken by a television address on 4 November 1960, in which the president inserted two words into his text – 'Algerian republic'. When Debré protested, de Gaulle responded: 'Anyway, that's how it will end.' Looking to 'an Algeria which will be emancipated, where responsibility will lie in the hands of Algerians'. He told his audience on both sides of the Mediterranean that this Algeria would have its own government and laws. Extremists set off fifteen explosive charges in a single night in Paris.

A ministry for Algeria was set up under the solid figure of Louis Joxe, a loyal Gaullist since 1943. Its task was to conduct negotiations, reporting to the Élysée and by-passing Matignon. In an interview with a newspaper editor from Oran, the president said everything separated the majority population of Algeria from the French. The Muslims wanted to govern themselves and he had to build his policy on such facts. Continuing the war led nowhere given the way in which the Muslim population would increase in the next five or ten years. Not that he was optimistic for an independent Algeria – 'it will be a bloodbath.'

At the end of the year, he paid his last visit across the Mediterranean at a moment when fighting in Algiers between Europeans, Muslims and police forces killed 100 people. He was the target of four separate unsuccessful assassination plots during the trip. But when the proposal for self-determination for Algeria was put to a referendum on 8 January 1961, 75 per cent of those who voted were in favour. At 23.5 per cent, the abstention rate was higher than in previous ballots, giving the General the support of 56 per cent of the total registered electorate. The issue was more divisive than the foundation of the new republic, but the proposal had the support of most of the mainstream political parties – though Communist opposition to the regime meant that the PCF refused to come out for a 'yes' vote despite its calls for independence. In Algeria, 42 per cent of voters stayed away from the polls in line with an FLN instruction; 40 per cent said 'yes' and 18 per cent 'no'.

Having been beaten at the polls, the Ultras formed an extremist

group, the *Organisation de l'Armée Secrète* (OAS) and two fervent officers, Antoine Argoud and Joseph Broizat, plotted a putsch. Massu
refused to join them but the recently retired *pied noir* air force boss,
Edmond Jouhaud, signed up as did another general, André Zeller, and
Maurice Challe, the former commander in Algeria who had retired
from the army thinking he had been badly done by. Another unhappy
man, Raoul Salan, who had also quit the forces feeling humiliated after
being removed from his command in Algeria, held a press conference
in Paris at which he denounced de Gaulle and offered himself as leader
of Algérie française. Going to Spain, he conferred with Lagaillarde and
Susini, and met with Pierre Poujade.

The conspirators made further attempts to enlist Massu who asked
them if they would kill de Gaulle if they had the opportunity. 'Without
hesitation,' they replied. The paratrooper looked at them without saying
anything, but later told them that what they were planning was mad.
However, they grew even more determined when agreement was
reached to hold peace talks in the Alpine city of Évian, which the
Algerians would be able to reach easily from the safety of Switzerland.

Swinging into action in Algeria, they mobilised columns of lorries carrying paratroopers in camouflage uniforms. Loyalist generals were
arrested along with Jean Morin, Delouvrier's successor as Delegate
General, and the Minister of Public Works, Robert Buron, who had just
arrived to inaugurate a technical college. By dawn, the rebels controlled
the capital city's main administrative buildings. Awakened at 2.30 a.m.
with news of what was going on, de Gaulle summoned Louis Joxe, the
Minister for Algeria, and told him to cross the Mediterranean to restore
order. President Kennedy offered any help that was needed, an offer
that annoyed the General, who did not think he required assistance and
regarded the putsch as an internal matter.

Salan flew from Spain to Algiers with Susini. But the putsch was
already losing ground. The plotters made no attempt to rouse the civilian European population. Some key units refused to join them; most
senior officers waited to see what would happen. The navy remained
loyal to Paris, and the air force flew planes back to the mainland to keep
them safe. The plotters had no cash reserves. There was almost unani-
mous condemnation in metropolitan France.

At a cabinet session that afternoon, de Gaulle was at his most haughtily dismissive – 'You know what is grave in this affair?' he said. 'That it is not serious.' Still, troops were ordered to move from bases in West Germany to defend Paris, and the President of the Republic assumed emergency powers under Article 16 of the constitution. At 8 p.m. on 23 April, the General deployed his rhetorical prowess in one of his greatest performances. He belittled the rebels as 'a quartet of retired generals ... partisan, ambitious and frenetic officers' who had attempted a Latin American-style military *pronunciamiento*. If they succeeded, everything achieved since 1958 would be at risk.

Listening on their transistor radios, conscripts in Algiers had no doubt whose side they were on. Loyalist forces took the radio station and broadcast an announcement that order and legality would be restored. When Salan and his three co-conspirators appeared on the balcony overlooking the Forum, government agents cut the electric current, and they could not make themselves heard. The paratroopers marched back to their base camp singing Édith Piaf's '*Je Ne Regrette Rien*'. Challe and Zeller gave themselves up; Salan and Jouhaud fled in a truck to a military camp and went underground.

De Gaulle was remorseless in victory. A special military tribunal created outside the justice system sentenced Challe and Zeller each to fifteen years' imprisonment. Suspect groups were dissolved and their members arrested. There was an army purge. Left-wing critics suffered, too – the Communist daily, *L'Humanité*, was seized. Polls showed 84 per cent backing for the General and 78 per cent in favour of opening negotiations with the FLN.

The Évian talks opened on 20 May 1961. Joxe headed the French delegation, working in close collaboration with the Élysée chief of staff, Bernard Tricot. The GPRA delegation travelled each day by helicopter from Switzerland for the sessions at the Park Hotel on the banks of the lake, headed by foreign minister Krim Belkacem, who had been in the Algerian underground since 1946.

Seeing terror as its only weapon, the OAS assassinated the mayor of Évian and unleashed a wave of attacks that took more than a hundred lives in Algeria on the single day of 19 May. Its leading killer, Roger Degueldre, a hatchet-faced former paratrooper lieutenant who had been wounded at Dien Bien Phu, led a well-armed 500-man 'Delta Commando' force which spread terror against Muslims and French officials. The OAS turned the poor white district of Bab-el-Oued into a virtual no-go area for the police and regular army. It funded itself with cash stolen from government safes, banks raids and 'contributions' levied on the European population. In metropolitan France, it set off a plastic explosive charge that derailed a passenger train between Strasbourg and Paris, killing eighteen people and injuring seventy.

As leader of the secret army, Salan envisaged an apartheid-style society for Algeria on South African lines. Susini saw the OAS somehow gaining the backing of Muslims and eventually spreading its rule to France. Pérez presented the fight in Algeria as the last struggle of White Christianity. Degueldre told a fellow OAS member, 'Only violence will make us heard ... Unleash war on the authorities. Kill the traitors. It's the only solution remaining to us.'

OAS assassins slaughtered policemen while the security forces were blowing up cafés known to be haunts of the extremists. Nightlife in Algiers closed down. Cinemas were deserted. An attempt to raise a force of undercover operatives known as *barbouzes* (false beards) to fight the Secret Army collapsed after Degueldre led a commando attack on their headquarters on New Year's Eve, demolishing the building with rockets and machine gun fire, then setting an explosive booby trap that killed nineteen of them, and finally staging a siege that lasted for two days.

The Évian talks stalled and were further complicated by a confrontation with Tunisia, which asserted its right to land around the big French base at Bizerta; when Tunisian forces tried to occupy the zone, Paris sent in paratroopers, killing more than 700 people. De Gaulle fell into one of his periods of melancholia, telling Joxe he feared physical collapse, adding, 'There are two solutions: my resignation or my death.' At that point, he was the target of the first known assassination attempt in metropolitan France when a huge sheet of flame from a gas container exploded across the road from his black Citroën DS 21 as he was driven to Colombey. The chauffeur stamped on the accelerator and took the car clear, stopping 500 metres further on. 'How clumsy!' the president growled as he got out. A binoculars case was found at the scene. The man who had set off the blast was caught with the glasses. He gave the names of two OAS members; one was arrested, one escaped.

The FLN put on a show of strength in Paris where 30,000 of the Algerian community in the capital were mobilised to demonstrate. The police, under the control of the wartime collaborator Maurice Papon, reacted with savage repression. People living near commissariats heard screams; bodies were fished from the Seine bearing the marks of severe beatings. The total killed has never been established: some reports put it at a hundred or more while an expert investigation came up with a figure of between thirty and fifty.

There was some success in the fight against the OAS; information extracted under torture from a Secret Army courier enabled the authorities to smash parts of the network and arrest Degueldre's number two. But Bidault announced the creation of a *Conseil National de la Résistance* (CNR) – the name of the wartime council. The former MRP leader was its chief with Salan as commander-in-chief to conduct 'the fight against the abandonment of Algeria, Gaullist dictatorship and international Communism.' Argoud took charge of operations in metropolitan France, and Soustelle of activities elsewhere.

In Paris, an OAS bomb left at the Quai d'Orsay killed one person and injured eleven. Prominent journalists were targeted though none were hurt. A bomb aimed at Malraux's flat blinded the five-year-old daughter of a friend of his. Police kept to their strong-arm tactics against anybody seen to challenge public order. They drove a group of people from a 10,000-strong demonstration against the OAS down the staircase of the Charonne Metro station in Paris, where the gates had been closed; nine people were crushed to death. The funeral of the victims saw a mass turnout against both the brutality of the repression and the Secret Army.

Amid this volatility, de Gaulle sent three members of the government – Joxe, Robert Buron, who had been detained during the putsch in Algiers, and Jean de Broglie, a prominent independent conservative who was Secretary of State for the Sahara – to meet an FLN delegation at an Alpine chalet, Le Yéti. He told them to be flexible and open to concessions on France's oil and nuclear testing rights in the Sahara and on the status of military bases. On 19 February, the two delegations agreed on a text and, for the first time, shook hands.

The cabinet meeting to which the agreement was put was a sombre affair. The foreign minister, Couve de Murville, forecast that an independent Algeria would become a revolutionary, totalitarian regime with which cooperation would be difficult, but he remained a partisan of self-determination. Debré, who had been kept out of the negotiations because of his underlying sympathies for the cause of Algérie française, spoke at length about how his hopes that Algeria would be led to political maturity by France had been undermined by the division between the communities, the revolt of the Muslim world, and external forces. The president wound up the session by saying it had been indispensable to get France out of a situation that brought it so many ills.

The French and Algerian delegations launched the final negotiations on outstanding points leading to final agreement on 18 March 1962. De Gaulle went on television to announce 'the good sense solution' for a ceasefire in Algeria, which was to go into effect in twenty-four hours. The agreement provided for Algerians to vote on 1 July in answer to a single question asking if they wanted their country to become an independent state, cooperating with France on conditions laid down in the accord. The French in Algeria would be able to have double nationality for three years and would be represented in Algerian assemblies. French people wanting to leave Algeria could take their assets or the product of the sale of their belongings with them. In the Sahara, French companies would enjoy preferential treatment in the allocation of energy licences. France would keep a renewable fifteen-year lease on its naval and air base at Mers-el-Kébir, and retain a military position in the Sahara for five years, as well as three airfields on Algerian territory. Algeria would remain in the franc currency zone, and Paris undertook to maintain its financial aid at the existing level.

The sad outcome of peace

The OAS had staged more than a hundred operations during the final stage of the negotiations and now stepped up its attacks, killing twenty-five people by firing mortar shells into a Muslim crowd. It declared

Bab-el-Oued an 'insurrectional zone' prohibited to 'the occupation forces' – the French army. Six soldiers were killed and nineteen wounded when they refused to allow themselves to be disarmed. Twenty-seven more people died in the ensuing battle. The Secret Army called on the European population to march from the war memorial in the centre of Algiers to the suburb and shots broke out as the unarmed crowd surged down the big thoroughfare of the rue d'Isly. Forty-six Europeans died and 121 were injured. Nobody knew who had fired but the terrorists launched an 'Arab hunt' which killed thirty-four more.

A referendum in metropolitan France on the Évian agreement gave 90 per cent backing to the accords. At 24.4 per cent, the abstention rate was high, due to the number of people who were uncomfortable with the outcome but did not want to cast a ballot that might encourage the OAS, and to those on the left who could not oppose independence but objected to the General's use of referendums to rally support.

Degueldre was arrested on information given to the police by a captured Foreign Legion deserter. He was executed. Salan, who had dyed his hair and moustache, was also caught and sent to jail. But the killing went on. The FLN attacked bars used by Secret Army personnel, killing seventeen people and wounding thirty-five. European extremists embarked on a scorched earth campaign, burning schools, hospitals, buildings at the University of Algiers, the city's town hall and the oil refinery in Oran and claiming fifty-six Muslim lives in one day. Still, on 1 July 1962, the Évian settlement received 99.72 per cent backing in a referendum in Algeria. Two days later, France recognised the new independent state whose leadership was dominated by hard-liners.

A million Europeans crossed the Mediterranean; in keeping with their worst fears and contrary to the Évian agreement, they were allowed only two suitcases each for their belongings while their homes and assets were requisitioned. Most of the refugees were poor and disoriented in their new surroundings, forming a pool of anti-Gaullist discontent, particularly in cities along the Mediterranean coast. Some OAS members who had gained a taste for illegal enrichment established underworld gangs in France.

Most exposed were members of the Arab *harki* militia. Though some did cross the sea, a committee chaired by de Gaulle rejected the idea of allowing them to emigrate en masse to metropolitan France. Their slaughter began immediately. How many died remains uncertain – an inquiry by Jean Lacouture for *Le Monde* in late 1962 came out with the figure of 10,000; other sources speak of between 30,000 and 80,000. The new government in Algiers sent some, with children aged over twelve, to the border with Tunisia to set off mines planted there by the French. Men were reported to have been boiled alive or emasculated. Those *harkis* who managed to get out of Algeria found themselves crammed into insanitary camps in Provence, treated by the French state as the detritus of a struggle people wanted to forget. To this day, they agitate for proper treatment and recognition of their past services but Paris, mindful of relations with Algiers, prefers to ignore them, just as the majority of French people prefer to forget about the long poisonous struggle.

On 22 August 1962, de Gaulle left Paris after a cabinet meeting to travel by road to the airbase at Villacoublay before flying to Colombey. He was accompanied by his son-in-law Alain de Boissieu and an aide-de-camp. As they passed a crossroads in the suburb of Petit Clamart, their car was hit by fourteen bullets from a dozen gunmen under the command of Jean-Marie Bastien-Thiry, another of France's colonels disillusioned by what they saw as the General's treason on Algeria. De Boissieu told the driver to accelerate and called to the president 'Father, get down!' With two tyres burst, the gear box smashed and its interior sprayed with broken glass, the DS got across the crossroads and made it to the airfield, swaying 'like a motor canoe at sea' as de Boissieu put it. The General and his wife were covered with glass fragments. At the base, he reviewed the honour guard as though nothing had happened but remarked as he got into the plane, 'This time, it was close.' Telephoning Pompidou after he got to his country home, de Gaulle said, 'My dear friend, those people shoot like pigs.'

Bastien-Thiry made no attempt to flee. A devout Catholic, he had convinced himself that de Gaulle was a devil incarnate who deserved death for the 'genocide' of the *pieds-noirs*. Arrested, he was sentenced to death by a military tribunal. Two thousand police ringed the execution ground at a fort outside Paris in case of a rescue bid. Bastien-Thiry refused to be blindfolded and died holding his rosary.

The direct presidency

Once the referendum on Algeria was won, Debré resigned, tears in his eyes. Georges Pompidou took his place in an appointment that clearly signalled a new phase of the Fifth Republic. The portly, affable and cultured Pompidou had never run for any kind of election, and was chosen for his managerial skills, a chief of staff who would ensure that the government machinery functioned smoothly. 'I have no political life of my own, no voters, no clientele,' he told a government colleague. 'I don't even have any ideas of my own in political matters. I have only the General's ideas.' He had, however, a hinterland in the cultural life of Paris where he frequented artists and writers. Though the prime minister made a point of spending his weekends away from Matignon, ministers remarked that, when he left for his country home on Saturdays, his car was packed with dossiers.

To broaden the administration's support, de Gaulle agreed to appoint five MRP ministers, including the Free French spokesman Maurice Schumann, and the former premier Pierre Pflimlin. The rising star of the independent conservatives, Valéry Giscard d'Estaing, who had been promoted to finance minister at the beginning of the year, joined Pompidou in pressing for economic modernisation to develop companies that could compete internationally and to consolidate state firms.

Petit Clamart led de Gaulle to propose a major constitutional change – the election of the President of the Republic by direct suffrage in place of the existing college of 60,000 legislators, local representatives and other worthies. He reasoned that, while he had been able to base his rule on his historic legacy, a successor would need a broader base of legitimacy to preserve the new regime and prevent a return to parliamentary ascendancy. The new system which would be put to voters in a referendum responded to his desire to unite the country across political barriers, as when he told referendum voters the outcome was 'a matter between each of you and myself'.

The proposal aroused opposition stretching from the Communists to the extreme right. Mollet warned of dictatorship and civil war. The National Assembly approved a censure motion. Pompidou submitted his resignation, which the president did not accept. Instead, he dissolved parliament pending new elections. Going on television in mid-October, he said he would step down if there was a negative referendum vote, or even in the event of a weak 'yes' vote.

The ballot at the end of the month produced 62 per cent support on a 77 per cent turnout, meaning that the constitutional change had the backing of just 46 per cent of the total registered electorate. But Gaullists took 233 seats at the parliamentary election, putting them only nine short of the absolute majority, which they could reach with the support of thirty-six independent conservatives. The MRP did badly. Poujadist and pro-Algerie française candidates were wiped out. De Gaulle told the Cabinet he had 'broken the parties'.

The ever-evolving domestic agenda was accompanied by a foreign affairs roundabout as, in his early seventies, the president sought to assert France's influence on the global stage. In 1960, he hosted a Franco-American-British-West German summit in Paris on the running crisis with Moscow over Berlin, which was followed by a meeting under his chairmanship in the French capital with Khrushchev, Eisenhower and the British prime minister, Harold Macmillan. The proceedings were derailed before they started, however, by the shooting down of an American U2 spy plane over the USSR. The Soviet leader insisted on starting the meeting by reading out a denunciation of the US in a loud voice – 'the acoustics in this room are excellent,' de Gaulle broke in. The summit dissolved into squabbling, the Soviet leader becoming even more agitated, Eisenhower pink with anger, Macmillan increasingly ill at ease, the host showing lofty disdain. When Khrushchev walked out, the Frenchman went round the table to take the American president by the arm, telling him: 'I want you to know that I will be with you to the end.'

He was similarly supportive of John Kennedy during the Cuban missile crisis two years later, even if he feared that the outcome would buttress American aspirations to global hegemony against which he had warned for three decades. Kennedy's visit to Paris in May 1961 was a gala affair, the General noting the charm of the president's French-speaking wife and praising her husband's energy, drive, intelligence and courage. However, nothing of substance emerged as de Gaulle warned that Indochina would be 'a bottomless military and political quagmire'. The French leader regarded his visitor as a novice while the American thought his host cared only for the 'selfish' interests of France and 'seemed to prefer tension instead of intimacy in his relations with the United States as a matter of pride and independence'. 'Rather quickly, the Kennedy administration reached a point where we simply did not care what de Gaulle thought except on those matters over which he had a veto,' secretary of state Dean Rusk recalled in his memoirs. 'We learned to proceed without him.'

The General's European policy and his long-held suspicion of Britain as a Trojan Horse for the US put him at odds with proponents of greater federal unity, led by Paul-Henri Spaak of Belgium and Josef Luns of the Netherlands. The General saw Europe as a means of increasing France's influence, not as a substitute for it. His intransigent stance led to the resignations of the five MRP members of the government after he warned that enlargement of the community would lead to the continent's national languages being replaced by 'Esperanto or Volapük'. Nearly 300 deputies, a clear majority of the Assembly, signed a declaration critical of the administration's Common Market policies.

The president set off a crisis with such foreign leaders when he vetoed Britain's application to join the Common Market, fearing that this would lead to 'a colossal Atlantic community ... under American dependence and control which would soon swallow up the European community'. Meetings on each side of the Channel with the British prime minister, Harold Macmillan, got nowhere. When Macmillan signed an agreement with Kennedy by which the US would sell Britain its Polaris underwater missile technology as the basis of a multilateral NATO nuclear force, de Gaulle reacted with a press conference in January 1962, at which he announced his veto of UK membership of the European community. London was left floundering. Macmillan said in a broadcast that France 'seems to think that one nation can dominate Europe and, equally wrongly, that Europe can or ought to stand alone.' Privately, he reflected that 'the French always betray you in the end.' The Foreign Office depicted the General as 'an almost impossible ally'. But all Britain could do in response was to cancel a visit to Paris by Princess Margaret for a film premiere.

Having delivered his negative blow, de Gaulle had a brilliant positive follow-up. As prime minister in 1958, he had invited West German chancellor Konrad Adenauer to Colombey. Despite his long-standing negative view of France's eastern neighbour, he recognised that the Federal Republic's revival meant he had to get its acquiescence to France's leadership of the West European community. That was even more the case given the potential rifts following his veto on UK membership. The answer was the Franco-German Friendship Treaty signed at the Élysée on 22 January 1963. It provided for regular meetings between the leaders of the two countries, and created a Franco-German youth organisation, which would arrange visits between the two countries by hundreds of thousands of young people in the coming decades. The agreement was among the most important post-war accords in signalling an end to the key European hostility stretching back to 1870 – this time at the initiative of a French leader who had survived Verdun and entered history by refusing to accept Hitler's victory of 1940.

DECLINE AND FALL

Another leader might have used this heady period to prepare for his retirement, but it was not in de Gaulle's character to step back, or moderate his policies and personalised leadership. He wanted the consecration of election by the French people to crown his achievement. Before that, he had much business to supervise.

There were tough negotiations over European farm policy from which Paris got most of what it wanted. The president stepped up his resistance to the US, especially over proposals for a multilateral Western military force. He proposed neutrality for Indochina, refused to sign the ban on nuclear tests in the atmosphere agreed by Washington and Moscow, criticised the United Nations as an instrument for American power and a threat to the world of nation states, cut off military cooperation with Israel, recognised Communist China and urged Latin American countries to stand up for themselves against the US and form an entente with France. At the funeral of Kennedy, who had been assassinated on his birthday, he made his way to sit at the very front despite having been placed in the eighth row. 'Right, we can start,' he told a protocol official when he had got to a position appropriate to his view of his country's status.

Drive for national independence

All this was broadly popular at home in asserting national independence, restoring global prestige and drawing on not always so latent anti-Americanism – an opinion poll showed that only 29 per cent of those questioned thought French interests were close to those of America. But the practical effects were thin. Adenauer's successor, Ludwig Erhard, the 'father' of West Germany's recovery, was an Atlanticist unwilling to line up with Paris against Washington – in a private note, de Gaulle later acknowledged a 'growing difficulty' between the two countries which he attributed to the fact that 'the Germans are no longer the polite and decent defeated power seeking to gain the favour of the victor.' Lyndon Johnson, for whom the General had little time, plunged ever deeper into the war in Vietnam, France's former Asian colony. The US continued to dominate Latin America politically and economically. No other power followed his example over NATO. Moscow regarded France simply as a useful spoiler in the West. Walt Rostow, Johnson's national security adviser, recalled that the president decided that when dealing with de Gaulle in public the administration would 'ignore him and never be aggressive'.

The drive for national independence brought state support for the Concorde supersonic airliner being developed with Britain, a French colour television system, a national computer plan and restrictions on foreign investments, particularly from across the Atlantic. But the economy was losing its sheen. The budgetary rigour introduced in 1958 was fraying, in part because of the cost of helping the *pieds-noirs* who had crossed to France. The money supply was growing twice as fast as in West Germany. Strikes hit the coal industry, railways, the electricity system and rubbish collectors. Rising inflation led to demands for wage increases that would set off a further spiral. There was a crisis over dairy over-production and growing discontent in the public sector where wages fell below those in private companies; protestors called out '*Charlot, des sous!*' (Charlie, cash!) on the president's provincial tours.

The tilt to the right by Pompidou and Giscard increased wealth disparity – an IFOP poll showed that 64 per cent of people thought they had become less well-off while up to 70 per cent were unconvinced by the government's social policies. The high sales tax penalised poorer consumers. Corporate profits were held down by big social security contributions. Despite regional development plans, the old disparities were still evident – France above a line drawn from Le Havre to

Grenoble housed two-thirds of the population and most advanced industry.

Bypassing parliament in a display of executive authoritarianism, the government introduced a six-month economic stabilisation plan to block prices, tighten credit and cut state spending. The result was positive but the plan had to be extended for twenty-eight months, holding back expansion and provoking recurrent strikes, protests and grumbling among small shopkeepers and artisans. Inveighing against the primacy of the dollar, de Gaulle ordered that France should build up its gold stocks and insist that the US settle 80 per cent of its trade payments for French goods in the metal. But when he told a press conference that there had to be a return to the pre-war gold standard to replace the dominance of the dollar, London and Bonn joined Washington in rejecting the idea; France found itself isolated, and unable to proceed.

All this took its physical toll. Meeting the president after he had a prostate operation in 1964, the British diplomat, Gladwyn Jebb, found him looking 'old, tired, and ill'. Even if there was little doubt as to what he would do, de Gaulle took his time declaring that he would seek re-election in 1965. His wife was not keen. 'Charles, you have done enough,' she told him. 'It is time to leave things to somebody younger than you.' But, a month before the first round of the poll on 5 December 1965, he announced his candidacy, expecting to win an absolute majority on the first round.[1]

An initial attempt to field Gaston Defferre, the former Socialist minister and long-time mayor of Marseilles, as the main candidate against the General fell apart because of disunity among the opposition. Mitterrand then engineered a coalition encompassing Socialists, Communists and Radicals, with the backing of Mendès France. The third main candidate, the Christian Democrat senator, Jean Lecanuet, was an attractive new-face campaigner in his forties; he appealed to centrists and those alienated by de Gaulle's foreign policies, especially after the General ordered France's place at Common Market meetings to be left empty while he pursued a joust with the commission in Brussels, which he saw as too integrationist. The one-time Vichyite and Algérie française lawyer, Jean-Louis Tixier-Vignancour, ran for the far right. As the election campaign gathered pace, a nasty reminder of the underside of the regime came to light with the kidnapping of Mehdi Ben Barka, a Moroccan opposition leader picked up by police in Paris and taken to a villa outside the city where he was tortured before being flown to Morocco and killed.

Buoyed by polls showing more than 60 per cent support, de Gaulle initially stayed above the electoral fray, declining to appear on television or hold meetings while his opponents criss-crossed the country and enjoyed a freedom on broadcasting media previously denied to them by state control. When he finally agreed to go on television at the end of November, he delivered one of his worst performances, looking old and out-of-touch. Far from a national endorsement, he got only 44.6 per cent of the vote, and so was forced into a second round against Mitterrand who had tallied 31.7 with Lecanuet scoring 15.5. De Gaulle spoke later of a 'wave of sadness that nearly carried me away'. He put his failure to win an overall majority down to the way in which 'fear has disappeared. Necessary national measures have annoyed interest groups. The feudal political groups are hostile.' But he rejected the idea of walking out as he had done in 1946. Preserving his republic was too important for that.

The General revived for the second round campaign, though he still refused to address public meetings. Interviewed on television, he was animated and spoke of everyday concerns in a manner he had never done before. He was cutting about Mitterrand, who was having trouble placating the varied coalition behind him, and knew that most of Lecanuet's voters would back him for fear of a president supported by the PCF. His core message was simple – me or chaos. On 19 December, he was re-elected with 54.5 per cent of the vote. But the Olympian Constable had been shown to be human while the left had been given hope that the Fifth Republic did not have to be eternally Gaullist.

Leaving Pompidou to get on with the week-to-week business of domestic affairs, the president pursued a determined foreign policy. The 'empty chair' crisis in Europe was settled with a solution that safeguarded France's interests. De Gaulle then announced that, while remaining 'the ally of our allies', France would withdraw from the integrated military structure of the NATO alliance. 'The subordination known as integration will end, so far as we are concerned,' he declared.

Non-French military personnel would leave France and their installations would be shut down. The alliance's headquarters would move from outside Paris to Brussels. Lyndon Johnson told Dean Rusk to ask de Gaulle if he wanted the American dead of two world wars to be removed as well.

Pressing his crusade against American influence and policies, the General spoke on a visit to Cambodia of the 'national resistance struggle' in Vietnam and castigated 'a detestable war'. He flirted increasingly with Moscow as he ordered that the nuclear *force de frappe* [strike force] should be targeted in all directions not just to the east, and promoted the idea of a Europe stretching 'from the Atlantic to the Urals'. On a ten-day visit to the USSR in June 1966, he praised the 'peaceful ardour' of his hosts and of a 'new alliance of Russia and France'. The outcome was minimal. The Soviets agreed to adopt the French colour television system and let Renault set up a plant in the USSR but Leonid Brezhnev told Polish leaders that de Gaulle remained 'an enemy' whose use was to weaken the US in Europe.

This activity abroad did not answer the basic complaints of the French about wage depression and rising prices. A strike wave hit the post and telephone services, a big shipyard outside Marseilles, the Paris public transport system, the national railways and the electricity and gas network. Though annual growth was a more than respectable 5 per cent, unemployment hit its highest level for a decade. Industrial output faltered. Profit margins were low. The budget deficit grew. Major state companies announced big losses.

The left built on the 1965 election with a pact between Mitterrand's Socialist-Radical grouping and the PCF where reformists were urging 'EuroCommunist' thinking. Lecanuet formed a new party, the *Centre Démocrate*, appealing to voters put off by de Gaulle's intransigence on the international scene. Giscard d'Estaing, still only forty, claimed autonomy for his Independent Republican conservative party.

In legislative elections in March 1967, the Gaullists got only 42.6 per cent of votes cast at the decisive second round while the main opposition parties took 46.4 per cent. The president's warning that victory for the left would bring 'utter ruin' cut less ice than in the past and voting discipline between the Communists and Mitterrand's grouping was tight. In the National Assembly, the government depended on the support of the 44 Independent Republicans, but Giscard started to criticise 'the solitary exercise of power' and to define his position as 'yes, but'.

The opposition launched a series of violent attacks on the government during stormy debates, which led to a Gaullist fighting a duel with swords with Defferre who had treated him as an idiot. (The Gaullist was slightly wounded in one arm.) The administration had to use decrees to push through measures, provoking fresh strikes. Three parliamentary censure motions were only narrowly defeated. De Gaulle told Pompidou to focus on schemes for worker participation in companies and an alliance of labour and capital; the prime minister was not enthusiastic and nothing much was done.

Increasingly irate, de Gaulle blocked a new attempt by Britain to enter the Common Market, and, on a visit to Canada, made his provocative cry of '*Vive le Québec libre! Vive le Canada français! Et vive la France!*'. He tried to act as an honest broker in the Middle East, only to alienate Israel when he told the foreign minister, Abba Eban: 'If Israel is attacked we shall not let it be destroyed, but if you attack we shall condemn your action.' When the Six Day War broke out between Israel and its Arab neighbours, the refusal of the Israelis to accept his advice rankled deeply. To his aide, Jacques Foccart, he remarked that they were 'unbearable'. France voted with the Soviet bloc countries for an unsuccessful UN resolution demanding Israel's unconditional withdrawal from territories occupied during the conflict.

This attitude did not help the president politically at home. Giscard signed a statement of solidarity with Israel along with Mitterrand and Lecanuet. An opinion poll showed 60 per cent support for Israel. But de Gaulle set off a storm at a press conference in November 1967, by referring to Jews as 'an elite people, sure of themselves and domineering' who, once gathered into a 'warrior state', were destined to show 'burning and conquering ambition'.

As accusations of anti-Semitism flew, de Gaulle wrote to the former Israeli leader, David Ben-Gurion, insisting he had meant nothing disparaging; on the contrary, the characteristics he had attributed to the Jews were the key to their survival through the centuries. France's Grand Rabbi thought him genuinely surprised by the fuss he had caused; he said his words had been intended as praise. But he told a Jewish Gaullist, Léo Hamon, that he had been shocked by pro-Israel statements on the war by the Rothschilds, and 'thought also of the Dassaults and those like them who do not even have the pride to keep their names', a remark his visitor could not have appreciated since his name had originally been Goldberg. The most crushing verdict came from Debré, grandson of a chief rabbi, who judged that the General displayed 'an infantile-psychological-senile' attitude.

Turning back to domestic matters, he bombarded Pompidou with notes on everything from aid for repatriated *pieds-noirs* to judicial reform, from the removal of the food market of Les Halles from central Paris to the need to raise the birth rate and increase farm productivity. He pressed for the implementation of a selection process in universities to reduce overcrowding and produce more science graduates. There were reasons for pride – the Concorde supersonic airliner, the expansion of the motorway network, a major oil and gas accord with Algeria and the creation of a single Common Market for grain on favourable terms for France. Decentralisation of authority was being pursued for cities like Toulouse, Marseilles and Grenoble where the Winter Olympics were to be held in February 1968. Preparations were going ahead for France's first test of a thermonuclear device in the South Pacific. But growth was still slowing, the franc was too strong for the good of exports, the value of the minimum wage continued to fall and there was a sharp increase in youth unemployment. The result was, inevitably, a fresh rise in workplace militancy, a partial stoppage in the public services and fighting between strikers and police at several factories.

Student discontent was spurred by overcrowding and the selection process backed by de Gaulle and the government. The faculty in the Paris suburb of Nanterre became the fulcrum of agitation stemming initially from anger at rules in sexually segregated hostels where students were not allowed to receive visitors in their rooms or to make any alterations, such as hanging pictures. A galaxy of groups mobilised, calling for a new social and human order with a greater place for the individual. In November 1967, 5,000 students marched in Paris. In January 1968, the Minister for Youth and Sport, François Missoffe, went to

Nanterre to inaugurate a swimming pool. When he had finished his speech, he was confronted by a red-haired, baby-faced German student, who attacked the government for making no mention of young people's sexual problems in a 600-page report on education. The swimming pool, he added, was an attempt to divert sexual energies into sport. 'With a head like yours you must have problems in that department,' the minister replied. 'You can always jump into the pool to let off steam.' 'That's a fascist response,' the 23-year-old Daniel Cohn-Bendit shot back.

Five thousand students at Bordeaux boycotted the university canteen. Police called in to Nanterre were forced to retreat. A hundred young women occupied a university hostel for men at Nantes. The urbane Pompidou took a relaxed view; 'Let them sleep together,' he said over a lunch at Matignon. 'While they're doing that, they won't cause us any worries.' De Gaulle, a man steeped in traditional morality was unable to understand that the order and conformity he so prized was at odds with an increasingly plural society. 'The hostels are anarchic,' he said. 'This agitation is the result of the weakness of those in charge. Everybody lies down. Nobody has the courage to resist.'

In the tenth year of his governance of France, the 77-year-old president had lived for too long in his own cocoon; how could he grasp the appeal of the teachings of Herbert Marcuse, the Structuralists and the other gurus of the protestors. As they got on a plane for a visit to Poland, Madame de Gaulle asked him joyously, 'So, it's true, you are going to ban miniskirts?' Told that such a measure would not be feasible, she showed deep disappointment. Her husband said nothing; a watching minister thought he sympathised with 'Tante Yvonne'.

In March 1968, radicals stormed the American Express office in central Paris; then Nanterre students started to occupy campus premises. The following month, 2,000 young people marched through the Latin Quarter on the Left Bank of the Seine waving red flags and throwing stones at police cars. There was fighting between the main student organisation, UNEF, and right-wingers after which Cohn-Bendit was arrested but released for lack of proof. Pompidou remained relaxed. 'We cannot make fools of ourselves by locking up a student because of a prank,' he told the interior minister, Christian Fouchet. Seeing the demonstrators as dangerously radical, the Communist Party came out against them, denouncing 'false revolutionaries' who had to be 'fought energetically'.

The Ides of May[2]

1 May 1968. Given the PCF's attitude, Pompidou authorised the traditional trade union march from the Place de la République to the Bastille on Labour Day for the first time in 14 years and saw no reason to put off a visit to Iran and Afghanistan. In his absence, the protests swelled, with big demonstrations proclaiming '*Dix ans, c'est assez*' (Ten years, that's enough). The Nanterre faculty of letters was closed because of the continuing disorder.

3 May. Students occupied the courtyard of the Sorbonne, France's most prestigious university establishment; it took CRS riot police three hours to take them away, amid fighting joined by pupils of neighbouring schools. Police staged violent charges and fired tear gas; made sinister by their visored helmets, batons and shields, they were denounced by protestors as 'CRS = SS'.

Pitched battles erupted in the streets and across the Place Saint-Michel, and surged up to the Luxembourg Gardens. The barricades of 1830, 1848 and 1870 re-appeared. The CRS beat down anybody in their path. The Sorbonne was closed. When Cohn-Bendit was temporarily re-arrested, the cry went up, 'We are all German Jews!'

4 May. 'No weakness!' de Gaulle told his ministers. 'Those who want to attack the state and the nation must be resisted.'

6 May. Violent clashes continued round the Sorbonne with radio stations relaying blow by blow accounts as demonstrators smashed shop windows, trashed cars and hurled paving stones, metal from torn-down fences and anything else to hand. The police reaction was even more violent with tear gas, truncheons and high-velocity water cannons. What started as a student rebellion over campus regulations had turned into something resembling an insurrection in Paris and nine provincial cities, bringing into question the regime's ability to cope and its leader's understanding of how society was changing.

8 May. 'Tonight, we take the Sorbonne,' a student leader, Alain Geismar, declared on the radio. A telegram from five French Nobel Prize-winners, including François Mauriac, called on de Gaulle to amnesty the jailed students and open the faculties. 'Contemptible demagogy,' the General reacted. 'Neither truncheons nor tear gas should be spared.' But the challenge grew as the Communist-led CGT trade union federation, and the leftist CFDT labour group, declared their solidarity with the 'struggle of the students and teachers'.

10 May. Amid the chaos, delegates to Vietnam peace talks agreed to open negotiations at the conference centre on the Avenue Kléber. That night, more than 10,000 demonstrators marched down the Boulevard Saint-Michel towards the Sorbonne, and put up barricades of cars, railings, chunks of metal, paving stones and tree branches. If the authorities had used maximum force, they could have rolled them over, but the Paris prefect of police, Maurice Grimaud, was intent on avoiding any loss of life.

On the other side of the world, Pompidou received a telephone call at the French embassy in Kabul from Michel Jobert, his chief of staff at Matignon, urging him to return to Paris. The prime minister took the advice. He concluded that de Gaulle did not grasp the situation and that the ministers concerned could not reach an agreed position.

11 May. Police went into action against the Boulevard Saint-Michel barricades. Advancing in solid lines, they fired more than 5,000 tear gas grenades, some containing chemicals that could cause blindness. One by one the barriers were taken, though some needed ten assaults. Demonstrators threw back paving stones and projectiles of all kinds, watched from their windows by local inhabitants. Having taken the barricades, the police indiscriminately beat people in the streets and stormed late-night cafés. The official casualty toll of 367 injured including 251 policemen hugely minimised the reality. The CGT and CFDT decided to call a strike in protest at the police action.

12 May. At a 6 a.m. meeting at the Élysée, de Gaulle asked if the army should be called in. The answer was negative. Arriving back in Paris, Pompidou told ministers he was going to order the reopening of the Sorbonne. When it was pointed out that this was contrary to the president's wishes, the prime minister replied, according to the historian Éric Roussel: 'The General doesn't exist anymore; de Gaulle is dead.' Going to the palace, Pompidou threatened to resign if his plan was not accepted. 'If you win, so much the better,' the president told Pompidou. 'France will win with you. If you lose, too bad for you.'

The premier recorded a television and radio address before going off for a good dinner. When it was transmitted at 11.10 p.m., he stepped out of de Gaulle's shadow, expressing 'deep sympathy for the students and trust in their common sense', pledging university reform and calling on 'everybody to reject the provocations of a few professional agitators and to cooperate in the rapid and complete [restoration of] calm'. Surrounded by a tight knot of aides, he took over decision-making in the justice, the interior and education ministries. 'Say nothing, do nothing, I will handle everything,' he said.

13 May. The Sorbonne opened its gates. The result was not what Pompidou had hoped for. Students immediately occupied the college, which became their base, the 'citadel of the revolution' and its 'ideological drugstore', as Pierre Viansson-Ponté of *Le Monde* put it.

Each evening an 'Occupation Committee' was elected which ran things for the next twenty-four hours. There was endless talk on how to construct an ideal world in marathon debates in the lecture halls. Sexual liberation was taken for granted. A poster culture proclaimed, 'It is forbidden to forbid', 'Be realistic, ask for the impossible', and 'I am a Marxist, Groucho faction'. It was, as the writer, Claude Roy, put it 'a revolution that is something of a party, a party that is something of a revolution'.

Seeing the weakness of the administration, the trade union federations swung into action. Transport and electricity workers went on strike in Paris. A vast procession marched to the Place de la République, accompanied by big demonstrations in other major cities, proclaiming that power lay in the street and attacking the man in the Élysée with cries of 'Goodbye de Gaulle. Goodbye de Gaulle. Goodbye'. The student and labour leaders were in the vanguard, with the politicians of the left well behind.

14 May. Despite the crisis, de Gaulle decided to go ahead with a scheduled visit to Romania; he saw the country, which seemed to be showing some independence from the Soviet Union, as an important element in his policy of breaking down the divisions between East and West. He could hardly allow the students to interfere with his role of the global statesman. But he may also have wanted to be away from a situation he could not control.

As he flew east, workers concerned with pay and conditions rather than freedom went into action, occupying Renault factories and two aviation plants.

15–17 May. In danger of being outflanked by factory floor militants, the CGT had to move into the struggle. Occupations and the sequestration of management added a revolutionary tinge to the movement, evoking echoes of the Popular Front thirty-two years earlier. The most militant areas were at the Renault plant in Boulogne-Billancourt and around Toulouse, Lyons, Grenoble and Nancy, as well as northern coalmines. There were big demonstrations in Le Mans, Clermont-Ferrand and Nantes, where protestors attacked the prefecture. Work stopped at a big shipyard on the Seine. The railways and postal services were affected and broadcasts on the state ORTF network were hit.

There was a clear distinction between the approaches of the two main labour federations involved. Under Communist leadership, the CGT drew a line between workers and students; it stressed the classic demands for improved pay and conditions and made a point of exercising all the control it could over the strikers. Renault workers at Billancourt closed the factory gates against a delegation from the Left Bank, and there were scornful jibes about young people from the Sorbonne driving to demonstrations in sports cars and wearing cashmere sweaters. The politically independent CFDT, on the other hand, showed an interest in broader social and workplace reform, and had talks with the students.

18–19 May. The president was highly irate when he got back to France – 'Playtime is over,' he told ministers who welcomed him at Orly. The authority and dignity of the state had been ridiculed and his efforts over the previous ten years had been undone in five days, he complained. 'It's a shambles,' he exclaimed to Pompidou, who offered to resign. Shrugging his shoulders, de Gaulle replied: 'No question of that!'

The General ordered that the Sorbonne and the occupied Odéon theatre be cleared immediately. The interior minister, Christian Fouchet, pointed out that this would involve use of firearms. There might be deaths and the unrest would gain a fresh impetus as a result.

Raising his arms in exasperation, de Gaulle conceded that action should be taken only at the Odéon – but straight away. The Sorbonne could wait. Before the meeting ended, the General gave the information minister, Georges Gorse, a sentence to relay to journalists: '*La réforme, oui; la chienlit, non*'. He meant '*chienlit*' in its long forgotten eighteenth-century sense of a carnival or masquerade, but the term was unknown to most people, some of whom assumed it meant 'shit in bed' – *chie en lit*. The president had been too erudite by half.

20 May. The number of strikers was estimated to have reached 6 million; in the following week it would rise to 10 million. Households stocked food, and petrol became scarce. Wealthy people headed for Switzerland with cash and valuables. The gap between the president and prime minister widened. De Gaulle spoke to his faithful follower, Alexandre Sanguinetti, of forming a 'combat government'. A new approach was needed, he said, based on the vague notion of 'participation' to get the population to feel more involved in the destinies of the nation.

But the head of government had decided on his own strategy based on an agreement with the PCF and CGT, which he saw as 'the last guarantors of a peaceful solution'. His protégé, Jacques Chirac, established contact with the number three in the CGT, Henri Krasucki. The union leader told him to go to a square near the Place Pigalle. Chirac drove there in his own car rather than using an official vehicle. A man smoking a pipe approached and gave an agreed password. Chirac told him the government was ready to open talks on wages and welfare payments. After further exchanges, he drove to a hotel in a poor part of northern

Paris with a revolver in his pocket because of worries that the Communists might try to kidnap him. Police agents watched from a distance. Led to a room on the third floor where Krasucki was waiting, Chirac began to hammer out a settlement to the strikes.

24 May. De Gaulle tried to gain the initiative with a broadcast promising a referendum on 'participation', a theme much pushed by left-wing Gaullists such as the jurist René Capitant who disliked Pompidou's market-oriented policies. But the speech fell flat, only provoking a major student demonstration that ended in street battles on both banks of the Seine; fighting also flared in Strasbourg and Bordeaux. In Brittany and central France, farmers set up roadblocks and waged a five-hour fight with police in Nantes. The first fatalities of the unrest came in Paris, where a young man died, probably as the result of being hit by a tear gas grenade, and in Lyons, where a lorry set rolling by demonstrators crushed a policeman.

The president sat up all night in the Élysée listening to radio reports of the violence. 'It's my departure they are calling for,' he acknowledged. He could only stand aside as Pompidou presided over the opening of talks to end the strikes at the Ministry of Social Affairs and Labour on the rue de Grenelle, the eighteenth-century *hôtel particulier* which had housed the Austrian embassy in Apponyi's day and had been given to the church by Napoleon III before being taken by the state under the anti-clerical measures at the start of the century.

27 May. At 4 a.m., a deal was reached between government, unions and employers for an average salary increase of 10 per cent and a small reduction in working hours to come into force in 1970. Strikers would be given half pay for the time they had been off the job.

As with his opening of the Sorbonne, Pompidou's emollient approach initially backfired. Renault workers at Billancourt voted to continue the strike. Thirty thousand people attended a meeting at the Charléty Stadium in Paris organised by the small but highly active PSU left-wing party whose patron saint, Mendès France, watched silently from the stands. Demonstrators stormed the prefecture in Toulouse and withdrew only when the Prefect apologised to them. Though banned from France, Cohn-Bendit made his way back to Paris and popped up at the Sorbonne with dyed hair and a broad grin. After Communist leaders went to see him, Mitterrand said he would stand for the presidency if de Gaulle resigned, and called for a provisional government headed by Mendès France.

The CGT announced a massive demonstration for the next day. Pompidou ordered an 'armoured gendarmerie' of 1,000 men with tanks to move to the Paris suburbs, and canvassed the idea of a general election. Shopping at the Madeleine, Yvonne de Gaulle was insulted by a group of shop workers and a motorist. 'Things can't go on like this,' she said on her return to the Élysée. 'It is becoming infernal.' She went on about it so much that her husband left the dining room that evening and had his meal served in an adjoining salon. Opinion polls showed support for the president slumping while backing for Pompidou rose by 25 per cent. The old man said he had not slept for three days, at times he changed this to six.

29 May. The Communist daily, *L'Humanité*, called for 'a government of the people and a democratic union with Communist participation'. Mendès France had said he was ready to head a new cabinet as proposed by Mitterrand. De Gaulle called off a cabinet meeting and told his staff he was going to Colombey. He telephoned Pompidou to say that he needed to clear his mind; he would be back the following afternoon. 'I am old, you are young, and it is you who represent the future,' he added and then, in an uncharacteristically personal sign-off, added '*Je vous embrasse.*' There was immediate speculation that, as in 1946, he was quitting. In a television interview a week later, he admitted that 'Yes! On the twenty-ninth of May I was tempted to retire ... I questioned myself.'

In fact, executing a well-laid plan, he was driven to a military base at Issy-les-Moulineaux outside Paris and then disappeared. 'We've lost any trace of the General,' Tricot, the Élysée secretary general, told Pompidou in the early afternoon after arriving unannounced at Matignon, white as a sheet. 'He's not at Colombey.' It was just as he had written in his 1934 book on military theory – 'Surprise has to be organised ... under a thick veil of deception.'

His destination was French army headquarters in Baden-Baden, West Germany. He wanted to sound out the commander there, Jacques Massu, on the loyalty of the army. But his main purpose was to deliver a mass psychological shock, as he told his son-in-law Alain de Boissieu with whom he had conferred before leaving Paris. 'I want to plunge the French, including the government, into a state of doubt and worry in order to be able to take control of the situation once again. I will win them back through fear.'

Accompanied in two helicopters by his wife and son, a military aide, a bodyguard, a doctor and a police inspector, the General landed at the base outside Baden in the early afternoon. The aide telephoned Massu who said he was having a siesta after staying up late the previous night drinking vodka with a visiting Soviet delegation. De Gaulle flew on to touch down on the lawn of Massu's villa.

'Everything is done for,' the president told the general.

'Don't think that way, *mon Général*,' the long-time loyalist replied. 'A man of your standing still has means of action.'

Sitting with Massu while their wives went off elsewhere, the president lamented how the Communists had paralysed France and how he was not wanted any more. As was his habit, he was really seeking encouragement from a straight-talking soldier he trusted. '*Mon Général*, what do you want? You're in the shit and you have to stay in it a bit longer,' Massu said. 'Go back. There is nothing else to do. You are still in the game; you've got to stay in it.' Hearing this, the General's spirits seemed to revive and he murmured 'Go on, go on ...' He got up and walked towards his host. 'I'm going,' he said. 'Tell my wife.'

Reaching Colombey, he telephoned Pompidou to say he had been on a 'tour', without giving details. Everything had gone well, he added. He wanted to rest and reflect, and hoped to get a good night's sleep. '*Mon Général*, you have won,' the prime minister replied. 'After the scare the French had in seeing you disappear, we are going to see a prodigious psychological reversal.' Dining at Colombey that evening, the General seemed happy, reciting a poem he had written as a young man about the Rhine and drafting a speech to the nation.

The CGT demonstration in Paris brought out several hundred thousand protestors but passed peacefully. Moscow did not want regime change in France. Washington was more ready for a switch. The CIA predicted a presidential election which would take Mitterrand to the Élysée at the head of an administration which would be 'more positive, less grandiose and more in harmony with American policy'.

30 May. Returning to the capital in the morning, de Gaulle broadcast his speech – only on radio as the television service was on strike. His combativeness was in striking contrast to his unconvincing appearance six days earlier. Banging his fist on the desk in front of him, shaking the microphone, he denounced the 'intimidation, intoxication and the tyranny of groups organised from afar, and by a party which is a totalitarian enterprise'. He called for 'civic action' to combat the PCF, which was playing on the 'ambition and hatreds of politicians on the scrapheap'. Saying he intended to continue his mandate, he announced a general election and said the referendum on participation would be delayed. 'No, the Republic will not abdicate,' he concluded.

The civic action took the form of a huge crowd of tricolour-waving supporters who marched down the Champs-Élysées from the Arc de Triomphe, headed by Malraux and Debré. Outside the presidential palace, 50,000 cried 'De Gaulle, you are not alone.' Unconvinced, CIA director Richard Helms told Lyndon Johnson France was on the brink of disaster and possible civil war.

'At last, I have slept,' de Gaulle told Pompidou when they met before a cabinet session. But the gulf between the president and prime minister had been further widened by the way in which the former had not told the latter about his movements. 'I had been treated with what seemed to me at that moment as a particular off-handedness,' Pompidou wrote in his memoirs. However, de Gaulle again waved aside his offer of resignation and the prime minister stayed in office at the head of a reshuffled government. Strikes and street violence continued into June when workers called off the occupation of the Renault plants and accepted the Grenelle agreements.

The General redux

The turmoil left an indelible mark on France which was echoed by events elsewhere – the Prague Spring, which would be put down by

Soviet tanks, the campus revolts and anti-Vietnam demonstrations in the United States and cries for freedom on their own terms by young people in many other countries, primarily in the developed world. The unfolding of events in France was largely accidental but was rooted in the nation's immediate discontents and the tradition of street protests dating back 170 years. The Gaullists in their newly renamed party, the *Union des Démocrates pour la République* (UDR), were intent on making the most of the fear factor and plumbing the anti-revolutionary tradition. Pompidou engineered a 'red scare' election campaign in which Mitterrand and Mendès France were portrayed as having been ready to stage a Communist-backed power grab. De Gaulle said he had stayed on because otherwise 'subversion threatened to sweep away the Republic'. An amnesty to OAS plotters placated the extreme-right while opposition centrists wanted to separate themselves from the Communists.

The UDR and Independent Republicans won 354 of the 487 National Assembly seats, a gain of 112 over 1967. Mitterrand's federation lost 64 seats to hold 57 and the PCF dropped by 34 to 39. The great upheaval from the left thus ushered in the biggest majority of the right since 1918. The old tug-of-war between revolutionary change and conservatism had led, once again, to victory for the latter.

De Gaulle was now free to get rid of Pompidou, the man who had implicitly challenged him in May–June and had organised the electoral triumph. The prime minister was ready to step down, to get away from government and 'to make myself wanted' as he positioned himself for the succession. The president's abrupt action in flying secretly to Baden had shaken the younger man and left him with the feeling he had 'ashes in [his] mouth'.

Maurice Couve de Murville, the long-time foreign minister who had moved briefly to the finance ministry, became prime minister. A ramrod-straight Protestant bureaucrat who liked to eat simple omelettes at a dowdy restaurant on the Boulevard St-Germain, he would implement the General's orders faithfully, but had little to add either in the way of policies or of popular appeal. Edgar Faure, who became education minister, put through reforms which conservative Gaullists did not like but de Gaulle realised were necessary. The cabinet lacked lustre. As the Gaullist speaker of the Assembly, Jacques Chaban-Delmas, put it, 'we have never had a government team made up of such serious and competent men but also so far from reality, so un-political.' That put de Gaulle in the front line even more and, despite the electoral victory, the circumstances were hardly promising, especially for a man approaching his seventy-eighth birthday.[3]

He had to abandon his referendum on participation because it did not fall within the constitutional requirements for such a vote. Instead, he sought to rally support with proposals for reform of the Senate and regional government, vowing to step down if the vote went against him. But the nation was not much interested. Internationally, the Soviet invasion of Czechoslovakia ruined the Gaullist dream of a Europe transcending Cold War barriers with France in a key balancing position. Relations with Israel deteriorated further as Paris imposed an arms embargo after an air raid on Beirut in response to a terrorist attack. In Washington for Eisenhower's funeral, the General had to ask to be received at the White House.

The core problem was the domestic economy. The Grenelle agreements were highly inflationary and led to costs that made French companies less competitive internationally. Devaluation was narrowly avoided and interest rates had to be raised, increasing corporate pressures. The president instructed Couve to cut public spending after the deficit grew. There were fresh strikes. Farm incomes fell. Shopkeepers demonstrated against supermarkets.

A murky affair involving the murder of a Yugoslav gangster, Stephan Markovic, produced rumours of the involvement of Pompidou's wife, Claude, and the actor Alain Delon; the left-wing anti-Pompidou Gaullist, René Capitant, who had become justice minister, did nothing to head off the smears; Couve did not keep his predecessor informed as he had said he would. Leaks from the judicial inquiry stirred the pot. Pompidou became so enraged that he demanded a meeting with the President at which de Gaulle was less than convincing about stopping the stories.

In that context, a remark to journalists by the former premier during a visit to Rome that he would probably be a candidate for the presidency when the General retired set off a flurry of speculation about his ambitions. By dropping Pompidou, the head of state had created a situation in which a trusted figure stood ready to take over; 'me or chaos' no longer rang true. He had alienated too many people, and younger figures like Giscard d'Estaing saw the need for a change at the Élysée and backed a 'no' vote in the referendum.

As the vote approached in late April 1969, de Gaulle told Michel Debré, 'The French want to see me leave. I will go to the end ... But I have no more illusions.' After watching the playback of his last television appeal to the country, he said simply 'We're fucked.' His belongings were packed up and he drove with his wife to Colombey where a presidential official called him at 10 p.m. on the night of 27 April to say that the 'no' vote had 54 per cent support. At ten minutes past midnight, the French news agency issued his statement: 'I cease to exercise my functions as President of the Republic. This decision takes effect today at midnight.' Asked by Malraux at the end of the year why he had gone over such a minor issue, he replied 'because of the absurdity.'

The Fifth Republic would continue to this day. But, without its founder, it steadily abandoned the attempt to unite France above the gap spawned by the heritage of 1789. Charles de Gaulle had, indeed, been a revolutionary figure in his way, but even he could not set a lasting template for a nation so immured in its own history. The political system he introduced endured, but, without him, it was a lesser beast that would prove, over time, difficult to manipulate as old forces dating back to the end of the eighteenth century resurfaced.

THE BANKER, THE PRINCE
AND THE FLORENTINE

Since de Gaulle's resignation in 1969, France has had six presidents and eighteen prime ministers. On two occasions, legislative elections have returned a majority from the opposite political camp to the head of state but he has stayed in office. Municipal, regional and European elections have regularly shown big votes for the opposition. The left, under François Mitterrand, held the presidency for fourteen years from 1981 to 1995, starting with an agenda of economic and social change to rival that of the post-war government, but then being forced to make a major U-turn to orthodoxy. Administrations of the right took various forms – corporatist, technocratic and survivalist verging on Fourth Republic compromise – but rarely showed a sustained taste for reform. The deep-rooted inheritances from the past, the strength of innate conservatism and belief in the special nature of *l'exception française*, together with the divisions bred by revolution and reaction, obstructed change and the compromises needed to move ahead to face a changing world and economic challenges. The result was a series of administrations that lost vigour – and often public support – within a short time of being elected and crafted policies to try to gain re-election. Mainstream parties lost credibility as extremists gained ground and social tensions rose.

This process reached its nadir after the election of the Socialist François Hollande in 2012. By the autumn of 2014, his popularity rating in opinion polls fell to 13 per cent as he failed to deliver on his election promises; growth was sluggish, competitivity declined and unemployment remained stubbornly high at 10 per cent (22 per cent for people aged under twenty-five). Municipal and European elections that year saw big gains for the opposition while Marine Le Pen of the far right National Front party outpolled both Hollande and orthodox right-wing leaders. Only the shock of terrorist killings in Paris in early 2015 and the president's resolute reaction temporarily boosted his standing, but that soon faded as the front advanced further: 'I fear for my country,' the Socialist prime minister said. [1]

In the previous decades, electoral switchbacks had become a recurrent phenomenon which undermined the stability needed for evolution and resolution of political leaders. The Socialists and their allies lost both municipal and European elections within two years of Mitterrand becoming the first president of the left in 1981. Though he won re-election easily in 1988, the Socialist vote slumped to 17.6 per cent in the 1993 legislative elections. The French elected the neo-Gaullist Jacques Chirac president on a programme of job creation and tax cuts in 1995 but, when the government reduced the state spending to try to cope with a yawning budget deficit, voted it out of office. The elder Le Pen, Jean-Marie, finished ahead of the Socialist candidate in the first round of the presidential election of 2002.

The mainstream parties were divided by a deadly combination of infighting and complacency. Centrists, and their efforts to promote reasonable compromise, were repeatedly crushed by the big battalions on either side of them. All the while, France's position as a global leader came under threat as it faced Germany's rise to predominance in Europe. Its economic health lagged behind other leading Western nations with a steadily shrinking share of world output and an increasingly unsustainable level of state spending which had been similar in France and Germany at the end of the twentieth century; a decade-and-a-half later it was ten points higher on the west of the Rhine than on the east. Tax and welfare payments to the state were unusually high and dragged down companies as public debt rose steadily as a proportion of GDP. Unemployment became a constant problem, rising to 10 per cent in the mid-1980s, hitting 12 per cent in the late

1990s and running at 9.5 per cent in 2004–6 before going back into double digits.

The result was what is known as '*morosité*', bringing widespread disillusion and alienation from conventional politics as voters plumped for extremes. Abstention rates soared and presidents lost authority as the holders of the most powerful elected post in the West failed repeatedly to grasp the challenges the nation faced, as if paralysed by the legacy of the past and unwilling to chart a new future for the country.

Rule of the Pompom

Georges Pompidou's appearance epitomised him. His cheeks were full, his body plump as befitted a man who savoured life, both earning him the nickname 'Pompom'. A patron of the arts as was his wife, Claude, he usually had a cigarette in the corner of his mouth, his eyes habitually hooded and calculating. Born in the Auvergne, he excelled as a student and became a teacher of literature. Lacking the wartime pedigree of other Gaullist stalwarts, he made his mark by his administrative skills in the prime minister's office after the Liberation and then ran the foundation set up by de Gaulle and his wife in memory of their daughter Anne. Forging a career for himself, he went into the Rothschild bank, becoming its general manager from 1956 to 1962, when he was appointed to Matignon.

His victory in the presidential election that followed de Gaulle's resignation was a foregone conclusion. Mitterrand did not run and the left-wing ticket of the moderate Socialist Gaston Defferre and Mendès France took only 5 per cent of the vote, a quarter of the score of the Communist Jacques Duclos who finished just behind the top opposition candidate, the roly-poly centrist president of the Senate, Alain Poher. Pompidou was the man to offer some relaxation from the rigours of the General without abandoning his inheritance, and he romped home in the second round with 58 per cent of the vote.

Foreign policy grew more relaxed. Britain was allowed into the Common Market. The dashing Resistance hero, Jacques Chaban-Delmas, became prime minister, pledging a 'New Society' to make France a fairer place. His government included some centrists who had backed Lecanuet in 1965. Taking on advisers from the centre-left, such as Jacques Delors and Simon Nora, the prime minister tried to encourage social dialogue, increased welfare provisions, raised the minimum wage and relaxed control of the media. Giscard d'Estaing's backing for the 'no' vote in the referendum was overlooked and he returned to the finance ministry. Growth was strong. Business was favoured as the administration drove industrial modernisation and the consolidation of big groups that could compete internationally was encouraged; by 1974 the 319 biggest enterprises controlled 4,000 subsidiaries and 25 per cent of jobs in the commercial non-farming sector.

Paris was given an overhaul. The wholesale food market at Les Halles was moved to Rungis in a southern suburb and replaced with shopping malls and clothes stores – and with a cultural centre that would take Pompidou's name. Real estate boomed. An expressway was driven along the Right Bank of the Seine. The fifty-nine-storey Tour Montparnasse went up. As in the days of Haussmann, fortunes were made. The power of money was heightened as the state and big business worked together, underwriting big projects including the Franco-British Concorde airline, a technological breakthrough that never made commercial sense.

A gulf opened up between the Élysée and Matignon, where conservatives round Pompidou suspected Chaban of trying to build up a centrist power base. The prime minister was hit by accusations of tax evasion in the whistle-blowing weekly, *Le Canard Enchaîné*. He won a confidence vote in the National Assembly but, in July 1972, Pompidou replaced him with a Gaullist stalwart, Pierre Messmer, who had fought for the Free French in Africa and been defence minister for nine years.

De Gaulle remained aloof from public affairs, visiting Spain and Ireland but never commenting on his successor, until his death in November 1970 at the age of seventy-nine – he suffered a massive aneurism as he played patience while waiting to watch the evening news at his country home. Pompidou declared that France had been widowed. The funeral, held in the parish church at Colombey as the General wished, was restricted to old companions from the Resistance and members of the armed forces, though a crowd of 40,000 watched from outside. The Constable was buried in the same tomb as his daughter, Anne.

The Pompidou administration faced discontent from workers, notably in the dramatic occupation of the Lip watch factory in eastern France, and a rising challenge from the *Parti Socialiste* (PS) headed by Mitterrand who forged an agreement with the Communists. The centrists were, predictably, split between a group that became part of the presidential majority and a smaller faction that sidled up to the sinuous Mitterrand while trying to keep its distance from the PCF and its pugnacious Stalinist leader Georges Marchais. At legislative elections in 1973, the left staged a dramatic revival, increasing its Assembly seats by eighty-four with 44 per cent of the second round vote. The administration held on, but France was ready for change.

The alternative triumphs

Pompidou was suffering from cancer, which killed him in April 1974. Voters faced three alternatives – a radical swing to the left proposed by the common programme with Mitterrand as sole candidate; Giscard d'Estaing's liberal, free market technocracy; or a more inclusive form of Gaullism offered by Chaban-Delmas who was, however, tied to the past by the barons of the old order. The race narrowed down when forty-three Gaullists headed by Pompidou's protégé, Jacques Chirac, lined up behind Giscard. In the first round of voting, Mitterrand won 43 per cent, Giscard 33 per cent and Chaban only 11 per cent.

Fear of the PCF was still an important electoral factor and Giscard d'Estaing ran a smooth campaign as the man who would bring 'change in continuity'. Though he had been a minister often enough, he was nine years younger than Mitterrand who carried with him more than a whiff of the Fourth Republic – in the first-ever television debate between the two candidates, the finance minister made much of his economic expertise and dismissed Mitterrand as a man of the past. Still, the result was extremely close. Giscard's winning margin was 1.6 per cent of the vote.

The new president appointed Chirac as prime minister. With the two men aged forty-eight and forty-one, the country seemed in for serious rejuvenation. Divorce, contraception and abortion were liberalised. The age of majority was lowered from twenty-one to eighteen. The TGV high-speed train project was launched along with an ambitious nuclear power programme. More motorways were built. Telecommunications were modernised and the prototype internet system, the Minitel, was made available to all households. Giscard cut an impressive international figure, notably when he invited the heads of government of the US, Britain, West Germany, Italy and Japan to a summit at Rambouillet, to form the Group of Six economic powers. He worked easily with the US, backed European cooperation and formed a formidable partnership with West German Chancellor Helmut Schmidt in launching the European Monetary System, though this soon turned into a zone founded on the West German mark with the franc playing a subsidiary role.

However, there were some nasty worms in the bud. Giscard's own Independent Republican party was the junior partner in the parliamentary coalition – he depended on the Gaullists elected to the National Assembly in the 1973 election for a majority to approve legislation and they were generally conservative. The president seemed to assume that he knew best on all subjects and interfered constantly in government business. As a result, Chirac was increasingly frozen out of top-level decision-making. He was instructed to walk three paces behind the head of state and consulted on a cabinet reshuffle only after Giscard had decided who to promote and who to sack. In August 1976, he resigned. His closest advisers, the hard line Pierre Juillet and Marie-France Garaud, who saw Giscard as a dangerously soft liberal out to destroy Gaullism, propelled him to form a neo-Gaullist party, the *Rassemblement Pour la République* (Rally for the Republic), named in obvious echo of the General's post-war *Rassemblement du Peuple Français*.

Its deputies launched a running parliamentary war against the new government led by the economist Raymond Barre. Chirac attacked the pro-European Giscardians as 'the party of the foreigners' and added to his challenge by winning election against one of the president's close associates, Michel d'Ornano, to the newly created post of Mayor of Paris. (The job had been abolished after the

The Prince Who Crashed to Earth

Handsome in a tall, slim, balding way, Valéry Giscard d'Estaing set out to be a president in tune with his age, a Gallic Kennedy who offered to modernise France and build a progressive and reasonable political majority, cleaving to the market economy and accepting the leadership of technocrats like himself. He was photographed stripped to the waist in a sports changing room in his native Auvergne. He invited dustmen to breakfast at the Élysée. There were stories about him crashing into a milk van while driving himself back to the Élysée in the early hours after a romantic assignation.

But, as his presidency wore on, much of what he did could be summed up by the dismissive phrase of a Gaullist critic – 'gadgets'. Even the aristocratic *d'* in his family name turned out to have been acquired only in 1922 as a result of a distant connection with nobility. His family style aroused public scorn. When the Head of State tried the common touch by dining in ordinary homes, he made known that his preferred dish was scrambled eggs with truffles.

Born in 1926 in Germany, where his father was a civil servant with the occupation forces, Giscard was one of those brilliant individuals who shot through the upper reaches of France's education system to run the country. He joined the prime minister's staff at the age of twenty-eight, won election to the National Assembly by the time he was thirty and was a junior member of the government three years later. He became finance minister a month before his thirty-sixth birthday, spoke for hours in parliament without notes and led the Independent Republic party to become an important part of the governing coalition. Though he had to bow to Georges Pompidou as the General's successor, there was never any doubt of his presidential ambition.

Commune for fear of the power that somebody running the capital would enjoy.) Chirac now had command of a mass party with the largest bloc of deputies in the Assembly and control of France's greatest city.

The president also had other problems to worry about. Nationalists staged a running fight with the authorities in Corsica. Giscard was buffeted by recurrent rumours that he had accepted diamonds from the self-proclaimed Emperor Jean-Bedel Bokassa of Central Africa. The administration was embarrassed when the complicity came to light of the budget minister, Maurice Papon, in the deportation of Jews from Bordeaux between 1942 and 1944 when he was a senior civil servant in the city – he had later headed the Paris police who killed scores of Algerians in a crackdown in the capital under de Gaulle.

But the biggest challenge was from the economy. Growth had dropped off at the start of Giscard's presidency as a result of an abrupt increase in the price of oil. After recovery in the middle of the decade, the second oil shock of 1979 halved growth. Inflation rose to 13 per cent and unemployment increased. State finances deteriorated – the last year with a balanced budget was 1974. Barre proposed orthodox austerity measures to cut the deficit and the administration's unpopularity shot up as taxes and social security contributions rose.[2]

The man in the Élysée came to epitomise the growing inequality, out-of-touch with the concerns of ordinary people as he radiated an air of superiority. He lived an aristocratic life and concerned himself with high policy, attracting the nickname of 'His Smugness'. Though his supporters finished marginally ahead of the left at legislative elections in 1978, helped by disunion between Socialists and Communists and fear of the PCF, his big lead in the opinion polls for the 1981 presidential race narrowed sharply as voting approached. His reforms had not been enough to gain success in the centre-left while they had sown doubts on the right; Chirac's challenge underlined to Gaullists that Giscard was not their man. Some of his modernising measures and his technocratic style grated with a population which still clung to traditions, real or imagined – *la Mère Denis*, a stout, ruddy-faced washerwoman from Brittany in her seventies, became an advertising icon for Vedette washing machines as she symbolised, in the words of historian Sarah

Farmer, 'the fantasy of combining the charms of outmoded rural life with the desires and demands of modern consumer society'. Mitterrand's marketing guru, Jacques Séguéla, knew what he was doing when he had the 64-year-old candidate shown on campaign posters against the background of a tranquil country village with the slogan 'The quiet force'.[3]

Mitterrand's expensive folly

The Socialist candidate put up a better performance than in 1974, appearing this time as an elder statesman against a ruler who had not delivered on his promise. The alliance with the Communists was given a progressive spin in order not to deter centrist voters. The challenger concealed his lack of interest in the vital matter of the economy and drew a curtain over the taste for Machiavellian intrigue that had won him his nickname 'the Florentine' – his supporters now called him Tonton – Uncle.

Chirac was the decisive factor in a knife-edged campaign. The left-wing vote was dispersed, with the Communists and four other candidates running in the first round as well as Mitterrand – Marchais got 15.3 per cent of the vote to the Socialist's 26 per cent. With four fringe candidates, votes for the centre-left totalled about 50 per cent. The neo-Gaullist former premier took 18 per cent in the first round; adding that to Giscard's 28 per cent and the votes two minor rightist candidates gave the president almost 50 per cent. Using the power of the incumbent and the official machine, he should have been able to win re-election.

But Chirac was not going to fall into line. While he had to back Giscard in public, he made it clear in private that he did not support his former boss. He had a secret dinner with Mitterrand; as they parted Mitterrand told him 'if Giscard wins, you will have problems. I would not like to be in your shoes. He won't do you any favours.' He then sent an emissary to assure Chirac he would not implement changes in the electoral system promised in his programme that would have hurt the RPR. In a televised debate with Giscard, he quoted criticism of the head of state by his former prime minister ten times.

Left-wing unity held for the second round but Giscard failed to hold all the right and totalled 48.2 per cent of the vote. With 51.7 per cent, Mitterrand became president of the Republic he had decried ever since its foundation 13 years before. The veteran Socialist mayor of Lille, Pierre Mauroy, moved into Matignon. The left erupted in joy; the streets around the Socialist headquarters in Paris were filled with exulting crowds on the night of 10 May convinced that a page had been turned in the nation's history, which would enable them to recover the promise of the Revolution under the emblem of the red rose of the left.

The left swept legislative elections in June 1981. Four Communists joined the government, though not in key positions. A dozen major firms were nationalised, including the big banks. Trade union powers were strengthened. Immigration laws were relaxed. Welfare benefits were increased along with the minimum wage, pensions and family allowances. The budget for healthcare rose. The retirement age was lowered to sixty. The working week was cut from 40 to 39 hours and continuous shift work to 35 hours. Laws were introduced against gender discrimination. Entitlement to paid holidays went up from four to five weeks.

A wealth tax was introduced. The death penalty was abolished.* At the interior ministry, Gaston Defferre pushed through decentralisation legislation to give regions more authority. Spending on social housing was increased by 40 per cent. Nearly 15,000 new education posts were established and teachers' salaries went up. The Minister of National Solidarity, Nicole Questiaux, wondered why she should have to keep to her budget – she saw her job as being to spend money and earned the nickname of 'Queen of Hearts' for her profligacy. The pipe-smoking foreign minister, Claude Cheysson, a man known for his lack of diplomacy, promised a new approach at the Quai d'Orsay with greater attention to the developing world. The culture minister, the exuberant theatre director Jack Lang, launched a big programme of artistic expansion including a national celebration of music. Though he did not take a government post, Mendès France was hailed as the patron saint of the new order.

* The last execution had been carried out in 1972.

At a Socialist conference that summer, delegates compared rich people who had gone abroad to émigrés fleeing the Revolution. When the finance minister, Jacques Delors, a moderate Socialist who had been on Chaban-Delmas's staff in the early 1970s, suggested it might be time for a pause in the pace of reform, nobody took any notice. Mitterrand responded to critics of the reckless economic expansion by saying there was nothing wrong with dreaming.

Communist backing for the new administration induced panic in some people as rumours flew of political commissars checking on citizens and a few businessmen smuggled their money over the Swiss border in suitcases. The head of the French Rothschilds went into exile in New York with the bitter comment that he was 'a traitor under Vichy, a pariah under Mitterrand'.

Giscard took his defeat very hard. He bade farewell to the nation with a melodramatic television appearance in which, when he had finished speaking, he rose from his seat and walked off the set while the camera stayed symbolically focused on the empty chair. He could not bring himself to read the newspapers and was said to avoid looking in the mirror. After returning to politics by winning a by-election in the Auvergne, he led the UDF Party from 1988 to 1996, but was short-circuited from office by his successors on the centre-right and suffered a humiliating defeat when he ran for the mayoralty of Clermont-Ferrand. Instead, he turned to Europe, working for greater cooperation in the Community and occasionally popping up domestically in his eighties as a grand old man of politics with sage advice of which nobody took much notice.

The price of Mitterrand's reverie was inescapable. In thirteen months, the franc was devalued twice. Inflation rose to 18 per cent and, despite reflation measures, unemployment hit 2 million. The boom in purchasing power boosted imports as domestic manufacturers failed to keep pace and wage and high welfare contributions sent up corporate costs.

France had to borrow billions of dollars to cover soaring debts. By March 1983, the pressure had become unbearable as the franc skidded further downwards and the economic performance gap with West Germany widened. Some ministers urged Mitterrand to pull France out of the European system and pursue socialism behind protectionist barriers. The president decided to stay with the European course as urged by Delors and to accept the cost in reversing his original policies in return for a big loan backed by West Germany.[4]

Two years after the blooming of the rose, the new revolution ground to a halt and reaction, with Social Democratic characteristics, set in. As Delors introduced an austerity plan with job cuts and reduced state spending, the Socialist elite swallowed the change of course with neither apology for what they had done nor resignations in protest at the policy reversal. Holding government office was what counted most. Mauroy remained at Matignon, though now watched by an emissary from the finance ministry. Cheysson stayed at the Quai d'Orsay and Defferre at the interior. The Communist Charles Fiterman continued to run the transport ministry, which took charge of the project to build a tunnel under the Channel with Britain.

Though he had no prior experience in foreign affairs, the president became a major international player, no doubt finding it a relief from the gloom at home as industry contracted and unemployment soared. He earned the gratitude of the US, which had looked askance at the election of an administration linked to the PCF, by backing deployment of new US missiles as part of a pro-Western Cold War policy course. Friendship with West Germany became a keystone of his foreign policy, helped by the Gaullien belief that he could retain political leadership of the European Community for France. The relationship with the Christian Democrat Helmut Kohl was particularly important; the photograph of the two men holding hands at Verdun in 1984 was an epochal image in the tradition of de Gaulle and Adenauer. France supported the inclusion of Spain and Portugal in the Community and promoted both the Single European Act of 1986 and the Maastricht Treaty six years later. But Mitterrand was not keen on German unification because he could see the impact on France's primacy, and agreed only if Bonn accepted the euro common currency, which Paris thought it could manipulate to its advantage.

Delors was offered the premiership. But he went too far in demanding to hold on to the finance ministry as well, which would have made

The Great Seducer

Asked late in life if he had any regrets, François Mitterrand replied 'None. Not everything was perfect in my life; who can claim that it was? But everything I did, I can be proud of. I mean to say, as a man, I never bowed the knee in front of anything or anybody.' Shortly before his death at the beginning of 1996 at the age of seventy-nine, he was asked what he expected if he met God. A confirmed agnostic who had rejected his Catholic upbringing, he answered, 'Now you know.'

That self-assurance characterised an outstandingly amoral politician – and one with extraordinary perseverance and huge powers of seduction. His career stretched from simultaneously working from Vichy – Pétain decorated him for his services – and joining the Resistance to standing for the presidency as the standard bearer of the left and then accepting rigour that would have delighted Poincaré.

Having denounced the Fifth Republic, he found its presidential powers suited him well when he got to the Élysée at his third attempt. In power from 1981 to 1995, he presided over a string of scandals and ran a secret family with his mistress and their daughter while his wife had a live-in lover, who he brought breakfast croissants.[5]

Born into a conservative family in south-west France in 1916, Mitterrand joined extreme right-wing leagues after going to Paris to study. He was taken prisoner by the Germans in 1940 but escaped from his Stalag. After his equivocal war record and marriage in 1944, he held a variety of Fourth Republic posts as the head of a small party needed to make coalitions. De Gaulle's return to power banished him to the margins but he clawed his way back over the following twenty-three years, a cultured cynic with a biting pen for whom power was an end in itself but who, when he did get to the top, was told he had prostate cancer which he nursed in secret, not telling even his wife for ten years.

him too powerful for the president's taste, so he went to Brussels instead to head the European Commission. A young Socialist star from a rich Parisian antique dealer family, Laurent Fabius, became prime minister in 1984. The Communists were dropped from the new government; having used their voters to win power, Mitterrand let them go.

A presidential loyalist, Pierre Bérégovoy, a one-time gas fitter with Ukrainian family roots, moved to the finance ministry – receiving journalists for lunch, he was unabashedly proud of how he had risen in the world; his official notepaper was headed 'Former Mechanic, Minister of the Economy and Finance'. He readily shouldered responsibility for policies which caused pain at home but made him a pin-up boy of international finance as inflation dipped and the franc strengthened. But the economic U-turn brought the left's defeat at National Assembly elections in 1986 when Mitterrand altered the voting system to help the far right National Front in a typically unprincipled bid to drain support from the mainstream right; where Chirac and the conservative Raymond Barre feuded, flanked by a renascent Giscard, who had shed his widow's weeds to attempt a comeback after winning a parliamentary seat.

Cohabitation

Mitterrand appointed the RPR leader to form a government for the first period of 'cohabitation' between a head of the executive from one party and a prime minister from the other side of politics. It was not a happy experience for the neo-Gaullist, though he pushed through some economic measures, including the first privatisation of firms taken over by the state only five years earlier.

Chirac stood as the main candidate of the right in the 1988 presidential election but staged a poor campaign and was hit by the split in the centre-right. Barre insisted on running but, lacking an electoral machine, was eliminated on the first round with only 16.5 per cent of the vote. In the run-off, Mitterrand beat Chirac by a handsome 54 to 46 per cent margin. The president regained his freedom to name the prime minister when National Assembly elections produced a moderately good result for the left. He gave Matignon to the leading Social Democratic figure, the slight, intense Michel Rocard, who wanted to build a modern left-centre movement and shed the Marxist trappings that still enfolded the party. He was the greatest threat to Mitterrand on the left and his appointment was probably a calcu-lated gamble that he would fail and be relegated to the sidelines. In private, the president was cutting about him saying he had 'neither the capacity nor the character for the job but since the French wanted him, they'll get him' – and reflecting that they would never accept a 'man who weighs 40 kilos'. Rocard lacked internal support from parties of the left and his earnest manner won few public enthu-siasts. Economic policy stayed tight, unemployment rose and taxes remained high.[6]

The Socialists did very badly at European elections and tore them-selves apart at a fratricidal party congress. It was time for another change at Matignon. Mitterrand turned first to Delors who decided to stay in Brussels. So the president named France's first woman pre-mier, Édith Cresson, who failed to impose herself and lasted for only eleven months before being forced out by bad regional election results in 1992. 'When I appointed her prime minister, I told her she would have to make herself unpopular,' Mitterrand reflected later. 'I did not think she would succeed so well.' Finally it was the turn of the faithful Bérégovoy, but he crashed to earth when the Socialists lost 80 per cent of their seats at legislative elections in the spring of 1993. The RPR emerged as the largest party with 242 deputies and the born-again Giscard had good reason for pleasure, with 207 seats for his UDF party.[7]

Bérégovoy retreated to the central city of Nevers where he was mayor. He telephoned the Élysée, but Mitterrand would not speak to him. On May Day, he told his driver to take him to a canal outside the city, slipped his bodyguard's pistol from the glove compartment of the car and shot himself in the temple. He was flown to Paris in a critical state. Mitterrand rushed to the hospital. Bérégovoy was dead on arrival. The president's voice choked when he blamed the critical media as dogs who had hounded an honest man to his grave.

The legislative election result meant that Chirac could have claimed

Matignon, but his eyes were fixed on the presidential poll two years later, so he stood aside while another one-time Pompidou aide, the urbane Édouard Balladur, took the job. Prospects for 1995 looked good. After fourteen years of rule by Mitterrand, it would be time for a swing to the right. Disillusion was widespread with the man whose economic illusions had inflicted huge cost on the nation and who seemed to be in the grip of megalomania, as he ignored the condition of state finances to pursue a building programme of 'great projects' including a new opera house at the Bastille and a national library that went six times over budget. This sentiment was compounded by a tide of scandals lapping round him and his associates that came to light as his fourteen-year reign drew towards a close.

François's friends

One of the president's closest associates, Roger-Patrice Pelat, with whom he liked to take walks around Paris, was involved in the insider dealing of shares in a company controlled by the state, along with a presidential aide. Another old pal, Roland Dumas, who had become foreign minister, was caught up in a murky affair of slush funds to grease the sale of frigates to Taiwan. Dubious dealings enveloped the state oil company, Elf, which had been headed by a Socialist apparatchik who used his corporate credit card liberally.

Mitterrand's party was found to have run an ingenious campaign to skim off cash from municipal contracts; when this was brought to light, the Élysée blocked the investigation and those being pursued were quietly granted an amnesty. There was also controversy over the military and financial aid France supplied to the Hutu regime in Rwanda in its genocide of the Tutsis through a special African 'cell' headed by Mitterrand's son, Jean-Christophe. It was revealed that Mitterrand had personally authorised the bombing in 1985 of the Greenpeace ship, *Rainbow Warrior*, which was preparing to sail from New Zealand to protest at French nuclear tests in the South Pacific – a photographer was killed in the incident.

The author Pierre Péan published a book in 1994 detailing Mitterrand's engagement with the far right during his student days and his service in the Vichy regime. When the president's long friendship with René Bousquet, the collaborationist police chief who had organised the big round-up of Jews in 1942, came to light, it seemed all too much part and parcel of a man without an ethical compass, even if he had been elected twice as leader of the centre-left which lauded republican values.

To make matters worse, the newspaper *Libération* disclosed that, between 1982 and 1986, an 'anti-terror cell' installed at the Élysée had illegally recorded 3,000 telephone conversations of 150 journalists, politicians and others. The main motive appeared to be the president's desire to keep secret his mistress, art historian Anne Pingeot, and their daughter Mazarine, as well as his cancer. He got his doctor to issue two bulletins a year giving him a clean bill of health. But, every day for eleven years, he received secret medical attention; on foreign trips, he had treatment at night – the needles and bottles of liquid for his injections were sealed in special suitcases and sent back to France in diplomatic bags for destruction. The truth began to emerge after he had an operation the following year, but it was massaged to reassure the public that the country was not being run by a sick man – in the later stages of his second term, he went straight to bed when he arrived at the Palace at 9.30 a.m. from his private home on the Left Bank and rested for most of the day.

Hanging over the late Mitterrand period was the increasingly unpalatable miasma of what was known as *la gauche caviar*, made up of supposed leftists enjoying the high life, epitomised by the silver-tongued lawyer, Dumas, whose mistress bought him an 11,000-franc pair of shoes on her Elf company credit card. Another Mitterrand operative, François de Grossouvre, a dapper seventy-year-old who had acted for him since 1965 and earned himself an office in the Élysée though he had no official function, made nice money by acting as a go-between for French, Middle Eastern and African interests. In April 1994, he was found shot dead by his own Magnum pistol in his office; the head of the security detail at the palace suspected a dirty deed against a man who knew too much and had grown indiscreet.

De Grossouvre probably took his own life but his death seemed all too much part of the piece, coming after all the other murky affairs surrounding France's Florentine ruler who ran through seven prime ministers in fourteen years, switched policies as it suited him and ger-rymandered the electoral system to help the National Front, a man for whom secrecy and manipulation became ends in themselves; asked by an associate how much of his life might be known by somebody close to him, he replied a third.[8]

His personal appeal applied to both sexes, though for men, it was the opium of politics and power – his actor brother-in-law observed: 'Mitterrand aroused even more loving feeling among men than among women', which, given his sexual conquests, was saying quite something. 'So, yes, I was married to a seducer. I had to make do,' said his wife, Danielle. 'He couldn't go into a bar or a restaurant without seeking out the face of a woman, and giving his famous wink,' said a journalist whom the president picked to chronicle his last days.

In his favour, Mitterrand bequeathed monuments and made a sub-stantial contribution to the construction of Europe. He has a place in history as the first president of the Fifth Republic to be elected from the left who ushered in social reforms and abolished the death penalty. But he left an economic record that bore down on the French for three decades – or more. The state debt, which had stood at 8 per cent in 1974, reached 32 per cent in 1994 and went on rising under its own inbuilt dynamic. If the trade balance improved, with a surplus of 19 billion francs in 1992, that reflected a severe contraction of domes-tic demand for imports as the result of a tight monetary policy. The economist François Caron aptly described the outcome as 'stagfla-tion'.[9]

'I work in shades of grey,' Mitterrand once said. 'There are black threads and white threads. I weave them together and with that I make grey.' His approach, honed over the decades, powerfully fuelled the lack of popular trust in politics and politicians. Not surprisingly, Socialists called for 'a right of inventory' after he left office, by which they meant that they should be free to choose which parts of Mitterrand's record they wanted to remember. He had been forced to switch policies after 1983 but had no coherent plan, allowing the forces of finance to take control as he concentrated on maintaining his per-sonal authority in his shades of grey regardless of who got hurt so long as he remained on top – be it Pierre Bérégovoy and other faithful followers he discarded at will or the millions of unemployed. The result was a downward legacy for the country and rising public cynicism and disenchantment, which, in the short run, made a victory for the right at the presidential election of 1995 inevitable. The only question was who would grab the crown.[10]

BULLDOZER, BLING AND NORMAL

In a system that rewards political longevity, the presidential succession to Mitterrand should have fallen automatically to Jacques Chirac given his long career at the forefront of French politics, his two premierships, his leadership of the RPR and his position as mayor of Paris where he had won a sweeping re-election. But there was a serious impediment in the shape of the man who had gone to Matignon two years earlier.

Chirac and Édouard Balladur met when the first was Pompidou's dashing lieutenant and the second the president's chief of staff. Pompidou promoted Chirac to be Minister for Relations with Parliament (where he was a disaster), then agriculture minister (where he ferociously defended French interests), and finally to the interior ministry, where he took office a month before his patron died. The death was a huge blow. 'I had the feeling of suddenly being an orphan,' he wrote. At the memorial mass for Pompidou, he sobbed uncontrollably. As finance minister in the first cohabitation government, Balladur implemented privatisations and financial liberalisation. The Gaullist leader regularly sent drafts of his speeches to him for comment and approval, but they made an odd couple. Son of a rich trading family from the Turkish city of Smyrna, Édouard Balladur was the epitome of a discreet gentleman in contrast to the other man's cavalier manner. Three years older than Chirac at sixty-five, he preferred steamed sole while the other man went for earthy country dishes like calf's head*. Balladur drank fine wines

---

* A restaurant in Chirac's department of the Corrèze offers 'calf's head as liked by you know who'.

while the RPR leader quaffed beer. He moved as if on roller skates and hated loud noise, though when surprised he could resemble an agitated chicken, while the younger man loved hubbub and plunged into crowds shaking every hand he could grasp. Mitterrand remarked privately that his prime minister practised 'the technique of an Ottoman strangler; he is soft, he insinuates himself, he neutralises you and, then, when the moment comes, bang.'[1]

At Matignon, Balladur lulled the nation into a sense of peace. Big business loved him and he rose from peak to peak in the polls. When he gave in to the threat of strikes, he won plaudits for statesmanship. By avoiding decisions, he became a hero; the *Financial Times* made him its man of the year. Ambitious young politicians such as Chirac's protégé, Nicolas Sarkozy, calculated the odds and changed camp – it was, after all, only what Jacques had done in 1974. The deal Chirac thought they had, that he would be the sole RPR presidential candidate, unravelled. After a party congress in La Rochelle, where Balladur had avoided his eye, he 'understood that the presidential election might well not turn out as planned'.

Indeed, the polls showed Balladur as clear favourite to move from Matignon to the much grander residence across the Seine. But this was to underrate the power of the RPR party machine, Chirac's canvassing powers and the debts he had to call in. Knowing this was his last bid for the presidency, he hurled himself into a no-holds-barred campaign in which coherence had no place. He made policy on the run, arms in the air, rictus smiles freezing his face. He promised wage rises but lower inflation, swore European fidelity but talked of a fresh referendum on the Maastricht Treaty, backed modern business but sought the support of Pierre Poujade.

The smooth, reasonable Balladur was left trailing, cutting a poor figure on the hustings. Satirists punned on the third syllable of his name to call him Ballamou rather than Balladur (Balla-soft, not Balla-hard). Down in the Rouergue, a lamb urinated on his jacket and the farmers chuckled. Electioneering in a café, he was visibly ill at ease if he had to touch anybody. A satirical television show which shaped public perceptions had great fun with skits in which His Smugness washed his hands after each electoral handshake and told his wife that he had discovered some charming new words – '*tu*' and '*le peuple*'. His government's best cutting-edge, foreign minister Alain Juppé, remained true to Chirac whom he had first served in the Paris city government in 1983. Alain Madelin, the apostle of free market economics, stayed loyal. The main Gaullist Eurosceptic, the bloodhound-faced president of the National Assembly, Philippe Séguin, decided that, despite their differences, Chirac was the man who should win the election.

As the battle moved into top gear, Giscard d'Estaing – or Monsieur Ex as he had come to be known – considered his options. There would be no place for him under Balladur; they were too similar. But he might yet cut a deal with the politician he had humbled two decades earlier. So, as spring blossomed on the hillside behind his fine country home in the Massif Central, Giscard announced his support for the man whose rivalry had cost him the presidency.

The first round of the election duly propelled Jacques Chirac into the decisive run-off, though with only 20 per cent of the vote, and eliminated Balladur. Lionel Jospin, the schoolmasterish Socialist candidate who got the nomination after Delors ruled himself out, put up a more than respectable show to win 23.3 per cent of the first round vote, to 20.8 for Chirac, 18.5 for Balladur and 15 per cent for Jean-Marie Le Pen. But the combined score for the right doomed the left to defeat at the second round. So Chirac became head of state at his third attempt with 54.6 per cent of the second round vote.

The problems of power

'Now our difficulties start,' Alain Juppé told his staff after he was appointed prime minister. The problem was that, as the political editor of *Le Monde* put it, Chirac's only real election programme had been 'no to Balladur' and the new president had little idea what to do next. As so often during this post-Pompidou period, the key problem was the economy. The new government evaluated the budget deficit as 50 billion francs more than it had been led to believe (a charge indignantly denied by Balladur). Privatisation revenue was a good deal less than expected. 'What is not working is our public finances,' as Chirac noted.

Though the franc was strong, markets began to ask if the policies of rigour pursued by successive governments and strongly endorsed by the Bank of France were sustainable in a country where the high jobless rate threatened public order. Chirac lamented that, for all his high standing in international financial circles, Jean-Claude Trichet, the erudite poetaster head of the Treasury and then governor of the Central Bank, seemed to know all the words in the language except for 'unemployment'.

The EU Maastricht Treaty requirements for budget discipline added to the problems. Maintaining low inflation and trying to live up to Euro-orthodoxy meant low growth. But this kept down government revenue, made deficit reduction more difficult and turned promised tax cuts into a chimera. To boost its income, the government raised the sales tax, which hit the poor and the unemployed while the parliamentary scene was complicated by the presence of a large Balladurian block in the National Assembly.

Once in the Élysée, as *Le Monde* put it, Chirac was like an unidentified flying object – 'one no longer knows quite who he is, where he is, what he wants.' Like Mitterrand, he found refuge in foreign affairs, developing a closer relationship with the US and NATO while maintaining links with West Germany, even if he found the Social Democrat Gerhard Schröder, who became chancellor in 1996, less easy to get on with than his predecessor. He ordered the resumption of nuclear weapons testing in the South Pacific setting off a wave of protests in the region. At home, the president took a courageous initiative by brushing aside the equivocations of his predecessors to publicly recognise France's responsibility for the deportation of Jews to their deaths during the Second World War. 'The criminal folly of the occupiers was seconded by the French,' he said on the fifty-third anniversary of the big round-up in Paris in 1942. 'These dark hours forever sully our history and are an insult to our past and our traditions.'

Juppé, another of France's superbly trained technocrats, who had worked with Chirac at the Paris mayoralty, put logic ahead of popular sentiment as he drew up a programme to reform welfare and state spending without any of the traditional consultations with bodies representing those affected. He got rid of Alain Madelin as finance

The Bulldozer

Jacques Chirac was Georges Pompidou's political son. Born in 1932 into a comfortable upper-middle-class family, he trained as a cavalry officer (he acquired the nickname of *Le Hussard* – as for a Hungarian cavalryman) and spent a summer in America, where he studied at Harvard, won a certificate from a Howard Johnson ice-cream parlour for his skill in making banana splits and gave a southern belle Latin lessons and her first kiss. After a flirtation with the left during which he sold the Communist newspaper *L'Humanité* in the street and signed a Moscow-inspired anti-nuclear petition, he turned into a dyed-in-the-wool Gaullist, joining the prime ministerial staff – Pompidou called him his 'bulldozer'.

As well as working at Matignon, he was despatched to the Corrèze *département* in France's agricultural heartland to conquer it for the Gaullists: Chirac and his wife, Bernadette, drove through the night from Paris each Friday or took the train that arrived at 4.10 a.m. to campaign through the weekend in the markets and charcuteries. He still held the constituency when he became president two decades later but also had a passion for Japan, including sumo wrestling, and for African art.

A Bonapartist seeking a direct link with the people, he was in constant motion, living off the political land, using concentrated force to achieve his ends – but then not knowing what to do with victory. He picked up ideas like lint, dodging from one side of the political spectrum to the other, often horse-trading in a Fourth Republic manner, moving from one top job to another in a manner that led one author to dub him the 'Resident of the Republic'.

A dashing figure, his love life became a matter of gossip, especially after his former chauffeur wrote a book referring to his quickie sessions at the RPR headquarters that gave rise to a saying among female staff: 'Three minutes, shower included'. He was also alleged to have dipped into secret state funds for personal use.[2]

minister after a disagreement. But mass demonstrations and crippling strikes forced him to step back as the antagonism towards reforms which would harm vested interests surfaced once more. 'The truth is that we live in a profoundly conservative country and it is very difficult to change things,' the president lamented. The chief of staff at the Élysée, Dominique de Villepin, another elite product of the top administrative finishing school, proposed to meet the administration's problems with the traditional Gaullist recipe of a referendum. Instead, Chirac called a legislative election in the early summer of 1997, 'I will lose a hundred deputies, but they will be easier to handle,' he told the Chinese premier Li Peng on a visit to China. 'And Juppé will put everything in order.'

However, under the leadership of the evidently capable Lionel Jospin, the Socialists held out the comfort blanket of promises that the French wanted to hear, but also radiated an impression of managerial competence as the team mostly broke with the Mitterrand era, bringing in Martine Aubry, the tough and able daughter of Jacques Delors, and Dominique Strauss-Kahn, a worldly economist with a fluent manner. Their campaign made the most of the government's weaknesses and Juppé's unpopularity – even if their pledges made little sense as they undertook to create hundreds of thousands of jobs without upsetting public finances, cut the working week to thirty-five hours without any reduction in pay, stop privatisations and meet the requirements of the Communists, the Greens and any other allies they could find. Modest and approachable after shedding the superior airs that marked him when he was a senior minister under Mitterrand, Jospin struck a welcome contrast to the technocracy of Juppé and de Villepin, putting on a human face for the electoral battle after remarrying – the nickname of 'Yo-Yo' given to him by a satirical television programme became rather endearing.

At the first round of voting, the combined left took 45 per cent of the vote and the orthodox right got its lowest score under the Fifth Republic with 36.5 per cent – only one minister won an outright victory. Abstentions soared to 32 per cent. The National Front recorded its highest score at 15 per cent. The following night, Juppé went on television to announce that, whatever happened at the decisive second round six days later, he would step down. The next Sunday, 1 June, the Socialists doubled their National Assembly representation to 225 with the left as a whole taking 320 of the 557 seats to 139 for the RPR and 112 for the centre-right UDF group headed by Giscard. Jospin became head of the government in France's third experience of cohabitation.

Despite the strong majority in parliament, the combined forces of the left still fell slightly short of a majority of popular votes. Even though Jean-Marie Le Pen's National Front won only one seat and saw its vote slump between the two rounds, it had been enough to harm the orthodox right, as its divisiveness became a recurrent factor in the politics of the Fifth Republic. By rejecting Juppé so emphatically, voters had humiliated the Élysée and Chirac recognised this, even if he reminded reporters that the constitution assured him of 'pre-eminence' and 'something of the last word'. *Le Canard Enchaîné* quoted a friend of his as saying: 'He's doing what he always does when things go against him. He's eating a lot of charcuterie, drinking a lot of beer and watching a lot of television.' When he asked his former finance minister what his followers were saying about him, Alain Madelin was reported to have replied: 'They say that you always lead us to failure, Jacques. They believe you bring bad luck.'

Living with the enemy

Chirac had what one reporter described as 'a fixed smile of resignation' at the first cabinet meeting of the new government as he listened to Jospin outline his plans to stimulate growth, create jobs and prepare the country for the European common currency. The prime minister was relaxed; privately he told colleagues not to attack the president, even adding a little joke – 'I forbid you to speak ill of our benefactor.' His twenty-six-strong government had Aubry as its second-ranking member with the job of introducing the thirty-five-hour working week. Strauss-Kahn, who enjoyed reasonable relations with business, took the finance ministry, while the Quai d'Orsay went to Hubert Védrine, who had been Mitterrand's foreign affairs adviser. Dominique Voynet, leader of the Green Party, became Minister for the Environment and Regional Planning.

The new government made a businesslike start, helped by an improvement in the economic environment that brought down unemployment by almost one million. It kept its commitment to the Maastricht budgetary requirements and Jospin declared that he wanted France to be a society of work, not charity. The Socialists got union backing for wage increases limited to 1.3 per cent for two years. Taxes were cut and, despite campaign cries of 'no to privatisation', sale of state assets was increased. To balance this there was the shorter working week and increased social security coverage. A system known as PACS legalised civil partnerships between unmarried people of both sexes. Women's rights were promoted. The presidential term was cut from seven to five years.

Following up on Chirac's honesty about the role of France in the deportation of Jews to Nazi concentration camps, the former minister and civil servant, Maurice Papon, was put on trial. He remained unrepentant, portraying himself as a scapegoat for national guilt and exuding what Robert Graham of the *Financial Times* aptly described as 'the irritation of a self-important man interrupting a weekend in the country to attend an unwelcome business meeting'. In April 1998, the jury found him guilty. Papon, eighty-seven, was sentenced to ten years' imprisonment and payment of 4.6 million francs in damages and costs. One of the few who dissented from the verdict was the National Front leader, Jean-Marie Le Pen, who called the trial an example of 'Judeo-centrism' by which 'history must compulsorily order itself by events which affect the Jewish community'.

Regional elections in March 1998 had confirmed the disfavour that had fallen on the right, but were not a complete disaster, with presidential supporters winning 36 per cent of the vote to the mainstream left's 40 per cent – though less than two-thirds of registered voters turned out, showing the continuing disillusion with politics. The president was hit by a series of allegations about his conduct as mayor of Paris, a job he had handed on in 1995 to Jean Tiberi, a Corsican who had been the long-serving mayor of the capital's 5th *Arrondissement*. The allegations pressed by a forceful Socialist deputy, Arnaud Montebourg, included vote rigging, the award of contracts to favoured firms without proper tendering and payment from municipal funds to people supposedly employed by the city but actually working for the RPR. Chirac enjoyed immunity from prosecution under a decision by the Constitutional Council, headed by the former Socialist minister Roland Dumas, who had to retire subsequently from the post because of his implication in the Elf Aquitaine scandals under Mitterrand. Juppé took the partial rap for his boss on the jobs scam, getting a fourteen-month suspended sentence.

However, Chirac regained popularity as he added to his foreign forays with a round of provincial tours, positioned himself above the daily governmental fray and ensured that nobody from his own side would obstruct his re-election bid in 2002. Seeing Jospin as his main opponent, he hardened his tone towards the government as the poll approached. But voters seemed bored. Opinion polls showed the president marooned at his usual first round score of around 20 per cent while Jospin was put at 17–19 per cent and Le Pen was credited with 12–14 per cent.

The great shock

Despite the numbers and their decent record in government, the Socialists ran a disjointed, complacent campaign. Jospin seemed strangely disconnected from the everyday worries of voters. As a result, the television screens at 8 p.m. on the night of the first round of voting showed the unthinkable – Le Pen would be Chirac's second round opponent, having taken 16.8 per cent of the vote to Jospin's 16.1 (and Chirac's 19.8).

The prime reason for Jospin's failure to get to the second round had been the fragmentation of the left, with candidates running regardless of the effect on the outcome as personal ambition combined with the political elite's myopia. The Socialist leader faced ten other candidates vying for the centre-left-ecologist vote, ranging from the serious centrist François Bayrou to three Trotskyites; the most egregious was the Mitterrand-era minister, Jean-Pierre Chevènement, who presented himself as a true 'republican', and defender of French sovereignty against 'the Chirac-Jospin pair'. The high abstention rate of 28 per cent did not help but the centre-left still won 37 per cent of the first round vote;

Chevènement's 5 per cent on its own would have been enough to put the Socialists well ahead of Le Pen.

It was the moment the leader of the *Front National* had been waiting for, ever since the 1950s when he became the youngest member of the National Assembly for a Paris constituency at the age of twenty-eight as a supporter of Algérie française. He had established himself as the braggart of French politics, a master at pandering to the fears of crowds, playing on immigration and insecurity. Undaunted by repeated reverses, he had built up a double-digit vote at the two previous presidential polls and now benefitted from the disenchantment of a growing slice of electors with the mainstream parties. Controversy always surrounded him – had he been a party to the use of torture as a paratrooper in Algeria? Had *le Chef*, as he was known to his supporters, lost his left eye as he said, when he was beaten by opponents in a 1958 electoral battle or had it been the other eye and the result of illness? How had he inherited his luxurious home outside Paris from an alcoholic acquaintance?

What was underrated, apart from his appeal to the fears of a substantial section of voters, was the organisation his supporters had built up; it was much more than a group of bullyboys nostalgic for Algeria, with groups to cater for young people, women, pensioners, ex-servicemen and farmers, police and prison officers. It held summer teach-ins, an annual march in central Paris on Joan of Arc Day and put on a 'Blue, White and Red' festival in the outskirts of Paris each year – one year, an effigy of Chirac was a target in the shooting gallery.

At the run-off, non-FN voters rallied behind the incumbent whatever their reservations about him – 'Vote for the crook, not the Fascist' went the cry. Even if Le Pen had no chance, France was shocked by what it had done – the abstention rate fell from 28 per cent at the first round to 20 per cent for the second as France rallied behind the Republic. The president, who had always abhorred the Front, refused to debate with Le Pen and got 25.5 million votes to his opponent's 5.5 million, which meant Le Pen attracted only a quarter of those who had supported minor right-wing candidates in the first round. Despite that crushing result, the mainstream had been put on notice. As Chirac reflected, 'it was not only the Socialist candidate who had just been sanctioned, but the whole political class.' Seventy per cent of the French said they recognised Le Pen as a danger to democracy, but approval for his ideas jumped by half in two years at the turn of the century to 28 per cent of those questioned – a figure that rose to one-third when it came to immigration and law and order.

The questioning of the political establishment coincided with a drop in national self-confidence which had been brewing for some time. A survey of the years between 1980 and 1993 showed that most people regarded the period as having been 'bad times'. The level of satisfaction the French said they felt with their lives was under half that in Britain, Denmark and Belgium. The suicide rate increased, as did consumption of tranquillisers. The World Health Organization reported that the French were more likely to suffer a 'major depressive episode' than inhabitants of eighteen others countries it looked at.

However, the FN promptly ran into difficulties, both external and internal. A new electoral system halved the number of its councillors in France's regions and weakened it in the European Parliament. The party faced financial pressures; Le Pen sold his home and headquarters in the fancy Paris suburb of Saint-Cloud and his personal armour-plated car. He split with his principal lieutenant, Bruno Mégret, an intense ideologue who wanted his own space. Above all, *le Chef* was approaching eighty.

Yet, it was clear how the Front had bitten into working-class voters who had previously backed the Communists against the system and who worried about unemployment, insecurity, Europe, loss of national identity – and, above all, immigration, which had become the major social fissure in the country.

Immigration and unrest

For more than a century, France had encouraged the arrival of foreign workers, first from Italy, then from Eastern Europe, then from Spain and Portugal but mainly from its former colonies. By the 1990s, they and their children constituted a large pool of discontent, living largely outside mainstream society and sometimes in angry, violent opposition to it, especially in the sprawling rabbit hutch housing estates that ringed big cities and satellite towns. Though the term could also refer to leafy middle-class suburbs, these became known as the *banlieues*, heirs to the shantytowns outside the city limits, their tower blocks inspired by urban planners whose dreams of 'streets in the sky' on the model laid down by Le Corbusier had turned into soulless concrete jungles.

Most of the post-war immigrants came from North and West Africa but some were from Southern and Eastern Europe and Turkey and a few from further afield, such as Southern Asians in the rag trade sweatshops of the Sentier district of Paris. Forty per cent lived in the Paris region of the Île-de-France with other large concentrations in and around Lyons and Marseilles. They were expected to conform to French ways and that was that. Some did but others did not and many became prisoners of the virtual ghettos of the housing projects in the suburbs or in run-down districts of big cities. Their children grew up often feeling excluded and found it hard to get jobs. Integration was slow. It was not until 2006 that the main television channel, TF1, appointed its first non-white news presenter, Harry Roselmack, born in Tours to immigrant parents. Zinédine Zidane, born to Algerian immigrant parents in Marseilles, established himself as probably the world's best footballer of the time when France's World Cup-winning team of 1998 awakened brief hopes for a '*bleu, blanc, beur*' nation, but the impact was fleeting.

The unemployment rate was twice as high among immigrants as among non-immigrants. Jobs that were available tended to be at the bottom of the pile, as Chirac said in a television address during urban riots in 2005. 'We are all aware of discrimination. How many CVs are thrown in the wastepaper basket just because of the name or the address of the applicant?'

Though no racist, and a firm opponent of the National Front, he also spoke of his understanding of what ordinary French people felt about the noise and smells of their immigrant neighbours.

Terrorist attacks by Islamic fundamentalists on other targets added to the toxic mix in the mid-1990s. In Algeria, five people died in an attack on French diplomatic quarters, a French bishop was blown up and seven French Trappist monks had their throats slit after being kidnapped by the main fundamentalist group amid a vicious civil war. A French airliner was hijacked across the Mediterranean. Then the rail network, a school, public places and famous landmarks became targets; the worst attack caused eight deaths and eighty injuries when a gas bottle was set off at the Saint-Michel station in the capital. Gas bottles that exploded at three other Métro stations in Paris wounded forty-two people. A bomb at the Arc de Triomphe wounded seventeen. At the start of the new century, police foiled a planned al-Qaeda bomb attack on Strasbourg Cathedral during the Christmas market of 2000.

The combination of terrorist bombs and the threatening cloud of violence in suburban housing estates, sometimes linked to organised crime and drug trafficking, made it easy for the far right to warn of France being swept by a murderous horde from the Maghreb, poised to cross the Mediterranean and join up with their brothers in Corbeil, Vaulx-en-Velin or Marseilles. Brigitte Bardot, who married a National Front supporter as her fourth husband, said she might have to emigrate because 'we have to submit against our will to this overflow ... Year by year, we see mosques flourish across France while our church bells fall silent.'

The gulf between a North African family in a *banlieue* tower block and a conventional French family became immeasurably deeper because the feeling of non-acceptance was mutual. Increasingly, immigrants asked what France was going to do for them. The jobs that brought them north were drying up, but they did not want to leave. For some, there was the visceral back story of French colonialism and the vicious war in Algeria. Religion was the only rallying point in which they could have confidence but it tended to set them even further apart from mainstream society. When a right-wing interior minister spoke of developing a 'French Islam', an imam from northern Paris countered: 'What is being asked of us is not integration but assimilation, which requires us to leave our identity behind. Individuals can be assimilated, a community cannot ... the arrival in France of Protestants and Jews required changes in French society; now it is the time of the Muslims.'

Riots erupted regularly after incidents ranging from local scuffles to police killings of immigrants fleeing from suspected crime scenes, or simply running away for their own safety. Towns outside Lyons had a history of disturbances reaching back to the 1970s with buildings and vehicles torched, and shopping centres looted. In 1995, police killed a young Arab, Khaled Kelkal, whose fingerprints had been found on a device used in an unsuccessful attempt to blow up a TGV high-speed train; his death was filmed by a television crew who accompanied the security forces.

The drama made Khaled a martyr among the youths of the *banlieues*. In the two days after his death, fifty cars were set on fire, telephone kiosks and bus shelters were smashed, and shops set alight. After violence that followed the death in the same region of a passenger on a motorcycle chased by police, a local resident wrote: 'Barricades, sirens, skeletons of burned vehicles, masked groups looting shops, men in balaclavas burning buildings, five hundred inhabitants of a run-down district facing squadrons of the forces of order. Such images are not from a far-away guerrilla war; this is what is happening right now, to the north-east of Lyons.'

Almost a thousand cars were set alight in the Seine-Maritime *département* of Normandy during 1997, and some 550 were burned in the Strasbourg area. Elsewhere in eastern France, buses and municipal buildings were torched and public transport employees shot at. In the country centre of Laval, shops were smashed and a cafeteria set on fire after police shot dead a young Arab who, they said, had grabbed one of their guns and tried to escape. In Fontainebleau, a youth who tried to crash through a police road barricade was killed with a bullet in the head and his companion beaten until a passing motorist intervened; a week of rioting shook the dead man's home town of Melun.

A report by a senior police officer identified 700 'sensitive' districts and focused on eighteen where there was 'collective rebellion and premeditated attacks against police, ambushes, throwing of paving stones and metal balls, Molotov cocktails, shots from firearms'. At the funeral of an immigrant killed by police outside Paris, the priest spoke of 'a generation of young people who have no chance, without work, without housing, without money, facing a world of adults who judge, condemn and exclude them without understanding'. Some gangs were made up of eight- to ten-year-olds. In the first decade of the new century, the violence spread to centres from Montauban in the south-west to Montbéliard in the east, from Strasbourg to Nîmes. Chirac spoke on television of 'a crisis of identity'. The government declared a three-week state of emergency in November 2005 to restore order. At the interior ministry, Nicolas Sarkozy talked tough, as usual, but little changed.

The Jewish community, the largest in Western Europe at some 600,000, faced a recrudescence of anti-Semitism. In the early 1980s, four people were killed and more than forty injured in an attack on a synagogue in central Paris followed by a bombing and shooting assault on the celebrated Jo Goldenberg restaurant in the old Jewish district of the Marais in Paris, which killed six people – including two American tourists – and injured twenty-two. Education minister Luc Ferry told parliament in 2003 that the Middle East conflict had 'entered our schools', a year after a group of teachers concluded that dealing with the Holocaust was impossible in some classes because students of Arab origin were so hostile towards the subject.

A stand-up comic, Dieudonné M'bala M'bala, son of a father from Cameroon and a white French painter, appeared on television with a sketch depicting an Israeli farmer as a Nazi and attracted audiences with increasingly anti-Semitic routines. In 2006, a gang consisting mainly of immigrant youths from Ivory Coast kidnapped a 23-year-old man 'because he was a Jew, so his family would have money' but, failing to get a ransom, tortured him to death. Roger Cukierman, head of the CRIF council of Jewish organisations, remarked that 'traditional extreme-right anti-Semitism has not got worse in France – anti-Jewish acts committed for the last year have clearly been situated in areas where Muslim and Jewish communities are neighbours.'

Rioters in the *banlieues* were not the only ones to defy the republican state. Separatists in Corsica staged a series of attacks on government buildings and security forces along with straightforward crime. At the 2002 French football cup final, supporters of the team from Bastia whistled at the national anthem in Chirac's presence.

The president had some reason for comfort, however, when his supporters won a majority in parliamentary elections in the summer of 2002 under the banner of a new party, the *Union pour la Majorité Présidentielle* (UMP), while the Socialists and centrists lost significant ground. Jean-Pierre Raffarin, an affable provincial politician from the Poitou-Charentes region of western France whom his boss addressed as *tu*, became prime minister. Dominique de Villepin moved from the Élysée to the Quai d'Orsay, carving out an international position in voicing France's opposition to the US-led invasion of Iraq, which earned the administration popularity at home even if French fries served in Congress were renamed as 'freedom fries' and vice-president Dick Cheney denounced the lack of support from Paris as an 'unpardonable crime'.

At home, the government responded to concerns about security by creating 13,500 new police posts and promising tougher legal enforcement especially against young offenders. Legislation was introduced to modify the thirty-five-hour working week. The retirement age for civil servants was raised, bringing strikes and demonstrations. The government stood firm and earned unpopularity.

Other problems surrounded the president as he entered his seventies. EU talks on immigration and border controls broke down. A right-wing extremist suffering from depression fired two shots at him during the Bastille Day parade in Paris; they went well wide. In regional elections in March 2004, the left took 49.9 per cent of the second round vote compared to 36.8 for the UMP and 12.4 per cent for the National Front. The government was reshuffled with Sarkozy becoming finance minister and de Villepin interior minister. There was some improvement on the economic front, with unemployment heading down to 8 per cent and the state debt shrinking to 2.5 per cent of GDP. But in a referendum in May 2005, 55 per cent of voters rejected a new EU constitution on a turnout of only 66 per cent. That made a change at the Matignon inevitable and Chirac plumped for de Villepin. But his own rating fell further to a historic low of 22 per cent, there were fresh urban riots and a general strike forced the prime minister to abandon an attempt to reform the labour laws.

Yet another murky affair surfaced involving the accusation that de Villepin had instructed a French espionage agent to conduct investigations into the alleged involvement of Sarkozy in a corruption affair stemming from the sale of French frigates to Taiwan. Chirac went on television to defend his chosen dauphin and declared that 'the Republic is not a dictatorship of rumours, a dictatorship of lies.' The president, who suffered a minor stroke in 2005, looked increasingly like a monarch who had outlived his time. It surprised nobody when he appeared on television in March 2007 to announce that he would not run for a third term. He did not endorse any candidate to succeed him.

Though Chirac's memoirs painted Sarkozy as 'irritable, rash, impetuous, disloyal, ungrateful, and un-French', the thrusting younger man's time had come, especially against the aristocratic, poetry-writing prime minister who could not hope to appeal to the everyday concerns of the French. But the electoral cycle meant France was due to turn to the left. To retain power, the right needed a scrappy, hard-charging politician who, asked by a television interviewer if he thought about becoming president when he shaved in the morning, replied with a smile, 'Not only when I shave.'

The right unites, the left less so

After the upset of the 2002 presidential election, the battle in 2007 was far more straightforward for the centre-right. After getting 98 per cent backing from a UMP Congress, Sarkozy ran on a platform that promised to boost economic growth and employment by reducing taxes and deficits, tough law-and-order measures and tighter immigration controls. Things were somewhat more complicated on the left.

The initial Socialist front-runners were the urbane, social democratic former finance and economics minister, Dominique Strauss-Kahn, Martine Aubry, the party secretary who had overseen the introduction of the thirty-five-hour working week in the Jospin government, and Laurent Fabius, prime minister under Mitterrand and leader of the successful 'no' campaign at the 2005 European referendum. But they were all outpaced by Ségolène Royal, president of the regional council of Poitou-Charentes in western France, who had spent a year as environment minister in the early 1990s and had four children with the Socialist first secretary, François Hollande. Known for her authoritarian streak, she called for an expansion of the state sector and public spending and set herself against the party's 'dinosaurs' by stressing the need for new ideas – Jospin denounced her 'pure demagoguery'. An assiduous user of social media and the internet with a site called Désirs d'Avenir (Desires for the Future), Ségo was a tireless and charismatic campaigner who showed not a shred of self-doubt as she won a series of internal debates and got 60 per cent of the vote of Socialist Party members when they named their preferred candidate.

Her opponent in the race for the Élysée aroused dislike bordering on hatred among many on the left. The hammer of the *banlieues*, Sarkozy was a short fuse prophet of law and order whose desire to get things done gave him the appearance of a bully. He sought a wider audience with calls for changes in economic policies, castigating past governments of right and left; he told *Le Monde* that the French had been misled for thirty years by false promises. He called for a simpler and fairer tax system with a maximum total payment of 50 per cent of revenue, reduction of welfare payments to the unemployed who did not take up offers of work, and a reduction in the state deficit. He celebrated the way in which France was finally getting over the 1968 upheaval 'and all its slogans'. Advocating immigration quotas to admit only skilled workers and tighter selection of students from abroad, his language was direct – 'Nobody has to live in France' he said in early 2007. 'But when you live in France, you respect its rules.'

Still, Sarkozy was more muted than usual during the campaign and not simply because advisers told him to control his temper. His second wife, Cécilia, who had acted as his personal aide with an office alongside his at the interior ministry, had left him for a French businessman living in New York. De Villepin intoned that 'a man who cannot keep his wife cannot look after his country'. Sarkozy himself was reported to have had several romantic liaisons.

Though Cécilia returned to Paris as her husband geared up for his presidential bid, she told Sarkozy she wanted a divorce, arranging for him to move out of the conjugal home to stay with a friend during the campaign and resisting his frequent telephone calls to try to get her to change her mind. To go to vote with his wife, the former minister had to sneak into a parking lot under their residence, go up to the apartment and emerge with her.[3]

In the first round of the election on 22 April 2007, Sarkozy headed the poll with 31 per cent to 26 per cent for Royal, 19 per cent for the centrist François Bayrou and 10 per cent for Marine Le Pen, who had taken over from her father as leader of the National Front*. The Communist Party hit its nadir with 1.9 per cent and the Greens did even worse with 1.5 per cent. Turnout was high at 84 per cent with an unusually intense degree of commitment as the right sought a new start and the left proclaimed 'anybody but Sarkozy'. The Socialist establishment ruled out the obvious tactical move, an alliance with Bayrou; the party wanted a clean win on its own. However, Royal telephoned the centrist's home to propose that, in return for his backing, she would make him prime minister if she won. Bayrou was not in at the time, and did not reply to the message she left on his answerphone, probably calculating that she would lose and perhaps not savouring the idea of serving under her.

When the two candidates met in a televised debate, Sarkozy remained cool while Royal went on the offensive, failing, however, to land a decisive blow. With 53 per cent in the second round, he took the presidency at his first attempt. His victory set off riots in Paris and other cities with more than a thousand cars torched and government buildings attacked. Five hundred people were arrested. A celebration arranged that night by Cécilia at the plush Fouquet's restaurant on the Champs-Élysées set the tone for the new administration – though a few politicians were invited, the guest list was crammed with tycoons and showbusiness stars.

Despite setting up the event, Madame Sarkozy only attended after a pleading mobile telephone call from her husband. He went on to a celebratory rally on the Place de la Concorde at which he declared that 'The French have chosen to break with the ideas, habits and behaviour of the past. I will restore the value of work, authority, merit and respect for the nation . . . I want to give French people back the pride of being French – to finish with repentance, which is a form of self-hate.'

Watching on television in the nearby Élysée Palace with his family,

---

* With the founder remaining as Honorary President and his granddaughter, Marion Maréchal-Le Pen playing a prominent role after being elected to the National Assembly in 2012, the party sometimes seemed like a family business, complete with tension between Marine and her father.

Chirac waited for a mention of himself. None came. 'I held back from showing the slightest reaction,' the outgoing president recalled. 'But deep inside I was affected and I knew what to expect.'

As the victor spoke, his wife sidled on to the platform, looking bored, pale and drawn. A Gaullist minister had to take the couple's hands in hers and raise them in a gesture of triumph. When she returned to Fouquet's, Cécilia was in tears. The following morning, after a night in a Parisian hotel, the Sarkozys flew off together for a Mediterranean vacation on a luxury yacht owned by one of their very rich friends, the industrialist and corporate raider Vincent Bolloré. The image spread of the new head of state as an enthusiast for conspicuous consumption of the most expensive kind, a crony of the wealthy who became known as 'President Bling' and who, in what the French call *la psychologie de concierge*, may have been making up for a childhood in which he was less well-off than his companions. 'I want to reform France; then I will earn a lot of money,' he said. He seemed afraid of running short of material goods, buying ten Lacoste sports shirts at a time.

In the inauguration ceremony, the new president declared, 'There is a demand for change. Never have the risks of inertia been so great for France.' He spoke of his desire to foster a 'Mediterranean Union', which France would lead as a new regional grouping to balance the power of Germany and the north European states. He promised to make 'the defence of human rights and the struggle against global warming priorities of France's diplomatic action in the world', concluding: 'The task will be difficult and it will take time.'

Not living up to promises

Sarkozy named François Fillon, a former labour and education minister who had been a campaign adviser, as prime minister. The head of government was a contrast with his boss, a provincial conservative heir to the socially conscious stream of Catholicism and Gaullism. He had been the youngest deputy in the National Assembly when first elected in 1981 at twenty-seven and became a minister at thirty-nine. He never appeared to be in a hurry, casting a reassuring aura around him, drawing on his roots in the deeply rural department of the Sarthe and

The sum of his humiliations

'I am a man of action,' Sarkozy told French journalists when he visited the USA as interior minister. 'I do as I say and I try to be pragmatic.' Self-belief and pride verging on arrogance, a taste for secrecy and drama, a forceful speaking style and a need to show that he was best in class had been the hallmarks of the new president for the past three decades. He made hasty judgments and did not follow through. He would be the hardest working president of the Fifth Republic, but dissipated his energies and lacked persistence – in the words of biographer Catherine Nay 'a fearful daredevil' who flashed a bad-boy smile.

Born in 1955, he grew up in the elegant 17th Paris *arrondissement* in a mansion owned by his maternal grandfather, a Greek Jew converted to Catholicism and a staunch Gaullist. He saw little of his father, a Hungarian aristocrat who founded a successful advertising agency. He suffered at school from being short of stature. 'What made me who I am now is the sum of all the humiliations I suffered in childhood,' Nay quoted him as saying. He failed to graduate from his college, the Institut d'Etudes Politiques de Paris (Sciences Po). Instead he studied law and specialised in business and family cases.

He began his political ascension by attracting Chirac's attention as a young councillor in the right-wing fiefdom of Neuilly run by the Gaullist warhorse Charles Pasqua. When Pasqua fell ill, Sarkozy moved in to claim the post for himself in 1983, becoming the youngest mayor of a town with a population of more than 50,000. Elected to the National Assembly for the area in 1988, he rose to be budget minister in the Balladur government. His backing for the prime minister in the 1995 election earned him a period in the wilderness when Chirac won the Élysée. But he was not a politician who could be kept down and, apart from a brief passage as finance minister, made the interior ministry his own with his law-and-order message and strident support for the police.[4]

keeping to himself his private life with his Welsh wife and their five
children. He was said to have remarked of himself and the new president: 'He will be the legs and I will be the head.'

In keeping with that image, Sarkozy was seen in shorts and trainers running up the stairs at the Élysée with his cell phone glued to his ear. He and
Fillon jogged together in the Bois de Boulogne as a symbol for a more
dynamic and representative cabinet, half of whose members were women,
with only two *énarques*. Putting his conviction for mishandling public
funds behind him, Alain Juppé was named as the second-ranking government minister – for ecology, sustainable development and planning.
The centrist Jean-Louis Borloo, who had made his name as the socially
aware mayor of the depressed northern town of Valenciennes, became
Minister of the Economy, Finance and Employment. Michèle Alliot-Marie
was appointed as the first woman interior minister charged with implementing the president's pet theme of law and order. A new ministry for
immigration, integration, national identity and co-development was created under Sarkozy's close associate, Brice Hortefeux.

Borloo set a target of cutting unemployment to 5 per cent by the
end of the presidential mandate in 2012 while only a third of retiring
civil servants were to be replaced to slim the state payroll. Citing de
Gaulle's admonition that 'France is not the right; France is not the
left; France is all the French people', Sarkozy also broadened his
administration, notably by appointing as foreign minister Bernard
Kouchner, a popular figure as founder of the Médecins Sans
Frontières aid organisation and health minister under both Jospin
and Mitterrand, who had backed Royal; he was promptly expelled
from the Socialist Party. Another Socialist, Jean-Pierre Jouyet, godfather to one of the Hollande-Royal children, was given responsibility
for European affairs. Two immigrant women joined the administration. Rachida Dati, a good friend of Cécilia Sarkozy, became justice
minister, the youngest person ever to hold that post at the age of
forty-one, while Rama Yade, from a small moderate party, was the new
junior Minister for Human Rights.

Sarkozy ran the administration in an extremely hands-on manner – 'I
want to be minister of everything,' he declared. The Élysée staff, headed
by the omnipresent secretary general, Claude Guéant, intervened in

government business as it wished. The president unfurled plans to reform agriculture, social policy and the state. He criticised Russia and China, annoyed Beijing by meeting the Dalai Lama, and spoke of a possible bombing of Iran if it continued its nuclear programme. His administration obtained the liberation of five Bulgarian nurses from Libya where they had been sentenced to death, accused of injecting more than 400 children with the AIDS virus. The president's wife went to bring them out, but the state of their marriage was no better. On a trip to the US, Cécilia refused to join Nicolas at a burger and hot dog lunch with George W. Bush, pleading a severe sore throat though she was seen out shopping the next day. The state of his marriage put the president on edge; he arrived for meetings with tell-tale red blotches on his face and exploded in anger at small failings of those around him. Divorce came the following year.

Still, his supporters captured 45.6 per cent of the vote at the first round of elections for a new National Assembly to the left's 35.6 per cent. But then, Borloo talked of a possible increase in VAT indirect taxation to improve public finances. At the second round of voting, in which the abstention rate soared to 40 per cent, the left made the most of the gaffe and took 227 seats, 184 of them for the Socialists. Sarkozy's followers still headed the poll with 346 deputies but it was not the expected triumph and the president was furious – 'If I don't do things myself, it doesn't work,' he exclaimed as the results came in. But he retained his top team led by Fillon, though Juppé had lost his parliamentary seat in Bordeaux and so had to step down. Despite his gaffe, Borloo was promoted to be second ranking member of the government while Christine Lagarde, a lawyer who had been successively in charge of foreign trade and agriculture, stepped up as Minister of the Economy, Industry and Employment.

For all his rhetoric about change, Sarkozy acted in lawyerly fashion to seek compromise solutions to disputes with powerful vested interests, including the public sector trade unions. Mindful of Juppé's fate when he tried to force the pace after 1995, he pushed through no meaningful reduction in spending; this led to an increased budget deficit, which earned the disapproval of the EU Commission in Brussels. Some real successes were achieved, notably in raising the retirement age in the state sector and reducing privileges enjoyed by railway workers. But the public was not greatly impressed and proposals for a partial ending of the inheritance tax and top-end income tax reductions created the impression of an administration run for the benefit of the rich, including the tycoons Sarkozy frequented. The left made much of the Treasury's reimbursement of 30 million euros from her tax payments to Liliane Bettencourt, ranked as the third richest woman in the world. Nor did the president's decision to double his own salary help, even if this took him only to parity with Fillon, whose long parliamentary career entitled him to significant benefits.

In September 2007, a 54–37 per cent majority of respondents in a poll for the leftist newspaper *Libération* said they were dissatisfied with the administration's record on growth while the margin was even larger, 65–31, when it came to the standard of living. In a typical display of inconsistency, the global economic crisis, which broke that year and deepened in 2008, led Sarkozy to shed the free market leanings he had proclaimed so loudly at his election. 'Laissez-faire capitalism is over,' he declared, denouncing the 'dictatorship of the market' and promising to create 100,000 state-subsidised jobs. 'Have I become a Socialist?' he asked himself in an interview. 'Perhaps,' he answered.

Sarkozy played a major role in Europe's reaction to the economic crisis though he and German chancellor Angela Merkel often did not see eye-to-eye and the Frenchman was forced to recognise the other country's economic primacy. France's presidency of the EU in the second half of 2008 was a success, even if he infringed on the preserves of the European Central Bank and the EU Trade Commission, and his insistence on rejecting Turkey's adhesion annoyed those who thought otherwise. He championed action against Colonel Gaddafi in Libya (despite having lavished attention on the Colonel on a visit to France in 2007 during which the Libyan pitched Bedouin tents at the bottom of the Champs-Élysées and signed deals to buy 10 billion euros' worth of aircraft and nuclear power equipment). He acted as peacemaker in the war between Russia and Georgia, pressed for a stronger European security and defence policy and took France back into the integrated military structure of the NATO alliance, which it had quit under de Gaulle. Visiting Washington, he received eight standing ovations during a speech to Congress. Personally, he found happiness in marriage to the Italian supermodel turned singer, Carla Bruni, though this only heightened his bling image; a majority in an opinion poll said he should live in a style more fitting for a head of state.

The depression of the economy

The economy exercised a grinding depression on the administration as growth fell, unemployment increased and the social security deficit rose to unsustainable levels. The parliamentary majority became restive. At municipal elections in March 2008, the left gained control of big cities; in Paris mayor Bertrand Delanoë's Socialists took 99 of the 163 council seats. The president's response was to opt for stimulus measures regardless of their impact on the state deficit and to become the champion of France's system of social protection, which he had criticised in his election campaign. Increasingly, he was the voice of the status quo – a politician reaching out for any branch that would win him re-election.

For all his activity, a poll placed him only thirty-second among the most admired political figures in the country; top of the list was Chirac whose reputation was, however, soon tarnished when he became the first former head of state since Pétain to be put on trial – for misuse of public money while mayor of Paris, by authorising the payment of cash from municipal funds, nominally for twenty-eight non-existent jobs, but actually to be used for party political purposes. Found guilty, he was given a two-year suspended jail sentence; he did not attend the trial because of neurological problems. Sarkozy also faced persistent allegations, pursued by a dogged investigating magistrate, that he had taken illicit funds for his presidential campaign from his Neuilly neighbour, Liliane Bettencourt, taking advantage of her poor mental health. The accusations were not finally put to rest legally till 2013.

There were rolling demonstrations against pension reform and university unrest about changes that made life more testing for students. Cantonal elections in 2011 gave the left 49 per cent of the vote to the right's 32 per cent with an astronomical abstention rate of 56 per cent – the National Front took 15 per cent of the first round vote. '*Malédiction*,' declared the cover of the news magazine, *Le Point*, after the results came in. Pollsters in Paris said the rating to watch was not Sarkozy's popularity but his unpopularity. One survey found that 63 per cent of respondents did not want him even to seek re-election. For all his rhetoric about law and order, insecurity remained a major concern of ordinary people. Youth crime increased and fear of immigrants with it. French Jews felt increasingly under attack; in March 2012, a French-Algerian, Mohammed Merah, shot dead seven soldiers and Jewish schoolchildren in Toulouse and Montauban. As police surrounded his flat, he ate food heated in his microwave and edited a video clip of his attacks on his laptop. Slipping through the cordon, he posted a memory stick with the video to the al-Jazeera television network (which did not show it). Then he returned home, where he was killed in a shoot-out with police. Alienation of Islamic immigrants increased when it was made illegal for people to cover their faces in public places – the main target was the burqa veil worn by Muslim women.

The Socialists, it seemed, had only to wait, with a winning candidate lined up when Dominique Strauss-Kahn, who had gone to head the IMF in Washington, prepared to return to lead them to end seventeen years of centre-right presidencies. He had a serious international reputation in the subject that most preoccupied the electorate, the economy; and enjoyed a 60 per cent approval rating in the polls. From a well-off Jewish family, DSK, as he was known, was the epitome of the 'caviar left' married to a celebrated television journalist, Anne Sinclair, heiress to an art fortune. He had built up a political base in the poor Paris suburb of Sarcelles and could count on the backing of most of his party. Known as an inveterate womaniser, he had been warned by Sarkozy before leaving for Washington to be careful about his sexual activities since 'the Americans, you know, are not like the French'.

That warning sounded all the more prescient in May 2011, when a maid in the Sofitel Hotel in Manhattan alleged that DSK had sexually assaulted her as she went in to clean his suite. After being subjected to a 'perp-walk', he was indicted, put on $1 million bail, plus a $5 million bond and held under armed guard in his New York apartment. A DNA test matched semen found on the maid's shirt with a sample submitted by the Frenchman. After doubts had been raised about the maid's testimony, the charges were abandoned. He admitted 'inappropriate' behaviour but said he had not used violence, and reached a settlement with the maid. It was the end of his political career as other allegations emerged and he was charged with 'aggravated pimping' for a prostitution ring in Lille – the trial in early 2015 produced lurid evidence about his 'animal' sexual tastes but he pleaded that he had attended only four orgies a year because he was too busy 'saving the world as head of the IMF'. He was acquitted. By then he had sought a new career by creating a hedge fund but his financial partner committed suicide amid accusations of unauthorised trading with money from a client. Still, an opinion poll in 2015 reported that 37 per cent of respondents thought he would make a good presidential candidate for the 2017 election.

The Socialist primary handed the nomination to François Hollande, the party's former first secretary, who was preferred to Aubry. He was credited in the opinion surveys with a margin of up to ten points over Sarkozy. The president played on his opponent's lack of experience in government and pointed to his own international activism. This was, indeed, significant in defending the euro, getting Germany to relax its austere absolutism, chairing an important meeting of the G20 nations in Cannes that helped towards a stabilisation of the global financial situation after the 2007–8 crisis – plus his role in pushing for the attack on Libya that overthrew the Gaddafi regime (overlooking the way he had earlier feted the Colonel on his state visit to Paris). Tacking to the right on social issues, especially immigration, he argued that the economy would have been in even worse straits without him.

In contrast, the Socialist platform called for higher taxation for big companies and the rich, banking reforms, help for industry, 60,000 more teaching posts and the reversal of Sarkozy's extension of the retirement age. Hollande stepped up calls for an easing of EU austerity and championed public spending to create jobs. He pledged to be a 'normal' president in tune with the nation. The real fight was over the judgment voters would make of the two men, the mercurial but experienced attack dog president and his more reassuring but untested rival who promised to be a 'normal' leader.

Ten candidates ran in the first round of the 2012 presidential election. Apart from the president and Hollande, the principal contenders were Marine Le Pen and Jean-Luc Mélenchon, a minister under Mitterrand who had quit the Socialists in 2008 to found his own Left Party. Both favoured protectionism and were hostile to the EU and the common currency. While softening her father's style, Le Pen hammered away about the need for 'national preference' for access to jobs and social welfare, a 95 per cent cut in immigration and the restoration of the death penalty. The swaggering Mélenchon, backed by what remained of the Communists, proposed a 100 per cent income tax for earnings above 360,000 euros a year, full state reimbursement of health costs, easier immigrant naturalisation rules, a reduction of presidential powers in favour of the legislature and proportional representation with gender parity for candidates.

Between them, the two won nearly a third of the vote – 17.9 per cent for Le Pen, ahead of her father's 2002 score, and 11 per cent for Mélenchon. Hollande took 28.6 per cent and Sarkozy 27.2. The eternally hopeful centrist François Bayrou slumped to 9.1 per cent. Though Angela Merkel intervened to say she supported Sarkozy and saw nothing 'normal' in Hollande, the Socialist ran a cool, competent campaign that contrasted with Sarkozy's efforts both to keep mainstream backing and to appeal to National Front voters. His typically energetic campaign won him back some support and enabled him to take 48 per cent on the run-off, but the new president was Hollande who told journalists that he wanted to 'pacify' France with reasonable policies for the population at large.

A president promises to set an example

To mark his divorce from the days of 'bling', Hollande cut ministers' salaries and told them to sign a code of ethics. He vowed to be an 'exemplary' president with a strict separation between his public and personal lives. As in the Jospin era, Green Party leaders joined the government. But what mattered most was the economy, which he had promised to spur into higher growth. Here the new administration fell significantly short. Tax increases took the fiscal burden to nearly 46 per cent of GDP, compared to 41 per cent in 2009, which put France at the top of the EU table. The electoral pretence that only the rich would be hit dissolved as ordinary households were affected and the purchasing power needed for reflation contracted.

Hollande could be decisive in foreign affairs. He took speedy action

Monsieur Normal

Born into a middle-class family with an extreme right-wing doctor father in the Norman city of Rouen, François Hollande moved with his parents when he was thirteen to Neuilly, the smart Paris suburb, which would be Sarkozy's electoral fief. Joining the Socialist Party while at ENA, he worked on Mitterrand's losing presidential campaign in 1974, and became a government adviser after the 1981 victory. He won a National Assembly seat in Chirac's Corrèze *département* in 1988 but remained primarily a party manager, preaching unity between the different factions to little avail as Ségolène Royal went down to defeat in 2007, for which he bore a part of the blame as the main organiser.

She and Hollande had met at ENA and lived together without marrying for three decades, having four children, before announcing after the 2007 campaign that they were splitting up. By the end of that year, he and journalist Valérie Trierweiler had become an established couple; she moved in to the Élysée. But, in 2014, a magazine reported that he had begun an affair with actress Julie Gayet, visiting her at night wearing a crash helmet on a motor scooter driven by a presidential aide. Trierweiler moved out.

As a candidate, Hollande had known how to tune the Socialist machine. He had few enemies. His personal style was reassuringly human, peppered with jokes and buttressed by his provincial experience in the Corrèze. He performed well in debates and was adequate at rousing audiences at mass rallies. But, as president, he alternated between intervening in matters he should have left to the government and adopting a Zen-like calm which could all too easily be seen as evidence that he did not know what to do. He lost weight after a prostate operation and cracked fewer jokes. His personality and style simply did not fit; the nature of the presidency of the Fifth Republic did not lend itself to ordinariness.

when Islamist militants threatened Bamako, capital of the former colony of Mali, establishing a 3,000-strong force to hold back the al-Qaeda allies. French special forces then went into action in Libya. The president had declared himself ready to join in the bombing of the Assad regime as civil war ripped through Syria, only to be isolated when the US and Britain demurred. In 2014, France sent arms to help the Kurds against ISIS. Delivery of two warships being built for Russia was cancelled to penalise Moscow for its intervention in Ukraine, where Hollande helped to broker a ceasefire. (They were later sold to Egypt.)

But, at home, retreats in the face of demonstrations earned disrespect both for the initial measures and then for the later surrender to protests. When Hollande made an attempt in 2013 to get on better with business and persuade entrepreneurs he was not hostile to them, a substantial number of the Socialist Party faithful made it plain they preferred an unreconstructed view of society and economics. Ministers squabbled over policies in public. There was a scandal when the budget minister was found to have a secret bank account in Switzerland.

In Brittany, farmers, fishermen, shopkeepers, industrial workers, owners of small businesses and traders donned red bonnets of the kind worn by protestors against royal taxes in the seventeenth century, set fire to piles of hay by roadsides and brought down bridges in protest against a transport tax which they feared would harm their livelihoods. In the city of Quimper, they fought with riot police and used heavy vehicles to break through the fence of a government building – this in a region where the Socialist held twenty-two of the twenty-seven seats in the National Assembly. Other farmers blocked roads round Paris to protest against the tax and against changes in European subsidies that worked to their disadvantage – a policeman was killed in an accident at one blockade. Less vocal households watched their disposable incomes dwindling and increased the savings they had set aside for a rainy day, further depressing demand, while the number of homeless rose steadily.

Hollande's popularity plummeted and contributed to a terrible showing at municipal elections in 2014. The Socialists managed to hold on to Paris, where Anne Hidalgo became the first female mayor of the capital, but lost Amiens, Limoges, Reims, Saint-Étienne, Toulouse and Tours. The abstention rate reached 39 per cent overall. 'France finds itself in a pre-revolutionary situation,' the news magazine *Le Point* warned. The prime minister, Jean-Marc Ayrault, was replaced with the popular interior minister, Manuel Valls, who was, however, suspect to the Socialist left for his supposedly Sarkozyist toughness on law and order. Ministers from the Green Party quit when the government reached a supply side 'responsibility pact' with companies, under which they were to get tax cuts of 40 billion euros over three years, and public spending was to be cut by 50 billion. 'I love enterprise,' the prime minister cried out at a meeting of employers, noting that this would raise eyebrows in Socialist ranks.

The National Front led the field in European elections in May 2014, with 25 per cent of the vote. The Socialists crashed to 14 per cent, but the results were most damaging for the UMP, which should have capitalised on the administration's unpopularity but finished four points behind the Front. The disarray was compounded by a funding scandal that led the UMP president Jean-François Copé to resign. His great rival, ex-prime minister Fillon, had not established himself as a leader and Juppé announced that he would stand for the presidency in 2017. The man everybody was watching, Sarkozy, was embroiled in allegations that he had taken campaign cash from Gaddafi and had tried to influence a judge. He was re-elected leader of the UMP at the end of 2014, but with only 65 per cent of the vote compared to the 85 per cent he had won in the past. As one of his rivals said, the party was no longer afraid of the former president, who reflected that the 'level of hatred' within the UMP was 'grotesque'.[5]

There were other reasons for the growing public alienation from those who ruled the country. A court launched a formal investigation into one of the few figures of the right who had stayed above the fray, the former finance minister Christine Lagarde, who had succeeded Strauss-Kahn at the IMF, on suspicion of negligence in a political scandal during the Sarkozy administration involving the maverick businessman Bernard Tapie. Lagarde denied culpability, but the case was front-page news.

Then the government was embarrassed when a junior minister, who had been at the forefront in denouncing tax exiles, was found to have failed to declare income to the tax authorities, and had to resign after just nine days in his post. To make matters worse, Hollande's former partner, Valérie Trierweiler, published her memoirs telling of his distant, crushing manner, how he mocked poor people as 'toothless' and how he had scrapped with her in the bedroom when she tried to take pills after reading in the press of his affair with another woman.[6]

By the autumn of 2014, the president's positive public opinion rating stood at a record low of 13 per cent while Valls had plummeted to 30 per cent. 'Never has a head of state been so devalued,' commented the left-wing daily, *Libération*. At a NATO summit in Wales, Hollande appeared grim-faced and flat-voiced as he denied his former partner's allegations, insisted that he had always had the greatest concern for the least well-off members of society, and vowed to continue to the end of his mandate in 2017. But there was no simple way out of the quagmire in which he found himself as the national mood was driven by ever-rising unhappiness mixed with anger. The economic and social challenges were such that the mainstream right could not be eager to form a new government. Only one politician could feel satisfied from all this – Marine Le Pen, of whom an opinion poll in September 2014 showed that she would beat Hollande by 60–40 if a presidential election were to be held then.[7]

The dangerous lady

France has regularly thrown up protest movements on the extremes of its political life: the revolutionaries and extreme royalists of the nineteenth century followed by the anarchists and General Boulanger, the quasi-fascist leagues and Green Shirt farmers of the 1930s, Pierre Poujade's anti-tax movement of the 1950s and then the Secret Army. A decade on from her father's shock performance in the 2002 presidential election, Marine Le Pen appeared set to outdo such predecessors. In the summer of 2013, she declared that the movement she headed would win power within ten years, taking over from the Socialists and the mainstream right whom she labelled as yesterday's men and women, incapable of addressing the nation's core concerns.

That might have been dismissed as typical bravado from an ambitious politician with everything to play for. But election results between 2012 and 2014 at local and national level gave resonance to her claims and frightened the political mainstream on the right, where the Front ate into UMP support, and the left, where it replaced the Communists as the main vehicle for protest. A lawyer by training and a twice-divorced mother of three, Le Pen softened the rough edges which had been her father's delight. Husky voiced from smoking (though she switched to electronic cigarettes), she appeared reassuringly normal as she reflected the broad disdain for mainstream politicians, dismissing the principal parties as an amalgam of the 'UMPS' living in a cocoon that took no account of everyday concerns. To broaden the Front's appeal, she evolved policies on every subject under the sun, though immigration, law and order, 'French first' employment policies and protectionist fear of Europe constituted its core appeal. She recruited a senior aide from ENA, widened her movement geographically and fielded smart young enthusiasts. In the spring of 2015, she reached a point of no return with her father, accusing him of 'a political strategy between scorched earth and political suicide' after an interview in which he defended his comment that Nazi concentration camps were a 'detail' of history, referred to Valls as 'the immigrant' and said Pétain had been treated too harshly. Withdrawing party support from him in regional elections, she accused him of 'vulgar provocations seemingly designed to damage me but which unfortunately hit the whole move-ment'. The patriarch agreed not to stand as head of the Front list in Provence-Alpes-Côte-d'Azur region, but remained a baleful reminder of the party's past. The Front won support among the gay and bisexual communities; one survey found a quarter of gay Parisians voted for it.[8] At the beginning of May 2015, Jean-Marie Le Pen was suspended from the party he had founded. He called her behaviour scandalous and hoped she would marry so that she would no longer shame his name. The row fitted her attempt to de-diabolise the party so well that some cynics wondered if she welcomed it.

It was all a mess, with no evident exit. The high abstention rates at elections showed the degree of public disaffection. Interest groups mobilised to defend their privileges – taxi drivers, tobacconists and hotel owners. Trade unions rose in protest against Sunday shop trading even if many of the workers involved said they wanted to earn some more cash. Factory workers took the law into their own hands to try to stop plant closures. There were fresh outbreaks of urban violence – a riot in the northern city of Amiens lasted for two days and caused damage put at 10 million euros.

Surveys reported that a growing number of people felt their standard of living was slipping and that they could no longer count themselves as belonging to the middle class.

Though an increasing number of immigrant actors appeared in hit films and a vibrant musical culture grew out of French rap, racism was still evident. When Hollande appointed a black justice minister, Christiane Taubira, in 2012, she was abused by demonstrators waving banana skins at her as they shouted 'Who is the banana for? It is for the monkey.' Najat Vallaud-Belkacem, the Moroccan-born education minister named in the post two years later was the target of a flood of racist and sexist attacks.

Anti-Semitism rose further; in May 2014, four people were shot dead at the Jewish Museum in Brussels and a Frenchman of Algerian descent, who was thought to have fought with Islamic radicals in Syria, was arrested for the crime. Israel's reprisal attack on Gaza that summer unleashed attacks on eight synagogues, a kosher supermarket and a pharmacy owned by a Jew. Some participants in pro-Palestinian demonstrations chanted 'Death to Jews' and 'Slit Jews' throats'. Valls denounced 'intolerable' anti-Semitic acts. Yonathan Arfi, vice-president of the Jewish CRIF organisation, said anti-Semitism had become 'a portmanteau for a lot of angry people; radical Muslims, alienated youths from immigrant families, the far right, the far left' and pointed to 'a process of normalisation by which anti-Semitism is being made somehow acceptable'. The comedian Dieudonné was found guilty of encouraging racial hatred and his show banned; but visits to his social media site increased and supporters paraded at a Jewish memorial in Bordeaux giving the 'reverse quenelle', a gesture mirroring the Nazi salute.

Amid these rising ethnic, cultural and religious tensions, education became a battleground far removed from the original ideal of it being the unifying keystone of the Republic. Though the government set out the first mission of schools as being 'to share among pupils the values of the Republic', a growing number of immigrant children rejected mainstream teaching and classroom violence rose. As the journalist Henri Astier noted in 2014, the education system was 'no longer the crucible of national identity; it has become a battleground fought over by strident communities.'[9]

It's the economy, stupid

The economy, the centre of popular concerns, remained resistant to the administration's efforts to promote growth, which was non-existent in the first half of 2014. Having declared in the spring of 2014 that the target of cutting the budget deficit to 3.8 per cent of GDP was 'unmovable', the finance minister Michel Sapin acknowledged four months later that this would not be met. Paris asked, once again, for leniency from Brussels; a Commission spokesman made a pointed reference to the better performance from countries which had pushed through reforms. The head of the German Bundesbank said flatly that France should set an example.[10]

Profit margins of non-financial firms were 12 points below those in Germany, while corporate social security contributions were more than double those across the Rhine. Net earnings at small and medium-sized enterprises were 20 per cent below 2008, with a 40 per cent drop for the construction industry. France slipped to twenty-third place among twenty-five major exporting nations. Unemployment remained stubbornly high; 84 per cent of new jobs in the summer of 2014 were short-term contracts. Job cuts were announced at a range of big companies, but the general morose mood meant that, after flare-ups in 2012–13, they were increasingly met with resignation and declining levels of anger from workers.[11]

Hollande and Valls's policy reversal brought a pledge of 40 billion euros of supply-side tax cuts and reductions in public spending of 50 billion euros. But when the president organised a round table on labour sector reforms, the two main trade union leaders walked out after delivering their speeches. The economics minister, Arnaud Montebourg, attacked government policy and castigated the way in which EU policy was led by Germany. After a couple of his particular outspoken declarations in August 2014, Valls issued an ultimatum to the president – he or Montebourg had to go. The minister was dropped and replaced by a former Rothschild banker who declared himself a liberal social democrat.

Despite this, Hollande and his prime minister looked increasingly isolated as 2015 dawned in the face of the mainstream right, the National Front and the Socialist Party, many of whose members agreed with Montebourg and longed for reflation and further delay in structural change. Such political uncertainty was all the more a matter of concern given the depth and breadth of the problems confronting France as, two hundred years after the Revolution and Empire had ended with the restoration of the Bourbons, the country of Joan of Arc, Louis XIV, Napoleon and de Gaulle found itself increasingly outside its comfort zone but still reluctant to alter its historical character acquired since the storming of the Bastille.

Then came a huge national shock in January 2015, when French Islamic extremists of Algerian origin shouting 'Allahu akbar' (God is great) stormed the Paris office of the satirical magazine Charlie Hebdo, which had run cartoons of the Prophet Mohammed as well as regularly lampooning other religions. It had been the target of previous assaults but continued with its irreverent, anarchic style. Wielding Kalashnikov automatic rifles, two of the terrorists killed twelve people in the office, including the editor and some of France's best-known cartoonists. Outside, they also shot dead a policeman, himself a Muslim, who pleaded for mercy. A third member of the group quickly surrendered; he appeared to have been the driver of their car.

The other two, Said and Cherif Kouachi, who had gone into the offices and committed the murders, were tracked down by a huge police manhunt in a printing works outside the capital where they had taken refuge. Hundreds of armed officers and snipers surrounded the building, with helicopters flying overhead. After eight hours, the brothers, who had vowed to die 'martyrs' deaths', came out firing as they ran. Both were killed and two policemen were injured. Another Islamist, Amedy Coulibaly, linked to them, shot a policewoman dead in the southern suburb of Montrouge and then attacked a kosher supermarket in the district round the Porte de Vincennes, taking nineteen hostages and murdering four before being killed when police attacked the building.

Hollande reacted fast and firmly. He went immediately to the Charlie Hebdo office and declared that 'France is today in shock, in the face of a terrorist attack. We need to show that we are a united country. We have to be firm, we have to be strong.' The government announced tougher anti-terror procedures. In a ringing speech to the National Assembly, where deputies stood to sing the national anthem, Valls said France was 'at war ... against terrorism, Jihadism and radical Islamism'. He not only condemned the attacks but went to the heart of the rising anti-Semitism in France in declaring: 'How can one accept that one hears cries of death of Jews in France, where the Jews were emancipated two centuries ago and was one of the lands of its martyrdom seventy years ago ... there is a historic anti-Semitism, but there is also this new anti-Semitism born in our districts against the background of the internet, of parables, of wretchedness on the base of a detestation of the State of Israel and which preaches hatred of the Jew, of all the Jews. We have to say that. We have to use words to fight this unacceptable anti-Semitism ... Without the Jews of France, France would not be France.'[12]

Demonstrations in cities across the country brought out nearly 4 million people, half of them in Paris where Merkel, British prime minister David Cameron, Israeli prime minister Benjamin Netanyahu, Palestinian president Mahmoud Abbas and EU president Donald Tusk joined the march from the Place de la République to the Place de la Nation. 'Paris is the capital of the world today,' Hollande said. The organisers barred Marine Le Pen from participating. When this became known, the Élysée tried to get the decision reversed but she made the most of the snub by saying that, if she was not wanted, she would hold her own event, in one of the Front's southern strongholds.

Marchers held up placards proclaiming '*Je suis Charlie*' and waved pencils which had become the symbol of solidarity with the slain journalists. Similar demonstrations were held in Berlin, Washington, London and other capitals. A few of those present had banners reading '*Je suis Juif*' or '*Je suis Charlie, Je suis Juif*'. The next edition of the magazine printed 4 million copies which sold out. Big demonstrations against the magazine and its cartoon of the prophet unfurled in Muslim countries and, in France, some Muslim pupils refused to respect a nationwide silence in schools following the killings; teachers reported that some teenagers from Muslim families had taken the side of the killers.[13]

A poll a week after the attacks reported that Hollande's popularity had more than doubled to 40 per cent while Valls rose to 61 per cent. The president told *Le Monde* that France and his presidency had emerged stronger from the terrorism 'ordeal' which had strengthened its values. 'The country has changed the way it regards my presidency,' he added. It was a sobering sign that it had taken such an atrocity to create a sense of national union around the values of the Republic.

Within two months, Hollande's favourable ratings in the polls had fallen from 67 to 25 per cent (and Valls to 45). One survey reported that just 23 per cent believed the president was capable of solving the problems facing the country. In departmental elections in March 2015, the UMP led by Sarkozy staged a striking comeback, increasing the number of councils it controlled from forty to sixty-seven while the Socialists dropped from sixty-one to thirty-four. Though it failed to win control of any councils and was at a disadvantage because of its lack of local organisation in some areas, the National Front still took 25 per cent of the first round vote ahead of the Socialists' 22 per cent. It dropped to 22 per cent support at the second round, where it had fewer candidates compared to 25 per cent for the president's party and 36 per cent for his predecessor's movement, but there was no mistaking the way it had broken through into mainstream politics. The Socialists, fragmented between supporters of reform and traditionalists, lost both Hollande's department of the Corrèze and Valls's base of the Essonne, as well as the traditionally left-wing Nord department, where the Front made gains.

The prime minister pledged to end 'social and ethnic apartheid' affecting immigrants but, when he visited a depressed district of Marseilles, gunfire broke out. Pupils from migrant families at dozens of schools were reported to have disrupted a one-minute's silence decreed in memory of the victims of the January attacks. Ten thousand soldiers were deployed to guard Jewish schools, social centres and synagogues as well as media offices – an assailant attacked one such military protection unit in Nice. More than a hundred graves were desecrated at a Jewish cemetery in eastern France by young people shouting Nazi slogans. A novel by the writer Michel Houellebecq, *Soumission* (*Submission*), depicting a France ruled by a Muslim president who stealthily Islamises the country, became an instant best-seller as debate swirled round multiculturalism and the integrity of the republic.

The attacks of November 2015 greatly accentuated all these issues, as described in the prologue. Apart from the scale of the slaughter and the questions about republican identity, Muslim radicalisation and citizenship, there was a chilling realisation of how national security had been breached, of the mobility which modern communications gave the attackers and the fear that, as Hollande said after the capture of Salah

Abdelsam following a four-month manhunt, the terrorist threat remained very much present, and would do so for long to come. In regional elections the following month, the National Front won 28 per cent of the first round vote compared to 23 per cent for the Socialists and 26 per cent for the Republican Party under the former president, Nicolas Sarkozy, who had taken an uncompromising line against multi-culturalism. At the second round, the Front was well placed to take two key regions – Nord-Pas-de-Calais-Picardie where Marine Le Pen headed the campaign and Provence-Alpes-Côte d'Azur where her firebrand niece, Marion Maréchal Le Pen, led the charge. The Socialist Party's decision to withdraw its third-placed candidates to enable the Republicans to win, plus a higher turn-out, meant that the Front ended up with control of no regions and only 18 per cent of votes in local assemblies, leading to Marine Le Pen to denounce a political caste which was conspiring to 'keep seats, positions, subsidies'.[14]

Though their score rose to 41 per cent of the second round and they took control of seven regions, the Republican leaders were feuding before voting ended. Alain Juppé, who had resurrected his political career after crashing to defeat as prime minister at the legislative election of 1995, set out what amounted to a presidential programme, as did François Fillon. But the former president controlled the party machine and was not a man to give up a fight; admitting to errors as head of state, he promised to do a better job if he was granted another chance. But he was a highly divisive figure, strongly disliked by a lot of people, and Juppé, whose poise contrasted with his attack-dog persona, soared above him in the opinion polls. With that division shaping up on the centre-right, Hollande could find hope in the thought that, if he maintained the unity of the Socialist Party behind him, he could finish second in the first round of the 2017 battle for the Élysée and count on voters rallying against the National Front, as they had in 2002, to give him another five years in office.

THE WEIGHT OF HISTORY

The central argument of this book is that, while justly proud of the nation's achievements since the Revolution, the French have become prisoners of the heritage of their past. The idea of the Hexagon as a model for the world is not one which many people could objectively defend in the twenty-first century, but it remains a potent reason to repel change or foreign influences. The French want to see their country as the bearer of a special mission bequeathed by their history, the Gallic cockerel crowing proudly to the world as they proclaim the historic virtues of the republican civil religion, on the basis of institutions dating back two centuries. If present reality contradicts such a vision, if they prefer to reject economic modernisation in favour of defence of tradition, if their nation has fallen behind its neighbour across the Rhine, if polls in the summer of 2014 showed that 90 per cent of respondents did not believe their elected president could handle the problems facing them, this leaves them feeling deprived of what they feel should be theirs by historic right and opens them to the temptation of extremist illusions.

They prize national unity but also the divisions which fragment it – as André Malraux observed, 'When the French fight for mankind, they are wonderful. When they fight for themselves, they are nothing.' Compromise is suspect; factional, personal and ideological conflicts are more in the tradition of a history marked by discord and periodic recourse to violence even if it is often minimised for the sake of the republican tradition. De Gaulle's remark about the difficulty of governing a country with so many cheeses strikes home*.[1]

The accepted narrative is the one enunciated by Thiers in 1870 when he hailed the Republic as the regime that divides the French least. But the multiplicity of parties that characterised the Third and Fourth Republics was based on catering to local and sectional interests, with regionalism playing an important role even if government was centralised on Paris. Royalist dreams of a restoration after 1848 were dashed not only by the stupidity of the main pretender but by rivalry between competing Bourbon factions. A century-and-a-half later, the self-indulgent fragmentation of the left at the first round of the 2002 presidential election opened the door to Le Pen. Despite Hollande's unpopularity, the mainstream right was split between competing ambitions a dozen years later.

There are two main national honours systems – the *Légion d'honneur* and the *Ordre National du Mérite*. Three major trade union federations compete for members, flanked by several smaller groups. The Islamic and Masonic movements have each been upset by internal political rifts. Rival organisations of hunters put up competing lists at regional elections. Though Basque and Breton separatists quietened down as the twentieth century ended, Corsican nationalists kept up their decades-old agitation and violence to press for autonomy from the Republic.

Occasionally, an exceptional figure, such as Charles de Gaulle, can reconcile the different strands embedded in national life and attitudes round a strong state, though he was always suspect to the left and Vichyite right and seven years was enough to see the waning of his attempt to achieve his 'certain idea' of France. For most of the period covered by this narrative there has been an underlying tension about the way France should go and recurrent challenges to the 'unfinished republic', sometimes spilling over into violence in the supposed home of enlightened reason, notably in the risings of the nineteenth century, Napoleon III's coup, the Commune, the street violence of the 1930s, the fight between collaboration and resistance, the Communist Party's use

---

* According to de Gaulle's wartime associate, General Catroux, the remark about cheese originated with Churchill (Gault et Millau, Guide Gourmand de la France, p. xii Hachette, 1970).

of its labour muscle in the late 1940s, the excesses of Algérie française and the OAS, the student riots and strikes of May–June 1968 – and, in a somewhat different mode, the immigrant tensions of recent decades.

The republican ideal, harking back to the 'good' elements of the Revolution, assumes that France is a nation of progress on the side of the secular angels. But the various narratives of the last two centuries have shown that the country invariably opts for right over left with occasional eruptions to prove that its revolutionary legacy is not dead. Thus, 1830 was followed by the bourgeois monarchy when those unhappy with the system were told that the answer to their complaints of exclusion was to enrich themselves as conservatism was entrenched under Guizot's golden mean. Within four months of the revolution that created the Second Republic, troops were liquidating the worker barricades of the June Days and, in 1851, Louis-Napoleon staged his coup. Twenty years later, the Commune was suppressed with equal bloodshed. The Third Republic was slow to introduce social reforms, shied away from an income tax for decades and denied the vote to half the population. While introducing historic and lasting changes, the Popular Front collapsed after two years and Paul Reynaud set to work to chip away at its legacy.

After the surge of social and economic measures following the Liberation, fear of the Communist Party became an integral element in the Fourth Republic and a powerful anti-republican tide surfaced on the right. The strikes and student riots of 1968 were followed by a massive conservative score at the general election and an administration friendly to big business before more rigorous economic times threatened the inflationary expansion which had underpinned the post-war *trente glorieuses*. When a majority of the electorate found that unacceptable, they opted for the left in 1981 but, within two years, the initial Mitterrand experiment gave way to orthodox monetary economics that exacted a long-term price.

To set against such flaws are the many achievements chronicled in this book which are more than sufficient reasons for national pride. Nor has the more recent story been all negative by any means. An 'anti-declinist' school of thought has pointed to the country's strengths, to its long holidays, short working week, good healthcare, big pensions, long lives and seventy decades of peace after three European wars. The American

Nobel Prize-winning economist and columnist, Paul Krugman, became a cheerleader for the 'France isn't so bad' school. Valls insisted that all the country had to do was to 'throttle declinism'. On the award of Nobel Prizes in 2014 to novelist Patrick Modiano and economist Jean Tirole, the prime minister sent out a tweet declaring 'What a way to thumb one's nose at French bashing! #ProudofFrance.'

Sarkozy's disinclination to bite the austerity bullet in 2008–9 meant that France was hit less hard by the global crisis than its neighbours, its GDP dropping by 3 per cent compared to 5 per cent in Germany. The country managed repeatedly to evade its obligations to the EU to cut its deficit and seemed to enjoy the status of being 'too big to fail' – or to be called to account.

The birth rate was strong. France exercised its military muscle in Africa against Islamic extremists and showed its disapproval of Vladimir Putin's action in Ukraine by suspending delivery of a warship to Russia despite the cost in jobs. Hollande joined Merkel in pressing Moscow to back a ceasefire between the warring parties in Ukraine at the start of 2015. Despite the image of the Hexagon as a nation sunk in the economic doldrums and the effect of the 35-hour week, hourly productivity remained high by international standards and the country housed major companies – if only one was in the global top fifty, thirty-five others figured in the Fortune 500. US investors increased their holding of French stocks by $1.9 billion in the first half of 2014 and the state was able to borrow money at low rates on international markets. Paris fashion houses and luxury-goods makers retained a high degree of chic appeal.

France had major global banks in BNP, Société Générale and Crédit Agricole. It was one of the biggest producers of electricity in the European Union, even if not everybody was happy at the dependence on nuclear power. It ranked third among European vehicle makers and its big car companies reported improving results in 2014 after a series of swingeing cost reductions. The Hexagon stood third among global arms suppliers, clinching big deals with Egypt and India in 2015, proudly announced by Hollande when he received the leaders of those countries in Paris. The Accor group was Europe's biggest hotel chain. France remained a major agricultural power with companies like Danone selling food products all over the world. It had world-class high-tech entrepreneurs; in 2014, maverick telecoms boss Xavier Niel set out to spread his low-cost mobile telephone business to the United States. The state welfare system provided comprehensive care. France was second in Europe for spending on research and development, patents taken out and university doctorates earned.[2]

For all its people's reputation for grumpiness, and the deterrent effect of the terrorist attacks, France retained allure for foreigners; on top of the Hexagon's own attractions, the European Disneyland opened outside Paris in 1992 and, denounced as a 'cultural Chernobyl',* claimed to be the most visited tourist attraction on the continent. The Tour de France was one of the great sports festivals on earth. Despite intense international rivalry, French food was far from suffering the decline attributed to it by enthusiasts for other gastronomic power houses. The nation's villages, towns and cities, its variety of landscape and local cultures are unequalled in their appeal for a country its size.

*

However, for almost every plus advanced by the 'anti-declinists' there was a minus. The shock of the 2008 crisis may have been felt less in France than elsewhere but growth in the first dozen years of the twenty-first century as a whole was extremely slow, and average incomes rose only from 26,100 euros in 2000 to 27,600 in 2013. When the numbers came in for 2014 as a whole they showed growth at 0.4 per cent, consumption rising by the same proportion and investment dropping by 0.5 per cent. For all his enthusiasm for France's anti-austerity policies, Krugman noted regretfully in a 2014 *New York Times* column headed 'Capitulation' that 'once in office, Mr Hollande promptly folded, giving in completely to demands for even more austerity' – a verdict which apparently ignored the trajectory of the first two years of his administration. France's repeated failure to meet its EU deficit targets spurred growing resentment among its partners, especially smaller states which had bitten the austerity bullet. While US investors bought French stocks,

---

* The phrase, originally attributed to theatre director Ariane Mnouchkine, was taken up by a number of commentators.

domestic finance houses sold twice as much in the first half of 2014 and the low interest rates paid by Paris were due to cheap money from central banks rather than a love affair on the part of bond dealers.[3]

The argument that the country's woes with unemployment reflected a national choice for security over opportunity ignored the corrosive effect of high long-term joblessness and spoke of a deep selfishness which ran counter to the nation's claims to be the home of equality and fraternity. It resulted in the paradox that, at a time of high unemployment, one-third of small and medium-sized enterprises (PMEs) said they suffered from having too few workers – but would not hire for fear of not being able to fire if things turned bad. It was also a safe bet that few members of the optimistic camp resided in the depressed former industrial areas where local sentiment seemed better reflected by the increased vote for the National Front.[4]

There might be a lot of babies but fewer and fewer young people could find permanent employment. Too many of the best and brightest business people chose to work abroad, mainly in California or London. A parliamentary survey in 2014 reported that 80 per cent of young people offered jobs in France or abroad preferred to leave the Hexagon while the number of those aged over sixty who had gone to live outside France rose by 10 per cent between 2011 and 2013.

Despite the reputation of state care, 80 per cent of respondents in a poll in late 2014 put health top of their list of concerns and 8 million used private services. Expenditure cuts threatened services. As increasing numbers of doctors moved into the private sector, state hospitals made growing use of interim staff whose charges put further strain on their finances. A scandal erupted in early 2015 over a big hospital in the city of Roanne which had accumulated debts of 173 million euros on a development plan, but which had only half its dozen operating theatres in action, two thousand square metres of its buildings unused and wards without toilets or showers.[5]

Three-quarters of those aged between twenty-five and thirty-five told pollsters they worried about their life-work balance. France had the biggest ratio of welfare to GDP among developed nations, but attempts to spread the burden ran into widespread opposition.[6]

Big firms increasingly drew growing revenues from operations outside

France – and outside Europe as the euro-zone was gripped by deflation. A Renault subsidiary, Dacia, became the continent's fastest-growing car brand in 2014 but it was located in Romania and applied work practices and a cost structure that French unions would not have accepted. While a new boss pulled Peugeot-Citröen back from the brink, he acknowledged that 'we have joined the pack but we haven't overtaken anybody yet.' Accor's healthy 2014 profits came from foreign operations – revenue in France grew by just 0.4 per cent. Manufacturing capacity in the Hexagon in 2014 was 9 per cent below the level of 2007. Corporate margins were low.[7]

The banks ran into major problems, with BNP paying a $9 billion settlement in the US over allegations of sanctions busting, SocGen caught in a big insider trading scandal and the Crédit Agricole plunging into losses. Another prominent French company, the engineering giant Alstom, agreed to pay a $772 million fine to the US Justice Department for having falsified its books and proffered bribes. In early 2016, the Total oil group was ordered to pay 7.5 million euros for siphoning cash from the UN 'oil-for-food' programme for Iraq. Xavier Niel's $15 billion bid to buy the fourth biggest US mobile network, T-Mobile US, was turned down by its owner, Deutsche Telekom. Luxury goods firms were subject to the vagaries of demand in China and other emerging markets.

The state-owned nuclear power developer, Areva, racked up losses of 2 billion euros in 2015, was unable to deliver on a major project in Finland and overpaid for uranium assets in Africa. Its acquisition by the electricity group EDF ran into problems over who would assume responsibility for the Finnish flop and for a six-year delay on another power station in France. EDF, in which the state held an 82 per cent stake, was, itself, in deep financial trouble. It dropped out of the index of 40 top stocks on the Paris bourse, and announced 3,000 job cuts while preparing to sell 10 billion euros of assets. It was also forced to postpone a decision on going ahead with a nuclear project in Britain amid concerns that the funding involved would be beyond it.[8]

No French label figured in a list of fourteen leading global brands drawn up in 2014. At 121,000, the number of small and medium-sized enterprises involved in exports was less than half that in Germany and had stagnated in the twenty-first century while rising by 50 per cent across the

Rhine. France's share in global trade in goods and services fell from 4.7 per cent in 2000 to 3.2 per cent in 2013, less than half that of Germany. While occupying second European place for patents, doctorates and research and development spending, France ranked far below Germany.[9]

The tourist lead was narrowing with the number of visitors remaining static in 2014, ending steady annual increases since 2008. Such was the level of assaults on Chinese visitors to Paris that there was talk of bringing police from the People's Republic, an idea that was dropped when it was realised what it would say about France. The great couture houses might still attract fashionistas to Paris but many of the top designers hailed from outside France. Disneyland Paris ran into fresh financial problems as visitor numbers and their spending fell. The Tour de France was besmirched by recurrent doping scandals.

Questioned about Nobel winner Modiano's work, the culture minister was unable to name any of his books and added that she did not have time to read literature. Commenting on the celebration over the 2014 Nobel awards, philosopher Alain Finkielkraut, a leading critic of what he attacked as France's decline into conformity and multiculturalism, said it only showed the country's desperation – 'There is an economic crisis. There is a crisis of integration. I am not going to be consoled by these medals made of chocolate.' Robert Frank, a history professor at the Sorbonne, suggested that the official response reflected a country lacking in self-confidence; in earlier centuries, he noted, the prize had been greeted as something natural for a great nation.[10]

The ceasefire Hollande helped to broker for Ukraine in 2015 proved fragile and, while the axis between Paris and Berlin had been revived for the occasion, their differences on economic policy remained sharp. In general, France's international political clout was constrained globally except in former colonial territories in Africa. Not everybody took comfort from its position among the top global arms suppliers given that the big contract signed at the start of 2015 was with a repressive military government in Cairo. Its leadership of the European project established in the 1950s and reinforced by de Gaulle, Giscard and Mitterrand had been severely undermined by the ascent of Germany. The inability of both Sarkozy and Hollande to resist the imposition of austerity policies on Europe at Berlin's behest was all the more galling because they knew that Merkel and her colleagues were going too far and choking off the growth revival which France so badly needed for the sake of domestic opinion across the Rhine.[11]

*

One by one, the icons that underpinned the nation for so long fell by the wayside. The franc gave way to the euro common currency in 2002 and supervisions of monetary policy moved to the European Central Bank in Frankfurt. Churches cut services and France counted more psychiatrists than priests. Even with state subsidies of 400 million euros a year, newspapers suffered even more than their peers elsewhere.

The status of the French language had declined from the days when it was the lingua franca of diplomacy and denoted international smartness. The number of posts in French on the United Nations website was one-fifteenth of those in English. The Polish politician, Donald Tusk, who became president of the EU Council in 2014, did not speak French. The mix of English and French terms known as Franglais became so entrenched that television news bulletins tell of planes which have *crashé* while beauticians offer un *relookage**.

Despite government protection of *l'exception culturelle*, the arts were not what they had been. While French cinema remained strong on the back of state subsidies, the country ranked only twelfth in the world book publication stakes as recorded by the United Nations. A survey of 20,000 readers conducted by the magazines *Foreign Policy* in the US and *Prospect* in Britain that listed leading global public intellectuals named just two Frenchmen, the philosopher and sociologist Alain Finkielkraut and Jean Baudrillard – Baudrillard had lamented that, 'We accept only what we invented . . . There are no more French intellectuals.' As the literary historian, Antoine Compagnon, put it, 'We have long thought ourselves the best, but France these days is an average cultural power, a good average cultural power.' This might be all that could be expected

_____

* This was not the first time the French had adopted English terms; it was smart to do so in the mid-eighteenth century when words such as *rosbif, paquebot, partenaire* and *budget* were adapted from over the Channel. (Rey et al. p. 116).

for a mid-sized state but it fitted badly with the image the French have of the home of Descartes, Flaubert, Balzac, Hugo, Proust, the Impressionists and all the other national icons.

The massed battalions of organised labour are long gone with trade union membership of just 8 per cent of workers. Graduates of the top finishing schools led by the École Nationale d'Administration (ENA) set up by de Gaulle's faithful follower, Michel Debré, remained unmatched in superior brilliance, but the education system at the heart of the republican model had run into difficulties. It failed to adapt to the demands of society as a whole and functioned largely to produce a thin slice of bright pupils while leaving the mass of students wallowing behind. Free tertiary education was open to all and 37 per cent of young people entered universities but 41 per cent then dropped out, compared to 20 per cent in Britain and 30 per cent in Germany.

The teaching trade unions have resisted reform and enjoyed powerful political backing from the Socialist Party to which they contributed most of their votes. Vocational training was poor, especially in comparison to Germany. There was increasing tension between parents and teachers as the traditional republican idea of education acting as a means of social ascension frayed and the becalmed jobs markets made it more difficult for graduates to find employment. Enrolment at private schools rose steadily to reach 2 million nationally in 2014, accounting for 29 per cent of all pupils in Paris and 40 per cent in Rennes.[12]

Or look at a traditional source of French pride – food. Though the oft-proclaimed death of French cuisine was nonsense, restaurants increasingly used ingredients from industrial suppliers to reduce costs and balance the rising price of labour; one estimate put at one-third the number of establishments serving meals made entirely or partly outside. Eighty per cent of croissants were reckoned to be made in food plants in the early twenty-first century. Some 13,000 bakers shut in the previous three decades – the head of the national bakers' institute said in 2014 that 60 per cent of apprentices in the trade wanted to work abroad.

Cafés closed in growing numbers and those that survived were less frequented than before; the old customs of having a few glasses of wine or beer or *apéritifs* after work fell out of fashion as people hurried home or simply saved cash. Fast-food outlets proliferated – McDonald's had 1,300 outlets in France in 2014, one of the highest levels in Europe; inhabitants of a northern town took to the streets that summer to demand that the local authorities lift a ban on the opening of a branch. A leading Paris chef estimated that the tax and labour laws meant that it was almost twice as expensive to run a restaurant in France as in Britain.[13]

As for drink, in 2014, France exported more vodka than cognac. Only 17 per cent of the population drank wine nearly every day – Chirac had preferred beer (Mexican before he switched to Kronenbourg) while Sarkozy was a teetotaller. A survey the following year reported that only 3 per cent of those polled said they were well versed on the subject of wine while 43 per cent replied that they knew nothing at all about it. As for two other emblematic elements of French cuisine – imports made up 80 per cent of the estimated 40,000 tons of snails consumed annually in the Hexagon while most of the 3–4,000 tons of frogs' legs eaten each year came from abroad.[14]

In 2005, Chirac remarked of the British that 'you can't trust people whose cuisine is so bad'; a decade later, Marks & Spencer had ten stores in Paris selling food, and planned to double the number – it sold 70,000 Indian ready-meals a year from one outlet. Despite the lack of accents in its name, the British fast food chain Pret A Manger enjoyed similar expansion while the French bought 22,000 tons of cheese from over the Channel in 2013.[15]

For those who still smoked cigarettes, pungent Gauloises and Gitanes, those hallmarks of café life and French films, had been replaced by lighter brands. By 2014, there was only one factory making the traditional headgear of the beret worn down the ages by farmers, soldiers, printers, right-wing militias and the Bouncing Basque tennis star, Jean Borotra. The 164-year-old Norman biscuit and cake maker which had provided Proust's madeleines went into liquidation at the end of 2013 and was only preserved after its twenty-five workers occupied the premises and raised 59,000 euros by crowd funding. Similarly, donations were needed to save the country's oldest accordion factory, on Hollande's home turf of Tulle, including one from Arsenal football player Laurent Koscielny, who was born there.[16]

One thing that did not change was the readiness to strike, the weakness of unions hampering German style workplace agreements. In the autumn of 2014, professions ranging from taxi drivers and law court officials to driving instructors and temporary showbusiness workers took action against government measures to reduce their welfare entitlements or remove their privileged positions and open them up to market competition. Chemists closed their shops to protest at proposals to end their monopoly on selling even the simplest patent medicines. Highly paid pilots at Air France (16 per cent owned by the state) staged a two-week stoppage against plans by the company to develop its low-cost airline with lower pay for staff – this ended inconclusively but the cost was put at 416 million euros for a firm that had lost 1.8 billion euros the previous year. When two railway employees were suspended for drinking rum punch while operating signals, the union called a strike in their defence.

All of which reflected deepening disaffection. Too many people had the nagging sense that the country was not living up to itself and that they were the victims. The left, meant to be the vanguard of progress, had become infused with a conservative, corporatist spirit that put defence of privileges above social justice. The mainstream right was divided and unsure where it stood in a changed world. All of which could only encourage a search for comfort at the political extremes.

'Society dreams of revolution but, in fact, is repelled by change,' in the words of the Giscardian minister and historian Michel Poniatowski. Or, as the old truism has it, the French wear their hearts on the left, their wallets on the right. The resulting conservatism stretched throughout society when privileges came under attack. Each group always had an argument against change but this selfishness sat ill with the broader idea of fraternity and social cohesion that the Republic was meant to embody. It also damaged France's ability to compete in a world in which low-growth developed nations such as the Hexagon were vulnerable to the challenges of globalisation and the rise of Asia. French consumers were hit, too – a study in 2014 showed that prices in sectors protected from foreign competition rose by 25 per cent between 2000 and 2010 while those exposed to competition fell by 10 per cent.

A Gallup Poll in 2013 found the French to be among the most depressed people on earth. The following year, the international organisation UNICEF published a survey reporting that 43 per cent of adolescents in France suffered from psychological difficulties; 41 per cent consumed alcohol and 32 per cent drugs. Homelessness rose by 50 per cent between 2001 and 2012. France stood in forty-fifth place in the World Economic Forum's index of gender equality in 2013. That year, a poll in *Le Monde* reported that three-quarters of respondents thought French democracy was not working well, that 62 per cent saw politicians as corrupt and that more than 70 per cent wanted a 'true chief' for the nation. The abstention rate showed the degree of disillusion with orthodox politics – at regional elections in 2015 it hit 50 per cent.[17]

For many, the fact that France was not what it used to be – or what they imagined it used to be was cause for a sadness that went beyond transient disgruntlement, and was given a special edge by the conviction that history had granted the Hexagon a special role as what Chirac called 'a beacon' for humanity. On all sides, present realities conflicted with that aspiration, fostering a melancholy that could turn visceral when exploited by extremist politicians, bolstered by the disjunction between the ruling elite and the mass of the population.

The transformation affected all parts of the nation. The rise of the National Front reflected more widespread worries among those from outside the immigrant community about the increasingly multi-ethnic nature of society, which successive governments either ignored or were unable to assuage. Even before the 2015 terrorist attacks, concern about law and order was widespread – data in early 2014 showed reported cases of physical violence increasing by more than 10 per cent since the same period of 2013, with an average of 100 attacks a day in Paris.

A much-needed plan to redraw the administrative map of France into fourteen regions to lessen the multi-layered millefeuille of local government produced nostalgia for familiar old names and an unwillingness to share costs; a survey found that 77 per cent said they did not want to see their existing region disappear. Despite the central and generally cherished role of the state, there was growing hostility towards its central actors, the 2.2 million civil servants who were seen both as unproductive and as imposing unpopular measures on behalf of out-of-touch authorities. A 2013 poll reported that reducing their numbers and making them undertake longer working hours were two of the most popular potential policies with the public.

As ethnic tensions rose, a survey in 2014 reported that people thought immigrants made up 31 per cent of the population, nearly four times the actual proportion. Polling of voters for the UMP centre-right party that year showed the proportion which believed there were too many immigrants in France had risen to 87 per cent, from 62 per cent in 2006 – those who felt they lived in conditions of insecurity had increased from 38 to 73 per cent in the same period.[18]

Demonstrations against Israel spilled over into attacks on synagogues and Jewish individuals and property. Instead of being fomented by classic extreme right-wing agitators with their roots stretching back to Dreyfus and Panama, anti-Semitism was now driven by mainly young immigrants with Arab and North African roots, the very people whom the far right saw as the main threat to national identity. Experts charted at least three waves of anti-Semitic violence in France since 1980, coinciding with heightened tension between Israel and its neighbours. As a contributor to *Le Monde* put it in 2012 this 'confirms a grim reality; there are groups in France determined on violence against Jews'. Israel's reprisals on Gaza after Hamas rocket attacks in 2014 unleashed assaults on eight synagogues, a kosher supermarket and a pharmacy owned by a Jew.

Interior ministry figures showed that anti-Semitic attacks and threats had nearly doubled in France in the first seven months of 2014 to 529 compared to 276 for the same period of 2013. Jewish organisations expressed 'growing unease that oppresses Jews in France each day and overshadows their future'. As CRIF's vice-president, Yonathan Arfi, noted, anti-Semitism had become 'a portmanteau for a lot of angry people; radical Muslims, alienated youths from immigrant families, the far right, the far left' amid 'a process of normalisation by which anti-Semitism is being made somehow acceptable'. Seven thousand French Jews emigrated to Israel in 2014, and, after the Paris attacks the following January, Benjamin Netanyahu appealed to others to follow suit, arousing criticism from Jewish leaders and the Hollande administration.

The government promised tougher measures. But it was hard to see how the poison could be lanced without a far deeper rethinking of France's immigration policy and it was probably too late for that. Muslims resented the fact that while anti-Semitism is outlawed as hate speech, France's secular tradition means that blasphemy is not, with no sanctions against anti-Islamic language. Dieudonné might be found guilty of encouraging racial hatred and his show banned; but he continued to play to packed halls, fans said they saw him as primarily anti-establishment rather than anti-Semitic but his message remained unwavering. After the 2015 attack on the kosher store in Paris, he posted a message on Facebook declaring 'I feel like a supermarket killer.'

In May 2014, a Frenchman of Algerian descent who was reported to have fought with the Islamic State in Syria was arrested after the murder of four people at the Jewish Museum in Brussels. There were estimated to be 1,400 radicals from France with the extremist forces in Syria/Iraq or on their way there, far more than from Britain and Germany. A Socialist deputy from the Paris *banlieue*, Sébastien Pietrasanta, who had worked for an anti-racist organisation, noted that 'for some young people, the feeling of having a religious affiliation is stronger than the feeling of belonging to the Republic.'[19]

Then came the attacks in Paris in January 2015. They represented an obvious challenge to the values of the secular Republic, a theme very evident in the huge demonstrations that followed. But they also brought out the extent of the growth of Islamic fundamentalism within that secular Republic which no demonstrations were going to dispel – and raised questions about how the authorities were dealing with people they knew could turn to terrorism as well as providing a tragic illustration of how immigration policy had not worked, how dysfunctional life was for many children of those who had come to work in France in the previous century.

The Kouachi brothers who carried out the massacre at *Charlie Hebdo* had been part of a jihadist group of young men whose families had emigrated from North Africa, which met in the Buttes-Chaumont park in northern Paris. In their early twenties, they had been to a local school but had poor educational records. They lived in a world of petty crime, drugs and gang warfare. They came under the influence of a young man from the local mosque who led what *Le Monde* called 'the first jihad school in France'. Chérif Kouachi, a pizza delivery man, had been stopped by police as he tried to board a plane to Damascus in 2005. Brought to court, he said he had not really wanted to join the fighters in Iraq, but was afraid of being regarded by his peers as a coward. He described himself to police as a 'ghetto Muslim', according to *Le Monde*. A French television documentary on radicalised youth showed him talking about how he learned that 'it's written in the texts that it's good to die as a martyr'. He was given an eighteen-month suspended prison sentence. He married and got a job at a supermarket fish counter.

A source who knew Chérif Kouachi at the time of his arrest told the *Guardian*: 'He was abandoned very young ... he was put in care homes early – before the age of ten.' When he emerged as a young man, the source went on, 'he was living almost like a homeless person ... very clearly marginalised. He was immature, just out of adolescence. He wasn't vindictive ... He went to the mosque, but went clubbing, made rap music, smoked hash, drank.' The preacher at the mosque 'made him feel important, he listened to him, recognised him as an individual ... Chérif Kouachi was fragile, looking for a family ... he didn't have a family he could turn to for support.'[20]

His elder brother Saïd, who did most of the shooting in the *Charlie Hebdo* attack, had spent time in Yemen where he was believed to have fought for al-Qaeda. He was questioned by French police about the Buttes-Chaumont jihadi cell in 2005 and was kept under surveillance. But this was lifted seven months before the assault since the counter-intelligence agency had no evidence that he was planning anything and had other priorities tracking young Muslims going to fight in the Middle East.[21]

The attacks brought out how French jails act as an incubator for extremism; Muslims constituted 60 per cent of prison inmates in 2013, according to a parliamentary report, compared to 7.5 per cent of the total population. Between his arrest while trying to fly to Damascus and his court appearance, Chérif Kouachi was held on remand in Fleury-Mérogis prison south of Paris. A huge decaying structure, it holds 3,800 people in its men's section – 150 per cent overcrowding – and was known for its violence between inmates, drugs, suicides, insalubrity and attacks on warders. After the conditions had been publicised through a video smuggled out, a renovation programme was launched.

One of the prisoners involved in the video was Amedy Coulibaly, an armed robber on his third sentence, son of parents from Mali who was born in a housing estate at La Grande-Borne, south of Paris, described by a local parliamentary deputy as a 'social dustbin' marked by 40 per cent unemployment, crime, poverty, trafficking of drugs and weapons, arson and attacks on police. Coulibaly and Kouachi met in prison where they became friends. They also found a mentor, Djamel Beghal, who had once been a regular worshipper at Finsbury Park Mosque in London and a disciple of radical preachers there. He was serving a ten-year sentence for a plot to bomb the US embassy in Paris.

After his release, Coulibaly was among those invited to the Élysée to meet President Sarkozy at an event on the perennial problem of youth unemployment. 'At least he might be able to help me get a job,' Coulibaly told a newspaper. But a police investigation into a suspected plot to free an Algerian convicted of bombing a Paris station showed that the two men had been visiting Beghal, who was under house arrest in central France; there Coulibaly photographed his wife who was wearing a niqab costume and firing a crossbow. The two were detained and Coulibaly was sentenced to five years in prison for the escape plot – Kouachi was released for lack of evidence.

Coulibaly left prison in 2014 and staged the attack on the kosher supermarket the following year after killing a policewoman in the suburbs; he had kept in touch with the Kouachis by telephone messages on the day of the assaults in Paris. Press reports said that an earlier examination of him by police diagnosed an 'immature and psychopathic personality', a lack of a sense of morality and a desire to be 'all powerful'. After shooting four hostages, he made himself a sandwich from the supplies in the store, telling the remaining captives to do the same.

Reacting to the revelations about prison contacts, the government said Islamist detainees would be housed separately from the rest of the prison population. It announced the launch of civic education courses in schools aiming to strengthen patriotism, respect for all religions and the country's secular tradition. Politicians lined up to denounce the terrorism. Hollande acknowledged that the national mood of unity expressed by the mass demonstrations after the attacks could prove fragile, but told *Le Monde*, 'My own belief and pride in the values of our republic have been reinforced.' Marine Le Pen said people should not confuse the terrorists with peaceful Muslims, but also repeated her call for the reintroduction of the death penalty. 'Our country has never experienced so much barbarism for decades,' she said. 'The nation is united to say that we, the French people, regardless of our origins, will not accept this attack against our freedoms and against our lives ... but we have enough intelligence to know that those attacks against us are not the consequences of fate. These are trained men with a deadly ideology who are murdering millions across the world.'

Her message had traction. A month after the attacks, the National Front candidate finished ahead of a UMP rival in a by-election in eastern France. Despite the short-lived jump in Hollande's support, the first opinion poll to be published after the killings reported that Le Pen would win the most votes if a presidential election were held immediately – 30 per cent. The president, the poll predicted, would be knocked out in the first round. The terrorist shock with its dramatic demonstration of home-grown jihadism in contravention of all the values of the Republic had not banished the broader concerns of the nation, even while underlining the depth of the immigration problem the Republic had failed to handle. That became ever more starkly clear after the attacks in November 2015, described, with their repercussions, in the prologue to this book.

*

A sociological study in 2014 reported that the standard of living of those in their thirties had declined by 17 per cent compared to those twice their age. The Pew Research Center in 2013 found that only 9 per cent of the French thought their children would be better off than the previous generation. The number of French people taking foreign jobs doubled to 1.6 million in the two decades up to 2013. A quarter of graduates told pollsters they saw their futures as lying outside the Hexagon; those who went abroad were, unsurprisingly, the most qualified – 53 per cent had higher education compared to 12.5 per cent of the total population.[22]

Politics offered no escape; very much the contrary, even if France's political class remained highly entrenched and numerous – with twice as many members of its legislatures as in the USA. Some of those who recognised the need for change clung to the status quo. The loss of presidential authority and status removed an essential element of the Fifth Republic – to the point at which, before the January attacks and his impressive response, commentators compared Hollande to René Coty of whom it had been said that his only job was to open flower shows. For all its new-found enthusiasm for reform, the administration was constrained by its desire not to provoke a massive movement of rejection, as the president battled to preserve his electoral base on the left for the 2017 election.

'We have lived beyond our means for the last forty years,' the prime minister acknowledged, but he also insisted that the social system, prime cause of that over-spending, would be defended. In early 2016, in the face of street and trade union protests, the administration swiftly pulled back from its proposals to free up the labour market to go with a relaxation of the thirty-five-hour working week. The pledge to spur growth looked increasingly like an electoral mirage put up by a president who lacked substance and would always opt for half measures.

When the Valls government advanced steps to open up some economic sectors, the modesty of the changes reflected both the power of entrenched interests and the desire not to upset established ways of life, on the left as much as on the right. While a prohibition of long-distance bus services to safeguard the railways was lifted, pharmacies were left with monopoly powers to sell simple patented medicines and notaries kept their privileged position. The measure which attracted the most attention, the liberalisation of trading on Sundays, ended up by still capping the number of days permitted at twelve a year, with total freedom restricted to major tourist areas in Paris. Still, unions protested in the name of the workers and a rebellion by left-wing deputies forced the Prime Minister to push the legislation through without a parliamentary vote in early 2015; the rebels came into line when the opposition put down a censure motion but the degree of resistance to change in Socialist ranks was evident*.

At the summit of its republican politics, France was caught in a never-ending and divisive fight for the presidency which was meant to stand for the nation but had become the object of partisan rivalries and con-tinual equivocations – as Giscard remarked in 2014, 'if you tell the French the truth and propose a remedy, you are sure to be beaten.' People, he added, imagined they could continue to live as a century ear-lier, without taking into proper account the transformation that had occurred since then. Understandably, they found it hard to accept that, every year since 2005, Germany had recorded a trade surplus rising to a record 217 billion euros in 2014 while, in the same period, France had been steadily in deficit. Or that the state deficit which the government said would fall to 0.7 per cent of GDP by 2019 was forecast by the state audit commission to rise steadily. When the national statistical office reported in February 2015, that growth for the previous year had amounted to 0.4 per cent, with a major drop in demand and invest-ment, the Finance Minister, Michel Sapin, was reduced to taking comfort from the fact that the figure was the same as the government's forecast for the first time for a long period.[23]

Once in the Élysée, heads of state saw their popularity crumble, most strikingly in the case of Hollande. That could only strengthen their underlying belief that the French people were, at heart, regicides who should be pacified for fear that their attachment to the notion that they had the right to overthrow regimes from below would lead to a rerun of 1789, 1830, 1848 or 1870. So they coddled the population to protect them from the reality that the *Trente Glorieuses* were long gone and that the world had become a harsher, more competitive place.

The idea of national unity round the head of state which underlay the

---

* The fact that the Economics Minister who drew up the proposals, Emmanuel Macron, had been an investment banker before joining Hollande's staff and replacing the left-wing standard bearer, Arnaud Montebourg, as a minister did nothing to endear him or his ideas to colleagues of the left of the Socialist party.

establishment of the Fifth Republic was ridiculed by the degree of divisions and the disdain in which many held the men elected to France's top post in 2007 and 2012, a feeling reinforced by the unpresidential demeanour of both Sarkozy and his Socialist successor who went to visit a mistress at night on the back of a motor scooter. Just as Sarkozy had veered away from his electoral programme of reform soon after winning power, so Hollande's zigzagging left his administration 'without a spine', in the words of one academic observer. After more than three decades of abdication of leadership at the top, France risked becoming 'a state emptied of its power' as Jacques Attali, presidential adviser to Mitterrand, Sarkozy and Hollande put it.[24]

When Sarkozy proposed to stage a return to power on the back of a broad centre-right coalition, a poll showed that 80 per cent of his potential supporters wanted him to retain the platform the electorate had rejected in 2007, or to move further in that direction. For all the ex-president's ambitions, the right was in bad shape with internal divisions and scandals. Le Pen offered a different recipe, harking back to a Napoleonic idea of direct contact between ruler and ruled, bypassing the representative institutions of the Republic. Her mix of policies might be distinctly questionable but the Front threatened to upset the traditional dominance of mainstream conservatism, claiming that its stronger version of the state was the way to correct the country's ills, a seductive offer at a time when fourth-fifths of non-left wing voters told pollsters they backed tougher immigration and penal measures.

The Front's appeal to mainstream politicians of the right was shown vividly in the number of them holding local government positions who backed its candidates in the 2014 Senate elections – in the depressed northern department of the Aisne, where the Front had won 40 per cent of the European election vote and held thirty-six elected local government posts, it got the backing of 131 electors from other parties. The Front won no regions in the elections the next year but topped the first round poll with 28 per cent of the vote.[25]

The Fifth Republic seemed to have become dysfunctional, but there was no mainstream figure to engineer a change towards a new form of politics, only the prospect of the continuing rise of the Front and its savvy chief. The perennial nature of the political class led to a feeling that

France was run by a self-enclosed elite impervious to rejection – if Mitterrand had set a long-distance record with the thirty-four years that elapsed between his first ministerial post and his successful presidential bid of 1981, both he and Chirac had two tilts at the Élysée before becoming president; Sarkozy's defeat in 2012 did not stop him aspiring to get back the top job five years later; Hollande had been a political operative since 1981. As Alain Juppé, who had come back from extreme unpopularity and a suspended prison sentence for mishandling public funds as a senior minister and opinion poll favourite for the presidency in 2017, once observed, in French politics 'only physical death counts, otherwise there is always the possibility of resurrection.'

There was a basic question stretching back more than two centuries over the nature of the system which had ruled France under republics, monarchy and empire. Was French democracy 'unfinished', as the historian Sudhir Hazareesingh has put it, and the republican tradition far less deeply rooted than the popular consensus believed? What place was there for popular revolt against the state of the kind epitomised by the act consecrated in the major national holiday? Was it the case, as the historian François Furet wrote, that 'the reason we are so unhappy today is that we no longer have a revolutionary idea. It is as if our political civilization has been truncated.'[26]

Amid the protests against Hollande's policies and the administration's inability to handle them, the editor of the middle-of-the-road news magazine, L'Express, was moved to speculate in 2013 about the possibility of a broad revolution in which working people would dodge tax, managers would refuse to fill up forms and the unemployed would revolt against a system which did little to help them find jobs. As the head of one opinion poll firm noted, 'One sees very different social groups mobilising against the central authority, and the traditional remedies have reached their limits. It is as if grassroots France is in rebellion against the central state.' A writer in Le Figaro in 2014 noted that, while France housed 66 million inhabitants, it had '99 million subjects of unhappiness' ranging from high unemployment and frozen civil service salaries to women earning 19 per cent less than men in equivalent jobs and 8.7 million living below the poverty line.

Valls signified the shift of policy by announcing that the 75 per cent tax on top incomes would be abolished, but this had always been a symbolic matter with little actual impact on the economy. The EU Commission called on France to revise its budget for 2015 to reduce the forecast budget of 4.3 per cent, nearly 50 per cent higher than the target set by Brussels. Hollande and Valls hoped for a common pro-growth front with Italy and the prime minister proclaimed that France would not redraft its budget to satisfy the EU Commission since 'we are a great nation ... France is a sovereign country'.

The prospect was for either deeper cuts that reached into the local government services the French had taken for granted, along with the continuing strain of slower growth, or a deepening of national anxieties. For all Valls's brave words, the budget was shaved to placate Brussels and sovereignty was once more compromised by France's economic weakness. A book entitled *Le Suicide Français* became a runaway bestseller in 2014 as it proclaimed that 'France is dying, France is dead', killed by 'a vast subversive project' driven by globalisation, immigration, feminism and the EU bureaucracy. For those able to afford it there might be a certain masochistic satisfaction to be drawn from the situation in which the country found itself; 'bleak is chic', as the *Economist* put it. But not for the ranks of the unemployed and the growing mass of people whose loyalty to the historic system was bound to be put under strain by the failure of leaders who so repeatedly did not live up to their promises.[27]

It is all too easy to draw parallels with the pre-1789 era when Louis XVI's minister, Charles Alexandre de Calonne, remarked that it was 'impossible to increase taxes, disastrous to keep on borrowing and not enough to cut expenses'. In the middle of the second decade of the twenty-first century, as in the 1780s, France had an unpopular ruler playing with reform but constrained by defenders of the status quo, an indebted economy falling behind that of a northern neighbour, a discontented middle class and unhappy workers, all against the backdrop of radical challenge from those who wanted systemic change. Then it faced a rising rival with a stronger economy in the shape of Britain; today that role is played by Germany where the cumulative growth between 2005 and 2014 was almost twice that within the Hexagon.[28]

Both past and present point to the need for adaptation, and respondents in some polls showed a greater readiness to consider change – but for others, not themselves. The die was certainly not cast on the side of positive change, as reflected in the sharp drop in the popularity of reformist prime minister Valls, the influence of the unchanging left in the ruling party, the high standing of the National Front and the continuing caution of Hollande. Successive presidents and governments had applied a self-serving logic in refusing structural reform to the economy – if times were hard and growth was low, it was held to be impossible; if things were going better and there was expansion, there was no need to change anything. It was an evasion of reality, and of necessity, which sat ill with the supposed rationality of national Cartesian thought. But it was politically convenient just as the Bourbon manoeuvres of the eighteenth century had suited the king and his court while leading to their disaster.

The level of unhappiness two centuries after the Revolution and the Empire ended with the restoration of the monarchy was, at base, rooted in a determination to stick to an image of the French nation which had been outpaced by the changing world that encompasses the Hexagon. Old assumptions no longer worked, especially when confronted by the open-ended 'war' with terrorism and the new forms of social division which had become ever more evident in the twenty-first century. But a realistic alternative acceptable to a majority of the French people was absent and there was a signal lack of politicians ready, and able, to rally the country behind a new course. France had become the prisoner of its history and its many embedded narratives.

NOTES

SOURCE NOTES

Econ – Economist, FH – French History (Oxford), FS – French Studies (Oxford), FT – Financial Times, Gdn – Guardian, Mon – Le Monde, Fig – Le Figaro, NYT –New York Times, PM – Paris Match, WSJ – Wall Street Journal,

PROLOGUE: A REPUBLIC AT WAR

1 Barometer: *Econ*, 21 Dec 2013.
2 Hollande: Grigny, *Gdn*, 23 Oct 2015.
3 Buttes-Chaumont: *Mon*, 19 Nov 2015.
4 Trévidic: *PM*, 28 Sept 2015; Senate report: AFP, 8 April 2015; Jails: Reuters, 22 Jan 2015.
5 Poll: Ipsos, April 2015.
6 Emigration: Saint-Denis, 17th arrondissement, *Jerusalem Report*, 5 Jan 2016, http://www.jpost.com/Jerusalem-Report/Jewish-World-On-the-Move-438342
7 Official: *Al Jazeera*, 14 Nov 2015; Trévidic: *PM*, 28 Sept 2015.
8 *Libération*, 15 Nov 2015.
9 Blood: BBC Radio Five, 14 Nov 2015.
10 Policeman: *Mon*, 17 Nov 2015.
11 Officer: RTL, 14 Nov 2015.
12 Attacks: 2015 – 17-18 Nov, *Gdn*, 21 Feb, TFI, France 2 television, BBC; other sources as indicated above; 2016 – Belgian gunfight and arrests, *Mon*, 19 March, *Gdn* 19 & 21, March; French security report, *NYT*, 19 March; Twitter, *Journal du Dimanche*, 7 Feb.
13 *Metro*, 23 Dec 2015.
14 Hollande : http://www.elysee.fr/declarations/article/discours-du-president-de-la-republique-devant-le-parlement-reuni-en-congres-3/
15 Sarkozy: *Mon*, 19 Nov 2015; Italy: *Econ*, 28 Nov 2015.
16 *Mon*, *Gdn*, 19, 21 Nov 2015.

17 *Journal du Dimanche*, 7 Feb 2016.
18 Experts, Juppé: *FT*, 17 Nov 2015; Heisbourg: *Econ*, 28 Nov 2015; Keppel: *Econ*, 21 Nov 2015.
19 Poll: TNS/Sofres/*Mon*, Feb 2015.
20 Senik: *Econ*, 21 Dec 2013; Suicides: INSEE.
21 *Mon*, 5 Feb 2016.
22 France–Germany comparisons: *Econ*, 25 April 2015.
23 Exports French customs figures: 4 Feb 2016.
24 *FT*, 11 Aug 2015, 19 Jan 2016, *Mon*, 10 July 2015.
25 Hollande: TFI interview, 7 Sept 2014.
26 Survey: Ipsos, *Fig*, 3 Feb 2016.
27 Valls: *FT*, 12 Dec 2015.
28 56 per cent: TNS/Sofres/*Mon*, 6 Feb 2016.
29 Journalist Simon Kuper, *FT*, 30 Jan 2016; 4 per cent, *Gdn*, 21 Jan 2016.
30 Polls: *Fig*, Oct 2012, Radio France Internationale, 24 November 2015, TNS/Sofres, 14–15 Dec 2015, IFOP, 14–17 Dec 2015; *Fig*, 3 Feb 2016.
31 Les français c'est les autres: France 2, 5 Feb 2016.
32 Deaths: *Econ*, 7 Nov 2015; Valls: *Libération*, 11 Sept 2014.
33 Security services: *Mon*, 5 Feb 2016; warnings: *Mon*, France 2, 17–18 Nov, *FT*, 18 Nov; borders: *FT*, 16 Nov 2015.
34 UN: UN News Center, 19 Jan 2016.
35 Valls: New Year press reception, 20 Jan 2015.
36 Avignon: *Mon*, 7 Feb 2016.
37 Todd: see Bibliography.
38 Badinter: *Mon*, 6 Feb 2016.
39 Minister: *Gdn*, 21 Jan 2016.
40 Valls, Bianco, sociologist: *Fig*, 19 Jan 2016; Bianco: *FT*, 29 Jan 2016.
41 Official, Valls: France 24, 12, 23 Jan 2016.
42 Tourism, plays: *FT*, 27 Jan 2016; Hotels: *Mon*, 7 Feb 2016.

INTRODUCTION: THE LASTING LEGACY OF THE REVOLUTION

1 Ferro, *Histoire de la France*, pp. 259–62, gives a good summary of the changes.
2 Maistre: Davies, *Europe*, p. 704.
3 Julliard, *Les Gauches Françaises*, pp. 565–695.
4 *Déclaration des Droits de la Femme et de la Citoyenne*, Paris, 1791: en.wikipedia.org/wiki/Declaration_of_the_Rights_of_Woman_and_the_Female_Citizen#mediaviewer/File:DDFC.jpg.
5 Declaration of the Rights of Man: www2.assemblee-nationale.fr/decouvrir-l-assemblee/histoire/histoire-de-l-assemblee-nationale/le-temps-de-l-invention-1789-1799. Citizenship: William Rogers Brubaker, *The French Revolution and the Invention of Citizenship* (Cambridge MA, Harvard Belknap Press, 1989), pp. 34 *et seq.*
6 Adolescent: Blum, Jerome, *The European World*, p. 454
7 Doyle, *France and the Age of Revolution* – gives a piercing analysis of the fall of

the Bourbons. See also Swann & Félix, *The Crisis of the Absolute Monarchy*.

8 Views in Israel, Furet and see discussion in Roger Chartier, *The Cultural Origins of the French Revolution* (Durham NC, Duke University Press, 1991).

9 The necklace affair is well told by Beckman.

10 Breteuil: Marseille, *Nouvelle Histoire de la France*, p. 667.

11 Grégoire: Morgan, *France*, Vol. I, p. 328.

12 See Spang, *Stuff and Money in the Time of the French Revolution*, for *assignats*.

13 Méot, Mellot, p. 7.

14 Carnot: Davies, *Europe*, p. 715.

15 Brunswick: Elizabeth Cross, 'The Myth of the Feign Enemy? The Brunswick Manifesto and the Radicalization of the French Revolution', *FH* (2011/2) – which argues that the impact of Brunswick's appeal has been overstated given the radicalisation already taking place in France.

16 Duty: Howarth, *Citizen King*, p. 77.

17 Townshend, *Terrorism*, pp. 37–42, gives an excellent summary of the Terror.

18 The morality argument is advanced in Marisa Linton, *Choosing Terror* (Oxford, 2013). Coachman, America: Howarth, *Citizen King*, pp. 75, 78. Character assassination: Mette Harder in Martijn Icks and Eric Shiraev (eds), *Character Assassination Throughout the Ages* (London, Palgrave Macmillan, 2014), p. 177.

19 Davies, *Europe*, p. 705.

20 Lyons: Latreille, *Histoire de Lyon et du Lyonnais*, pp. 292–303, 307.

21 Marseilles: Baratier (ed.), *Histoire de Marseille*, pp. 282–8.

22 Agulhon, *Histoire de Toulon*, pp. 179–92.

23 Dauphiné, Stendhal, Alps: Bligny (ed.), *Histoire du Dauphiné*, p. 346. Périgord: Arlette Higounet-Nadal, *Histoire du Périgord* (Toulouse, Privat, 1983), p. 261.

24 For public and private spheres, see Lynn Hunt's essay 'Women' in Perrot (ed.), *History of Private Life*, Vol. IV, p. 45.

25 Massacres: Stephen Clay, 'Vengeance, Justice and the Reactions in the Revolutionary Midi', *FH* (2009/1). Robespierre: Mette Harder in Icks & Shiraev (eds), *Character Assassination Throughout the Ages*, pp. 176, 180. Colin Jones, 'The Overthrow of Maximilien Robespierre', *American Historical Review* (2014); 'The Fall of Robespierre', *History Today* (8 Aug 2015).

26 Fleet: John Molony, *Penguin History of Australia*, (Ringwood VIC, Penguin, 1988), p. 53.

27 Jugular: Paul Schroeder quoted by William Doyle, *FT* (4 Oct 2014).

28 Among the mountain of books on Napoleon one might mention the excellent recent works by Gueniffey (*Bonaparte*), Forrest (*Napoleon*) and Broers (*Napoleon: Soldier of Destiny*), the latter making first use of Bonaparte's full correspondence. Former prime minister Lionel Jospin expresses a critical view in his work *Le Mal Napoléonien*.

CHAPTER 1: RESTORATION

1 See, for instance, Dwyer, *Citizen Emperor*.

2 Two Frances, Paris: Charle, *Histoire Sociale*, pp. 18–19, 23, 29, 36.

3 10 per cent: Fouché, *Authentic Memoirs*, p. 21; Lesur, *La France et les Français en 1817*, p. 469.

4 Health: Lever, *Louis XVIII*, pp. 557–8, Mansel, *Louis* XVIII, pp. 404, 407. Reputation, Cayala: Maillé, *Souvenirs des Deux Restaurations*, pp. 52, 60, 84, 110. Chateaubriand, Vol. 4, p.8.

5 Horne, *Seven Ages*, p. 241. Troops, Wellington: Lever, *Louis XVIII*, pp. 406, 420. Bridge: Lawday, *Napoleon's Master*, p. 299.

6 Greeks: Baratier (ed.), *Histoire de Marseille*, pp. 319–20.

7 Caron, François, *Histoire Économique*, pp. 36–7, 38, 51, 95, 159.

8 Priests, land, choice: Magraw, *France 1815–1914*, pp. 24, 29, 30.

9 Perrot (ed.), *History of Private Life*, Vol. IV, pp. 104–5.

10 Toulon, Stendhal: Robb, *The Discovery of France*, p. 8, photo insert after p. 302; Heine, *Works* Vol. 8, p. 143.

11 Bourdonnaye: Bonin & Dider, *Louis XVIII, Roi de Deux Peuples, 1814–1816*, p. 118. White Jacobin: Maillé, *Souvenirs des Deux Restaurations*, p. 69.

12 Barings: Ziegler, *The Sixth Great Power*, pp. 78–85. Staël: Longford, Elizabeth, *Wellington* (Abacus, 2012) p. 37.

13 Chateaubriand, Vol. 4, p. 10. Laziness: Mansel, *Louis XVIII*, p. 369; Lesur, *La France et les Français en 1817*, p. 369.

14 *Ibid.* p. 469.

15 Opportunists, no middle ground: Fabian Rausch, 'The Impossible Gouvernement Représentatif', *FH* (2013 (2)).

16 Wolff (ed.), *Histoire du Languedoc*, p. 491.

17 Duchess: Hillerin, *La Duchesse de Berry*. Bathing: Castelot, *Louis-Philippe le Méconnu*, p. 182. Affair: Maillé, *Souvenirs*, pp. 177–8.

18 Reconciliation: Lucas-Dubreton, *Le Comte d'Artois, Charles X*, p. 133.

19 Death: Maillé, *Souvenirs*, pp. 124–6, 130; Lever, *Louis XVIII*, pp. 555–6; Mansel, *Louis XVIII*, pp. 407–8. Talleyrand: Lawday, *Napoleon's Master*, p. 325.

CHAPTER 2: REACTION AND REVOLUTION

1 Polignac: Lucas-Debreton, *Le Comte d'Artois, Charles X*, pp. 176–7.

2 Journal: Tombs, *France*, p. 34; Chateaubriand, Journal, Cabanis, *Charles X, Roi Ultra*, p. 405.

3 Volcano: Cabanis, *Ibid.* p. 423.

4 Horne, A *Savage War of Peace*, p. 9.

5 The following account of the July Days draws on: Lucas-Dubreton, *Le Comte d'Artois, Charles X*, pp. 179, 195–9, 255; Cabanis, *Charles X, Roi Ultra*, p. 427; Castelot, *Louis-Philippe le Méconnu*, pp. 195, 198; Pinkney, *The French Revolution of 1830*, p. 93; Blessington, Vol. 2, pp. 150–1, 168–9; Chateaubriand, *Correspondance Générale*, Vol. VIII, pp. 425–7; Brillat-Savarin, *Physiologie du goût*. Introduction, p. 11, (English edition, London, Penguin, 1970); Apponyi, Vol. I, pp. 309, 313; Howarth, *Citizen King*, p. 178; Lawday, *Napoleon's Master*, pp. 327–8.

CHAPTER 3: CITIZEN KING

1 Trove: *Le National* (1 Aug 1832); Mass, shops: Allies, *Journal in France, 1845 & 1848*, p. 41.

2 Government: Heine, *Works* Vol. 7, p. 39; Proudest: Howarth, *Citizen King*, p. 239.

3 Legitimists: de Broglie, *La Monarchie de Juillet 1830–1848*, pp. 59–60. Marseilles: Baratier (ed.), *Histoire de Marseille*, p. 323.

4 Legitimists: de Broglie, *La Monarchie de Juillet 1830–1848*, pp. 59–60. Bottle, affair: Howarth, *Citizen King*, p. 204.

5 Maillé, *Mémoires 1832–1851*, p. 108; Castelot, *Louis-Philippe le Méconnu*, pp. 255–9.

6 Chateaubriand on fall of Charles X, letter to Madame Récamier, 29 July 1830, *Correspondence* Vol. 8, (Paris, Gallimard, 2010).

7 In this and next para – Apponyi, Vol. 1, pp. 416–35.

8 Victor Hugo, *Les Misérables*, (Arvensa Editions, 2014) Vol. 2, p. 372.

9 Wilson: Mollier, *Scandale*, pp. 253–4.

10 Paris conditions. Wealth, Charle, *Histoire Sociale*, pp. 29, 36, Daumard, p. 119; Horne, *Paris*, pp 242–52; Hazan, pp. 64–5, 83; Seminaries, rats Balzac, Jones, pp. 318, 319, 341, Lazare, Félix et Louis, *Dictionnaire des rues et monuments de Paris*, Paris, 1855; Galleries, *Illustrated Guide to Paris*, 1852; Saint-Antoine, Lava, Reader, p. 2 *et seq.*

11 Heine, *Works*, Vol 7, pp. 319–21.

12 The street is now part of the rue Beaubourg. See Maïté Bouyssy, *L'Urgence, l'Horreur, la Démocratie: Essai sur le Moment Frénétique Français 1824–1834* (Paris, Publications de la Sorbonne, 2012) pp. 222–71.

13 Howarth, *Citizen King*, pp. 212, 259; Karl Marx, *The Civil War in France* (London, Penguin, 1974), pp. 191–2.

14 Heine, *Works*, Vol. 7, p. 159; King: Howarth, *Citizen King*, p. 253.

15 Algeria colonisation is well charted in Gallois, *A History of Violence in the Early Algerian Colony*.

16 Tombs, *France*, pp. 364–5.

17 Heine, *Works*, Vol. 7, p. 39.

18 Knife: Howarth, *Citizen King*, p. 291.

19 Queen Victoria, *Letters*, ed Arthur Christopher Benson, (John Murray, 1908) Vol. III, p. 122.

20 Dauphin: Castelot, *Louis-Philippe le Méconnu*, pp. 325–7; Nemours: Apponyi, Vol. 4, p. 63.

CHAPTER 4: SHARPENING THE KNIFE

1 Attempt: Steiner, *Language and Silence*, p. 291.

2 Music, pianos, de Broglie, *La Monarchie de Juillet 1830–1848*, p. 84; Heine, *Works*, Vol. 8, p. 108.

3 *Hernani*: Fourcassié, *Toulouse*, p. 176.

4 Philipon: Kerr, *Caricature and French Political Culture 1830–48*.

5 Agoult, writing as Daniel Stern, *Essai sur la Liberté*, (Paris, Amyot, 1847), p. 103.

6 Railways, British: Wolmar, *Blood, Iron and Gold*, pp. 22–5; Jenks, *The Migration of British Capital to 1875*, pp. 141–50.

7 Heine: Hazan, *The Invention of Paris* pp. 257–8.

8 Dickens: Walter & Arqué, *The World in 1900*, p. 64, Ligou, *Montauban*, pp 288–9.

9 Michelet, Stendhal: Gildea, *Children of the Revolution*, pp. 77–8. Balzac, *La Comédie humaine*, Vol 8, *Les Paysans*, (Gallimard, 1955), p. 71

10 Trade, industry: Caron, François, *Histoire Économique*, pp. 93–4. Banks: de Broglie, *La Monarchie de Juillet 1830–1848*, p. 318.

11 Society: Caron, François, *Histoire Économique*, p. 144.

12 Agriculture: Charle, pp. 62–3; Caron, François, *Histoire Économique*, pp. 28, 33.

13 Scandals: Apponyi, Vol. 4, pp. 61, 78, 83–4; de Broglie, *La Monarchie de Juillet 1830–1848*, pp. 381–3; Castelot, *Louis-Philippe le Méconnu*, p. 355.

14 Reactions: de Broglie, *La Monarchie de Juillet 1830–1848*, p. 398; Howarth, *Citizen King*, pp. 304–5, 310.

15 Hot water: Howarth, *Ibid.* p. 296.

16 *Gazette de France*, 16 Jan 1848.

17 Banquets: Vincent for full account. Also Daniel Stern, *Histoire de la Révolution de 1848*, pp. 32, 258, 262, 264–7; Heine, *Works*, Vol. 8, p. 51; Zeldin, *France 1848-1945, Politics and Anger* , pp. 117–19.

18 The following account draws on these main sources: Castelot, *Louis-Philippe le Méconnu*, pp. 347–99; Daniel Stern, *Histoire de la Révolution de 1848*, Vol. 1, Chp. VII–XV; Howarth, *Citizen King*, pp. 317–25, 328–35; Apponyi, Vol. 4, pp. 137, 142–50, 154, 158, 207–8; Price, *Archbishop Darboy and Some French Tragedies*, pp. 52–6, 58, 62; de Tocqueville, *Recollections*, p. 71; Maillé, *Mémoires*, p. 215; Heine, *Works*, Vol. 8, pp. 515, footnote 1 – 516.

CHAPTER 5: THE IMPOSSIBLE DREAM

1 Victoria: A. N. Wilson, *Victoria: A Life* (London, Atlantic, 2014), pp. 247–8.

2 Weber, *Peasants into Frenchmen*, p. 245.

3 *Chambres*: Spencer, *A Tour of Inquiry through France and Italy*, Vol. I, pp. 31–2.

4 Demonstrators: Tombs, *France*, p. 23.

5 Eighteen-year-old: Laura O'Brien, 'Cette Nouvelle Transformation du Gamin de Paris', *FH* (2011 (3)).

6 Garde: O'Brien, *Ibid.*

CHAPTER 6: FROM PRINCE PRESIDENT TO EMPEROR

1 Description: Farat, *Persigny*, p. 82.

2 Périgord: Arlette Higounet-Nadal, *Histoire du Périgord* (Toulouse, Privat, 1983), p. 301.

3 *Montagne* programme: Kayser, *Les Grandes Batailles du Radicalisme 1820–1901*, pp. 316–17.

4 *Revue des Deux Mondes*, Chronique, 1849.

5 All or nothing: Apponyi, Vol. 4, p. 367.

6 Goncourt, Vol. 2, p. 754.

7 Apponyi, Vol. 4, pp. 367–9.

8 Slips: Ferro, *Histoire de France* p. 289 has full text of instruction. Rural rallying: Caron, François, *Histoire de France*, p. 292.

9 Baratier (ed.), *Histoire de Marseille*, pp. 345–7.

10 Ferguson, Niall, *The World's Banker* (Weidenfeld & Nicholson, 1998) pp. 560-1

CHAPTER 7: THE OPPORTUNISTIC EMPIRE

1 Victor Hugo, *Actes et Paroles, Avant l'Exile* (Paris, Michel Lévy, 1875), p. 330; Marx & Engels, *Selected Works*, p. 93; Charles Baudelaire, *The Essence of Laughter* (New York, Meridian, 1956), p. 185.

2 Health is fully dealt with by Williams, Roger – see last chapter for conclusions. Also Wellesley & Sencourt, *Conversations with Napoleon III*, pp. 350–1 for late visitor on health.

3 Duff, *Eugenie and Napoleon III*, p. 96; Goncourt, Vol. 2, pp. 632–3, 657.

4 Richardson, *The Courtesans* (Weidenfeld & Nicolson, 1967), pp. 32–1, 39; Belenky, *La Morale à la Carte*; Goncourt, Vol. 1, p. 738.

5 Morny, *France*, Tombs, p. 397.

6 See Zeldin's superb account of the political system in *Political System* especially pp. 127–8, 146, 167, 177, 183–4, and *France, Politics and Anger*, p. 175. Also Charle, *Hauts Fonctionnaires* p. 82; Williams, Roger, p. 21.

7 Empress quote: McMillan, *Napoleon III*, p. 55.

8 Godillon: Ingrid Sykes, 'Gender and Musical Performance in Mid-19th-Century France', *FH* (2010 (4)).

9 Marseille, *Nouvelle Histoire de la France*, p. 786.

10 Laon, beetroots: Bur, p. 237.

11 Agulhon (ed.), *Histoire de la France Urbaine, Tome 4*, pp. 174–9.

12 Silk: Junko Thérèse Takeda, *FH* (Vol. 28 (2), June 2014). Landes: Robb, *The Discovery of France*, p. 270.

13 Dumas: Marseille, *Nouvelle Histoire de la France*, p. 788.

14 Godin: Perrot (ed.), *History of Private Life, Vol. IV*, pp. 407–12.

15 Wilson, Schneider: Mollier, *Panama*, pp. 252–7; Dutch art: Perrot (ed.), *History of Private Life, Vol. IV*, p. 542.

16 Ferrières: *Le Monde Illustré*, 27 Dec 1862; *The Times*, 10 Dec 1862; Stern, Fritz, pp. 172–3.

17 Mirès, Millaud, Iffla: D. Barjot & N. Stoskopf, *Mirès, Millaud, Iffla* (Paris, Picard, 2002); Laurent Aiglon, 'Jules Isaac Mirès, entre Jacques Coeur et l'Affaire Dreyfus', *Cévennes Magazine* (2004); Iffla, Jarrassé, Dominique. *Osiris.* (Editions of Aesthetic Miscellaneous, 2009)

18 Menier: Perrot (ed.), *History of Private Life*, Vol. IV, pp. 414–17.

19 Milza gives a good account of Italian policy in *Napoléon III*, Chp. 12, as does McMillan, pp. 80–93.
20 Japan: Junko Thérèse Takeda, *FH*, (Vol. 28/2), June 2014).

CHAPTER 8: REFORM AND DISASTER

1 Morny: Wellesley & Sencourt, *Conversations with Napoleon III*, p. 132.
2 Eugénie: *Lettres Familières de l'Impératrice Eugénie*, pp. 146 *et seq.*
3 Ambassador: Wellesley & Sencourt, *Conversations with Napoleon III*, p. 138.
4 March: Zeldin, *The Political System of Napoleon III*, p. 101.
5 Vizier: McMillan, *Napoleon III*, p. 122.
6 Richelieu: Zeldin, *France, Anger and Politics*, p. 185.
7 Musset, Taine, Flaubert: quoted by Rupert Christiansen, *Offenbach's Paris*, Garsington opera programme, 2014.
8 Belleville programme: Kayser, *Les Grandes Batailles du Radicalisme 1820–1901*, pp. 318–20.
9 Napoleon, Ambassador: McMillan, *Napoleon III*, pp. 129–30.
10 Prince: Wellesley & Sencourt, *Conversations with Napoleon III*, pp. 350–1.
11 Bismarck: Caron, François, *Histoire de la France*, p. 16.
12 Eugénie, *Lettres Familières de l'Impératrice Eugénie*, p. 225.
13 Guedella, *The Second Empire*, pp. 332–4.
14 Interviews: Wellesley & Sencourt, *Conversations with Napoleon III*, pp. 369–70, 371–5.

CHAPTER 9: THE BLOODY WEEK

1 Dordogne: Higounet-Nadal, p. 292.
2 Voisin: Mellot, *Paris Disparu*, p. 8.
3 Bismarck: Stern, Fritz, pp 148–50.
4 Bleichroder: Stern, Fritz, p. 154.
5 Thiers: Marseille, *Nouvelle Histoire de la France*, p. 812.
6 *Le Rappel* (30 March 1871).
7 Heritage: Caron, *Histoire Sociale*, p. 137.
8 Delescluze: Gildea, p. 243.
9 McCullough, p. 324.
10 Zola: Marseille, *Nouvelle Histoire de la France*, p. 814. Marseille repeats 20,000. Ferro's *Histoire de France* cites 17–35,000.
11 'Rapport d'ensemble de M. le Général Appert sur les opérations de la justice militaire relatives à l'insurrection de 1871', Assemblée Nationale, annexe au procès-verbal de la session du 20 juillet 1875 (Versailles, 1875). Tombs explains his 6–7,500 figure in a 2011 paper, www.h-france.net/Salon/Salonvol3no1.pdf. Higher figure in Prosper-Olivier Lissagaray, *Histoire de la Commune de 1871* (Paris, Maspero, 1876, reprinted 1972). See bibliography

and Zeldin, France, Politics and Anger, p. 380. Karine Varley, www.h-france.net/Salon/Salonvol3no3.pdf. MacMahon, Déposition du M. le maréchal Mac-Mahon (28 August 1871) in Enquête parlementaire sur l'insurrection du 18 mars 1871 (Paris, Libraire Législative, 1872), p. 183.

CHAPTER 10: A GOOD LITTLE REPUBLIC

1 Divides, Thiers election platform March 1873: Ferry quoted in Ferro, *Histoire de France*, p. 281.
2 Quadrupled: Hobsbawm, *The Age of Empire 1875–1914*, p. 175.
3 Agulhon (ed.), *Histoire de la France Urbaine, Tome 4*, pp. 25, 48, 56, 123, 124. Marseilles: Anon, *French Home Life*, p. 239. Toulouse: Wolff (ed.), *Histoire du Languedoc*, pp. 501–2.
4 See Jeanneney, *L'Argent Caché*.
5 Seignobos: Goguel & Grosser, *La Politique en France*, p. 98.
6 Superiority, Barthélemy, on the right: Goguel & Grosser, *Ibid.* pp. 32–3.
7 Slums: Aghulon (ed.), *Histoire de la France Urbaine, Tome 4*, p. 326
8 Illegitimacy: Agulhon (ed.), *Ibid.* p. 305. Infant mortality: *Ibid.* p. 276. Diseases: *Ibid.* pp. 277 *et seq.*
9 Poincaré: Tardieu, *La Profession Parlementaire*, p. 43. Ferry speech: Bordeaux, 30 Aug 1885.
10 Hazareesingh, FH. 2009/2, Renan, Hazareesingh, p. 211 from conference on 'Qu'est ce qu'une nation', 1882; Caillaux, *Mes Mémoires*, p. 33.
11 Patriotism is analysed in Weber, *Peasants into Frenchmen*, p. 100 *et seq.*
12 A right: Ferry to Chamber of Deputies, 28 July 1885.
13 Weber, *Peasants into Frenchmen*, describes the process with his usual array of telling examples, pp. 203–9.
14 Ministry: Peter Jackson, 'Tradition and Adaptation', *FH* (2010/2).
15 Gildea, *Children of the Revolution*, pp. 294–301.
16 Ardèche, Cholvy (ed.), pp. 244–5.
17 Tim Verhoeven, 'The Satyriasis Diagnosis', *FH* (2013/4).
18 Bishop: Christina de Bellaigue, 'Only What Is Pure and Exquisite', *FH* (2013/2).
19 80,000: Horne, *Seven Ages*, p. 330.
20 Greffulhe: see Hillerin, *La Comtesse Greffulhe*.
21 Henry James, *A Little Tour in France*, p. 1.
22 Allais: Gagnière, *Pour Tout l'Or des Mots*, pp. 50–6.
23 Exhibition: Musée du Luxembourg, Paris, 2014; National Gallery, London, 2015; *FT, Gdn*, 21 Feb 2015.
24 Anon, *French Home Life*, pp. 138–9.
25 O'Fallowell: Jones, *Paris*, p. 232. Coubertin: Buruma, *Voltaire's Coconuts or Anglomania in Europe*, Chp. 8.
26 Le Tréport: Walter & Arqué, *The World in 1900*, p. 56. Northern Europeans on Riviera: Nice, Cannes, Nelson, Chp. 4

27 Cransac: poster in Musée de la Mine, Aubin.

28 André: see Monnier, *Édouard André.*

29 Alps, turbines, Grenoble: Bligny (ed.), *Histoire du Dauphiné*, pp. 378–9. Vivarais: Cholvy (ed.), *Histoire du Vivarais*, p. 208.

30 Bread: Weber, *France, Fin de Siècle*, p. 64.

31 Weber, *Ibid.* p. 111; Ousby, *Occupation*, pp. 154, 156–8.

32 Ratios: Anon, *French Home Life*, p. 321. France and Germany: Earle, *Modern France*, p. 317; Zola, FS, (Vol. LXVII/2 April 2014).

33 Immigrants: Agulhon (ed.), *Histoire de la France Urbaine, Tome 4*, pp. 295–6.

34 Proust: *Fig*, 8 Nov 2013. Alcohol: Perrot (ed.), *History of Private Life, Vol. IV*, pp. 620–2.

35 White, *French Divorce Fiction from the Revolution to the First World War.* Attendance: Weber, *France, Fin de Siècle*, p. 92.

36 Meat, bread, wine: Weber, *Peasants into Frenchmen*, pp. 133, 135, 142, 144. This magnificent book and the same author's equally compelling *France, Fin de Siècle* are the best guides to the variety of France during the nineteenth century and form an essential counterpoint to politics in Paris.

37 Betham-Edwards, *France of To-day*, p. 277.

38 Weber, *France, Fin de Siècle*, p. 56. Landes, photograph, butcher's shop in Rignac, Aveyron. Communities: Bouyé, *Les Enfarinés de Cassaniouze.* Chestnut country: Maison de la Châtaigne at Mourjou, Cantal.

39 Talabot, washing: Mercadié, *Marie Talabot*, pp. 277, 279. Wash houses: Agulhon (ed.), *Histoire de la France Urbaine, Tome 4*, p. 362.

40 Renters: Scott Haine, p. 41.

41 Housing, cafés, prostitution: Ibid, pp. 38–9, 126, 135; Agulhon (ed), *Histoire de la France Urbaine, Tome 4*, pp. 305–6.

42 Rothschild: Earle, *Modern France*, p. 47.

43 Ministers: Caron, François, *Histoire de France*, pp. 250, 260.

CHAPTER 11: THE MEN OF THE MIDDLE

1 Zeldin, *France, Politics and Anger*, has excellent portrait of Thiers, pp. 242–7. Bury & Tombs, *Thiers, 1797–1877*, focus on the 1870s and the crisis with MacMahon.

2 Cartoon: Bury & Tombs, *Thiers, 1797–1877*, p. 221.

3 Wolmar, *Blood, Iron and Gold*, p. 103.

4 Gambetta: Bury & Tombs, *Thiers, 1797–1877*, p. 461.

5 Cobban, History, p. 24.

6 Kayser, *Les Grandes Batailles du Radicalisme 1820–1901*, has a useful list of governments from 1879–99 and the reasons for their fall, pp. 375–9.

7 Mayeur, *Léon Gambetta*, gives full account of Gambetta's life. Mistress, letters: Susan Foley, *FH* (2012/2).

8 Ferry, Clemenceau: Kayser, *Les Grandes Batailles du Radicalisme*, p. 109, including letter from Ferry to Mme Scheurer-Kestner; Tombs, *France*, p. 447.

9 Radicals: Kayser, *Les Grandes Batailles du Radicalisme*, p. 388 and map at end.

10 First driver, songs, soap, aperitif: Tombs, *France*, pp. 448, 450.

11 Lombroso: Edward Erickson, *FH*, (2008/1).

12 Zeldin, *France, Politics and Anger*, p. 290; Chp. 8 of this book is devoted to solidarism.

13 Leroy-Beaulieu, Péguy, Earle, pp. 48–9, 130.

CHAPTER 12: FROM THE AFFAIR TO WAR

1 Voltaire: Simon Schama, *FT*, 24 Jan 2015. Proudhon anti-Semitism: www.marxists.org/reference/subject/economics/proudhon/1847/jews.htm.

2 Péguy: Schuker, Stephen A., Origins of the 'Jewish Problem' in the Later Third Republic, pp. 149–51, https://www.academia.edu/8381887/Origins_of_the_Jewish_Problem_in_the_Later_Third_Republic_in_The_Jews_in_Modern_France_ed._M._Malino

3 Panama is best covered in Mollier, *Le Scandale de Panama*, which is excellent on the wider financial–political nexus of the times. Also Diesbach, *Ferdinand de Lesseps*.

4 Blacker's involvement is laid out in Maguire, *Ceremonies of Bravery*.

5 Waldeck: Edward Whiting Fox in Earle, *Modern France*, pp. 130–2; Cobban, *History*, pp. 56–9; Zeldin, *France, Politics and Anger*, pp. 307–15.

6 Brittany: Brustein, *The Social Origins of Political Regionalism*, p. 167.

7 Ligou, *Montauban*: pp. 263, 270.

8 Combes: Merle's *Émile Combes* is the best biography; see also Zeldin, *France, Politics and Anger*, pp. 321–7; Cobban, History, pp. 60–3; Viviani in Cobban, p. 63.

9 Clemenceau: National Assembly speech, 8 March 1918; Keynes on Clemenceau: Robinson, Elizabeth & Moggridge, Donald, *Collected writings of John Maynard Keynes*, Vol. 2. (Cambridge, 2012) pp. 18, 20.

10 The best biography is Winock's *Clemenceau*. Also Zeldin, *France, Politics and Anger*, pp. 334–40; Cobban, *History*, pp. 65–6; Keynes, *The Economic Consequences of the Peace* (BiblioLife, 2008) Chp. 3.

11 Poincaré: Fenby, *The General*, p. 84.

12 Ambassador, Bleichröder: Stern, Fritz, pp. 330–1.

13 Colonial policy: Ferro, *Histoire de France*, pp. 307–14 and at greater length in his *Histoire des Colonisations*.

14 In *July 1914* McMeekin argues strongly for Russian responsibility given its desire to break up the Ottoman Empire, but it is difficult to accept his conclusion that France was as eager for war as Germany and that the latter went into war 'kicking and screaming as the Austrian noose snapped shut around their necks' since Berlin had given Vienna a blank cheque to act in the Balkans. For Franco-British talks, see Owen, *The Hidden Perspective*.

15 Steel: Caron, François, *Histoire Économique*, p. 153. Joffre's order is commemorated on the plinth of the equestrian statue of him outside the École de Guerre in Paris, which shows him pointing the way to victory.

16 Mother: Fenby, *The General*, p. 60.

17 De Gaulle, *Lettres, Notes et Carnets*, Vol. I, pp. 111, 133, 205–8, 213, 218, 227–8, 242, 276, 284, 416–7, 421.

18 Horne, Verdun, pp. 34–6, Winter pp. 88–9.

19 Serrigny p. 45, Williams, Charles, *Pétain*, pp. 125–6

20 Horne, Alistair, *The Price of Glory, Verdun 1916*, (Penguin, 1993), pp. 148, 174; Williams, Charles, *Pétain*, pp. 134–9; Ousby, *Occupation*, p. 16; Brown, *The Embrace of Unreason*, p. 164; Fenby, *The General*, pp. 63–4.

21 The best account is Guy Pedroncini, *Les Mutineries de 1917* (Paris, Publications de la Sorbonne, Presse Universitaires de France, 1983).

22 Briand, Painlevé: Stevenson, *1914–18*, p. 360.

23 Clemenceau: Stevenson, *With Our Backs to the Wall*, p. 87.

24 Mon-archie: Goguel & Grosser, *La Politique en France*, p. 221.

25 Stevenson, *With Our Backs to the Wall*, p. 87, Ch 2.

26 Offensives: Stevenson, *Ibid.* Chp. 2.

CHAPTER 13: THE TROUBLED PEACE

1 Losses: Pedrocini, Guy, *Histoire militaire de la France, Tome 3 : De 1871 à 1940* (PUF, 1997) p. 323 ; Giraudoux, Mood: Weber, Eugen, *The Hollow Years*, pp. 12-16; Chastenet, pp. 213, 220, 224.

2 Population, Farms: Larkin, *France Since the Popular Front*, p. 4-5, 7, 9, Syphilis: Brendon, p. 128, Nord: Claudine Wallart, head curator of heritage at the Archives départementales du Nord, www.remembrancetrails-northern-france.com/learn-more/the-department-of-nord-and-the-coal-basin-under-germanoccupation/nord-in-the-aftermath-1918.html. Sheep: Jones, *History*, p. 248.

3 Economy: Caron, *Histoire Économique*, pp. 178–9, 186, 248–9.

4 Barr, *A Line in the Sand* gives a good account of the Middle East.

5 Agulhon (ed.), *Histoire de Toulon* – a photograph opposite p. 353 shows the beard in all its glory.

6 Maginot: Weber, *Hollow Years*, p. 8.

7 Evolutionary liberalism and analysis of Wilson and US policy: Tooze, *The Deluge*.

8 Profits, Bourse: Caron, *Histoire Économique*, p. 194.

9 Contraction: Caron, *Histoire Économique*, pp. 193–8, Rist quoted on p. 194.

10 The Israeli historian Zeev Sternhell has depicted the leagues as constituting a new fascistic movement on the right to go with Legitimism, Orléanism and Bonapartism, but work by Bertrand Joly has shown that, for all the street violence some of their members espoused, they were conservatives rather than fascist. For summary of the argument, see *L'Express*, 7 May 2014, p. 94.

CHAPTER 14: TOUT VA TRÈS BIEN, MADAME LA MARQUISE

1 Procession, Renault: Maclean, *Eastern Approaches*, pp. 14–15. Laon: Bur *et al.*, pp. 253 *et seq.*
2 The Popular Front has been much written about. Among the best accounts are Lacouture, *Le Front Populaire* and Margairaz, *et al.*, *Le Front Populaire*, Larkin, *France Since the Popular Front*, pp. 59–60, 67; and Jackson. For industrialists, Jeanneney, *L'Argent Caché*, pp. 39–40.
3 Bonnet: Brendon, Piers, *The Dark Valley* (Vintage, 2002), p. 508.
4 Caron, *Histoire Économique*, pp. 197–8.
5 Intelligence: www.livresdeguerre.net/forum/contribution.php?index=49343A
6 Albert Speer, *Inside the Third Reich* (Weidenfeld & Nicolson, 1970) pp. 171–2.

CHAPTER 15: TWO FRANCES

1 Claudel: www.contreculture.org/AG%20Claudel.html.
2 In *Pétain*, Vergez-Chaignon gives an excellent analysis of the old man.
3 Feeble: Cobban, *History*, p. 177.
4 Pétain's role in the anti-Jewish laws is laid out in Vergez-Chaignon, *Pétain*.
5 *Mon*, 18 Feb 2015.
6 Henriot: Kay Chadwick, 'Radio Propaganda and Public Opinion Under Endgame Vichy', *FH* (2011/2). Food: Kenneth Mouré, 'Food Rationing and the Black Market in France (1940–44)', *FH*, (2010 (2)).
7 Cultural life under the Occupation is excellently covered in Alan Riding's fine book *And the Show Went On*.
8 Semelin, *Persécutions et Entraides dans la France Occupée.*
9 De Gaulle, *Lettres, Notes et Carnets*, Vol. 1, pp. 336–7; Guy, *En Écoutant de Gaulle*, p. 71.
10 Bankrupt, shape: Williams, *The Last Great Frenchman*, pp. 170–1.

CHAPTER 16: LIBERATION

1 Resistance deaths: Marcot *et al.*, *Dictionnaire Historique de la Résistance.* I am grateful to Bernard Edinger for his help on these points.
2 Pétain: Don Cook, *Charles de Gaulle* (Secker & Warburg, 1984), p. 286.
3 The regime's last months have been described in several books, notably : Rousso, Henri, *Un château en Allemagne: La France de Pétain en exil, Sigmaringen 1944-5* (Fayard, 2012) and in Pierre Assouline's novel, *Sigmaringen* (Gallimard, 2014).
4 Among many accounts on the liberation of Paris, see Muracciole, Jean-François, *La Libération de Paris* (Editions Tallandier, 2013). Lapierre, Dominique and Collins, Larry, *Paris, brûle-t-il ?* was a bestseller in the 1990s and was subsequently turned into a film.

CHAPTER 17: SEEKING A NEW COURSE

1 Dissolution, reeds: C. Mauriac, *Un Autre de Gaulle*, (Hachette, 1970) p. 45.
2 C. Mauriac, *Ibid.* pp. 31–4, 45–6.
3 Claudel, www.contreculture.org/AG%20Claudel.html.
4 Caron, *Histoire Économique*, pp. 253 *et seq.*
5 Grosser, *Affairs Extérieures*, p. 34; Lacouture, *De Gaulle*, Vol. II, p. 227.
6 De Gaulle, *Mémoires*, p. 869; Moch, *De Gaulle*, pp. 121–2; *Une si longue vie*, pp. 311–12; Lacouture, *De Gaulle*, Vol. 2, p. 235.

CHAPTER 18: THE UNLOVED REPUBLIC

1 Miller, Henry, *Paris Review* (Summer, 1961); Baldwin, www.nytimes. com/2014/01/19/travel/james-baldwins-paris.html?_r=0.
2 Goguel, *Géographie des Élections Françaises*, pp. 171, 173, 175, 177, 179, 181, 184.
3 For maps of the 1956 results see Goguel, *Ibid.* pp. 142–62.
4 'Politicians': Windrow, *The Last Valley*, p. 128.
5 Mayer, poll: Windrow, *Ibid.* pp. 205–6.
6 Reynaud: Windrow, *Ibid.* p. 208. 'Dien Bien Phu': Windrow gives a full account of battle, also see Fall's two books on the war.
7 Defence plan: see Victor Gavin, 'Power through Europe?', *FH*, (2009/1).

CHAPTER 19: THE END OF A REPUBLIC

1 For the early history of FLN, see Harbi, *Aux Origines du FLN.*
2 Torture: Alleg, *La Question.* Protests, Mendès: Evans, *Algeria*, pp. 163, 167–8. Goutte: Sarah Howard, 'Three Cats and a Watermelon', *FH*, (2013/3).
3 Algeria, Archives Nationales, AGM 83–94; Mollet, Guy, *Bilan et perspectives socialistes* (Plon, 1958).
4 Suez: Archives Nationales (AGM79).
5 Massu gives his account in *La Vrai Bataille d'Alger.* Also see Bromberger, *Les Rebelles Algériens*; Alleg; both books, Evans, *Algeria*; Horne, *Savage War.*
6 Emmanuel, *Atlantic Monthly* (June 1958).

CHAPTER 20: NEW REGIME, NEW TIMES

1 Effervessence: Julliard, *IVe République*, p. 72.
2 Productivity, exports: Caron, François, *Histoire Économique*, pp. 274, 311.
3 Caron, François, *Histoire Économique*, develops the thesis of the division between protected and open sectors, pp. 262 *et seq.*

CHAPTER 21: DECLINE AND FALL

1 Election covered in Fenby, *The General*, pp. 534-40; Viansson-Ponté, II, pp. 177-83; De Gaulle, *Lettres*, 1964-6, pp. 217-8, 220-1, 237, 241, 271; Peyrefitte, III, pp. 42-7; Lacouture, III, pp. 628-32; Bernstein, *Gaullisme*, pp. 269-70, 295, 303, 320-1; Roussel, II, pp. 410-5.
2 Demonstrations and strikes, Viansson-Ponté, II, pp. 439-40, 449-50, 452-3; Peyrefitte, pp. 467-75, 484-6, 498-9, 520, 546-52, 561; Fenby, *The General*, Chp. 35. *Le Monde* and other French newspapers, May-June, 1968.
3 Chaban-Delmas, Viansson-Ponté, *Histoire de la République Gaullienne*, Vol. II, p. 598.

CHAPTER 22: THE BANKER, THE PRINCE AND THE FLORENTINE

1 This account of the Pompidou, Giscard and Mitterrand presidency draws on the authors; experience as a correspondent in Paris for Reuters, *The Times* and The *Economist* and on French newspapers of the epoch. For Pompidou, see Roussel, Eric, *Georges Pompidou, 1911-1974* (Tempus, 2004); Giscard: Bernard, Mathias, *Valéry Giscard d'Estaing: Les ambitions déçues*, Mitterrand: Winock, Michel, *François Mitterrand* (Gallimard, 2015), Short, Cotta, Michèle, *Le monde selon Mitterrand* (Tallandier, 2015). Prime minister: *Gdn* (19 March 2015).
2 Economy: Caron, François, *Histoire Économique*, pp. 394–7.
3 Sarah Farmer, 'Memoirs of French Peasant Life', *FH* (2011/3).
4 Caron, François, *Histoire Économique*, pp. 397–404.
5 Lover: Short, *Mitterrand*, p. 210.
6 Mitterrand on Rocard, *Le Point* (12 Feb 2015).
7 Mitterrand, *Ibid.*
8 A third: Marc Lambron, *Ibid.*
9 Caron, François, *Histoire Économique*, pp. 410–3.
10 Grey: Short, *Mitterrand*, p. 567.

CHAPTER 23: BULLDOZER, BLING AND NORMAL

1 Mitterrand, *Le Point* (12 Feb 2015).
2 This account of the Chirac, Sarkozy and Hollande years is drawn from the author's experience covering France. See also on Chirac, Baque, Chirac, Nay, *La double méprise*, Fenby, *On the Brink*, Chp. 13.
3 Nay, *L'Impétueux*, Chp. 1.
4 Best account of Sarkozy is Nay *op cit.* Also Fenby, *On the Brink*, Ch 14.
5 *Econ*, Déjà vu, (6 Dec 2014).
6 Trierweiler, *Merci pour ce moment.*
7 Poll: *Fig* (4 & 5 Sept 2014).

8 www.breitbart.com/london/2015/01/30/front-nationals-le-penconsoli-dates-lead-in-first-presidential-poll-since-charlie-hebdo/.

9 Astier, *Times Literary Supplement* (15 Aug 2014).

10 *FT* (15 Aug 2014); *WSJ* (15–17 Aug 2014).

11 Survey, Boston Consulting Group, *Fig* (5 May 2014). Margins, construction, *Les Echos* (18 Nov 2013).

12 www.lepoint.fr/societe/charlie-hebdo-valls-la-menace-estaussi-interieure-13-01-2015-1896194_23.php.

13 www.independent.co.uk/news/world/europe/paris-attacks-francoishol-lande-sees-his-popularity-ratings-double-in-wake-of-strong-french-responseto-charlie-hebdo-killings-9988775.html#.

13 *Fig* (18 Feb 2015).

14 Sarkozy speech, Schiltigheim, Alsace, 25 Nov, 2015; Le Pen, *FT* (12 Dec, 2015).

CHAPTER 24: THE WEIGHT OF HISTORY

1 Malraux, *Penguin Dictionary of Quotations* (New York, Viking, 1993), p. 248.

2 US investors: *WSJ* (15 Oct 2014). Research and development etc.: *Mon* (15 Oct 2014).

3 *Ibid.*

4 Summed up in Simon Kuper, *FT* (13 & 14 Sept 2014); 'PMEs': *Fig Magazine* (10 Oct 2014).

5 Roanne': France 3 television, Pièces à conviction, *Fig* & *Mon* (18 Feb 2015).

6 Health: *Fig,* (14 Oct 2014). Opposition: *Fig,* (19 Sept 2014).

7 Dacia: *Gdn,* (22 Oct 2014). Peugeot: *Les Echos* (19 Feb 2015).

8 Areva: *Mon* (12 Jan 2012); www.liberation.fr/politiques/2012/01/17/anne-lauvergeon-accuse-l-elysee-de-destabilisation-systematique_788957.

9 Brands: *Econ* (30 Aug 2014). Companies, exports, research: *Mon,* (9 Sept 2014).

10 NYT, Oct 14, To French Nobel Prize win shows talk of decline is premature.

11 Germany, austerity: Martin Wolf, *The Shifts and the Shocks* (London, Allen Lane, 2014).

12 Universities: www.ucd.ie/geary/static/publications/workingpapers/geary wp200944.pdf. Teachers: *Mon* (12 Oct 2014). Private schools: *Fig Magazine* (10 Oct 2014).

13 McDonald's: www.telegraph.co.uk/news/worldnews/europe/france/10862560/ French-town-protests-to-demand-McDonalds-restaurant.html. Twice as expensive: *FT* (11 Feb 2015).

14 Vodka: *Fig* (12 Feb 2015). Survey: *Terre de Vins* (Sept 2014). Snails: www.snail-breeding.net/snail-consumption/. Frogs: *WSJ* (Europe) (5–7 Sept 2014).

15 *Gdn* (31 Oct 2014).

16 For berets, see Jouvion, *Le Béret.*

17 UNICEF: *Mon* (24 Sept 2014).

18 Survey: *Gdn* (29 Oct 2014). Polls, IFOP in *Fig* (24 Sept 2014).

19 Pietrasanta: *Mon* (16 Sept 2014).

20 *Mon* (12–18 Jan 2015), www.theguardian.com/world/2015/jan/12/-sp-charlie-hebdo-attackers-kids-france-radicalised-paris.

21 *NYT* (18 Feb 2015).

22 Study, *Mon* (10 June 2014). Abroad: *Mon* (11 Mar 2014).

23 Giscard: *PM* (17 July 2014). Audit: *Fig* (12 Feb 2015). GDP: *Mon* (14 Feb 2015).

24 Attali: *Mon* (14 Oct 2014).

25 Polls: *Fig* (21 Sept 2014). Aisne: *Mon* (14 Oct 2014).

26 Unfinished: Sudhir Hazareesingh, *FH* (2009/2), p. 215. Furet, *Lies*, p. 37.

27 Eric Zemmour, *Le Suicide Français* (Paris, Albin Michel, 2014); *Econ* (21 Dec 2013).

28 Growth: *WSJ* (20 Oct 2014).

BIBLIOGRAPHY

All books in French published in Paris, all in English in London/New York unless otherwise stated.

Aaslestad, Katherine & Joor, Johan. *Revisiting Napoleon's Continental System* (Palgrave Macmillan, 2015)

Agulhon, Maurice. *De Gaulle: Histoire, Symbole, Mythe* (Hachette, 2001)

— (ed.). *Histoire de la France Urbaine, Tome 4* (Seuil, 1983)

— (ed.). *Histoire de Toulon* (Toulouse, Privat, 1980)

— *The Republican Experiment, 1848–1852* (Cambridge, 1983)

— *La République au Village* (Plon, 1970)

— *La République de Jules Ferry à François Mitterrand* (Hachette, 1990)

— & Bonte, Pierre. *Marianne, Les Visages de la République* (Gallimard, 1992)

Alexandre, Philippe. *Le Duel de Gaulle-Pompidou* (Grasset, 1970)

— *L'Elysée en Péril* (Fayard, 1959)

— *Paysages de Campagne* (Grasset, 1988)

Alleg, Henri. *La Guerre d'Algérie* (Actuel, 1981)

— *La Question* (Éditions de Minuit, 1958)

Allies, Thomas. *Journal in France, 1845 & 1848* (Longman, British Library, 2010)

Amann, Peter H. *Revolution and Mass Democracy: The Paris Club Movement in 1848* (Princeton, 1975)

Amouroux, Henri. *La Vie des Français sous l'Occupation* (Éditions De Borée, 2011)

Anglade, Jean. *La Vie Quotidienne des Immigrés en France de 1919 à Nos Jours* (Hachette, 1976)

Anon. *French Home Life* (William Blackwood, 1873)

Anon. *Le Petit Livre Rouge du Président Chirac* (Collection du Ravi, 2002)

Apponyi, Rodolphe. *Vingt-cinq ans à Paris*, 4 vols. (Plon, 1913–1926)

Aron, Jean-Paul. *Le Mangeur du XIXe Siècle* (Robert Laffont, 1973)

Asselain, Jean-Charles. *Histoire Économique de la France* (Seuil, 1984)

Attali, Jacques. *Urgences Françaises* (Fayard, 2013)

— *Verbatim*. 2 Vols. (Fayard, 1993–6)

Auclair, Marcelle. *La Vie de Jean Jaurès* (Seuil, 1954)

Bacqué, Raphaëlle. *Chirac ou le Démon du Pouvoir* (Albin Michel, 2002)

— *Jacques Chirac* (Michel Lafon, 2003)

— & Saverot, Denis. *Seul comme Chirac* (Grasset, 1997)

Baratier, Édouard, (ed.). *Histoire de Marseille* (Toulouse, Privat, 1973)

Barjot, D. Stoskopf, N. *Mirès, Millaud, Iffla: Les Patrons du Second Empire* (Picard, 2002)

Barr, James. *A Line in the Sand* (Simon & Schuster, 2011)

Barrès, Philippe. *Charles de Gaulle* (Plon-Cartier, 1945)

Barthez, E. *The Empress Eugénie and Her Circle* (T. Fisher Unwin, 1912)

Baverez, Nicolas. *Réveillez-vous!* (Fayard, 2012)

Beaunier, André. *Visages d'Hier et d'Aujourd'hui* (Plon, 1911)

Becker, Jean-Jacques & Wieviorka, Annette. *Les Juifs de France* (Éditions Liana Levi, 1998)

Beckman, Jonathan. *How to Ruin a Queen* (John Murray, 2014)

Beevor, Antony. *D-Day* (Penguin, 2012)

— & Cooper, Artemis. *Paris After the Liberation 1944–1949* (Penguin, 1994)

Belenky, Masha. *La Morale à la Carte* (George Washington University, 2013)

Benamou, Georges-Marc. *Le Dernier Mitterrand* (Plon, 1997)

Benda, Julien. *La Trahison des Clercs* (Grasset, 2003)

Berenson, Edward, Duclert, Vincent & Prochasson, Christopher (eds). *The French Republic* (Cornell, 2011)

Berstein, Serge. *Les Cultures Politiques en France* (Seuil, 1999)

— *Histoire de Gaullisme* (Perrin, 2002)

— *Nouvelle Histoire de la France Contemporaine: La France de l'Expansion, La République Gaullienne (1958–1969)* (Seuil, 1989)

— & Rioux, Jean-Pierre. *Nouvelle Histoire de la France Contemporaine. La France de l'Expansion, l'Apogée Pompidou (1969–1974)* (Seuil, 1998)

Betham-Edwards, M. *France of To-day* (Rivington Percival, 1894)

Bidault, Georges. *D'Une Résistance à l'Autre* (L'Harmattan, 2006)

Blessington, Countess of. *The Idler in France.* 2 Vols. (Henry Colburn, 1841)

Bleton, Auguste. *Petite Histoire Populaire de Lyon* (Lyon, Ch. Palud 1885)

Bligny, Bernard (ed.). *Histoire du Dauphiné* (Toulouse, Privat, 1973)

Blom, Philipp. *The Vertigo Years* (Weidenfeld & Nicolson, 2008)

Blum, Jerome. *The European World* (Little, Brown, 1966)

Blum Léon. *À l'Échelle Humaine* (Gallimard, 1945)

— *L'Oeuvre de Léon Blum (1947–50)* (Albin Michel, 1963)

Bodley, J. E. C. *France* (1898, reissued 2012 by Ulan Press)

Boisard, Pierre. *Le Camembert, Mythe National* (Calmann-Lévy, 1992)

Bonin, Jacques, & Didier, Paul. *Louis XVIII, Roi de Deux Peuples, 1814–1816* (Albatros, 1978)

Bourgin, Georges & Hubert. *Le Régime de l'Industrie en France de 1814 à 1830* (Picard, 1912)

Bouvier, Jean, Furet, François & Gillet, Marcel. *Le Mouvement du Profit en France au XIXe Siècle* (EHESS, 1965)

Bouyé, Édouard. *Les Enfarinés de Cassaniouze* (Éditions du Veinazès, undated)

Bredin, Jean-Denis. *L'Affaire* (Julliard, 1983)

Brigouleix, Bernard. *Histoire Indiscrète des Années Balladur* (Albin Michel, 1995)

Brocheux, Pierre & Hémery, Daniel. *Indochina: An Ambiguous Colonization* (Berkeley, 2009)

Broers, Michael. *Napoleon: Soldier of Destiny* (Faber, 2014)

Brogan, Denis. *The Development of Modern France* (Hamish Hamilton, 1967)

Broglie, Gabriel de. *La Monarchie de Juillet 1830–1848* (Fayard, 2011)

Bromberger, Serge. *Les Rebelles Algériens* (Plon, 1958)

Bromberger, Merry et Serge; Elgey, Georgette & Chauvel, J. F. *Barricades et Colonels* (Fayard, 1960)

Brown, Frederick. *The Embrace of Unreason: France, 1914–1940* (Knopf, 2014)

Brustein, William. *The Social Origins of Political Regionalism: France 1849–1981* (University of California, 1988)

Bur Michel. *Histore de Laon et du Laonnois* (Toulouse, Privat, 1987)

Buruma, Ian. *Voltaire's Coconuts or Anglomania in Europe* (Weidenfeld & Nicolson, 1999)

Bury, J. P. T. *Gambetta and the Making of the Third Republic* (Longman, 1973)

— & Tombs, R. P. *Thiers, 1797–1877. A Political Life* (Allen & Unwin, 1986)

Bynum, Helen. *Spitting Blood* (Oxford, 2012)

Cabanis, José. *Charles X, Roi Ultra* (Gallimard, 1972)

Caillaux, Joseph. *Mes Mémoires 1863–1909* (Plon, 1942)

Campa, Laurence. *Guillaume Apollinaire* (Gallimard, 2013)

Camus, Albert. *Chroniques Algériennes* (Gallimard, 1958)

Candar, G. & Becker, J-J. *Histoire des Gauches en France* (La Découverte, 2004)

Carmona, Michel. *Haussmann* (Fayard, 2000)

Caron, François. *Histoire de France: La France des Patriotes de 1851 à 1914* (Fayard, 1985)

— *Histoire Économique de la France XIXe–XXe Siècles* (Armand Colin, 1995)

Caron, J-C. *L'Été Rouge* (Aubier, 2002)

Cars, Jean des. *Haussmann* (Perrin, 1978)

Castelot, André. *Louis-Philippe le Méconnu* (Perrin, 1994)

Castries, Duc de. *Monsieur Thiers* (Perrin, 1983)

Chapman, Brian. *The Prefects and Provincial France* (George Allen & Unwin, 1955)

Charle, Christophe. *Les Hauts Fonctionnaires en France au XIXe Siècle* (Gallimard, 1980)

— *Histoire Sociale de la France au XIXe Siècle* (Seuil, 1991)

Chateaubriand, François-René de, *Mémoirs d'Outre-tombe*. 5 Vols. (Méline, Brussels, 1849)

— *Correspondance Générale*, 7 Vols. (Gallimard, 1903)

Chirac, Jacques. *La France pour Tous* (NiL Éditions, 1994)

— *Mémoires* (NiL, 2009)

— *Le Temps Présidentiel. Mémoires* (NiL, 2011)

— with Jean-Luc Barré. *Chaque Pas Doit Être un But. Mémoires* (NiL, 2009)

Cholvy, Gérard (ed.). *Histoire du Vivarais* (Toulouse, Privat, 1988)

Clark, C. & Kaiser, W. (eds). *Cultural Wars* (Cambridge, 2003)

Clark, Christopher. *The Sleepwalkers* (Harper, 2013)

Clément, Pascal. *Persigny* (Perrin, 2006)

Cobb, Matthew. *Eleven Days in August* (Simon & Schuster, 2013)

Cobb, Richard. *French and Germans, Germans and French: A Personal Interpretation of France under Two Occupations 1914–1918/1940–1944* (Brandeis, 1985)

— *The Police and the People: French Popular Protest, 1789–1820* (Oxford, 1972)

— & Jones, Colin. *The French Revolution: Voices from a Momentous Epoch, 1789–95* (Simon & Schuster, 1988)

Cobban, Alfred. *A History of Modern France, Vol. III* (Cape, 1965)

— *France Since the Revolution* (Cape, 1970)

Cole, Simon. *Suspect Identities* (Harvard, 2001)

Colombani, Jean-Marie. *La France sans Mitterrand* (Flammarion, 1992)

— *Le Résident de la République* (Stock, 1998)

Conlin, Jonathan. *Tales of Two Cities* (Atlantic, 2013)

Crackanthorpe, David. *Marseille* (Signal, 2012)

Dansette, Adrien. *Louis Napoléon à la Conquête du Pouvoir* (Hachette, 1973)

Darnton, Robert. *The Forbidden Best-sellers of Pre-Revolutionary France* (Fontana, 1997)

— *The Great Cat Massacre and Other Episodes in French Cultural History* (Basic, 2009)

Daumard, Adeline. *Les Fortunes Françaises au XIXe Siècle* (Mouton, 1973)

Davies, Norman. *Europe* (Oxford, 1996)

Deligny, Henri. *Chirac ou la Fringale du Pouvoir* (Alain Moreau, 1977)

Delwasse, Liliane. *Dr Fillon et Mr Sarkozy* (Archipel, 2012)

Diesbach, Ghislain de. *L'Abbé Mugnier* (Perrin, 2003)

— *Ferdinand de Lesseps* (Perrin, 1998)

Domenach, Nicolas & Szafran, Maurice. *Le Roman d'un Président* (Plon, 1997)

Douglas, Allen. *From Fascism to Libertarian Communism* (California, 1992)

Doyle, William. *France and the Age of Revolution* (I. B. Tauris, 2013)

— *Origins of the French Revolution* (Oxford, 1999)

— *Oxford History of the French Revolution* (Oxford, 2002)

Drumont, Édouard. *La France Juive, Vols 1 and 2* (C. Marpon & E. Flammarion, no dates)

— *La France Juive devant l'Opinion* (C. Marpon & E. Flammarion, 1886)

— *Le Testament d'un Antisémite* (É. Dentu, 1891)

Dubief, Henri. *Le Déclin de la IIIe République 1929–1938* (Seuil, 1976)

Duclert, Vincent. *Alfred Dreyfus, l'Honneur d'un Patriote* (Fayard, 2006)

Duff, David. *Eugenie and Napoleon III* (Collins, 1978)

Duhamel, Alain. *Le Complexe d'Astérix* (Gallimard, 1985)

— *Portraits, Souvenirs* (Plon, 2012)

— *La République de Monsieur Mitterrand* (Gallimard, 1982)

— *La République Giscardienne* (Gallimard, 1980)

Dumas, Roland. *Politiquement Incorrect* (Cherche Midi, 2015)

Duroselle, Jean-Baptiste. *Clemenceau* (Fayard, 2007)

Dwyer, Philip. *Citizen Emperor: Napoleon in Power* (Bloomsbury, 2014)

— *Napoleon: the Path to Power* (Yale, 2008)

Earle, Edward Mead. *Modern France* (Princeton, 1951)

Edgeworth de Firmont, Henry. *Memoirs* (Kessinger Reprints, 2010)

Evans, Martin. *Algeria: France's Undeclared War* (Oxford, 2011)

— & Godin, Emmanuel. *France 1815–2003* (Arnold, 2004)

Fall, Bernard. *Hell in a Very Small Place* (Vintage, 1961)

— *Street Without Joy* (Pall Mall Press, 1964)

Farat, Honoré. *Persigny: Un Ministre de Napoléon III 1808–1872* (Hachette, 1957)

Fedida, Jean-Marc. *L'Affaire Maurras* (L'Age d'Homme, 2015)

Fenby, Jonathan. *Alliance* (Simon & Schuster, 2006)

— *The General* (Simon & Schuster, 2010)

— *On the Brink* (Little, Brown; Skyhorse, 1998 and 2014)

Ferguson, Niall. *The World's Banker* (Weidenfeld & Nicolson, 1998)

Ferniot, Jean. *De Gaulle et le 13 Mai* (Plon, 1965)

Ferro, Marc. *La Grande Guerre 1914–1918* (Gallimard, 1968)

— *Histoire de France* (Odile Jacob, 2001)

— *Histoire des Colonisations* (Seuil, 1994)

— *Pétain* (Fayard, 1987)

Ferry, Jules. *Lettres* (Calmann-Lévy, 1914)

Figes, Orlando. *Crimea, The Last Crusade* (Allen Lane, 2010)

Forrest, Alan. *Napoleon* (Quercus, 2011)

Forrester, Viviane. *L'Horreur Économique* (Fayard, 1996)

Fouché, J. *Authentic Memoirs* (H. Colburn, 1818)

Fourcassié, Jean. *Toulouse* (Plon, 1953)

Fralon, José-Alain. *A Good Man in Evil Times* (Viking, 2000)

Frémont, Armand. *Portrait de la France* (Flammarion, 2001)

Furet, François. *La Gauche et la Révolution au Milieu du XIXe Siècle* (Hachette, 1986)

— *Lies, Passion and Illusions: The Democratic Imagination in the Twentieth Century* (University of Chicago, 2014)

— *Penser la Révolution Française* (Gallimard, 1985)

— *Revolutionary France 1770–1880* (Oxford: Blackwell, 1992)

— *La Révolution de Turgot à Jules Ferry* (Gallimard, 1988)

Gagnière, Claude. *Pour Tout l'Or des Mots* (Laffont, 1997)

Gaillard, Jean-Michel. *Jules Ferry* (Fayard, 1989)

Gallois, William. *A History of Violence in the Early Algerian Colony* (Basingstoke, Palgrave Macmillan, 2013)

Gaulle, Charles de. *Discours et Messages* 5 Vols. (Plon, 1970–10)

— *Le Fil de l'Épée* (Bourg-la-Reine, Lubineau, 1963)

— *Lettres, Notes et Carnets* 12 Vols. (Plon, 1980–8)

— *Mémoires* (Gallimard, 2000)

Giesbert, Franz-Olivier. *François Mitterrand, ou la Tentation de l'Histoire* (Seuil, 1987)

— *François Mitterrand: Une Vie* (Seuil, 1997)

— *Jacques Chirac* (Seuil, 1987)

— *Le Président* (Seuil, 1990)

Gilbert, Martin. *A History of the Twentieth Century* (William Morrow, 1997)

Gildea, Robert. *Fighters in the Shadows* (Faber, 2015)

— *Children of the Revolution* (Allen Lane, 2008)

— *France 1870–1914* (Longman, 1996)

— *France Since 1945* (Oxford, 1997)

— *The Past in French History* (Yale, 1994)

Gille, Bertrand. *Histoire de la Maison Rothschild.* 2 Vols. (Geneva, Librairie Droz, 1965–7)

Giscard d'Estaing, Valéry. *Démocratie Française* (Fayard, 1976)

— *Deux Français sur Trois* (Flammarion, 1984)

— *Le Pouvoir et la Vie* (Interforum, 1988)

Goguel, François. *Géographie des Élections Françaises sous la Troisième et la Quatrième République* (Armand Colin, 1970)

— & Grosser, A. *La Politique en France* (Armand Colin, 1972)

Goncourt, Edmond et Jules de. *Journal: Mémoires de la Vie Littéraire 1866–86,* 3 Vols. (Fasquelle et Flammarion, 1956)

Grenville-Murray, E. C. *High Life in France Under the Republic* (Vizetelly, 1884)

Grosser, A. *Affaires Extérieures* (Flammarion, 1984)

Groult, Benôite et Flora. *Journal à Quatre Mains* (Denoël Ligugé, 1962)

Gubler, Claude. *Le Grand Secret* (Plon, 1996)

Guedalla, Philip. *The Second Empire* (Hodder & Stoughton, 1932)

Guéhenno, Jean. *Journal des Années Noires* (Gallimard, 1947)

Gueniffey, Patrice. *Bonaparte* (Gallimard, 2013)

Guy, Claude. *En Écoutant de Gaulle* (Grasset, 1996)

Haine, W. Scott, *The World of the Paris Café* (Baltimore, John Hopkins Press, 1999)

Harbi, Mohammed. *Aux Origines du FLN* (Christian Bourgois, 1975)

Hause, Steven & Kenney, Anne. *Women's Suffrage and Social Politics in the French Third Republic* (Princeton, 1984)

Haussmann, Georges. *Mémoires.* 2 Vols. (Durier, 1979)

Hayward, Jack. *Fragmented France* (Oxford, 2007)

Hayward, Susan & Vincendeau, Ginette. *French Film* (Routledge, 1990)

Hazan, Eric. *The Invention of Paris* (Verso, 2010)

Hazareesingh, Sudhir. *How the French Think* (Allen Lane, 2015)

— *The Legend of Napoleon* (Granta, 2005)

— *Le Mythe Gaullien* (Gallimard, 2010)

— *Political Traditions in Modern France* (Oxford, 1994)

Heine, Heinrich. *Works Vols 7 and 8* (Heinemann, 1893)

Higounet-Nadal, Arlette. *Histoire du Périgord* (Toulouse, Privat, 1983)

Hillerin, Laure. *La Comtesse Greffulhe* (Flammarion, 2014)

— *La Duchesse de Berry* (Flammarion, 2010)

Hobsbawm, E. J. *The Age of Capital 1848–1875* (Abacus, 1975)

— *The Age of Empire 1875–1914* (Abacus, 1987)

Hoffbauer, M. F. *Paris à travers les Âges* (Inter-Livres, 1993)

Hole, S. Reynolds. *Nice and her Neighbours* (Sampson Low, Marston, Searle, & Rivington, 1889)

Horne, Alistair. *The Fall of Paris* (Penguin, 2007)

— *A Savage War of Peace* (Papermac, 1996)

— *Seven Ages of Paris* (Macmillan, 2002)

— *To Lose a Battle: France, 1940* (Macmillan, 1969)

Horricks, Raymond. *Marshal Ney* (Tunbridge Wells, Midas Books, 1982)

Howard, Michael. *The Franco-Prussian War* (Routledge, 2001)

Howarth, T. E. B. *Citizen King: The Life of Louis-Philippe* (Eyre & Spottiswoode, 1961)

Hugo, Victor. *Souvenirs Personnels (1848–1851)* (Gallimard, 1952)

Hunt, Lynn & Censer, Jack. *Liberty, Equality, Fraternity* (Pennsylvania, 2001)

Hussey, Andrew. *The French Intifada* (Granta, 2014)

Imbert, Claude & Julliard, Jacques. *La Droite et la Gauche* (Laffont, 1995)

Irvine, William. *The Boulanger Affair Reconsidered* (Oxford, 1989)

Jackson, Julian. *The Fall of France* (Oxford, 2003)

— *France: The Dark Years 1940–1944* (Oxford, 2001)

— *The Politics of Depression in France 1932–1936* (Cambridge, 1985)

— *The Popular Front in France: Defending Democracy 1934–1938* (Cambridge 1988)

James, Colin. *France* (Cambridge, 1994)

James, Henry. *A Little Tour in France* (Heinemann, 1900)

Jamet, Dominique. *Demain le Front?* (Bartillat, 1995)

Jarreau, Patrick. *Chirac, la Malédiction* (Stock, 1997)

— *La France de Chirac* (Flammarion, 1995)

— & Kergoat, Jacques. *François Mitterrand: 14 Ans de Pouvoir* (Éditions Le Monde, 1995)

Jaume, Lucien. *L'État Administratif et le Libéralisme* (Fondation pour l'Innovation Politique, 2009)

— *L'Individu Effacé ou le Paradoxe du Libéralisme Français* (Fayard, 1997)

Jeanneney, Jean-Noël. *L'Argent Caché* (Fayard, 1981)

Jenks, Leland Hamilton. *The Migration of British Capital to 1875* (Cape, 1938)

Johnson, Douglas. *Guizot* (Greenwood, 1976)

Johnson, Michael. *French Resistance* (Cassell, 1996)

Jones, Colin. *Cambridge Illustrated History of France* (Cambridge, 1999)

— *Paris: Biography of a City* (Allen Lane, 2004)

— *The Smile Revolution* (Oxford, 2014)

Jospin, Lionel. *Je M'Engage* (L'Atelier de Campagne, 2002)

— *Le Mal Napoléonien* (Seuil, 2014)

Jouvion, Philippe. *Le Béret* (Rodez, Éditions du Rouergue, 1998)

Julliard, Jacques. *La Cinquième République* (Seuil, 1976)

— *La IVe République (1947–1958)* (Calmann-Lévy, 1968)

— *Les Gauches Françaises* (Flammarion, 2012)

Karabell, Zachary. *Parting the Desert: The Creation of the Suez Canal* (John Murray, 2003)

Kauffmann, Grégoire. *Édouard Drumont* (Perrin, 2008)

Kavanagh, Julie. *The Girl Who Loved Camellias* (Knopf, 2013)

Kayser, Jacques. *Les Grandes Batailles du Radicalisme 1820–1901* (Marcel Riviere & Cie, 1962)

Kedward, Rod. *La Vie en Bleu* (Allen Lane, 2005)

Kelly, Christine & Fillon, François. *Le Secret et l'Ambition* (Éditions du Moment, 2007)

Kelly, Debra & Cornick, Martyn. *History of the French in London* (London University, 2013)

Kelly, Ian. *Cooking for Kings: Antonin Carême* (Short Books, 2003)

Kerr, David. *Caricature and French Political Culture 1830–1848* (Oxford, 2000)

Kirkland, Stephane. *Paris Reborn* (Picador, 2013)

Klein, Richard. *Cigarettes are Sublime* (Picador, 1995)

Kley, Dale Van. *The French Idea of Freedom* (Stanford, 1994)

Labrousse, Ernest. *Aspects de la Crise et de la Dépression de l'Économie Française au Milieu du XIXe Siècle, 1815–1851* (Société d'Histoire de la Révolution, 1848–1956)

Lacouture, Jean. *De Gaulle*. 3 Vols. (Seuil, 1984–1990)

— *Le Front Populaire* (Actes Sud, 2006)

— *Léon Blum* (Seuil, 1979)

— *Pierre Mendès France* (Points Histoire, 2010)

Landes, David. *The Wealth and Poverty of Nations* (Little, Brown, 1998)

Larkin, Maurice. *France Since the Popular Front* (Oxford, Clarendon Press, 1988)

Latreille, André (ed.). *Histoire de Lyon et du Lyonnais* (Toulouse, Privat, 1978)

Lavigne Family. *Cousins d'Auvergne* (Aurillac, Association Cousins d'Auvergne, 1995)

Lawday, David. *Danton* (Cape, 2009)

— *Napoleon's Master: A Life of Prince Talleyrand* (Cape, 2006)

Le Bras, Hervé & Todd, Emmanuel. *L'Invention de la France* (Pluriel, 1981)

Lefebvre, Georges. *The French Revolution* (Routledge, 2001)

— & Tackett, Timothy. *The Coming of the French Revolution* (Princeton, 2005)

Le Monde. La Droite sans Partage: Élections Législatives, 1993 (Éditions Le Monde, 1993)

Le Monde hors-série, 'Une présidence sous tension, les années Sarkozy' (2012)

Lenotre, G. *The Tuileries, The Glories and Enchantments of a Vanished Palace* (Herbert Jenkins, 1934)

Lentz, Thierry. *100 Questions sur Napoléon* (La Boétie, 2013)

Lesseps, Ferdinand de. *Souvenirs de Quarante Ans, Vols 1 and 2* (Paris Nouvelle Revue, 1887)

Lesur, C. L. *La France et les Français en 1817* (De l'Imprimerie d'Ange, 1817)

L'Etat de la France, Édition 1992 (La Découverte)

Lettres Familières de l'Impératrice Eugénie (Le Divan, 1935)

Lever, Évelyne. *Louis XVIII* (Fayard, 1988)

Lévy, Claude & Tillard, Paul. *La Grande Rafle du Vél d'Hiv* (Laffont, 1967)

Ligou, Daniel. *Historie de Montauban* (Privat, Toulouse, 1992)

Lucas-Dubreton, J. *Le Comte d'Artois, Charles X* (Hachette, 2000)

McCauley, Elizabeth Anne. *Industrial Madness: Commercial Photography in Paris 1848–1871* (Yale, 1994)

McKay, Donald C. *The National Workshops* (Harvard, 1933)

Maclean, Fitzroy. *Eastern Approaches* (Penguin, 1991)

McLynn, Frank. *Napoleon* (Jonathan Cape, 1998)

McMeekin, Sean. *July 1914: Countdown to War* (Icon, 2013)

McMillan, James F. *Napoleon III* (Longman, 1991)

MacMillan, Margaret. *Peacemakers* (John Murray, 2003)

— *The War that Ended Peace* (Profile, 2013)

Madelin, Louis. *Fouché* (Librairie Académique Perrin, 1969)

Magraw, Roger. *France 1815–1914* (Fontana, 1987)

Maguire, J. Robert. *Ceremonies of Bravery: Oscar Wilde, Carlos Blacker and the Dreyfus Affair* (Oxford, 2013)

Maillé, Duchesse de. *Mémoires 1832–1851* (Librairie Académique Perrin, 1989)
— *Souvenirs des Deux Restaurations* (Librairie Académique Perrin, 1984)
Maîtres Cuisiniers de France. *Les Recettes du Terroir* (Laffont, 1984)
Malka, Solomon and Victor. *Le Grand Déssaroi* (Albin Michel, 2016)
Mancoff, Debra. *Fashion in Impressionist Paris* (Merrell, 2012)
Mansel, Philip. *Louis XVIII* (Blond & Briggs, 1981)
— *Paris Between Empires, 1814–1852* (Phoenix, 2003)
Marcot, François *et al. Dictionnaire Historique de la Résistance* (Laffont, 2006)
Marcus, Paul. *Jaurès et Clemenceau* (Privat, 2014)
Margadant, Ted. *French Peasants in Revolt: The Insurrection of 1851* (Princeton, 1979)
Margairaz, Michel, Tartakowsky, Danielle & Lefeuvre, Daniel. *Le Front Populaire* (Paris Larousse, 2009)
Marmin, Michel. *Napoléon, au Delà de la Légende* (Chronique, 2012)
Marseille, Jacques. *Nouvelle Histoire de la France* (Perrin, 1999)
Marsh, David. *The Euro: The Politics of the New Global Currency* (Yale, 2009)
Martel, Gordon. *The Month That Changed the World: July 1914* (Oxford, 2014)
Martin-Fugier, Anne. *Les Salons de la IIIe République* (Perrin, 2003)
Marx, Karl. *The Eighteenth Brumaire of Louis Bonaparte* (www.marxists.org/archive/marx/works/1852/18th-brumaire/)
— and Engels, Frederick. *Selected Works* (Lawrence & Wishart, 1968)
Maspero, François. *Les Passagers du Roissy-Express* (Seuil, 1990)
Massu, Jacques. *La Vrai Bataille d'Alger* (Plon, 1971)
Mauriac, François. *De Gaulle* (Grasset, 1964)
Mayeur, Jean-Marie. *Léon Gambetta, la Patrie et la République* (Fayard, 2008)
Maza, Sarah. *The Myth of the French Bourgeoisie* (Harvard, 2003)
McCullough, David. *The Greater Journey: Americans in Paris* (Simon & Schuster, 2011)
Mellot, Philippe. *Paris Disparu* (Michèle Trinckvel, 1996)
Mercadié, Louis. *Marie Talabot* (Rodez, Éditions du Rouergue, 2007)
Merle, Gabriel. *Émile Combes* (Fayard, 1995)
Mermet, Gérard. *Francoscopie* (Larousse, 1994)
Merriman, John. *Massacre: The Life and Death of the Paris Commune of 1871* (Yale, 1994)
Milza, Pierre. *L'Année Terrible: Vol. 2, La Commune* (Perrin, 2009)
— *Napoléon III Mars–Juin 1871* (Perrin, 2004)
Minc, Alain. *La France de l'An 2000* (Odile Jacob, 1994)
Mine, Alain & the Commissariat General du Plan. *La France de l'An 2000* (Odile Jacob, 1994)
Mitterrand, Danielle. *En Toutes Libertés* (Ramsay, 1996)
Mitterrand, François. *Le Coup d'État Permanent* (Plon, 1964)
— *Ma Part de Vérité* (Fayard, 1969)
— *La Paille et le Grain* (Flammarion, 1975)
— *La Rose au Poing* (Flammarion, 1973)
Moati, Serge. *Le Pen, Vous et Moi* (Flammarion, 2014)
Moch, Jules. *Rencontres avec de Gaulle,* (Plon, 1971)
— *Une si longue vie* (Robert Laffont, 1976)

Moïsi, Dominique. 'The Trouble with France' in *Foreign Affairs* (New York, May/June, 1998)

Mollet, Guy. *Bilan et Perspectives Socialises* (Plon, 1958)

Mollier, Jean-Yves. *La Cinquième République* (Editions Le Monde, 1995)

— *Le Scandale de Panama* (Fayard, 1991)

Monnet, Jean. *Mémoires* (Fayard, 1976)

Monnier, Virginie. *Édouard André* (Alcide, 2014)

Montagnon, Pierre. *La France Coloniale. La Gloire de l'Empire* (Pygmalion, 1988)

Montaldo, Jean. *Mitterrand et les 40 Voleurs* (Albin Michel, 1994)

Moorehead, Caroline. *Village of Secrets* (Chatto & Windus, 2014)

Moreau, Émile. *Souvenirs d'un Gouverneur de la Banque de France* (Genin, 1954)

Morgan, Lady. *France.* 2 Vols. (Henry Colburn, 1818)

Morrison, Donald & Compagnon, Antoine. *The Death of French Culture* (Polity, 2010)

Muir, Rory. *Wellington: The Path to Victory* (Yale, 2014)

Nadeau, Jean-Benoît & Barlow, Julie. *Sixty Million Frenchmen Can't Be Wrong* (Robson, 2004)

Nay, Catherine. *La Double Méprise* (Grasset, 1980)

— *L'Impétueux* (Grasset, 2012)

— *Le Noir et le Rouge* (Grasset, 1984)

— *Un Pouvoir Nommé Désir* (Grasset, 2007)

Nelson, Michael. *Queen Victoria and the Discovery of the Riviera* (Tauris Parke, 2007)

Nora, P. *Les Lieux de Mémoire.* 2 Vols. (Gallimard, 1984–1986)

Nourrisson, Didier. *Crus et Cuites: Histoire du Buveur* (Perrin, 2013)

O'Ballance, Edgar. *The Indo-China War 1945–54* (Faber, 1964)

L'Observatoire Français des Conjonctures Économiques. *L'Economie Française, 1997* (La Découverte, 1997)

Orléans, Louis-Philippe de. *Mon Journal,* 2 Vols. (Michel Lévy Frères, 1845)

Otte, T. G. *July Crisis: The World's Descent into War, Summer 1914* (Cambridge, 2014)

Ousby, Ian. *Occupation* (John Murray, 1997)

Owen, David. *The Hidden Perspective* (Haus, 2014)

Ozouf, Mona. *De Révolution en République* (Gallimard, 2015)

— *La Fête Révolutionnaire* (Folio, 2013)

— *Jules Ferry* (Gallimard, 2014)

Paxton, Robert. *French Peasant Fascism* (Oxford, 1997)

— *Vichy France* (Columbia, 2002)

Péan, Pierre. *Une Jeunesse Française: François Mitterrand, 1934–1947* (Fayard, 1994)

Pelletan, Camille. *La Semaine de Mai* (Dreyfous, 1880)

Perrot, Michelle (ed.). *History of Private Life, Vol. IV* (Harvard, Belknap Press, 1990)

Peyrefitte, Alain. *C'était de Gaulle* (Fallois-Fayard, 1997-9)

— *Le Mal Français* (Plon, 1977)

— *Quand la Rose se Fanera* (Plon, 1983)

Philip, André. *Le Socialisme Trahi* (Plon, 1957)

Pilbeam, Pamela. *The Constitutional Monarchy in France, 1814–48* (Routledge, 1999)

Pingeot, Mazarine. *Premier Roman* (Julliard, 1998)

Pinkney, David. *The French Revolution of 1830* (Princeton 1972)

Pisani-Ferry, Fresnette. *Le Général Boulanger* (Flammarion, 1969)

Poincaré, Raymond. *Au Service de la France* (Plon, 1926–33)

Polèse, Mario, Shearmur, Richard & Terral, Laurent. *La France Avantagée* (Odile Jacob, 2014)

Pollard, Miranda. *Reign of Virtue: Mobilizing Gender In Vichy France* (Chicago, 1998)

Pompidou, Georges. *Pour Rétablir une Vérité* (Flammarion, 1982)

Popkin, Jeremy. *A History of Modern France* (Prentice Hall, 2005)

Price, Lewis C. *Archbishop Darboy and Some French Tragedies 1813–1871* (George Allen & Unwin, 1915)

Price, Munro. *Napoleon, The End of Glory* (Oxford, 2014)

Price, Roger. *1848 in France* (Thames & Hudson, 1975)

— *The French Second Republic: A Social History* (Batsford, 1972)

— *People and Politics in France, 1848–1870* (Cambridge, 2009)

Reader, Keith. *The Place de la Bastille: The Story of a Quartier* (Liverpool, 2011)

Rémond, René. *La Droite en France de 1815 à Nos Jours* (Aubier, 1954)

— *Les Droites Aujourd'hui* (Points histoire, 2007)

— *Les Droites en France* (Aubier-Montaigne, 1992)

— *Introduction à l'Histoire de Notre Temps*. 3 Vols. (Points Histoire, 2014)

— *La Vie Politique en France*. 2 Vols. (Pocket, 2005)

Rey, Alain, Duval, Frédéric & Siouffi, Gilles. *Mille Ans de Langue Française* (Perrin, 2007)

Rey, Marie-Pierre. *Alexandre I* (Northern Illinois University Press, 2012)

Reynaud, Paul. *Au Coeur de la Mêlée* (Flammarion, 1951)

Richardson, Joanna. *The Bohemians, La Vie de Bohème in Paris 1830–1914* (Macmillan, 1969)

— *The Courtesans* (Castle Books, 2004)

Riding, Alan. *And the Show Went On* (Duckworth Overlook, 2011)

Rioux, Jean-Pierre. *La France de la Quatrième République, l'Expansion et l'Impuissance, 1952–1958* (Seuil, 1983)

— *La France de la Quatrième République, l'Ordeur et la Nécessité 1944–1952* (Seuil, 1980)

— *Jean Jaurès* (Librarie Académique Perrin, 2008)

— *La Révolution Industrielle, 1780–1880* (Seuil, 1989)

Risse, Jacques. *Le Petit Père Combes* (Harmattan, 2000)

Robb, Graham. *The Discovery of France* (Picador, 2007)

Robert, Vincent. *Le Temps des Banquets* (Sorbonne, 2010)

Roberts, Andrew. *Napoleon the Great* (Allen Lane, 2014)

Roberts, Mary Louise. *What Soldiers Do* (Chicago, 2013)

Röhl, John. *Kaiser Wilhelm II* (Cambridge, 2014)

Rol-Tanguy, Henri & Bourderon, Roger. *Libération de Paris* (Hachette, 1994)

Rosanvallon, Pierre. *L'État en France de 1789 à Nos Jours* (Seuil, 1990)

— *Le Modèle Politique Français* (Seuil, 2004)

— *Le Moment Guizot* (Gallimard, 1985)

— *Le Peuple Introuvable* (Folio, 1998)

Rosbottom, Ronald. *When Paris Went Dark* (John Murray, 2014)

Ross, George, Hoffmann, Stanley & Malzacher, Sylvia. *The Mitterrand Experiment* (Oxford, Polity, 1987)

Roupnel, Gaston. *Histoire de la Campagne Française* (Plon, 1981)

Rousell, Eric. *De Gaulle,* 2 Vols. (Perrin, Tempus, 2007)

Rousso, Henry. *Le Syndrome de Vichy* (Fayard, 1990)

— & Conan, Eric. *Vichy, un Passé qui ne passe pas* (Fayard, 1994)

Rudé, George. *The Crowd in the French Revolution* (Oxford: Clarendon Press, 1959)

— *The French Revolution* (Weidenfeld & Nicolson, 1988)

Sarkozy, Nicolas. *Témoignage* (Fixot, 2006)

Schama, Simon. *Citizens* (Penguin, 2004)

Scurr, Ruth. *Fatal Purity* (Vintage, 2007)

Seager, Frederic. *The Boulanger Affair* (Cornell, 1969)

Sée, Henri. *La Vie Économique de la France 1815–1848* (Félix Alcan, 1927)

Seignobos, Charles. *La Révolution de 1848 – Le Second Empire (1848–1859)* (Hachette, 1921)

Semelin, Jacques. *Persécutions et Entraides dans la France Occupée* (Arènes-Seuil, 2013)

Seward, Desmond. *Eugénie: The Empress and her Empire* (Stroud, Sutton, 2004)

Shafer, David A. *The Paris Commune* (Palgrave Macmillan, 2005)

Short, Philip. *Mitterrand* (Bodley Head, 2013)

Smith, William. *Second Empire and Commune* (Longman, 1996)

Spang, Rebecca. *The Invention of the Restaurant* (Harvard, 2000)

— *Stuff and Money in the Time of the French Revolution* (Harvard, 2015)

Spencer, Edmund. *A Tour of Inquiry through France and Italy.* 2 Vols. (Hurst and Blackett, 1853)

Staël, Madame de. *Considérations sur la Révolution Française* (Kessinger Reprints, 2010)

Steiner, George. *Language and Silence* (Faber, 1967)

Stern, Daniel (Comtesse d'Agoult). *Histoire de la Révolution de 1848.* 3 Vols. (Sandre, 1850–3)

— *Mémoires* (Calmann-Lévy, 1927)

Stern, Fritz. *Gold and Iron* (Allen & Unwin, 1977)

Stevenson, David. *1914–18: The History of the First World War* (Allen Lane, 2011)

— *With Our Backs to the Wall* (Allen Lane, 2011)

Stoeckl, Agnes. *King of the French: A Portrait of Louis-Philippe* (John Murray, 1957)

Swann, Julian & Félix, Joël. *The Crisis of the Absolute Monarchy* (Oxford, 2013)

Tackett, Timothy. *The Coming of the Terror in the French Revolution* (Harvard, 2015)

— *When the King Took Flight* (Harvard, 2003)

Tardieu, André. *La Profession Parlementaire* (Flammarion, 1937)

Taylor, A. J. P. *The Struggle for Mastery in Europe* (Oxford, 1971)

Thiers, Adolphe. *Memoirs of M. Thiers* (George Allen & Unwin, 1915)

Thureau-Dangin, Paul. *Histoire de la Monarchie de Juillet.* 6 Vols. (Plon, 1884–1892)

Todd, Emmanuel. *Qui est Charlie?* (Seuil, 2015)

Tocqueville, Alexis de. *The Old Regime and the Revolution* (Chicago, 1998)

— *Recollections* (Anchor, 1975)

Tombs, Robert. *France, 1814–1914* (Longman, 1996)

— *The War Against Paris, 1871* (Cambridge, 1981)

— & José Chatroussat. *Paris, Bivouac de Révolutions* (Libertalia, 2014)

Tooze, Adam. *The Deluge: The Great War and the Remaking of Global Order* (Allen Lane, 2014)

— *The Wages of Destruction* (Allen Lane, 2006)

Touchard, Jean. *La Gauche en France depuis 1900* (Seuil, 1977)

Tournoux, Jean-Raymond. *Jamais Dit* (Plon, 1971)

— *Le Mois de Mai du Général* (Plon, 1969)

— *Pétain et de Gaulle* (Plon, 1964)

— *Secrets d'État* (Plon, 1960)

— *La Tragédie du Général* (Plon, 1967)

Townshend, Charles. *Terrorism* (Oxford, 2011)

Trierweiler, Valérie. *Merci pour ce Moment* (Les Arènes, 2014)

Truesdell, Matthew. *Spectacular Politics* (Oxford, 1997)

Tudesq, André-Jean. *Les Grands Notables en France, 1840–1849* (Faculté des Lettres et Sciences Humaines, 1964)

Valence, Georges. *Haussmann le Grand* (Flammarion, 2000)

Vergez-Chaignon, Bénédicte. *Pétain* (Perrin, 2015)

Viansson-Ponté, Pierre. *Histoire de la République Gaullienne.* 2 Vols. (Fayard, 1980, Pluriel, 1991)

Vidal-Naquet, Pierre. *Face à la Raison d'État* (La Découverte, 1989)

Vigée, Louise-Elisabeth. *Mémoires* (H. Fournier, 1837)

Vincendeau, Ginette. *Bardot* (Palgrave Macmillan, 2013)

Vinen, Richard. *A History in Fragments* (Little, Brown, 2000)

Wagret, Paul (ed.). *Histoire de Vendôme et du Vendômois* (Privat, 1984)

Walter, Marc & Arqué, Sabine. *The World in 1900* (Thames & Hudson, 2007)

Weber, Eugen. *France, Fin de Siècle* (Harvard, 1986)

— *The Hollow Years* (W.W. Norton, 1996)

— *Peasants into Frenchmen* (Chatto & Windus, 1977)

Weill, Georges. *Histoire du Parti Républicain en France, 1814–1870* (Alcan, 1928)

Weiner, Robert & Sharpless, Richard. *An Uncertain Future* (Toronto, 2012)

Wellesley, Sir Victor & Sencourt, Robert. *Conversations with Napoleon III* (Benn, 1934)

Werth, Alexander. *De Gaulle* (Penguin, 1965)

White, Nicholas. *French Divorce Fiction from the Revolution to the First World War* (Oxford, Legenda, 2013)

Willard, Claude. *La France Ouvrière* (Editions Ouvrières, 1995)

Williams, Andrew J. *France, Britain and the United States in the Twentieth Century (1900–1940)* (Palgrave Macmillan, 2014)

Williams, Charles. *The Last Great Frenchman* (Little, Brown, 1993)

Williams, Kate. *Josephine: Desire, Ambition, Napoleon* (Hutchinson, 2014)

Williams, Philip & Harrison, Martin. *Politics and Society in De Gaulle's Republic* (Longman, 1971)

Williams, Roger L. *The Mortal Napoleon III* (Princeton, 1971)

Wilson, Colette E. *Paris and the Commune, 1871–78* (Manchester, 2007)

Wilson, Derek. *Rothschild* (Deutsch, 1988)

Windrow, Martin. *The Last Valley* (Weidenfeld & Nicolson, 2004)

Winock, Michel. *La Belle Epoque* (Perrin, 2002)

— *Clemenceau* (Perrin, 2011)

— *La Gauche en France* (Tempus, 2006)

— *Gustave Flaubert* (Galimard, 2013)

— *Histoire de l'Extrême Droite en France* (Seuil, 1993)

— *Parlez-moi de la France* (Plon, 1995)

— *La République se Meurt* (Seuil, 1978)

Wolff, Philippe (ed.). *Histoire du Languedoc* (Toulouse: Privat, 1967)

Wolmar, Christian. *Blood, Iron and Gold: How the Railways Transformed the World* (Atlantic, 2009)

Wright, D. G. *Napoleon and Europe* (Longman, 1984)

— *Revolution and Terror in France 1789–1795* (Longman, 1990)

Yon, Jean-Claude. *Le Second Empire: Politique, Société, Culture* (Armand Colin, 2012)

Zamoyski, Adam. *Phantom Terror* (Collins, 2014)

— *Rites of Peace* (Harper, 2007)

Zeldin, Theodore. *France 1848–1945.* 3 Vols. (Oxford, 1982)

— *The French* (Collins Harvill, 1983)

— *The Political System of Napoleon III* (Macmillan, 1958)

Ziegler, Philip. *The Sixth Great Power: Barings 1762–1929* (Collins, 1988)

ACKNOWLEDGEMENTS

This book is drawn from half a century of personal and professional involvement with France. During that time, I have benefitted from meeting with scores of people who have illuminated the country's history. For the period since 1965, when I first went to work as a correspondent in Paris, I have drawn on my experiences as a journalist for Reuters, *The Times* and the *Economist* and am particularly grateful to the late André Passeron for his insights into high politics. Apart from the assistance of such contacts and of historians of modern France, I have been fortunate enough to have family links which have illuminated many corners of the nation's life for me over the decades.

I am indebted to the staff at the National Archives and the Bibliothèque Nationale, as well as to Musée de la Presse, the Fondation Charles de Gaulle and, for the nineteenth century, the Musée d'Orsay. In London, the extensive French archives at the London Library were an extremely useful source of books over the centuries. For the contemporary passages I drew on French and foreign media, especially the excellent reporting on the 2015 terrorist attacks and their ramifications by *le Monde*, *le Figaro*, French broadcasting stations, the *Financial Times* and Angelique Chrisafis and her colleagues of the *Guardian* and *Observer*. As an inveterate flâneur, I have picked up many of the details on Paris while strolling through this most walkable of cities. Provincial France also provided a rich source of material, from city museums to those devoted to regional life, the Camisards, Breton sailors and the agriculture, industries and mines of different regions. Among other unexpected treasure troves, the Garrison Library in Gibraltar provided a rich range of nineteenth-century travel books and memoirs and I am grateful to the director, Dr Jennifer Ballantine Perera, for her help in accessing them.

I owe a special debt to André Villeneuve for his encouragement and detailed research into various subjects of interest around 1900. I am grateful to Dr Sudhir Hazareesingh for his assistance, especially his thesis of the 'unfinished republic'. Annie Besnier, Ginette Vincendeau, Simon Caulkin and Peter Graham provided valuable assistance as always, while no book would be complete without spells writing in Mourjou in the Cantal, Belcastel in the Aveyron and the home of Peter and Jenny Thomas in the Gard. The shelves of Susan and Rick Walters were a very useful vein of information on Paris. Timothy McFarland provided stimulating ideas and knowledge even from his hospital bed. Ludovic de Montille was illuminating on the Orléanist tradition as well as having relevant cartoons on his walls. Bernard Edinger provided much pertinent information on both past and present, while I am grateful to Professor Robert Tombs for pointing out errors in the first edition which have been corrected here. Graham Webb provided further exemplary corrections for which I thank him.

At Simon & Schuster, Mike Jones took up the commission and Iain MacGregor and his team saw the book through editing into publication; I am especially grateful to Sally Partington for her expert copy editing, to Clare Hubbard for her highly diligent proofreading especially of the notes, to Jo Whitford, Charlotte Coulthard and Harriet Dobson for their editing and for seeing the text through to the printer with high efficiency and good humour down to finding a shared enthusiasm for the best couscous restaurant in Paris. Simon & Schuster's art department did its usual fine job with the cover. Christopher Sinclair-Stevenson was, yet again, a source of support and counsel.

But, as ever, my overwhelming debt is to my wife who brought her knowledge and judgement to bear as well as being the best first reader I could imagine.

INDEX